VHDL
for
Programmable Logic

VHDL
for
Programmable Logic

VHDL
for
Programmable Logic

Kevin Skahill

Cypress Semiconductor

CONTRIBUT

Jay Legenhause
Ron Wade
Corey Wilner
Blair Wilson

Cypress Semiconductor

▲▲ **ADDISON-WESLEY**

An imprint of Addison Wesley Longman, Inc.

Reading, Massachusetts ▪ Menlo Park, California ▪ New York ▪ Harlow, England
Don Mills, Ontario ▪ Sydney ▪ Mexico City ▪ Madrid ▪ Amsterdam

Acquisitions Editor: Tim Cox
Executive Editor: Dan Joraanstad
Assistant Editor: Laura Cheu
Editorial Assistants: Anne Gavin, Susan Slater
Production Editor: Lisa Weber
Projects Manager: Ray Kanarr
Art Supervisor: Kelly Murphy
Design Manager: Don Kesner
Composition and Film Manager: Lillian Hom
Composition and Film Coordinator: Vivian McDougal
Marketing Manager: Sanford Forte
Marketing Coordinator: Anne Boyd
Copy Editor: Elizabeth Gehrman
Proofreader: Holly McLean-Aldis
Indexer: Nancy Kopper
Text Designer: Lisa Jahred
Illustrators: Bert Koehler, Karl Miyajima
Compositor: Rex Wolf
Film and Printing: Maple Press
Cover Designer: Yvo Riezebos

Library of Congress Cataloging-in-Publication Data

Skahill, Kevin.
     VHDL for programmable logic / Kevin Skahill;
contributors, Jay Legenhausen . . . [et al.].
     p.   cm.
     Includes bibliographical references and index.
     ISBN 0-201-89573-0
     1. VHDL (Computer hardware description
language) 2. Logic design-Data processing.
3. Programmable logic devices--Design--Data
processing. I. Legenhausen, Jay. II. Title.
TK7885.7.S55   1996
621.39'5--dc20
                                          96-16472
                                              CIP

0-201-89586-2

3 4 5 6 7 8 9 10—MA—00 99 98 97

The cover was printed using soy-based inks.

Addison-Wesley Publishing Company, Inc.
2725 Sand Hill Road
Menlo Park, CA 94025

Table of Contents

Preface

Audience and Approach

VHDL for Programmable Logic is appropriate for courses in VHDL, advanced logic design, and ASIC design, as well as for professional engineers and graduate students interested in updating their design methodologies to include both VHDL and programmable logic devices.

The objectives of this book are to equip the reader with:

- the skills to write VHDL code that can be synthesized to efficient logic circuits,

- an understanding of the VHDL and programmable logic design process—from design description through synthesis, placement, and routing, to the creation of test benches for design verification,

- a knowledge of design trade-offs that can be made, and

- a toolbox of techniques that can be modified and used to solve unique design problems.

To achieve these objectives, the book covers VHDL by:

- emphasizing real-world examples rather than abstract theories,

- including design topics such as state machine design, area versus performance tradeoffs, parameterized components, hierarchy and libraries, pipelining and resource sharing,

- using numerous examples reduced through synthesis to logic gates,

- demonstrating options for synthesizing, fitting, placing, and routing logic circuits within CPLDs and FPGAs,

- introducing breakout exercises that reinforce design topics and quickly bring the reader up to speed with using the included Warp software, and

- including over 80 design files on the enclosed CD-ROM, some for use with the problem sets and hands-on experience with synthesizing, fitting, placing, and routing.

The philosophy of this text is to thoroughly involve readers in numerous synthesis and design issues so that they nearly forget they are simultaneously learning a new design language and methodology. This text teaches by showing how VHDL models are synthesized for implementation in programmable logic devices—which are in turn explained through a series of design issues, examples, and techniques. This is in contrast to focusing on syntax and language structure—an abstract and theoretical approach that tends to emphasize building simulation models that cannot necessarily be synthesized, because the designs are either physically meaningless or contain constructs that are not particularly well suited for synthesis.

Many exercises encourage hands-on use of synthesis software in order to reduce theory to practice. This also helps readers to understand how abstract VHDL descriptions are reduced to digital logic. It is also expected that with practice, readers will write code that can be synthesized to efficient digital logic circuits.

Understanding and executing the design objectives is also emphasized. The reader is challenged to make decisions about requirements such as time-to-market, cost, design features, performance, and manufacturing capabilities.

Content and Organization

Chapter 1 examines the motivation for a design methodology that includes VHDL and programmable logic devices. It presents the process of designing with VHDL and programmable logic devices, including the EDA tool flow. A Breakout Exercise introduces the reader to the Warp2 tool flow.

Chapter 2 is a programmable logic primer that brings the reader from an understanding of simple logic gates and discrete devices to an appreciation for the capabilities of PALs, simple PLDs, CPLDs, and FPGAs. The chapter presents several device architectures and their features, and outlines the decisions that go into selecting an appropriate device for an application.

Chapter 3 introduces the basic building blocks of VHDL design. The behavioral, dataflow, and structural architecture description styles are introduced and explained vis-à-vis synthesis efficiency. The chapter explores the simulation cycle and the differences between processing code for simulation and synthesis, and ends with a discussion of data objects and types.

Chapter 4 describes how to use VHDL language constructs to build combinational and synchronous logic. Sequential statements such as `if-then-else` and `case-when`, as well as concurrent statements such as `when-else` and `with-select-when`, are compared and reduced to logic gates to illustrate the synthesis process.

The chapter also uses design examples to illustrate the concept of overloaded operators; this provides a good context for introducing the IEEE 1076.3 `numeric_std` and `numeric_bit` packages. Other topics include: creating flip-flops, control logic, three-state outputs, bidirectional outputs, and implicit memory. The chapter ends with the design of a FIFO.

Chapter 5 explains how to easily translate state flow diagrams to equivalent VHDL state machine descriptions. Several state machine implementations are examined to determine effects of implementation on resource usage, setup times, clock-to-output times, and maximum operating frequency. Discussions of state encoding schemes, including one-hot, focus on area versus speed trade-offs and on fault-tolerance.

Chapter 6 introduces large designs and VHDL's capabilities to deal with hierarchy, as well as design libraries and their components. Generics are used to create parameterized components. Packages containing type declarations and components are compiled into a library for use with two large designs developed in this chapter. The first is the design of an AM2901 microprocessor slice. The second is the design of the core logic for a 100 BASE-T4 network repeater, a "real world" 8,000-gate design that illustrates the complexity of designs that programmable logic devices and VHDL synthesis tools are intended to handle. Product-term clocks, synchronization of asynchronous signals, and communicating state machines are design issues explored through this case study.

Chapter 7 illustrates how to create and use subprograms (functions and procedures) effectively in designs intended for synthesis. Subprograms are used for type conversion and as a substitute for component instantiation; examples of overloaded functions, procedures, and operators are given for both various types and various numbers of operands. The concept of module generation is introduced and compared to standard operator overloading. The subprogram body for the `std_match` function of the 1076.3 `numeric_std` package is explained.

Chapter 8 uses the FLASH370 architecture for a case study in synthesis and fitting to CPLD architectures; the pASIC380 is used for a case study in synthesis, placement, and routing to FPGA architectures. The strengths and weaknesses of both types of devices are explored, with special emphasis on how designs are realized in architectures, and how device resources can and cannot be used. Issues include routing into logic blocks, product-term distribution, clocking schemes, and loading.

Chapter 9 illustrates several techniques for optimizing datapaths, including pipelining, resource sharing, and choosing either area- or speed-optimized versions of components, such as adders, comparators, and counters. Emphasis in this chapter is on altering the design topology to meet area and speed objectives for a design.

Chapter 10 illustrates the concept of a test bench, using three methods for implementation. The first implementation uses a record to hold a table of test vectors. The second reads test vectors from a file and writes output vectors to another file. The third is a procedural approach that uses sequential statements to compute test vectors. Overloaded read and write procedures are given in the text (and in the enclosed CD-ROM) for use in reading and writing `std_logic` and `std_logic_vectors` to files.

Appendix A contains instructions for installing Warp from the CD-ROM and gaining access to on-line documentation; Appendix B contains a list of VHDL reserved words; and Appendix C contains a VHDL quick reference guide.

The organization of the book follows an emphasis on synthesis and design issues. The chapter on creating test benches is last in order to maintain this focus. Readers who wish to learn how to write test benches earlier may wish to read Chapter 10 after Chapter 4; this will equip them to write both design models and their test benches for the remainder of the exercises in the text.

Instructional Materials

Software. The text includes Cypress Semiconductor's Warp2 CPLD and FPGA synthesis, fitting, and placing and routing software. It also includes an interactive waveform simulator that performs functional simulation of CPLDs based on a JEDEC programming file.

Use of Warp is integrated into the text, but the text is not tied to the use of this software. Readers who have access to another VHDL processing tool can benefit equally from this text. Of course, some of the Breakout Exercises and end-of-chapter Problems will need modification to suit these readers' particular software environments.

Solutions Manual. A solutions manual for the problems at the end of each chapter is available to instructors through Addison-Wesley's ftp site at ftp.aw.com/cseng/authors, or through our World Wide Web site, http://www.aw.com/.

Suggestions

The reviewers helped root out inaccuracies during various stages of this manuscript. The accountability for any remaining errors lies with me. If you find any errors or have suggestions for improvement for this text, please forward them via e-mail to aw.eng@aw.com or through our World Wide Web site, http://www.aw.com/. New examples and exercises (with solutions) are also welcome.

Acknowledgments

It is a pleasure to recognize the many individuals who helped me in all phases of this project. Without their help, I would not have finished this project, or even started it. So, to begin with, I wish to thank Barry Fitzgerald for providing the impetus to get this book off the ground. Once off the ground, I relied heavily on David Johnson and Terri Fusco to manage schedules and enlist the support of others. A special debt of gratitude is owed to David Johnson for creating nearly every drawing in the text and providing guidance and assistance while I finished the book.

For the version of this text that went to reviewers, I relied on Garett Choy to capture many of the initial drawings, Krishna Rangasayee to supply additional exercises, Caleb Chan to type the quick reference guide and generate the table of contents, and Nancy Schweiger to edit. Steve Klinger performed the difficult job of indexing while also reviewing the text. For the final manuscript delivered to Addison-Wesley, Bert Koehler put the finishing touches on format and figures, and Rich Kapusta provided the glossary and technical edit.

To those colleagues who generously offered their advice and counsel on issues of VHDL, programmable logic, and design, I am especially grateful: Haneef Mohammed, Alan Coppola, Chris Jones, Jeff Freedman, John Shannon, John Nemec, Larry Hemmert, Jay Legenhausen, Tim Lacey, and Krishna Rangasayee. Chris Jones also reviewed the manuscript, providing many suggestions for improvement, and Krishna Rangasayee supplied resource material to help with Chapter 9. I wish to express my appreciation to the Warp software development group for their quick response to my questions and suggestions.

I am grateful to Greg Somer for providing the Verilog code for the 100BASE-T4 network repeater design and explaining its operation to me. A special thanks to the contributing authors: Jay Legenhausen for developing and writing much of Chapter 5, and Corey Wilner, Ron Wade, and Blair Wilson for providing material for and working on the outlines of Chapters 2, 3, and 4, respectively. Jay and Corey also provided the Solutions Manual.

Ross Smith of Configured Energy Systems, Diane Rover of Michigan State University, Bob Reese of Mississippi State University, Ralph Carestia of Oregon Institute of Technology, Tom Chiacchira, and Daniel Harmon reviewed the manuscript and provided valuable constructive criticism and advice to help improve the text. I hope they are pleased with the result.

The team at Addison-Wesley was instrumental through the development of this book. Tim Cox lent his support from the book's conception. He and Laura Cheu acquired reviewers and provided feedback to improve the text and integrate the use of the software into the text. Lisa Weber lead me through the production process, Elizabeth Gehrman performed a careful copy edit, and many others behind the scenes helped produce this book.

I would also like to recognize the support I received from the management at Cypress Semiconductor while I worked on this project. Thanks to John Hamburger, David Johnson, Al Graf, David Barringer, and J. Daniel McCranie.

Thanks most of all to my wife Karen for her encouragement, patience, and support throughout this long process.

Kevin Skahill
Sunnyvale, California
March, 1996

⚠ Addison-Wesley Tech Support

To the Student

Addison-Wesley provides help for students with installation issues, or if you feel you have received a defective product. We do not provide assistance with "how to" questions. Please consult with your instructor if you have a question on how to use the software, or if it appears a particular command or function does not give the expected results.

To the Instructor

We will be happy to provide assistance to adopters of Warp with any issue that may arise. Please understand that on some occasions we may need to consult with the software developer for answers to specific problems, but we will make every attempt to obtain a rapid answer for you.

Before You Call Tech Support

- Please take time to consult the Warp manuals in the Acrobat files on the CD and any release notes that came with the software. These items might answer your questions.

- Please document the problem if you are receiving error messages. When do they occur? What is the exact message? Can you recreate it?

- Check that your computer hardware setup meets or exceeds the minimum system requirements printed on the back cover of this book. Please take a moment to compare your hardware against the system requirements. Are your hardware and peripherals set up correctly and are all cables attached securely?

- Verify that your CD drive can read the CD correctly. A quick way to check this is to view the directory of the CD. Do you see files?

- Be prepared to state the specifics of your computer hardware setup and the release of Warp that you are using so we can answer your questions efficiently.

Reaching Addison-Wesley Tech Support

Voice: (617) 944-2630   Monday–Friday, 9:00 a.m. to 4:30 p.m., EST
Fax: (617) 944-9338   Anytime
Email: techsprt@aw.com   Anytime

Chapter 1

Introduction

In the first half of the 1990s, the electronics industry experienced an explosion in the demand for personal computers, cellular telephones, and high-speed data communications devices. Vying for market share, vendors built products with increasingly greater functionality, higher performance, lower cost, lower power consumption, and smaller dimensions. To do this, vendors created highly integrated, complex systems with fewer IC devices and less printed-circuit-board (PCB) area. The submicron semiconductor process, PCB manufacturing, and surface-mount packaging technologies supported increased integration. The bottleneck for some vendors appeared to be the ability of designers to deal with the increasing complexity of designs, given the existing electronic design automation (EDA) tools and accelerated time-to-market schedules. This situation fostered the need for widespread adoption of modern methodologies in design and test. Both high-density programmable logic devices (PLDs) and VHDL, the Very High Speed Integrated Circuit (VHSIC) Hardware Description Language, became key elements in these methodologies.

Higher density programmable logic devices, including complex PLDs (CPLDs) and field programmable gate arrays (FPGAs), can be used to integrate large amounts of logic in a single IC. Semicustom and full-custom application specific integrated circuit (ASIC) devices are also used for integrating large amounts of digital logic, but CPLDs and FPGAs provide additional flexibility: they can be used with tighter schedules, for low volume products, and for first production runs even with high-volume products. They are also attractive for projects requiring low nonrecurring engineering (NRE) expenses.

VHDL is particularly well suited for designing with programmable logic devices, and it is gaining in popularity. Designing with larger capacity CPLDs and FPGAs of 500 to more than 100,000 gates, engineers can no longer use Boolean equations or gate-level descriptions to quickly and efficiently complete a design.

1

VHDL provides high-level language constructs that enable designers to describe large circuits and bring products to market rapidly. It supports the creation of design libraries in which to store components for reuse in subsequent designs. Because it is a standard language (IEEE standard 1076), VHDL provides portability of code between synthesis and simulation tools, as well as device-independent design. It also facilitates converting a design from a programmable logic to an ASIC implementation.

Simple PLDs of fewer than 500 gates have been used successfully for some time now for design flexibility and integration on a smaller scale. Traditional design techniques, such as Karnaugh maps, are typically used to generate design equations that are implemented in a PLD. Using a simple language with a syntax for entering combinational and registered equations, the designer enters design equations in a data file. The equations are then synthesized by software, which produces a data file to use in programming the PLD.

For larger systems that use CPLDs, FPGAs, or ASICs, the traditional design methodology described above is not feasible: Generating equations with traditional techniques is time-consuming and prone to mistakes. Tracking errors in equations can also be difficult. Schematic capture offers several advantages. For example, it provides a graphical view of the design, and with software tools that support schematic hierarchy, it provides for design modularity. But as a means for capturing large designs, even pure schematic capture has its drawbacks:

- control logic must still be generated using traditional design techniques;
- schematics can be difficult to maintain because the intent of the design is often clouded by its implementation;
- a schematic must often be accompanied by documentation to describe a design's functionality, yet descriptions in English or any other spoken language are open to interpretation;
- schematic capture environments are proprietary, so a designer who works in a schematic capture environment for one project may not be able to reuse material when working on a new project that requires the use of a new schematic capture environment;
- the simulation environment supported by the PLD schematic capture tool may not fit with the system design environment, making design verification difficult at best.

A more appropriate design methodology is one that increases the efficiency of designers. At a slightly more detailed level, it facilitates capturing, understanding, and maintaining a design; it is not open to interpretation, but is well defined; it is an open—not proprietary—standard accepted by industry; it allows designs to be ported from one EDA environment to another, so that modules can be packaged and reused; it supports complex designs with hierarchy and gate-level to system-level design; it may be used for the description, synthesis, and simulation of logic circuits; and it supports multiple levels of design description.

At this time only two languages satisfy these requirements for digital logic design: VHDL and Verilog. Verilog is considered less verbose than VHDL, but one can argue that this is at the expense of language richness and features. For the combined purposes of documentation, synthesis, and simulation for both devices and systems, VHDL is an excellent choice.

VHDL is a product of the VHSIC program funded by the Department of Defense in the 1970s and 1980s. When the language was first developed, it was intended to be a standard means to document complex circuits so that a design documented by one contractor could be understood by another. It was also intended to be used as a modeling language that could be processed by software for simulation purposes. VHDL was established as the IEEE 1076 standard in 1987. In 1988, MilStd454 required that all ASICs delivered to the Department of Defense be described in VHDL, and in 1993, the IEEE 1076 standard was updated and an additional VHDL standard, IEEE 1164, was adopted. In 1996, IEEE 1076.3 became a VHDL synthesis standard.

Today VHDL is an industry standard for the description, modeling, and synthesis of digital circuits and systems. In 1993, the market for VHDL simulators exceeded the Verilog simulator market, according to *Electronic Engineering Times*. A primary driving force behind the growth in the use of VHDL has been **synthesis**— the reduction of a design description to a lower-level circuit representation (such as a netlist). The entire synthesis market has reached approximately $100 million, with a growth rate of 20 to 30 percent a year. Because of this, engineers in many facets of the electronics industry—from ASIC designers to system level designers—must learn VHDL to increase their efficiency.

Because it has such wide-ranging capabilities, VHDL is a language that serves the needs of designers at many levels. This book presents VHDL within the context of synthesis and design. We explore a number of applications of VHDL for designing with programmable logic, in contrast to focusing on syntax and language structure, an abstract and theoretical approach that tends to emphasize VHDL models that cannot be synthesized, because the designs are either physically meaningless or contain constructs that are not particularly well suited for synthesis. We present VHDL in the context of synthesis and design for two reasons. First, this approach provides an effective framework to facilitate learning the language. It stresses active learning in which the reader is asked to use the language to create designs. Second, it allows the reader to use the language as it is used on the job. What this text teaches about VHDL is also applicable to other uses of VHDL. At times our discussion will draw on modeling concepts in order to clarify what it means to a design engineer to write VHDL code for synthesis versus simulation.

1.1   Why Use VHDL?

Every design engineer in the electronics industry should soon learn and use a hardware description language to keep pace with the productivity of competitors. With VHDL, you can quickly describe and synthesize circuits of five, 10, or 20 thousand gates. Equivalent designs described with schematics or Boolean equations at the register-transfer level can require several months of work by one person. In addition, VHDL provides the capabilities described below.

1.1.1   Power and Flexibility

VHDL has powerful language constructs with which to write succinct code descriptions of complex control logic. It also has multiple levels of design description for controlling design implementation. It supports design libraries and the creation of reusable components. It provides for design hierarchies to create modular designs. It is one language for design *and* simulation.

1.1.2   Device-Independent Design

VHDL permits you to create a design without having to first choose a device for implementation. With one design description, you can target many device architectures. You do not have to become intimately familiar with a device's architecture in order to optimize your design for resource utilization or performance. Instead, you can concentrate on creating your design. (Though this, of course, does not eliminate the need for datapath optimization techniques, such as pipelining, which we will discuss in Chapter 9.) VHDL also permits multiple styles of design description. For example, Figure 1-1 illustrates four ways to describe a 2-bit comparator.

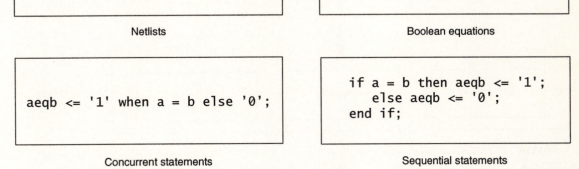

```
u1: xor2 port map(a(0), b(0), x(0));
u2: xor2 port map(a(1), b(1), x(1));
u3: nor2 port map(x(0), x(1), aeqb);
```

Netlists

```
aeqb <= (a(0) XOR b(0)) NOR
        (a(1) XOR b(1));
```

Boolean equations

```
aeqb <= '1' when a = b else '0';
```

Concurrent statements

```
if a = b then aeqb <= '1';
   else aeqb <= '0';
end if;
```

Sequential statements

Figure 1-1   VHDL permits several classes of design description

1.1.3   Portability

VHDL's portability permits you to simulate the same design description that you synthesized. Simulating a several-thousand-gate design description before synthesizing it can save considerable time: a design flaw (bug) discovered at this stage can be corrected before the design implementation stage. Because VHDL is a standard, your design description can be taken from one simulator to another, one synthesis tool to another, and one platform to another. This means that VHDL design descriptions can be used in multiple projects, and that your skills in using one EDA tool are useful with another. Figure 1-2 illustrates that the source code for a design can be used with any synthesis tool, and that the design can be implemented in any device that is supported by a synthesis tool.

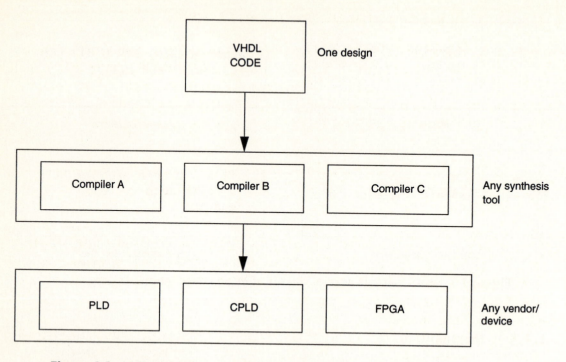

Figure 1-2 VHDL provides portability between compilers and device-independent design

1.1.4   Benchmarking Capabilities

Device-independent design and portability allow you to benchmark a design using different device architectures and different synthesis tools. You no longer have to know before you start a design which device you will use or whether it will be a CPLD or an FPGA. You can take a completed design description and synthesize it, creating logic for an architecture of your choice. You can then evaluate the results and choose the device that best fits your design requirements. The same can be done for synthesis tools in order to measure the quality of the synthesis.

1.1.5   ASIC Migration

The efficiency that VHDL generates allows your product to hit the market quickly if you synthesize the design to a CPLD or FPGA. When production volumes reach appropriate levels, VHDL facilitates the development of an ASIC. Sometimes, the exact code used with the PLD can be used with the ASIC. And because VHDL is a well defined language, you can be assured that your ASIC vendor will deliver a device with the expected functionality.

1.1.6   Quick Time-to-Market and Low Cost

VHDL and programmable logic pair well together to facilitate a speedy design process. VHDL permits designs to be described quickly. Programmable logic eliminates NRE expenses and facilitates quick design iterations. Synthesis makes it all possible. VHDL and programmable logic combine as a powerful vehicle to bring your products to market in record time.

1.2   Shortcomings

Design engineers express three common concerns about VHDL: (1) You give up control of defining the gate-level implementation of circuits that are described with high-level, abstract constructs, (2) the logic implementations created by synthesis tools are inefficient, and (3) the quality of synthesis varies from tool to tool.

There's not a direct way around the first "shortcoming." In fact, the intent of using VHDL as a language for synthesis is to free the engineer from having to specify gate-level circuit implementation. However, if you understand how the compiler synthesizes logic, you're likely to realize that the compiler will optimally implement most constructs, and you will have little need or desire to dictate implementation policy. Most synthesis tools allow the designer to use synthesis directives to obtain some level of control over implementation, especially to make area-efficient versus speed-efficient implementation choices. Many synthesis tools also allow designers to specify technology-specific, gate-level implementations. Descriptions of these types, however, are neither high-level nor device-independent.

The concern that logic synthesis is inefficient is not without warrant. VHDL compilers will not always produce optimal implementations, especially because the optimal solution depends on the design objectives. Compilers use algorithms to decide upon logic implementations, following standard design methodologies. An algorithm cannot look at a design problem in a unique way. Sometimes, there is no substitute for human creativity, and when this is the case you will want to code your design in a way that lets you control the design implementation. The complaint that synthesis provides poor implementations is also commonly the result of inefficient code. Like inefficient C code, which results in slow execution times or poor memory utilization, inefficient VHDL code results in unneeded, repetitive, or nonoptimal logic.

The third shortcoming is being addressed by the marketplace. Fortunately, VHDL synthesis for CPLDs and FPGAs is emerging from its infancy, the competition is growing, and synthesis technology is maturing in a process similar to what C compilers went through. Not long ago, a typical C compiler may have produced executable code that in some cases was so inefficient that it was worth a designer's time to write assembly code instead. Today, while there are still cases in which assembly code is appropriate, the vast majority of code must be written at a higher level. C compilers have matured to the point where the average engineer often can't write as efficient executable code. Certainly, the engineer's time is usually better spent elsewhere, considering the massive size of today's software programs.

If you still believe that these shortcomings are too large to make it worthwhile to use VHDL at this point, take heed of the larger picture. As an engineer you should resist the temptation to believe that the details of a design's implementation are as important as the design objectives: fulfilling the design requirements, meeting the price-point, and getting the product to market quickly. Meeting design objectives is essential; the implementation is secondary.

1.3   Using VHDL for Design Synthesis

The design process can be broken into the six steps below. We'll explain each briefly in this section.The remainder of the text will focus primarily on steps 2 and 4; Chapter 10 will focus on steps 3 and 5.

1. Define the design requirements
2. Describe the design in VHDL (formulate and code the design)
3. Simulate the source code
4. Synthesize, optimize, and fit (place and route) the design
5. Simulate the post-layout (fit) design model
6. Program the device

1.3.1   Define the Design Requirements

Before launching into writing code for your design, you should have a clear idea of the design objectives and requirements. What is the function of the design? What are the required setup and clock-to-output times, maximum frequency of operation, and critical paths? Having a clear idea of the requirements may help you to choose a design methodology and the device architecture to which you will initially synthesize your design.

1.3.2   Describe the Design in VHDL

Formulate the Design. Having defined the design requirements, you may be tempted to jump right into coding, but we suggest that you first decide upon a design methodology. By having an idea of how your design will be described, you will tend to write more efficient code that is realized, through synthesis, to the logic implementation you intended.

You're probably already familiar with the methodologies: top-down, bottom-up, or flat. The first two methods involve creating design hierarchies, the latter involves describing the circuit as a monolithic design.

The top-down approach requires that you divide your design into functional components, each component having specific (but not always unique) inputs and outputs and performing a particular function. A top-level module is created to tie the design components together, as in a netlist, then the components themselves are designed. The bottom-up approach involves just the opposite: defining and designing the individual components, then bringing the pieces together to form the overall design. A flat design is one in which the details of functional components are defined at the same level as the interconnection of those functional components.

Flat designs work well for small designs, where having details of the underlying definition of a functional block does not distract from understanding the functionality of the chip-level design. For many of the smaller designs in this text, a flat approach is used. Hierarchical schemes prove useful in large designs consisting of multiple complex functional components. Levels of hierarchy can clarify the interconnection of components. Avoid using too many levels of hierarchy, however, because excessive levels make it difficult to understand the interconnection of design elements and the relevance to the overall design.

Code the Design. After deciding upon a design methodology, you can reference your block-, dataflow-, and state diagrams as you code your design, being careful of syntax and semantics. If you're like many engineers, you will simply follow or edit an existing example to meet your particular needs. The key to writing good VHDL code is to think in terms of hardware. More specifically, think as the synthesis software "thinks" to understand how your design will be realized. A good portion of this book is devoted to helping you think like synthesis software so that you will write efficient code.

1.3.3   Simulate the Source Code

For large designs, simulating the source code with a VHDL simulator will prove time-efficient. The process of concurrent engineering (performing tasks in parallel rather than in series) brings circuit simulation (once a late-stage task) to the early stages of design. With source code simulation, flaws can be detected early in the design cycle, allowing you to make corrections with the least possible impact to the schedule. For small designs, it is sometimes unnecessary or inefficient to simulate the source code. However, for larger designs, for which synthesis and place and route can take a couple of hours, you can significantly reduce your design iteration and debugging cycle times by simulating your source code before synthesis. Also, large designs are usually hierarchical, consisting of several subdesigns or modules. This modularity allows you to verify and debug each subdesign before assembling the hierarchy, potentially saving considerable time over verifying and debugging a monolithic design. Initially, you should not spend a lot of time simulating the source code, because after synthesis, you may discover that you need to modify your design (by introducing a pipeline stage, for example) in order to meet performance objectives. In this case, time spent with an exhaustive verification of the source code would be ill spent, since a new verification would be required after the design change.

1.3.4   Synthesize, Optimize, and Fit the Design

Synthesis. We have already used the word synthesis several times now, and given a brief definition—it is the reduction of a design description to a lower-level circuit representation (such as a netlist). In other words, synthesis is the process by which netlists or equations are created from design descriptions, which may be abstract. It is a process that should be described as taking a design description as input and producing output (logic equations or netlists). For brevity, however, we may at times drop either the input or output, and use phrases such as "synthesize logic descriptions," "synthesize logic," and "logic synthesis."

VHDL synthesis software tools convert VHDL descriptions to technology-specific netlists or sets of equations. Synthesis tools allow designers to design logic circuits by creating design descriptions without necessarily having to perform Boolean algebra or create technology-specific, optimized netlists. A designer presents an abstract description of his or her design, specifying the function of the digital circuit, and the synthesis software produces a set of equations to be fitted to a PLD/CPLD or a netlist to be placed and routed in an FPGA.

Synthesis should be technology-specific. In other words, the rendering of a netlist from a VHDL description may be different for one device architecture than it is for another. Figure 1-3 illustrates the synthesis and optimization processes. Before synthesis, a software tool must read the design and parse it, checking for syntax errors and possibly a few semantic errors as well. The synthesis process then converts the design to internal data structures, translating its "behavior" to a register-transfer level (RTL) description. RTL descriptions specify registers, signal inputs, signal outputs, and the combinational logic between them. Other RTL elements depend on the specific features of a device architecture. (For example, some programmable logic devices contain XOR gates.) At this point, the combinational logic is still represented by internal data structures. Some synthesis tools will search the data structures for identifiable operators and their operands, replacing these portions of logic with technology-specific, optimized components. These operators can be as simple as identifying the use of an XOR gate for an architecture that has one, or as complicated as inferring a 16-bit add operation. Other portions of logic that are not identified are then converted to Boolean expressions that are not yet optimized.

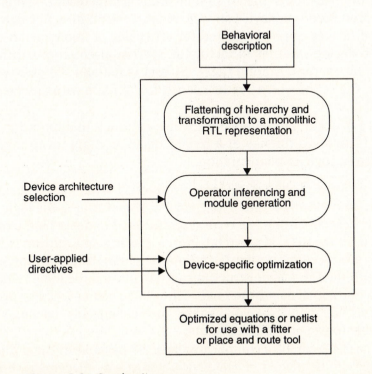

Figure 1-3 Synthesis process

Optimization. The optimization process depends on three things: the form of the Boolean expressions, the type of resources available, and automatic or user-applied synthesis directives (sometimes called **constraints**). Some forms of expressions may be mapped to logic resources more efficiently than others. For example, whereas a minimal sum of products can be implemented efficiently in a PAL, a canonical sum of products can be mapped more efficiently to a multiplexer or RAM. Sometimes a canonical or minimal product of sums may be the best representation for the target technology. Other user or automatic constraints may be applied to optimize expressions for the available resources. These constraints may be to limit the number of appearances of a literal in an expression (to reduce signal loading), limit the number of literals in an expression (to reduce fan-in), or limit the number of terms in an expression.

Optimizing for CPLDs usually involves reducing the logic to a minimal sum of products, which is then further optimized for a minimal literal count. This reduces the product-term utilization and the number of logic block inputs required for any given expression. These equations are then passed to the fitter for further device-specific optimization. Optimizing for FPGAs typically requires that the logic be expressed in forms other than a sum of products. Instead, systems of equations may be factored based on device-specific resources and directive-driven optimization goals. The factors can be evaluated for efficiency of implementation. Criteria can be used to decide whether to factor the system of equations differently or keep the current factors. Among these criteria is usually the ability to share common factors, the set of which can be cached to compare with any newly created factors.

Another method for optimizing does not involve as much manipulation of Boolean expressions; it involves the use of a binary decision diagram to map a given equation to a specific logic implementation.

Fitting. **Fitting** is the process of taking the logic produced by the synthesis and optimization processes, and placing it into a logic device, transforming the logic (if necessary) to obtain the best fit. Fitting is a term typically used to describe the process of allocating resources for CPLD-type architectures. **Placing and routing** is the process of taking logic produced by synthesis and optimization, transforming it if necessary, packing it into the FPGA logic structures (cells), placing the logic cells in optimal locations, and routing signals from logic cell to logic cell or I/O. For brevity, we will use the terms "fit" and "place and route" interchangeably, leaving you to discern when we mean to use one or both terms.

Fitting designs in a CPLD can be a complicated process because of the numerous ways in which logic can be placed in the device. Before any placement, however, the logic equations are further optimized, again depending upon the available resources. For example, some macrocells permit the configuration of a flip-flop to be D-type or T-type, and also allow the output polarity to be selected. In such a case, logic expressions for the true and complement of both the D-type and T-type should be generated. The optimal implementation can then be chosen from the four versions for each expression. After all equation transformations, expressions that share scarce resources (perhaps resets and presets, clocks, output enables, and input macrocells) can be grouped together. Expressions are also grouped together based upon user constraints such as pin assignment. The groups can then be examined to verify that they can be placed together in a logic block. Thus the collective resources of the group must be evaluated: number of required macrocells, independent resets and presets, output enables, unique product terms, clocks (and clock polarity), total input signals, and total output signals. If any of the groups cannot fit within the physical limitations of a logic block, they are adjusted. Next, an initial placement is attempted. If a legal placement is not found, the grouping process may start over, possibly based on a different scarce resource. Once locations are found for all of the logic elements, routing between inputs, outputs, and logic cells is attempted. If routing cannot be completed with the given placement, the router may suggest a new grouping. Once a routing solution has been found, a fit has been achieved.

Place and Route. Place and route tools have a large impact on the performance of FPGA designs. Propagation delays can depend significantly on routing delays. A "good" placement and route will place critical portions of a circuit close together to eliminate routing delays. Place and route tools use algorithms, directives, user-applied constraints, and performance estimates to choose an initial placement. Algorithms can then iterate on small changes to the placement to approach a layout that is expected to meet performance requirements. Routing may then begin, with global routing structures used first for high-fanout signals or signals that must route over large distances. Local routing structures may then be used to route local inter-logic cell and I/O signal paths.

Figure 1-4 on page 14 shows the process of synthesizing, optimizing, and fitting the following equality comparator into a CPLD and an FPGA:

```
aeqb <= '1' when (a = b) else '0';
```

There are many synthesis tool vendors on the market today. Among the most popular are Synopsys, Cadence, Mentor Graphics, Viewlogic, Data I/O, Synplicity, and several programmable logic vendors that provide their own device-specific synthesis. Each synthesis vendor uses different, proprietary algorithms for synthesizing logic, so resulting logic implementations from one vendor to another will vary (but be functionally equivalent), just as the results of compiling C code with different compilers differ. Nonetheless, there are some fundamental synthesis policies that apply across synthesis tools, making a general discussion of synthesis possible.

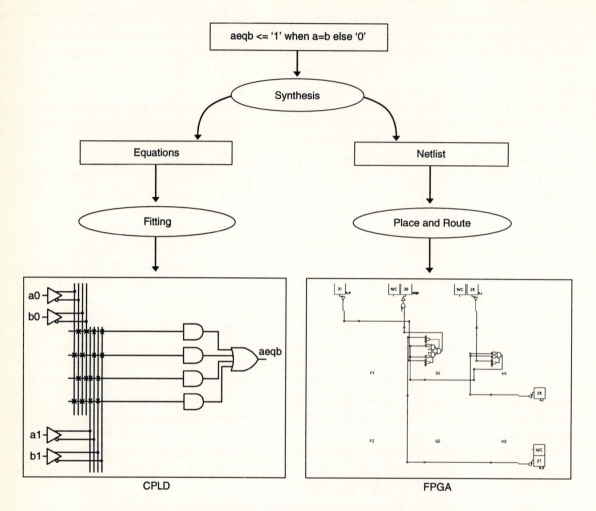

Figure 1-4 The process of synthesis to design implementation

1.3.5   Simulate the Postlayout Design Model

Even if you have performed a presynthesis simulation, you will want to simulate your design after it has been fitted (or placed and routed). A postlayout simulation will enable you to verify not only the functionality of your design but also the timing, such as setup, clock-to-output, and register-to-register times. If you are unable to meet your design objectives, then you will need to either resynthesize and fit your design to a new logic device, massage (using compiler directives) any combination of the synthesis or fitting processes, or choose a different speed grade device. You may also want to revisit your VHDL code to ensure that it has been described efficiently and in such a way as to achieve a synthesis and fitting result that meets your design objectives.

1.3.6 Program the Device

After completing the design description, synthesizing, optimizing, fitting, and successfully simulating your design, you are ready to program your device and continue work on the rest of your system design. The synthesis, optimization, and fitting software will produce a file for use in programming the device.

1.4 Design Tool Flow

Having covered the design process, we are now ready to present the EDA tool flow. The tool flow diagram of Figure 1-5 shows the inputs and outputs for each tool used in the design process.

The inputs to the synthesis software are the VHDL design source code, synthesis directives, and device selection. Synthesis directives may be explicit directives used to influence the synthesis and fitting processes, or they may be default options passed by the graphical user interface (GUI) to the underlying synthesis software. Device selection is required at this stage in order to perform device-specific synthesis and optimization.

The output of the synthesis software—an architecture-specific netlist or set of equations—is then used as the input to the fitter (or place and route software, depending on whether the target device is a CPLD or FPGA). Directives may be passed from the synthesis to the fitter software by embedding information in the intermediate file. The fitter or place and route software then performs the task of fitting or placing and routing. The outputs of this tool are information about resource utilization, static, point-to-point, timing analysis, a device programming file, and a postlayout simulation model. The resource utilization and static timing information are used by the designer to see whether synthesis and fitting yielded the desired results. The device programming file is used with a device programmer and other software to program a PLD. The postlayout simulation model may be a VHDL model that can be simulated (but not synthesized, for reasons that will be explained in Chapter 3), or some other format, including Verilog. Multiple formats are typically supported by a vendor so that they can fit into the numerous system environments of its customers.

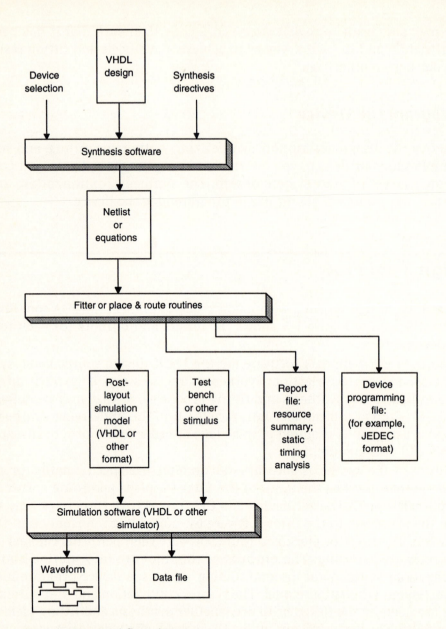

Figure 1-5   Tool flow diagram

The simulation model, along with a test bench or other stimulus format, is used as input to the simulation software. Many simulators provide for interactive simulation. That is, they allow you to apply stimulus, advance simulation time, observe results, and iterate on this process. The outputs of simulation software are often waveforms or data files.

1.5   Our System

We will be using Cypress's Warp2 VHDL synthesis software to synthesize, optimize, and fit designs to CPLD and FPGA devices. A copy of this software is
included with this text. As mentioned in the preface, the use of this software is
integrated into the body of the text; however, the body of the text is not tied to the
use of Warp. Any VHDL synthesis software will suffice for applying the concepts
illustrated throughout the text.

The Warp2 Release 4.0 software consists of

- VHDL synthesis software for use with several PLDs, CPLDs, and FPGAs;
- fitter software for PLDs and CPLDs;
- place and route software for use with FPGAs;
- a JEDEC format simulator for functional simulation of PLD and CPLD
  implementations;
- a static timing analyzer for use in the place and route tool.

The fitter will output VHDL models in case you already have access to a
VHDL simulator. Warp3, which is not included with this text, includes a VHDL simulator, as well as a schematic capture tool, both based on Viewlogic.

The first breakout exercise follows the next section. It will have you install
the software and run through the tutorial described in the on-line documentation.
This exercise will acquaint you with the tool flow and the GUI.

1.6   Font Conventions

In this book, VHDL code listings and code within text are printed in monospaced
font to distinguish them from regular text. The following paragraph illustrates the
use of this font convention.

The lack of an `else` after `elsif enable` implies that `cnt` will retain its
value if neither of the previous conditions (`load` or `enable`) is true.

In this paragraph, `else`, `elsif enable`, `cnt`, `load`, and `enable` are in monospaced
font because they represent VHDL code; in code listings, reserved words and
predefined attributes appear in bold. Bold regular text is used to identify new
terms, and italic regular text is used for emphasis.

▼

Breakout Exercise 1-1

Purpose: To learn the Warp tool flow.

Read each step completely before performing any operations. You should resist the temptation to select options other than those prescribed until after you have completed the exercise.

1. Install the Warp software on your PC. Refer to Appendix A for installation instructions. For this exercise, we will assume that you have installed the software in the default installation directory, `c:\warp`.

2. Create the directory `c:\vhdlbook` and copy the contents of `c:\warp\examples\vdhlbook` to `c:\vhdlbook`. For all Breakout Exercises in this text, we will assume that you have completed this step.

3. Start Windows. Double-click on the Galaxy icon in the Warp2 program group. This will launch Galaxy, the GUI for the Warp software.

4. A dialog box will appear, prompting you for the name of a new project. Enter the name `c:\vhdlbook\ch1\break1` (Figure 1-6). This will create a project named `break1`, for Breakout Exercise 1-1, in the `c:\vhdlbook\ch1` directory. A Galaxy project will appear, with the project name listed in the title bar of the window (Figure 1-7).

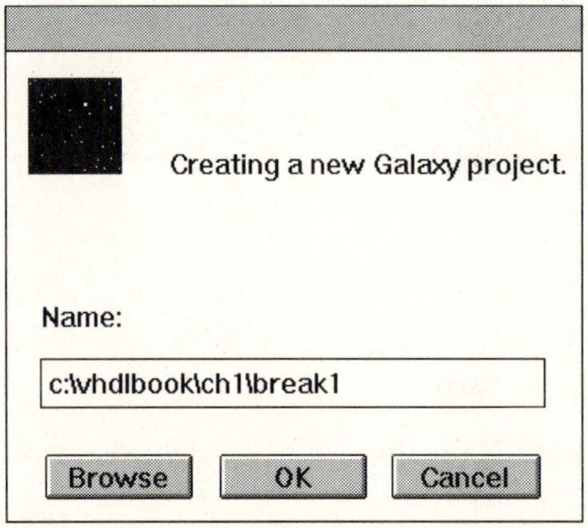

Creating a new Galaxy project.

Name:

c:\vhdlbook\ch1\break1

Browse   OK   Cancel

Figure 1-6 Creating a new project

Project: c:\vhdlbook\ch1\warp

Project   Files   Info   Search   Tools   Font   Help

Edit
  Selected   New

Compile
  Selected   Smart

Synthesis options
  File   Generic
  Set top   Device

Top design: <none>   Device:

Figure 1-7   Project window

5. From the **Files** menu, select **Add All**. The file name `simple.vhd` will appear in the project file list. It will be highlighted in blue, indicating that it is selected.

6. Click on the **Selected** button in the **Edit** panel. This opens Warp's text editor and automatically loads the selected file (in this case, `simple.vhd`). View the VHDL code. It is not important at this time for you to understand the syntax and semantics of the code. The design describes the logic of Figure 1-8.

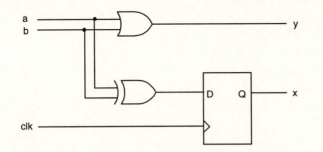

Figure 1-8   Logic described in `simple.vhd`

7. Select **Close** from the **File** menu of the text editor. If you have modified the file, *do not* save changes.

8. Click on **Set top** in the **Synthesis options** panel. The status bar on the bottom left will indicate that this is the top-level design. This tells the synthesis compiler that the design is intended to be implemented in a device, not compiled to a library.

9. Click on **Device** from the **Synthesis options** panel. This brings up a dialog box. Select C371 from the device scroll list (Figure 1-9). We will be synthesizing and fitting this design to a CY7C371 FLASH370 CPLD. Also, select 1164/VHDL from the post-JEDEC simulation scroll list. This will cause the fitter to produce a VHDL file that can be used with a VHDL simulator for postfit functional and timing verification. Leave all other selections with their default values, and click the **OK** button.

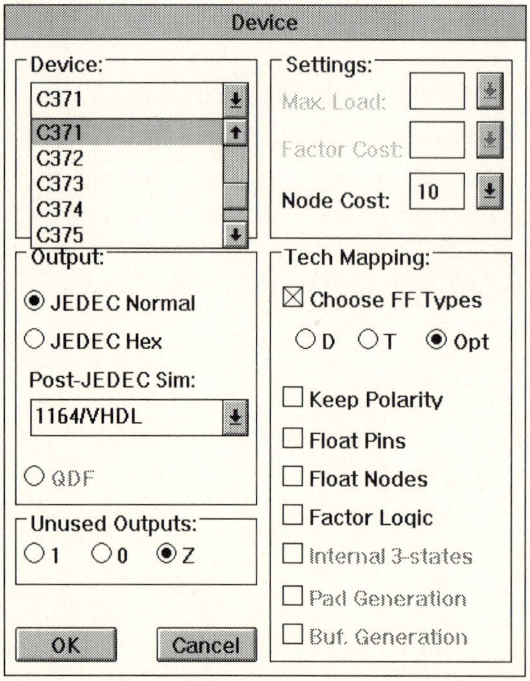

Figure 1-9 Device selection

10. Click the **Smart** button from the **Compile** panel. This will cause a compilation window to appear and the synthesis software to process the VHDL code (Figure 1-10). After synthesis is complete, the fitter software will be invoked automatically. Once the design is successfully synthesized and fitted to the CY7C371, the software also produces a postfit simulation model. When this is complete, the status bar in the lower-left of the compilation window will indicate a successful compilation. At this point, select **Close** from the **File** menu of the compilation window.

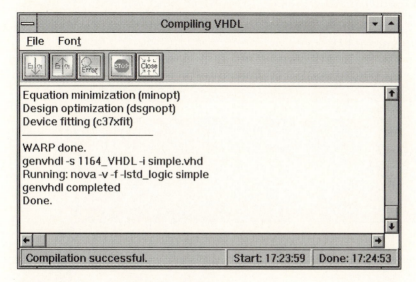

Figure 1-10 Compilation window

11. Verify that the JEDEC file, `simple.jed`, used for programming the CY7C371, was created and placed in the project directory. Also verify that a subdirectory named `c:\vhdlbook\ch1\break1\vhd` was created and the file `simple.vhd` was placed in it. Although this file has the same name as the source code, its contents are different. It contains a postfit model of the design as implemented in the CY7C371.

12. Warp2 does not have a VHDL simulator. Instead it has a functional simulator that simulates the JEDEC file produced by the synthesis and fitting software. This simulator is called Nova. From the **Tools** menu, select **Nova** to start the simulator.

13. In Nova, select **Open** from the **File** menu. Select the file name `simple.jed`.

14. Several traces will appear in the Nova window. Click once on the button for signal c1k. This will cause the c1k trace to turn light blue, indicating that it is selected. Select **clock** from the **Edit** menu. This brings up a dialog box. Click on **OK** to accept the default values.

15. Next, place the cursor over the trace for signal a. Click and hold the left mouse button, dragging it to the right over a portion of the signal trace a. Release the button. Type 1 on the keyboard, or select **High** from the **Project** menu. Refer to Section 6.5, "The Edit Menu," of Warp's on-line user's guide, if you need further instructions on this procedure.

16. Select **Execute** from the **Simulate** menu. The output traces x and y will be updated (Figure 1-11).

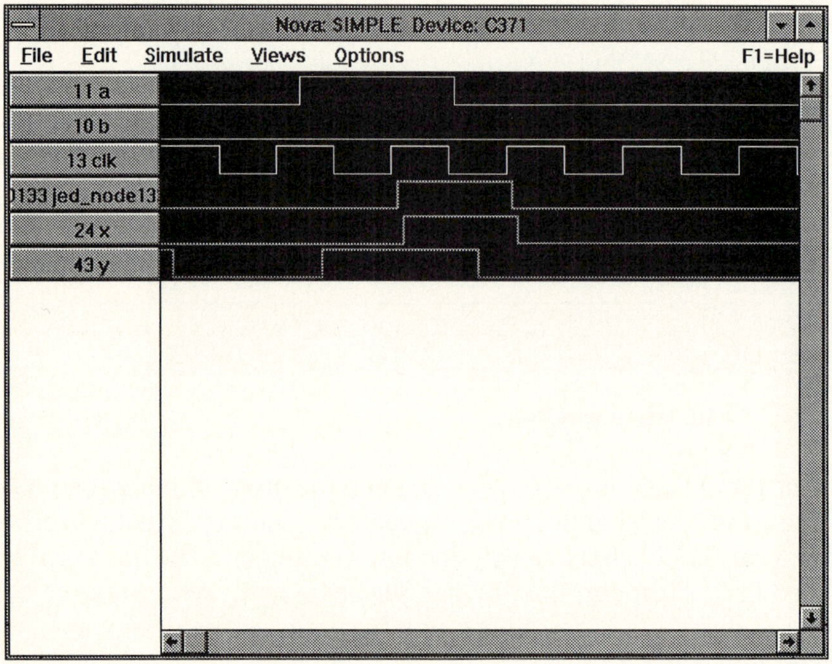

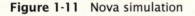

Figure 1-11   Nova simulation

17. Verify that the output waveforms are accurate for the circuit of Figure 1-8. (Traces other than for a, b, c1k, x, and y are internal device nodes. These signals may be removed from the trace window using the **Edit Views** option in the **Views** menu.)

18. Select **Exit** from Nova's **File** menu.

19. Select **Save** from Galaxy's **Project** menu. This will save break1 as a project that contains the simple.vhd design with the options currently selected.

This completes the tool flow for synthesizing and fitting a design to a CPLD within the Warp2 design environment. Do not delete the files created by the software during this exercise. We will be using one of these files in a Breakout Exercise in the next chapter, where we will also synthesize, place, and route a design in an FPGA.

1.7   Summary

In this chapter we outlined the scope of this text, described some of the benefits of using VHDL, and enumerated the design process steps, providing brief explanations of each. In the next chapter, we discuss programmable logic devices and their architectures. In the chapters after that, we introduce VHDL as well as synthesis, optimization, and design issues.

Problems

1.1. What are the advantages and benefits of using VHDL?

1.2. Give two design examples for which it is appropriate to skip source code simulation, in favor of synthesizing and fitting the design first, and simulating only the postlayout model.

1.3. Give two design examples for which it is appropriate to perform source code simulation in addition to postlayout simulation.

1.4. What are some concerns that designers voice when using VHDL? List 10 words or phrases that indicate VHDL's strengths as a language for design synthesis.

1.5. How would the descriptions in Figure 1-1 change if the output were altb (*a* less than *b*)?

Chapter 2

Programmable Logic Primer

2.1   Introduction

This chapter establishes a context for learning VHDL and shows that our purpose is to implement designs in programmable logic. In this chapter, we explain the motivation for using programmable logic as well as the programmable logic design process, and illustrate how device resources may be utilized. Important data-sheet timing specifications are also explained. If you are already familiar with simple PLD architectures, you may wish to skip to the sections on CPLDs and FPGAs, in which we introduce the defining features of these architectures and of many popular devices, as well as the decisions that go into selecting an appropriate device for an application.

2.2   Why Use Programmable Logic?

Not long ago, Texas Instruments' TTL Series 54/74 logic circuits were the mainstay of digital logic design for implementing "glue logic": combinational and sequential logic for multiplexing, encoding, decoding, selecting, registering, and designing state machines and other control logic. These SSI and MSI logic circuits include discrete logic gates, specific boolean transfer functions, and memory elements, as well as counters, shift registers, and arithmetic circuits. Table 2-1 describes just a few of the members of the 54/74 Series.

Table 2-1   TTL Series 54/74 logic circuits

54/74 Series	Description
7400	Quadruple 2-input positive-NAND gates: $Y = \overline{AB}$
7402	Quadruple 2-input positive-NOR gates: $Y = \overline{A + B}$
7404	Hex inverters: $Y = \overline{A}$
7408	Quadruple 2-input positive-AND gates: $Y = AB$
7430	8-input positive-NAND gates: $Y = \overline{ABCDEFGH}$
7432	Quadruple 2-input positive-OR gates: $Y = A + B$
7451	Dual AND-OR-INVERT gates: $Y = \overline{AB + CD}$
7474	Dual D-type positive-edge-triggered flip-flops with preset and clear
7483	4-bit binary full adder with fast carry
7486	Quadruple 2-input exclusive-OR gates: $Y = A \oplus B$
74109	Dual J-K positive-edge-triggered flip-flops with preset and clear
74157	Quadruple 2-to-1 multiplexers
74163	Synchronous 4-bit counter with synchronous clear
74180	9-bit odd/even parity generator/checker
74374	Octal D-type flip-flops

2.2.1   Designing with TTL Logic

Armed with this inventory of TTL logic, digital designers could attack a problem following the standard design flow of Figure 2-1. Suppose, for example, that we were designing a network repeater consisting of four communication ports A, B, C, and D. A collision signal X must be asserted if more than one port's carrier sense is active at a time. Signal X is to be synchronized to the transmit clock.

From the design specifications, we can generate a truth table (Figure 2-2). Each row of the truth table in which X takes on the value 1 denotes a product (AND) term, for a total of 11 product terms. Using Boolean algebra or a Karnaugh map, we can reduce the expression for X to six product terms. An expression for the complement of X can be reduced to four product terms.

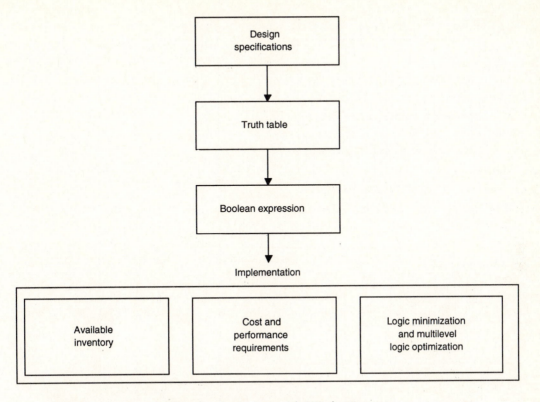

Figure 2-1 Design flow for designing with TTL logic

In determining how to implement the equation for X in TTL logic, we will want either to minimize the number of devices required, to minimize the number of levels of logic in order to minimize total propagation delay, or strike a balance between the two, depending on the performance and cost requirements of the design. Although the expression for $\overline{X}$ requires fewer product terms than the expression for X, the expression for $\overline{X}$ requires the use of 3-input AND gates. Examining our inventory of TTL logic, we see that the AND functions have a fan-in of only two. Creating wider AND gates would require cascading the 2-input AND gates. This cascading and the inverters that would be necessary to implement the complements of signals would unnecessarily increase the device count and levels of logic, thereby increasing cost and decreasing performance. If we implement the expression for X as a sum of products, the design will require two 7408s and two 7432s. In all, six levels of logic will be required: one level to produce each of the six

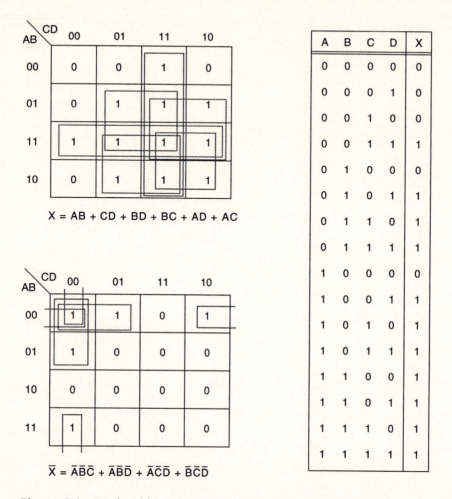

$$X = AB + CD + BD + BC + AD + AC$$

$$\overline{X} = \overline{A}\,\overline{B}\,\overline{C} + \overline{A}\,\overline{B}\,\overline{D} + \overline{A}\,\overline{C}\,\overline{D} + \overline{B}\,\overline{C}\,\overline{D}$$

Figure 2-2   Truth table and Karnaugh maps for collision signal

AND terms and five to produce the 6-input OR function by cascading the 2-input OR gates of the 7432. The product of sums implementation

$$X = (A + B + C)(A + B + D)(A + C + D)(B + C + D)$$

also requires several devices and levels of logic. An implementation that requires fewer devices and levels of logic (that is, one that costs less and has better performance) is the NAND-NAND implementation. The equation

$$X = AB + CD + BD + BC + AD + AC$$

may be rewritten in NAND-NAND form as

$$X = \overline{(\overline{AB} \cdot \overline{CD} \cdot \overline{BD} \cdot \overline{BC} \cdot \overline{AD} \cdot \overline{AC})}$$

This implementation requires two 7400s and one 7430, for a total of two levels of logic. Finally, to synchronize this signal to the transmit clock, we will use one 7474, wiring the circuit as shown in Figure 2-3. Depending on our current inventory of TTL devices, we could have implemented this design in one of several different ways.

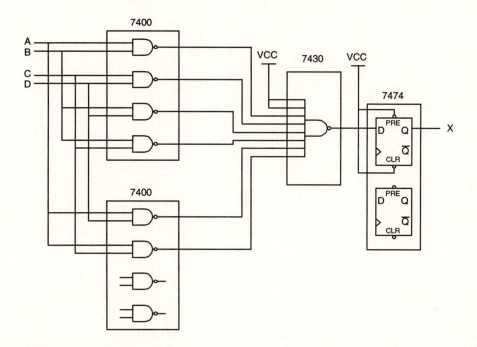

Figure 2-3   TTL logic implementation

How is implementing this design in programmable logic any different? Before we can answer that question, we need to understand what programmable logic is.

2.3   What Is a Programmable Logic Device?

PAL (programmable array logic) devices, or PALs, are the simplest of programmable logic devices that are readily available in today's market. PALs consist of an array of AND gates and an array of OR gates in which the AND array is programmable and the OR array is fixed. Before proceeding, we will review PAL logic notation.

Figure 2-4(a) illustrates the standard gate symbol for a 3-input AND gate and the equivalent PAL logic diagram. The single line extending from the AND gate is used to represent several inputs. The vertical lines represent the signals A, B, and

C. An asterisk represents a programmed connection between an input signal A, B, or C and an input of the AND gate. The programmed connections are made via EPROM cells or another programming technology. EPROM, EEPROM, and FLASH programming technologies are discussed later in this chapter.

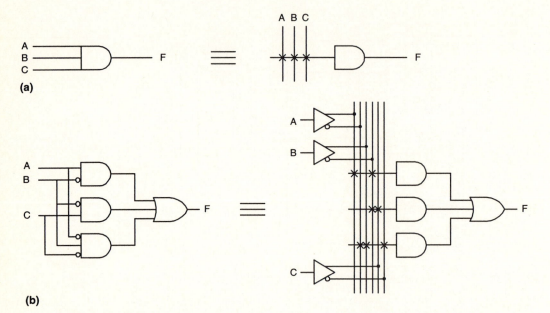

Figure 2-4   (a) Standard gate symbol and equivalent PAL diagram; (b) schematic and PAL diagram equivalence

The schematic diagram and equivalent PAL diagram for the Boolean function

$$F = A\bar{B} + \bar{B}C + \bar{A}B\bar{C}$$

are shown in Figure 2-4(b). This time, each of the vertical wires is shown connected to an input signal or its complement. The appropriate connections are made to establish connections to the inputs of the three AND gates, and the OR gate sums all of the product terms.

To understand PAL architectures, consider the PAL 16L8 device shown in Figure 2-5. The 16L8 is available from several programmable logic vendors, including Advanced Micro Devices, Cypress Semiconductor, Lattice Semiconductor, National Semiconductor, and Texas Instruments. The 16L8 is so named because there are 16 inputs into the AND array and 8 outputs. The *L* in 16L8 is for *logic* array.

Eight of the inputs to the array are dedicated device inputs. Another eight are from the I/O pins. If a three-state inverter associated with an I/O pin is enabled, then the input to the logic array is actually a feedback associated with an OR gate.

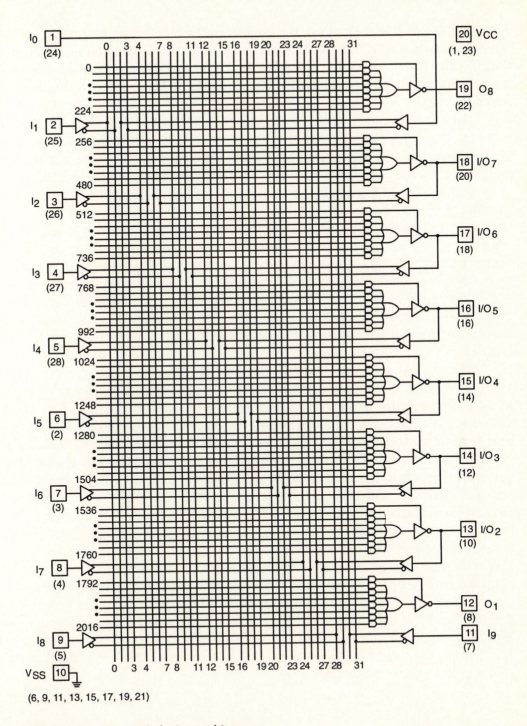

Figure 2-5 PAL 16L8 device architecture

This feedback is inverted; hence the bubble on the three-state inverter. That is, the signal source is not from an I/O input buffer; rather, it is from an inverting buffer, which is driven by an OR gate. If a three-state inverter is not enabled, then an I/O pin is working as an input. That is, the input to the logic array in this case originates off-chip.

The programmable AND array consists of 64 AND gates, each of which may be used to create a product of any of the 16 inputs, or their complements. The OR array is fixed; each of its eight gates sums seven products. The remaining eight product terms are used for the enables of the three-state inverting buffers.

Each of the three-state inverting buffers is controlled by a product term. Each product term may be programmed for a function of the inputs and their complements, or to ensure that the buffer is always on or always off. If it is always on, then the associated I/O pin functions as an output only. If it is always off, then the associated pin functions as an input only. If the I/O pin is controlled by a product term, then it can be used as a three-state output for use on an external bus or for bidirectional signal flow. In bidirectional mode, an I/O pin may be driven externally by a signal to be used internally in the logic array (when the output enable is deasserted), or driven with the function at the OR gate (when the output enable is asserted).

Next, consider the PAL 16R8 device architecture shown in Figure 2-6. Like the 16L8, this industry-standard architecture has 16 inputs to a logic array consisting of 64 product terms. In this architecture, eight of the logic array inputs are from device inputs and eight are from register feedbacks. These feedbacks are important to creating functions of the state of the flip-flops for use in generating next-state logic, state machine outputs, counters, shifters, and so forth. Each of the OR gates sums eight product terms, and this sum is then registered by one of the output flip-flops. The *R* in 16R8 is to indicate the presence of registers. The clock for the flip-flops is from a dedicated pin. The outputs cannot be configured as inputs, but may be configured as three-state outputs for use on an external bus. The three-state outputs are controlled by a dedicated pin rather than a product term.

Whereas the 16R8 provides registers, the 16L8 does not. Instead, it provides combinatorial output, more flexible output-enable control, and the capability to use more device pins as inputs. Two additional industry-standard architectures, the 16R6 and the 16R4, balance these differences. The 16R6 includes six registers, leaving two combinatorial output structures with individual three-state control. The 16R4 is the compromise between the 16L8 and 16R8, with four registered and four combinatorial output structures.

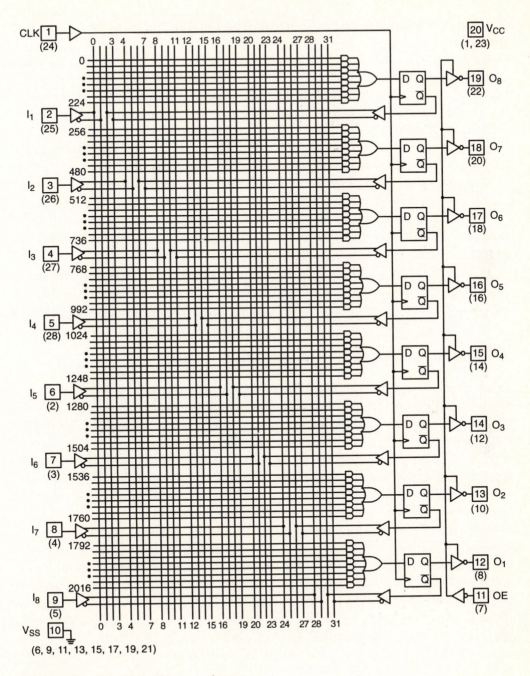

Figure 2-6 PAL 16R8 device architecture

2.3.1   Designing with Programmable Logic

Consider, again, the design of the network repeater collision signal, X, for which an expression is given in Figure 2-2. Because this signal must be registered, of the PALs we have discussed, we can use the 16R8, 16R6, or 16R4 to implement this design. In order to obtain X as an output, the logic implementation for the Boolean expression for the complement of X should be implemented in the AND-OR array. This is because the inverting three-state buffer complements the output of the OR gate. This implementation will require six device inputs (A, B, C, D, TXCLK, and the enable connected to logic high) and one output (X). Only four of the eight product terms allocated to the register are required to implement the expression. There is considerably more logic available in the PAL to consolidate any additional functionality. Additional logic may be independent of A, B, C, and D, but does not need to be.

This example highlights the difference between TTL logic and programmable logic implementations. The design process for programmable logic shown in Figure 2-7 is also different from that of TTL logic, which is illustrated in Figure 2-1.

2.3.2   Advantages of Programmable Logic

Programmable logic provides several advantages, many of which have been illustrated through our simple example. Clearly, fewer devices are used: In our example, one 20-pin DIP (dual in-line package), PLCC (plastic leaded chip carrier), or LCC (leadless chip carrier) 16R8 device replaced four 14-pin devices. The design used only a portion of the device, so one PAL could easily replace 10 or more TTL devices, which makes the PAL implementation more cost-effective, even though one TTL device may be less expensve than a PAL. Additionally, the cost structure for producing many simple TTL logic devices today is inefficient, and is absorbed by the end user. Today the largest portion of cost associated with TTL logic is packaging and testing. The manufacturing cost of a small PAL is close to that of many TTL logic devices because the amount of die area required to implement the TTL logic functions using today's technology is smaller than the minimum die area required for the pads (I/O buffers), rendering the designs of TTL logic pad-limited. That is, additional logic resources could be added to a die without increased manufacturing cost because the number of dice per wafer would remain the same. In our example, it would be cost-effective to use a PAL over discrete TTL components even if the rest of the PAL went unused.

Besides saving on parts, programmable logic saves valuable board space, or "real estate," power, and debug time. It also increases performance and design security. The integration provided by the PALs results in lower power requirements, particularly because a PAL implementation requires fewer I/Os. A TTL implementation requires several TTL devices, each with several inputs and outputs switching; a PAL implementation requires fewer total I/Os and fewer switching outputs, resulting in lower standby and switching currents. This savings can help the power budget or make it possible to use a smaller power supply. Integration increases design reliability because there are fewer dependencies on the interconnection of devices. This can yield debug-time savings, which can lower costs. Integration also increases performance by reducing the number of I/O delays and levels of logic. An additional feature of most PLDs is a security fuse, which can be used to protect proprietary intellectual property. Logic implemented with TTL devices is easily discernible, but the fuse map of a programmable logic device with a blown security fuse cannot be read back.

Perhaps the greatest advantage of programmable logic is flexibility, which is absent with discrete logic components. Once you have developed your board-level design, any change will necessitate jumpers and/or drilling the boards. If the board is to be produced in high volume, it will have to be redesigned, resulting in additional NRE costs and lost time-to-market. The same design with a PAL provides a fallback: The boards can be used as they are. Rather than making and breaking connections on the board, you can modify the connections inside the PAL. This concept will become more clear as we discuss other device architectures.

An additional advantage is that programmable logic allows you to use design tools that help automate the process. Rather than manually producing several equivalent Boolean expressions to determine which will work best with an inventory of TTL devices, we can produce one design description, leaving the logic synthesis and optimization software to determine an adequate implementation. Compare the manual method of Figure 2-1 with that of Figure 2-7. The only real work in the programmable logic design process is in producing the design description from the design specification. The rest of the steps are automated with software. The design description can be captured in a number of languages, including VHDL and Verilog, as well as proprietary languages such as ABEL. The output of the software is a fuse map that is used to program a device.

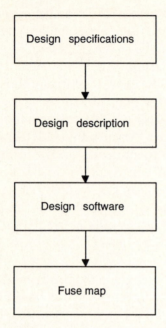

Figure 2-7   The programmable logic design process

2.3.3   Programming Technologies

EPROM, EEPROM, and FLASH technologies are commonly used in PLDs and CPLDs to establish the programmable connections such as those shown in Figure 2-4.

EPROM. Figure 2-8 shows how EPROM cells are used to create a wired-AND function. It is actually a wired-NOR function, but if the complements of signals are available (as they are in PLDs), then the equivalent AND function can be implemented. For example:

$$\overline{(a + b)} = \bar{a} \cdot \bar{b}$$

The product-term wire is initially pulled high by a pull-up mechanism. If any of the transistors conduct, then the product term is pulled to ground.

The transistor used in an EPROM cell has two gates, a select gate and a floating gate. The structure of this transistor is illustrated in Figure 2-9. Charge can be accumulated and trapped on the floating gate by a mechanism called *avalanche injection,* or *hot electron injection.* This mechanism is induced by applying programming voltages to the drain and select gates of the transistor. The large electric field from the drain to source gives electrons more energy. The higher voltage on the gate attracts the high-energy electrons, some of which gain enough energy to

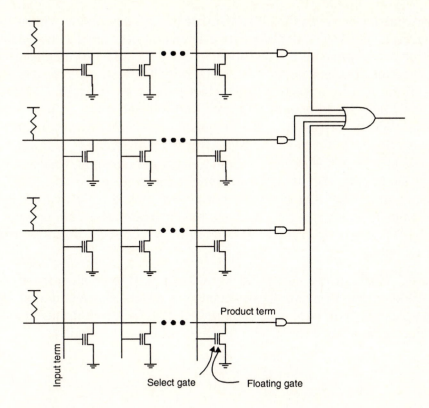

Figure 2-8 Creating a wired-AND with EPROM cells

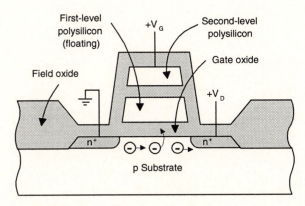

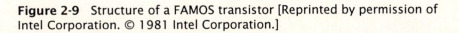

Figure 2-9 Structure of a FAMOS transistor [Reprinted by permission of Intel Corporation. © 1981 Intel Corporation.]

cross the energy barrier between the silicon substrate and gate oxide. These transistors are referred to as FAMOS, floating gate avalanche-injection MOS transistors. The electrons that are trapped on the floating gate have the effect of increasing the threshold of the transistor as seen by the select gate. Thus, in normal operating mode, even if an input term applied to the select gate of a programmed FAMOS transistor is held high, the transistor will not conduct. Without a charge on the floating gate, the FAMOS transistor acts as a normal n-channel transistor in that when a voltage is applied to the gate, the transistor is turned on.

EPROM cells provide a mechanism to hold a programmed state, which is used in PLDs and CPLDs to establish, or not establish, a connection. To erase the cell (remove charge from the floating gate), the device is exposed to ultraviolet light. Electrons will jump the energy barrier back to the substrate after gaining enough energy from the UV radiation. Typical erasure time is about 35 minutes under high-intensity UV light.

EEPROM. Figure 2-10 illustrates how E^2PROM cells are used to create a wired-AND function. The E^2PROM cells consist of two transistors each, the select and storage transistors. The product-term wire is initially pulled high by a pull-up mechanism. If any of the cells conduct, then the product-term is pulled to ground.

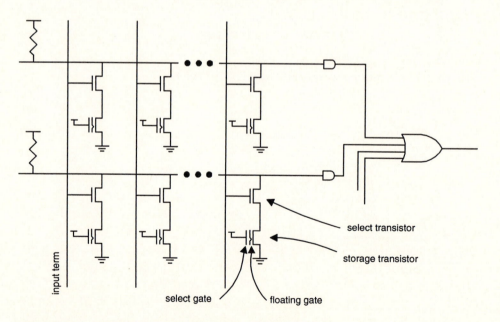

Figure 2-10   Creating a wired-AND with E^2PROM cells

Like the FAMOS transistor, the storage transistor has two gates, a select gate and a floating gate. The structure of the storage transistor is illustrated in Figure 2-11. It is similar to the FAMOS transistor except that the oxide region over the drain is considerably smaller—less than 100 angstroms, compared to as much as 200 angstroms for the FAMOS. This allows charge to be accumulated and trapped on the floating gate by a mechanism called Fowler-Nordheim tunneling. By applying a programming voltage to the select gate and keeping the drain voltage at ground, a tunnel current through the oxide of low-energy electrons charges the floating gate. This process can be reversed by applying a sufficiently high voltage to the drain and grounding the select gate. These transistors are referred to as FLOTOX, floating gate tunnel oxide transistors.

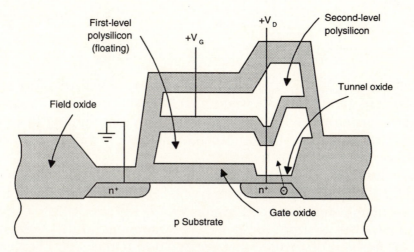

Figure 2-11   Structure of a FLOTOX transistor [Reprinted by permission of Intel Corporation. © 1981 Intel Corporation.]

E^2PROM cells require a select transistor because when the floating gate does not hold a charge, the threshold voltage of the FLOTOX transistor is negative. Thus, an unprogrammed FLOTOX transistor could conduct a current between the source and the drain if the input term were connected to the select gate and the input term potential were at ground. Because we want the transistor to conduct only when the input term is high and the floating gate is not charged, a select transistor is included. The select gate of the FLOTOX transistor is held at a voltage that will turn it on fully if the floating gate is not charged or keep it off if the floating gate is charged. The input term is then attached to the gate of a normal MOS transistor. If the input term is high and so is the cell, then the state of the FLOTOX storage transistor determines whether or not the product-term line is brought low. Figure 2-12 illustrates the four possible states of the two transistors in each pull-down path for a given product term.

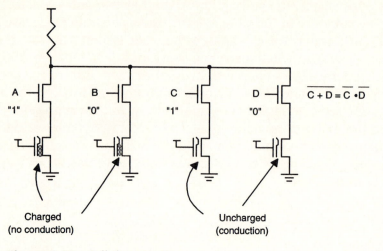

$$\overline{C + D} = \overline{C} \cdot \overline{D}$$

Charged
(no conduction)

Uncharged
(conduction)

Figure 2-12   Pull-down paths

FLASH. Like E²PROM cells, FLASH cells also consist of two transistors, the select and storage transistors, and they create wired-AND functions in a similar manner.

The storage transistor is a FAMOS transistor, so programming is accomplished via hot electron injection. However, the floating gate is shared by an erase transistor that takes charge off it via tunneling.

The primary difference between these technologies for the end user is that E²PROM and FLASH allow for electrical erasing, while EPROM requires UV erasing, which is time consuming and, therefore, expensive. Clearly, electrically erasable technologies can pave the way for in-system reprogramming, while UV erasable cannot. These features will be covered in more detail in "Other CPLD Features," later in this chapter.

2.4   Simple PLDs: The 22V10

There are several popular industry-standard PLDs, such as the 16V8, 20G10, and 20RA10, but we will limit our discussion of small PLDs to the 22V10 for brevity. Once you understand the 22V10 architecture described below, you should be able to quickly compare its architectural features with those of other PLDs by comparing architecture diagrams found in PLD vendor data sheets.

The 22V10 architecture of Figure 2-13 represented a breakthrough: It included a programmable macrocell and variable product-term distribution.

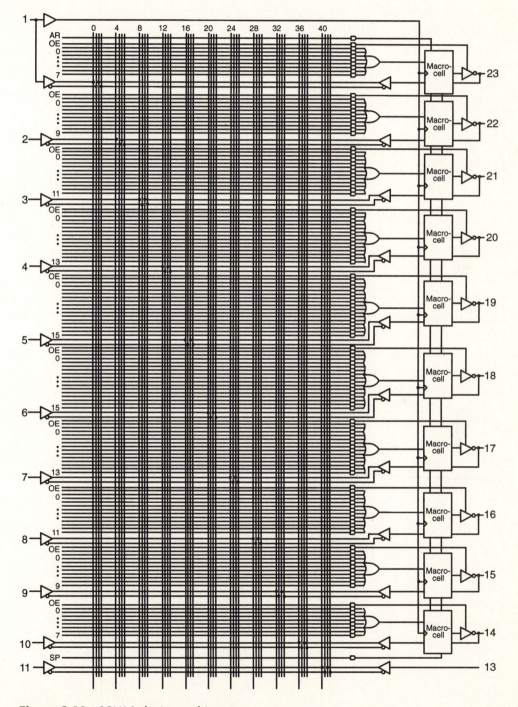

Figure 2-13   22V10 device architecture

Each macrocell (see Figure 2-6) may be individually configured—see Table 2-2—by programming the state of configuration bits. Configuration bits allow a macrocell input, which is a sum of products, to either be registered or pass directly to the output buffer. The polarity of the macrocell output is also selectable. With polarity control, the true or the complement of an expression may be used. Either the true or the complement may require fewer product terms than the other. For example, the complement of a large sum of individual terms

$$X = A + B + C + D + E + F$$

may be expressed as one product term

$$\overline{X} = \overline{A}\overline{B}\overline{C}\overline{D}\overline{E}\overline{F}$$

Because a wide AND gate uses more device resources than a wide OR gate, it is more efficient to implement $\overline{X}$. The complement of X, namely $\overline{X}$, can then be obtained by inverting at the output buffer:

$$X = (\overline{\overline{X}})$$

The output polarity selection of the macrocell enables software to perform logic optimization on an expression and its complement and to select the one that requires the fewest logic resources.

The programmable macrocell also allows feedback for use as input to the logic array. The feedback can be directed from the register or the I/O buffer, depending on whether or not the register is bypassed (that is, whether or not the signal is registered or combinational). Additionally, an output-enable product term can be programmed such that an output is always disabled, allowing an I/O to be used as a device input.

Table 2-2   22V10 macrocell configuration table

C_1	C_0	Description
0	0	Registered/active low
0	1	Registered/active high
1	0	Combinational/active low
1	1	Combinational/active high

The other innovation in the 22V10 is variable product-term distribution. Recognizing that in typical applications some logic expressions require more product terms per OR gate than others, the architects of the 22V10 (the *V* is for variable) varied the number of product terms per OR gate from 8 to 16 (Figure 2-13). The top and bottom macrocells are allocated 8 product terms, the middle macrocells are allocated 16 product terms, and the others are allocated 10, 12, or 14, depending on location. The 22 in 22V10 is for the 22 inputs to the logic array; the 10 is for the 10 outputs.

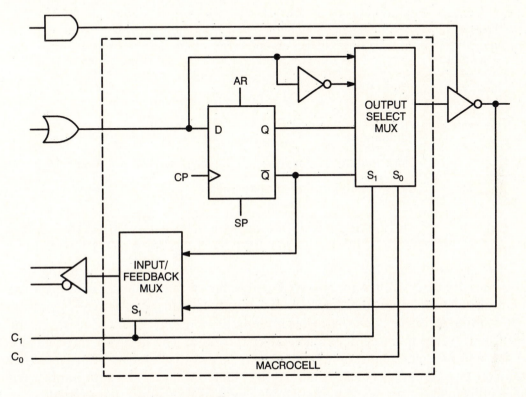

Figure 2-14   22V10 macrocell

Why did the architects of the 22V10 not allocate 16 product terms to every macrocell? The most likely reason is that doing so would increase the cost to manufacture the device (the increased die size would result in fewer dice per wafer and, therefore, higher unit costs). Because many applications do not require more product terms, the additional product terms per macrocell would usually go unused, in which case the additional cost would not provide additional functionality.

2.4.1   Timing Parameters

Although there are additional data-sheet timing parameters (such as minimum clock width, input to output enable delay, and asynchronous reset recovery time), the basic timing parameters most frequently referenced are propagation delay

(t_{PD}), setup time (t_S), hold time (t_H), clock-to-output delay (t_{CO}), clock-to-output delay through the logic array (t_{CO2}), and system clock to system clock time (t_{SCS}), which is used to determine the maximum frequency of operation. Table 2-3 shows these basic parameters for a 4-nanosecond 22V10 (a 22V10 with a t_{PD} of 4 ns).

Table 2-3   Sample data-sheet parameters for a 22V10

Parameter	Description	Min.	Max.
t_{PD}	Propagation delay		4 ns
t_S	Setup time	2.5 ns	
t_H	Hold time	0	
t_{CO}	Clock-to-output delay		3.5 ns
t_{CO2}	Clock-to-output delay (through logic array)		7 ns
t_{SCS}	System clock to system clock delay		5.5 ns

The propagation delay is the amount of time it takes for a combinational output to be valid after inputs are asserted at the device pins. The setup time is the amount of time the input to a flip-flop must be stable before the active edge of the clock is applied to the clock pen. Hold time is the amount of time for which the input to a flip-flop must be held stable after the clock. The designer must ensure that the setup time and hold time requirements are not violated—in this case, that data must be valid at least 2.5 ns before the clock. Violating the setup and hold-time requirements may cause a metastable event: the flip-flop may transition to the wrong value, remain indeterminate, or oscillate for an indeterminate (but statistically predictable) period of time. (The reader interested in more detail about metastability in PLDs can refer to Dingman or Cheney, et al., both listed in the bibliography.) Clock to output delay is the amount of time after which the clock input is asserted at a device pin that the output becomes valid at another device pin. These timing parameters are illustrated in Figure 2-15.

The parameter t_{CO2} represents the clock to output delay for an output that does not route directly from a register to its associated output pin (that is, t_{CO}); rather, it represents the clock to output delay for a signal that is fed back from the register through the logic array, through a macrocell configured in combinational mode, and to a device pin (Figure 2-15, bottom left). This configuration is often used in decoding registers (to produce a state machine output, or to generate a terminal count output from the logical AND of several counter bits stored in regis-

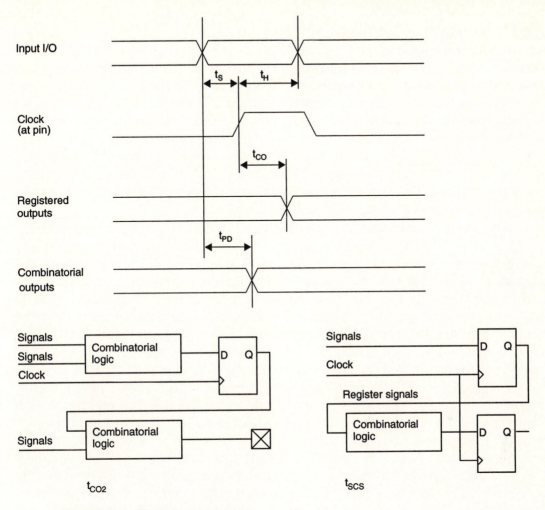

Figure 2-15   Timing parameters

ters, for example). A sequential circuit is shown at the bottom right of Figure 2-15. The second bank of registers may be clocked t_{SCS} after the first bank. The parameter t_{SCS} indicates the minimum clock period if register-to-register operation is required, and accounts for the amount of time from when the clock is asserted at the registers until the output of one register is valid at the input of another (or the same) register, in addition to the setup time for that register. The parameter t_{SCS} is used to calculate the maximum frequency of operation:

$$f_{max} = 1/t_{SCS}$$

2.4.2   **Designing with the 22V10**

Here, we discuss a few design implementation issues. We use a simple design spec-ification to generate a set of equations to implement in the 22V10, and discuss which resources can be used for implementation and focus on the post-fit (post-implementation) timing characteristics. This will introduce you to the task of a software **fitter,** and to help you understand the timing issues involved with design implementation in programmable logic. The task of a fitter is more fully developed in Chapter 8, "Synthesis and Design Implementation." In this chapter we will not discuss how to use VHDL to create such a design; the design equations we present will be generated using truth tables and Karnaugh maps.

Suppose, as an example, that you are asked to design a three-bit synchronous counter with an enable. The design has two additional outputs—one that is asserted when the present count is greater than three, and one that is asserted when the count is equal to six. We can determine the expressions for each of the counter bits and outputs by creating a table with the present-state (PS), next-state (NS), and present-state outputs, respectively, using Karnaugh maps to find the minimal sum of products for each expression, as illustrated in Figure 2-16. There are two inputs (the clock and enable, e) and five outputs (a, b, c, x, and y). If all macrocells are configured for active high logic, then the $\overline{Q}$-output for each flip-flop must be multiplexed to the inverting output buffers. This allows positive-logic implementations for A, B, and C. Signals A, B, and C are the D-inputs to the flip-flops associated with output signals a, b, and c. Figure 2-17 indicates that signal A requires four product terms, B three, and C two. Output x does not require any additional logic because it is equivalent to output a. In fact, one output pin can be used for both signals a and x. Signal y requires one product term. Because the product-term requirement associated with each of the outputs is less than eight, the signals can be implemented with *any* of the macrocells. This is equivalent to saying that the output signals can be placed on any of the I/O pins. A schematic of this design implementation is shown in Figure 2-17.

PS	In	NS	Out
a b c	e	A B C	x y
0 0 0	0	0 0 0	0 0
0 0 0	1	0 0 1	0 0
0 0 1	0	0 0 1	0 0
0 0 1	1	0 1 0	0 0
0 1 0	0	0 1 0	0 0
0 1 0	1	0 1 1	0 0
0 1 1	0	0 1 1	0 0
0 1 1	1	1 0 0	0 0
1 0 0	0	1 0 0	1 0
1 0 0	1	1 0 1	1 0
1 0 1	0	1 0 1	1 0
1 0 1	1	1 1 0	1 0
1 1 0	0	1 1 0	1 1
1 1 0	1	1 1 1	1 1
1 1 1	0	1 1 1	1 0
1 1 1	1	0 0 0	1 0

$$x = a$$
$$y = ab\bar{c}$$

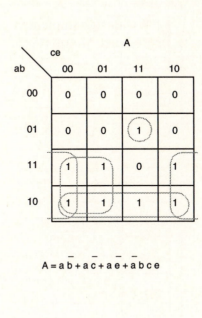

$$A = a\bar{b} + a\bar{c} + a\bar{e} + \bar{a}bce$$

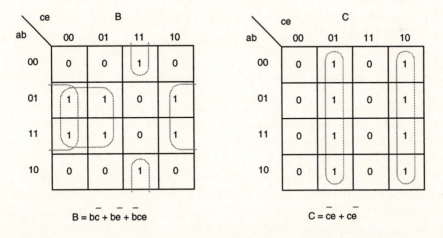

$$B = b\bar{c} + \bar{b}\bar{e} + \bar{b}ce$$

$$C = \bar{c}e + c\bar{e}$$

Figure 2-16   Truth table, Karnaugh maps, and expressions for a 3-bit counter

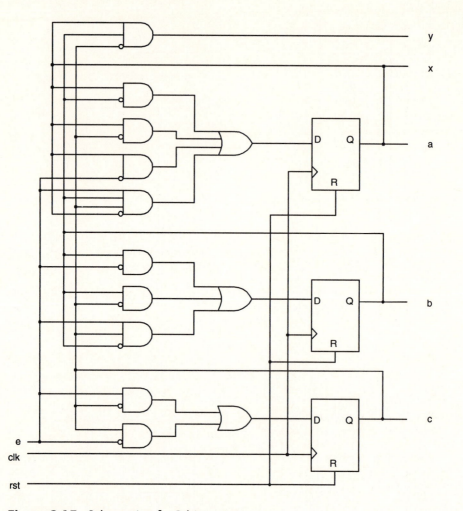

Figure 2-17   Schematic of a 3-bit counter

Figure 2-18 illustrates the resulting waveforms for this design. Signal e (enable) is the only input to the device that has a setup-time requirement. It must be valid and stable at least 2.5 ns before the clock is asserted at the pin. Although this signal does not change immediately when the clock is asserted, it could, because there is a zero-ns hold-time requirement. Outputs a, b, c, and x are valid at the output pins 3.5 ns, t_{CO}, after the clock input transitions. Output y is valid at its output pin 7 ns, t_{CO2}, after the clock input transitions. More time is required for y to be valid because the outputs of the counter must be decoded to produce it. The decoding is made possible by the outputs of the counter feeding back into the logic array and using a product term associated with another macrocell. This

PS a b c	In e	NS A B C	Out x y
0 0 0	0	0 0 0	0 0
0 0 0	1	0 0 1	0 0
0 0 1	0	0 0 1	0 0
0 0 1	1	0 1 0	0 0
0 1 0	0	0 1 0	0 0
0 1 0	1	0 1 1	0 0
0 1 1	0	0 1 1	0 0
0 1 1	1	1 0 0	0 0
1 0 0	0	1 0 0	1 0
1 0 0	1	1 0 1	1 0
1 0 1	0	1 0 1	1 0
1 0 1	1	1 1 0	1 0
1 1 0	0	1 1 0	1 1
1 1 0	1	1 1 1	1 1
1 1 1	0	1 1 1	1 0
1 1 1	1	0 0 0	1 0

$$x = a$$
$$y = ab\overline{c}$$

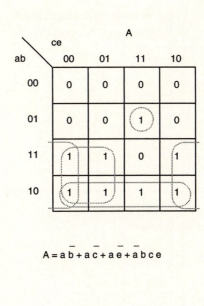

$$A = a\overline{b} + a\overline{c} + a\overline{e} + \overline{a}bce$$

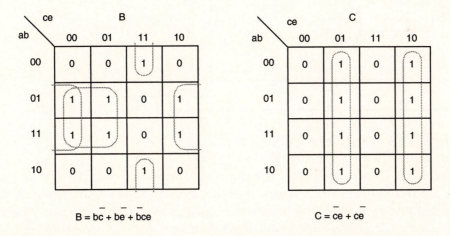

$$B = \overline{b}c + \overline{b}e + b\overline{c}\overline{e}$$

$$C = \overline{c}e + c\overline{e}$$

Figure 2-16 Truth table, Karnaugh maps, and expressions for a 3-bit counter

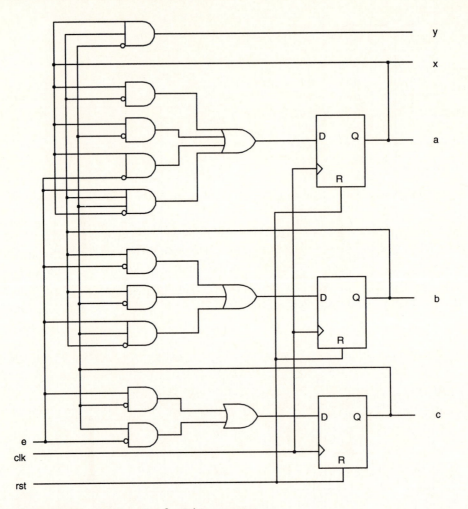

Figure 2-17 Schematic of a 3-bit counter

Figure 2-18 illustrates the resulting waveforms for this design. Signal e (enable) is the only input to the device that has a setup-time requirement. It must be valid and stable at least 2.5 ns before the clock is asserted at the pin. Although this signal does not change immediately when the clock is asserted, it could, because there is a zero-ns hold-time requirement. Outputs a, b, c, and x are valid at the output pins 3.5 ns, t_{CO}, after the clock input transitions. Output y is valid at its output pin 7 ns, t_{CO2}, after the clock input transitions. More time is required for y to be valid because the outputs of the counter must be decoded to produce it. The decoding is made possible by the outputs of the counter feeding back into the logic array and using a product term associated with another macrocell. This

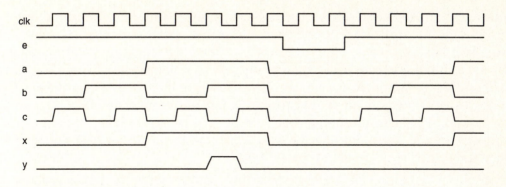

Figure 2-18   Timing diagram for counter design

decoding causes an additional delay of 4 ns over t_{CO}. The maximum clock frequency at which this circuit may be clocked is usually dictated by the amount of time it takes for the output of one flip-flop to propagate to the input of another as well as the setup time requirement for the second flip-flop. This frequency is the reciprocal of t_{SCS} (5.5 ns), or 180 MHz. In this case, however, the design cannot be clocked at this frequency because the output y takes 7 ns to propagate to an output pin. If the circuit were clocked at 180 MHz, the output y would never be valid. Theoretically, this circuit could be clocked at the rate of the reciprocal of 7 ns (143 MHz), and you would find a valid output at the device pin for y. However, the output is guaranteed to be valid only for an instant in time. In order to sample the output, you will need to include any trace delay and setup time of the sampling device in determining the maximum clock frequency for the system.

2.4.3   Using More Than 16 Product Terms

Although the largest number of product terms associated with any macrocell in the 22V10 is 16, you can implement expressions that require more than 16 product terms by using two passes through the logic array. For example, to sum 20 product terms, two macrocells can sum 10 product terms each and a third macrocell can sum the macrocell feedbacks of the first two macrocells. This **sum-splitting** technique requires two product terms for the third macrocell. Sum-splitting can also be accomplished with the third macrocell using only one product term: If a and b are the outputs of the first two macrocells, and y is the output to be propagated to the device pin, then the expression for $\overline{y}$, $\overline{y} = \overline{a} \cdot \overline{b}$, can be implemented with the third macrocell using only one product term. The complement of $\overline{y}$, namely y, can be obtained with the macrocell polarity control. Yet another sum-splitting technique is to use one of the center macrocells to sum 16 product terms and another to sum the feedback of the first macrocell and the remaining four product terms (for a total of five product terms for this second macrocell). Either way, two passes through the logic array are required, and this will increase the propagation delay from input pins to output for combinational functions, or will increase the setup time for signals to be registered. If the data sheet does not provide a specification for a propagation delay from input, through the logic array twice, and to an output pin, then the sum of $t_{PD} + t_{PD}$ is a safe worst-case estimate. Likewise, if a setup time for two passes through the logic array is not specified, then $t_{PD} + t_S$ provides a safe estimate.

2.4.4   Terminology

The 22V10 architecture is shown in block diagram form in Figure 2-19 for the purpose of assigning terms to the various blocks, or features of the 22V10 architecture. We will use these terms in our discussion of CPLDs.

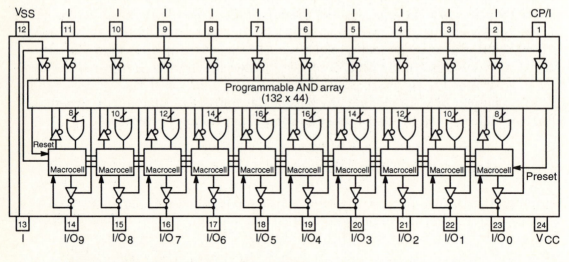

Figure 2-19   Block diagram of the 22V10

The term **logic array inputs,** or simply **inputs** refers to all of the signals that are inputs to the logic array. These inputs include dedicated device inputs, feedbacks from macrocells, and inputs from I/Os that are configured as device inputs. The term **product-term array** describes the programmable AND gates (product terms). The **product-term distribution scheme** is the mechanism for distributing product terms to the macrocells. Macrocells typically contain a register (flip-flop) and combinational path with polarity control as well as one or more feedback paths. **I/O cells** is a term used to describe the structure of the I/O buffers and flexibility of the output enable controls.

Breakout Exercise 2-1

Purpose: To gain additional experience with the Warp2 tools, particularly the functional simulator Nova.

Read each step completely before performing any operations.

1. Start Galaxy.

2. Select **New** from the **Project** menu to create a new project. Enter the name c:\vhdlbook\ch2\break1. This will create a project named break1 in the c:\vhdlbook\ch2 directory. (If you have two projects, or Galaxies, open at this time, you may close the old one by selecting **Close** from the **Project** menu of *that* Galaxy window.)

3. From the **Files** menu select **Add All**. The file name 3bcount.vhd will appear in the project list. It will be selected.

4. Click on the **Selected** button in the **Edit** panel. This loads the selected file into Warp's text editor. View the VHDL code. It is not important that you understand the syntax, but you should recognize that this is the design of the 3-bit counter shown in Figures 2-16 and 2-17.

5. Select **Close** from the **File** menu of the text editor. If you have modified the file, *do not* save changes.

6. Click on **Set top** in the **Synthesis options** panel. This tells the synthesis compiler that the design is intended to be implemented in a device, not compiled to a library.

7. Click on **Device** from the **Synthesis options** panel. This brings up a dialog box. Select C371 from the device scroll list (Figure 1-9). We will be synthesizing and fitting this design to a CY7C371 FLASH370 CPLD. Leave all other selections with their default values, and click the **OK** button.

8. Click the **Smart** button from the **Compile** panel. This will cause a compilation window to appear and the synthesis software to process the VHDL code. After synthesis is complete, the fitter software will be invoked automatically. When this is complete, the status bar in the lower left of the compilation window will indicate *Compilation Successful*. Select **Close** from the **File** menu of the compilation window.

9. Select **Nova** from the **Tools** menu to start the Nova functional simulator.

10. In Nova, select **Open** from the **File** menu. Select the file name 3bcount.jed.

11. Several traces will appear in the Nova window. Select **Simulation Length** from the **Options** menu. Increase the simulation length to 1024.

12. Edit the rst, clk, and e waveforms to provide stimulus for the counter. Refer to Chapter 6, section 6.5, "The Edit Menu," of the Warp user's guide on-line documentation set for instructions on editing waveforms within Nova.

13. Select **Execute** from the **Simulation** menu and verify that the counter is reset when rst is asserted, that the counter increments each clock cycle that e is asserted (provided that rst is not asserted simultaneously), that x is asserted when the counter value is 4 or more, and that y is asserted when the counter value is 6.

14. Select **Edit Views** from the **Views** menu to place the traces in the order you wish. Eliminate any unneeded (internal) nodes. Refer to Chapter 6, section 6.7, "The Views Menu," of the Warp user's guide on-line documentation set for instructions on editing a view.

15. Using the on-line documentation for Nova as a reference, select **Create Bus** from the **Edit** menu and create a bus for the counter bits.

16. Modify the input stimulus and execute simulation.

17. Experiment with Nova; you will need to become proficient. Use the on-line documentation as a reference.

18. Exit Nova when you are finished.

19. Save the project, and then exit Galaxy.

2.5   What Is a CPLD?

Complex PLDs (CPLDs) extend the concept of the PLD to a higher level of integration to improve system performance; they also use less board space, improve reliability, and reduce cost. Instead of making the PLD larger with more inputs, product terms, and macrocells, a CPLD contains multiple logic blocks, each similar to a small PLD like the 22V10. The logic blocks communicate with one another using signals routed via a programmable interconnect (Figure 2-20). This architectural arrangement makes more efficient use of the available silicon die area, leading to better performance and reduced cost.

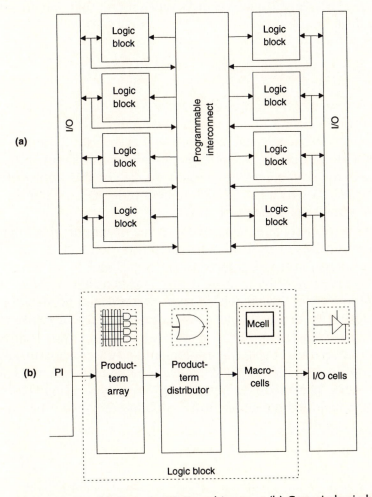

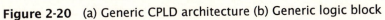

Figure 2-20   (a) Generic CPLD architecture (b) Generic logic block

In this section, we present an overview of CPLDs, examining their makeup and indicating the features of some specific families of popular CPLDs. This section does not include a comprehensive examination of all of the CPLDs on the market today or an in-depth examination of all the features that are present in the architectures we will discuss. For this, we strongly recommend that you obtain the data sheets for these devices.

2.5.1   Programmable Interconnects

The programmable interconnect (PI) routes signals from I/Os to logic block inputs or from logic block outputs (macrocell outputs) to the inputs of the same or other logic blocks. (Some logic blocks have local feedback so that macrocell outputs used in the same logic block do not route through the global programmable interconnect; later we'll discuss the advantages and disadvantages of this approach.) As with a PLD such as the 22V10, which has a fixed number of logic array inputs, each logic block has a fixed number of logic block inputs.

Most CPLDs use one of two implementations for the programmable interconnect: **array-based interconnect** or **multiplexer-based interconnect.** Array-based interconnect allows any signal in the PI to route to any logic block (see Figure 2-21). Each term in the PI is represented by a vertical wire and is assigned as an input (through a sense amp) to a given logic block, so there is one PI term for each input to a logic block. An output from a logic block can connect to one of the PI terms through a memory element (such as an EPROM cell). Device inputs can connect to PI terms as well. This interconnect scheme implements a full crosspoint switch; that is, it is fully **routable:** any input to the programmable interconnect can be routed into any logic block, provided that not all of the inputs to a logic block are already being used. Although highly flexible, full routability may be at the expense of performance, power, and die size.

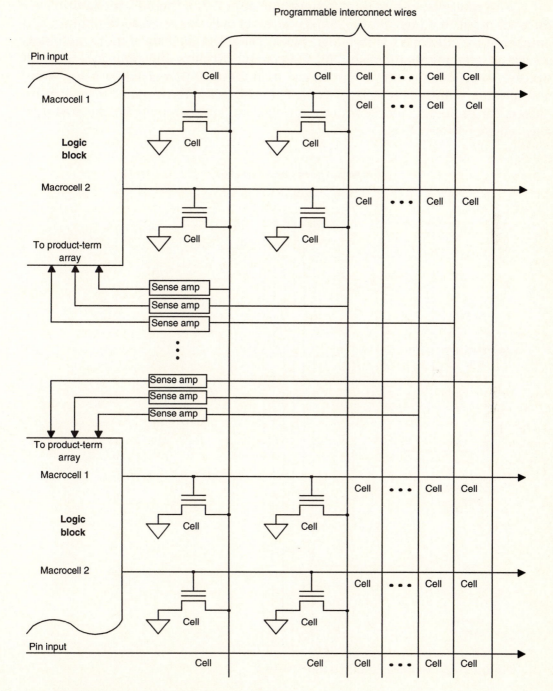

Figure 2-21   Array-based interconnect

With multiplexer-based interconnect (Figure 2-22), there is one multiplexer for each input to a logic block. Signals in the PI are connected to the inputs of a number of multiplexers for each logic block. The selection lines of these multiplexers are programmed (with flash cells, for example) to allow one input for each multiplexer to propagate into a logic block. Routability is increased by using wider multiplexers, allowing each signal in the PI to connect to the input of several multiplexers for each logic block. Wider multiplexers, however, increase die area (and may reduce performance).

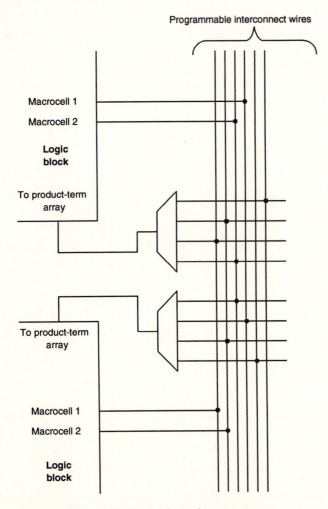

Figure 2-22 Multiplexer-based interconnect

2.5.2 Logic Blocks

A logic block is similar to a PLD such as the 22V10: Each has a product-term array, a product-term distribution scheme, and macrocells. I/O cells are sometimes considered to be part of a logic block, but we will consider these to be separate, as in Figure 2-20. The size of a logic block is a measure of its capacity—how much logic can be implemented in it. It is typically expressed in terms of the number of macrocells, but also important are the number of inputs to the logic block, the number of product terms, and the product-term distribution scheme. Logic blocks usually range in size from 4 to 20 macrocells. Sixteen or more macrocells permit 16-bit functions to be implemented in a single logic block, provided that enough inputs from the PI to the logic block exist. For example, a 16-bit free-running counter can fit in a logic block that has 16 macrocells, 15 inputs (one for each bit except the most significant), and a sufficient number of product terms, assuming that the macrocell outputs propagate through the PI. If T-type flip-flops are used, then fewer product terms are required. A 16-bit counter with synchronous load and asynchronous reset requires a logic block with 16 macrocells and 33 inputs to the logic block (one for each counter bit, plus 16 for the load inputs, plus one for the asynchronous reset). This function could fit in a CPLD that has fewer macrocells or inputs per logic block only with signals propagating between multiple logic blocks and through multiple passes of the logic array, resulting in slower performance. Logic blocks with few inputs also tend to use logic block resources inefficiently. This is because if one expression using a macrocell requires all the available inputs to a logic block, then other expressions cannot be placed in the other macrocells in that logic block unless they use a subset of the signals required for the first expression.

2.5.3 Product-Term Arrays

There is little difference between the product-term arrays of the different CPLDs. Of course, the size of the array is important because it identifies the average number of product terms per macrocell and the maximum number of product terms per logic block.

2.5.4 Product-Term Distribution

Different CPLD vendors have approached product-term distribution with different schemes. The MAX family ("family" meaning several devices with the same architecture) of CPLDs, jointly developed by the Altera Corporation and Cypress

Semiconductor, was the first family of CPLDs on the market. (Altera named it the MAX5000 family, Cypress, MAX340.) Rather than using the variable product-term distribution scheme of the 22V10 (which allocated a fixed but varied number of product terms—8, 10, 12, 14, or 16—per macrocell), the MAX family allocated four product terms per macrocell while allowing several **expander product terms** to be allocated individually to any macrocell or macrocells (Figure 2-23). With expander product terms, the additional product terms are allocated only to those macrocells that can make use of them. The concept that a product term can be used by a particular macrocell is termed **product-term steering,** and the concept that the same product term may be used by multiple macrocells is termed **product-term sharing.** An additional delay is incurred for signals that use the expander product terms, because the output of the expander product term must pass through the logic array before propagating to a macrocell.

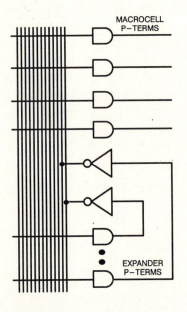

Figure 2-23   Product-term distribution in the MAX340 and MAX5000 families of devices

The MACH families offered by Advanced Micro Devices allow product terms to be steered in groups of four product terms and used in another macrocell without an additional delay (Figure 2-24). For each group of macrocells that must be steered, one macrocell is left unusable. This product-term distribution scheme does not provide product-term sharing.

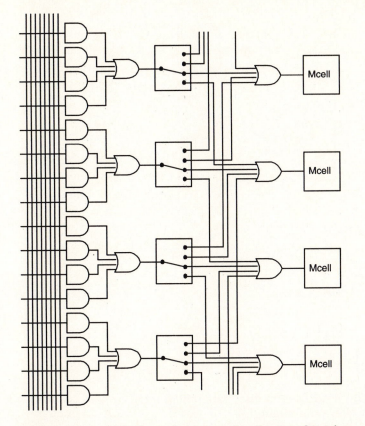

Figure 2-24   MACH3 product-term distribution [© Advanced Micro Devices, Inc. (Fall 1994) Reprinted with permission of copyright owner. All rights reserved.]

The MAX7000 family offered by Altera Corporation improved the product-term distribution scheme of the MAX5000 family (Figure 2-25). In addition to the expander product terms, which may be individually steered or shared, the new architecture also includes a product-term steering mechanism in which five product terms may be steered to a neighboring macrocell—which in turn can be steered to a neighboring macrocell. Steering in this way adds a significantly shorter delay because the signal does not propagate through the product-term array, as it does with an expander product term. This steering does prevent the product terms from being shared, unlike with the expander product terms.

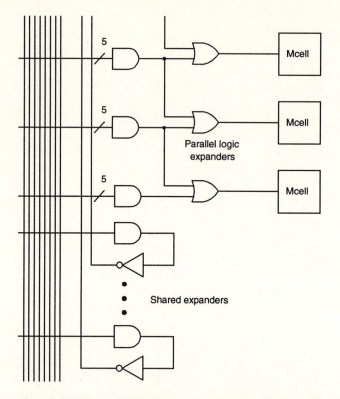

Figure 2-25 MAX7000 product-term distribution [Reprinted by permission of Altera Corporation. © 1993 Altera Corporation.]

The FLASH370 family offered by Cypress Semiconductor provides yet a different scheme (Figure 2-26). Each macrocell is allocated from zero to 16 product terms, depending on the requirements of the logic expression implemented at a given macrocell; however, adjacent macrocells cannot be allocated 16 *unique* product terms each. Each product term may be individually steered (that is, a product term can be allocated to a particular macrocell). This steering scheme does not render a macrocell unusable or result in an incremental delay. Most product terms (except for some used by the first and last macrocell in a logic block) can also be shared with up to four neighboring macrocells without additional delay.

The product-term distribution schemes of these architectures provide flexibility for the designer. More important, these schemes provide flexibility for software algorithms that will ultimately choose how to use logic resources. The design engineer should understand how logic resources may be used and the trade-offs among architectures, but engineering design automation software should automatically select the optimal implementation, leaving the designer to provide innovation to his or her system design.

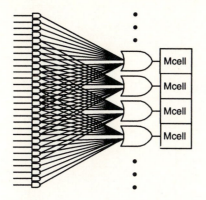

Figure 2-26   FLASH370 product-term distribution

2.5.5   Macrocells

As with simple PLDs, complex PLDs include macrocells that provide flip-flops and polarity control. Polarity control enables the implementation of either the true or complement of an expression—whichever uses the fewest product terms. CPLD macrocells offer more configurability than do 22V10 macrocells. For example, many include flip-flops that can be configured for D- or T-type operation, again in order to allow the efficient implementation of an expression. In addition, CPLDs often have I/O macrocells, input macrocells, and buried macrocells. A 22V10 has only an I/O macrocell (a macrocell associated with an I/O). An input macrocell, as you may have deduced, is associated with an input pin. A buried macrocell is usually similar to an I/O macrocell except that its output cannot propagate directly to an I/O. Rather, its output is fed back to the PI.

I/O and Buried Macrocells. Figure 2-27 illustrates the I/O macrocell of the MAX340 family of devices. It provides more configurability than the 22V10 macrocell. There are several inputs to this macrocell. The sum-of-products input is used as one input to the XOR gate. The other input to the XOR gate is an individual product term. The XOR gate can be used in arithmetic expressions (comparators and adders make good use of it) or to complement the sum-of-products expression. If the array is programmed such that the individual product term is always deasserted, then the output of the XOR gate is the same as the sum-of-products expression on the other input of the XOR gate. If the individual product term is always asserted, then the output of the XOR gate is the complement of the sum of products, which thereby allows the expression (complemented or uncomplemented) that uses the fewest number of product terms to be implemented in the product-term array. That is, the XOR gate serves the same function as the output

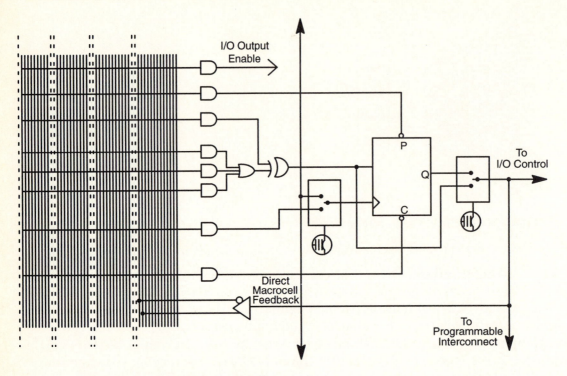

Figure 2-27   MAX340 macrocell

polarity multiplexer found in the 22V10 macrocell, but it can also be used to implement logic, especially arithmetic logic, or to configure a flip-flop for T-, JK-, or SR-type operation. The preset and clear are individual NAND terms, and the clock can be either the system clock or an internally generated (product-term) clock. The flip-flop may be clocked by one of two clocks. The system clock provides the best performance, and the product-term clock provides flexibility. Product-term clocks should be used sparingly and carefully because they can easily cause timing problems; for example, race conditions can cause glitches in the clock. The use of product-term clocks will be explained in Chapters 6 and 8. The output of the macrocell can be configured as registered or combinational. Feedback is from either the combinational or registered signal, depending on the macrocell configuration. This architecture provides both local feedback (that is, the macrocell feedback does not use the PI and is not available to other logic blocks) and global feedback through the PI. The advantage of local feedback is quicker propagation to other macrocells in the logic block. The disadvantage of having local in addition to global feedback is a more complicated timing model and redundant resources. Buried macrocells for this family are identical to the I/O macrocells except that their outputs are used only as feedback and do not drive I/O cells.

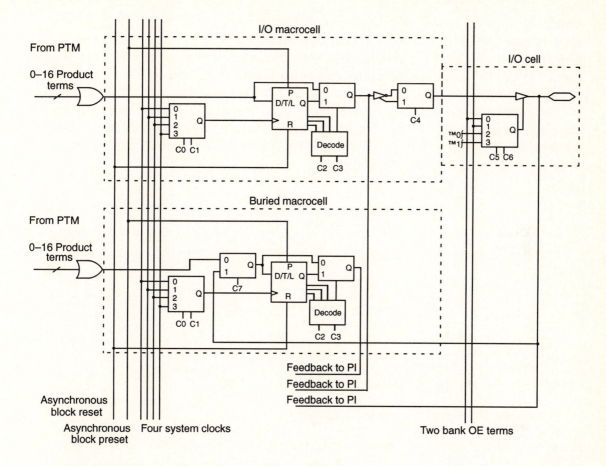

Figure 2-28 FLASH370 I/O and buried macrocells

Figure 2-28 represents the I/O and buried macrocells of the FLASH370 architecture. The macrocell input can be programmed for 0 to 16 product terms. This input can be registered, latched, or passed through as a combinational signal. If it is configured as a register, the register can be D-type or T-type. The clock for the register/latch can be one of four clocks available to a logic block (the polarity of a clock is determined on a logic-block-by-logic-block basis). The output polarity control permits the polarity optimization of an expression. The macrocell has a feedback separate from the I/O cell to permit the I/O cell to be configured as a dedicated device input while still allowing the I/O macrocell to be used as an internal macrocell, in either a registered or combinational mode. (Contrast this with the functionality of a 22V10 macrocell.) The buried macrocells are nearly the same as the I/O macrocells, except that the output feeds back to the PI. Additionally, a buried macrocell can be configured to register the input associated with a neighboring I/O cell.

Input Macrocells. Input macrocells, such as the one shown in Figure 2-29, are used to provide additional inputs other than those associated with I/O macrocells. The figure shows that for this architecture these inputs can be used as clocks, inputs to the PI, or both. The inputs can be combinational, latched, registered, or twice registered. (A signal that is asynchronous to the system clock is sometimes synchronized with two flip-flops to increase the MTBF—mean time between failure— for a metastable event.) If registered or latched, the register/latch can be clocked by another clock input, but not itself—this would surely lead to metastable events if delays were not carefully controlled!

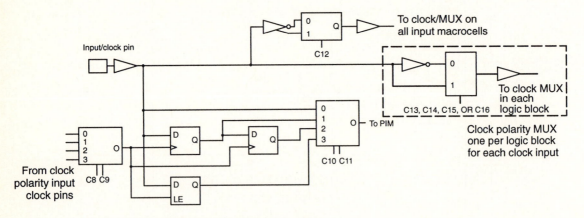

Figure 2-29 FLASH370 input macrocell

2.5.6   I/O Cells

Most I/O cells are used only to drive a signal off of the device, depending on the state of the output enable, and to provide a data path for incoming signals, as shown on the right-hand side of Figure 2-28. With some architectures, like that of the MACH 3 family, however, I/O cells contain switch matrices or output-routing pools in which a one-to-one connection is made between an I/O macrocell output and an I/O (see Figure 2-30). The advantage to this scheme is flexibility in determining where logic can be placed in a logic block in relation to where the I/O cell is located. The disadvantage is an incremental delay associated with the programmable routing structure and the increased die size.

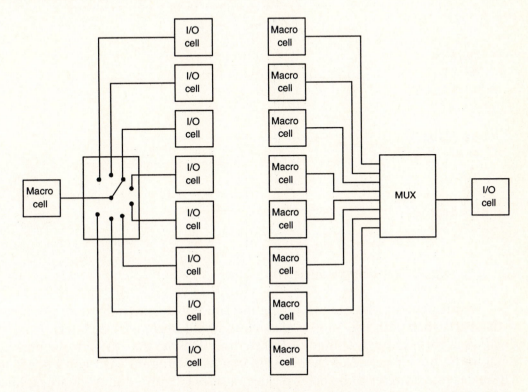

Figure 2-30 I/O cell with switch matrix [© Advanced Micro Devices, Inc. (Fall 1994) Reprinted with permission of copyright owner. All rights reserved.]

2.5.7 Timing Parameters

The timing specifications for CPLDs that are of most interest are the same for those of a 22V10: propagation delay, setup, clock-to-output, and register-to-register times (Figure 2-31).

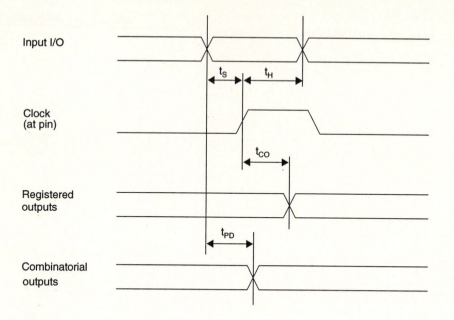

Figure 2-31 Key timing parameters

Postdesign implementation timing information is generally more predictable with CPLDs than with FPGAs (for reasons that will become clear later). For some designers, this is an advantage of CPLDs over FPGAs: that prior to beginning a design, the performance of that design can be estimated with good precision. These designers prefer to be able to select a device before doing any work, knowing that in the end it will perform as expected.

With a 22V10, the performance of a design can be estimated before you start if you have an accurate understanding of how many passes through the product-term array any logic expression will require. Any expression of more than 16 product terms will require additional passes. An expression of up to 112 product terms $(16 + 16 + 14 + 14 + 12 + 12 + 10 + 10 + 8 = 112)$ can be implemented in two passes. Of course, it is easier to predict with some certainty, based on your knowledge of the design, whether a given expression will require a 0–16 or 17–112 product terms versus a multiple of one product term. For example, if you believe the largest expression required for a state machine you are designing may take 14 product terms, then you could safely estimate that it would take no more than a maximum of two passes. An additional pass was added to **guard-band** (buffer) the estimate. If the number of passes for an expression can be accurately predicted, then the timing parameters can also be accurately predicted.

Estimating performance in some CPLDs is as easy as it is for a 22V10, but it is more complicated for many others. Compare the timing models for the MAX340 and FLASH370 (Figure 2-32). Performance in the former is highly dependent upon resource utilization. It may be difficult to determine the achievable performance prior to implementing the design in a CPLD with a timing model similar to that of the MAX340. Nonetheless, it is more predictable than with an FPGA.

MAX340 Timing Model

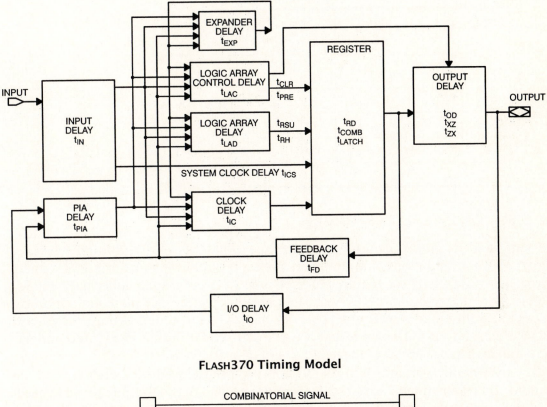

FLASH370 Timing Model

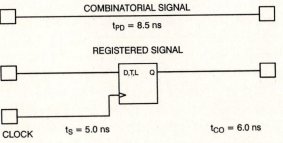

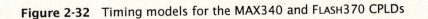

Figure 2-32   Timing models for the MAX340 and FLASH370 CPLDs

Like the 22V10, the CY7C371-143 CPLD has a simple timing model and will be used as the target architecture for the synthesis and fitting of many design examples. Its timing specifications are listed in Table 2-4. Its full datasheet is contained on the CD-ROM included with this text. See Appendix B for instructions on viewing and printing datasheets.

Table 2-4 Timing specification of the CY7C371-143 CPLD

Parameters	Min.	Max.
t_{PD}	—	8.5 ns
t_S	5 ns	—
t_H	0 ns	—
t_{CO}	—	6 ns
t_{CO2}	—	12 ns
t_{SCS}	7 ns	—

2.5.8   Other CPLD Features

Besides logic resources, routing mechanisms, product-term distribution schemes, macrocell configurations, and timing models, a few other features set CPLDs apart from one another. These features include in-system programmability (ISP), in-system reprogrammability (ISR), 5V/3.3V operation, test access port and boundary scan capability that is IEEE 1149.1 (JTAG, or Joint Test Action Group) compliant, and input and output buffers that are PCI (Peripheral Component Interconnect) compliant. Devices are also offered in a variety of packages.

In-system programmability is the ability to program a device while it is on the board. This mainstreams the manufacturing flow, and may save time because parts do not have to be handled for programming. This is particularly important for today's packages with fine-pitched pin spacing. Also, it eliminates the need for inventories of both programmed and unprogrammed parts. Instead, devices need to be handled only once—to place and solder on a board. Programming can then be accomplished via a card connector or automatic test equipment (ATE).

In-system reprogrammability is the ability to reprogram a device while it is in a circuit; it can be used for prototyping, field upgrades, or even to alter the functionality of the device during system operation. For a device advertised as ISR to be truly useful, it must be able to support logic changes while remaining in the same pinout and maintaining the requisite speed. Whether or not a device can meet these constraints is often dictated by the architecture of the programmable interconnect, logic block, and IO cells. A critical requirement for ISR is that an architecture allows a signal, whether it originates from a device pin or macrocell feedback, to route into a specific logic block, specific macrocell, and specific pin. Routing into a logic block depends upon both the number of inputs allowed into a logic block and whether that signal and other requisite signals can get into the logic block with the paths provided by the interconnect structure. Once inside the logic block, a specific macrocell can be used only if it is not already required for another function and if enough product terms (dedicated, steered, or shared) are available.

The JTAG specification defines a method to test device functionality and connections to other devices on the board through a test access port and boundary scan. By shifting data through the boundary scan, interconnections to other devices can be verified and vectors can be applied to a device's internal logic (Figure 2-33). JTAG is a methodology that may be used for testing and quality

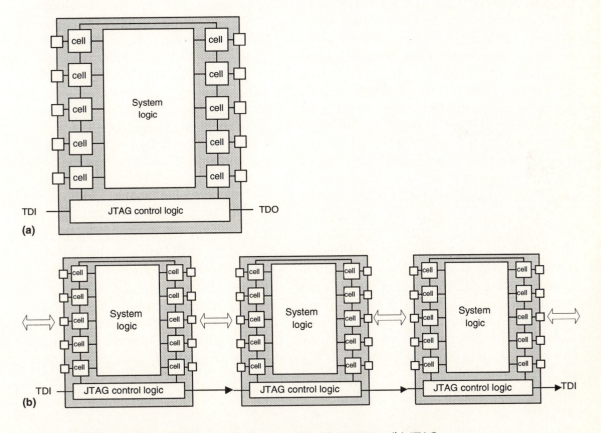

Figure 2-33   (a) JTAG used to test internal circuitry, (b) JTAG used for external testing of connections to other JTAG devices.

assurance or for debugging. To limit the number of vectors that need to be clocked through the scan path, JTAG also specifies a BIST (built-in self-test) mode. A device placed in this mode generates pseudorandom test-vectors as stimuli, compares internal outputs against expected results, and indicates success or failure.

The Peripheral Component Interconnect (PCI) bus is a local bus standard intended to support high-bandwidth applications such as full-motion video, networking, and data storage. It also supports plug-and-play operation. The PCI specification includes an electrical components checklist with requirements such as AC switching current. Because the PCI bus specification has become popular quickly, vendors of programmable logic have rushed to electrically characterize their devices and declare them PCI compliant.

An important feature of any PLD is packaging. Through-hole packages such as DIPs (dual in-line packages) and PGAs (pin-grid arrays) are used for a number of reasons. Sometimes they are used because the end user's board-manufacturing process may not support the newer surface-mount devices. They are also considerably easier to test: pins are typically spaced farther apart and test clips are readily available. Military customers often prefer DIPs and PGAs because the through-hole soldering is highly reliable in cases where the device will undergo acceleration (as in tank, aircraft, missile, or shipboard applications). DIP and PGA packages may have better thermal characteristics than their surface-mount counterparts: these packages are in direct contact with the board, allowing heat to dissipate not only through the package to the surrounding air, but also through the package and pins to the board. Many board materials also have a different coefficient of expansion than the devices. That is, the board will expand at a different rate than the device during temperature changes. Devices with "legs," such as DIPs and PGAs, can bend to accommodate these differences.

DIP packages, however, are being used less in favor of the surface-mount packages such as the SOIC (small outline IC), PLCC (plastic leadless chip carrier), LCC (J-leaded chip carriers), PQFP (plastic-quad flatpack), CQFP (ceramic-quad flatpack), and BGA (ball-grid array), ranging in I/O densities from 20 to 352 pins. The need for these packages arises not only from the need for high pin-count (through-hole devices could not have such fine-pitch pin spacing such as 0.65 mm for a QFP), but also from the need for higher board integration. Fewer and smaller boards in a system usually means lower costs and higher reliability. In addition, the booming portable and hand-held applications market requires high integration. The military has also found many applications in which it can use the ceramic flatpacks and J-leaded carriers. Figure 2-34 shows several packages and their relative sizes.

Our discussion of programmable logic to this point has followed the natural progression from TTL logic to higher levels of integration, through small PALs to CPLDs. We continue the progression and discuss FPGAs next.

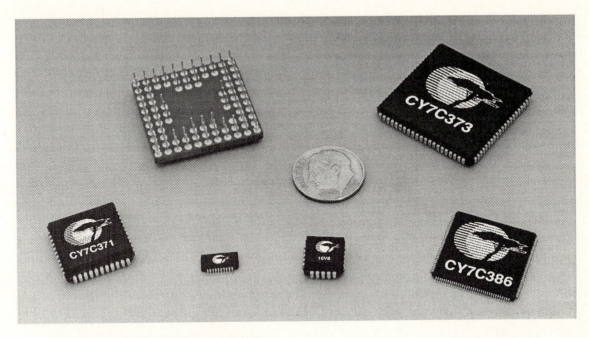

Figure 2-34 Packaging options

Breakout Exercise 2-2

Purpose: To become familiar with reading CPLD report files for resource utilization and timing analysis.

Perform the following steps carefully.

1. For this exercise we will return to the design in Breakout Exercise 1-1. If you have not completed that exercise, you will need to before proceeding.

2. Start Galaxy.

3. Select **Open** from the **Project** menu. To open the project, type `c:\vhdlbook\ch1\break1.wpr` or use the **Browse** button to traverse the directories, find, and select the `break1.wpr` file.

4. Select **Report file** from the **Info** menu. This will invoke Warp's text editor with the file `simple.rpt`, the report file that was created by Warp during Breakout Exercise 1-1. Maximize the window to create a larger viewing area.

5. Select **Find** from the **Search** menu. In the dialog box, type `design equations` and select **OK**. This will forward you to a section in the report file that is similar to the following:

```
DESIGN EQUATIONS                    (23:18:26)
    /y =
            /a * /b
    x.D =
            a * /b
          + /a * b
    x.AP =
            GND
    x.AR =
            GND
    x.C =
            clk
```

The / notation indicates inversion. It is similar to the bar notation commonly used. Thus, $/y = \bar{y}$ The /y notation indicates that the logic for the complement of y was implemented in the logic array and that y is obtained at the output pin by using the output polarity multiplexer in the macrocell of the CY7C371. The /y implementation was chosen by the optimization software because it requires one fewer product term. The * notation indicates a logical AND. The + notation indicates a logical OR. The order of precedence follows the normal precedence in Boolean algebra—AND before OR.

Whereas y is the output of a combinational function, x is the output of D-type flip-flop, as indicated by the .D extension in x.D. Signal x, used in other equations, is referred to as x.Q to indicate the Q output of the x flip-flop. The expressions for the .AP, .AR, and .C extensions represent the asynchronous preset, asynchronous reset, and clock input expressions, respectively. In this case, the asynchronous preset and reset of the flip-flop are grounded. The clock for the flip-flop comes from the signal clk.

6. Search for (Available). This will bring you to a section in the report file similar to the following:

	Required	Max (Available)
CLOCK/LATCH ENABLE signals	1	2
Input REG/LATCH signals	0	5
Input PIN signals	2	5
Input PINs using I/O cells	0	0
Output PIN signals	2	32
Total PIN signals	5	38
Macrocells Used	2	32
Unique Product Terms	3	160

This illustrates the resources that the design required compared to those available. In particular, it shows that:

- one clock signal was required;
- no input signals required registering or latching (this includes double registering);
- two signals were placed on input pins (they could just as easily have been placed on the I/O cells rather than on the dedicated inputs, but the fitter software chose to place them on the input pins);
- no input signals were placed on the I/O cells;
- two output signals were placed on the I/O cells;
- five total signals (clk, a, b, x, and y) were placed on pins;
- two macrocells were required (one for x and one for y);
- three unique product terms were required.

Obviously, this design does not stress the available resources of the 32 macrocell CY7C371 device.

7. Search for `timing path analysis`. This will bring you to a section in the report file similar to the following:

```
TIMING PATH ANALYSIS          (23:18:27) using Package: CY7C371-143JC
Messages:
-----------------------------------------------------------------------
Signal Name | Delay Type  |   tmax   | Path Description
-----------------------------------------------------------------------
reg::x[24]
inp::a
              tS            5.0 ns      1 pass
out::x
              tCO           6.0 ns
-----------------------------------------------------------------------
cmb::y[43]
inp::a
              tPD           8.5 ns      1 pass
-----------------------------------------------------------------------
Worst Case Path Summary
-----------------------
              tPD = 8.5 ns for y
               tS = 5.0 ns for x.D
              tCO = 6.0 ns for x.C
```

This portion of the report file indicates point-to-point delays. The first one is for the registered signal x, placed in the macrocell associated with pin 24. The worst-case path for setup time is from a to the input of the flip-flop, which requires one pass through the logic array (5 ns). In fact, the path from b also requires one pass. The fitter simply chose one signal to illustrate the worst-case path. If the path from b were to require two passes, then it would be shown instead of a. The worst-case clock-to-output time is 6.0 ns. This reflects the propagation delay for the clock to the flip-flop, in addition to the intrinsic clock-to-output delay of the flip-flop and the propagation delay from the flip-flop output to an output pin. In this case the signal propagates directly to the pin associated with the macrocell. This does not require any passes through the logic array. Other times, the worst-case delay may be associated with a signal that must be decoded from the state of flip-flops. This will require one or more passes through the logic array, and, hence, an incrementally larger clock-to-output delay (t_{CO2}).

The path for the combinational signal y takes one pass through the logic array, a propagation delay of 8.5 ns. The worst-case paths are summarized here. For this design there were so few paths that a summary wasn't really necessary. Soon, however, we will implement designs with hundreds of paths and we will want to be able to quickly identify the worst-case setup and clock-to-output times, as well as propagation delay.

8. Review the remainder of the report file to see what other useful information you can find. Refer to Chapter 6 of the on-line reference manual if you find something of particular interest that you want to understand in greater detail.

2.6   What Is an FPGA?

A field programmable gate array (FPGA) architecture is an array of logic cells that communicate with one another and with I/O via wires within **routing channels** (Figure 2-35). Like a semi-custom gate array, which consists of an array of transistors, an FPGA consists of an array of logic cells. In a gate array routing is customized, without programmable elements. In an FPGA, existing wire resources that run in horizontal and vertical columns (routing channels) are connected via programmable elements. These routing wires also connect logic to I/Os. Logic cell and rout-ing architectures differ from vendor to vendor. In general, logic cells have less functionality than the combined product terms and macrocells of CPLDs, but large functions can be created by cascading logic cells. We will compare CPLDs with FPGAs briefly in the section "PREP Benchmarks" at the end of this chapter, and revisit the topic at the end of Chapter 8, "Synthesis and Design Implementation."

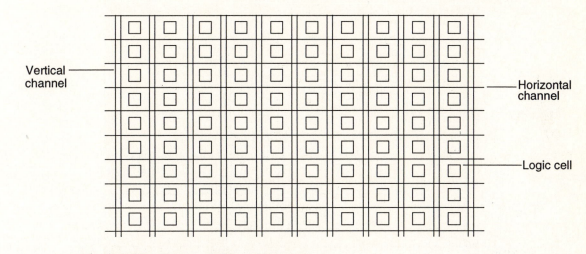

Figure 2-35 Generic FPGA architecture

To gain a more concrete understanding of how FPGAs work, consider the design of the three-bit counter of Figure 2-16 and Figure 2-17. This design can be implemented in an FPGA, as shown in Figure 2-36, which depicts a zoomed view of a portion of an FPGA architecture. All routing and logic cell resources are shown: Used resources are shown with solid lines. Unused resources are shown with dot-ted lines. Output C is the least significant bit of the counter, and is placed on pin 59. Tracing the signal back to its source, we find that the flip-flop for the C output is in the bottom-right corner. Examining the logic of this cell, we find that two inputs control a four-two-one multiplexer. The two inputs come from the enable on pin 56 and from the C output itself. We leave you to verify that the flip-flop will toggle when the enable is held high.

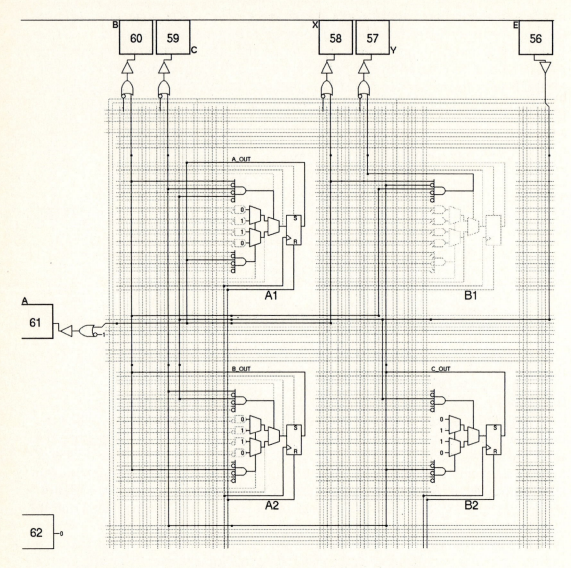

Figure 2-36 Implementation of a three-bit counter in an FPGA

2.6.1   Architecting an FPGA

As with other programmable logic products, FPGAs are developed to meet market needs. A market-driven vendor will survey not only what FPGAs are currently used for (predominately data-path, I/O-intensive, and register-intensive applications) but also what system designers would like to use FPGAs for or what they believe that they will use FPGAs for in the near future (high-performance applications such as a PCI bus target interface operating at 33 or 66 MHz, a DRAM controller with a 3 ns setup time, a DMA controller with a 6 ns clock-to-output delay, and networking applications involving Ethernet and ATM, among others). Among the top few market needs that FPGAs currently attempt to serve are:

1. Performance—the ability for real system designs to operate at increasingly higher frequencies;

2. Density and capacity—the ability to increase integration, to place more and more in a chip (system in a chip), and use all available gates within the FPGA, thereby providing a cost-effective solution;

3. Ease of use—the ability for system designers to bring their products to market quickly, leveraging the availability of easy-to-use software tools for logic synthesis as well as place and route, in addition to architectures that enable late design changes that affect logic, routing, and I/O resources without a significantly adverse effect on timing; and

4. In-system programmability and in-circuit reprogrammability—the ability to program or reprogram a device while it is in-system, mainstreaming manufacturing and inventories as well as allowing for field upgrades and user configurability.

After completing the list of market needs, a vendor must choose or develop a technology that it believes will satisfy the most important market needs. As with much of product development, there are trade-offs. Presently, there are two technologies of choice for use in developing FPGAs—SRAM and antifuse—each of which can satisfy a subset of the market needs. SRAM technology is presently used by Altera, Lucent Technologies, Atmel, Xilinx, and others. Antifuse technology is presently used by Actel, Cypress, QuickLogic, and Xilinx. We'll briefly explain each technology and its impact on device architectures, and summarize which market needs are best addressed with each technology.

2.6.2   **Technologies and Architecture Trade-offs**

Once a technology has been selected, it influences the choice of routing architectures. The routing architecture, in turn, influences the design of the logic cells.

Routing. The choice of technology has a significant impact on the routing architecture for one very simple reason: The physical dimensions of an SRAM cell are an order of magnitude larger than those of an antifuse element.

An **amorphous-silicon antifuse** can be deposited in the **via,** or the space between two layers of metal, as shown in Figure 2-37. In a semi-custom gate array, the top and bottom layers of metal make direct contact through a metal-interconnect via. In an amorphous-silicon-based FPGA, the two layers of metal are separated by amorphous (uncrystallized) silicon, which provides electrical insulation. A programming pulse of 10V to 12V and of necessary duration can be applied across the via, causing the top and bottom layers of metal to penetrate the amorphous silicon, creating a bidirectional conductive link (with a resistance of about 50 ohms), also shown in Figure 2-37. Because the size of an amorphous-silicon antifuse element is the same as that of a standard metal interconnect via, the programmable elements can be placed very densely, limited only by the minimum dimensions of the metal-line pitch, as shown in Figure 2-38. Once programmed, an antifuse element cannot be erased or reprogrammed.

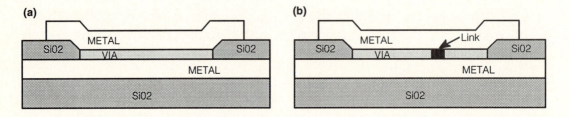

Figure 2-37   (a) An unprogrammed antifuse element and (b) a programmed antifuse element

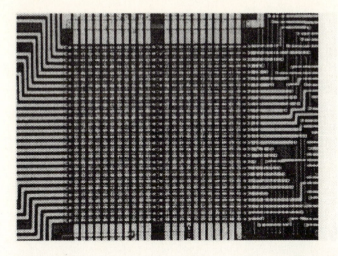

Figure 2-38   An array of amorphous-silicon antifuse elements

To program an antifuse element, a voltage differential must be applied across the antifuse element. Each antifuse element is isolated by with pass transistors so that other elements are not inadvertently programmed. These programming transistors, as well as the associated logic for addressing the antifuse locations, constitute the programming circuitry overhead.

The Actel FPGA products make use of an **oxide-nitride-oxide (ONO) antifuse,** which consists of three layers (Figure 2-39): the top, a conductor made of polysilicon, is electrically connected to one layer of metal; the middle has an oxide-nitride-oxide chemical composition and is an insulator; and the bottom is a conductive layer of negatively doped diffusion. Unprogrammed, the ONO antifuse insulates the top layer of metal from the bottom layer. The fuse is programmed in a manner similar to that of an amorphous-silicon antifuse: A programming voltage is applied, allowing the insulator to be penetrated by the top and bottom layers and establishing an electrical connection of fairly low resistance (about 300 ohms).

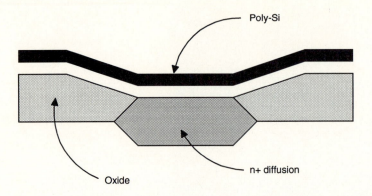

Figure 2-39 ONO antifuse element [*Field-Programmable Devices, Technology, Applications, Tools* by Stephen D. Brown. Published by Stan Baker Associates, ©1995.]

Because antifuse elements can be placed very densely, FPGAs that use this technology typically have flexible routing architectures, which allow the electrical connection of wires at nearly every intersection. Figure 2-40 illustrates a routing architecture of an antifuse-based FPGA. The open boxes at the intersections of wires indicate a programmable antifuse. The inputs and outputs of the logic cell can connect to any vertical wire (except the clock structure, which in this figure connects only to the clock, set, and reset of the flip-flop). Wires within a vertical channel may connect with those in a horizontal channel where they intersect. Some wires (segmented ones) extend the length of only one logic cell. These may connect to the segmented wires of the logic cells above and below but on the same layer of metal through a programmed antifuse, called a **pass link,** shown as an x in the figure. A routing architecture made up of entirely segmented wires would provide the greatest routing flexibility. However, using segmented wires for long routes would require several antifuse elements to be programmed, each adding an additional resistance (about 50 ohms for amorphous-silicon antifuse, about 300 ohms for ONO antifuse) to the signal path. Greater resistances result in slower performance. Therefore, other wires extend further distances (four logic cells or the entire length or width of the array), and are optimized for either local or global routing.

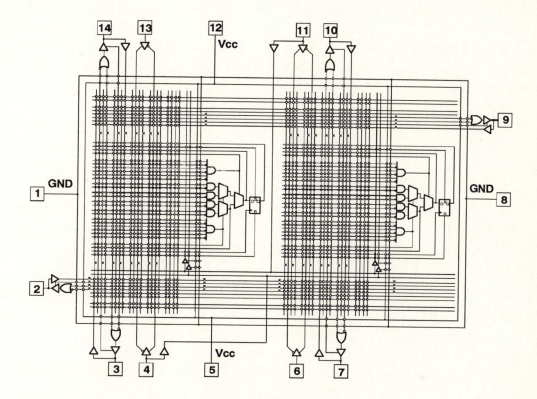

Figure 2-40 The Cypress pASIC380 routing structure

Static RAM (SRAM) cells may be used to control the state of pass transistors, which can establish connections between horizontal and vertical wires. Figure 2-41 shows six pass transistors that allow any combination of connections of the four wires (N, S, E, W). The source-to-drain resistance of such a pass transistor is about 1,000 ohms. SRAM cells can also be used to drive the select inputs of multiplexers that are used to choose from one of several signals to route on a given wire source.

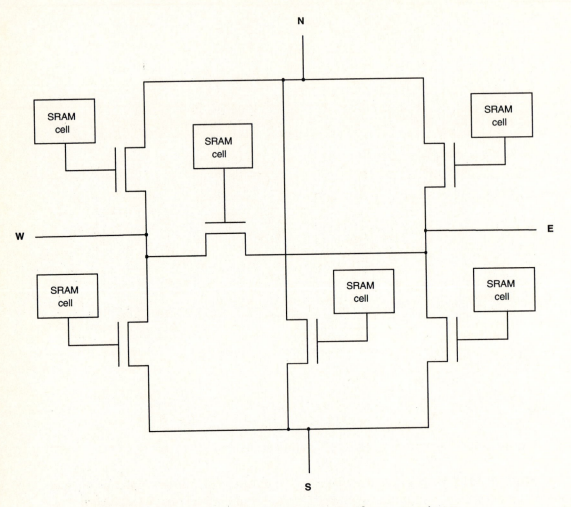

Figure 2-41   SRAM cells used to control states of pass transistors

An SRAM memory cell consists of five transistors (Figure 2-42): two for each of the two inverters making up the latch and one for addressing (used to select the memory cell for programming). An SRAM cell is reprogrammable, unlike antifuse elements, which are physically altered when programmed. SRAM cells are volatile, however, meaning that the states of the memory cells are lost when power is not applied. SRAM-based FPGAs must be programmed (usually from a serial EPROM) each time the circuit is powered up. As with antifuse elements, the programming circuitry for SRAM elements must include the addressing and data registers (programming circuitry overhead).

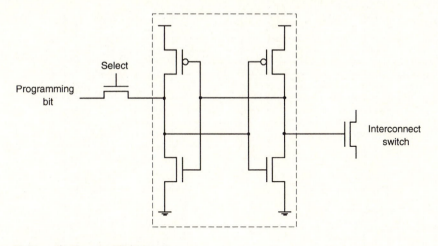

Figure 2-42 An SRAM cell

An SRAM cell and associated pass transistor is considerably larger than an antifuse element and associated programming transistor. These programming elements cannot be placed as densely as antifuse elements. SRAM FPGAs therefore do not have routing architectures for which there is a programmable element at nearly every intersection; having them would increase the metal spacing and overall die size, limiting density, increasing cost, and slowing performance. Instead, programmable elements are strategically placed to provide a trade-off between routability, density, and performance. As with antifuse FPGAs, some wires may extend the length of one logic cell and others may extend further, again balancing routing flexibility with density and performance.

Figure 2-43 illustrates the Xilinx XC4000 interconnect. This figure shows only those wires that extend the length of one cell (called **single-length wires** for this architecture). Programmable elements exist at the intersection of the logic cell (named **configurable logic block,** or CLB, by Xilinx) inputs and single-length wires. The outputs can connect to some of the single-length wires. For one CLB to communicate with another or with an I/O via single-length wires, wires can connect through the switch matrices. Each wire on one side of a switch matrix can connect to a wire on each of the other three sides of the matrix, as illustrated by dots indicating where connections can be established. The XC4000 architecture also includes double-length and long lines (not shown) for longer routes and greater routing flexibility.

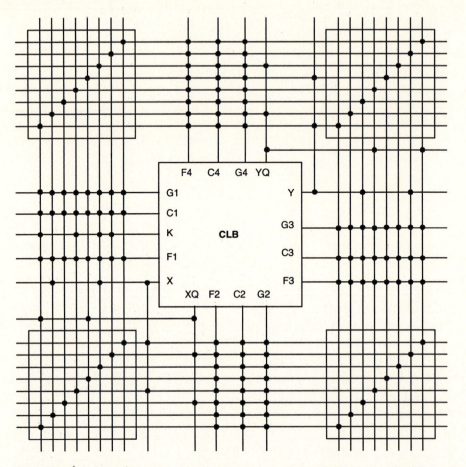

Figure 2-43 XC4000 Interconnect [Figure courtesy of Xilinx, Inc. © Xilinx, Inc. 1995. All rights reserved.]

Logic Cell Architecture. Logic cell architectures are influenced by routing resources: FPGAs that have routing structures with many wires and many programmable connections tend to have smaller logic cells with more inputs and outputs relative to the number of gates in the logic cell. These are typically antifuse

FPGAs. FPGAs that have routing structures with fewer wires and programmable interconnections tend to have larger logic cells with fewer inputs and outputs relative to the number of gates in the logic cell. These are typically SRAM FPGAs.

Antifuse FPGAs may use logic cells with more inputs and outputs because of the availability of wires to transport signals and the availability of fuses, which allow nearly any wire to connect to any other wire. Routing does not usually pose a problem or limitation for these FPGAs. Antifuse FPGAs may also use smaller logic cells to increase efficiency, since small functions (such as a 2-input AND gate) do not waste logic cell resources, and large functions can be built from multiple logic cells. An architecture with small logic cells enables you to utilize the full capacity of the device. If a logic cell is too small, however, most functions will require multiple levels of logic cells, with each level incurring a propagation delay as well as a routing delay associated with the wire capacitance and fuse resistance and capacitance. To balance efficiency with performance, antifuse FPGAs may use medium-sized logic cells with multiple outputs that can implement multiple independent functions.

SRAM-based FPGAs typically use larger logic cells with fewer inputs and outputs. These logic cells can implement larger functions without incurring routing delays, which can be more significant because of the larger resistance and capacitance of the programmable element. But, because they tend to have fewer outputs as a ratio of the number of gates in the logic cell, they tend to be less efficient for implementing small functions. Again, the trade-off is made between efficiency and performance, and is closely tied to the routing architecture.

Figure 2-46 through Figure 2-48 illustrate the logic cells of Actel's ACT3, Lucent Technologies' ORCA, Cypress's pASIC380, Xilinx's XC4000, and Altera's FLEX 8000 families of FPGAs. The first two are logic cells of antifuse FPGAs; the remainder are from SRAM FPGAs.

The ACT3 logic cell (**logic module,** or **LM**) has eight inputs and one output. There are two types of logic modules in the ACT3: combinational and sequential (one includes a flip-flop, and the other does not). The logic is based on multiplexers, which are universal logic modules (that is, a 2^n to-1 multiplexer can implement any function of $n + 1$ or fewer variables, using 0, 1, the true, and the complement of the variables as select lines and inputs to the multiplexer). As such, the modules can implement any of several hundred functions of the inputs. Larger functions can be built by cascading logic cells.

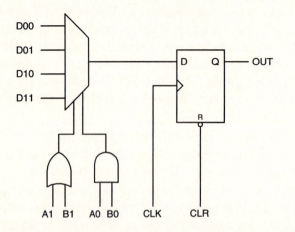

Figure 2-44   The ACT3 logic module [© Actel Corporation. Reprinted by permission.]

The ORCA logic cells, or **programmable function units (PFUs),** have 14 inputs and 5 outputs. Each PFU can be configured as four 4-input LUTs (look-up tables), two 5-input LUTs, or one 6-input LUT, which can implement a function of up to 11 inputs. Each PFU has four flip-flops and can be configured for arithmetic circuits or read/write RAM.

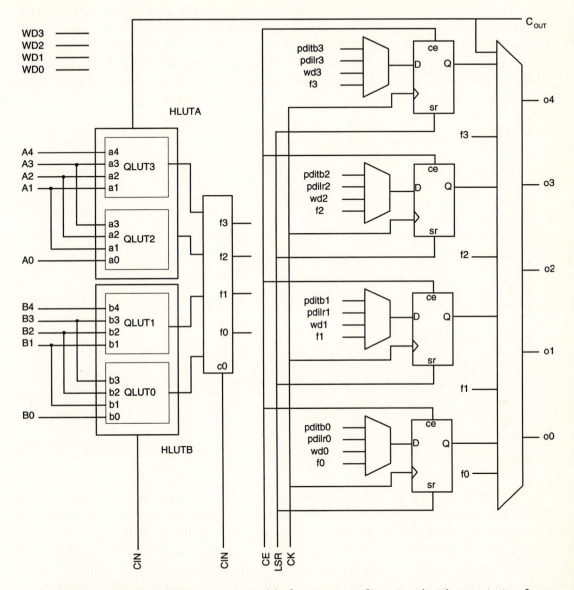

Figure 2-45 The ORCA programmable function unit [Reprinted with permission from Lucent Technologies, Inc.]

The pASIC380 logic cell has 23 inputs and 5 outputs and can implement multiple independent functions. The 4-to-1 multiplexer can implement any function of three variables, and the wide AND gates also allow gating functions of up to 14 inputs. Exclusive OR gates, OR gates, a sum of three small products, and counter macros can be implemented. Larger functions can be built by cascading logic cells. All logic cells include a flip-flop.

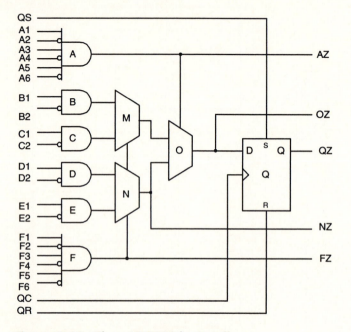

Figure 2-46   The pASIC380 logic cell

The XC4000 CLB has 13 inputs and 4 outputs. It is a complex cell: two 4-input LUTs feed another 3-input LUT. Each CLB can implement any function of four or five variables and some of up to nine variables. Alternatively, a CLB can be configured to implement two functions of four variables, or one of two variables and another of five. Each CLB has two flip-flops. The CLB can also be configured for special arithmetic circuits, such as a two-bit adder with carry-in and carry-out, or as a read/write RAM of 16 bits for storing data.

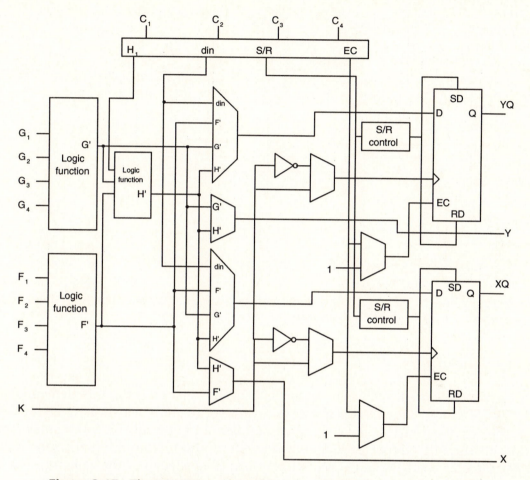

Figure 2-47   The XC4000 configurable logic block [Figure courtesy of Xilinx, Inc. © Xilinx, Inc. 1995. All rights reserved.]

Altera markets the FLEX 8000 as a CPLD, as indicated in the caption of Figure 2-48. We will consider it to be a hybrid CPLD/FPGA architecture, because it addresses the SRAM routing issues differently from both CPLDs and FPGAs. In this architecture, the logic cells (**logic array blocks,** or **LABs**) are made up of eight **logic elements (LEs).** Each LAB has a local interconnect in which any LE can connect to any other LE. The local interconnect and the relatively large size of the LABs (compared to FPGA logic cells) reduce the routing congestion on the inter-LAB and I/O routing channels. Each LE has a four-input LUT and can implement a single function of four variables. An LE also has carry circuitry for arithmetic circuits, as well as a flip-flop.

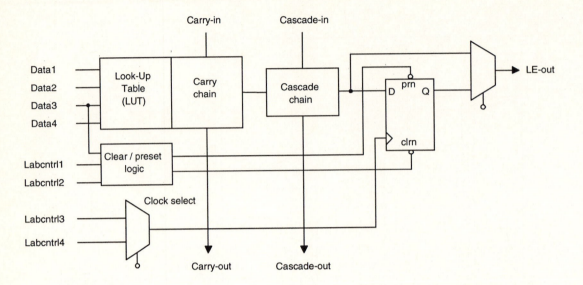

Figure 2-48   The FLEX8000 CPLD logic element [Reprinted by permission of Altera Corporation. © 1993 Altera Corporation.]

2.6.3   Timing

Timing cannot be predicted easily for any but the simplest of designs implemented in FPGAs. Signal propagation delays are a function of the number of cascaded logic cells, the signal path in the logic cells, the number of programmable interconnects through which the signal propagates (as well as the technology—antifuse or SRAM), fan-out, and I/O cell delays. Without prior knowledge of the value of each of these variables (how many logic cells, how many programmable interconnects, fan-out, and so forth)—that is, without a knowledge of how the design will be placed and routed—the propagation delays and system performance cannot be predicted with precision. This is not unlike the dilemma faced when developing a semi-custom gate array. For systems that do not have high-performance requirements, any FPGA will do.

Place and route tools typically include static timing analyzers, which are used to calculate setup times, clock-to-output delays, and maximum operating frequency. These timing analyzers enable you to find delays for signals that propagate between the output of one register and the input of another, as well as delays from input buffers to input registers and registers to output buffers. Figure 2-49 is an example of the type of timing data that a path analyzer can provide.

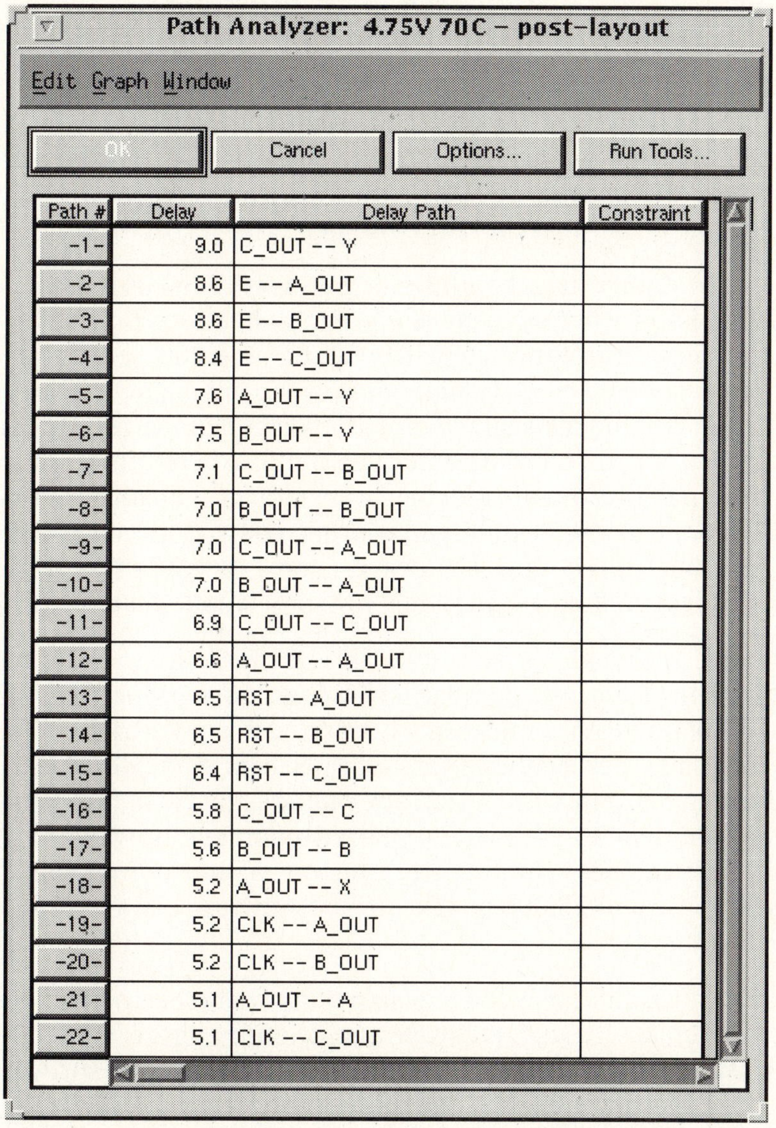

Path #	Delay	Delay Path	Constraint
-1-	9.0	C_OUT -- Y	
-2-	8.6	E -- A_OUT	
-3-	8.6	E -- B_OUT	
-4-	8.4	E -- C_OUT	
-5-	7.6	A_OUT -- Y	
-6-	7.5	B_OUT -- Y	
-7-	7.1	C_OUT -- B_OUT	
-8-	7.0	B_OUT -- B_OUT	
-9-	7.0	C_OUT -- A_OUT	
-10-	7.0	B_OUT -- A_OUT	
-11-	6.9	C_OUT -- C_OUT	
-12-	6.6	A_OUT -- A_OUT	
-13-	6.5	RST -- A_OUT	
-14-	6.5	RST -- B_OUT	
-15-	6.4	RST -- C_OUT	
-16-	5.8	C_OUT -- C	
-17-	5.6	B_OUT -- B	
-18-	5.2	A_OUT -- X	
-19-	5.2	CLK -- A_OUT	
-20-	5.2	CLK -- B_OUT	
-21-	5.1	A_OUT -- A	
-22-	5.1	CLK -- C_OUT	

Path Analyzer: 4.75V 70C – post–layout

Edit Graph Window

OK   Cancel   Options...   Run Tools...

Figure 2-49   Path analyzer provides point-to-point delay information

Understanding the technologies as well as the routing and logic cell architectures can help a designer choose an FPGA for a particular application. Additionally, HDLs like VHDL and Verilog allow relative design independence, permitting a designer to benchmark design performance from one architecture to the next without reentering a design.

2.6.4   Comparing SRAM to Antifuse

Vendors of SRAM and antifuse FPGAs attempt to service the same market. However, the choice in technology forces a conscious and deliberate decision to focus on a segment of that market. Below, we list again those issues that architects of FPGAs must consider, and compare SRAM and antifuse-based products, to see which best services a particular market requirement.

Performance. Many designs push the limits of FPGA system performance, and designers often like to know where to start. Some generalizations may be made: (1) At present, peak system performance achievable from an 8,000 gate FPGA is less than 50 MHz (despite what advertisers claim) and for most designs it is around 35 MHz. Of course, design techniques such as pipelining can help achieve higher performance. (2) Presently, antifuse FPGAs offer the highest performance for most designs, due, in large part, to the smaller resistance of programmable links (50 ohms versus 1,000) as well as the flexibility in routing, which does not prohibit signals from taking the most direct paths. However, some SRAM FPGAs have dedicated carry logic to provide better performance for some applications.

Density and Capacity. Although the size of an antifuse FPGA logic cell is typically smaller and the number of outputs as a ratio of the number of logic cell gates is greater than those for its SRAM counterpart, which allows these logic cells to implement more user logic per available gate (greater capacity), SRAM FPGAs are presently available at higher densities. AT&T, for example, has a 40,000-gate FPGA. Most vendors of SRAM-based FPGAs have plans to achieve upward of 50,000 usable gate densities in the next three years, whereas vendors of antifuse-based FPGAs plan to reach upward of 25,000 usable gates. For massive integration, SRAM FPGAs provide the solution.

Ease of Use. The designer must develop a design quickly and easily. This requires the availability of both easy-to-use software and friendly and forgiving device architectures. The availability of software varies from one silicon or software vendor to the next. Those that have been in the market longer tend to have the most support. Friendly, forgiving architectures make it easy to implement structures efficiently (anything from simple AND gates to counters, arithmetic circuits, and state machines), have routing flexibility so that software tools can automatically place and route a design, and can accommodate design changes without changing pinout and performance.

Antifuse-based architectures, for the most part, have the lead in this area: Routable architectures make it easy for software to be developed so that placing and routing can be done automatically and design changes can still fit in the same pinout by rerouting (the routing limitations of some SRAM FPGAs make it impossible or difficult for a design to fit with the same pinout, since placing and routing may have to be done by hand). Design changes in antifuse FPGAs usually can be accommodated with little impact on timing, provided that multiple logic cell delays are not added. This is because routing changes that require additional programmable links cause only incremental delays.

In-System Programmability (ISP) and In-System Reprogrammability (ISR). Antifuse FPGAs are OTP (one-time programmable) devices. While it is clearly not possible to reconfigure such a device, it is possible to program such a device in-system, but the programming yield and times of antifuse FPGAs currently make ISP cost prohibitive. (Scrapping one device in a hundred usually is not a problem, particularly if the device can be replaced without charge, but scrapping one board or system in a hundred is usually too costly). Because the ability to program an SRAM device can be verified before the device is delivered to the customer, SRAM FPGAs have significantly higher programming yields, allowing ISP for all and ISR for some. In-system programmability is used to mainstream the manufacturing flow, although in-system programmability usually requires an on-board serial EPROM or a card connector. With ISP, fewer parts and inventories need to be handled. In-system reprogramming is also an emerging need: it is the ability to reconfigure an FPGA in its system for prototyping, or even for field upgrades. Reprogramming could be performed by a technician or an end user, from a serial EPROM or perhaps from data downloaded from a disk. Reconfiguring in the field is feasible only if the design can fit, route, and use the same pinout. For some device architectures, this requirement is an obstacle.

2.6.5 Other FPGA Features

Some FPGAs also include I/O cells with input or output registers, or both. These are included to increase flip-flop count, efficiently use flip-flops as opposed to entire logic cells for input and output registering, and provide good setup and clock-to-output times. Special-purpose inputs are commonly included in FPGAs, and are used to drive large internal loads while minimizing skew. Although they may have limitations as to which routing resources may be used, they are particularly useful for control signals that affect a large portion of a circuit. Nearly all FPGAs will include low-skew clock-distribution networks, which allow a clock to be distributed to all flip-flops quickly and with minimal skew between when the clock arrives at one logic cell and when it arrives at another. Low skew is critical to high-performance design.

Some vendor logic cells or routing structures include internal three-state buffers, which allow signals to share a common unidirectional or bidirectional bus.

Busing techniques may be used in conjunction with register files to efficiently perform arithmetic or other datapath operations. We'll cover this topic in the context of design examples.

As with CPLDs, FPGAs may offer 5V/3.3V operation, lower power consumption options, JTAG-compliant boundary scan, on-chip RAM (used to efficiently implement register files or FIFOs), and PCI-compliant I/Os.

Vendors of FPGAs and CPLDs specify power differently—there isn't a common measuring stick, so you should read the fine print if low power is critical. This can also be true of performance.

Vendors may use the term "PCI-compliant" loosely: it usually means that the device meets the requirements of the PCI components electrical checklist for a specified range of temperature, but it often does not necessarily mean that a real-world PCI interface design can operate from dc to 33 MHz, as required by PCI.

▼

Breakout Exercise 2-3

Purpose: To become acquainted with the FPGA tool flow process, including using the static timing analyzer.

Read each step completely before performing any operations.

1. For this exercise we will return to the design in Breakout Exercise 2-1.

2. Start Galaxy.

3. Select **Open** from the **Project** menu, and open the project
   c:\vhdlbook\ch2\break1.wpr either by typing the name or by using the
   Browse button to traverse the directories, find, and select the break1.wpr
   file. The Galaxy window will appear with 3bcount.vhd in the project list. If it
   is not listed, it is probably because you did not save the project settings
   before closing the project at the end of Breakout Exercise 2-1. In this case,
   select **Add All** from the **Files** menu. Then set the file to be the top-level
   design.

4. Click on **Device** from the **Synthesis options** panel. This brings up a dialog
   box. Select C381A from the device scroll list. We will resynthesize this design
   for a pASIC380 FPGA. Leave all other selections with their default values, and
   click the **OK** button.

5. Click the **Smart** button from the **Compile** panel. This will cause a compilation
   window to appear and the synthesis software to process the VHDL code. The
   synthesis process will create a netlist, contained in the file 3bcount.qdf.

6. Close the compilation window.

7. From the **Tools** menu in Galaxy, select **SpDE** to start the place and route tool for the pASIC380 FPGAs. Maximize this window for the largest viewing area.

8. In SpDE, click the open folder icon in the toolbar (do not choose File->Open; this is not the same). Traverse the directories to the `c:\vhdlbook\ch2` directory. Select the file `3bcount.qdf`.

9. Select **Run Tools** from the **Tools** menu. Click on **Run**. The place and route tools will run. A dialog box will appear when all tools have completed. Click **OK**.

10. Select **Full Fit** from the **View** menu. This will give you a view of the design layout on the chip. Select **Zoom In** from the **View** menu, click, and drag the mouse to form a square around the portion of the layout that you want to zoom.

11. After you have zoomed in on a portion of the circuit, choose **Preferences** from the **View** menu. Select the boxes for Draw Routing Resources and Draw Cell Resources. Choose **OK**. You should see an image similar to that of Figure 2-36. The used resources will be in color. The unused resources will be in light gray. Before zooming out, deselect the viewing preferences; otherwise, when you zoom out, the layout view will become a mess of gray.

12. Select **Utilization** from the **Info** menu. This brings up a resource utilization summary. In particular, it summarizes the utilized logic cell, I/O cell, and interconnect resources. For more detailed information about the synthesis, place, and route of this design, choose **Report File** from the **Info** menu.

13. Read completely section 5.5, "SpDE Analysis Tools" of the Warp user's guide on-line documentation set. Use the information under "Key Calculations" to calculate the worst-case setup time, register-to-register delay, and clock-to-output delay. Clock-to-output delay is measured as the sum of the delay from the clock pad to flip-flops and flip-flops to output pads. Which of these parameters limits maximum operating frequency? (Remember, if the clock-to-output delay plus the setup time of the sampling device is greater than the register-to-register delay, then it is the limiting factor.)

2.7   PREP Benchmarks

The Programmable Electronics Performance Company (PREP) is a nonprofit corporation that is in essence a consortium of programmable logic vendors. Its goal is to provide a standard means to benchmark, compare, and analyze CPLD and FPGA device architectures. One of the primary reasons PREP aspires to this goal is that the average engineer does not have time to study the individual features of each vendor's offerings to determine which CPLD or FPGA best suits his or her application.

The member vendors of PREP defined a set of nine simple circuits:

1. A datapath circuit consisting of a 4-to-1 multiplexer, a register, and a shift register (all 8 bits wide).

2. A timer/counter circuit consisting of two registers, a 4-to-1 multiplexer, counter, and comparator (all 8 bits wide).

3. A small state machine consisting of 8 states, 8 inputs, and 8 outputs.

4. A large state machine consisting of 16 states, 8 inputs, and 8 outputs.

5. An arithmetic circuit consisting of 4-by-4 multiplier, an 8-bit adder, and an 8-bit register.

6. A 16-bit accumulator.

7. A 16-bit counter with synchronous load and enable.

8. A 16-bit prescaled counter with load and enable. The counter does not have to begin counting until several clock cycles after the a value has been loaded.

9. A 16-bit address decoder.

Individual vendor companies may then implement these circuits in a device and report performance and the number of instances of a given benchmark circuit that can fit in the device. When more than one instance of a circuit can be implemented in a device, the outputs of one instance are tied to the inputs of the next instance. PREP collects, verifies, and publishes vendor data.

Table 2-5 is an example of the type of information that is provided by a vendor to PREP. For each of the nine benchmark circuits, a row in the table lists the number of "reps," or instances, of that benchmark that can fit in a device. It also indicates the worst, best, and mean performance of the instances. In addition, it indicates the external performance, which is a measure of how fast the circuit could operate if the outputs of the last instance were tied externally via pins to the inputs of the first instance. External performance is the sum $t_{CO} + t_S$. Other information indicates whether the implementation was optimized for capacity or performance, the name of the tool used for benchmarking, the version of the tool, whether automatic place and route was used, and other notes.

Table 2-5   Sample vendor benchmark submission to PREP

Device	BM#	Description	Capacity		Performance (MHz)				Optimized		Tools used					Notes
			Reps	Reps%	Worst	Best	Mean	Ext	Cap	Perf	Tool Name	Rev	APR	Crit	HM	
CY7C371-143	1	Datapath	2	100	143	145	143	91	X	X	Warp2	3.2	X			1
CY7C371-143	2	Timer/counter	1	78	87	87	87	87	X	X	Warp2	3.2	X			
CY7C371-143	3	Small state machine	3	84	143	143	143	91	X	X	Warp2	3.2	X			
CY7C371-143	4	Large state machine	1	41	65	65	65	65	X	X	Warp2	3.2	X			
CY7C371-143	4	Large state machine	2	81	87	87	87	65	X	X	Warp2	3.2	X			2
CY7C371-143	5	Arithmetic	0	103	0	0	0	0	X	X	Warp2	3.2	X			
CY7C371-143	6	16-bit accumulator	1	100	50	50	50	50	X	X	Warp2	3.2	X			
CY7C371-143	7	16-bit counter	1	50	91	91	91	91	X	X	Warp2	3.2	X			
CY7C371-143	7	16-bit counter	2	100	143	143	143	91	X	X	Warp2	3.2	X			
CY7C371-143	8	16-bit prescaled counter	1	50	91	91	91	91	X	X	Warp2	3.2	X			
CY7C371-143	8	16-bit prescaled counter	2	100	143	143	143	91	X	X	Warp2	3.2	X			
CY7C371-143	9	Memory map	3	84	143	143	143	91	X	X	Warp2	3.2	X			

Notes:
(1) Alternate Step and Repeat used to avoid pin constraints
(2) Required 103.12 percent of device to fit

PREP has not gained as much acceptance as the SPEC marks used for the computing industry. This is partly because the programmable logic market is considerably smaller, but also for a variety of other reasons, including vendor misuse of the benchmark results. Although PREP does not endorse averaging or manipulating the numbers, some vendors do so, and claim that they "win" the benchmarks. This has happened enough that some engineers doubt the usefulness of the benchmarks.

Engineers may also ponder whether or not someone who is not an expert in the architecture can achieve the results that are published. That is, the benchmark data does not adequately indicate how easy it is to use a particular device and the software to achieve these results. The large amount of data can lead to confusion, particularly for those who have not been told what the data represents. Although one of the ideas behind having so much data is to allow engineers to see for themselves how a particular device performs for a given type of application, the PREP data lacks the simplicity of the SPEC marks.

PREP has received varying degrees of support from vendors as well. Xilinx, for instance, pulled its data out of version 1.3 of the benchmarks; Altera certified a large number of their devices, and Cypress certified just four. Obviously, some vendors may believe the PREP benchmarks to be a valuable marketing tool, and others may not. Some of the vendor's reluctance may be due to vendor misuse of the data, and some of the reluctance may be due to concerns about the benchmarks themselves. One complaint has been that the benchmarks do not adequately measure performance and capacity in larger devices. This is because the PREP benchmarks provide data only for the same circuit replicated over and over, rather than using a more realistic system. In addition, some of the circuits do not actually perform any function when connected together. The state machines, for example, quickly become stuck in states, with outputs never changing when the outputs of one instance are connected to the inputs of another.

With all their shortcomings, the PREP benchmarks do provide useful data. However, you should carefully analyze the data and not necessarily rely on vendors' summaries. At the least, the data can give you a ballpark feel for how well a device will perform for a particular application. The alternative is to create your own benchmark circuits and gather data for yourself. This would not only be time consuming but also costly. As a consortium and a nonprofit company, PREP continues to try to improve its services to engineers in order to promote and improve the programmable logic industry. One of PREP's considerations is to define a set of synthesis benchmarks to help engineers compare and analyze synthesis and EDA vendors. PREP can be reached via the World Wide Web site: http//www.prep.org. There, you can find out more about PREP and the benchmarks, and download the benchmark data for all certified devices.

Choosing a Device. When you select a device for a given design, it should be based on several points:

- The design goals. You need to know how fast the design must run, the maximum setup time and clock-to-output delay. You also need to have an idea for how much logic the design takes—100 gates, 1,000 gates, or 10,000 gates? Having a ballpark figure will help narrow the choices.

- Architectural features. How many clocks are required? What sort of output enable control is required? How many resets? How many critical signals? Understanding which type of resources is required may help to eliminate a few architectures and highlight a few others.

- Useful benchmark data. What type of application will you be implementing— state machines, counters, datapath, arithmetic, glue logic? Knowing the types of design units you want to implement in a PLD and having some benchmark data can help you to select the most appropriate architectures.

- Benchmarking. Although many designers must choose a device so that board design may continue in parallel with the PLD design, sometimes there is enough time to test a design in several PLDs. This gives a designer the best understanding of how well architectures perform, before selecting a device.

2.8   Future Direction of Programmable Logic

We do not have a crystal ball that shows the future of programmable logic, but that won't keep us from making predictions, some of which are obvious.

- Performance and density requirements will increase. Three-layer metal technology as well as smaller processes such as 0.35 micron CMOS (most programmable logic is presently on 0.65 micron CMOS) will help both performance and density. As performance improves at higher densities, FPGAs will take some of the ASIC market because they provide several advantages: They have small NRE costs (resulting in lower initial and low volume costs), designing is less risky (multiple cycles are acceptable), the design cycle is rapid (simulation can be less exhaustive, and manufacturing is not part of the total design time), working with an ASIC vendor is eliminated (interfacing with another company can be time consuming), and fewer resources are required (one person rather than a team).

- The 3.3V market will continue to grow.

- Large devices may incorporate on-board PLLs (phase-locked loops) to control clock skew, and perhaps to purposely introduce clock skew in output flip-flops to achieve short clock-to-output delays. PLLs are already used in some ASICs.

- In-system programming will continue to be used to mainstream manufacturing.

- In-circuit reprogrammability will lead to innovative designs, which will fuel the need for more devices that are truly reconfigurable. Reprogrammability, however, requires robust routing resources and a reprogrammable technology. These two requirements may be at odds with each other and with end-user performance requirements. It may take a few years for reconfigurability to be viable in a large percentage of systems, but if it takes hold, it could change design methodologies to include programmable and reprogrammable systems.

- The distinction between CPLDs and FPGAs may become less clear as programmable logic vendors experiment with FPGAs partitioned into blocks of logic with dedicated routing resources.

- The use of on-board RAM and other dedicated functions and interfaces may proliferate.

Breakout Exercise 2-4

Purpose: To become proficient with all GUIs in the Warp design environment.

Starting with the Breakout Exercises in Chapter 3, we will no longer provide explicit directions for navigating menus. We will assume that you are familiar with the GUI. To become more accustomed to the GUIs of Galaxy, SpDE, and Nova, we suggest that you read Chapters 4, 5, and 6 of the on-line user's guide. You may also want to work through the tutorial in Chapter 3 of the user's guide.

Problems

2.1. Noactivity is a signal that is asserted if none of the ports in a 4-port network repeater are active. (a) Draw the circuit diagram required to implement the logic for noactivity using the TTL inventory listed at the beginning of the chapter. (b) Draw the circuit diagram required to implement the logic for noactivity in a PAL16R4. (c) Compare the implementations: How many TTL devices are required? How many of the 16R4 product terms are required? How many macrocells? Compare the levels of logic. Qualitatively compare the total propagation delays and standby power requirements.

2.2. What resources of the 16R4 (I/Os, product terms, and macrocells) are required to implement the collision signal X (described at the beginning of the chapter) and noactivity (see exercise above) in the same 16R4?

2.3. After producing several production units of a board, a design change is required: The logic for collision and noactivity must change because it is discovered that the input signals are active low. Describe the corrective action for the next production run of the board if (a) TTL devices are used, and (b) a PAL is used.

2.4. Determine the Boolean expressions required to implement a 10-bit counter in a 22V10. How can resources be allocated in order for this design to fit? What is the maximum frequency of operation, given the timing specifications of page 44? Can resources be allocated for a 10-bit counter with synchronous load?

2.5. Odd is a registered signal that is the exclusive OR of A, B, C, D, E, and F. How can this expression be implemented in a 22V10? What setup and hold times must be met? What is the clock-to-output delay?

2.6. Implement a 4-bit counter with synchronous enable in a 22V10. What are the setup and hold-time requirements? What is the clock-to-output delay and maximum frequency of operation?

2.7. Describe the features of a 16V8 in relation to those of a 16L8 and 22V10.

2.8. Implement the following functions in each of the logic cells of Figures 2-44 through 2-48 and compare efficiency:

   a. two-input AND

   b. seven-input AND

   c. two-bit counter

   d. one-bit full adder (hint: start with a truth table)

   e. two input OR

   f. eight input XOR (parity generator)

2.9. Illustrate how to implement the following functions in a four-to-one multiplexer. You can use 1, 0, the true and complement of each signal as inputs and select lines to the multiplexer:

   a. $a + \bar{b} + c$

   b. $a + b\bar{c}$

   c. $a + \overline{bc}$

   d. $a \oplus b \oplus c$

2.10. Illustrate how to implement the following equations in a eight-to-one multiplexer:

   a. $a\bar{b} + b\bar{c} + c\bar{d}$

   b. $\overline{a\bar{b} + b\bar{c} + c\bar{d}}$

   c. $\overline{a \oplus b \oplus c \oplus d}$

2.11. Rewrite the equations in Figure 2-16 using the report file equation format described in Breakout Exercise 2-2. Rewrite the expressions in Problems 2.9 and 2.10 using the report file equation format (expand the XOR expressions into two-level AND-OR logic).

2.12. Compile the 3bcount.vhd design described in Breakout Exercises 2-3 to a CY7C371. Examine the report file and compare equations to the ones that you generated in Problem 2.11. Determine the setup time, clock-to-output delay, and register-to-register delays. Which parameter limits the maximum operating frequency?

2.13. What size multiplexer is required to implement a function of three signals, four signals, n signals? How many unique functions of three, four, and n signals are there?

2.14. List features that are used to classify a device as a PAL, CPLD, FPGA, or an ASIC.

2.15. List major differences in the I/O and buried macrocell structures of the Cypress MAX340 and the Cypress FLASH370 CPLDs.

2.16. List major differences in the logic cell structures of the Xilinx XC4000 and the Cypress pASIC380 FPGAs. Refer to the data sheets, which may be obtained from the Web pages of the respective companies, if necessary.

2.17. Create your own 256-macrocell CPLD. What issues are you concerned with? What architectural features would you include? Justify your choices.

2.18. Create your own 20K gate Antifuse FPGA. What issues are you concerned with? What architectural features do you include? Design the logic cells, I/O cells, and routing architecture. Justify your choices. Would you choose to use this device as opposed to an ASIC? Why?

2.19. Create your own 20K gate SRAM-based FPGA. What issues are you concerned with? What architectural features do you include? Design the logic cells, I/O cells, and routing architecture. Justify your choices. Would you choose to use this device as opposed to an ASIC? Why?

2.20. Obtain the latest PREP benchmark data from the World Wide Web. Compare any two 32 macrocell devices. For each benchmark, determine which device can hold more reps and which has better performance. Explain the types of applications for which you would use one device over another. What other features, not measured by PREP, would you consider?

2.21. Obtain the latest PREP benchmark data from the World Wide Web. Compare any two 2,000-gate FPGAs. For each benchmark determine which device can hold more reps and which has better performance. Explain the types of applications for which you would use one device over another. What other features, not measured by PREP, would you consider?

Chapter 3

Entities and Architectures

3.1 Introduction

In Chapter 2 we introduced programmable logic devices, focusing on CPLDs and FPGAs. Our primary motivation for learning VHDL is to create working logic designs to implement in programmable logic devices. In this chapter, we discuss the basic building blocks of VHDL design, the **entity declaration** and the **architecture body.** We explain three basic coding styles, making analogies to schematic design entry and high-level programming languages to help place VHDL concepts into a familiar framework. We must be careful not to overstate the analogies, however, because VHDL coding is very different from coding in a computer programming language. An important concept to keep clear as you write VHDL code is that you are designing for hardware: Your descriptions in VHDL code will be synthesized into digital logic for a programmable logic device.

Simulation concepts and the simulation cycle are also explained in this chapter, to acquaint you with nuances in VHDL semantics for synthesis and simulation. The last section of the chapter deals with identifiers, data objects, data types, and attributes.

3.2 A Simple Design

The code example below is a VHDL description of a 4-bit equality comparator. It is divided into two sections: an entity declaration and an architecture body. Line numbers are *not* part of a VHDL description—they are used here to help us identify specific lines of code in our discussion. In this example, the boldface words are

VHDL **reserved** words, which have special meaning in the language. The other words are identifiers furnished by the designer. This 4-bit equality comparator demonstrates the basic framework of entity declarations and architecture bodies. Following the code listing is a line-by-line explanation.

```
 1 -- eqcomp4 is a four bit equality comparator
 2 entity eqcomp4 is
 3    port   (a, b: in bit_vector(3 downto 0);
 4            equals:out bit);    -- equals is active high
 5 end eqcomp4;
 6
 7 architecture dataflow of eqcomp4 is
 8 begin
 9    equals <= '1' when (a = b) else '0';
10 end dataflow;
```

Listing 3-1 Dataflow design of a 4-bit comparator

The dashes in line 1 (--) introduce a comment; their appearance at the beginning of the line indicates that line 1 is a comment line. Comments help to document your design; they are for you and other readers, but are ignored by the compiler. The comment continues to the end of the line. To continue a comment on another line, you would need to start the line with another double-dash. Comments can also start anywhere in a line, as shown in line 4. Everything to the right of the double-dash is part of the comment; all new code must start on a new line. Lines 2 through 5 describe the I/O of a 4-bit equality comparator called eqcomp4. Lines 2 and 5 begin and end the entity declaration for eqcomp4. Line 3 begins a port, or pin, declaration, and the right-parenthesis and semicolon at the end of line 4 complete the port declaration. Ports are points of communication for the entity to communicate with other entities. On line 3 of this example, we declare two ports, a and b. These are inputs to the design and are 4-bit buses, or bit_vectors. Each member of a bit_vector—a(0), for instance—is a bit, which means it may have the value of '0' or 1' (single quote marks must be used with the character literals, 0 and 1, of type bit; double quote marks are used with the values of bit_vectors, as in "0101"). Finally, equals is declared as an output in line 4. The entity declaration has a schematic symbol equivalent, as shown in Figure 3-1.

Lines 7 through 10 describe what our entity, eqcomp4, does. This is called the architecture body; it begins on line 7 with the reserved word architecture, and ends on line 10. In line 7, we give the architecture a name, dataflow, and identify the entity declaration with which it is paired: of eqcomp4. (The name that we give an architecture is our choice. We chose dataflow for this one because it falls into

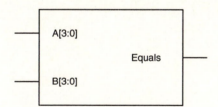

Figure 3-1   Schematic symbol equivalent of `eqcomp4` entity

the style of dataflow descriptions. We'll explore this and other styles of architectural descriptions later in the chapter.) An **architecture declarative part** can be included before the reserved word `begin`. Signal, type, component, and other declarations can be made in this declarative region, as we will see in this and subsequent chapters. The **architecture statement part** appears after the reserved word `begin` at line 9, where the function of the design is described. This simple architecture describes an equality comparator. The semantics of line 9 indicate that when the value of bus a is equal to the value of bus b, then the signal `equals` is assigned '1'; otherwise `equals` is assigned '0'. Read from left to right: "`equals` is assigned '1' when a equals b, else '0'." The <= symbol is used to indicate signal assignment, and may be read as "is assigned to." The comparison is bitwise from left to right; that is, a(3) is compared to b(3), a(2) is compared to b(2), and so forth.

We will make a point of ordering vectors in descending order by using the keyword `downto`, as in `bit_vector(3 downto 0)`, in order to indicate that we wish to interpret the bit with the highest index as the most significant bit (MSB). For example, we will consider a(3) and b(3) to be the most significant bits of their respective vectors. Alternatively, we could define the vectors in ascending order, as in `bit_vector(0 to 3)`. In this case, a(3) and b(3) are the least significant bits (LSBs). We will use ascending order occasionally to illustrate specific points.

3.3   Design Entities

The design example above illustrates that a VHDL design entity is a pairing of an entity declaration and an architecture body (Figure 3-2). An entity is an abstraction of a design that could represent a complete system, board, chip, small function, or logic gate. An entity declaration describes the design I/O, and as you will see later, that may include parameters used to customize an entity. An architecture body describes the function of a design entity. An architecture can contain any combination of behavioral, structural, or dataflow descriptions to define an entity's function.

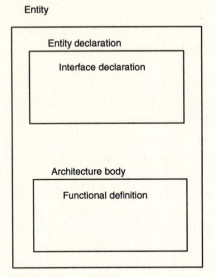

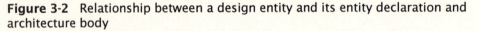

Figure 3-2   Relationship between a design entity and its entity declaration and architecture body

Next, we look in greater detail at the syntax and semantics of the code that makes up design entities. To have correct syntax, you must follow the rules of whatever language you are using to create meaningful statements. If we were to reverse the words of this sentence, the sentence would not be syntactically correct—it would not be meaningful. To have the correct semantics, the code you write must have the correct meaning. If you were to write, "Coming out of the subway station, the sun was blinding," your sentence would be syntactically correct (it would have meaning), but semantically incorrect (it would have the wrong meaning). The sentence contains a misplaced modifier that implies the sun came out of the subway station; this is a semantic error. To correct the sentence, you could write, "Coming out of the subway station, *I* was blinded by the sun."

We could start with a detailed discussion of identifiers, data objects, and data types, but you'll benefit more by first gaining a broad understanding of how VHDL designs are constructed before delving into the details of data. If you prefer, read the section "Identifiers, Data Objects, Data Types, and Attributes" later in this chapter before returning here.

3.3.1   Entity Declarations

An entity declaration describes the inputs and outputs of a design entity. It can also describe parameterized values, but we will defer that discussion to the next chapter. The I/O could be the I/O of an entity in a larger, hierarchical design, or—if the entity is a device-level description—the I/O of a chip. The entity declaration is analogous to a schematic symbol, which describes a component's connections to the rest of a design. A schematic symbol for a 4-bit adder (add4) is shown in Figure 3-3. You can see that the 4-bit adder has a name (add4), two 4-bit inputs (a and b), a carry-in input (ci), a 4-bit output (sum), and a carry-out output (co). These items are also contained in an entity declaration:

```
entity add4 is port(
      a, b:   in std_logic_vector(3 downto 0);
      ci:     in std_logic;
      sum:    out std_logic_vector(3 downto 0);
      co:     out std_logic);
end add4;
```

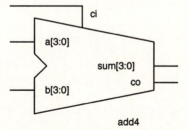

Figure 3-3   Symbol equivalent of entity add4

3.3.2   Ports

Each I/O signal in an entity declaration is referred to as a **port,** which is analogous to a pin in a schematic symbol. A port is a data object. Like other data objects, it can be assigned values and used in expressions. We'll investigate other data objects in the next section of the chapter. The set of ports defined for an entity is referred to as a **port declaration.** Each port you declare must have a name, a direction (**mode**), and a data type. The first part of the declaration, the port name, is self-explanatory. Legal VHDL identifiers (names) are described on page 139.

Modes. The mode describes the direction in which data is transferred through a port. The mode can be one of four values: in, out, inout, or buffer. If the mode of a port is not specified, then the port is of the default mode in. The use of these modes is illustrated in Figure 3-4 and described below.

- **In.** Data flows only into the entity. The driver for a port of mode in is external to the entity. Mode in is used primarily for clock inputs, control inputs (like load, reset, and enable), and unidirectional data inputs.

- **Out.** Data flows only from its source to the output port of the entity. The driver for a port of mode out is inside the entity. Mode out does not allow for feedback because such a port is not considered readable within the entity. Mode out is used for outputs such as a terminal count output (a terminal count is asserted when the value of a counter reaches a predefined value).

- **Buffer.** For internal feedback (that is, to use a port also as a driver within the architecture), you will need to declare a port as mode buffer, or declare a separate signal for use within the architecture body (an internal signal). A port that is declared as mode buffer is similar to a port that is declared as mode out, except that it does allow for internal feedback. Mode buffer does not allow for bidirectional ports because it does not permit the port to be driven from outside of the entity.

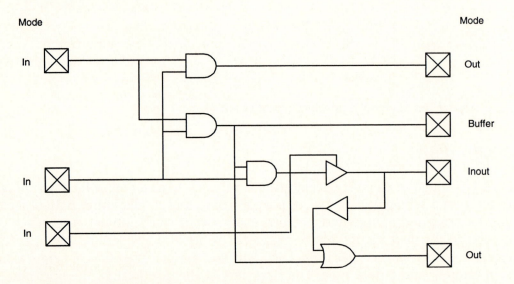

Figure 3-4   Modes and their signal sources

Two additional caveats apply to the use of mode `buffer`: (1) a port of mode buffer may not be multiply driven. Multiple drivers will be explained on page 134. (2) A port of mode `buffer` may connect only to an internal signal or to a port of mode `buffer` of another entity. It cannot connect to a port of mode out or inout of another entity, except through an internal signal.

Mode `buffer` is used for ports that must be readable within the entity, such as the counter outputs (the present state of a counter must be used to determine its next state, so its value must be in the feedback loop, which necessitates a mode other than just out).

- **Inout.** For bidirectional signals, you must declare a port as mode `inout`, which allows data to flow into or out of the entity. In other words, the signal driver can be inside or outside of the entity. Mode `inout` also allows for internal feedback.

  Mode `inout` can replace any of the other modes. That is, `in`, `out`, and `buffer` can all be replaced by mode inout. Although using only mode `inout` for all ports would be legal, it would reduce the readability of the code, making it difficult to discern the source of signals. A more appropriate use for mode `inout` is for signals that are truly bidirectional, such as the data bus of a DMA controller.

Because large designs may be developed by a team of engineers, it is important to determine in advance the interface between design units. For example, a team may decide to use **buffer** for all output ports, regardless of whether the ports require internal feedback. This can simplify the interconnection of design units because the second caveat listed above for mode **buffer** would be eliminated. This convention could be used, however, only if the first caveat—that signals cannot be multiply driven—can be met. Another convention would be to use only mode **out** and create internal signals where mode **buffer** would otherwise be required. Examples of this will be shown in Chapter 6.

Types. In addition to specifying identifiers and modes for ports, you must also declare the data types for ports. The types provided by the IEEE 1076/93 standard that are most useful and well-supported *and* that are applicable to synthesis are the data types Boolean, `bit`, `bit_vector`, and `integer`. The most useful and well-supported types for synthesis provided by the IEEE std_logic_1164 package are the types `std_ulogic` and `std_logic`, and arrays of these types. As the names imply, "standard logic" is intended to be a standard type used to describe circuits for synthesis and simulation. For simulation and synthesis software to process these types, their declarations must be made visible to the entity by way of `library` and use clauses. Thus, the entity declaration above for add4 cannot be processed by software tools until it is modified as follows:

```
library ieee;
use ieee.std_logic_1164.all;
entity add4 is port(
        a, b:   in std_logic_vector(3 downto 0);
        ci:     in std_logic;
        sum:    out std_logic_vector(3 downto 0);
        co:     out std_logic);
end add4;
```

Many of the examples throughout this book will use the std_logic type to reinforce the idea that it is a standard. However, you should be aware that you are not restricted from using other types. We'll defer a more detailed discussion of data types to page 143.

3.3.3   Architecture Bodies

Every architecture body is associated with an entity declaration. An architecture describes the contents of an entity; that is, it describes an entity's function. If the entity declaration is viewed as the engineer's "black box," for which the inputs and outputs are known but the details of what is inside the box are not, then the architecture body is the internal view of the black box. VHDL allows you to write your designs using various styles of architecture, and to mix and match these styles as you see fit. The styles are behavioral, dataflow, and structural descriptions, or any combination thereof. These styles allow you to describe a design at different levels of abstraction, from using algorithms to gate-level primitives. The name given to an architecture style is not important, and often the style of design description that you use for synthesis is not important. However, the terms will give us a common vocabulary.

```
 1 library ieee;
 2 use ieee.std_logic_1164.all;
 3 entity eqcomp4 is port(
 4     a, b:      in std_logic_vector(3 downto 0);
 5     equals:   out std_logic);
 6 end eqcomp4;
 7
 8 architecture behavioral of eqcomp4 is
 9 begin
10 comp: process (a, b)
11     begin
```

```
12          if a = b then
13              equals <= '1';
14          else
15              equals <= '0';
16          end if;
17      end process comp;
18  end behavioral;
```

Listing 3-2 Behavioral architecture description for eqcomp4

Behavioral Descriptions. Listing 3-2 is an example of a **behavioral description,** as is Listing 3-1. What makes it behavioral? After reading the code listing, you may already have an idea. Simply put, it's because of the algorithmic way in which the architecture is described. Behavioral descriptions are sometimes referred to as high-level descriptions because of their resemblance to high-level programming languages. Rather than specifying the structure or netlist of a circuit, you specify a set of statements that, when executed in sequence, model the function, or behavior, of the entity (or part of the entity). The advantage to high-level descriptions is that you don't need to focus on the gate-level implementation of a design; instead, you can focus your efforts on accurately modeling its function.

Lines 1 and 2 are required to make the std_logic and std_logic_vector types visible to this entity. Lines 3 through 6 contain the entity declaration for this 4-bit comparator. Lines 8 through 18 contain the architecture body, which uses an algorithm to describe the design's function. A **process statement** is one of VHDL's design constructs for embodying algorithms. A process statement begins with an optional label (comp in this case), followed immediately by a colon (:), then the reserved word process and a sensitivity list. A **sensitivity list** identifies (for a simulator) which signals will cause the process to execute. Thus, in our example, a change in signal a or in signal b will cause the process to be executed. Lines 12 through 16 include **sequential statements** that when executed model a 4-bit comparator. An if statement is used to indicate that equals should be asserted when a is equal to b. The process statement is completed with the reserved words end process and optionally the process label.

If you've noticed that Listing 3-2 is just another way to describe the 4-bit equality comparator of Listing 3-1, then you've discovered one of VHDL's greatest strengths: the ability to describe the same circuit using different styles. We'll consider three more ways to describe a 4-bit equality comparator as we continue to discuss behavioral, structural, and dataflow design descriptions.

Processes, like the one in the architecture of Listing 3-2, permit you to describe circuits using **processes** and **sequential statements,** or algorithms. Although hardware is concurrent, or parallel, and executing simultaneously, you can model it by a series of sequential statements that define how outputs react to inputs. An architecture body can contain more than one process, and each process is concurrent with the others. The architecture of Listing 3-2 can be rewritten as shown in Listing 3-3.

```
 1 architecture behavioral of eqcomp4 is
 2 begin
 3    comp: process (a, b)
 4       begin
 5          equals <= '0';
 6          if a = b then
 7             equals <= '1';
 8          end if;
 9       end process comp;
10 end behavioral;
```

Listing 3-3 Alternative implementation of eqcomp4; equals has a default value of '0'

The ordering of the statements in this process is important because each statement is executed in the order in which it appears. This process indicates that as a default, equals should be assigned '0', but that if a is equivalent to b, then equals should be assigned '1'. If the statement equals <= '0'; were placed after line 8, then this design would take on a completely different meaning: equals would always be '0'. We will take a brief look at how processes are executed during simulation later in the chapter. For now, we move on to discuss the other styles of architectures.

Dataflow Descriptions. Listing 3-1 is a dataflow description; Listing 3-4 is the same dataflow description, with the data types of the ports changed.

```
-- eqcomp4 is a four bit equality comparator
library ieee;
use ieee.std_logic_1164.all;
entity eqcomp4 is
port (a, b:     in std_logic_vector(3 downto 0);
        equals:   out std_logic);
end eqcomp4;

architecture dataflow of eqcomp4 is
begin
    equals <= '1' when (a = b) else '0';    -- equals is active high
end dataflow;
```

Listing 3-4 Dataflow architecture description for eqcomp4

This is a dataflow architecture because it specifies how data will be transferred from signal to signal and input to output without the use of sequential statements. Some authors distinguish between behavioral and dataflow architectures, and others lump them together as behavioral descriptions. The primary difference is that one uses processes and the other does not. They are both clearly *not* structural. We will use the term dataflow when we wish to be specific.

You will likely use dataflow descriptions in cases where it is more succinct to write simple equations, conditional signal assignment (when-else) statements, or selected signal assignment (with-select-when) statements rather than a complete algorithm. On the other hand, when you need to nest structures, sequential statements are preferable. For the most part, it is simply a matter of style—use what you're most comfortable with.

If you're like most people, you will develop a comfortable coding style as you first start to write VHDL code. As you gain familiarity with some constructs, you'll explore other constructs and techniques.

Listing 3-5 shows a style that many logic designers are already comfortable with.

```
library ieee;
use ieee.std_logic_1164.all;
entity eqcomp4 is port(
    a, b:      in std_logic_vector(3 downto 0);
    equals:    out std_logic);
end eqcomp4;

architecture bool of eqcomp4 is
begin
    equals <=          not(a(0) xor b(0))
                and    not(a(1) xor b(1))
                and    not(a(2) xor b(2))
                and    not(a(3) xor b(3));
end bool;
```

Listing 3-5 Dataflow architecture for eqcomp using Boolean equations

Listing 3-5 is also a dataflow description because it describes the way in which data flows from signal to signal. Writing Boolean equations, particularly for the description of a comparator, is unnecessarily cumbersome. Suppose that the size of ports a and b were increased. The architecture of Listing 3-5 would require modification: The expression for equals would have to change. However, the architectures described previously, which also describe the comparator, are independent of the size of a and b, and would not require modification. Nonetheless, there are times when Boolean equations provide the most concise and clearly defined interaction of signals.

Dataflow architectures use **concurrent signal assignment statements** rather than processes and their sequential statements. To illustrate the difference between these types of statements and other types, consider the statements of Listing 3-2 and Listing 3-4 (or Listing 3-5). The signal assignments in Listing 3-2 are sequential, and the assignment in Listing 3-4 is concurrent. Concurrent statements lie outside of process statements. Whereas the order of sequential signal assignment statements in a process can have a significant effect on the logic that is described, the order of concurrent signal assignment statements doesn't matter. An architecture can have multiple signal assignment statements, and the statements will execute concurrently. You will notice, as you read further, that concurrent statements may be expressed using a process statement. We will take a closer look at how concurrent signal assignments differ from sequential signal assignments after discussing the last style of architectural descriptions.

Structural Descriptions. Read through Listing 3-6 and observe what makes this description structural:

```
library ieee;
use ieee.std_logic_1164.all;
entity eqcomp4 is port(
    a, b:    in std_logic_vector(3 downto 0);
    aeqb:    out std_logic);
end eqcomp4;

use work.gatespkg.all;
architecture struct of eqcomp4 is
    signal x : std_logic_vector(0 to 3);
begin
    u0: xnor2 port map (a(0),b(0),x(0));
    u1: xnor2 port map (a(1),b(1),x(1));
    u2: xnor2 port map (a(2),b(2),x(2));
    u3: xnor2 port map (a(3),b(3),x(3));
    u4: and4 port map (x(0),x(1),x(2),x(3),equals);
end struct;
```

Listing 3-6 Structural description of eqcomp4

This design requires that and4 and xnor2 components be defined in a package, and that this package be compiled into a library. We have accessed these components by including a use clause, which allows us to instantiate components from the gatespkg package found in the work library. (Libraries and packages are discussed in Chapter 6.)

Structural descriptions consist of VHDL netlists. These netlists are very much like schematic netlists: Components are **instantiated** and connected together with signals. To instantiate a component is to place it in a hierarchical design. An instantiation is therefore either (1) an act of instantiating (placing) a component or (2) an *instance* of a component—that is, a particular occurrence of a component.

Structural designs are hierarchical. In this example, separate entity declarations and architecture body pairs are created for the and4, xnor2, and eqcomp4 design entities. The eqcomp4 design contains instances of the xnor2 and and4 components (when an entity is used inside of another entity, it is referred to as a **component**). Figure 3-5 illustrates the hierarchy. The entity declarations and architecture bodies for the xnor2 and and4 are not contained in the same design file for our eqcomp4 entity. They are accessed (made visible) by way of a use clause.

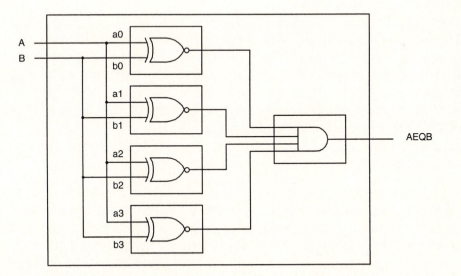

Figure 3-5 Hierarchical schematic representation of Listing 3-6

A structural description for a 4-bit equality comparator probably is not an appropriate use of structural descriptions, because it is more cumbersome than necessary. Large designs, however, are best decomposed into manageable subcomponents. Multiple levels of hierarchy may be called for, with the underlying components netlisted (connected) at each level of the hierarchy. Hierarchical design allows the logical decomposition of a design to be clearly defined. It also allows each of the subcomponents to be easily and individually simulated.

3.3.4   Comparing Architectural Descriptions

We've examined behavioral, dataflow, and structural architectures, and we created five different design descriptions for the same function (a 4-bit comparator). We can think of a couple of other descriptions for a 4-bit comparator, and you may be able to as well. This demonstrates the flexibility of VHDL, but begs the question of how the synthesis and fitting of one design description differs from synthesis and fitting of another. That is, will different PLD resources be used depending on which description is synthesized? For example, if you want the 4-bit comparator to be realized in a 22V10, will the same 22V10 device resources be used regardless of which description is synthesized?

Fortunately, for simple design descriptions (such as those for our 4-bit comparator), almost any description will most assuredly be realized with the same device resources. However, this is not true of more complex design descriptions. Synthesis software must interpret complex design descriptions and attempt to minimize the logic of your circuit. The synthesis software and fitter—or place and route—software must then determine how to implement that logic to make the best use of available resources in the target logic device.

There are three reasons that different design descriptions for complex designs can result in different device resources being used:

- The VHDL code may not accurately describe an optimal function. For example, it is possible to describe a design that produces a functionally correct circuit but that has unneeded logic that is accurately synthesized from the code. For example, if the logic shown on the left-hand side of Figure 3-6 is described in your code, it may not be optimized to the logic shown on the right-hand side, depending on the "intelligence" built into the synthesis tool. With many synthesis tools, the bordering points for logic minimization are flip-flops and I/O buffers. Synthesis based on this type of optimization is called RTL (register transfer level) synthesis.

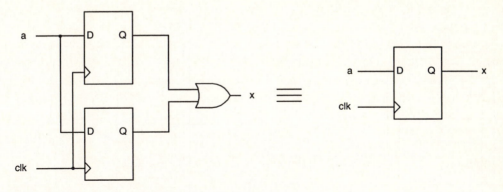

Figure 3-6 Unneeded logic may not be detected

• Synthesis software may perform poorly while attempting to make good use of a device's architectural resources. For example, some synthesis tools produce sum-of-products logic equations and pass those equations to the placer and router without having optimized the logic for the target architecture. Sum-of-products equations cannot easily be mapped to just any architecture (FPGAs in particular). Therefore, if the synthesis software does not present (to the place and route software) logic in a form that is representative of a device's architectural resources, then more resources than necessary may be used, unless the place and route software can compensate for the lack of optimization in the synthesis tool. In this scenario, the VHDL description that more closely resembles a netlist of RTL components representative of device resources will synthesize to a more optimal implementation (provided that the designer reduced the logic). For example, it is easier to see how to implement the logic on the bottom left of Figure 3-7 into the logic cell on the right than it is for the logic on the top left. Mature synthesis tools will have built-in algorithms that will find the optimal, or near optimal, solution regardless of the form of the description. "Optimal" will be defined more fully in Chapter 8.

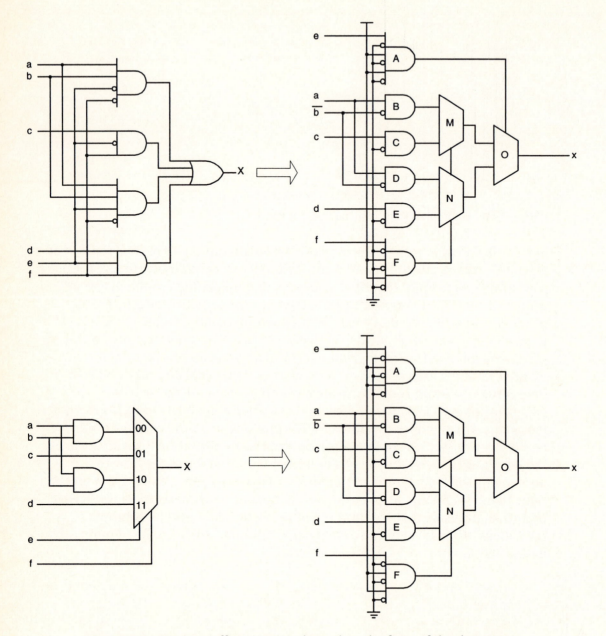

Figure 3-7 Mapping efficiency may depend on the form of the description

• The fitter tool may not make the appropriate choices for using device resources. If the appropriate heuristics are not embedded within the fitter software, then the fitter may not find a solution to fit a design even though the synthesis software has presented optimized logic and there is a theoretical solution for fitting the design.

In summary, different design descriptions can produce different, but functionally equivalent, design equations resulting in different circuit implementations. Mature VHDL synthesis tools should, however, produce nearly equivalent, optimal circuits. In the pages to follow, we will point out where there is danger in the form of the description resulting in a nonoptimal implementation.

A structural design methodology is often used to decompose a design into manageable units. Each entity can be developed separately, perhaps by different individuals or teams. A structural design methodology is also used to attain a higher degree of control over synthesis. That is, it is sometimes used to build a design out of vendor-specific library components, where the library components map efficiently to the target device architecture. Most synthesis tools or silicon vendors provide libraries you can use to instantiate components that represent device-specific resources and optimized structures. For example, a library may contain an adder that will map efficiently for a specific device.

Using vendor-specific components should be avoided, if possible, for several reasons, unless it is the only way to access a required feature of a device or achieve the requisite area and operating-frequency requirements. Instantiating vendor-specific components may eliminate the device independence of the design. Unless the library component has an underlying VHDL description that can be synthesized to any architecture or simulated with a VHDL simulator, it is not device-independent. Another reason to avoid using or overusing these components is that doing so requires an inordinate amount of time; it provides little, if any, benefit over schematic-based design, and it may require that you build functions from small-device resources. Using device-primitive components, you may inadvertently create logic that is not optimal for the architecture or that is in error. It can be an arduous task to find a logic error in a convoluted netlist. Computers can run through algorithms much faster than any human, and carefully constructed algorithms can produce optimal implementations. Finally, behavioral and dataflow descriptions are easier to read, understand, and maintain than a netlist of vendor-specific components, which is precisely why the HDL synthesis markets are growing.

We return to the trade-off discussed in Chapter 1: meeting design requirements versus controlling a design's implementation. In the chapters ahead, we'll identify how circuits will be realized in logic devices to give you an idea of when it will be most suitable to use behavioral, dataflow, or structural design descriptions. For the most part, you will want to start out with behavioral and dataflow design descriptions, adding structure only where the design is naturally decomposed into units. Behavioral and dataflow descriptions are usually the quickest and easiest way to describe designs. If after you've synthesized the behavioral design description, the design implementation meets your performance and cost requirements, then you have completed your design in the shortest possible time. If at that point you have not met your requirements, then you will want to use directives with the synthesis tool or constraints with the place and route tool to help influence those processes and achieve the design goals. If the desired results still are not achieved, you can introduce RTL descriptions or vendor-specific library components to optimize critical portions of your design. Next time, you will be more aware of what portions of your design to describe with the different coding styles. As the state of the art in VHDL synthesis improves, you'll be able to describe larger portions of your designs with fewer vendor-specific primitives.

Breakout Exercise 3-1

Purpose: To compare results of synthesizing different architectural descriptions for the same entity.

Perform the following steps.

1. Create a project named `break1` in the `c:\vhdlbook\ch3` directory. Select **Add** from the **Files** menu to add the file `behave.vhd` to the project list, set it to be the top-level design, select C371 as the target device, and compile the design.

2. Either (a) create separate projects (`Boolean` and `dataflow`) in the same directory to compile the designs `boolean.vhd` and `dataflow.vhd`, or (b) use the same project, but remove `behave.vhd` from the project list before adding the next design file, setting it as top, and compiling it.

3. We will not compile the structural description of Listing 3-6 because it requires that components have been compiled to the work library. We will discuss libraries in Chapter 6.

4. Open the report files for each design. Compare the equations for `equals`. Compare the resource utilization summaries and timing path analysis. Do you find what you expected?

3.3.5 Modeling for Synthesis versus Modeling for Simulation

It will now be instructive to explore briefly a few differences between modeling for synthesis and modeling for simulation. The stated purpose of this text is to teach VHDL with an emphasis on synthesis and design issues. Nonetheless, understanding how a VHDL simulator processes code can help to clarify the semantics of some VHDL statements. Having a firm grasp of semantics will enable you to write accurate code. Ignoring nuances in semantics can lead to poor coding and to frustration with synthesis and simulation software tools and VHDL itself.

VHDL contains a few language constructs that are more specific to simulation and verification than to synthesis. Synthesis software may ignore such constructs, or rules. However, we want the functional results of simulating code to match the functionality of hardware specified by synthesis, particularly if we will be using both simulation and synthesis tools with the same code. Therefore, as designers, we must take care to ensure that the models we create for use with synthesis tools are semantically correct for simulation software as well.

Consider the following analogy. Suppose you were to leave a message for two friends stating, "Arriving home from work, a cold beer would be nice." This sentence has a semantic error—a misplaced modifier. The sentence, read literally, means that a cold beer is arriving home from work. In reality it is *you* who are arriving home from work. You could correct the sentence by saying, "Arriving home from work, I would like a cold beer." Your friend, Synthesis, understands either sentence. Another friend, Simulation, is a strict grammarian and understands only the second sentence. If you want the message to be understood by either friend and want to make sure there's a cold beer waiting for you when you arrive home, you will use the sentence that Simulation will understand.

Process Statement Execution. A process is either being executed or suspended. It is executed when one of the signals in its sensitivity list has an **event,** a change in value. When this happens, the sequential statements inside are executed in succession. Depending on the evaluation of control statements such as `case` statements, `if` statements, and `loop` statements, execution may branch to different sets of sequential statements within the process. A process continues to execute until the last statement is reached. At this point, the process suspends itself and is executed again only when there is an event on a signal in the sensitivity list. An explicit sensitivity list is not required: A `wait` statement can also be used to suspend a process. However, synthesis software typically supports `wait` statements only at either the beginning or end of a process. A `wait` statement at the beginning of the process, used to describe a flip-flop, will be illustrated in Chapter 4. The following two processes show the equivalence of a sensitivity list and an explicit wait statement.

```
proc1: process (a, b, c)
    begin
        x <= a and b and c;
    end process;

proc2: process
    begin
        x <= a and b and c;
        wait on a, b, c;
    end process;
```

Both of these processes will execute when a change in value of signal a, b, or c occurs. The semantics of the sequential signal assignment x <= a and b and c; is that the value of the logical AND of a, b, and c at the current simulation time, T_c, is scheduled for assignment to signal x one **delta delay** after the current simulation time, $T_{c+\delta}$. Think of a delta delay as an infinitesimally small delay that implies a **delta cycle** (explained below) must be run. A delta delay is used because an after clause was not present to specify a delay, as in

```
proc3: process (a, b, c)
    begin
        x <= a and b and c after 5 ns;
    end process;
```

However, an after clause is not specified in our original process because we are writing our models for synthesis, and synthesis tools do not typically support after clauses. After clauses are usually ignored by synthesis software, not only because there is not a standard to define how to interpret them for synthesis but also because it would be difficult to guarantee the results of such delays. For example, should the standard be to interpret this as the minimum or maximum propagation delay? How can synthesis software guarantee such propagation delays even if it is tightly coupled with the place and route software? What should the software do if it cannot match a delay specified in code?

Incomplete Sensitivity Lists. Some (not all) synthesis tools may not check for sensitivity lists. Instead, these synthesis tools may assume that all signals on the right-hand side of sequential signal assignments are in the sensitivity list. Thus these synthesis tools will interpret the following two processes to be the same:

```
proc4: process (a, b, c)
    begin
        x <= a and b and c;
    end process;

proc5: process (a, b)
    begin
        x <= a and b and c;
    end process;
```

Any synthesis tool should interpret proc4 as a 3-input AND gate. Some synthesis tools will also interpret proc5 as a 3-input AND gate, even though when this code is simulated, it will not behave as a 3-input AND gate. While simulating, a change in value of signal a or b will cause the process to execute, and the value of the logical AND of a, b, and c will be assigned to x. However, if c changes value, the process is not executed, and x is not updated.

Because it is not clear how a synthesis tool should build a circuit for which a transition in c does not cause a change in x, but for which a change in a or b causes x to be the logical AND of a, b, and c, synthesis software will either (1) interpret proc5 as proc4 (with a sensitivity list that includes all signals to the right of any signal assignment statement within the process), or (2) issue a compile-time error stating that the process cannot be synthesized without a completed sensitivity list. The latter implementation is preferable, because it will have you modify the code so that the functionality of the synthesized hardware will match the functional simulation of the VHDL code. (In Release 4.0, Warp does the former.) Synthesis tools will not generate the circuit of Figure 3-8 for proc5. This is for good reason: product-term clocking should be avoided because race conditions can cause false clocks and because it unnecessarily complicates system timing.

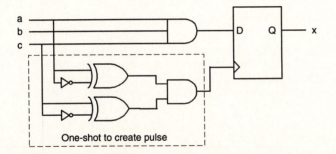

One-shot to create pulse

Figure 3-8 Dangerous interpretation of proc5

Although it is syntactically legal to have a process without a sensitivity list or `wait` statement, such processes never suspend. Therefore, if you were to simulate such a design, the simulation time would never advance because the initialization phase, in which all processes are executed until suspended, would never complete.

Signal Drivers. As previously explained, if a, b, or c changes value, then `proc1` causes the value of the logical AND of a, b, and c at the current simulation time, T_c, to be scheduled for assignment to signal x one delta delay after the current simulation time, $T_{c + \delta}$. An event is said to be scheduled for the **signal driver** for x. A signal driver is represented by a **projected output waveform.** Each time a signal assignment is made, that signal's projected output waveform is updated. A projected output waveform is a set of transactions that specify new values for a signal and the times at which the signal will assume the new values. When simulating models written for synthesis, there are essentially two transactions that need to be maintained for any given signal: the current transaction specifying the current value and time, and the next transaction, if it exists, specifying the new value to be assumed at the next delta delay.[1] However, this does not mean that a maximum of two delta cycles will be required before the next simulation time. We will illustrate this when we simulate a model with several concurrent statements. For now, we will illustrate that two transactions may be kept in the projected output waveform. For example, executing `proc1` results in a signal driver for x as shown in Figure 3-9.

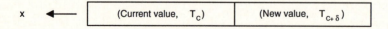

x ◄─── | (Current value, T_c) | (New value, $T_{c+\delta}$) |

Figure 3-9 Signal driver for *x* represented by a projected output waveform

If b and c are '1' and a changes from '0' to '1' at 5 ns, as in Figure 3-10, then `proc1` will execute when the simulation time is 5 ns. At this time, the current value of x is '0', and a transaction is added to the signal driver for x: ('1', 5 ns + δ), where δ is an infinitesimally small delay. When the current simulation time, T_c, passes 5 ns, the only transaction left on the driver for x is ('1', T_c).

---

[1] This discussion of signal drivers, projected output waveforms, transactions, and delta delays is for conceptual purposes only. Vendors of VHDL simulators may implement these concepts differently than described here. VHDL simulators need only comply with the operational specifications defined in the *Language Reference Manual* (IEEE Standard 1076). The implementation is vendor-specific.

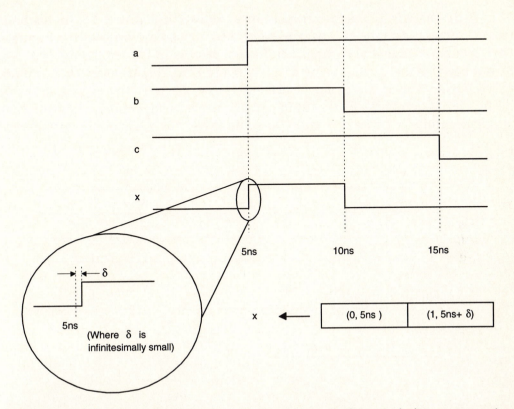

Figure 3-10 Timing diagram and projected output waveform, including a transaction with a delta delay, for signal x

Next, consider a process in which there are two assignments to the same signal:

```
interesting: process (a, b, c)
    begin
        x <= '0';
        if (a = b or c = '1') then
            x <= '1';
        end if;
    end process interesting;
```

If the signals a, b, and c transition as shown in Figure 3-11, then when the current simulation time is 5 ns, the event on b causes the process to execute. The first sequential signal assignment statement results in the transaction ('0', 5 ns + δ), but because the current value of x is already zero, this transaction is not added to the driver. The if statement is evaluated next. Because the expression is false, no further statements are executed and the process suspends. When the current simulation time is between 5 and 10 ns, the driver for x has only one transaction,

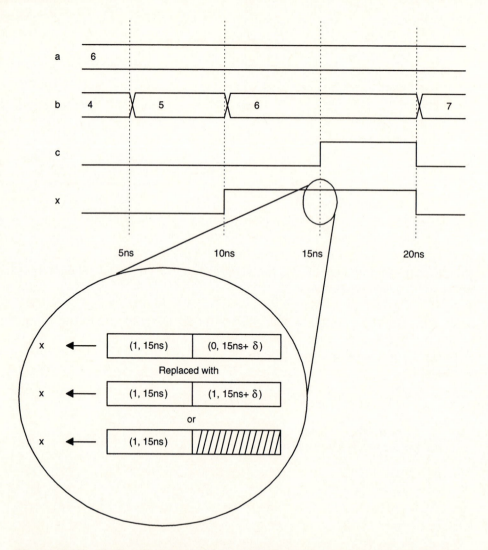

Figure 3-11   Timing diagram for interesting process; second sequential assignment causes deletion of transaction

('0', T_c). At 10 ns, signal b transitions, and the process is executed again. As previously, the first sequential statement results in no transaction being added to the driver (that is, the projected output waveform is not updated). However, this time when the if statement is evaluated, the expression is true. The signal assignment statement x <= '1'; is executed, causing a new transaction, ('1', 10 ns + δ), to be generated and added to the driver for x. When the simulation time reaches 15 ns, c transitions, causing the interesting process to execute. The first statement causes the transaction ('0', 15 ns + δ) to be added to the driver. But because the if statement evaluates true, the next signal assignment statement overrides the current transaction, replacing it with ('1', 15 ns + δ). Because the value '1' is the same as the current value, this transaction need not replace the last transaction, ('0', 15 ns + δ), in the projected output waveform, provided that the last transaction is deleted. When the simulation time is 20 ns, b and c transition, causing the process to execute once again. The first statement causes the transaction ('0', 15 ns + δ) to be added to the projected output waveform. The if statement evaluates false, and the process suspends.

A Simple Interpretation. A simple way to interpret signal assignments in a process is to assume that all expressions are based on the *current* value of the signals on the right-hand side of the <= symbol, that a signal will be updated with the value in the last assignment, and that all signals will be updated only at the end of the process, when it suspends. This is true only if after clauses are not included. We will show a simple example of how to use this interpretation with Listing 3-8 later in the chapter.

Concurrent Statement Execution. A concurrent signal assignment statement has an implicit sensitivity list that includes all signals on the right-hand side of the <= symbol. Concurrent statements execute any time a signal in the implicit sensitivity list transitions. When there are multiple concurrent statements, they do not execute sequentially. In the next section, we'll explain how multiple concurrent statements execute when the evaluating expressions contain signals that are being updated by another statement.

Simulation Cycle. When a model is simulated, it goes through an initialization phase and then repeated simulation cycles. The initialization phase starts with the current simulation time set to 0 ns. In general, if an explicit initialization value is not specified for a signal, then the signal will have the initial value '0' if it is of type bit or 'U', the uninitialized value, if it is type std_logic. Next, each process is executed until it suspends. Because concurrent statements can be rewritten with process statements, they are considered as processes in this context and will also execute.

After the initialization phase, simulation cycles are run, and each consists of the following steps:

- Signals are updated. Updating will cause signals to transition and events to occur on these signals.

- Each process that is sensitive to a signal that has had an event on it in the current simulation cycle is executed.

- The simulation time of the *next* cycle, T_n, is determined. It is either (1) the next time that a signal has a new value, based on its projected output waveform, or (2) the time at which a process resumes (used in models written for simulation and test benches, not synthesis)—whichever is earlier. If the simulation time for the next cycle is a delta delay or multiple delta delays from the current simulation time, then the current simulation time, T_c, remains the same and a **delta cycle** consisting of the same steps as above is executed (hence, a delta delay is actually zero delay—it is only conceptually convenient to think of it as being a small delay). Otherwise, the current simulation time is set to the next simulation cycle time ($T_c = T_n$).

The following design will be useful in illustrating the simulation cycle. Implementation of the simulation cycle is vendor-specific. Our discussion here is useful to conceptualize simulation. Vendors of simulators will have different implementations, but the simulator output (for example, waveforms) will be equivalent.

```
1 entity delta is port(
2             a, b, c, d:        in bit;
3             u, v, w, x, y, z:  buffer bit);
4 end delta;
5 architecture delta of delta is
6 begin
7     z <= not y;
8     y <= w or x;
9     x <= u or v;
10    w <= u and v;
11    v <= c or d;
12    u <= a and b;
13 end delta;
```

Listing 3-7 A simple design to illustrate the simulation cycle

The initialization phase will set all signals to '0'. Next, each concurrent statement is executed. The order of concurrent statement appearance and execution is not important, so we will demonstrate this by executing the statements from last to first. The signal drivers are updated according to Figure 3-12, and one delta cycle is required to update the signals before the current simulation time can advance. Next, observe what happens when the inputs transition as shown in Figure 3-13(a). When the current simulation time reaches 100 ns, a simulation cycle begins. The signals are updated: a transitions from '0' to '1'. This causes the signal assignment statement for u (line 12) to be executed. The value of u does not change, so the simulation cycle is complete: simulation time can advance. When the current simulation time reaches 200 ns, a new simulation cycle begins. The signals are updated: b transitions from '0' to '1'. This causes line 12 to be executed. A new transaction ('1', 200 ns + δ) is added to the driver for u. A delta cycle is required, so simulation time does not advance. During the delta cycle, u is updated with its new value. This causes lines 10 and 9 to execute (in either order, but during the same delta cycle). A new transaction is not added for w, because its value will remain '0'. However, a new transaction is added to the signal driver for x, ('1', 200 ns + δ). A second delta cycle is required. During this delta cycle, x is updated with its new value, which causes line 8 to execute. A new transaction is added to the driver for y, ('1', 200 ns + δ). A third delta cycle is required to update y and add the transaction ('1', 200 ns + δ) to the driver for z. A fourth delta transaction is required to update z, after which the current simulation time may advance. Figure 3-13(b) shows the simulation and delta cycles required for simulating this design through 400 ns.

It is worth repeating that regardless of the number of delta cycles required, the order of concurrent signal assignment statements is of no consequence.

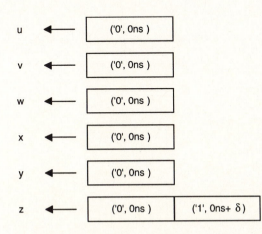

Figure 3-12 Projected output waveforms

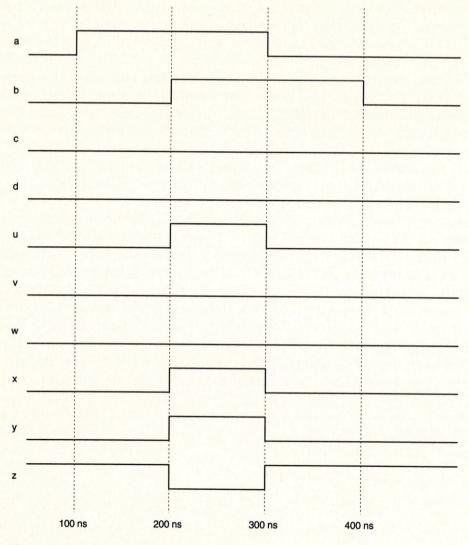

Figure 3-13   (a) Input/output waveforms

sim cycle	ns	δ	a	b	c	d	u	v	w	x	y	z
1	000	+0	0	0	0	0	0	0	0	0	0	0
	000	+1	0	0	0	0	0	0	0	0	0	1
2	100	+0	1	0	0	0	0	0	0	0	0	1
3	200	+0	1	1	0	0	0	0	0	0	0	1
	200	+1	1	1	0	0	1	0	0	0	0	1
	200	+2	1	1	0	0	1	0	0	1	0	1
	200	+3	1	1	0	0	1	0	0	1	1	1
	200	+4	1	1	0	0	1	0	0	1	1	0
4	300	+0	0	1	0	0	1	0	0	1	1	0
	300	+1	0	1	0	0	0	0	0	1	1	0
	300	+2	0	1	0	0	0	0	0	0	1	0
	300	+3	0	1	0	0	0	0	0	0	0	0
	300	+4	0	1	0	0	0	0	0	0	0	1
5	400	+0	0	0	0	0	0	0	0	0	0	1

Figure 3-13 (continued)   (b) Simulation cycle and delta cycle listing

Our next example uses Listing 3-8 to show how someone unfamiliar with the concepts of event scheduling and the simulation cycle may expect to write code to logically AND all bits of a bus.

```
entity my_and is port(
    a_bus:     in bit_vector(7 downto 0);
    x:         buffer bit);
end my_and;
architecture wont_work of my_and is
begin
anding: process (a_bus)
    begin
        x <= '1';
        for i in 7 downto 0 loop
            x <= a_bus(i) and x;
        end loop;
    end process;
end wont_work;
```

Listing 3-8 Inaccurate model of an 8-bit AND gate; initialization and scheduling causes output to always be '0'

As the architecture name indicates, this process won't work as the designer intends. The designer wants the output x to equal the logical AND of all of the bits in a_bus, but running this design through simulation verifies that this model is not what the designer had in mind.

Let's step through the simulation of this design. Initialization will set x to '0' and a_bus to "00000000". The process will execute until suspended, and then simulation cycles may continue. However, the result of running this process during initialization will yield the same result as it would at any other time during simulation, regardless of the value of a_bus. Suppose, for example, that when the simulation time is 100 ns, a_bus transitions to "11111111". The designer now expects that x will be '1', but it won't. We execute the process to find out why. The event on a_bus causes the process to resume. The first statement results in the transaction ('1', 100 ns + δ) being added to the signal driver for x, but remember the complete projected output waveform for x still has a transaction for the current simulation time. The projected output waveform for x is

$$x \leftarrow [('0', 100 \text{ ns}), ('1', 100 \text{ ns} + δ)]$$

and the *current* value of x is still '0'. This means that for each iteration of the loop, the expression on the right-hand side of the <= symbol evaluates to '0'. Thus, the previous transaction is deleted, or overridden with the transaction ('0', 100 ns + δ). Signal x will always be '0'. Synthesis software must ensure that the logic it produces will match the functionality of simulation, so output x is hard-wired to '0', which is not what the designer desired.

The simple interpretation of this process is to assume that a signal is not updated until the end. So, even though the sequential signal assignments cause transactions to be scheduled, it is only the last transaction that has an effect. The last transaction is x <= a_bus(0) and x;, where x is '0'.

The design can be corrected to produce the desired results easily, by introducing a variable into the process. Variables will be explained later in this chapter, and our architecture of Listing 3-8 will be reworked. We conclude our discussion of simulation issues after a brief discussion of resolution functions.

Multiple Drivers and Resolution Functions. VHDL does not permit a signal to have more than one driver unless it has an associated resolution function. A resolution function is used to compute a value for a signal based on multiple drivers. For example, Figure 3-14 illustrates a case in which a signal has two drivers. Depending on the current driving values of the two gates, the logic value for x could be '0', '1', or 'X', where 'X' is an indeterminate state. 'X' is not a don't-care value as it is often used with logic minimization. Rather, it is a don't-know value. The logic of Figure 3-14 can be written in VHDL as

```
architecture multiply_driven_signal of my_design is
begin
    y <= a and b;
    y <= a or b;
end multiply_driven_signal;
```

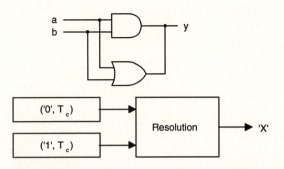

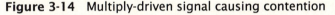

Figure 3-14   Multiply-driven signal causing contention

In this example, two concurrent signal-assignment statements cause two drivers to be created for y. Although two sequential signal assignments to the same signal *in the same process* do not create separate drivers (it simply causes transactions on the same driver), sequential signal assignments to the same signal in *separate* processes would have the same effect as the two concurrent signal-assignment statements illustrated here. A resolution function must be associated with the signal y. This function is used to compute a value for y based on the values of the drivers. The concept of resolving two drivers is illustrated in Table 3-1. If the two drivers are the same, the output is known; otherwise it is not.

Table 3-1   Truth table to resolve multiply-driven signal

a	b	a AND b	a OR b	y
0	0	0	0	0
0	1	0	1	X
1	0	0	1	X
1	1	1	1	1

It is not likely that you would ever intentionally write code such as the fragment on page 135 in which you knowingly place the drivers in conflict. But one of the more common applications for which resolution functions are used is busing. Figure 3-15 illustrates multiple entities driving the same signal, or data. To avoid bus contention, no two entities can drive the data bus at the same time. However, if two entities do drive the bus at the same time with opposing logic levels, it is useful for simulators to be able to indicate contention by computing an appropriate value such as 'X'. A resolution function for signal y in the code fragment on page 135 may conceptually be modeled by the following code.

```
function compute_value(a, b: X01) return X01 is
begin
    if a /= b    then return('X');
                 else return(a);
end;
```

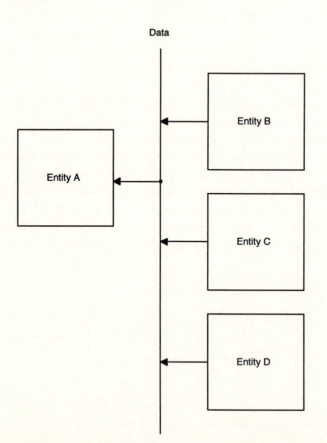

Figure 3-15   Using a resolved signal for busing

Functions are discussed in Chapter 7. The point we wish to make here is that if signal y is a resolved type for which this function applies, then if two drivers are in conflict, the output will be assigned 'X'. The don't-know value 'X' is not, however, very meaningful for synthesis. For example, you would not write,

```
architecture not_meaningful of synthesis_example is
begin
    y <= 'X'
end not_meaningful;
```

Synthesizing this code would not yield a meaningful result. Synthesis tools would issue errors. At this point, it should be clear that although all code written for synthesis can be simulated, not all code that is written for simulation can be synthesized.

Uses for Synthesis. There are some nonbinary values that are useful with synthesis. Nonbinary values may be referred to as **metalogical values** because they do not represent a logic level. Two metalogical values that are particularly useful for synthesis are the don't-care and high-impedance values. We will use '-' to denote don't-care and 'Z' to denote high-impedance. We use the don't-care value in the following code fragment to ensure that the logic synthesized is minimized.

```
architecture useful of good_synthesis is
begin
logic_minimization: process (s)
    begin
        if s = "00" or s = "11" then -- s is std_logic_vector
            y <= '1';
        elsif s = "01" then
            y <= '0';
        else
            y <= '-';
        end if;
    end process;
end;
```

The don't-care value in this code will ensure that synthesis produces the minimized logic equation

$$y = s_1 + \overline{s_0}$$

rather than

$$y = \overline{s_1}\,\overline{s_0} + s_1 s_0$$

Simulation, however, will show that y actually has the value '-' (not '0' or '1') if s is not "00", "01", or "11". This is because simulation treats '-' as a value, whereas synthesis treats it as a wild card that can represent '0' or '1'. The above code fragment should be used only if "10" is an invalid input combination and you want to ensure that this is a don't-care condition; otherwise, you may find a simulation and synthesis mismatch.

The metalogical value 'Z' is often used to describe three-state buffers, as in

```
y <= output_signal when output_enable = '1' else 'Z';
```

This concurrent signal-assignment statement indicates that the signal y will be assigned the value of signal `output_signal` when the value of signal `output_enable` is asserted. Otherwise, y will be assigned the metalogical value 'Z'. This code fragment, when synthesized, will result in a three-state buffer being produced. More will be said about three-state drivers in Chapter 4.

We cover one final example in this section—the use of multiple drivers to increase the drive of a signal. Some synthesis tools permit two drivers for a signal *if the drivers are identical*. Synthesis tools may create multiple buffers in order to increase driving current, if the device supports this (Figure 3-16). While supported for ASIC designs, it is not often supported in synthesis for programmable logic. The following code could be used to describe two buffers as drivers for signal y.

```
architecture multiple_drivers of creating_buffers is
begin
    y <= a and b;
    y <= a and b;
end multiple_drivers;
```

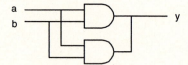

Figure 3-16   Multiply-driven signal used to increase driving current

Although this code can be interpreted by synthesis software to produce two buffers for signal y, synthesis **directives** are usually a better approach, they help guide synthesis in optimizing a design for area or speed goals. Synthesis directives and goals are discussed in Chapter 8.

Breakout Exercise 3-2

Purpose: To illustrate the use of the don't-care value '-' in synthesis.

Separately synthesize the designs `docare.vhd` and `dontcare.vhd`, targeting the CY7C371. Compare design equations found in the report files.

3.4   Identifiers, Data Objects, Data Types, and Attributes

We will now discuss some details about identifiers, data objects, data types, and attributes, using examples to help move the discussion along and provide a context for understanding basic concepts. You may wish to use this material primarily for reference, rather than reading for detail the first time.

3.4.1   Identifiers

Basic identifiers are made up of alphabetic, numeric, and/or underscore characters. The following rules apply:

- The first character must be a letter.
- The last character cannot be an underscore.
- Two underscores in succession are not allowed.

VHDL reserved words are listed in Appendix B and may not be used as identifiers. Uppercase and lowercase letters are equivalent when used in identifiers. The following are equivalent:

```
txclk, Txclk, TXCLK, TxClk
```

The following are all legal identifiers:

```
tx_clk
Three_State_Enable
sel7D
HIT_1124
```

The following are *not* legal identifiers:

```
_tx_clk        -- an identifier must start with a letter
8B10B          -- an identifier must start with a letter
large#number   -- letters, digits, and underscores only
link__bar      -- two underscores in succession are not allowed
select         -- keywords (reserved words) cannot be used as identifiers
rx_clk_        -- last character cannot be an underscore
```

3.4.2   Data Objects

Data objects hold values of specified types. They belong to one of four classes: constants, signals, variables, or files, and must be declared before they are used.

Constants. A constant holds a value that cannot be changed within the design description. This value is usually assigned upon declaration. Constants are generally used to improve the readability of code, and may also make it easier to modify code—rather than changing a value each place that it is used, you need change only the value of the constant. For example, the following constant may represent the width of a register:

```
constant width: integer := 8;
```

The identifier width may be used at several points in the code. However, to change the width of the FIFO requires only that the constant declaration be changed and the code recompiled (resynthesized).

Constants must be declared in package, entity, architecture, or process declarative regions. A constant defined in a package can be referenced by any entity or architecture for which the package is used; one defined in an entity declaration is visible only within the entity; one defined in an architecture is visible only to that architecture; and one defined in a process declarative region is visible only to that process.

Signals. Signals can represent wires, and can therefore interconnect components. Ports are signals; in fact, ports can be specifically declared as signals. As wires, signals can be inputs or outputs of logic gates; we have already seen them used for such purposes. Signals can also represent the state of memory elements.

```
signal count: bit_vector(3 downto 0);
```

Count may represent the current state of a counter. As such, it represents memory elements, or at the least wires attached to the outputs of those memory elements (Figure 3-17). Initial values may be assigned to signals but are rarely meaningful for synthesis. It is a misconception to believe that when you assign an initial value to a signal the memory element will power-up in that initialized state. For example, the following initialization is usually meaningless for synthesis.

```
signal count: bit_vector(3 downto 0) := "0101";
```

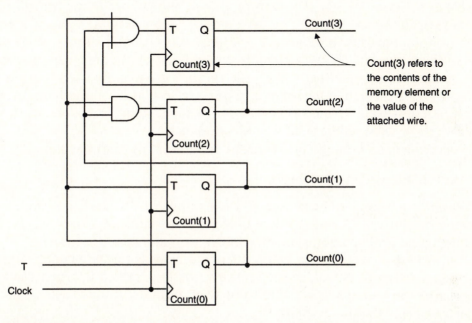

Figure 3-17 A signal can refer to the memory elements or the wires attached to the outputs of the memory elements

The := symbol indicates immediate assignment and is used to indicate the initial value of the signal. For simulation, this initialization ensures that the signal is initialized to "0101", but will not necessarily match the power-on state of the memory elements. To determine the state of memory elements on power-up, refer to the data sheets of the target device. Many devices, such as FLASH370 devices, power-up with flip-flops in the reset state. If, however, a macrocell and its associated product terms are configured to implement the complement of a function, then the output pin associated with that macrocell will indicate a logic level of high. In general, to ensure that memory elements are in the proper state, apply reset or preset during power-up. This is required for the pASIC380 devices for which the flip-flops power-up in an unknown state. Alternatively, clock in known data after power-up.

For designs that are to be synthesized, signals are most commonly declared in the entity and architecture declarative regions. Whereas signals declared as ports have modes, locally declared signals do not; they are both readable and writable. Signals may also be declared in a package.

As illustrated earlier in the chapter, the <= symbol is used to indicate signal assignment, which may modify the signal's projected output waveform.

Variables. Variables are used only in processes and subprograms (functions and procedures), and must therefore be declared in the declarative region of a process or subprogram (shared variables are not discussed). Unlike signals, variables do not represent wires or memory elements. In simulation models, variables can be used for high-level modeling. For synthesis, they are usually used for computational purposes. Although variables can be used in high-level modeling, variable synthesis is not well defined. Therefore, we avoid using variables in this text except when we can predict results with confidence.

Following is an example of a variable declaration and initialization.

```
variable result: std_logic := '0';
```

Variable assignments are immediate, not scheduled. Variables do not have projected output waveforms, so they hold only one value at a time. The variable assignment and initialization symbol := indicates immediate assignment.

For synthesis, the most common use of variables is for index holders and the temporary storage of data. The scope of a variable declared in a process is that process. For the value of a variable to be used outside of a process, it must be assigned to a signal of the same type.

Listing 3-8 contained an incorrect model of an AND gate. This model did not work because signal x is initialized to '0' and the effect of all but the last signal assignment is discarded. A new architecture using variables can correct the model, as shown in Listing 3-9.

```
architecture will_work of my_and is
begin
anding: process (a_bus)
      variable tmp: bit;
   begin
      tmp := '1';
      for i in 7 downto 0 loop
         tmp := a_bus(i) and tmp;
      end loop;
      x <= tmp;
   end process;
end will_work;
```

Listing 3-9 An 8-bit AND gate; assignments to variables are immediate

A variable, tmp, is declared in the process-declarative region. It must be initialized each time the process is activated so that it will not retain its previous value. The := symbol is used here to indicate immediate variable assignment. Thus, tmp is immediately assigned a value of '1', and iterations of the loop result in immediate, not scheduled, assignment to tmp. The last statement in the process is an assignment to x. Thus, an event on x is scheduled for zero delay. It will assume the value equivalent to the logical AND of all bits of a_bus after the current simulation time. The current simulation time is over once the process suspends.

Using tmp as a variable, and assigning the value of this variable to a signal at the end of the process, solved this problem. You may have also noticed that we used another variable, i, that we did not declare. When a variable is used only in a loop, the variable is implicitly declared. As long as it is not used elsewhere in the process, it does not have to be explicitly declared (but it can be).

Files. Files contain values of a specified type. We will use files to read in stimulus and write out data when using test benches in Chapter 10.

Aliases. Aliases are not data objects, but are discussed here nonetheless. An alias is an alternate identifier for an existing object; it is not a new object. Referencing the alias is equivalent to referencing the original object. Making an assignment to the alias is equivalent to making an assignment to the original object. An alias is often used as a convenient method to identify a range of an array type. For example, to identify fields in an address:

```
signal address: std_logic_vector(31 downto 0);
alias top_ad: std_logic_vector(3 downto 0) is address(31 downto 28);
alias bank: std_logic_vector(3 downto 0) is address(27 downto 24);
alias row_ad: std_logic_vector(11 downto 0) is address(23 downto 12);
```

3.4.3 Data Types

Here, we discuss the categories of data types that are most useful for synthesis, **scalar** and **composite** types. We will not discuss **access** and **file** types, both of which are used in models written primarily for simulation.

VHDL is a strongly typed language, meaning that data objects of different base types cannot be assigned to one another without the use of a type-conversion function (discussed in Chapter 7, "Functions and Procedures"). A base type is either a type itself or the type assigned to a subtype. Thus, if a and b are both integer variables, the assignment

```
a <= b + '1';
```

would illicit a compile-time error because '1' is a bit and cannot be used as an operand for addition unless the + operator is **overloaded.** An overloaded operator is one for which there is a user-defined function that handles the + operation for various data types. Many overloaded operators are also defined in the IEEE 1164 and 1076.3 standards. We will discuss how to use overloaded operators in Chapter 4, how to write functions to overload operators in Chapter 7, and the implementation of arithmetic operators in Chapter 9.

Scalar Types. Scalar types have an order, which allows relational operators to be used with them. There are four categories of scalar types: enumeration, integer, floating, and physical types.

Enumeration Types. An enumeration type is a list of values that an object of that type may hold. You may define the list of values. Enumeration types are often defined for state machines:

```
type states is (idle, preamble, data, jam, nosfd, error);
```

A signal can then be declared to be of the enumeration type just declared:

```
signal current_state: states;
```

The physical implementation of an enumeration type is application-specific. For example, `current_state` may represent a set of memory elements that hold the current state of a state machine. The state encoding can be user-assigned, as we will see in Chapter 5.

As a scalar type, an enumeration type is ordered. The order in which the values are listed in the type declaration defines their relation. The leftmost value is less than all other values. Each value is greater than the one to the left and less than the one to the right. Thus, if the type `sports` is defined as

```
type sports is (baseball, football, basketball, soccer, bicycling,
                running);
```

and `your_sport` is declared to be of type sports,

```
signal your_sport: sports;
```

then a comparison of `your_sport` to the value basketball,

```
better_than_bball <= '1' when your_sport >= basketball else '0';
```

reveals whether your preference in sports meets my definition of sport superiority. That is, the values basketball, soccer, bicycling, and running for `your_sport` would result in `better_than_bball` being assigned a '1'.

There are two enumeration types predefined by the IEEE 1076 standard that are particularly useful for synthesis: `bit` and `Boolean`. They are defined as follows:

```
type boolean is (FALSE, TRUE);
type bit is ('0', '1');
```

The IEEE 1164 standard defines an additional type, `std_ulogic`, and several subtypes that are consistently used as standards for both simulation and synthesis. The type `std_ulogic` defines a 9-value logic system. The type declaration for `std_ulogic` is

```
type std_ulogic is ( 'U',    -- Uninitialized
                     'X',    -- Forcing   Unknown
                     '0',    -- Forcing   0
                     '1',    -- Forcing   1
                     'Z',    -- High Impedance
                     'W',    -- Weak      Unknown
                     'L',    -- Weak      0
                     'H',    -- Weak      1
                     '-'     -- Don't care
                   );
```

The subtype `std_logic` has `std_ulogic` as its base type, and the set of values for `std_logic` is the same. But this subtype also has a resolution function, named `resolved`, associated with it. Signal assignments for resolved signals were discussed back on page 134. This resolution function is defined in the `std_logic_1164` package of the IEEE 1164 standard. The subtype declaration for `std_logic` is:

```
subtype std_logic is resolved std_ulogic;
```

The values '0', '1', 'L', and 'H' are logic values that are supported by synthesis. The values 'Z' and '-' are also supported by synthesis for three-state drivers and don't-care values. The values 'U', 'X', and 'W' are not supported by synthesis.

In this text, we use `std_logic` for most designs. That is because, as its name implies, it is a standard data type useful for synthesis. It is more versatile than bit because it provides the high-impedance value 'Z' and the don't-care value '-'. `Std_logic` can also be used effectively with simulators. However, writers of simulation models may find `std_logic` too restrictive for higher-level modeling. Writers of large system models may avoid using a resolved type in order to increase simulation performance—use of a resolved type requires a call to the resolution function for each signal assignment, thereby slowing simulation. This is not a concern for us because we are more interested in synthesis, and our models are not large.

The IEEE 1164 standard defines arrays of std_ulogics and std_logics as std_ulogic_vector and std_logic_vector. The standard defines several other subtypes (such as X01 and X01Z), operator overloading functions, conversion functions, and strength strippers. To use these types, we simply place the following lines before an entity declaration so that the scope of the declarations in the package will extend across the entire entity.

```
library ieee;
use ieee.std_logic_1164.all;
```

One final note about enumeration types like std_logic: Although indentifiers are not case-sensitive, the interpretation of enumeration literals such as 'Z' and 'L' is case-sensitive. This means that 'z' is *not* equivalent to 'Z'.

Integer Types. Integers and the relational and arithmetic operators for integers are predefined by VHDL. Software tools that process VHDL must support integers in the range from –2,147,483,647, –$(2^{31}-1)$, to 2,147,483,647, $(2^{31}-1)$. A signal or variable that is an integer type and that is to be synthesized into logic should be constrained with a range. For example,

```
variable a: integer range -255 to 255;
```

An integer can be represented internal to a synthesis tool by a signed vector. The subtype natural can be represented in a synthesis tool by an unsigned vector, because the range of naturals is positive integers. Not all synthesis tools (especially for programmable logic) handle both signed and unsigned operations. Warp Release 4.0, for instance, does not. Therefore, in it, integers are represented by unsigned vectors.

Floating Types. Floating-point type values are used to approximate real numbers. Like integers, floating-point types can be constrained. The only predefined floating type is real, which includes, at minimum, the range –1.0E38 to +1.0E38, inclusive. Floating-point types are not often supported in synthesis tools (especially those for programmable logic) because of the large amount of resources required for implementation of arithmetic operations with them.

Physical Types. Physical type values are used as measurement units. The only predefined physical type is time. Its range includes, at minimum, the range of integers. Its primary unit is fs (femtoseconds) and is defined as follows (the range can exceed the minimum, and is tool-dependent):

```
    type time is range -2147483647 to 2147483647
units
  fs;
  ps = 1000 fs;
  ns = 1000 ps;
  us = 1000 ns;
  ms = 1000 us;
  sec = 1000 ms;
  min = 60 sec;
  hr = 60 min;
end units;
```

Physical types do not carry meaning for synthesis; they are discussed here only to round out the discussion of scalar types, and because they are used frequently in simulation. We will use them in creating test benches (see Chapter 10, "Creating Test Benches").

You could create another physical type based on another unit of measure such as meters, grams, ounces, and so forth. However, you can see that these units of measure have very little to do with logic design, but may bring to mind some interesting ideas of how VHDL can be used to simulate models of systems that do not represent logic circuits but some other type of system.

Composite Types. Data objects of scalar types can only hold one value at the current simulation time. Data objects of composite types, on the other hand, can hold multiple values at a time. Composite types consist of **array types** and **record types.**

Array Types. An object of an array type consists of multiple elements of the same type. The most commonly used array types are those predefined by the IEEE 1076 and 1164 standards:

```
type bit_vector is array (natural range <>) of bit;
type std_ulogic_vector is array (natural range <>) of std_ulogic;
type std_logic_vector is array (natural range <>) of std_logic;
```

These types are declared as unconstrained arrays: The number of bits, std_ulogics, or std_logics in them are not specified (range <>); rather, the arrays are bounded only by natural, the set of positive integers. These types are commonly used for buses, as in our previous code listings wherein these unconstrained arrays are constrained. For example,

```
signal a: std_logic_vector(3 downto 0);
```

However, a bus can also be defined with your own types:

```
type word is array(15 downto 0) of bit;
signal b: word;
```

If you define your own type, you may also need to define, or overload, operators for that type.

Two-dimensional arrays are useful in creating a truth table.

```
type table8x4 is array(0 to 7, 0 to 3) of bit;
constant exclusive_or: table8x4 := (
        "000_0",
        "001_1",
        "010_1",
        "011_0",
        "100_1",
        "101_0",
        "110_0",
        "111_1");
```

These entries are arranged vertically for readability, but of course they do not have to be. An underline character is inserted to distinguish between the input and output sides of the table. An underline character can be inserted between any two adjoining digits.

When using strings, a base specifier may be used to indicate whether the bit string is specified in binary, octal, or hexadecimal format. If the base specifier is binary, however, that string may be assigned to an object of type `bit_vector` but not `std_logic` vector. If the base specifier is octal, then the actual *value* of the bit string is obtained by converting the octal designator to its appropriate three-digit binary value. If the base specifier is hexadecimal, then the actual value of the bit string is obtained by converting the hexadecimal designator to its appropriate four-digit binary value. For example,

```
a <= X"7A";
```

requires that a be 8 bits wide, where a is a `bit_vector` or `std_logic` vector whose value becomes "01111010". The base specifier for hexadecimal is X, the base specifier for octal is O, and the base specifier for binary is B.

Record Types. An object of a record type has multiple elements of different types. Individual fields of a record can be referenced by element name. The following shows a record-type definition for `iocells`, objects declared as that type, and assignment of values:

```
type iocell is record
    buffer_inp: bit_vector(7 downto 0);
    enable:bit;
    buffer_out:bit_vector(7 downto 0);
end record;

signal busa, busb, busc: iocell;
signal vec: bit_vector(7 downto 0);

busa.buffer_inp <= vec;                  -- one bit_vector assigned
                                         -- to another
busb.buffer_inp <= busa.buffer_inp;      -- assigning one field;
busb.enable <= '1';
busc <= busb;                            -- assigning entire object
```

3.4.4 Types and Subtypes

We have already created new types for enumeration types. Other types can also be created. Take for instance the type `byte_size`:

```
type byte_size is integer range 0 to 255;
signal my_int: byte_size;
```

Although `byte_size` is based on the integer type, it is its own type. Type-checking rules require that operands or ports be of a specific type. If an integer is expected for an operand, type `byte_size` will not be allowed. For example, suppose signal `your_int` is defined as an integer:

```
signal your_int: integer range 0 to 255;
```

The following operation would produce a compile-time error:

```
if my_int = your_int then ...
```

The operands of this comparison operator are of type `byte_size` and integer resulting in a type mismatch.

A subtype is a type with a constraint. Subtypes are mostly used to define objects of a base type with a constraint. For example, byte below is defined as a subtype; objects can then be defined to be of this subtype. Compare

```
subtype byte is bit_vector(7 downto 0);
signal byte1, byte2: byte;
signal data1, data2: byte;
signal addr1, addr2: byte;
```

to the individual declaration of objects as constrained types:

```
signal byte3, byte4: bit_vector(7 downto 0);
signal data3, data4: bit_vector(7 downto 0);
signal addr3, addr4: bit_vector(7 downto 0);
```

In this case, the following code will not result in a compile-time error, because the base types are the same.

```
if byte1 = byte3 then ...
```

As we saw earlier, std_logic also uses a subtype to resolve a base type. Std_logic can still, however, be used in operations with the type std_ulogic. Four additional subtypes are declared in this standard:

```
subtype X01 is resolved std_ulogic range 'X' to '1';
                                  --('X','0','1')
subtype X01Z is resolved std_ulogic range 'X' to 'Z';
                                  --('X','0','1','Z')
subtype UX01 is resolved std_ulogic range 'U' to '1';
                                  --('U','X','0','1')
subtype UX01Z is resolved std_ulogic range 'U' to 'Z';
                                  --('U','X','0','1','Z')
```

Whereas different types will often produce compile-time errors for type mismatches, subtypes of the same base type can be interchanged. For example, suppose the subtype X01Z is expected for the port (a signal) of a given component. If a signal that is connected to that port is of subtype UX01, no compile-time error will occur. A simulation error or synthesis error will occur, however, if you attempt to pass the value of 'U' (defined by the subtype UX01 but not X01Z) to the component. Also, the following comparison will not produce a compile-time error:

```
signal mine: X01Z;
signal yours: UX01;
...
if yours = mine then ...
```

This is not a type mismatch because yours and mine are of the same base type.

IEEE Standard 1076.3 and the Types Signed and Unsigned. IEEE 1076.3, the *Standard VHDL Synthesis Package*, is a standard for synthesis. It defines two VHDL packages, `numeric_bit` and `numeric_std`. Both of these packages overload several operators and define new functions for the types `unsigned` and `signed`. Both cannot be used at the same time because they define the types differently. The `numeric_std` packge defines these types as:

```
type unsigned is array (natural range <>) of std_logic;
type signed is array (natural range <>) of std_logic;
```

The `numeric_bit` package defines these types as:

```
type unsigned is array (natural range <> ) of bit;
type signed is array (natural range <> ) of bit;
```

We will consider only `numeric_std`. The purpose of these two types is to represent signed and unsigned binary integers. For both types, the MSB is on the left. The type `signed` represents a 2's complement binary integer, and the type `unsigned` represents an unsigned binary integer. `Numeric_std` also defines several new functions and overloaded arithmetic, relational, and logical operators for these types. Because `signed`, `unsigned`, and `std_logic` are different types, they cannot be used interchangeably in arithmetic, relational, logical, and assignment operations. However, several type-conversion functions, such as `to_unsigned`, are defined for converting between the types. Use of the `numeric_std` package and these types will be explained in the next chapter.

3.4.5   Attributes

An attribute provides information about items such as entities, architectures, types, and signals. There are several predefined value, signal, and range attributes that are useful in synthesis.

Scalar types have value attributes. The value attributes are `'left`, `'right`, `'high`, `'low`, and `'length` (pronounce the apostrophe as "tick," as in tick-left, tick-right, tick-high, and so forth).

The attribute `'left` yields the leftmost value of a type, and `'right` the right-most. The attribute `'high` yields the greatest value of a type. For enumerated types, this value is the same as `'right`. For integer ranges, the attribute `'high` yields the greatest integer in the range. For other ranges, `'high` yields the value to the *right* of the keyword `to` or to the *left* of `downto`. The attribute `'low` yields the value to the *left* of to or the *right* of downto. The attribute 'length yields the number of elements in a constrained array. Some examples follow:

```
type count is integer range 0 to 127;
type states is (idle, decision, read, write);
type word is array(15 downto 0) of std_logic;
```

Table 3-2   Attributes and their return values

Return value	Attribute description
count'left = 0	'left yields leftmost value of type
states'left = idle	
word'left = 15	
count'right = 127	'right yields rightmost value of type
states'right = write	
word'right = 0	
count'high = 127	'high yields greatest value of type
states'high = write	
word'high = 15	
count'low = 0	'low yields the lowest value of type
states'low = idle	
word'low = 0	
count'length = 128	'length yields the number of elements in a constrained array
states'length = 4	
word'length = 16	

An important signal attribute useful for both synthesis and simulation is the 'event attribute. This yields a Boolean value of true if an event has just occurred on the signal for which the attribute is applied. It is used primarily to determine if a clock has transitioned.

A useful range attribute is the 'range attribute, which yields the range of a constrained object. For example,

```
signal word: std_logic_vector (15 downto 0);
word'range = 15 downto 0
```

3.5   Common Errors

There are several common errors that are worth mentioning. Identifying them early may prevent misconceptions about syntax and semantics. Following is a code example with several errors, some syntax and some semantic. See if you can identify them:

```
entity many_errors is port              --line 1
        a: bit_vector(3 to 0);          --line 2
        b: out std_logic_vector(0 to 3);  --line 3
        c: in bit_vector(5 downto 0);)  --line 4
end many_errors                         --line 5
                                         line 6
architecture not_so_good of many_errors --line 7
begin                                   --line 8
my_label: process                       --line 9
    begin                               --line 10
    if c = x"F" then                    --line 11
        b <= a                          --line 12
    else                                --line 13
        b <= '0101';                    --line 14
    end if                              --line 15
  end process;                          --line 16
end not_so_good                         --line 17
```

We'll take this design one line at a time because there are so many errors. The port declaration requires a left parenthesis at the end of line 1 or beginning of line 2. In line 2, to should read downto. The lack of the keyword in to identify the mode is acceptable. If the mode is not explicitly declared, then the default of in is assumed. Line 3 is OK, except that it declares a port of type std_logic_vector, and we have not made the IEEE library and std_logic_1164 package visible. A library and use clause are necessary. The semicolon on line 4 should appear after the close parenthesis. The omission of a semicolon is one of the most common syntax errors. A semicolon is required at the end of line 5. In line 6, the comment character "--" is required. Line 7 is missing the keyword is after the name of the entity. Line 8 is OK. The process sensitivity list is missing from line 9. This is syntactically OK, but gives the process the wrong meaning (a semantic error). Line 10 is OK. The comparison of line 11 will *always* evaluate to FALSE because x"F" represents "1111", not "001111"—six bits must be compared with six bits (this is a semantic error). In line 12, a signal of one type may be assigned to a signal only of the same base type, so we will have to change a or b to be of the same type. Line 13 is OK. The single quote marks (') of line 14 should be replaced with double quote marks ("). Line 15 requires a semicolon. Line 16 is OK. Line 17 requires a semicolon. The design is corrected and listed below.

```
library ieee;
use ieee.std_logic_1164.all;
entity many_errors is port(               --line 1
      a: std_logic_vector(3 downto 0);    --line 2
      b: out std_logic_vector(0 to 3);    --line 3
      c: in bit_vector(5 downto 0));      --line 4
end many_errors;                          --line 5
                                          --line 6
architecture not_so_good of many_errors is  --line 7
begin                                     --line 8
my_label: process(c, a)                   --line 9
   begin                                  --line 10
   if c = "001111" then                   --line 11
      b <= a;                             --line 12
   else                                   --line 13
      b <= "0101";                        --line 14
   end if;                                --line 15
 end process;                             --line 16
end not_so_good;                          --line 17
```

▼ Breakout Exercise 3-3

Purpose: To interactively work with Warp to correct syntax errors.

Attempt to synthesize the design `errors.vhd`, targeting a CY7C371. Use Warp's error messages to correct the code and achieve a successful compilation.

▲

Problems

3.1. Write the entity declaration for a 2-bit equality comparator.

3.2. Write the entity declaration for the following architecture, assuming that all signals in the architecture are ports:

```
architecture write_entity of exercise2 is
begin
    mapper: process (addr) begin
        shadow_ram_sel <= '0';
        sram_sel <= '0';
        if addr >= x"0100" and addr < x"4000" then
            shadow_ram_sel <= '1';
        elsif addr >= x"8000" and addr < x"C000" then
            sram_sel <= '1';
        end if;

        promsel <= '0';
        if mem_mapped = '0' and bootup then
            prom_sel <= '1';
        end if;
    end process mapper;

mem_mapped <= shadow_ram_sel or sram_sel;
end write_entity;
```

3.3. Write an entity declaration for each of the TTL devices in Table 2-1.

3.4. Write an entity declaration for a 4-bit magnitude comparator. Name the output port altb for "a less than b."

3.5. Write four architecture bodies for the entity declaration of Problem 3.4: one using an if-then-else statement, one using Boolean equations, one using a when-else statement, and one using component instantiation statements and components similar to the xnor2 and and4 components of Listing 3-5. (Hint: the < symbol is used as a relational operator for "less than.")

3.6. Compile and synthesize to a CY7C371 the entity/architecture pairs for each of the first three descriptions that you generated in Problem 3.5. Open the report files and compare equations.

3.7. Resynthesize the designs of Problem 3.6, this time targeting a CY7C381A FPGA. Place and route each design, and compare resource utilization and propagation delay with the CY7C371 implementations. That is, compare the number of macrocells and product terms in the CPLD implementations to the number of logic cells in the FPGA implementations. Also compare the propagation delays.

3.8. Which of the architecture bodies that you generated for Problem 3.5 will require modification if the comparator is changed to an 8-bit comparator? Make the necessary changes and use software to synthesize and fit the new designs to a CY7C371. Then compare utilization and performance results.

3.9. Identify errors in the following code:

```vhdl
entity 4to1_mux port(
        signal a, b, c, d: std_logic_vectors(3 downto 0);
        select: in std_logic_vector(1 downto 0);
        x: out bit_vector(3 downto 0);
end;
architecture of 4to1_mux
begin
p1: process begin
        if select = '00' then
            x <= a;
        elsif select = '10'
            x <= b;
        elsif select = '11'
            x <= c;
        else
            x <= d
        end if;
    end process;
end 4to1_mux;
```

3.10. Use the software to obtain a successful compilation of the code in Problem 3.9.

3.11. Show the waveforms and simulation/delta cycles for the following code, using the input waveforms shown in Figure 3-18.

```vhdl
entity delta is port(
            a, b, c, d:          in bit;
            u, v, w, x, y, z:     buffer bit);
    end delta;
architecture delta of delta is
```

```
begin
    z <= not y;      --line z
    y <= w or x;     --line y
    x <= u or v;     --line x
    w <= u and v;    --line w
    v <= c or d;     --line v
    u <= a and b;    --line u
end delta;
```

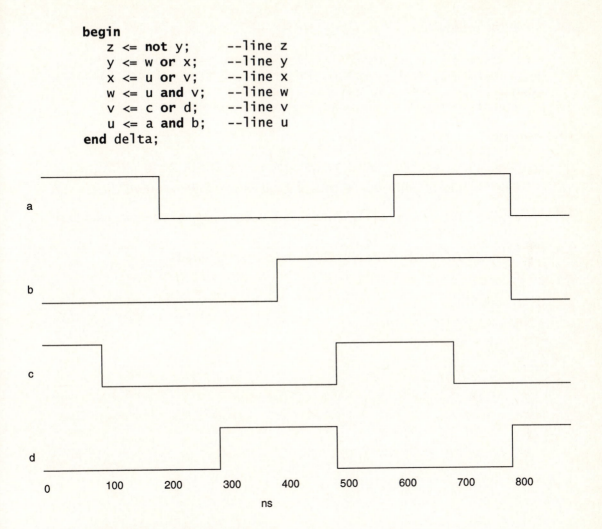

Figure 3-18 Input waveforms

3.12. Create a type declaration that has ampere declared as a physical type with a range from 0 to 1,000. Declare Nanoamps as your primary unit. Declare other units microamp, milliamp, amp, kiloamp, and megaamp.

3.13. Given the following,

> **type** groups **is** (Gin_Blossoms, Rembrandts, Hootie, REM, Mellencamp, U2, Rush, Anthrax, Metallica, Pantera, Black_Sabbath, Tesla, Alice_Cooper, Spinal_Tap, The_Who);
>   **signal** your_music, my_music, juke_box: groups;

evaluate:

a. `loud_music <= '1' **when** your_music > = Anthrax **else** '0';`

   Which values of your_music causes loud_music to be asserted?

b. `author_likes_best <= '1' **when** (juke_box  < Anthrax or juke_box = The_Who) else '0';`

   Of those listed, which groups does the author like best?

c. `groups'high`

d. `groups'low`

Chapter 4

Creating Combinational and Synchronous Logic

4.1   Introduction

In Chapter 3, we discussed the relationship between a design entity and its entity declaration and architecture body. We saw that an entity declaration consists of an interface list that contains ports. Ports are of a specific type and have a mode (direction of dataflow). We also saw that architecture bodies may be written in any of three styles or a combination of the three: behavioral, dataflow, and structural. In this chapter, we cover how to describe combinational and synchronous logic using the various styles of description. With small code examples, we will introduce several new language constructs, illustrating the results of synthesizing each. With these results, we will identify which constructs produce the most efficient circuits when describing particular types of logic functions. Understanding how a description will be synthesized will allow you to write efficient code—code that does not describe extraneous logic.

4.2   Design Example

We begin this chapter with a code listing that brings together several concepts from the previous chapters with concepts that will be developed by this chapter's end. The design of Listing 4-1 is an 8 by 9 FIFO (8 words deep, 9-bit wide, first-in, first-out buffer). The FIFO does not have the empty and full flags typically found in FIFOs. Instead, it is customized for a particular application that will be developed in Chapter 6.

The purpose of introducing this code listing so early in the chapter is to expose you to the types of language constructs you may find in designs of this complexity. Do not read Listing 4-1 for detail. Rather, read it to identify the new constructs and concepts. The syntax and semantics of these constructs, as well as an explanation of some of the design techniques, will be elucidated in this chapter. Near the end of the chapter we will bring the individual constructs and concepts together and revisit the FIFO design.

Two packages are used in this design: std_logic_1164 and std_arith. Std_logic_1164 is included so we can use the types std_logic and std_logic_vector; std_arith is a package we access to overload the + operator so that we can add integers to std_logic_vectors. Four processes are used for registering the data, controlling the read and write pointers, and controlling the three-state outputs. Some of the logic is combinational; other portions are synchronous.

```vhdl
library ieee;
use ieee.std_logic_1164.all;
use work.std_arith.all;

entity fifo8x9 is port(
        clk, rst:                   in std_logic;
        rd, wr, rdinc, wrinc:       in std_logic;
        rdptrclr, wrptrclr:         in std_logic;
        data_in:                    in std_logic_vector(8 downto 0);
        data_out:                   out std_logic_vector(8 downto 0));
end fifo8x9;

architecture archfifo8x9 of fifo8x9 is
  type fifo_array is array(7 downto 0) of std_logic_vector(8 downto 0);

  signal fifo: fifo_array;
  signal wrptr, rdptr: std_logic_vector(2 downto 0);
  signal en: std_logic_vector(7 downto 0);
  signal dmuxout: std_logic_vector(8 downto 0);

begin

-- fifo register array:
reg_array: process (rst, clk)
  begin
        if rst = '1' then
                for i in 7 downto 0 loop
                        fifo(i) <= (others => '0');   -- aggregate
                end loop;
```

```vhdl
            elsif (clk'event and clk = '1') then
                    if wr = '1' then
                            for i in 7 downto 0 loop
                                    if en(i) = '1' then
                                            fifo(i) <= data_in;
                                    else
                                            fifo(i) <= fifo(i);
                                    end if;
                            end loop;
                    end if;
            end if;
    end process;

-- read pointer
read_count: process (rst, clk)
    begin
            if rst = '1' then
                    rdptr <= (others => '0');
            elsif (clk'event and clk = '1') then
                    if rdptrclr = '1' then
                            rdptr <= (others => '0');
                    elsif rdinc = '1' then
                            rdptr <= rdptr + 1;
                    end if;
            end if;
    end process;

-- write pointer
write_count: process (rst, clk)
    begin
            if rst = '1' then
                    wrptr <= (others => '0');
            elsif (clk'event and clk = '1') then
                    if wrptrclr = '1' then
                            wrptr <= (others => '0');
                    elsif wrinc = '1' then
                            wrptr <= wrptr + 1;
                    end if;
            end if;
    end process;

-- 8:1 output data mux
with rdptr select
            dmuxout <=          fifo(0) when "000",
                                fifo(1) when "001",
                                fifo(2) when "010",
                                fifo(3) when "011",
```

```
                        fifo(4) when "100",
                        fifo(5) when "101",
                        fifo(6) when "110",
                        fifo(7) when others;

-- FIFO register selector decoder
with wrptr select
        en <=   "00000001" when "000",
                "00000010" when "001",
                "00000100" when "010",
                "00001000" when "011",
                "00010000" when "100",
                "00100000" when "101",
                "01000000" when "110",
                "10000000" when others;

-- three-state control of outputs
three_state: process (rd, dmuxout)
  begin
        if rd = '1' then
                data_out <= dmuxout;
        else
                data_out <= (others => 'Z');
        end if;
  end process;

end archfifo8x9;
```

Listing 4-1 An 8 by 9 FIFO

4.3   Combinational Logic

Combinational logic can be described in several ways. In the FIFO design above, it is described by the signals dmuxout and en, as well as the three-state buffers. The signals dmuxout and en use dataflow constructs (with-select-when statements). The three-state buffers are described with behavioral code using if-then-else statements. In the following sections, we will examine how to write combinational logic with concurrent and sequential statements. Concurrent statements are used in dataflow and structural descriptions. Sequential statements are used in behavioral descriptions.

4.3.1   Using Concurrent Statements

As explained in the previous chapter, concurrent statements lie outside of a process. Conceptually, they execute concurrently. Therefore, their order is not important.

Here, we will first discuss three types of concurrent statements used in data-flow descriptions: concurrent signal-assignment statements with Boolean equations, selective signal-assignment (with-select-when) statements, and conditional signal-assignment (when-else) statements.

Boolean Equations. Boolean equations can be used in both concurrent and sequential signal-assignment statements. Here, we illustrate using Boolean equations in concurrent statements to describe combinational logic. Listing 4-2 describes a four-to-one multiplexer that multiplexes 4-bit buses (Figure 4-1).

```
library ieee;
use ieee.std_logic_1164.all;
entity mux is port(
        a, b, c, d:      in std_logic_vector(3 downto 0);
        s:               in std_logic_vector(1 downto 0);
        x:               out std_logic_vector(3 downto 0));
end mux;

architecture archmux of mux is
begin
    x(3) <=      (a(3) and not(s(1)) and not(s(0)))
            or   (b(3) and not(s(1)) and s(0))
            or   (c(3) and s(1) and not(s(0)))
            or   (d(3) and s(1) and s(0));

    x(2) <=      (a(2) and not(s(1)) and not(s(0)))
            or   (b(2) and not(s(1)) and s(0))
            or   (c(2) and s(1) and not(s(0)))
            or   (d(2) and s(1) and s(0));

    x(1) <=      (a(1) and not(s(1)) and not(s(0)))
            or   (b(1) and not(s(1)) and s(0))
            or   (c(1) and s(1) and not(s(0)))
            or   (d(1) and s(1) and s(0));

    x(0) <=      (a(0) and not(s(1)) and not(s(0)))
            or   (b(0) and not(s(1)) and s(0))
            or   (c(0) and s(1) and not(s(0)))
            or   (d(0) and s(1) and s(0));

end archmux
```

Listing 4-2 A 4-bit wide multiplexer

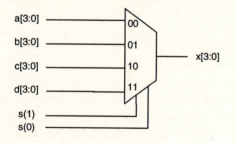

Figure 4-1   Block diagram of mux

Listing 4-2 is a cumbersome description that provides little advantage over some proprietary, low-level languages that have been popular in the past for use with PALs. However, for those functions most easily described with Boolean equations, VHDL provides for this capability. For example, in Listing 4-3 several signals are effectively defined using Boolean equations. In a case like this, using if-then-else statements (explained later in the chapter) would be cumbersome. We will illustrate more examples of where Boolean equations are most appropriate later in the chapter.

```
entity my_design is port (
        mem_op, io_op:      in bit;
        read, write:        in bit;
        memr, memw:         out bit;
        io_rd, io_wr:       out bit);
end my_design;

architecture control of my_design is
begin
        memw   <=   mem_op and write;
        memr   <=   mem_op and read;
        io_wr  <=    io_op and write;
        io_rd  <=    io_op and read;
end control;
```

Listing 4-3 Signals described with Boolean equations

Logical Operators. Logical operators are the cornerstone of Boolean equations. The logical operators and, or, nand, xor, xnor, and not are predefined for the types bit or Boolean, or for one-dimensional arrays of bit and Boolean. To use these operators (except not) with arrays of bits or Booleans, the two operands must be of the same length. The IEEE 1164 standard also overloads these operators for the types std_ulogic, std_logic, and their one-dimensional arrays. Overloaded operators are discussed on page 173.

The logical operators do *not* have an order of **precedence.** You may be accustomed to the precedence of operators in Boolean algebra: expressions in parentheses are evaluated first, followed by complements, AND expressions, and finally OR expressions. For example, with Boolean algebra, you expect the expression

A + B · C

to be evaluated as

A + (B · C)

However, in VHDL, no logical operator has precedence over another. Parentheses are required in multilevel logic equations. For example, parentheses are required to differentiate the above expression from

(A + B) · C

In fact, the code

```
X <= A or B and C;
```

will result in a compile-time error. Listing 4-2 shows that parentheses were used to group each AND expression. Parentheses were also used to identify that the NOT operator operated only on the signal to its immediate right, although in this case, parentheses were not needed and were included for clarity only.

with-select-when. The `with-select-when` statement provides **selective signal assignment,** which means that a signal is assigned a value based on the value of a selection signal. In the construct,

```
with selection_signal select
    signal_name <=  value_a when value_1_of_selection_signal,
                    value_b when value_2_of_selection_signal,
                    value_c when value_3_of_selection_signal, ...
                    value_x when last_value_of_selection_signal;
```

`signal_name` is assigned a value based on the current value of `selection_signal`. All values of `selection_signal` must be listed in the `when` clauses and will be mutually exclusive. So, if `selection_signal` has the value "value_2_of_selection_signal" then `signal_name` is assigned the value "value_b". In Listing 4-4, we use a selective signal-assignment statement to describe the multiplexer of Figure 4-1.

```
library ieee;
use ieee.std_logic_1164.all;
entity mux is port(
        a, b, c, d:        in std_logic_vector(3 downto 0);
        s:                 in std_logic_vector(1 downto 0);
        x:                 out std_logic_vector(3 downto 0));
end mux;

architecture archmux of mux is
begin
with s select
    x <= a when "00",
         b when "01",
         c when "10",
         d when others;
end archmux;
```

Listing 4-4 Selective signal assignment

Based on the value of signal s, signal x is assigned one of four values (a, b, c, or d). This construct enables a concise description of the four-to-one multiplexer. Three values of s are explicitly enumerated ("00", "01", and "10"). The reserved word others is used to indicate all other possible values for s. Others is specified instead of "11" for the following reason: s is of type std_logic_vector, and there are nine possible values for a data object of type std_logic. If "11" were specified instead of others, only four of the 81 values would be covered in the with-select-when statement. The values "1X", "Z0", "U-", "UU", and "LX" are just a few of the other possible values for s that include metalogic values. For hardware and synthesis tools, "11" *is* the only other meaningful value, but the code must be made VHDL-compliant. In simulation, there are indeed 77 other values that *s* can have. You *can* explicitly specify "11" as one of the values of s; however, others is still required to specify all possible values of s:

```
architecture archmux of mux is
begin
with s select
    x <= a when "00",
         b when "01",
         c when "10",
         d when "11",
         d when others;
end archmux;
```

The metalogical value "--" can also be used to assign the don't-care value to x, as in,

```
architecture archmux of mux is
begin
with s select
   x <= a when "00",
        b when "01",
        c when "10",
        d when "11",
        "--" when others;
end archmux;
```

The last when indicates that signal x will receive the value "--" if signal *s* takes on a value other than those explicitly listed. For synthesis, the results are the same for any of the three versions of the architecture, because hardware will dictate that x will be undefined if the elements of s are not of known logic levels. Results of synthesizing this design to a sum-of-products architecture (a CPLD, for instance) results in four equations similar to the following, which is for x(3):

```
x_3 =
      /s_1 * /s_0 * a_3
   +   s_1 * /s_0 * c_3
   +  /s_1 *  s_0 * b_3
   +   s_1 *  s_0 * d_3
```

A selective signal assignment describes logic based on mutually exclusive combinations of values of the selection signal. That is, the when conditions can only specify possible values of the selection signal. This is not necessarily true for conditional signal-assignment (when-else) statements. In the next section we will compare with-select-when statements to when-else statements.

when-else. The when-else statement provides for conditional signal assignment, which means that a signal is assigned a value based on a condition. In the construct,

```
signal_name <=  value_a when condition1 else
                value_b when condition2 else
                value_c when condition3 else ...
                value_x;
```

signal_name is assigned the value based on the evaluation of the conditions. Signal_name is assigned a value based on the first condition listed that is true. For example if condition1 is false and condition2 is true, then signal_name will be assigned the value "value_b". In Listing 4-5, we use a conditional signal-assignment statement to describe the multiplexer of Figure 4-1.

```
library ieee;
use ieee.std_logic_1164.all;
entity mux is port(
        a, b, c, d:      in std_logic_vector(3 downto 0);
        s:               in std_logic_vector(1 downto 0);
        x:               out std_logic_vector(3 downto 0));
end mux;

architecture archmux of mux is
begin
        x <= a when (s = "00") else
             b when (s = "01") else
             c when (s = "10") else
             d;
end archmux;
```

Listing 4-5 Conditional signal assignment

Whereas the when conditions in a with-select-when statement must specify mutually exclusive values of the selection signal, the when conditions in a when-else statement can specify any simple expression. However, in Listing 4-5, all of the conditions listed in the when-else statement *are* mutually exclusive. Thus the four Boolean transfer equations produced by synthesizing this design to a sum-of-products architecture reduce to one resembling the following, which is for x(3):

```
x_3 =
        s_1 *  s_0 * d_0
    +   s_1 * /s_0 * c_0
    + /s_1 *  s_0 * b_0
    + /s_1 * /s_0 * a_0
```

Because the when conditions were mutually exclusive, the equations for this design match those produced for the with-select-when description. However, if the conditions in a when-else statement are not mutually exclusive, logic ensures that the highest priority goes to the first when condition listed. Priorities to subsequent when conditions are based on order of appearance.

If used with mutually exclusive values of one signal, the when-else construct is slightly more verbose than the with-select-when construct (as in our multiplexer example). But this construct can also help you to succinctly describe priority encoders such as that of Listing 4-6.

```vhdl
library ieee;
use ieee.std_logic_1164.all;
entity priority is port(
        a, b, c, d, w, x, y, z: in std_logic;
        j: out std_logic);
end priority;

architecture priority of priority is
begin
j <= w when a='1' else
     x when b='1' else
     y when c='1' else
     z when d='1' else
     '0';
end;
```

Listing 4-6 Priority encoding with conditional signal assignment

This construct describes the logic of Figure 4-2 and results in the following equation for j:

```
j =    a *  w
   + /a *  b *  x
   + /a * /b *  c * y
   + /a * /b * /c * d * z
```

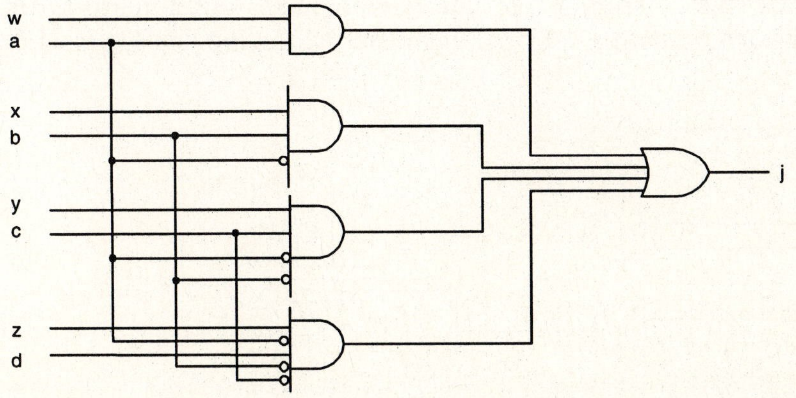

Figure 4-2   A priority encoder described with a when-else statement

This equation and the when-else statement indicate the priority that j is assigned the value of w when a is asserted, even if b, c, or d is asserted. Signal b holds priority over c and d, and signal c holds priority over d. If, however, a, b, c, and d are mutually exclusive (that is, if it is known that only one will be asserted at a time), then the code of Listing 4-7 is more appropriate.

```
library ieee;
use ieee.std_logic_1164.all;
entity no_priority is port(
        a, b, c, d, w, x, y, z: in std_logic;
        j: out std_logic);
end no_priority;

architecture no_priority of no_priority is
begin
        j <= (a and w) or (b and x) or (c and y) or (d and z);
end;
```

Listing 4-7 Selection without priority using a Boolean equation

This design ensures that the logic of Figure 4-3 is produced by synthesis. The logic requires AND gates with fewer inputs than that of Figure 4-2. Although using wider AND gates in a CPLD does not usually require additional resources, the wider AND gates could have an impact on the implementation in an FPGA. Wider AND gates could require additional logic cells and levels of logic. These designs are not functionally equivalent, however. In Listing 4-6, signals a, b, c, and d are not necessarily mutually exclusive, and if more than one is asserted at a time, there is a priority to determine which signal is selected. If signals a, b, c, and d are known to be mutually exclusive, then Listing 4-7 produces equivalent functionality with fewer resources. The design of Listing 4-8 does *not* describe the logic of Figure 4-3.

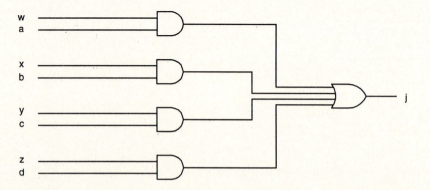

Figure 4-3 Selection of w, x, y, and z based on mutually exclusive signals a, b, c, and d

```vhdl
library ieee;
use ieee.std_logic_1164.all;
entity compares is port(
        a, b, c, d, w, x, y, z: in std_logic;
        j: out std_logic);
end compares;

architecture compares of compares is
    signal tmp: std_logic_vector(3 downto 0);
begin
    tmp <= (a, b, c, d);
    with tmp select
        j <=  w when "1000",
              x when "0100",
              y when "0010",
              z when "0001",
              '0' when others;
end;
```

Listing 4-8 Selection based on values of *a, b, c,* and *d* combined.

Listing 4-8 describes the logic of Figure 4-4. An **aggregate** is used to assign the values of a, b, c, and d to tmp. An aggregate is a list of elements, enclosed in parentheses and separated by commas. In this example, tmp(0) is equivalent to a, tmp(1) is equivalent to b, and so on. Signal j is assigned the value of w only if a is '1' and b, c, and d are each '0'. The following code, when synthesized, will also *not* result in the logic of Figure 4-3. It can be analyzed without error by simulation software, but will produce an error when compiled by synthesis software.

```vhdl
tmp <= (a, b, c, d);
with tmp select
    j <=  w when "1---",
          x when "-1--",
          y when "--1-",
          z when "---1",
          '0' when others;
```

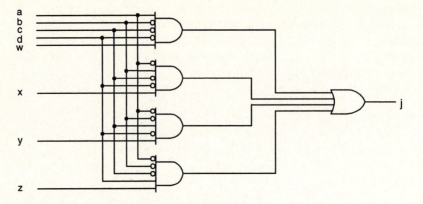

Figure 4-4   Logic described by Listing 4-8

Synthesis must attempt to produce logic that behaves as the simulation of this code. With simulation software, signal j is assigned the value of w only when a is '1' and b, c, and d are each '-'. Because '-' is a value that an object of type std_logic can have, simulation software will not assign j the value of w when b, c, or d is '1' (or any value other than '-'). That is, it will not treat '-' as a don't care, or wild card, where '-' can represent a '0' or a '1'. In order to avoid a mismatch between simulation and synthesis, synthesis software should not interpret '-' differently. Thus, synthesis tools treat when choices that contain a '-' as ones that won't occur, because in hardware, a signal will never have the value '-'.

Conditions as Simple Expressions. The when conditions in a when-else statement can also be simple expressions, as shown in the following code fragments. These types of conditions are not usually possible with with-select-when statements because the conditions must be values of the selection signal.

```
signal stream, instrm, oldstrm: std_logic_vector(3 downto 0);
signal state: states;
signal we: std_logic;
signal id: std_logic_vector(15 downto 0);;
...

    stream <="0000" when (state=idle and start='0') else
             "0001" when (state=idle and start='1') else
             instrm when (state=incoming) else
             oldstrm;

    we <= '1' when (state=write and id < x"1FFF") else '0';
```

Relational Operators. Relational operators are used for testing equality, inequality, and ordering. The equality and inequality operators (= and /=) are defined for all types discussed in this text. The magnitude operators (<, <=, >, and >=) are defined for scalar types or an array with a discrete range. Arrays are equivalent only if their lengths are equivalent and all corresponding elements of both arrays are equivalent. The result of any relational operation is Boolean (that is, true or false).

The types of operands in a relational operation must match. The following would produce an error because a is a `std_logic_vector`, and 3 is an `integer`:

```
signal a: std_logic_vector(7 downto 0)
      ...
if a = 3 then...
```

Overloaded Operators. However, as with other operators, relational operators may be overloaded. Overloaded operators permit you to use operators with multiple types (for which the operator is not predefined by the IEEE 1076 standard). Operators may be overloaded with user-defined functions, but many overloaded operators are defined in the IEEE 1164 and 1076.3 standards. For example, the IEEE 1076.3 standard defines functions to overload the = operator for the types `signed` and `integer`, as well as `unsigned` and `natural`. This overloaded operator will permit the code fragment below to be processed.

```
library ieee;
use ieee.std_logic_1164.all;
use work.numeric_std.all;
entity compare is port(
        a:      in unsigned(3 downto 0);
        x:      out std_logic;
end compare;
architecture compare of compare is
begin
    x <= '1' when a = 3 else '0';
end;
```

Listing 4-9 Overloaded = operator defined in `numeric_std`

The operator overloading functions are defined in the `numeric_std` package of the 1076.3 standard, and this package must be made visible to the design entity with a `use` clause. Many synthesis vendors also supply additional packages to overload operators for the type `std_logic`. Although not standards, these packages are often used by VHDL users because they were available well before `numeric_std` was adopted. Because they allow relational and arithmetic operations on the type std_logic, some perceive these packages as more useful than the numeric_std package. Certainly, they do not require the overhead of using two additional types (in addition to std_logic_vector) as well as type-conversion functions. When using one of these packages in arithmetic operations, a synthesis tool will interpret the std_logic_vector using an unsigned representation or one of several possible signed representations. The synthesis tool must then also produce the appropriate signed or unsigned arithmetic components. You will need to consult the documentation for a synthesis tool to determine how it represents std_logic_vectors in arithmetic operations.

Warp provides the std_arith package. It defines several new functions and overloads the arithmetic operators to handle the type std_logic_vector, interpreting it as unsigned. For example, it allows the following code to be processsed:

```
library ieee;
use ieee.std_logic_1164.all;
use work.std_arith.all;        --std_arith, rather than numeric_std
entity compare is port(
        a:      in std_logic_vector(3 downto 0);   --type std_logic_vector
        x:      out std_logic;
end compare;
architecture compare of compare is
begin
    x <= '1' when a = 3 else '0';
end;
```

Listing 4-10 Overloaded = operator defined in std_arith

For some examples in this text, we will use the numeric_std package to illustrate the use of the types, functions, and operators defined therein. We will also use the std_arith package in other examples to illustrate how the use of one array type, std_logic_vector, can reduce design overhead.

When transferring code from one synthesis tool to another, you should use the package provided by the particular vendor for overloading the std_logic or std_logic_vector types. Although one synthesis tool may be able to process the VHDL code of another synthesis vendor's proprietary package, that tool probably will not produce efficient arithmetic and logic structures because the package was not optimized for it.

The numeric_std and std_arith packages also contain another important function, std_match. This function is used to treat the '-' value of the std_logic type as a don't-care, or wild-card, value that can represent '0' or '1'. This standard function can be useful because the following comparison evaluates to false for all values of a except "1--1", which will never be true in hardware.

```
if a = "1--1" then ...-- always evaluates false in synthesis
```

Simulation and synthesis tools must interpret '-' as a value. Thus, the comparison will be true only when a is literally "1--1". Although '-' represents the don't-care value, the = operator cannot be used to identify don't-care conditions. The = operator will return a Boolean value of true if and only if the left-hand-side expression is equivalent to the right-hand-side expression. The don't-care value, '-', is the 'high value of the std_logic type. A comparison of '-' to '0' or '1' using the = operator always evaluates to false. The std_match function, on the other hand, returns true for the comparison of '-' to '0' or '1'. Using the std_match function, the comparison of "1--1" to a std_logic_vector(3 downto 0) evaluates to true if the first and last elements of the vector are '1', regardless of the value of the middle two:

```
if std_match(a, "1--1") then ...        -- true if a(3)=a(0)='1'
```

The numeric_std package also overloads the = operator to have a different meaning for the types signed and unsigned than is predefined by the 1076 standard for array types. For example, the default = comparison for the following code would alway result in a false evaluation because the size of a and the comparison string are not equivalent.

```
signal a: bit_vector(3 downto 0);
...
if a = "00001" then ...-- array sizes not the same; always false
```

With the overloaded relational operators of numeric_std, the following evaluation could be true if a had the value of "0001":

```
library ieee;
use ieee.numeric_std.all;
...
signal a: signed(3 downto 0);
...
if a = "00001" then ...-- doesn't matter that array sizes not the same
```

Component Instantiations. Component instantiations are concurrent statements that specify the interconnection of signals in the design. It is unlikely that you would use component instantiation to describe a 4-bit comparator as in Listing 4-11, but the code serves to illustrate that component instantiation can be used to implement combinational logic.

```
library ieee;
use work.std_logic_1164.all;
entity compare is port(
        a, b:    in std_logic_vector(3 downto 0);
        aeqb:    out std_logic);
end compare;

use work.gatespkg.all;
architecture archcompare of compare is
        signal c: std_logic_vector(3 downto 0);
begin
        x0: xor2 port map(a(0), b(0), c(0));
        x1: xor2 port map(a(1), b(1), c(1));
        x2: xor2 port map(a(2), b(2), c(2));
        x3: xor2 port map(a(3), b(3), c(3));

        n1: nor4 port map(c(0), c(1), c(2), c(3), aeqb);
end;
```

Listing 4-11 A 4-bit comparator described structurally

Gate components are not defined by the VHDL standard. This design requires that the gates xor2 and nor2 be defined in another package (created by you, a synthesis-tool vendor, or a PLD vendor). Sometimes, vendor-provided gates are technology-specific (device-dependent) and are provided so that you can access a particular feature. Using these components can reduce readability and eliminate the device-independence of the code, unless there are behavioral descriptions of the supplied component for use in retargeting or simulating the design.

For example, a synthesis tool may provide an adder component for instantiating. This component may not have an underlying behavioral or structural description; rather, it may be recognized directly by the synthesis tool and directly mapped to the target architecture. Although this ensures that your code will produce the best possible implementation of the adder, it prevents the code from being used to target another device architecture. It also prevents the source code from being simulated, unless, of course, there are also behavioral models of the code.

4.3.2   Using Sequential Statements

As explained in the previous chapter, sequential statements are those statements contained in a process, function, or procedure. Functions and procedures are described in Chapter 7. Here, we discuss sequential statements in processes. The collection of statements that make up a process (that is, the process itself) constitutes a concurrent statement. Electronic systems are "concurrent" and so are processes. If a design has multiple processes, then those processes are concurrent with respect to one another and to other concurrent statements within the architecture. Inside a process, however, signal assignment is sequential from a simulation standpoint, and the order in which signal assignments are listed *does* affect how logic is synthesized.

In this section, we discuss how to use processes and sequential statements to describe combinational logic. Do not confuse sequential statements with sequential logic (logic with memory, or clocked logic).

if-then-else. The if-then-else construct is used to select a set of statements to execute based on a Boolean evaluation (true or false) of a condition or set of conditions. In the following construct,

```
if (condition) then
    do something;
else
    do something different;
end if;
```

if the condition specified evaluates true, the sequential statement or statements (do something) following the keyword then are executed. If the condition evaluates false, the sequential statement or statements after the else (do something different) are executed. The construct is closed with end if. Because sequential statements are executed in order of appearance, the following processes are functionally equivalent.

```
signal step: std_logic;
signal addr: std_logic_vector(7 downto 0);
        .
        .
        .

similar1: process (addr)
    begin
        step <= '0';
        if addr > x"0F" then
            step <= '1';
        end if;
    end process;
```

```
similar2: process (addr)
   begin
      if addr > x"0F" then
         step <= '1';
      else
         step <= '0';
      end if;
   end process similar2;
```

With either of these processes, step will assume the value '1' if addr is greater than 0F hex, and '0' if it is less than or equal to that value. The process

```
not_similar: process (addr)
   begin
      if addr > x"0F" then
         step <= '1';
      end if;
   end process;
```

does not describe the same logic because neither a default value nor an else assignment is specified for step. The process not_similar implies that step should retain its value if addr is less than or equal to 0F (hex). This is referred to as **implied,** or **implicit memory.** Thus, once asserted, step will remain forever asserted as shown in Figure 4-5 and as defined by the following equation:

step = addr(3) * addr(2) * addr(1) * addr(0)
          + step

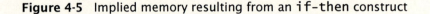

Figure 4-5   Implied memory resulting from an if-then construct

If you do not want the value of step to be "remembered," be sure to include a default value or complete the if-then with an else.

The `if-then-else` can be expanded further to include an `elsif` to allow for further conditions to be specified and prioritized. The syntax for this operation is

```
if (condition1) then
    do something;
elsif (condition2) then
    do something different;
else
    do something completely different;
end if;
```

For each signal x that is assigned a value based on a `condition`, synthesis will produce an equation. For example, the following code

```
if (condition1) then
    x <= value1;
elsif (condition2) then
    x <= value2;
else
    x <= value3;
end if;
```

results in this equation:

```
x =     condition1 * value1
        + /condition1 * condition2 * value2
        + /condition1 + /condition2 * condition3 * value3
        + ...
```

The `if-then-elsif-else` construct and the equation above clearly show that for x to be assigned `value3`, not only does `condition3` have to be true, but also `condition1` and `condition2` must be false. For x to be assigned `value1`, only `condition1` need be true, regardless of the evaluation of `condition2` and `condition3`. This indicates a clear order of precedence among the conditions. A `when-else` construct can be rewritten with an `if-then-else` statement. This is left as an exercise for the reader.

The 4-bit-wide four-to-one multiplexer can be described with an `if-then-elsif-else` construct, as shown in Listing 4-12.

```
architecture archmux of mux is
begin
mux4_1: process (a, b, c, d, s)
        begin
                if s = "00" then
                        x <= a;
                elsif s = "01" then
                        x <= b;
                elsif s = "10" then
                        x <= c;
                else
                        x <= d;
                end if;
        end process mux4_1;
end archmux;
```

Listing 4-12 Describing a multiplexer with an `if-then` statement

Because the conditions are mutually exclusive values of s, the logic described here synthesizes to the same for the previous implementations. However, because there is priority in the conditions (as in a `when-else` statement), an `if-then` statement is not the best choice when the conditions involve multiple signals that are mutually exclusive. Using an `if-then-else` statement in this case may cause additional logic to be synthesized to ensure that previous conditions are not true, as with the `when-else` statement. Instead, a Boolean equation, or `case-when` statement, may be more appropriate.

Signals a, b, c, d, and s are included in the process sensitivity list in the code fragment of Listing 4-12 because a change in any one of them should cause a change in (or evaluation of) x. If s were omitted from the sensitivity list, then x would not change with a change in s; only changes in a, b, c, or d would lead to a change in x, and this would not describe a multiplexer. The design equations produced by synthesizing this design description, or any of the other descriptions of the multiplexer found in this chapter, are the same for each bit of x:

$$x = \bar{s_1}\bar{s_0}a + \bar{s_1}s_0b + s_1\bar{s_0}c + s_1s_0d$$

If mapped to a PLD-like architecture, each bit of x can easily be implemented with one macrocell and four product terms. If mapped to an FPGA, it is up to the synthesis and optimization software to optimally map the equation to the device architecture. For device architectures with multiplexers, this design should fit nicely.

Listing 4-13 is an address decoder. The design takes in a 16-bit address, determines which portion of the address space (see Figure 4-6) is being addressed, and asserts the appropriate output. This design uses `if-then-else` constructs and relational operators to identify areas of memory and assert the correct signal. Because the address ranges (conditions) are mutually exclusive, only one product term per output signal is required, as verified by the design equations that follow the code.

```
library ieee;
use ieee.std_logic_1164.all;
entity decode is port(
        address:                in std_logic_vector(15 downto 3);
        valid, boot_up:         in std_logic;
        sram, prom, eeprom, shadow,
        periph1, periph2:       out std_logic);
end decode;
architecture mem_decode of decode is
begin
mapper: process (address, valid, boot_up) begin
        shadow  <= '0';
        prom    <= '0';
        periph1 <= '0';
        periph2 <= '0';
        sram    <= '0';
        eeprom  <= '0';
        if valid = '1' then
                if address >=x"0000" and address < x"4000" then
                        if boot_up = '1' then
                                shadow <= '1';
                        else
                                prom <= '1';
                        end if;
                elsif address >=x"4000" and address < x"4008" then
                        periph1 <= '1';
                elsif address >=x"4008" and address < x"4010" then
                        periph2 <= '1';
                elsif address >=x"8000" and address < x"C000" then
                        sram <= '1';
                elsif address >= x"C000" then
                        eeprom <= '1';
                end if;
        end if;
end process;
end mem_decode;
```

Listing 4-13 Address decoder

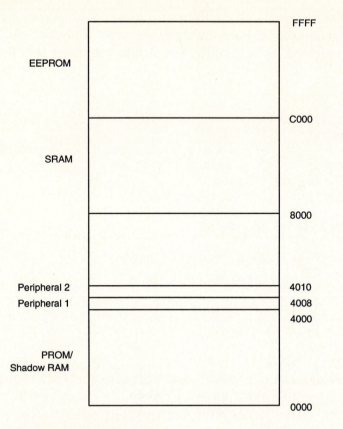

Figure 4-6   Memory map

The design equations on page 183 indicate the need for one product term for each output. This maps well to a CPLD architecture. The equations for `periph1` and `periph2` contain as many as 14 literals. CPLD logic blocks typically have many more inputs than FPGA logic cells, so there are still additional inputs to a logic block that can be used for other expressions. In an FPGA, these signals would likely require more than one logic cell (and therefore more than one level of logic) because of the wide fan-in and large AND gate required. The signals `valid`, `address(15)`, and `address(14)` would each have fan-outs of six.

```
sram =
   valid * address_15 * /address_14
prom =
   valid * /address_15 * /address_14 * /boot_up
eeprom =
   valid * address_15 * address_14
shadow =
   valid * /address_15 * /address_14 * boot_up
periph1 =
   valid * /address_15 * address_14 * /address_13 * /address_12 *
   /address_11 * /address_10 * /address_9 * /address_8 * /address_7*
   /address_6 * /address_5 * /address_4 * /address_3
periph2 =
   valid * /address_15 * address_14 * /address_13 * /address_12 *
   /address_11 * /address_10 * /address_9 * /address_8 * /address_7*
   /address_6 * /address_5 * /address_4 * address_3
```

Because the address ranges for the different memory selections are mutually exclusive, additional logic is *not* added to ensure that previous conditions are false. If the conditions were not mutually exclusive, then default values and separate if-then statements would ensure that the additional logic is not added.

case-when. Case statements are used to specify a set of statements to execute based on the value of a given selection signal. A case-when statement can be used, for example, as the equivalent of a with-select-when statement. In the following construct, a set of statements is executed based on the value of selection_signal.

```
case selection_signal is
   when value_1_of_selection_signal =>
      (do something)      --set of statements 1
   when value_2_of_selection_signal =>
      (do something)      --set of statements 2
   when value_3_of_selection_signal =>
      (do something)      --set of statements 3
   ...
   when last_value_of_selection_signal =>
      (do something)      --set of statements x
```

A case-when statement is used in Listing 4-14 to describe another address decoder.

```
library ieee;
use ieee.std_logic_1164.all;
entity test_case is
    port (address :  in std_logic_vector(2 downto 0);
             decode:     out std_logic_vector(7 downto 0));
end test_case;

architecture design of test_case is
begin
process (address)
    begin
        case address is
            when "001" =>  decode   <= X"11";
            when "111" =>  decode   <= X"42";
            when "010" =>  decode   <= X"44";
            when "101" =>  decode   <= X"88";
            when others => decode   <= X"00";
        end case;
    end process;
end design;
```

Listing 4-14 A different address decoder

The `case-when` statement describes how decode is driven based on the value of the input address. The reserved word `others` is used to completely define the behavior of the output decode for all possible values of address. When `others` covers the address input combinations "000," "011," "100," and "110," as well as all of the metalogical values. Although you may specify multiple statements to execute for each `when` condition, this example has just one signal-assignment statement per condition. The equations generated by synthesizing this design are:

```
decoded_7 =
      address_2 * /address_1 * address_0
decoded_5 =
      GND
decoded_4 =
      /address_2 * /address_1 * address_0
decoded_3 =
      address_2 * /address_1 * address_0
decoded_2 =
      /address_2 * address_1 * /address_0
decoded_1 =
      address_2 * address_1 * address_0
decoded_0 =
      /address_2 * /address_1 * address_0
```

```
decoded_6 =
        /address_2 * address_1 * /address_0
      + address_2 * address_1 * address_0
```

Many of these equations turn out to have common product terms. The 4 and 0 bits are equivalent, as well as the 3 and the 7. The 1 and 6 bits share a common product term, as well as the 2 and 6. In a CPLD, these common product terms may share resources. (Some architectures produce an incremental delay when shared product terms are used, in which case, depending upon the performance requirements of this design, you may not want to use shared product terms.) An implementation in an FPGA could take advantage of equivalent signals—the output of one logic cell could drive two I/O cells, such as decode(0) and decode(4). The shared gates between the 1, 2, and 6 bits probably would not provide an advantage in most FPGAs because an additional level of logic would likely be required; however, they can fit into the pASIC380 logic cell, as shown in Figure 4-7. The equations for decode(1) and decode(2) are placed on the select lines, each of which has its own unique output. If either select line is asserted, then the output for decode(6) is also asserted.

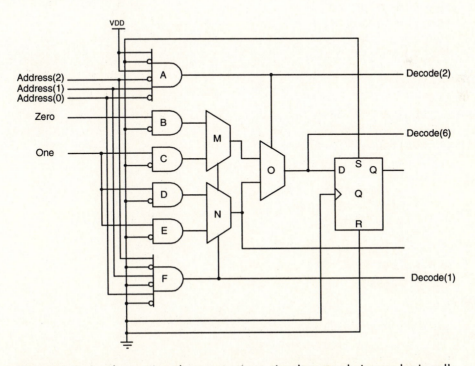

Figure 4-7   Implementing three equations simultaneously in one logic cell

Breakout Exercise 4-1

Purpose: To illustrate logic resource requirements for conditional versus mutually exclusive input conditions.

The code in Listing 4-15 can be found in the file c:\vhdlbook\ch4\cond.vhd. Compile and synthesize it to a CY7C371. The code in Listing 4-16 can be found in the file c:\vhdlbook\ch4\exclusiv.vhd. Compile and synthesize it to a CY7C371. Open the report files and compare design equations.

```vhdl
library ieee;
use ieee.std_logic_1164.all;
entity break1 is port(
    a, b, c, d:     in std_logic;
    j, k:           in std_logic;
    x:              out std_logic);
end break1;
architecture conditional of break1 is
    signal func1, func2, func3, func4: std_logic;
begin
    func1 <= j or k;
    func2 <= j and k;
    func3 <= j xor k;
    func4 <= j xnor k;

p1: process (a, b, c, d, j, k)
    begin
        if a = '1' then
            x <= func1;
        elsif b = '1' then
            x <= func2;
        elsif c = '1' then
            x <= func3;
        elsif d = '1' then
            x <= func4;
        else
            x <= '-';
        end if;
    end process;
end;
```

Listing 4-15 Conditional signal assignment

```vhdl
library ieee;
use ieee.std_logic_1164.all;
entity break1 is port(
    a, b, c, d: in std_logic;
    j, k:       in std_logic;
    x:          out std_logic);
end break1;
architecture exclusive of break1 is
    signal func1, func2, func3, func4: std_logic;
begin
    func1 <= j or k;
    func2 <= j and k;
    func3 <= j xor k;
    func4 <= j xnor k;

p1: process (a, b, c, d, j, k)
        subtype select_type is std_logic_vector(3 downto 0);
    begin
        case select_type'(a & b & c & d) is-- qualified expression
            when "1000" => x <= func1;
            when "0100" => x <= func2;
            when "0010" => x <= func3;
            when "0001" => x <= func4;
            when others => x <= '-';
        end case;
    end process;
end;
```

Listing 4-16 Signal assignment based on mutually exclusive signals

A subtype is defined in the process declarative region of Listing 4-16. This type is then used in a **qualified expression** (an expression that qualifies a value as a specific type) to ensure that the return of the concatenation operation is a constrained array.

4.4   Synchronous Logic

Programmable logic devices lend themselves well to synchronous applications. Most device architectures have blocks of combinational logic connected to the inputs of flip-flops as the basic building block for a CPLD macrocell or an FPGA logic cell. This section will show you how to write VHDL for synchronous logic, using both behavioral and structural descriptions.

The following code describes a simple D-type flip-flop, or DFF (Figure 4-8):

```vhdl
library ieee;
use ieee.std_logic_1164.all;
entity dff_logic is port (
    d, clk : in std_logic;
    q      : out std_logic );
end dff_logic;

architecture example of dff_logic is
begin
    process (clk) begin
        if (clk'event and clk = '1') then
            q <= d;
        end if;
    end process;
end example;
```

Listing 4-17 Description of a positive edge-triggered D-type flip-flop

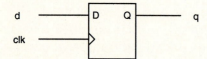

Figure 4-8   Block diagram of DFF

This process is sensitive only to changes in clk. Thus, a VHDL simulator activates this process only when clk transitions; a transition in d does not cause a sequencing of this process. Many synthesis tools, however, will ignore the sensitivity list.

The if clk'event condition is true only when there is a change in value—that is, an event—of the signal clk (recall that 'event is an attribute that when combined with a signal forms a Boolean expression that indicates when the signal transitions). The clk'event expression and the process sensitivity list are redundant—they both detect changes in clk—but because many synthesis tools ignore sensitivity lists, you should include the clk'event expression to describe edge-triggered events. Because the change in clk can be either from '0' to '1' (a rising edge) or 1 to 0 (a falling edge), the additional condition clk = '1' is used to define a rising-edge event. The statements inside of the if statement are executed only when there is a change in the state of clk from '0' to '1'—a synchronous event, allowing synthesis software to infer from the code a positive edge-triggered flip-flop. You can make this occur on the falling edge of the clock instead of the rising edge simply by changing

```
if (clk'event and clk = '1') then
```

to

```
if (clk'event and clk = '0') then
```

Also, you can describe a level-sensitive latch (see Figure 4-9) instead of an edge-triggered flip-flop. To do this, all you have to do is take away the clk'event condition and insert d in the process sensitivity list:

```
process (clk,d) begin
    if (clk = '1') then
        q <= d;
    end if;
end process
```

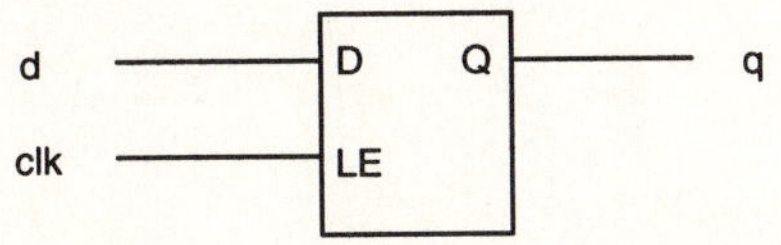

Figure 4-9   Block diagram of a D-latch

In this case, whenever clk is at a logic high level, the output q is assigned the value of input d, thereby describing a latch. In none of these cases (the rising-edge-triggered flip-flop, the falling-edge-triggered flip-flop, and the level-sensitive latch) is there an else condition indicating what assignments to make when the if conditions are not met. Without an else, there is implied memory (that q will keep its value), which is consistent with the operation of a flip-flop. In other words, writing:

```
if (clk'event and clk = '1') then
    q <= d;
end if;
```

has the same meaning for simulation as writing:

```
if (clk'event and clk = '1') then
    q <= d;
else
    q <= q;
end if;
```

This is exactly how a D-type flip-flop, and other synchronous logic, should operate. If there is a rising edge on the clock line, then the flip-flop output will get a new value based on the flip-flop input. If not, the flip-flop output stays the same. In fact, most synthesis tools will not handle an else expression following an if (clk' eventand clk = '1') because it may describe logic for which the implementation is ambiguous. For example, it is unclear how the following description should be synthesized:

```
if (clk'event and clk = '1') then
    q <= d;
else
    q <= a;
end if;
```

The following two examples show how a T-type flip-flop, or TFF (a toggle flip-flop) and an 8-bit register can be described. First is the T-type flip-flop shown in Figure 4-10 and described in Listing 4-18.

```
library ieee;
use ieee.std_logic_1164.all;
entity tff_logic is port (
    t, clk : in std_logic;
    q      : buffer std_logic
);
end dff_logic;
    architecture t_example of dff_logic is
begin
    process (clk) begin
        if (clk'event and clk = '1') then
            if (t = '1') then
                q <= not(q);
            else
                q <= q;
            end if;
        end if;
    end process;
end t_example;
```

Listing 4-18 Description of a T-type flip-flop

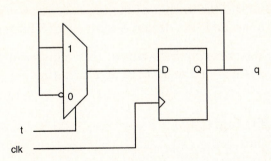

Figure 4-10 Implementation of a T-type flip-flop in a device that only has D-type flip-flops

All signal assignments in this process that occur after `if (clk'event and clk = '1')` are synchronous to the signal `clk`. The signal assignments in the process above—`q <= not(q)` and `q <= q`—are synchronous to the clock. The first signal assignment, which occurs if `t` is asserted, indicates that on the rising edge of the clock, `q` will be assigned the opposite of its current value. The second signal assignment, which occurs if `t` is deasserted, indicates that on the rising edge of the clock, `q` will retain its value. Figure 4-10 shows that combinational logic is described in this process (the multiplexer); however, all signal assignments (q) are synchronous. (This implementation is device-specific. A 22V10, for example, does not have multiplexers, so obviously it would not be implemented as shown—it would be implemented with a sum of product terms. The CY7C371 device has a macrocell for which the register can be configured as a TFF, and so would not require any additional resources.)

```
library ieee;
use ieee.std_logic_1164.all;
entity reg_logic is port (
    d   : in std_logic_vector(0 to 7);
    clk : in std_logic;
    q   : out std_logic_vector(0 to 7)
);
end reg_logic;

architecture r_example of reg_logic is
begin
    process (clk) begin
        if (clk'event and clk = '1') then
            q <= d;
        end if;
    end process;
end r_example;
```

Listing 4-19 Description of an 8-bit register

The architcture of Listing 4-19 is similar to that of Listing 4-17 except in this design, q and d are `bit_vectors`, not `bits`, and this design describes an 8-bit register.

Wait until statement. You can also describe the behavior of this registered circuit by using the `wait until` statement instead of the `if (clk'event and clk = '1')` statement:

```
architecture example2 of dff_logic is
begin
    process begin
        wait until (clk = '1');
            q  <=  d;
        end process;
end example2;
```

This process does not use a sensitivity list, but begins with a `wait` statement. A process that has a `wait` statement cannot have a sensitivity list (the `wait` statement implicitly defines the sensitivity list). For descriptions that are to be synthesized, the `wait until` statement must be the first in the process. Because of this, synchronous logic described with a `wait` statement cannot be asynchronously reset, as will be explained below.

If you interpret the code fragment above in terms of simulation, you will see that this process is suspended until the condition following the `wait until` statement is true. Once true, the signal assignments that follow the `wait` statement are made, after which the process once again waits for the clock to be asserted (even if it is still presently asserted). So, in this case, once the `clk` signal becomes equal to '1' (that is, on the rising edge of `clk`), q will be assigned the value of d, thereby describing a D-type flip-flop without an asynchronous reset or preset.

Rising_edge and falling_edge functions. The `std_logic_1164` package defines the functions `rising_edge` and `falling_edge` to detect rising and falling edges of signals. One of these functions can be used in place of the (`clk'event and clk = '1'`) expression if the `clk` signal is of type `std_logic`. These functions are preferred by some designers because in simulation the `rising_edge` function will ensure that the transition is from '0' to '1' and not some other transition such as 'U' to '1'. However, if the clock is an input signal, you will be able to easily control its transitions. These transitions will be only from '0' to '1' and from '1' to '0'. We will use the (`clk'event and clk = '1'`) and `rising_edge(clk)` expressions interchangeably. Listing 4-20 also describes a D-type flip-flop.

```
library ieee;
use ieee.std_logic_1164.all;
entity dff_logic is port (
    d, clk : in std_logic;
    q      : out std_logic );
end dff_logic;

architecture example of dff_logic is
begin
    process (clk) begin
        if rising_edge(clk) then
            q <= d;
        end if;
    end process;
end example;
```

Listing 4-20 Description of a D-type flip-flop using `rising-edge` function

4.4.1 Resets in Synchronous Logic

None of the examples above make reference to resets or initial conditions. The VHDL standard does not require you to reset or initialize a circuit. The standard specifies that for simulation, unless a signal is explicitly initialized, it gets initialized to the `'left` value of its type. So a signal of type `std_logic` will get initialized to 'U', the uninitialized state, and a bit will get initialized to '0'. In the hardware world, however, this is not always true—not all devices power up in the reset state, and the uninitialized state is physically meaningless. So, what if you want to have global and local resets to place the logic in a known state? You can describe resets and presets (as shown in Figure 4-11) with simple modifications to the code (see Listing 4-21):

```
architecture rexample of dff_logic is
begin
    process (clk, reset) begin
        if reset = '1' then
            q <= '0';
        elsif rising_edge(clk) then
            q <= d;
        end if;
    end process;
end rexample;
```

Listing 4-21 Describing an asynchronous reset

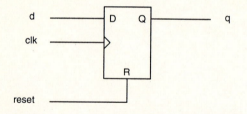

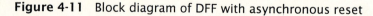

Figure 4-11   Block diagram of DFF with asynchronous reset

The sensitivity list indicates that this process is sensitive to changes in `clk` and `reset`. A transition in either of these signals will cause a simulator to sequence through the process. You'll find that this code accurately describes a D-type flip-flop with an asynchronous reset: The process is activated only by a change in `clk` or `reset`. If `reset` is asserted, then signal q will be assigned '0', regardless of the value of `clk`. If `reset` is not asserted and the clock transition is from '0' to '1', then the signal q will be assigned the value of signal d. This process template causes synthesis software to infer an asynchronous reset.

To describe a preset instead of a reset, you can simply modify the sensitivity list and write:

```
if (preset = '1') then
    q <= '1';
elsif rising_edge(clk) then ...
```

instead of:

```
if (reset = '1')
    then q <= '0'
elsif rising_edge(clk) then ...
```

You can also reset (or preset) your flip-flops synchronously by putting the reset (or preset) condition inside the portion of the process that describes logic that is synchronous to the clock, as shown in Listing 4-22.

```
architecture sync_rexample of dff_logic is
begin
    process (clk) begin
        if rising_edge(clk) then
            if (reset = '1') then
                q <= '0';
            else
                q <= d;
            end if;
        end if;
    end process;
end sync_rexample;
```

Listing 4-22 Describing a synchronous reset

Listing 4-22 describes a process that is sensitive only to changes in the clock; synthesis produces a D-type flip-flop that is synchronously reset whenever the `reset` signal is asserted and is sampled by the rising edge of the clock. Because most flip-flops in PLDs do not have synchronous sets or resets (the 22V10, with a synchronous set, is a notable exception), implementing synchronous presets and resets requires using additional product terms (see Figure 4-12).

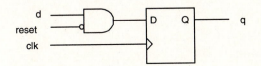

Figure 4-12 Additional logic resources are usually required for synchronous resets and sets

You can also describe a combination synchronous/asynchronous reset and/or preset in VHDL. Suppose, for example, that you want an 8-bit register to be asynchronously reset to all 0s whenever the signal `reset` is asserted, but synchronously preset to all 1s whenever the signal `init` is asserted and sampled by the rising edge of the clock. The code to implement this function is shown in Listing 4-23.

```vhdl
library ieee;
use ieee.std_logic_1164.all;
entity reg_logic is port (
    d                  : in std_logic_vector(0 to 7);
    reset, init, clk : in std_logic;
    q                  : out std_logic_vector(0 to 7) );
end reg_logic;

architecture fancy_example of reg_logic is
begin
    process (clk, reset) begin
        if (reset = '1') then
            q <= b"00000000";
        elsif (clk'event and clk = '1') then
            if (init = '1') then
                q <= b"11111111";
            else
                q <= d;
            end if;
        end if;
    end process;
end fancy_example;
```

Listing 4-23 An 8-bit register with asynchronous reset and synchronous initialization

Arithmetic Operators. We will digress for a moment to discuss the arithmetic operators: adding, subtracting, concatenation, sign, multiplying, dividing, modulus, remainder, and absolute value. The arithmetic operators most commonly used in designs created for synthesis are addition and subtraction, which are used in describing adders, subtracters, incrementers, and decrementers. All arithmetic operators are predefined for the types integer and floating. Therefore, the following code can be written for use with synthesis:

```
entity myadd is port (
        a, b : in integer range 0 to 3;
        sum: out integer range 0 to 6);
end myadd;

architecture archmyadd of myadd is
begin
        sum <=  a + b;
end archmyadd;
```

Here, the result of the addition is assigned to a data object of type integer. Most synthesis tools can handle this design, internally converting the integers to bit_vectors or std_logic_vectors. Nonetheless, using integers as ports poses a couple of problems: (1) In order to use the value of sum in another portion of a design for which the interface has ports of type std_logic, a type conversion must take place. (2) The same vectors applied during simulation of the source code cannot be used to simulate the post-fit (post-layout) simulation model. For the source code, the vectors will be integer values. The post-fit model will require std_logics.

Because the native VHDL + operator is not predefined for the types bit or std_logic, it must be overloaded before it can be used to add operands of these types (or mixed operand types). Operators may be overloaded with user-defined functions, but many overloaded operators are defined in the IEEE 1164 and 1076.3 standards. The IEEE 1076.3 standard defines functions to overload the + operator for the following operand pairs: (unsigned, unsigned), (unsigned, integer), (signed, signed), and (signed, integer). Overloaded for these operand types, the + operator may be used as shown in Listing 4-24.

The operator overloading functions are defined in the numeric_std package of the 1076.3 standard. This package must be made visible to the design entity with a use clause. Many synthesis vendors also supply additional packages to overload operators for the type std_logic. Although not standards, these are often used by VHDL users because they were available well before numeric_std was adopted. Because these packages allow relational and arithmetic operations on std_logic, some perceive them as more useful than the numeric_std package. Certainly, they do not require the overhead of using two additional types (in addi-

```vhdl
library ieee;
use ieee.std_logic_1164.all;
use work.numeric_std.all;
entity add_vec is port(
        a, b:           in unsigned(3 downto 0);
        sum1, sum2:  out unsigned(3 downto 0));
end add_vec;
architecture adder of add_vec is
begin
    sum1 <= a + b;
    sum2 <= c + 1;
end;
```

Listing 4-24 Adder described with the type unsigned and the `numeric_std` package

tion to `std_logic_vector`) as well as the type conversion functions used to convert between these types. When using one of these packages in arithmetic operations, a synthesis tool will interpret the `std_logic_vector` using an unsigned representation or one of several possible signed representations (usually 2's complement). The synthesis tool must then produce the appropriate signed or unsigned arithmetic components as well. You will need to consult the documentation of the synthesis tool to determine how it represents `std_logic_vectors` in arithmetic operations.

Warp provides the `std_arith` package. It defines several new functions and overloads the arithmetic operators to handle the type `std_logic_vector`, interpreting the `std_logic_vector` as unsigned. It allows the code shown in Listing 4-25 to be processsed.

```vhdl
library ieee;
use ieee.std_logic_1164.all;
use work.std_arith.all;          -- std_arith rather than numeric_std
entity add_vec is port(
        a, b:        in std_logic_vector(3 downto 0);     --type std_logic_vec
        sum1, sum2:  out std_logic_vector(3 downto 0));
end add_vec;
architecture adder of add_vec is
begin
    sum1 <= a + b;
    sum2 <= c + 2;
end;
```

Listing 4-25 Adder described with `std_logic_vectors` and the `std_arith` package

We will use the `numeric_std` package to illustrate how to use the types, functions, and operators defined in some examples in this text. In other examples we'll use the `std_arith` package to illustrate how the use of one array type, `std_logic_vector`, can reduce design overhead. When transferring code from one synthesis tool to another, you should use the package provided by the particular vendor for overloading the `std_logic` or `std_logic_vector` types.

The + operations in Listings 4-24 and 4-25 are for unsigned addition. Sum is only four digits wide, even though it could result in a value greater than 16. An extra bit would be required to indicate a carry or overflow. However, the + operator only returns a vector with the same number of elements as the larger of the two vector operands. This allows for the easy description of counters, which do not have carries or overflows:

```
count <= count + 1;
```

If you wish to increase the size of `sum` (see page 196) so that it will include a carry, then the adder may be described as in Listing 4-26.

```
library ieee;
use ieee.std_logic_1164.all;
use work.numeric_std.all;
entity add_vec is port(
        a, b:  in unsigned(3 downto 0);
        sum:   out unsigned(4 downto 0));
end add_vec;
architecture adder of add_vec is
begin
    sum <= ('0' & a) + b;
end;
```

Listing 4-26 Adder with carry

This time, one of the operands to + is (`'0'` & a). The & operator is the concatenation operator; here it results in an unsigned vector one bit greater than a, with a '0' prepended. Thus the result of this + operation will be a vector five digits wide, with the MSB as the carry-out. An alternative implementation is to create a temporary signal that is assigned the concatenation of '0' and a, and use it as an operand to the + operation.

The synthesis of arithmetic operators will be discussed in Chapter 9, "Optimizing Datapaths." In that chapter we will discuss implementations of adders, subtracters, and counters. For now, we will simply use these operators to describe such components.

4.4.2   Asynchronous Resets and Presets

Listing 4-27 describes an 8-bit counter with one asynchronous signal, which places it at the value "00111010". The counter also has a synchronous load and enable. A use clause makes the overloaded + operator in numeric_std package visible to this design entity. The data and cnt ports are of type unsigned, indicating that these binary numbers are considered positive.

```vhdl
library ieee;
use ieee.std_logic_1164.all;
use work.numeric_std.all;
entity cnt8 is port(
        txclk, grst:     in std_logic;
        enable, load:    in std_logic;
        data:            in unsigned(7 downto 0);
        cnt:             buffer unsigned(7 downto 0));
end cnt8;

architecture archcnt8 of cnt8 is
begin
count: process (grst, txclk)
  begin
        if grst = '1' then
                cnt <= "00111010";
        elsif (txclk'event and txclk='1') then
                if load = '1' then
                        cnt <= data;
                elsif enable = '1' then
                        cnt <= cnt + 1;
                end if;
        end if;
  end process count;
end archcnt8;
```

Listing 4-27 An 8-bit counter with one asynchronous signal to reset some flip-flops and set other flip-flops

The process count is sensitive to transitions in grst and txclk. If grst is asserted, then some of the cnt flip-flops are asynchronously reset and others are asynchronously preset (Figure 4-13). On the rising edge of txclk, the cnt registers are loaded if load is asserted, incremented if enable is asserted, and remain the same if neither load nor enable is asserted. The lack of an else after elsif enable implies that cnt will retain its value if neither of the previous conditions (load or enable) is true. Alternatively, you can explicitly include else cnt <= cnt.

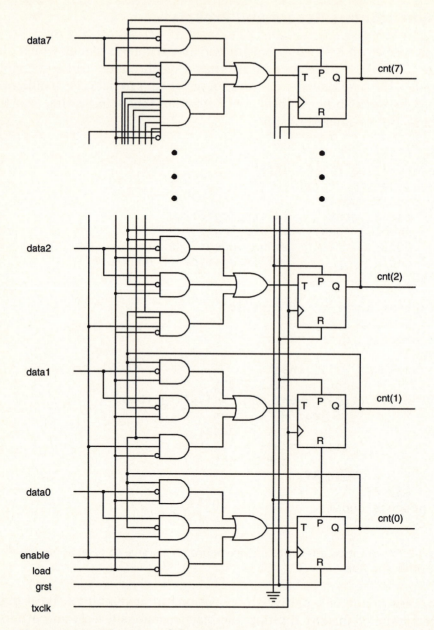

Figure 4-13 Schematic of the 8-bit counter of Listing 4-27, as implemented in the FLASH370 architecture

Combining Resets and Presets. Occasionally, a design may require two asynchronous signals: both a reset signal and a preset. How are both a reset and a preset described? Listing 4-28 shows our suggestion.

```
library ieee;
use ieee.std_logic_1164.all;
use work.numeric_std.all;
entity cnt8 is port(
        txclk, grst, gpst:        in std_logic;
        enable, load:             in std_logic;
        data:                     in unsigned(7 downto 0);
        cnt:                      buffer unsigned(7 downto 0));
end cnt8;

architecture archcnt8 of cnt8 is
begin
count: process (grst, gpst, txclk)
  begin
        if grst = '1' then
                cnt <= (others => '0');
        elsif gpst = '1' then
                cnt <= (others => '1');
        elsif (txclk'event and txclk='1') then
                if load = '1' then
                        cnt <= data;
                elsif enable = '1' then
                        cnt <= cnt + 1;
                end if;
        end if;
    end process count;
end archcnt8;
```

Listing 4-28 A counter with asynchronous reset and preset

The process shown in Listing 4-28 is sensitive to changes in grst, gpst, and txclk. Grst and gpst are both used to asynchronously assign values to the cnt registers. The reset/preset combination of Listing 4-28 poses a synthesis issue: As discussed earlier in the chapter, the if-then-else construct implies a precedence—that cnt should be assigned the value of all 1s (others => '1') only when gpst is asserted *and* grst is not asserted. The logic in Figure 4-14 assures that the counter will not be preset unless the reset signal is also low. What if this was not the intended effect? Some synthesis tools recognize that this may not be the intended effect and that flip-flops by design are either reset- or preset-dominant. Therefore, depending on the synthesis policy of your software tool, the code of

Listing 4-28 produces the logic of either Figure 4-14 or Figure 4-15. Many CPLDs with product-term resets and presets are able to fit either implementation. Likewise, most FPGAs have the resources to implement product-term resets and presets. However, while most FPGAs are set up to provide a high-performance, global, or near global reset or preset, most do not have the resources to provide a high-performance product-term reset or preset, in which case the implementation of Figure 4-15 is preferred.

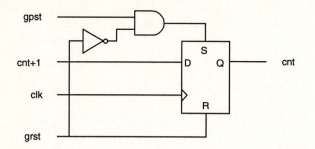

Figure 4-14   Logic assures that the reset is dominant

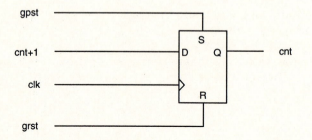

Figure 4-15   Synthesis result of Listing 4-28, assuming the reset is dominant

The (others => '0') represents an aggregate—a list of elements in parentheses, separated by commas—in which all elements of the vector are defined as '0'. In this case, it is equivalent to "00000000". Others must appear last in an aggregate. For example,

```
signal a: std_logic_vector(7 downto 0);
...
a <= ('1','0',others => '1')
```

would result in a being assigned the value "10111111".

Product-Term Resets. Sometimes you want a series of flip-flops to be reset to all 0s when asynchronously reset, and preset to a predetermined value (some 0s, some 1s) when asynchronously preset. Listing 4-29 is an example.

```
library ieee;
use ieee.std_logic_1164.all;
use work.numeric_std.all;
entity cnt8 is port(
        txclk, grst, gpst:      in std_logic;
        enable, load:           in std_logic;
        data:                   in unsigned(7 downto 0);
        cnt:                    buffer unsigned(7 downto 0));
end cnt8;

architecture archcnt8 of cnt8 is
begin
count: process (grst, gpst, txclk)
  begin
        if grst = '1' then
                cnt <= "00000000";
        elsif gpst = '1' then
                cnt <= "00111010";
        elsif (txclk'event and txclk='1') then
                if load = '1' then
                        cnt <= data;
                elsif enable = '1' then
                        cnt <= cnt + 1;
                end if;
        end if;
  end process count;
end archcnt8;
```

Listing 4-29 A counter with asynchronous preset and product-term reset

Assuming reset dominance, synthesis will cause cnt(7) to be asynchronously set to '0' if grst OR gpst is asserted, provided that the device supports an OR term asynchronous reset (see Figure 4-16).

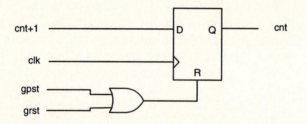

Figure 4-16   A flip-flop with an OR term asynchronous reset

All of the examples showing resets and presets in this chapter use the `if (signal_name'event and signal_name = '1')` or `rising_edge(signal_name)` construct to describe synchronous logic. You can also use the `wait until` statement to describe synchronous logic with resets and presets, but these resets and presets must be synchronous. This is because the `wait` statement must be the first statement in the process, and any statements that come after it describe synchronous logic.

Breakout Exercise 4-2

Purpose: To review resource and timing requirements of a complex reset function.

Compile, synthesize, and simulate the design `cntpt.vhd`. Review the design equations in the report file. Verify, in particular, that the reset equation requires a second pass though the logic array. If separate reset equations are given for each bit, search for the word `duplicate` to see if nodes were later combined. What effect does multiple passes for the reset signal have on timing? Functionally simulate the design with Nova.

4.4.3   Three-State Buffers and Bidirectional Signals

Most programmable-logic devices have three-state outputs or bidirectional I/Os. Output buffers are placed in a high-Z (high-impedance) state so they don't drive a shared bus at the wrong time (that is, to avoid bus contention), or so that bidirectional pins may be driven by off-chip signals. Additionally, some devices have internal three-state buffers. We will show how to describe three-state and bidirectional signals using both behavioral descriptions and structural instantiations of three-state and bidirectional I/O components. We will also show how three-state logic can be converted to multiplexer logic when retargeting a design that uses internal three-states to a device that does not have internal three-states.

Behavioral Three-States and Bidirectionals. The values that a three-state signal can have are '0', '1', and 'Z', all of which are supported by the type std_logic. We will modify the 8-bit counter example to have three-state outputs, and then discuss what code changes were necessary. Listing 4-30 contains the modifications. This time, we also use the std_arith package and the type std_logic_vector for data and cnt.

```vhdl
library ieee;
use ieee.std_logic_1164.all;
use work.std_arith.all;
entity cnt8 is port(
    txclk, grst:  in std_logic;
    enable, load: in std_logic;
    oe:           in std_logic;                       --output enable
    data:         in std_logic_vector(7 downto 0);
    cnt_out:      buffer std_logic_vector(7 downto 0)); -- cnt output
end cnt8;

architecture archcnt8 of cnt8 is
  signal cnt: std_logic_vector(7 downto 0);  -- cnt signal for counting
begin
count: process (grst, txclk)
  begin
    if grst = '1' then
        cnt <= "00111010";
    elsif rising_edge(txclk) then
        if load = '1' then
            cnt <= data;
        elsif enable = '1' then
            cnt <= cnt + 1;
        end if;
    end if;
  end process count;
```

```
oes: process (oe, cnt)                          -- three-state buffers
  begin
    if oe = '0' then
        cnt_out <= (others => 'Z');
    else
        cnt_out <= cnt;
    end if;
  end process oes;

end archcnt8;
```

Listing 4-30 A counter with three-state outputs

The process labeled oes is used to describe the three-state outputs for the counter. This process simply indicates that if oe is asserted, the value of cnt is assigned to cnt_out (the output port of this design), and if oe is not asserted, the outputs of this design are placed in the high-impedance state. The process is sensitive to changes in either oe or cnt, because a change in either signal causes a change in cnt_out. Two additional signals are used in this design compared to the design of Listing 4-27: oe was added as the three-state control and cnt_out was added as the output port. The signal cnt was changed from a port of this design to a signal declared in the architecture declarative region. The oes process description is consistent with the behavior of a three-state buffer (Figure 4-17).

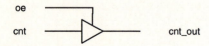

Figure 4-17   A three-state buffer

The three-state control can also be described with a when-else statement. In Listing 4-31, we add an additional output, collision, which is asserted when load and enable are asserted, provided that its output is also enabled.

```
library ieee;
use ieee.std_logic_1164.all;
use work.std_arith.all;
entity cnt8 is port(
    txclk, grst:    in std_logic;
    enable, load:   in std_logic;
    oe:             in std_logic;
    data:           in std_logic_vector(7 downto 0);
    collision:      out std_logic;              -- 3-state output
    cnt_out:        buffer std_logic_vector(7 downto 0));
end cnt8;
```

```vhdl
architecture archcnt8 of cnt8 is
  signal cnt: std_logic_vector;
begin
count: process (grst, txclk)
  begin
    if grst = '1' then
        cnt <= "00111010";
    elsif rising_edge(txclk) then
        if load = '1' then
            cnt <= data;
        elsif enable = '1' then
            cnt <= cnt + 1;
        end if;
    end if;
  end process count;
-- three-state outputs described here:
    cnt_out <= (others => 'Z') when oe = '0' else cnt;
    collision <= (enable and load) when oe = '1' else 'Z';
end archcnt8;
```

Listing 4-31 Three-state outputs defined with a when–else construct

Bidirectionals. Bidirectional signals are described with little modification of Listing 4-30 or 4-31. In Listing 4-32, the counter is loaded with the current value on the pins associated with the counter outputs, meaning that the value loaded when load is asserted may be the counter's previous value or a value driven onto the pins from another device, depending upon the state of the output enable.

```vhdl
library ieee;
use ieee.std_logic_1164.all;
use work.std_arith.all;
entity cnt8 is port(
    txclk, grst:    in std_logic;
    enable, load:   in std_logic;
    oe:             in std_logic;
    cnt_out:        inout std_logic_vector(7 downto 0));     -- inout req'd
end cnt8;
```

```vhdl
architecture archcnt8 of cnt8 is
  signal cnt: std_logic_vector(7 downto 0);
begin
count: process (grst, txclk)
  begin
    if grst = '1' then
        cnt <= "00111010";
    elsif (txclk'event and txclk='1') then
        if load = '1' then
            cnt <= cnt_out;          -- cnt now loaded from the cnt_out port
        elsif enable = '1' then
            cnt <= cnt + 1;
        end if;
    end if;
  end process count;

oes: process (oe, cnt)
  begin
    if oe = '0' then
        cnt_out <= (others => 'Z');
    else
        cnt_out <= cnt;
    end if;
  end process oes;

end archcnt8;
```

Listing 4-32 I/Os used bidirectionally

If you compare these listings closely, you'll find that the greatest difference is in the assignment of cnt when load is asserted. Another subtlety is that cnt_out *must* be of mode inout in this example, whereas it can be of mode buffer in the other listings. The remaining difference is that data is not a required signal for this listing because the load value is coming from the cnt_out.

Implicit Output Enables. In Listing 4-33, the output enable of a three-state buffer is implicitly defined.

The three-state buffers for the signal dram are enabled if the value of present_state is row_address, ras_assert, col_address, or cas_assert. The output buffers are not asserted for any other values of the present_state.

```
multiplexer: process (row_addr, col_addr, present_state)
    begin
        if (present_state = row_address or present_state = ras_assert) then
                dram <= row_addr;
        elsif (present_state = col_address or present_state= cas_assert) then
                dram <= col_addr;
        else
                dram <= (others => 'Z');
        end if;
    end process;
```

Listing 4-33 Implicit output enable control

4.4.4   Structural Three-States and Bidirectionals

As with any other structure, you can create a component for a three-state buffer.
You may want to instantiate three-state buffers rather than describe them behav-
iorally, to gain tighter control of their implementation or for ease of description.
The code fragment of Listing 4-33, for example, creates three-state buffers for
which the output-enable logic may be ambiguous. If you were to want to explicitly
define the output enable component, you could simply instantiate the component
(here, the component name is threestate):

```
    u0:threestate port map (cnt(0), oe, cnt_out(0));
```

For-Generate. If you use the threestate component to implement the three-state
buffers for a 32-bit bus, you may find it cumbersome to instantiate the component
32 separate times. The for-generate statement helps in this case:

```
gen_label:
    for i in 0 to 31 generate
        inst_label:threestate port map (value(i), read, value_out(i));
    end generate;
```

A generation scheme is implemented in the concurrent-statement portion of
an architecture, not within a process (loops, discussed later, are used in processes).
A generation scheme requires a generation label; in this case, gen_label. A generation scheme can also include conditional instantiations. For instance, suppose you

required 32 three-state signals, with each set of 8 having its own byte read, byte_rd, as an output enable (Figure 4-18). The following generation scheme could be used:

```
g1:    for i in 0 to 7 generate
           u0t7:   threestate port map (val(i), byte_rd(0), val_out(i));
           u8t15:  threestate port map (val(i+8), byte_rd(1), val_out(i+8));
           u16t23: threestate port map (val(i+16),byte_rd(2), val_out(i+16));
           u24t31: threestate port map (val(i+24), byte_rd(3), val_out(i+24));
       end generate;
```

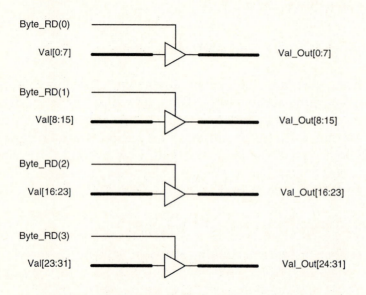

Figure 4-18 Three-state buffers with output enables for each byte

You can use more complicated generation schemes. The one shown below, which describes the same logic, is more complicated than necessary, but it is helpful in demonstrating the flexibility of generation schemes. The name of the component has been abbreviated to thrst.

```
g1:    for i in 0 to 3 generate
   g2:     for j in 0 to 7 generate
               if i < 1 then generate
                   ua: thrst port map(val(j), byte_rd(0), val_out(j));
               end generate;
               if i = 1 then generate
                   ub: thrst port map (val(j+8), byte_rd(1), val_out(j+8));
               end generate;
```

```
        if i = 2 then generate
            uc: thrst port map (val(j+16), byte_rd(2), val_out(j+16));
        end generate;
        if i > 2 then generate
            ud: thrst port map (val(j+24), byte_rd(3), val_out(j+24));
        end generate;
    end generate;
end generate;
```

The scheme above includes an if-then statement. When used in a generation scheme, an if-then statement may not include an else or elsif. Generation schemes can be used to instantiate any component, not just vendor-supplied or user-written three-state or bidirectional components.

4.4.5   Converting Internal Three-States to Multiplexers

Some FPGAs contain internal three-state buses. Others, such as the pASIC380 family of FPGAs, do not. However, designs that use internal three-state buses can be converted to designs using multiplexers. Some synthesis tools can automatically convert three-state buses to multiplexer logic. The process of converting three-state-buffers and their buses to multiplexer logic is illustrated in Figure 4-19. With only two three-state buffers on the bus, a two-to-one multiplexer provides the equivalent functionality, even if the enable signals are different. This is because the enable signals must be mutually exclusive. With four three-state-buffers, a four-to-one multiplexer is required. The select lines are controlled by a function of the enable signals.

If your target device does not have three-state enables, you should avoid describing internal three-states and use multiplexers or other logic instead. Describing internal three-states for a device that does not contain them may create unnecessary logic during automatic conversion, particularly if the output-enable controls are implicitly defined.

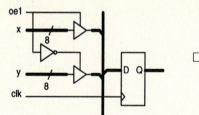
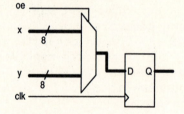

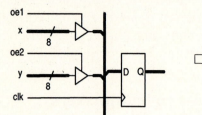
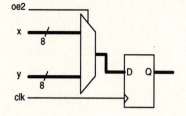

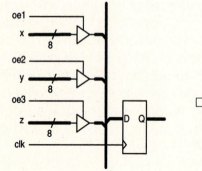
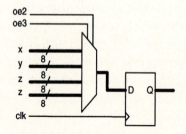

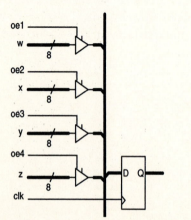
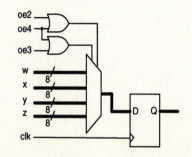

Figure 4-19   Converting internal three-state buses to multiplexer logic

4.5   Designing a FIFO

Having discussed how to create combinational and synchronous logic, and several design topics along the way, we are now ready to design the FIFO introduced at the beginning of the chapter. We wish to design an 8-deep, 9-bit wide FIFO. When a read signal, rd, is asserted, we wish to enable the output, data_out, of the FIFO. When it is not asserted, we want the output placed in the high-impedance state. When the write signal wr is asserted, we want to write to one of the 9-bit wide registers. Signals rdinc and wrinc are used to increment the read and write pointers that indicate which register to read and which register to write. Rdptrclr and wrptrclr reset the read and write pointers to point the first register in the FIFO. Data_in is the data to be loaded into one of the registers. Figure 4-20 is a block diagram of the FIFO.

Listing 4-1 gives the VHDL code for this design. The entity declaration is simple enough and does not introduce any new concepts. The type declaration fifo_array is the first interesting construct we encounter in this design. It is simply an array of eight std_logic_vectors that are each nine bits wide. Signal fifo is then declared to be of this type (a one-dimensional array of std_logic_vectors). We can therefore access eight std_logic_vectors by indexing fifo, as in fifo(3), fifo(7), fifo(1), and so on. The next new concept that we run across is the loop, though we saw them briefly in the previous chapter.

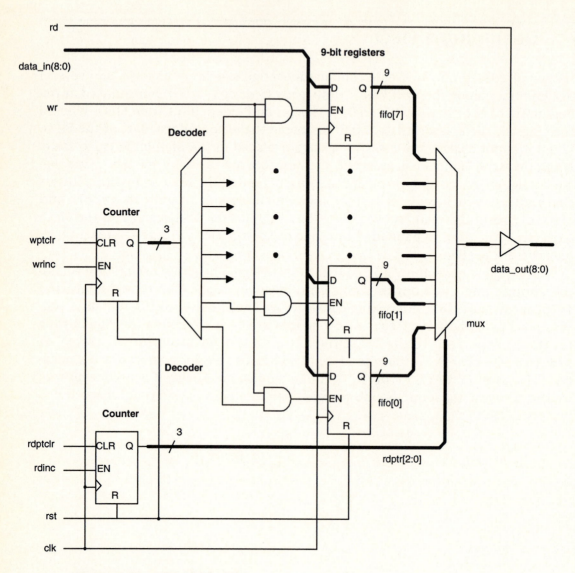

Figure 4-20 FIFO block diagram

4.5.1   Loops

Loop statements are used to implement repetitive operations, and consist of either for loops or while loops. The for statement will execute for a specific number of iterations based on a controlling value. The while statement will continue to execute an operation as long as a controlling logical condition evaluates true. An extra step is required to initialize the controlling variable of a while statement. Take, for instance, the loop used to asynchronously reset the FIFO array:

```
for i in 7 downto 0 loop
        fifo(i) <= (others => '0');
end loop;
```

This loop sequences through the eight std_logic vectors that make up the FIFO array, setting each element of the vectors to '0'. In a for loop, the loop variable is automatically declared. A while loop can be used here instead of a for loop, but it requires the additional overhead of declaring, initializing, and incrementing the loop variable. (The variable can be initialized upon declaration or within the process. Depending on how you use the variable, you may need to reinitialize it within the process. Warp requires that a variable be initialized in the process-statement region, not in the process-declarative region as shown here.)

```
reg_array: process (rst, clk)
    variable i: integer := 0;
  begin
        if rst = '1' then
                while i < 7 loop
                        fifo(i) <= (others => '0');
                        i := i + 1;
                end loop;
        ...
```

Conditional Iterations. The next statement is used to skip an operation based on specific conditions. Suppose, for example, that when rst is asserted, all of the fifo registers are reset except for the fifo(4) register:

```
reg_array: process (rst, clk)
  begin
        if rst = '1' then
                for i in 7 downto 0 loop
                    if i = 4 then
                        next;
                    else
                        fifo(i) <= (others => '0');
                end loop;
        ...
```

Or, as written with a while loop:

```
reg_array: process (rst, clk)
      variable i: integer;
   begin
       i := 0;
      if rst = '1' then
         while i < 8 loop
              if i = 4 then
                  next;
              else
                  fifo(i) <= (others => '0');
                  i := i + 1;
         end loop;
      ...
```

Exiting Loops. Above, we placed the variable initialization inside the process statement. An `exit` statement is used to exit a loop, and can be used to check for an illegal condition. The condition must be determinate at compile-time. Suppose, for example, that FIFO is a component that is instantiated in a hierarchical design. Suppose further that the depth of the FIFO was defined by a **generic,** or parameter (these will be discussed in Chapter 6, "Hierarchy in Large Designs"). You may wish to exit the loop when the depth of the FIFO is greater than a predetermined value. For instance,

```
reg_array: process (rst, clk)
   begin
      if rst = '1' then
        loop1: for i in deep downto 0 loop
               if i > 20 then
                   exit loop1;
               else
                   fifo(i) <= (others => '0');
            end  loop;
```

The above code fragment can also be written as

```
reg_array: process (rst, clk)
   begin
      if rst = '1' then
        loop1: for i in deep downto 0 loop
               exit loop1 when i > 20;
               fifo(i) <= (others => '0');
            end loop;
```

For clarity, a loop label was added. Loops have been used in a limited capacity here; however, they can be used to perform many functions. For example, the second loop in the FIFO design checks which register is being written to (the en signal is decoded from `wrptr`):

```
if wr = '1' then
        for i in 7 downto 0 loop
             if en(i) = '1' then
                    fifo(i) <= data_in;
             else
                    fifo(i) <= fifo(i);
             end if;
        end loop;
end if;
```

Now that we have discussed registered and combinational logic, including three-state and bidirectional signals, the remainder of the design provides no new challenges. The read and write pointers are simply three-bit counters that indicate which register in the `fifo` array to write to or read from. The dataflow constructs are used to decode the read and write counters, and the `three_state` process is used to control the three-state outputs.

4.5.2   Alternate Description

Now that you have mastered the basics, you are ready to move on to the topics covered in the remainder of this book, starting with state machines in the next chapter. But before we do that, we leave you with a modified version of our FIFO in which the width and depth are specified with a generic (parameter) and a constant in Listing 4-34. Additionally, the read and write pointers in this new implementation are not explicitly decoded, because their values are of type integer. Although this implementation is a more concise version of the FIFO, the use of integers can cause problems. A synthesis tool will be required to internally convert the integers to a binary value such that when the counter reaches its maximum value, it will roll over on the next count. A VHDL simulator, however, will not convert the integers to a binary value. Consequently, when the counter reaches its maximum value, incrementing it will cause the simulator to issue a run-time error indicating that the range for the counter signal (type `integer`) has been exceeded. You can work around this incompatibility between simulation and synthesis by forcing the value of the counter to roll over at the appropriate time. Alternatively, you can explicitly specify in the VHDL code that the counter is to return to zero after it reaches its maximum value. This is the preferred solution, as it maintains compatibility between the simulation and synthesis results and is unlikely to use additional resources in the PLD (depending on the compiler). We leave you to make this modification. Release 4.0 of Warp does not support the use of signals as indexes to arrays, though later releases may.

Listing 6-23 shows another way to implement a FIFO that uses hierarchy and structural design. It is discussed in detail in Chapter 6.

```vhdl
library ieee;
use ieee.std_logic_1164.all;
use work.std_arith.all;

entity fifoxbyy is generic (wide : integer := 32);      --width is 31 + 1
    port(
    clk, rst, oe:             in std_logic;
    rd, wr, rdinc, wrinc:     in std_logic;
    rdptrclr, wrptrclr:       in std_logic;
    data_in:                  in std_logic_vector(wide downto 0);
    data_out:                 out std_logic_vector(wide downto 0));
end fifoxbyy;

architecture archfifoxbyy of fifoxbyy is
  constant deep: integer := 20;--depth is 20 + 1
  type fifo_array is array(deep downto 0) of std_logic_vector(wide
downto 0);

  signal fifo: fifo_array;
  signal wrptr, rdptr: integer range 0 to deep;
  signal en: std_logic_vector(deep downto 0);
  signal dmuxout: std_logic_vector(wide downto 0);

begin

-- fifo register array:
reg_array: process (rst, clk)
  begin
    if rst = '1' then
        for i in fifo'range loop
            fifo(i) <= (others => '0');
        end loop;
    elsif rising_edge(clk) then
        if wr = '1' then
            fifo(wrptr) <= data_in;
        end if;
    end if;
  end process;
```

```
-- read pointer
read_count: process (rst, clk)
  begin
    if rst = '1' then
        rdptr <= 0;
    elsif rising_edge(clk) then
        if rdptrclr = '1' then
            rdptr <= 0;
        elsif rdinc = '1' then
            rdptr <= rdptr + 1;
        end if;
    end if;
  end process;

-- write pointer
write_count: process (rst, clk)
  begin
    if rst = '1' then
        wrptr <= 0;
    elsif rising_edge(clk) then
        if wrptrclr = '1' then
            wrptr <= 0;
        elsif wrinc = '1' then
            wrptr <= wrptr + 1;
        end if;
    end if;
  end process;

-- data output multiplexer
dmuxout <= fifo(wrptr);

-- three-state control of outputs
three_state: process (oe, dmuxout)
  begin
    if oe = '1' then
        data_out <= dmuxout;
    else
        data_out <= (others => 'Z');
    end if;
  end process;

end archfifoxbyy;
```

Listing 4-34 Modified FIFO design

▼

Breakout Exercise 4-3

Purpose: To compare CPLD and FPGA implementations of the FIFO design.

1. Compile the design fifo.vhd first to a CY7C375 CPLD. Save the report file with a new name, then recompile the design for a CY7C381A FPGA. Next, place and route the design using SpDE. Compare the resource utilization requirements and performance.

2. For the CPLD implementation, how many macrocells and product terms are required? What is the maximum operating frequency, and which timing parameter is the limiting factor for operating frequency?

3. For the FPGA implementation, how many logic cells are required? What is the maximum operating frequency, and which timing parameter is the limiting factor for operating frequency?

▲

4.6   Common Errors

The code in Listing 4-35 contains several errors. See if you can identify them.

```
library ieee;                                      --line 1
use ieee.std_logic_1164.all;                       --line 2
entity terminal_count is port(                     --line 3
   clock, reset, enable  in bit;                    --line 4
   data:                 in std_logic_vector(7 downto 0);  --line 5
   equals, term_cnt:     out std_logic);           --line 6
end terminal_count;                                 --line 7
architecture terminal_count of terminal_count is   --line 8
   signal count: std_logic_vector(7 downto 0);     --line 9
begin                                               --line 10
compare: process                                    --line 11
   begin                                            --line 12
      if data = count then                          --line 13
         equals = '1';                              --line 14
      end if;                                        --line 15
   end process;                                     --line 16
                                                    --line 17
counter: process (clk)                              --line 18
   begin                                            --line 19
      if reset = '1' then                           --line 20
         count <= "111111111";                      --line 21
```

```
        elsif rising_edge(clock) then                    --line 22
            count <= count + 1;                          --line 23
        end if;                                          --line 24
    end process;                                         --line 25
                                                         --line 26
    term_cnt <=  'z' when enable = '0' else              --line 27
                 '1' when count = "1-------" else        --line 28
                 '0';                                    --line 29
end terminal_count;                                      --line 30
```

Listing 4-35 Description with many errors

We find the first error in line 11. The process needs a sensitivity list, which should include count and data. The next error is on line 14. The = relational operator should be changed to the <= symbol, which indicates signal assignment. The next error is a semantic error, the lack of an else clause or initialization value for equals. Without an else clause or an initialization value for equals, a latch will be created to ensure that once asserted, equals remains asserted. The lack of an else statement describes implied memory. Another way to correct this problem is to use a when–else statement instead of a process:

```
equals <= '1' when data = count else '0';
```

The next error is with the process sensitivity list for the counter process. The signal clock is misspelled, and reset is missing from the list. Line 21 also contains an error: there is one extra 1 in the string "111111111". The next error is in line 22. To use the function rising_edge, the signal must be of type std_logic. So, we can either change clock to type std_logic or use the (clock'event and clock = '1') expression. The next error is at line 23. The + operator is not predefined for the types std_logic_vector or integer, so we must make the std_arith package visible to this design; it overloads the + operator for std_logic_vector and integer operands. Line 27 contains the next error. The enumeration literal 'z' must be capitalized. 'Z' is a value for an object of type std_logic; 'z' is not. The last error occurs in line 28. The comparison of count to "1-------" will always evaluate to false, because none of the elements of count will ever be '-', the don't-care value. In order to evaluate '-' as a wild card, the std_match function must be used. Alternatively, in this case, the statement could have been written as:

```
term_cnt <=  'z' when enable = '0' else
             '1' when count > "10000000" else -- or count > 127
             '0';
```

The corrected code is shown in Listing 4-36.

```vhdl
library ieee;
use ieee.std_logic_1164.all;
use work.std_arith.all;
entity terminal_count is port(
      clock, reset, enable:    in std_logic;
      data:                    in std_logic_vector(7 downto 0);
      equals, term_cnt:        out std_logic);
end terminal_count;
architecture terminal_count of terminal_count is
   signal count: std_logic_vector(7 downto 0);
begin
compare: process (count, data)
   begin
      if data = count then
         equals <= '1';
      else
         equals <= '0';
      end if;
   end process;

counter: process (clock, reset)
   begin
      if reset = '1' then
         count <= "11111111";
      elsif rising_edge(clock) then
         count <= count + 1;
      end if;
   end process;

   term_cnt <= 'Z' when enable = '0' else
               '1' when std_match(count,"1-------") else
               '0';
end terminal_count;
```

Listing 4-36 Corrected VHDL code of Listing 4-35

Next, we cover some more obscure errors or difficulties with descriptions used for synthesis.

4.6.1   Unintentional Registers

As explained in Chapter 3, a simple way to interpret signal assignments in a process is to assume that all expressions are based on the *current* value of the signals on the right-hand side of the <= symbol, and that signals will be updated only at the end of the process, when it suspends. This simple method can reveal hidden registers, or flip-flops, in the following code fragment:

```
seq: process (clk)
   begin
       if clk'event and clk='1' then
           b <= c;
           a <= b;
           h <= i;
           i <= j xor k;
       end if;
   end process;
```

Because the signal-assignment statements for b, a, h, and i appear after the if (clk'event and clk = '1') statement, these signals represent the states of flip-flops. In addition, because the signal assignments occur only on the rising edge of clk, this code does not describe logic in which b is equivalent to c and h is equivalent to i. Rather, synthesis infers from this code registers for each of the signal assignments, which produces the logic of Figure 4-21. If you don't want signals h and i to be registered, these sequential signal assignments should be removed from the process and made concurrent signal assignments, as shown.

```
seq: process (clk)
   begin
       if clk'event and clk='1' then
           b <= c;
           i <= j xor k;
       end if;
   end process;
       a <= b;
       h <= i;
```

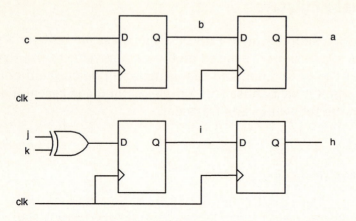

Figure 4-21 A process can describe interconnected flip-flops, depending on the order of signal assignment

Using the simulation cycle model, or the simple interpretation of signal assignments, you will notice that Listing 4-37 also contains a "hidden," or unintentional, register. Because signals do not take on their new values until the process is suspended, you should pay close attention when using a signal that is assigned in a process in an expression on the right-hand side of another signal-assignment statement or relational expression within that same process. Figure 4-22 illustrates the logic that this code listing describes.

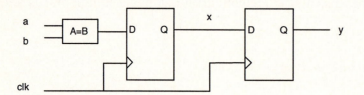

Figure 4-22 Logic of Listing 4-37

```
architecture careful of dangerous is
    signal x: bit;
begin
p1: process begin
    wait until clk = '1';
        x <= '0';
        y <= '0';
        if a = b then
            x <= '1';
        end if;
```

```
      if x = '1' then
          y <= '1';
      end if;
  end process p1;
  end careful;
```

Listing 4-37 A signal in an assignment and as an operand within the same process

In this process, signal x is used as the object of an assignment and as an operand in a comparison. Because the assignment to x is scheduled and not immediate, the subsequent comparison, if x = '1', compares the *present, not scheduled,* value of x. Thus, y is the registered version of x.

If x were a variable rather than a signal, the architecture could be written as shown in Listing 4-38, in which y is the output of a combinational comparison of a and b.

```
  architecture careful of dangerous is
  begin
  p1: process
    variable x: bit;
  begin
    wait until clk = '1';
    x := '0';
    y <= '0';
    if a = b then
        x := '1';
    end if;

    if x = '1' then
        y <= '1';
    end if;
  end process p1;
  end careful;
```

Listing 4-38 A registered equality comparator

Because x is a variable in this process, the assignment is immediate; hence, y is the output of an equality comparator (Figure 4-23). As a variable, x is only meaningful inside the process; to use the value outside of the process requires that its value be assigned to a signal as in the following code:

```
  architecture pass_variable of to_signal is
    signal vec: bit_vector(0 to 3);
    signal and_result: bit;
```

```
begin
proc: process (vec)
   variable result: bit := '1';
 begin
   for i in vec'range loop
      result := result and vec(i);
   end loop;
   and_result <= result;
 end process;
 output_enable <= wmask and and_result;
end pass_variable;
```

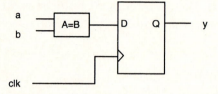

Figure 4-23 Logic described by Listing 4-38

This code demonstrates that `result` can be used for an immediate assignment, the value of which is passed to `and_result` at the end of the process. Placing the assignment statement for `and_result` at the beginning of the process would clearly produce a different result—it would always be assigned '1'.

4.6.2 Synthesis and Variables

Variables do not always represent wires or states of memory elements such as flip-flops, like signals do. In addition, variables are visible only in processes, functions, and procedures. Variables (except for shared variables, which are not discussed in this text) are available only to the processes in which they are declared. They do not have projected output waveforms, like signals do, and to use the value of a variable outside of a process, it must be assigned to a signal within that process. For all of these reasons, variable synthesis is not always well defined, particularly if the range is not known at compile time. Therefore, we will use variables primarily as index holders in loops.

Even though the following design can be synthesized and describes a counter, we will avoid such use because not all synthesis tools can handle variables used in this fashion or produce the same results.

```vhdl
library ieee;
use ieee.std_logic_1164.all;
use work.std_arith.all;
entity variable_synthesis is port(
    rst, clk:      in std_logic;
    count:         out std_logic_vector(3 downto 0));
end variable_synthesis;

architecture not_well_defined of variable_synthesis is
begin
count: process (rst, clk)
    variable cnt: std_logic_vector(3 downto 0);
  begin
    if rst = '1' then
        cnt := (others => '0');
    elsif (clk'event and clk='1') then
        cnt := cnt + 1;
    end if;
    count <= cnt;
  end process;
end;
```

Listing 4-39 Use of variables in counter design

If in doubt, consider whether a variable is really required, or useful, for what you are describing, and think about rewriting the description using a signal.

4.7   Test Benches

Having covered the basics of VHDL design, you may now be interested in knowing how to test your design. You can do this at two points in the design phase: (1) When you have completed the VHDL description, you can simulate the source code with a VHDL simulator. (2) When you have synthesized and fitted (placed and routed) the design in a device, the software can produce a simulation model (in a number of formats, including VHDL) for use with a simulator that processes models of the given format. Warp2 allows for post-fit simulations in a proprietary format, but not for VHDL source-code simulation. This is because Warp2 contains a

VHDL synthesizer but not a VHDL simulator. For the designs of the complexity we have covered so far, little time is lost in not performing the source code simulation. Warp3 and other EDA tools that contain VHDL simulators allow you to simulate both the source code—to verify its functionality before you spend time to synthesize and fit the design to a device—and a post-layout VHDL model.

VHDL simulators typically allow interactive simulations, wherein you can apply vectors either by editing waveforms or using commands provided by the simulator. However, the real power behind VHDL simulation is the ability to write test benches. A test bench is a self-contained VHDL entity used for generating and applying vectors to another VHDL model, and verifying the accuracy of its outputs.

If you have access to Warp3 or another VHDL simulator, you may now wish to spend time becoming familiar with its command language. Simulating a few of the listings of this chapter would suffice. If you have access to Warp3 or another VHDL simulator and you wish to now focus on test benches rather than design techniques, descriptions, and their implementations in programmable logic, you should read Chapter 10, "Creating Test Benches" before proceeding with Chapter 5.

Problems

4.1. Translate the following code to an `if-then-else` statement:

```
transmit <=  signal_a when state = idle else
             signal_b when state = incoming else
             signal_c when state = outgoing else
             signal_d;
```

4.2. Translate the following code to a `when-else` statement:

```
process (a, b, j, k)
   begin
      if a = '1' and b = '0' then
         step <= "0100";
      elsif a = '1' then
         step <= j;
      elsif b = '1' then
         step <= k;
      else
         step <= "----";
      end if;
   end process;
```

4.3. Translate the following code to a case-when statement:

```
with state select
        data <=   "0000" when idle | terminate,
                  "1111" when increase,
                  "1010" when maintain,
                  "0101" when decrease,
                  "----" when others;
```

4.4. Translate the following code to two with-select-when statements:

```
case state is
    when idle => a <= "11"; b <= "00";
    when terminate | increase => a <= "01"; b <= "--";
    when maintain | decrease => a <= "10"; b <= "11";
    when others => a <= "11"; b <= "01";
end case;
```

4.5. Write the code to describe an 8-bit wide, four-to-one mux using a case-when statement. Inputs: a[7:0], b[7:0], c[7:0], d[7:0], s[1:0]; Outputs: q[7:0].

4.6. Write the code to compare two 8-bit buses, a and b. The output signal is agrb for "a greater than b".

4.7. Build a 4-bit magnitude comparator with three outputs (equals, less than, and greater than) using:

a. logical operators

b. relational operators

c. structural instantiation

d. a when-else statement

e. an if-then-else statement

4.8. Compile, synthesize, and simulate each version of the design in Problem 4.7.

4.9. Write the code for a 4-bit register. Inputs: clk, enable, data; output: q.

4.10. Design a 32-bit register bank using D-type flip-flops. The register bank has three-state outputs, controlled by a common output enable. Inputs: clk, register_enable, output_enable, data[31:0]; output: q[31:0].

4.11. Build a 16-bit down-counter with synchronous load and asynchronous reset. The outputs are three-state outputs, controlled by two separate signals—one for the lower 8-bits and one for the upper 8-bits. Inputs: `clk, reset, load, data[16:0], upper_enable, lower_enable`; output: `count[15:0]`.

4.12. What are the names of the standard VHDL package and function necessary for the following comparison to not always evaluate to false?

```
signal a: std_logic_vector(4 downto 0)
if a= "0011" then...
```

4.13. Find the errors in the following code:

```
architecture has_errors of design
begin
p1: process
    begin
        if clk'event and clk = '1' then
            q <= a or b and c;
        end if;
    end;
end;
```

4.14. Write an entity declaration and architecture body pair for each of the TTL devices in Table 2-1.

4.15. Do all processes require sensitivity lists? Can you declare a clocked process without a sensitivity list?

Chapter 5

State Machine Design

5.1 Introduction

In the previous two chapters, we covered the basic building blocks and language constructs in VHDL. In this chapter, we apply these concepts to state machine design. We choose state machines because they are commonly implemented in programmable logic devices. Our focus is how state machines are described and synthesized so that you will be able to create designs that meet your performance and resource utilization (speed and area) goals.

We begin with a simple example showing that writing a behavioral state machine description in VHDL is simply a matter of translating a state flow diagram to `case-when` and `if-then-else` statements. Next, we examine how a state machine description, when synthesized, is realized in a PLD. Knowing which resources are used will enable us to determine performance characteristics (such as t_S, t_{CO}, and t_{SCS}) and area requirements. We will then explore variations of design descriptions that, when synthesized, use different device resources and consequently have different performance characteristics. From the various design descriptions, you'll be able to identify a style that best fits your design requirements.

Depending on the design requirements (time-to-market, performance, and cost), you may be concerned with more than just having a functionally accurate design description. That's why we will investigate methods for optimizing designs for speed or area. Some of the optimization techniques are more applicable to CPLD architectures than to FPGAs (or vice versa); others are device-independent. We will point out which techniques will be short-lived—needed only for working around the current state of the art in synthesis—and which will always be applicable. All of the techniques discussed will help you to understand not only the synthesis process and how to quickly find the optimal design solution as defined by your goals, but also how to get the most of CPLD and FPGA architectures. We conclude the chapter with a discussion of fault tolerance and ways to avoid problems when designing complex state machines.

5.2   A Simple Design Example

We will use the following problem description to design a state machine, first using traditional design methodologies, then with VHDL.

A controller is used to enable and disable the write enable (we) and output enable (oe) signals of a memory buffer during read and write transactions. The signals `ready` and `read_write` are outputs of a microprocessor and inputs to the controller. `we` and `oe` are outputs of the controller. A new transaction begins with the assertion of `ready` following a completed transaction (or upon power-up, for the initial transaction). One clock cycle after the commencement of a transaction, the value of `read_write` determines whether it is a read or write transaction. If `read_write` is asserted, then it is a read cycle; otherwise, it is a write cycle. A cycle is completed by the assertion of `ready`, after which a new transaction can begin. Write enable is asserted during a write cycle, and output enable is asserted during a read cycle.

5.2.1   Traditional Design Methodology

Traditional design methodology tells us that the first step is to construct a state diagram from which we can derive a state table. We can determine and eliminate equivalent states by matching rows of the state table and using an implication table, if necessary. We can then make state assignments and create a state transition table from which we can generate next-state and output equations based on the types of flip-flops used for implementation.

From the design description, we can produce the state, or bubble, diagram of Figure 5-1. This diagram shows that a read or write transaction commences with the assertion of ready, in which case the state machine transitions from the `idle` state to the `decision` state. Depending upon the value of `read_write` during the

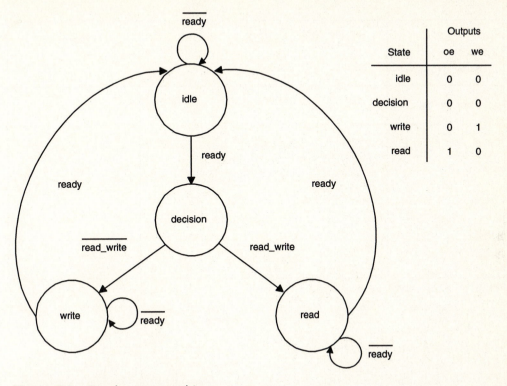

| State | Outputs | |
	oe	we
idle	0	0
decision	0	0
write	0	1
read	1	0

Figure 5-1 Simple state machine

next clock cycle, the transaction is either a read or write, and the state machine transitions to the appropriate state. A transaction is completed when ready is asserted, placing the controller back in the idle state. If ready is not asserted, then the controller remains in the current state.

There are no equivalent states in this machine; all states require different inputs to transition to the next state or have different outputs. We will combine the state assignment table with the state transition table (Figure 5-2); the state assignment is listed in the present-state (PS) column. We decided to use the fewest possible number of state registers, two. The next-state (NS) column shows transitions from present state to next state based upon the present value of the two inputs, read_write and ready. The combinations of values for these inputs are shown in a row as 00, 01, 11, and 10. They are listed in this order for easy translation to a Karnaugh map. The outputs are in the rightmost column.

| PS | | read_write ready | | NS Q_0Q_1 | | Outputs | |
State	q_0q_1	00	01	11	10	oe	we
idle	00	00	01	01	00	0	0
decision	01	11	11	10	10	0	0
write	11	11	00	00	11	0	1
read	10	10	00	00	10	1	0

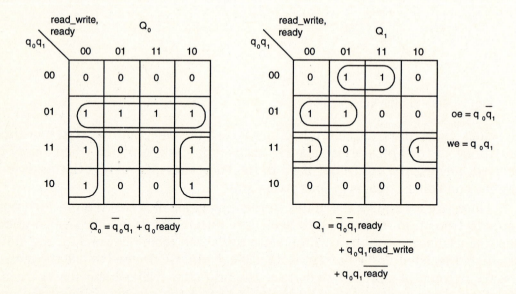

$$Q_0 = \overline{q_0}q_1 + q_0\overline{ready}$$

$$Q_1 = \overline{q_0}\,\overline{q_1}\,ready$$
$$+ \overline{q_0}q_1\,read\_write$$
$$+ q_0q_1\,\overline{ready}$$

$$oe = q_0\overline{q_1}$$

$$we = q_0q_1$$

Figure 5-2 Next-state and output equations

Next, we can determine the next-state equations for each of the two state bits (Figure 5-2). In the equations shown, Q_1 and Q_0 represent the next-state values, and q_1 and q_0 represent the present-state values. The Karnaugh maps can be generated easily from the state transition table: Each row corresponds to a state, each column corresponds to a combination of the inputs, and the entries in the Karnaugh maps correspond to the values of Q_1 and Q_0 found in the transition table. The Karnaugh maps are then used to find the minimal equations assuming D-type flip-flops. The outputs are functions of the present state only.

This implementation can then be used in a PLD that has D-type flip-flops, such as the 22V10. To optimize the design for another type of flip-flop requires a different set of Karnaugh maps based on the excitation equations for the flip-flops and the transition table of the state machine.

5.2.2 State Machines in VHDL

The state diagram shown in Figure 5-2 can be translated easily to a high-level VHDL description without having to perform the state assignment, generate the state transition table, or determine the next-state equations based on the types of flip-flops available. In VHDL, each state can be translated to a case in a `case-when` construct. The state transitions can then be specified in `if-then-else` statements. For example, to translate the state flow diagram into VHDL, we begin by defining an enumeration type, consisting of the state names, and declaring two signals of that type:

```
type StateType is (idle, decision, read, write);
signal present_state, next_state : StateType;
```

Next, we create a process. Next_state is determined by a function of the `present_state` and the inputs (`ready` and `read_write`). Thus, the process is sensitive to these signals:

```
state_comb: process (present_state, read_write, ready)
    begin
        ...
    end process state_comb;
```

Within the process we describe the state machine transitions. We open a `case-when` statement and specify the first case (`when` condition), which is for the `idle` state. For this case, we specify the outputs defined by the `idle` state and transitions from it:

```
state_comb: process (present_state, read_write, ready)
   begin
      case present_state is
         when idle =>
               oe <= '0'; we <= '0';
               if ready = '1' then
                  next_state <= decision;
               else                           --else not necessary
                  next_state <= idle;    --included for readability
               end if;
```

There are two options in this case (that is, when present_state is idle): (1) to transition to decision if ready is asserted or (2) to remain in the idle state. The else condition is not required. Without it, there is implied memory, and next_state remains the same. It is included to explicitly define state transitions. Coding of the remaining states requires following the same procedure: Create a branch of the case statement for each state (when state_name =>), specify that state's outputs, and define the state transitions with if-then-else statements. Below is the complete definition of the state transitions and outputs:

```
state_comb:process(present_state, read_write, ready) begin
   case present_state is
      when idle =>        oe <= '0'; we <= '0';
         if ready = '1' then
            next_state <= decision;
         else
            next_state <= idle;
         end if;
      when decision =>   oe <= '0'; we <= '0';
         if (read_write = '1') then
            next_state <= read;
         else          --read_write='0'
            next_state <= write;
         end if;
      when read =>       oe <= '1'; we <= '0';
         if (ready = '1') then
            next_state <= idle;
         else
            next_state <= read;
         end if;
      when write =>      oe <= '0'; we <= '1';
         if (ready = '1') then
            next_state <= idle;
         else
            next_state <= write;
         end if;
      end case;
   end process state_comb;
```

Two-Process FSM. The above process indicates what the next-state assignment will be based on the present-state and the present inputs, but it does not indicate when the next state becomes the present state. This happens synchronously, on the rising edge of a clock, as described in a second process, like the one shown below. Because this finite state machine (FSM) design is described with two processes, we will call it a two-process FSM description. The second process is:

```
state_clocked:process(clk) begin
   if (clk'event and clk='1') then
      present_state <= next_state;
   end if;
end process state_clocked;
```

The complete code for this two-process FSM follows.

```
entity example is port (
   read_write, ready, clk  : in bit;
   oe, we                  : out bit);
end example;

architecture state_machine of example is
   type StateType is (idle, decision, read, write);
   signal present_state, next_state : StateType;
begin
state_comb:process(present_state, read_write, ready) begin
   case present_state is
      when idle =>        oe <= '0'; we <= '0';
         if ready = '1' then
            next_state <= decision;
         else
            next_state <= idle;
         end if;
      when decision =>   oe <= '0'; we <= '0';
         if (read_write = '1') then
            next_state <= read;
         else          --read_write='0'
            next_state <= write;
         end if;
      when read =>        oe <= '1'; we <= '0';
         if (ready = '1') then
            next_state <= idle;
         else
            next_state <= read;
         end if;
```

```
        when write =>        oe <= '0'; we <= '1';
            if (ready = '1') then
                next_state <= idle;
            else
                next_state <= write;
            end if;
    end case;
end process state_comb;

state_clocked:process(clk) begin
    if (clk'event and clk='1') then
        present_state <= next_state;
    end if;
end process state_clocked;

end architecture state_machine;
                        --"architecture" is optional; for clarity
```

Listing 5-1 Design of a simple memory controller

Verifying Design Functionality. Now that we have described the state machine, we can examine the description to see if it accurately models the state machine behavior. To do this, we would typically use a VHDL simulator, but for instructional purposes and because this description is small enough, we will run through the simulation cycles manually.

The first part of simulation is the initialization phase: all signals without an explicit initialization value are initialized to the 'left value of their data types, and all processes are executed until suspended. This means that all bits are initialized to '0,' and the signals present_state and next_state are initialized to idle. Both processes are then executed, in either order.

When the state_comb process is evaluated, present_state is idle, and execution of the case statement jumps to the set of statements for when present_state is idle. The if condition is evaluated: The input ready is 0, so the statement next_state <= idle is executed. Execution jumps to the end of the case statement. No further assignments statements that would schedule a new value for next_state are executed, so at the end of the process, next_state retains the value of idle. When the process state_clocked is evaluated as part of initialization, the if condition evaluates false, and the process suspends. No new value for present_state is scheduled. After initialization, simulation time can be executed or inputs modified to effect a change in value of the circuit signals.

A process does not become active again until one of the signals in its sensitivity list changes value. The signals in the state_comb sensitivity list represent the present state and the state machine inputs. If any of these signals changes value, the process is executed. The `state_clocked` process is executed any time that `clk` changes value. This process is used for `present_state` to capture the present value of `next_state` on the rising edge of the clock. Figure 5-3 illustrates the input stimuli we will apply and the corresponding changes in state and outputs. The clock period will be 100 ns, with the first rising edge of the clock at 100 ns. Figure 5-4 shows the simulation and delta cycles that we will discuss next.

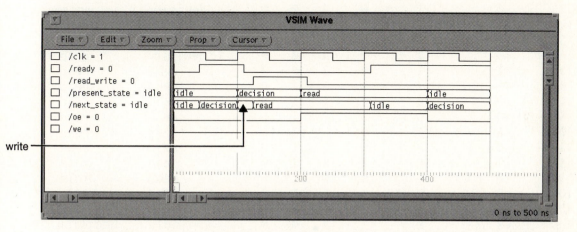

Figure 5-3 Functional verification of state machine [V-System Simulator Display printed with permission of Model Technology, Inc.]

When the current simulation time is 40 ns, the input `ready` is asserted. This transition causes the `state_comb` process to execute. Execution of the `case` statement jumps to the set of statements for when `present_state` is `idle`. The `if` condition is evaluated: The input `ready` is 1, so the statement `next_state <= write` is executed (thus, a new value is scheduled in the projected output waveform of `next_state`). Execution then jumps to the end of the `case` statement and the process suspends, causing `next_state` to be updated with its new value, `decision`.

At 50 ns, `clk` transitions from 1 to 0. This causes the `state_clocked` process to become active. The `if` condition evaluates false and the process suspends, with no new values scheduled for `present_state`.

At 100 ns, `clk` transitions from 0 to 1. This causes the `state_clocked` process to become active. The `if` condition evaluates true, so `present_state` is scheduled to assume the value of `next_state`, which is `decision`. When the process suspends, the current value of `present_state` becomes `decision`. The transition occurs one delta delay after 100 ns. This is because we are simulating the source code, not the postlayout model. When the design is implemented in a PLD, the state transition will occur not immediately, but after some propagation delay.

```
 ns   delta read_write  ready  clk  oe  we  present_state  next_state
  0    +0        0         0     0   0   0          idle        idle
 40    +0        0         1     0   0   0          idle        idle
 40    +1        0         1     0   0   0          idle    decision
100    +0        0         1     1   0   0          idle    decision
100    +1        0         1     1   0   0      decision    decision
100    +2        0         1     1   0   0      decision       write
110    +0        0         0     1   0   0      decision       write
125    +0        1         0     1   0   0      decision       write
125    +1        1         0     1   0   0      decision        read
150    +0        1         0     0   0   0      decision        read
200    +0        1         0     1   0   0      decision        read
200    +1        1         0     1   0   0          read        read
200    +2        1         0     1   1   0          read        read
210    +0        0         0     1   1   0          read        read
250    +0        0         0     0   1   0          read        read
300    +0        0         0     1   1   0          read        read
310    +0        0         1     1   1   0          read        read
310    +1        0         1     1   1   0          read        idle
350    +0        0         1     0   1   0          read        idle
400    +0        0         1     1   1   0          read        idle
400    +1        0         1     1   1   0          idle        idle
400    +2        0         1     1   0   0          idle    decision
450    +0        0         1     0   0   0          idle    decision
500    +0        0         1     1   0   0          idle    decision
500    +1        0         1     1   0   0      decision    decision
500    +2        0         1     1   0   0      decision       write
```

Figure 5-4   Simulation cycles for Listing 5-1

The change in value of present_state from idle to decision causes the state_comb process to be executed. Execution of the case statement jumps to the set of statements for when present_state is decision. Read_write is deasserted, so next_state is scheduled to assume the value of write. This happens two delta delays after 100 ns.

At 110 ns, ready is deasserted. This is a signal in the sensitivity list of process state_comb, so the process is executed. Execution of the case statement jumps to the set of statements for when present_state is decision (although next_state has changed value, present_state has not). Read_write has not changed value, and the next_state is presently write. Therefore, the signal-assignment statement next_state <= write does not cause a new value to be scheduled for next_state.

At 125 ns, `read_write` is asserted, so the `state_comb` process is executed. Execution of the `case` statement jumps to the set of statements for when `present_state` is `decision` (`present_state` has not yet changed). The `if` condition evaluates true because `read_write` is asserted. `Next_state` is scheduled to have the value of `read` upon termination of the process. The `else` is not executed, and execution jumps to the end of the `case` statement. The process suspends again.

At both 150 ns and 200 ns, the `state_clocked` process is executed due to a transition in `clk`. At the later time, `present_state` changes value from `decision` to `read`, which causes the `state_comb` process to be executed. Execution jumps to the set of statements for when `present_state` is `read`. A new value for oe is added to its projected output waveform. When the process suspends one delta delay after 200 ns, oe becomes 1.

At 210 ns, `read_write` is deasserted, causing `state_comb` to be executed. Execution jumps to the set of statements for when `present_state` is `read`. Ready is not asserted, so `next_state` retains its value.

At 250 ns the `state_clocked` process is executed due to a transition in `clk`. However, the transition is from 1 to 0, so the process suspends again. At 300 ns, the `state_clocked` executes anew. This time the `if` condition is true, but because the value of `next_state` is the same as the value of `present_state`, a new value is not assigned.

At 310 ns, `ready` is asserted, and `state_comb` is executed. Execution jumps to the set of statements for when `present_state` is `read`. The `if` condition is true (`ready` is asserted), so `next_state` is scheduled to assume the value `idle`.

On the next rising edge of `clk` (at 400 ns), the `state_clocked` process is executed, and `present_state` assumes the value of `idle`. This causes the `state_comb` process to execute; execution jumps to the set of statements for when `present_state` is `idle`. The signal oe is updated, as well as `next_state`.

We have partially verified that the behavior of our state machine description is consistent with expected behavior. We are now ready to synthesize the design and fit it to a PLD, after which we can simulate a postlayout model of the design.

Manual Synthesis. With the traditional design methodology, you are expected to perform the logic synthesis from problem description to logic equations. If you were to use VHDL to write design equations in order to implement the state machine in this way, you would write Boolean equations in place of the `state_comb` process, as in the following code fragment, which illustrates the assignment of one state register. (Remember that the logical operators do not carry precedence over each other, so the parenthesis between ANDs and ORs are required). Because VHDL is not case-sensitive, we cannot use q to represent the present state and Q the next state, as in the state transition table of Figure 5-2. Instead, we use x and y, respectively:

```
y(1) <= ((not q(0)) and (not q(1)) and ready) or
        ((not q(0)) and q(1) and (not read_write)) or
        (q(0) and q(1) and (not ready));

state_clocked:process(clk) begin
    if (clk'event and clk = '1') then
        x <= y;
    end if;
end process state_clocked;
```

Behavioral Synthesis. Describing the state machine in a behavioral style is not only easier but less prone to error. Synthesis of the behavioral design description will produce logic similar to that in the previous listing. Next, we review the results of synthesizing the design of Listing 5-1 to a FLASH370 CPLD using Warp. The report file produced by synthesis indicates that sequential encoding is used to encode the states of the state machine:

```
State variable 'present_state' is represented by a Bit_vector (0 to 1).
State encoding (sequential) for 'present_state' is:
    idle :=      b"00";
    decision :=  b"01";
    read :=      b"10";
    write :=     b"11";
Note:  No reset found for 'present_state'.
Device might not power up in a legal state.
```

Other encoding schemes can be used, either by modifying the code or using synthesis directives. Both approaches will be explained later in the chapter. Internally, the synthesis software represents the present state using a bit_vector with a width of two. The equations for the two state bits are given below as present_stateSBV_0.D and present_stateSBV_1.D. The .D extension indicates that these are the D-inputs to the flip flops. These are, in fact, the next_state equations. However, the .D equations were substituted for the next_state signals during synthesis, because they are equivalent:

```
Information: Process virtual 'next_stateSBV_0' ... expanded.
Information: Process virtual 'next_stateSBV_1' ... expanded.
```

The present_state signals in the VHDL code are represented in the report file by the signal names preceding the .Q extension. The outputs equations do not indicate the .D extension, and therefore represent combinatorial equations. The note ("No reset found…") indicates that there is no asynchronous reset to this state machine. Thus, we are relying on the flip-flops in the PLD powering up in known value and expecting that the power-up states will place the machine in a valid state. Compare the following equations to those of Figure 5-2.

```
DESIGN EQUATIONS
    oe =
            present_stateSBV_0.Q * /present_stateSBV_1.Q

    we =
            present_stateSBV_0.Q * present_stateSBV_1.Q

    present_stateSBV_0.D =
            present_stateSBV_0.Q * /ready
        + /present_stateSBV_0.Q * present_stateSBV_1.Q
    present_stateSBV_0.AP =
            GND
    present_stateSBV_0.AR =
            GND
    present_stateSBV_0.C =
            clk

    present_stateSBV_1.D =
            /present_stateSBV_0.Q * /present_stateSBV_1.Q * ready
        + /present_stateSBV_0.Q * present_stateSBV_1.Q * /read_write
        + present_stateSBV_0.Q * present_stateSBV_1.Q * /ready
    present_stateSBV_1.AP =
            GND
    present_stateSBV_1.AR =
            GND
    present_stateSBV_1.C =
            clk
```

The .AP, .AR, and .C extensions to the present_stateSBV equations indicate, respectively, the asynchronous reset, asynchronous preset, and clock for these registered signals.

State machines are clearly examples of the type of design that is best expressed with high-level constructs. A high-level description is easier to create, understand, and maintain. Additionally, as the number of inputs to or states of a state machine increases, generating the transition table and next-state equations would become increasingly tedious and difficult to manage, as is shown in our next example.

5.3   A Memory Controller

Our next design example is also a memory controller, but it is more practical and
has more functionality than the previous one. Figure 5-5 shows a block diagram of
a system that uses a state machine for a memory controller.

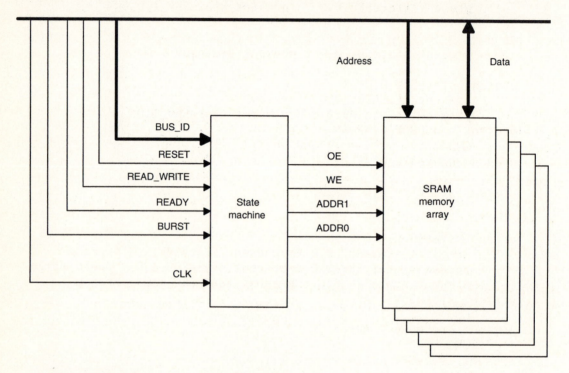

Figure 5-5   Memory controller block diagram

The system works like this: Other devices on the bus initiate an access to the
memory buffer by asserting its bus identification, F3 (hex). One cycle later, the
read_write signal is asserted to indicate a read from the memory buffer; the signal is deasserted to indicate a write to the memory buffer. If the memory access is
a read, the read may either be a single-word read or a four-word burst read. A

burst read is indicated by the assertion of burst during the first read cycle, following which the controller accesses four locations from the buffer. Consecutive locations are accessed following successive assertions of ready. The controller asserts oe (output enable) to the memory buffer during a read, and increments the lowest two bits of the address during a burst.

A write to the buffer is always a single-word write, never a burst. During a write, we is asserted, allowing data to be written to the memory location specified by address. Read and write accesses are completed upon assertion of ready.

Figure 5-6 is the state diagram for this memory controller. This diagram shows that a synchronous reset places the state machine in idle. When the memory buffer is not being accessed, the controller remains in idle. If bus_id is asserted as F3 (hex) while the controller is in idle, then the machine transitions to the decision state. On the next clock cycle, the controller transitions to either read1 or write, depending on the value of read_write. If the access is a read, the controller branches to the read portion of the state machine. A single-word read is indicated by the assertion of ready without the assertion of burst while in the read1 state. In this case, the controller returns to the idle state. A burst read is indicated by the assertion of both ready and burst while in the read1 state. In this case, the machine transitions through each of the read states, advancing on ready. Oe is asserted during each of the read cycles. Addr is incremented in successive read cycles following the first.

If the access is a write, it can only be a single-word write. Therefore, after determining that the access is a write (read_write = 0) in the decision state, the controller branches to the write portion of the state machine. It simply asserts we to the memory buffer, waits for the ready signal from the bus, and then returns directly to the idle state.

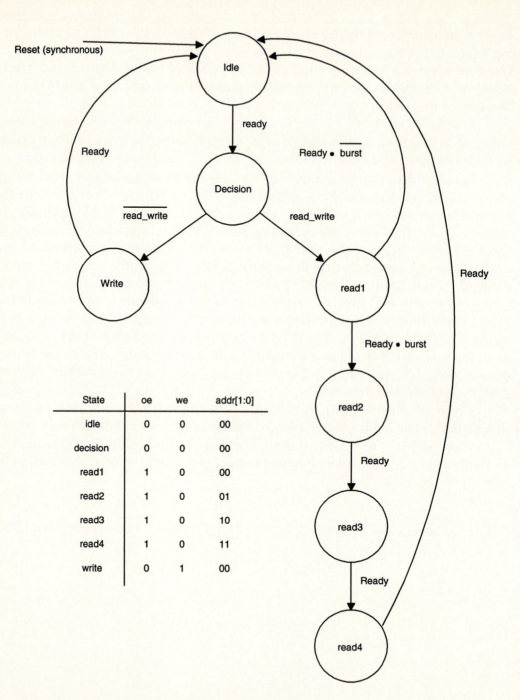

Figure 5-6 Memory controller state flow diagram

5.3.1   Translating the State Flow Diagram to VHDL

The state flow diagram can be translated easily to a series of cases in a case-when construct as follows (we are disregarding the synchronous reset for now):

```vhdl
case present_state is
    when idle     =>    oe <= '0'; we <= '0'; addr <= "00";
        if (bus_id = "11110011") then
            next_state <= decision;
        else
            next_state <= idle;
        end if;
    when decision=>    oe <= '0'; we <= '0'; addr <= "00";
        if (read_write = '1') then
            next_state <= read1;
        else                          --read_write='0'
            next_state <= write;
        end if;
    when read1    =>    oe <= '1'; we <= '0'; addr <= "00";
        if (ready = '0') then
            next_state <= read1;
        elsif (burst = '0') then
            next_state <= idle;
        else
            next_state <= read2;
        end if;
    when read2    =>    oe <= '1'; we <= '0'; addr <= "01";
        if (ready = '1') then
            next_state <= read3;
        else
            next_state <= read2;
        end if;
    when read3    =>    oe <= '1'; we <= '0'; addr <= "10";
        if (ready = '1') then
            next_state <= read4;
        else
            next_state <= read3;
        end if;
    when read4    =>    oe <= '1'; we <= '0'; addr <= "11";
        if (ready = '1') then
            next_state <= idle;
        else
            next_state <= read4;
        end if;
```

```
        when write   =>    oe <= '0'; we <= '1'; addr <= "00";
            if (ready = '1') then
                next_state <= idle;
            else
                next_state <= write;
            end if;
    end case;
```

As you can see, the section of code inside the `state_comb` process falls directly from the bubble diagram: Each state is simply one of the case statement branches. For each state, the state machine outputs are documented with sequential signal-assignment statements, and all of the state transitions are documented in `if-then-else` statements. Take `decision`, for example: Examining the state flow diagram, you see that the outputs are 0 for `we`, `oe`, and both bits of `addr`. In addition, there are two transitions from this state depending on the value of `read_write`. If `read_write` is asserted (a read operation), then `next_state` is `read1`; otherwise `next_state` is `write`. The remaining states are likewise coded.

Synchronous Reset in a Two-Process FSM. This state machine requires a synchronous reset. Rather than specifying the reset transition to the `idle` state in each branch of the case statement, we can include an `if-then-else` statement at the beginning of the process in order to place the machine in the `idle` state if `reset` is asserted. If `reset` is not asserted, then the normal state transitioning occurs, as specified in the `case` statement. We must also specify, in this `if-then-else` statement, what we want the outputs (`oe`, `we`, and `addr`) to be if `reset` is asserted. If we do not specify what we want the outputs to be for this condition, then we will see the effects of implied memory: latches will be created to ensure that when `reset` is asserted, the outputs retain their previous values. Because we do not want latches created, we will specify that we don't care what value the outputs are when `reset` is asserted. This will allow don't-care optimization in reducing the output equations. When `reset` is asserted, the state machine will transition to the idle state, and the outputs will be decoded from `present_state` and assigned according to their definition in the `idle` state. If we were to assign values to the outputs in this initial `if` statement, the outputs would become functions of `present_state` and `reset`, rather than of `present_state` alone. The code required for the reset is:

```
state_comb:process(reset, present_state, burst, read_write, ready)
begin
    if (reset = '1') then
        oe <= '-'; we <= '-'; addr <= "--";
        next_state <= idle;
```

```
else
   case present_state is
      ...
   end case;
end if;
end process state_comb;
```

Alternatively, the reset condition could come after the `case` statement, as the last statement in the `state_comb` process. This way, it could be a simple `if-then` statement, and only the state transition would be required. Defining the values of the outputs would not be required here because the `case` statement, in which the values of the outputs are defined, will not be part of the `else` statement. The code required for the reset in this case would be:

```
state_comb:process(reset, present_state, burst, read_write, ready)
begin
   case present_state is
      ...
   end case;
   if (reset = '1') then
      next_state <= idle;
   end if;
end process state_comb;
```

The complete code for the memory-controller state machine is shown in Listing 5-2.

```
library ieee;
use ieee.std_logic_1164.all;
entity memory_controller is port (
     reset, read_write, ready,
     burst, clk                  : in std_logic;
     bus_id                      : in std_logic_vector(7 downto 0);
     oe, we                      : out std_logic;
     addr                        : out std_logic_vector(1 downto 0));
end memory_controller;

architecture state_machine of memory_controller is
   type StateType is (idle, decision, read1, read2, read3, read4, write);
   signal present_state, next_state : StateType;
begin
state_comb:process(reset, bus_id, present_state, burst, read_write, ready)
```

```
begin
    if (reset = '1') then
        oe <= '-'; we <= '-'; addr <= "--";
        next_state <= idle;
    else
        case present_state is
            when idle    =>    oe <= '0'; we <= '0'; addr <= "00";
                if (bus_id = "11110011") then
                    next_state <= decision;
                else
                    next_state <= idle;
                end if;
            when decision=>    oe <= '0'; we <= '0'; addr <= "00";
                if (read_write = '1') then
                    next_state <= read1;
                else                       --read_write='0'
                    next_state <= write;
                end if;
            when read1    =>    oe <= '1'; we <= '0'; addr <= "00";
                if (ready = '0') then
                    next_state <= read1;
                elsif (burst = '0') then
                    next_state <= idle;
                else
                    next_state <= read2;
                end if;
            when read2    =>    oe <= '1'; we <= '0'; addr <= "01";
                if (ready = '1') then
                    next_state <= read3;
                else
                    next_state <= read2;
                end if;
            when read3    =>    oe <= '1'; we <= '0'; addr <= "10";
                if (ready = '1') then
                    next_state <= read4;
                else
                    next_state <= read3;
                end if;
            when read4    =>    oe <= '1'; we <= '0'; addr <= "11";
                if (ready = '1') then
                    next_state <= idle;
                else
                    next_state <= read4;
                end if;
            when write   =>    oe <= '0'; we <= '1'; addr <= "00";
                if (ready = '1') then
                    next_state <= idle;
```

```
            else
                next_state <= write;
            end if;
      end case;
   end if;
end process state_comb;

state_clocked:process(clk) begin
   if rising_edge(clk) then
      present_state <= next_state;
   end if;
end process state_clocked;

end state_machine;
```

Listing 5-2 Memory controller described as a two-process FSM

Listing 5-2 is a two-process FSM description. One process describes the combinational logic, and another describes synchronization of state transitions to the clock. This code structure is analogous to the architecture of a CPLD logic block, as illustrated in Figure 5-7. Decoding of `present_state` and inputs is performed in the combinatorial portion (product-term array) of the logic block just as it is described in the combinatorial process in the code. Synchronization of `next_state` is described in the `state_clocked` process, which describes a bank of registers such as the macrocells in a logic block.

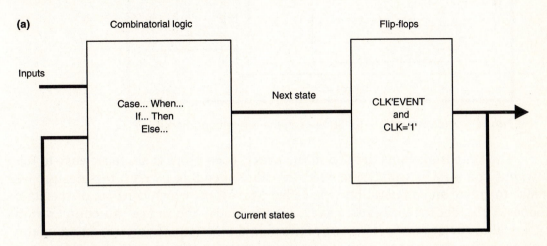

Figure 5-7   (a) The code structure of Listing 5-2

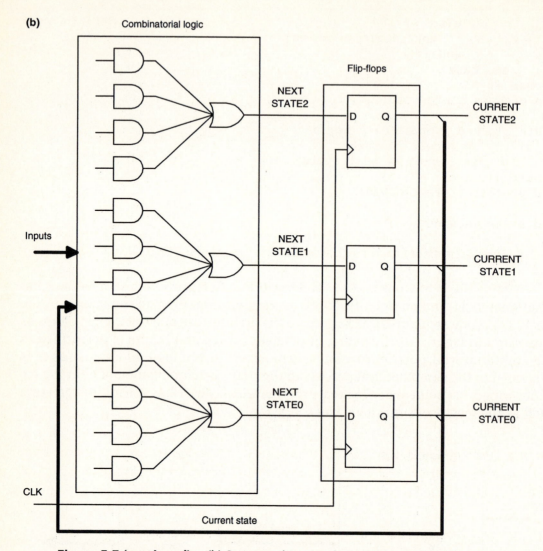

(b)

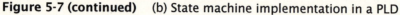

Figure 5-7 (continued)   (b) State machine implementation in a PLD

The state transitions defined in the state_comb process are fairly easy to follow, but you may be wondering what the state encoding is. With this design, we
chose to create an enumeration type called StateType, which consists of the state
names: idle, decision, read1, read2, read3, read4, and write. An enumeration
type makes the code easier to comprehend and maintain. If you use an enumeration type, the state encoding is determined by the synthesis software unless you
explicitly declare the state encoding with constants or by using a synthesis directive. Using synthesis directives for state encoding is explained later in the chapter,

and the use of synthesis directives, in general, is described in Chapter 8. As a default, most synthesis tools use sequential encoding, in which case three bits are used for the seven states: `idle` is 000, `decision` is 001, `read1` is 010, and so forth. Later in this chapter, we'll see how to set the state encoding with constants.

Asynchronous Reset in a Two-Process FSM. If an asynchronous reset is desired instead of a synchronous reset, then you can use the asynchronous reset template discussed in the previous chapter by rewriting the `state_clocked` process of Listing 5-2 as follows:

```
state_clocked:process(clk,reset) begin
    if reset= '1' then
        present_state <= idle;
    elsif rising_edge(clk) then
        present_state <= next_state;
    end if;
end process state_clocked;
```

If the reset signal is used only during initialization or system failure, then using an asynchronous reset may be better than a synchronous reset. This is mainly because a synchronous reset may require additional device resources (product terms, in the case of a CPLD); it also eliminates the possibility of inadvertently introducing implied memory.

This state machine is one that would be difficult to design and maintain using a traditional design methodology. For instance, if the polarity of `ready`, `burst`, or `read_write` is reversed, updating the VHDL code is a simple task. Regenerating next-state design equations manually is not, because this design has many combinations of inputs. A comparison of the relative ease of design is left as an exercise for the reader!

▼
Breakout Exercise 5-1

Purpose: To illustrate the effects of implicit memory.

The paragraph beginning "Synchronous reset" on page 248 indicates that if we remove the signal assignment statements for the reset condition, the description implies that the outputs will not change. This implied memory will cause latches to be created.

1. Compile and synthesize the design `c:\vhdlbook\ch5\memcont.vhd`, targeting a CY7C371.

2. Edit `memcont.vhd` to remove the signal assignment statements for `oe`, `we`, and `addr` under the reset condition. Save the file with a new name.

3. Compile and synthesize the new design, targeting a CY7C371.

4. Compare the new report file with that of the original design. Verify with the equations that implicit memory resulted in the creation of a combinatorial latch.

5. Simulate the newer design with Nova. What happens when `reset` is asserted?

5.3.2   An Alternate Coding Style

One-Process FSM. The code shown in Listing 5-3 is functionally equivalent to, and results in the same logic being produced as, the code in Listing 5-2, if it is modified to use an asynchronous reset. Listing 5-3 uses only one process to describe the state transitions and the synchronization of those transitions to the clock, so we call it a one-process FSM. Additional concurrent signal-assignment statements are used to describe the behavior of the outputs. The code follows (the entity declaration is the same, and is not reprinted).

```vhdl
architecture state_machine of memory_controller is
   type StateType is (idle, decision, read1, read2, read3, read4, write);
   signal state : StateType;
begin
state_tr:process(reset, clk) begin          -- one process fsm
   if reset = '1' then                      -- asynchronous reset
      state <= idle;
   elsif rising_edge(clk) then              -- synchronization to clk
      case state is                         -- state transitions defined
         when idle   =>
            if (bus_id = "11110011") then
               state <= decision;
            else                            -- not req'd; for clarity
               state <= idle;
            end if;
         when decision=>
            if (read_write = '1') then
               state <= read1;
            else                            --read_write='0'
               state <= write;
            end if;
```

```vhdl
        when read1   =>
            if (ready = '0') then
                state <= read1;
            elsif (burst = '0') then
                state <= idle;
            else
                state <= read2;
            end if;
        when read2   =>
            if (ready = '1') then
                state <= read3;
            end if;              -- no else state <= read2; implicit
        when read3   =>
            if (ready = '1') then
                state <= read4;
            else                 -- else not req'd; could use
                state <= read3;  -- implicit memory, as in read2 above
            end if;
        when read4   =>
            if (ready = '1') then
                state <= idle;
            else
                state <= read4;
            end if;
        when write   =>
            if (ready = '1') then
                state <= idle;
            else
                state <= write;
            end if;
        end case;
    end if;
end process state_tr;

-- combinatorially decoded outputs
  with state select
        oe <= '1' when read1 | read2 | read3 | read4,
              '0' when others;

  we <= '1' when state = write else '0';

  with state select
        addr <= "01" when read2,
                "10" when read3,
                "11" when read4,
                "00" when others;

end state_machine;
```

Listing 5-3 Memory controller described as a one-process FSM

In this design description, the state transition process state_tr is used for the next-state logic and for clocking the state registers. Only one signal, state, of type StateType, is required. The following statement implies that all subsequent signal assignments within the process occur on the rising edge of the clock:

```
elsif rising_edge(clk) then
```

The following collection of statements implies that the assignment of state is synchronous:

```
state_tr:process(reset, clk) begin
    .
    .
    .
    elsif rising_edge(clk) then
    case state is
       when idle    =>
          if (bus_id = "11110011") then
             state <= decision;
          else                              -- not req'd; for clarity
             state <= idle;
       end if;
```

Using this construct, if state presently has the value idle and the bus identification is F3 (hex), then on the next clock edge it will be assigned a new value of decision. The code fragment above can be read, "When the present state is idle, if bus_id is 11110011, then the new state will be decision; otherwise, the state will be idle." The comment to the right of else indicates that this statement else state <= idle; is not necessary: if it is omitted, it is implied that the state should retain its current value of idle. It is included only for clarity, so that it is easier to translate between the code and the bubble diagram.

The outputs shown in Listing 5-3 are described with concurrent signal-assignment statements that, when synthesized, result in combinational logic. Of course, the outputs could also be described in equivalent processes. When synthesized, Listings 5-2 and 5-3 will result in the same logic. We will see how these descriptions are synthesized in the next section.

Although Listing 5-3 uses one process and three concurrent signal-assignment statements to describe the state machine in a one-process FSM description, the entire design—state transitions and output values—could be captured in just one process. This would require that in addition to the state transitions, the outputs also be defined in the branches of the case statement. We find that one can easily become confused when doing this, because the outputs must be defined for the next state. Thus, the outputs must be defined for each transition, either in each branch of the `if-then-else` statements or by defining default values at the top of the process and indicating only where changes are necessary for the subsequent clock cycle (but defined in the `if-then-else` statements). We recommend the two-process FSM coding style of Listing 5-2, because it lets you easily identify the outputs and state transitions in one process statement. We find that the two-process FSM descriptions are easiest to create, understand, and maintain, particularly for large state machines, machines with many transitions, or machines with a large number of outputs. Listing 5-3 and the other state machines described in this paragraph, however, illustrate that the language is not tied to one style.

Next, we take four versions of this memory-controller design and analyze the results of synthesizing each. We'll compare which device resources are required, and the impact of each on different speed (timing) parameters.

5.4   Area, Speed, and Device Resource Utilization

The current state of the art in synthesis is largely based on RTL (register transfer level) optimization. Behavioral descriptions are broken down into explicitly declared or inferred registers and the logic between these registers. Optimization is then performed on the combinational logic between the registers and the I/O. In writing VHDL code, you must ensure that your descriptions synthesize to expected results. Synthesis directives can be used to influence how logic is optimized and registers are inferred, but coding style is also an important factor. One description may yield a faster circuit than another simply because the description is more efficient. Even with efficient descriptions, you may be able to trade speed for area. With speed-optimized designs, you may be able to further optimize for a particular timing parameter (t_{SU}, t_{CO}, or operating frequency).

Both setup and clock-to-output times are important in determining the maximum frequency of operation for a system, but one may be more important than another for a given device, depending on the timing parameters of interfacing devices. Area and speed often work against each other. Some implementations may require more flip-flops but fewer product terms (usually better for FPGAs), whereas others may require more product terms but fewer flip-flops (usually better for CPLDs).

Achieving the optimal implementation is not always a design objective. Rather, time-to-market and having easy-to-read code that facilitates quick design cycles often supercede the need for the most area-efficient or highest-performance design. In such cases, the following discussion may not be necessary. In cases that push the current limits of technology in terms of achievable silicon performance and the ability to use directives to influence synthesis choices, the following discussion will prove helpful.

You can get the optimal hardware implementation from a VHDL description by understanding how specific VHDL implementations synthesize to logic in CPLDs and FPGAs from RTL-based synthesis. With this understanding, you will be equipped to write code optimized for the particular timing and resource-utilization requirements of your design. In the following sections, we look at four techniques for generating state machine outputs for Moore machines:

- outputs decoded from state bits combinatorially,
- outputs decoded in parallel output registers,
- outputs encoded within state bits, and
- one hot encoding.

Each of these techniques produces a logic implementation with different timing characteristics. Some also impact gate-utilization as well.

5.4.1   **Outputs Decoded from State Bits Combinatorially**

Listings 5-2 and 5-3 describe outputs that must be decoded from the present state of the state bits (Figure 5-8). This combinatorial decoding can require additional levels of logic, resulting in slower propagation from the output of the state bits to the output signals at the device pins (and increased clock-to-output delay).

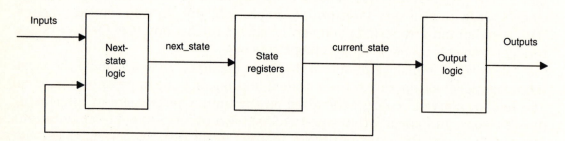

Figure 5-8   State machine with outputs decoded from state registers

Synthesis Results. The results of synthesizing the memory controller of Listing 5-2, modified so that it has an asynchronous reset, are shown below. The target device was the 32-macrocell CY7C371-143 CPLD.

State variable 'present_state' is represented by a Bit_vector (0 to 2).
State encoding (sequential) for 'present_state' is:
```
    idle :=      b"000";
    decision :=  b"001";
    read1 :=     b"010";
    read2 :=     b"011";
    read3 :=     b"100";
    read4 :=     b"101";
    write :=     b"110";
```

DESIGN EQUATIONS
```
    we =
          present_stateSBV_0.Q * present_stateSBV_1.Q

    addr_1 =
          present_stateSBV_0.Q * /present_stateSBV_1.Q

    oe =
          present_stateSBV_0.Q * /present_stateSBV_1.Q
        + /present_stateSBV_0.Q * present_stateSBV_1.Q

    addr_0 =
          present_stateSBV_1.Q * present_stateSBV_2.Q
        + present_stateSBV_0.Q * present_stateSBV_2.Q

    present_stateSBV_0.D =
          /present_stateSBV_0.Q * /present_stateSBV_1.Q *
          present_stateSBV_2.Q * /read_write
        + present_stateSBV_1.Q * present_stateSBV_2.Q * ready
        + present_stateSBV_0.Q * /present_stateSBV_1.Q *
          /present_stateSBV_2.Q
        + present_stateSBV_0.Q * /ready
    present_stateSBV_0.AP =
          GND
    present_stateSBV_0.AR =
          reset
    present_stateSBV_0.C =
          clk

    present_stateSBV_1.D =
          /present_stateSBV_0.Q * present_stateSBV_1.Q *
          /present_stateSBV_2.Q * burst
        + /present_stateSBV_0.Q * /present_stateSBV_1.Q *
          present_stateSBV_2.Q
        + present_stateSBV_1.Q * /ready
    present_stateSBV_1.AP =
          GND
```

```
present_stateSBV_1.AR =
     reset
present_stateSBV_1.C =
     clk

present_stateSBV_2.D =
     /present_stateSBV_0.Q * /present_stateSBV_1.Q *
     /present_stateSBV_2.Q * bus_id_7 * bus_id_6 * bus_id_5 *
     bus_id_4 * /bus_id_3 * /bus_id_2 * bus_id_1 * bus_id_0
   + /present_stateSBV_0.Q * present_stateSBV_1.Q *
     /present_stateSBV_2.Q * ready * burst
   + present_stateSBV_0.Q * /present_stateSBV_1.Q *
     /present_stateSBV_2.Q * ready
   + present_stateSBV_1.Q * present_stateSBV_2.Q * /ready
   + present_stateSBV_0.Q * present_stateSBV_2.Q * /ready
present_stateSBV_2.AP =
     GND
present_stateSBV_2.AR =
     reset
present_stateSBV_2.C =
     clk
```

The report file indicates that present_state was internally converted to a bit_vector of width 3. The equations for each of the state bits is given as present_stateSBV_*.D, where * is 0, 1, or 2. The .D extension indicates that these are equations for the D-inputs to the flip flops. The .D equations were substituted for the next_state signals during synthesis, because they are equivalent. The present_state signals in the VHDL code are represented in the report file by the .Q signal names. The output equations do not indicate the .D extension, and therefore represent combinatorial equations. The .AP, .AR, and .C extensions to the present_stateSBV equations indicate, respectively, the asynchronous reset, asynchronous preset, and clock for these registered signals.

Because the state bits must propagate through the programmable interconnect and the product-term array in order to be decoded, outputs we, oe, and addr appear at the pins 12 ns (t_{CO2}) after the rising edge of clk. The worst-case clock-to-output, setup, and t_{SCS} delays are:

```
Worst-Case Path Summary
-----------------------
              tS = 5.0 ns for present_stateSBV_2.D
            tSCS = 7.0 ns for present_stateSBV_2.D
             tCO = 12.0 ns for we
```

Had any outputs propagated straight from the flip-flops to the output pins without going through the additional level of combinational logic, they would change 6.0 ns (t_{CO}) after the rising edge of clk, worst case. See Table 2-4 for the CY7C371-143 timing specifications.

The VHDL code of Listing 5-2 is easy to comprehend and maintain. However, there may be a performance issue: The outputs of the state machine arrive t_{CO2} instead of t_{CO} after the rising edge of the clock. In many cases, this difference in delay will be acceptable in the overall system timing. In other cases, it may not. Until synthesis technology for CPLDs progresses, modification of the code will be required to achieve higher performance.

For example, let's revisit the design of the memory controller. Let's assume that for the data coming from the SRAM memory array to be ready in time for the device that is reading it, the addr outputs from the PLD must be available no more than 8 ns after the rising edge of the clock. In this particular implementation, they are not—they are available 12 ns after the rising edge of the clock. If we keep addr from requiring the additional pass through the logic array before going to the output pins, then it will be available in 6.0 ns (t_{CO} instead of t_{CO2}), and the system design requirements will be satisfied.

5.4.2   Outputs Decoded in Parallel Output Registers

One way to ensure that the state machine outputs arrive at the device pins earlier is to decode the outputs from the state bits *before* the state bits are registered, then store the decoded information in registers. This can be done with either a one-process or two-process FSM description. In either case, the assignments to addr must be described outside of the process in which the state transitions are defined. Instead of using the present_state information to determine the value for addr, we will use the next_state value to determine what addr should be during the next clock cycle. If in the next state of the machine addr(1) is a '1', we store a '1' into a flip-flop at the rising edge of clk. If the next_state value indicates that addr(1) is a '0', then we store a '0' into that flip-flop. The same technique can be used with oe and we, but since there isn't a clock-to-output requirement for these outputs, we leave them as is. We illustrate the concept of storing the values of outputs based on the value of next_state in Figure 5-9.

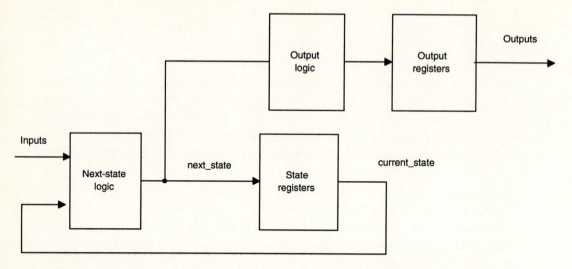

Figure 5-9 Moore machine with outputs decoded in parallel output registers

To modify the memory controller design to include outputs decoded in parallel output registers, we modify the Listing 5-2 as shown in Listing 5-4. Comments are used to indicate where there are differences in the code.

```vhdl
library ieee;
use ieee.std_logic_1164.all;
entity memory_controller is port (
    reset, read_write, ready,
    burst, clk                    : in std_logic;
    bus_id                        : in std_logic_vector(7 downto 0);
    oe, we                        : out std_logic;
    addr                          : out std_logic_vector(1 downto 0));
end memory_controller;

architecture state_machine of memory_controller is
    type StateType is (idle, decision, read1, read2, read3,
                       read4, write);
    signal present_state, next_state : StateType;
    signal addr_d: std_logic_vector(1 downto 0)   -- D-input to
                                                  -- addr f-flops
begin
state_comb:process(bus_id, present_state, burst, read_write, ready)
begin
    case present_state is                         -- addr outputs not
        when idle    =>    oe <= '0'; we <= '0'; -- defined here.
            if (bus_id = "11110011") then
                next_state <= decision;
```

```vhdl
                else
                    next_state <= idle;
                end if;
            when decision=>    oe <= '0'; we <= '0';
                if (read_write = '1') then
                    next_state <= read1;
                else                            --read_write='0'
                    next_state <= write;
                end if;
            when read1   =>    oe <= '1'; we <= '0';
                if (ready = '0') then
                    next_state <= read1;
                elsif (burst = '0') then
                    next_state <= idle;
                else
                    next_state <= read2;
                end if;
            when read2   =>    oe <= '1'; we <= '0';
                if (ready = '1') then
                    next_state <= read3;
                else
                    next_state <= read2;
                end if;
            when read3   =>    oe <= '1'; we <= '0';
                if (ready = '1') then
                    next_state <= read4;
                else
                    next_state <= read3;
                end if;
            when read4   =>    oe <= '1'; we <= '0';
                if (ready = '1') then
                    next_state <= idle;
                else
                    next_state <= read4;
                end if;
            when write   =>    oe <= '0'; we <= '1';
                if (ready = '1') then
                    next_state <= idle;
                else
                    next_state <= write;
                end if;
        end case;
end process state_comb;
```

```
    with next_state select              -- D-input to addr flip-flops
          addr_d <= "01" when read2,    -- defined here.
                    "10" when read3,
                    "11" when read4,
                    "00" when others;

  state_clocked:process(clk, reset) begin
     if reset = '1' then
        present_state <= idle;
        addr <= "00";                   -- asynchronous reset for addr flops
     elsif rising_edge(clk) then
        present_state <= next_state;
        addr <= addr_d;                 -- value of addr_d stored in addr
     end if;
  end process state_clocked;

end state_machine;
```

Listing 5-4 Addr outputs registered for improved t_{CO}

An additional signal, addr_d, is declared in this design. It is used to combinatorially decode what the value of addr should be in the next clock cycle. This is done by removing addr signal-assignment statements from the case statement, where they are based on present_state, and inserting a with-select-when concurrent signal-assignment statement, where the selection signal is next_state. This causes addr_d to be decoded from next_state rather than present_state. Next, the addr_d is captured by signal addr on the rising edge of clk. This is described in the state_clocked process. The with-select-when statement did not need to be placed between the two processes; it could have been before or after either of them.

Addr has the same values in the same clock cycle as it did in the previous implementations, but now it is available t_{CO} after clk (6.0 ns in the CY7C371-143 CPLD) instead of t_{CO2} (12.0 ns). The outputs are available in t_{CO} time because the value of the output address is held in flip-flops, and the outputs of these flip-flops may propagate directly to the device pins rather than first propagating through the logic array.

Synthesis Results. From the diagram of Figure 5-9, it may appear as if this implementation will have two unintended side effects: (1) that it will require two more flip-flops than the previous version, and (2) that the propagation of the state-bit signals to the addr flip-flops takes two passes through the combinational logic array (one for the next-state logic and one for the output logic), affecting the maximum frequency at which this design can operate. Both of these side effects may mum frequency at which this design can operate. Both of these side effects may exist depending on the specific CPLD or FPGA chosen to implement the design and the synthesis tool used. In the particular case of the CY7C371 and the Warp synthesizer, these side effects do not exist. The logic that determines the next_state signals and the logic that determines the outputs are combined into a single level of logic by the optimization algorithms in the synthesis software. The resulting logic uses fewer than the 16 product terms available to a CY7C371 macrocell, so the output decoding logic requires only a single pass through the logic array. The equations produced by synthesis are shown below (equations for clock, asynchronous reset, and asynchronous preset assignment are removed to save space):

```
DESIGN EQUATIONS
    we =
            present_stateSBV_0.Q * present_stateSBV_1.Q

    oe =
            present_stateSBV_0.Q * /present_stateSBV_1.Q
        + /present_stateSBV_0.Q * present_stateSBV_1.Q

    addr_1.D =
            present_stateSBV_1.Q * ready * present_stateSBV_2.Q
        + present_stateSBV_0.Q * /present_stateSBV_1.Q *
          /present_stateSBV_2.Q
        + present_stateSBV_0.Q * /present_stateSBV_1.Q * /ready

    addr_0.D =
            /present_stateSBV_0.Q * present_stateSBV_1.Q * ready *
            /present_stateSBV_2.Q * burst
        + present_stateSBV_0.Q * /present_stateSBV_1.Q * ready *
          /present_stateSBV_2.Q
        + present_stateSBV_0.Q * /present_stateSBV_1.Q * /ready *
          present_stateSBV_2.Q
        + /present_stateSBV_0.Q * present_stateSBV_1.Q * /ready *
          present_stateSBV_2.Q

    present_stateSBV_0.D =
            /present_stateSBV_0.Q * /present_stateSBV_1.Q *
            present_stateSBV_2.Q * /read_write
        + present_stateSBV_1.Q * ready * present_stateSBV_2.Q
        + present_stateSBV_0.Q * /present_stateSBV_1.Q *
          /present_stateSBV_2.Q
        + present_stateSBV_0.Q * /ready
```

```
present_stateSBV_1.D =
        /present_stateSBV_0.Q * present_stateSBV_1.Q *
        /present_stateSBV_2.Q * burst
    + /present_stateSBV_0.Q * /present_stateSBV_1.Q *
        present_stateSBV_2.Q
    + present_stateSBV_1.Q * /ready

present_stateSBV_2.D =
        /present_stateSBV_0.Q * /present_stateSBV_1.Q *
        /present_stateSBV_2.Q * bus_id_7 * bus_id_6 * bus_id_5 *
        bus_id_4 * /bus_id_3 * /bus_id_2 * bus_id_1 * bus_id_0
    + /present_stateSBV_0.Q * present_stateSBV_1.Q * ready *
        /present_stateSBV_2.Q * burst
    + present_stateSBV_0.Q * /present_stateSBV_1.Q * ready *
        /present_stateSBV_2.Q
    + present_stateSBV_1.Q * /ready * present_stateSBV_2.Q
    + present_stateSBV_0.Q * /ready * present_stateSBV_2.Q
```

Addr required two macrocells in this and the previous implementation, and this design requires the same total number of macrocells as the previous. More product terms are required in this implementation because the next state must essentially be decoded twice. Because the addr outputs can propagate directly from the macrocells to the output pins, the clock-to-output delay will be 6.0 ns:

```
Worst-Case Path Summary
-----------------------
                tS = 5.0 ns for present_stateSBV_1.D
              tSCS = 7.0 ns for present_stateSBV_1.D
               tCO = 6.0 ns for addr_1.C
```

5.4.3   Outputs Encoded within State Bits

Another way to acquire the state machine outputs in t_{CO} is to use the state bits themselves as outputs. A counter is an example of a state machine for which the outputs are also the state bits. This method may work better than the previous one for some criteria, but it requires that you choose your state encoding carefully: The outputs must correspond to the values held by the state registers, as shown in Figure 5-10. This approach makes the design more difficult to comprehend and maintain, so it is recommended only for cases that require specific area and performance optimization not provided by the synthesis tool, automatically or through directives.

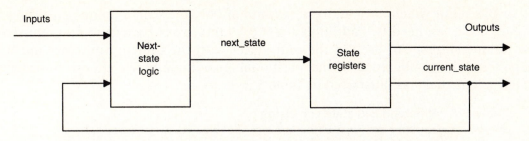

Figure 5-10   Moore machine with outputs encoded within state registers

We'll use the memory controller again to illustrate the concept of encoding the outputs within the state registers. With seven states in the machine, the fewest number of state bits we can use is three, but we may need additional bits to encode the outputs. We have two outputs, addr(1) and addr(0), that we would like to have propagated to the output pins in t_{CO} time, and another two that are not critical and can take t_{CO2} time. Altogether we need at most seven macrocells—three state bits, two registered outputs, and two combinatorial outputs. Our task now is to create a state encoding such that addr(1) and addr(0) are two of the state bits. To choose the encoding, we start by creating a table of the present state and outputs that we wish to encode. We use Table 5-1 as the starting point for our state encoding table.

Table 5-1   Outputs

State	addr(1)	addr(0)
idle	0	0
decision	0	0
read1	0	0
read2	0	1
read3	1	0
read4	1	1
write	0	0

Next, we examine the table, looking for the set of outputs that appears with the greatest frequency. Reading across the table, we see that the set of outputs 00 appears with the greatest frequency—four times. To create a state encoding table from here, we need to distinguish the state encodings for idle, decision, read1, and `write`, all of which have address outputs of 00. To create a unique encoding for each state, we need two additional bits (two bits are sufficient to distinguish four unique states). For each of the four states with the same outputs, we must assign a unique combination of the additional encoding bits. We choose to order the bits sequentially as illustrated in Table 5-2.

Table 5-2   Differentiated state encodings

State	addr(1)	addr(0)	st1	st0
idle	0	0	0	0
decision	0	0	0	1
read1	0	0	1	0
read2	0	1		
read3	1	0		
read4	1	1		
write	0	0	1	1

The remaining states have unique outputs, so we choose to fill in the encoding table with 00 for these entries, although any arbitrary pair of bits will do. Our final encoding scheme appears in Table 5-3.

Table 5-3   Completed state encodings

State	addr(1)	addr(0)	st1	st0
idle	0	0	0	0
decision	0	0	0	1
read1	0	0	1	0
read2	0	1	0	0
read3	1	0	0	0
read4	1	1	0	0
write	0	0	1	1

We now have a unique state encoding for each state. You can see that with this scheme we had to use more than the fewest possible number of state bits to encode seven states. But now two of the outputs, addr(1) and addr(0), are encoded in the state bits. If these had not been encoded (as in Figures 5-8 and 5-9), implementation of the design would require a total of seven macrocells: three for the state bits, two for the registered outputs addr(1) and addr(0), and two for the combinatorial outputs oe and we. Although in the new implementation we need to use more state bits, we need fewer total macrocells (six): four for the state encoding and addr outputs, and two for the oe and we outputs. This analysis assumes the design is implemented in a CPLD.

In an FPGA, the savings in logic resources is not as clear. Four registers and additional logic cells for the next-state logic, as well as the output logic for oe and we are required. Without determining the complexity of the next-state and output logic, we can only make educated guesses about the number of logic cells required. Thus, for an FPGA, there is no clear advantage to using this implementation over the previous one, in which the outputs are decoded in parallel output registers. The quickest way to find out is often to use software to synthesize the code and see first-hand what the setup, internal flip-flop to flip-flop, and clock-to-out delays are. Later in the chapter, we'll choose a method that will help us achieve an efficient implementation in an FPGA. In Chapter 8 we will also discuss how to use synthesis directives to tune an FPGA design. This state machine is small enough—it has few states, few inputs, and relatively simple transitions—that its implementation in an FPGA will not differ by much regardless of how it is described. For now, we'll proceed, assuming that we will target this design to a CPLD.

Because we're implementing this design in a CPLD, we will see if fewer total macrocells are required to encode all four state machine outputs in the state encoding. We start, as we did before, by creating Table 5-4 showing the present state and outputs.

Table 5-4   Outputs as a function of the present state

State	addr(1)	addr(0)	oe	we
idle	0	0	0	0
decision	0	0	0	0
read1	0	0	1	0
read2	0	1	1	0
read3	1	0	1	0
read4	1	1	1	0
write	0	0	0	1

Next, we examine the table, looking for the set of outputs that appears with the greatest frequency. If all outputs were unique, our state encoding would be complete. In this case, the set of outputs 0000 appears twice (once for `idle` and once for `decision`). We must distinguish between `idle` and `decision` by adding an additional bit (one bit is sufficient to distinguish two states). We arbitrarily choose 0 for `idle` and 1 for `decision`. Next we arbitrarily choose to fill the remaining entries in the table with 0. We could choose either 0 or 1 for any of these entries, because the state encoding would remain unique regardless of their values. The implications for choosing 0 or 1 are discussed at the end of the chapter. Our final state encoding appears in Table 5-5.

Table 5-5   Outputs encoded within the state bits

State	addr(1)	addr(0)	oe	we	st0
idle	0	0	0	0	0
decision	0	0	0	0	1
read1	0	0	1	0	0
read2	0	1	1	0	0
read3	1	0	1	0	0
read4	1	1	1	0	0
write	0	0	0	1	0

With five bits, the state registers are now able to hold all the outputs. This is a savings of one macrocell over the case in which only `addr(1)` and `addr(0)` are encoded, and a savings of two macrocells over the case in which the outputs are decoded either in parallel with or serially from the state bits. In general, macrocell savings depend upon the uniqueness of the state machine outputs on a state-by-state basis. Typically, the worst case will require that you use the same number of macrocells as when you're decoding the outputs in parallel registers. For state machines implemented in CPLDs, this technique will often produce the implementation that uses the fewest macrocells and achieves the best possible clock-to-out times.

We're now ready to design the state machine. Whereas earlier we simply indicated the states in an enumeration type, now we will have to explicitly declare the state encoding with constants. Listing 5-5 illustrates this point, in which `present_state` and `next_state` are declared as `std_logic_vectors`, rather than as the enumeration type `StateType`, and the state encoding is specified with constants. An explanation of the code follows the listing (the entity is the same and is not reprinted).

```vhdl
architecture state_machine of memory_controller is
-- state signal is a std_logic_vector rather than an enumeration type
    signal state    : std_logic_vector(4 downto 0);
    constant idle    : std_logic_vector(4 downto 0) := "00000";
    constant decision: std_logic_vector(4 downto 0) := "00001";
    constant read1   : std_logic_vector(4 downto 0) := "00100";
    constant read2   : std_logic_vector(4 downto 0) := "01100";
    constant read3   : std_logic_vector(4 downto 0) := "10100";
    constant read4   : std_logic_vector(4 downto 0) := "11100";
    constant write   : std_logic_vector(4 downto 0) := "00010";
begin
state_tr:process(reset, clk) begin
    if reset = '1' then
        state <= idle;
    elsif rising_edge(clk) then
        case state is                   -- outputs not defined here
            when idle    =>
                if (bus_id = "11110011") then
                    state <= decision;
                end if;                 -- no else; implicit memory
            when decision=>
                if (read_write = '1') then
                    state <= read1;
                else                    -- read_write='0'
                    state <= write;
                end if;
            when read1   =>
                if (ready = '0') then
                    state <= read1;
                elsif (burst = '0') then
                    state <= idle;
                else
                    state <= read2;
                end if;
            when read2   =>
                if (ready = '1') then
                    state <= read3;
                end if;                 -- no else; implicit memory
            when read3   =>
                if (ready = '1') then
                    state <= read4;
                end if;                 -- no else; implicit memory
```

```
        when read4    =>
            if (ready = '1') then
                state <= idle;
            end if;                        -- no else; implicit memory
        when write    =>
            if (ready = '1') then
                state <= idle;
            end if;                        -- no else; implicit memory
        when others =>
                state <= "-----";          -- don't care if undefined state
    end case;
  end if;
end process state_tr;

-- outputs associated with register values
  we  <= state(1);
  oe  <= state(2);
  addr <= state(4 downto 3);

end state_machine;
```

Listing 5-5 State machine with outputs encoded in state registers

This listing is a one-process FSM description, but it could just as easily have been written as a two-process FSM. One process is used to describe and synchronize the state transitions. This process, state_tr, is similar to that of Listing 5-3, but this time the case statement contains an additional branch: when others =>. This branch is required to cover all possible values of the state signal. Because state is a std_logic_vector of width 5, it has 9^5 (59,049) possible values. Most of these are metalogical and meaningless for synthesis; however, there are a total of 2^5 (32) possible binary values for state. Because there are only seven defined states, the other 25 binary values define illegal states, or states that we never expect the state machine to enter. (More about illegal states and fault tolerance later.) The reserved word others is used to cover all the combinations, binary or metalogical, not already listed in the case statement. The following code indicates that if the state machine enters an illegal state, we don't care where it transitions to. This will reduce the state transition logic.

```
    when others => state <= state "-----";
```

Because the state encoding was explicitly declared and was chosen to contain present state outputs, the outputs can be assigned directly from the `state` signal as follows:

```
-- outputs associated with register values
  we <= state(1);
  oe <= state(2);
  addr <= state(4 downto 3);
```

Accessing the outputs in this way (that is, directly from the state flip-flops) means that they will be available t_{CO} after the rising edge of the clock, instead of propagating through the programmable interconnect and product-term array and coming out in t_{CO2}, as was the case with the original implementation.

Synthesis Results. This new implementation ensures that no extra pass is needed to decode several state bits in generating the state machine outputs. Consequently, the outputs are available at the device pins sooner. In addition, this method typically requires fewer macrocells than does decoding the outputs in parallel output registers. Equations produced from synthesis are below. Only five equations are required, because none of the outputs need to be decoded. State bit names are replaced by the names of the outputs. A T-type flip-flop was selected as optimal for the `addr_1` equation because the CY7C371 macrocell can be configured for T-type flip-flop operation and this implementation will require the fewest product terms. This implementation requires considerably fewer product terms than the previous implementations, but that will not always be the case.

```
DESIGN EQUATIONS
   addr_1.T =
         ready * addr_0.Q

   addr_0.D =
         oe.Q * ready * /addr_0.Q * burst
      + ready * addr_1.Q * /addr_0.Q
      + /ready * addr_0.Q

   oe.D =
         oe.Q * /addr_0.Q * burst
      + state_0.Q * read_write
      + /addr_1.Q * addr_0.Q
      + oe.Q * /ready
      + addr_1.Q * /addr_0.Q
```

```
we.D =
      we.Q * /ready
    + state_0.Q * /read_write

state_0.D =
      /oe.Q * /state_0.Q * /we.Q * bus_id_7 * bus_id_6 * bus_id_5 *
      bus_id_4 * /bus_id_3 * /bus_id_2 * bus_id_1 * bus_id_0
```

Because the outputs propagate directly from the macrocells to the I/O pins, the timing t_{CO} is 6 ns.

```
Worst-Case Path Summary
-----------------------
                tS = 5.0 ns for oe.D
              tSCS = 7.0 ns for oe.D
               tCO = 6.0 ns for oe.C
```

We've spent considerable time explaining this design technique and its benefits, so we'll reiterate its drawbacks:

- Time and effort are required to choose a state encoding that maps well to the state machine's outputs.
- The code becomes more difficult to read due to the outputs being decoded from the state bits. This can increase debugging time and make it difficult to maintain the code.

Some synthesis optimization may already allow you to use the code of Listing 5-2 to achieve this implementation. If you are using a tool that does not presently do this type of optimization, you will have to decide when using this coding technique is appropriate. Next we discuss an implementation technique that is often used in FPGA designs.

State Encoding for Reduced Logic.   Earlier, we explained how to encode state machine outputs within state registers. In Table 5-6, we reprint the partially completed state encoding table for one of the examples.

In explaining how to choose the state encoding, we arbitrarily chose to complete the table by filling in the empty entries with 0. This encoding may not be optimal; another encoding may require fewer device resources. Choosing 0s may be adequate; at other times, you may need to experiment with the state encoding or use software that determines the optimal encoding for minimal logic (choosing an optimal state encoding is a not a trivial task). Some VHDL synthesis tools perform this function.

Table 5-6   Choosing an encoding for reduced logic

state	addr(1)	addr(0)	st1	st0
s0	0	0	0	0
s1	0	0	0	1
s2	0	0	1	0
s3	0	1		
s4	1	0		
s5	1	1		
s6	0	0	1	1

5.4.4   One-Hot Encoding

One-hot encoding is a technique that uses n flip-flops to represent a state machine with n states. Each state has its own flip-flop, and only one flip-flop is "hot" (holds a 1) at any given time. Decoding the current state is as simple as finding the flip-flop containing a 1. Changing states is as simple as changing the contents of the flip-flop for the new state from 0 to 1 and the flip-flop for the old state from 1 to 0.

The primary advantage of one-hot-encoded state machines is that the number of gates required to decode state information for outputs and for next-state transitions is usually much less than the number of gates required for those purposes when the states are encoded in other ways. This difference in complexity becomes more apparent as the number of states becomes larger. To understand this point, consider a state machine with 18 states that are encoded with two methods, sequential and one-hot, as shown in Table 5-7.

Eighteen flip-flops are required for one-hot encoding, whereas only five are required for the sequential encoding. With one-hot, only one flip-flop is asserted at a time. To continue our example, suppose that Figure 5-11 represents a portion of the state flow diagram that depicts all possible transitions to state 15.

Table 5-7   Sequential versus 1-hot encoding

State	Sequential	One-Hot
state0	00000	00000000000000001
state1	00001	00000000000000010
state2	00010	00000000000000100
state3	00011	00000000000001000
state4	00100	00000000000010000
state5	00101	00000000000100000
state6	00110	00000000001000000
state7	00111	00000000010000000
state8	01000	00000000100000000
state9	01001	00000001000000000
state10	01010	00000010000000000
state11	01011	00000100000000000
state12	01100	00001000000000000
state13	01101	00010000000000000
state14	01110	00100000000000000
state15	01111	00100000000000000
state16	10000	01000000000000000
state17	10001	10000000000000000

The code fragment that represents this state flow is:

```
case current_state is
    when state2 =>
        if cond1 = '1' then next_state <= state15;
        else ...

    when state15 =>
        if ...
        elsif cond3 = '0' then next_state <= state15;
        else ...
```

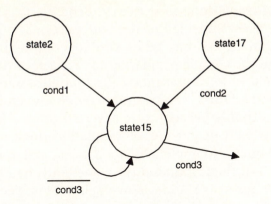

Figure 5-11   State flow diagram

```
when state17 =>
   if ...
   elsif cond2 = '1' then next_state <= state15;
   else ...
```

The if-then statements would be completed, of course, to specify the state transitions for conditions not shown in the diagram, but the code is suitable for our purpose of differentiating sequential and one-hot coding effects on state-transition logic.

We examine the next-state logic for sequential encoding first. We will call the sequential state vector s, which is five bits wide. The sequential encoding for state15 is 01111, or

$$s_4 s_3 s_2 s_1 s_0$$

Using the state flow diagram of Figure 5-11, we can write for each of the five bits of the vector s an equation that represents the conditions that cause that bit to be asserted due to a transition to state15:

$$
\begin{aligned}
s_{i,\,15} \;=\; & \overline{s_4} \cdot \overline{s_3} \cdot \overline{s_2} \cdot s_1 \cdot \overline{s_0} \cdot \text{cond1} \\
+\; & s_4 \cdot \overline{s_3} \cdot \overline{s_2} \cdot \overline{s_1} \cdot s_0 \cdot \text{cond2} \\
+\; & \overline{s_4} \cdot s_3 \cdot s_2 \cdot s_1 \cdot s_0 \cdot \overline{\text{cond3}}
\end{aligned}
$$

where $0 \le i \le 4$, s_i represents one of the 5-bits of vector s, and $s_{i,15}$ represents the equations that cause s_i to be asserted due to transitions to state15. The expression equated with s_4 is 0, because transitions to state15 do not cause this most significant bit to be asserted.

Although this equation defines s_i for transitions to state15, it is not sufficient to specify s_0, s_1, s_2, and s_3. For example, the equation for $s_{0,15}$ covers only the cases in which s_0 is asserted due to transitions to state15. The bit s_0 is also asserted due to transitions to eight other states (all of the odd states). The logic equations associated with these transitions may be of similar complexity to the equation for $s_{0,15}$ above. To obtain the complete equation for s_i, each of the $s_{i,x}$ equations (where x is an integer from 0 to 17, representing the 18 states) must be summed. As you might imagine, the logic for s_0 can be quite complex, even for a relatively simple state flow diagram, simply because s_0 is asserted for a total of nine states. The sequential encoding will create five complex equations for s_i.

Compare the amount of logic required to implement s_0, s_1, s_2, s_3, and s_4 for a sequentially encoded state machine to the logic required for a one-hot coded state machine, for which the decoding logic for state 15 is shown below. State vector t is used for one-hot encoding so as not to confuse the equation with that of s above. The vector t is 15 bits wide.

$$t_{15} = t_2 \cdot \text{cond1} + t_{17} \cdot \text{cond2} + t_{15} \cdot \overline{\text{cond3}}$$

The equation for t_{15} can easily be derived from the state flow diagram. Figure 5-12 shows the logic implementation for transitions to state15. Whereas the sequential encoding requires five complex equations for the next-state logic, the one-hot encoding requires 18 simple equations. Depending on the target logic device architecture, a one-hot coded state machine may require significantly fewer device resources for implementation of the design. Simple next-state logic may also require fewer levels of logic between the state registers, allowing for higher frequency of operation.

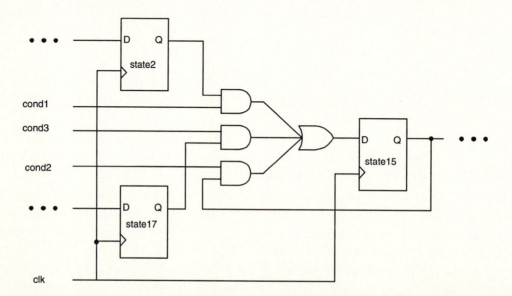

Figure 5-12   State transition logic for one-hot coded state machines is simple

One-hot encoding is not always the best solution, however, mainly because it requires more flip-flops than a sequentially encoded state machine. In general, one-hot encoding is most useful when the architecture of the programmable logic device you want to use has relatively many registers and relatively little combinational logic between each register. For example, one-hot encoding is most useful for state machines implemented in FPGAs, which generally have much higher flip-flop densities than CPLDs but fewer gates per flip-flop. One-hot encoding may be the best choice even for CPLDs when the number of states and input conditions are such that the next-state logic for an encoded machine requires multiple passes through the logic array.

Up to now, we have discussed only what one-hot encoding is and the motivation for using it, but not how to code one-hot state machines. Fortunately, using one-hot encoding requires little or no change to the source code, but depends on the synthesis software tool you are using. Many synthesis tools allow you to use a synthesis directive to one-hot encode a state machine. These synthesis directives may be in the form of VHDL attributes, command-line switches, or GUI options. VHDL allows user- or vendor-defined attributes to be applied to objects in order to convey user- or vendor-defined information about that object. With Warp, the state encoding synthesis directive is applied with a vendor-defined attribute, called `state_encoding`, applied to the enumeration type:

```
type StateType is (idle, decision, read1, read2, read3,
                    read4, write);
attribute state_encoding of StateType:type is one_hot_one;
signal current_state, next_state : StateType;
```

The remaining code is left unchanged.

Generating outputs for one-hot encoded state machines is similar to generating outputs for machines in which the outputs are decoded from the state registers. The decoding is quite simple, of course, because the states are just single bits, not an entire vector. The output logic consists of an OR gate because Moore machines have outputs that are functions of the state, and all states in a one-hot coded state machine are represented by one bit. The output decoding adds a level of combinational logic and the associated delay, just as it did before when the state bits were encoded. In an FPGA, the delay associated with the OR gate is typically acceptable and is an improvement upon decoding the outputs from an entire state vector. In a CPLD, the OR gate requires a second pass through the logic array, which means that the outputs will be available in t_{CO2} time. The outputs can also be generated using parallel decoding registers, as was described earlier. This will eliminate the level of combinational logic and associated delay.

If any outputs are asserted in one state only, they are automatically encoded within the state bits. For example, we (write enable) is asserted only during the state write:

```
we <= '1' when present_state = write else '0';
```

There is a flip-flop directly associated with write, so we will be the value of that flip-flop. Consequently, it will be available at the device pins or for internal logic without the additional delay associated with decoding.

Breakout Exercise 5-2

Purpose: To illustrate the advantage of one-hot encoding large state machines implemented in FPGA architectures.

1. Compile and synthesize the design c:\vhdlbook\ch5\onehot.vhd. Place and route the design. Record the number of logic cells required, the setup time, clock-to-output delay, and maximum operating frequency.

2. Now, edit the file onehot.vhd. Insert the "--" characters in front of the attribute to make this line of code a comment rather than a line processed by Warp. Compile, synthesize, place, and route the design. Record the number of logic cells required, the setup time, clock-to-output delay, and maximum operating frequency. Compare to the one-hot implementation.

5.5   Mealy State Machines

So far we have discussed only Moore machines in which the outputs are strictly functions of the current state. Mealy machines may have outputs that are functions of the present- state and present-input signals, as illustrated in Figure 5-13.

The additional work involved in describing Mealy machines versus Moore machines is minimal. To implement a Mealy machine, you simply have to describe an output as a function of both a state bit and an input. For example, if there is an

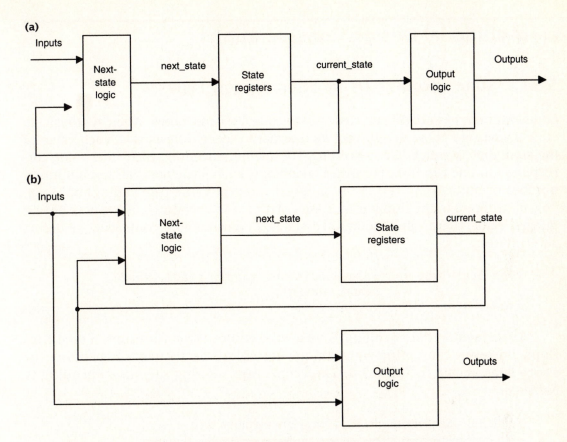

Figure 5-13   Difference between (a) Moore and (b) Mealy machines

additional input to the memory controller called `write_mask` that when asserted prevents we from being asserted, you can describe the logic for we as

```
if (current_state = s6) and (write_mask = '0') then
    we <= '1';
else
    we <= '0';
end if;
```

This makes we a Mealy output.

The design techniques used previously to ensure that the output is available in t_{CO} instead of t_{CO2} cannot be used with a Mealy machine because they are functions of the present inputs and the present state.

5.6   Additional Design Considerations

5.6.1   State Encoding Using Enumeration Types

Enumeration types provide an easy way to code state machines. When synthesized, state signals are converted to vectors internal to the synthesis tool. Each value of the state type is assigned an encoding. For one-hot encoding, each state value corresponds to one flip-flop. For other encodings, such as sequential, the minimum number of states required is the greatest integral value (the ceiling) of $\log_2 n$, $\lceil \log_2 n \rceil$, where n is the number of states. With these encodings, if $\log_2 n$ is not an integral value, there will be undefined states. In our memory controller, we define seven states:

```
type StateType is (idle, decision, read1, read2, read3,
                   read4, write);
signal state : StateType;
```

Using sequential encoding, state will require three flip-flops. Three flip-flops, however, can define eight unique states, so the sequential encoding for state is as shown in Table 5-8. The vector representing the state encoding is named q.

Table 5-8   Sequential encoding for an enumeration type

State	q_0	q_1	q_2
idle	0	0	0
decision	0	0	1
read1	0	1	0
read2	0	1	1
read3	1	0	0
read4	1	0	1
write	1	1	0
undefined	1	1	1

Implicit Don't Cares. For the examples in this chapter that make use of an enumeration type, synthesis assumes that the value 111 for q is a don't-care condition. No transitions into or out of this state are defined. If the state machine were ever to get into this undefined, or illegal, state, it would not function in a predictable manner. The behavior of the state machine, if placed in an illegal state, will depend on the state transition equations. The advantage in having transitions out of the illegal state as don't-care conditions is that additional logic is not required to ensure that the machine will transition out of this state. This additional logic can require substantial device resources for implementation, especially if there are many undefined states. The disadvantage of using these implied don't cares is that the state machine is less fault-tolerant. The designer should make a conscious decision about whether this is acceptable for a particular design.

Fault Tolerance: Getting Out of Illegal States. The state 111 is an illegal state for our memory controller, but in hardware, glitches, ground bounce, noise, power up, or illegal input combinations may cause one of the flip-flop values to change, causing the machine to enter an illegal state. If this happens, the state machine will not respond predictably, which may cause problems in your system. The machine may enter an illegal state and stay there permanently, or, among other possibilities, it may assert outputs that are illegal, or even harmful: Signals may cause bus-contention or may cause a device to sink or source too much current, thereby destroying it.

State machines can be made more fault-tolerant by adding code that ensures transitions out of illegal states:

- First, you will need to determine how many illegal states are possible—the number of illegal states is the number of states in the machine subtracted from the number of flip-flops used to encode the machine, raised to the power of two. For our memory controller, there is one undefined state.

- Next, you'll have to include a state name in the enumeration type for each undefined state. For example,

```
type StateType is (idle, decision, read1, read2, read3, read4,
                   write, undefined);
```

- Finally, a state transition must be specified for the state machine to transition out of this state. This can be specified as

```
case present_state is
    ...
        when undefined  => next_state <= idle;
end case;
```

This state transition will require additional logic resources. Compare the equations below to those produced by synthesizing Listing 5-2. These equations illustrate that more product terms are required.

```
DESIGN EQUATIONS
    present_stateSBV_0.D =
          /present_stateSBV_0.Q * /present_stateSBV_1.Q *
          present_stateSBV_2.Q * /read_write
        + /present_stateSBV_0.Q * present_stateSBV_1.Q *
          present_stateSBV_2.Q * ready
        + present_stateSBV_0.Q * /present_stateSBV_2.Q * /ready
        + present_stateSBV_0.Q * /present_stateSBV_1.Q * /ready
        + present_stateSBV_0.Q * /present_stateSBV_1.Q *
          /present_stateSBV_2.Q
    present_stateSBV_1.D =
          /present_stateSBV_0.Q * present_stateSBV_1.Q *
          /present_stateSBV_2.Q * burst
        + /present_stateSBV_0.Q * present_stateSBV_2.Q * /ready
        + present_stateSBV_1.Q * /present_stateSBV_2.Q * /ready
        + /present_stateSBV_0.Q * /present_stateSBV_1.Q *
          present_stateSBV_2.Q
    present_stateSBV_2.D =
          /present_stateSBV_0.Q * /present_stateSBV_1.Q *
          /present_stateSBV_2.Q * bus_id_7 * bus_id_6 * bus_id_5 *
          bus_id_4 * /bus_id_3 * /bus_id_2 * bus_id_1 * bus_id_0
        + /present_stateSBV_0.Q * present_stateSBV_1.Q *
          /present_stateSBV_2.Q * ready * burst
        + present_stateSBV_0.Q * /present_stateSBV_1.Q *
          present_stateSBV_2.Q * /ready
        + /present_stateSBV_0.Q * present_stateSBV_1.Q *
          present_stateSBV_2.Q * /ready
        + present_stateSBV_0.Q * /present_stateSBV_1.Q *
          /present_stateSBV_2.Q * ready
```

If multiple states are left undefined, you can follow the same process, adding several undefined states to the enumeration type:

```
type states is (s0, s1, s2, s3, s4, u1, u2, u3);
signal next_state, present_state: states;
...
case present_state is
   ...
   when others => next_state <= s0;
end case;
```

In this example, there are three undefined states (designated as u1, u2, and u3). Rather than specifying all three individual states, you may use when others to specify to transition to the s0 state if the state machine enters any of the illegal states.

Rather than returning to an idle or arbitrary state, you may have illegal states transition to error states that handle faults.

To have direct control over the state encoding and the enumeration of undefined states, you can use constants to define the state, as shown in Listing 5-5 and described in the next section.

5.6.2   Explicit State Encoding: Don't Cares and Fault Tolerance

State machine designs with explicit state encoding, such as the one of Listing 5-5, in which constants are used to define states, must explicitly declare don't cares. The following state encoding defines seven states (however, state can have 32 unique binary values and numerous more metalogical values):

```
signal present_state, next_state : std_logic_vector(4 downto 0);
constant idle    : std_logic_vector(4 downto 0) := "00000";
constant decision: std_logic_vector(4 downto 0) := "00001";
constant read1   : std_logic_vector(4 downto 0) := "00100";
constant read2   : std_logic_vector(4 downto 0) := "01100";
constant read3   : std_logic_vector(4 downto 0) := "10100";
constant read4   : std_logic_vector(4 downto 0) := "11100";
constant write   : std_logic_vector(4 downto 0) := "00010";
```

To create a more fault-tolerant state machine, specify a state transition for the other 25 unique states:

```
when others => next_state <= idle;
```

Explicit Don't Cares. In specifying that illegal states will transition to a known state, additional logic is required. However, the cost of the solution may not be worth the need for fault tolerance. In this case, rather than specifying that all other states should transition to a known state, explicitly declare that the state transition is a don't-care condition (that is, you don't care what state it transitions to because you don't expect the state machine to ever get in that state, and are not designing the state machine to be fault-tolerant). You can define the don't-care conditions for explicit encoding as:

```
when others => next_state <= "-----";
```

Five don't-care values are assigned to the signal `state`, which is a `std_logic_vector(4 downto 0)`. Whereas don't-care conditions are implicit in state machine designs that use enumeration types that don't specify all possible combinations of values, the don't cares must be explicitly defined for state machines designed with explicit state encoding. Using constants allows you to explicitly define both the don't-care conditions and the transitions from illegal states.

5.6.3   Fault Tolerance for One-Hot Machines

The potential for entering illegal states is magnified when you use outputs encoded within state bits or one-hot encoding. Both of these techniques can result in many more illegal, or undefined, states. With one-hot encoding, for example, there are 2^n possible values for the n-bit state vector. The state machine has only n states. Here we have a dilemma: One-hot encoding is usually chosen to achieve an efficient state machine implementation, but including logic that causes all of the illegal states to transition to a reset or other known state creates an inefficient implementation. To completely specify state transitions for a one-hot coded state machine that has 18 states, another 262,126 (2^{18}–18) transitions would have to be decoded. This is an enormous amount of logic. Alternatively, rather than adding logic to transition out of all possible states, you can include logic that detects more than one flip-flop being asserted at a time.

A collision signal can be generated to detect multiple flip-flops asserted at the same time. For eight states, the collision signal is as below. The same technique can be extended for any number of states. The states below are enumerated as `state1`, `state2`, and so forth:

```
colin           <= (state1 and (state2 or state3 or state4 or
                   state5 or state6 or state7 or state8)) or

                   (state2 and (state1 or state3 or state4 or
                   state5 or state6 or state7 or state8)) or

                   (state3 and (state1 or state2 or state4 or
                   state5 or state6 or state7 or state8)) or

                   (state4 and (state1 or state2 or state3 or
                   state5 or state6 or state7 or state8)) or

                   (state5 and (state1 or state2 or state3 or
                   state4 or state6 or state7 or state8)) or
```

```
(state6 and (state1 or state2 or state3 or
    state4 or state5 or state7 or state8)) or

(state7 and (state1 or state2 or state3 or
    state4 or state5 or state6 or state8)) or

(state8 and (state1 or state2 or state3 or
    state4 or state5 or state6 or state7)) ;
```

It may not be necessary for the collision signal to be decoded in one clock cycle, in which case you may want to pipeline such a signal. Pipelining is described in Chapter 9.

Entering an illegal state is usually a catastrophic fault in that it may require the system to be reset. Depending on the system requirements, it may not be necessary to reset the machine in one clock cycle, in which case the collision signal can be pipelined, if necessary, to maintain the maximum operating frequency. In all cases, you need to make a conscious design decision regarding fault tolerance. For one-hot encoding, fault tolerance is at odds with performance and resource utilization. You must decide how much speed or area (device resources) you can give up to make your design more fault tolerant, and if you decide not to include logic for fault tolerance, then you must be aware of the ramifications.

5.6.4 Incompletely Specified IF-THEN-ELSE Statements

In this section, we reiterate a point made in the previous chapter about the use of if-then-else statements and implied memory. We have shown several methods for decoding state machine outputs. If-then-else statements may be used to decode state machine outputs or to create combinational logic in general. When using if-then-else statements, be careful to explicitly assign the value of signals for all conditions. Leaving ambiguities implies memory: If you do not specify a signal assignment, then you imply that the signal is to retain its value. For example, consider the following, syntactically correct, code:

```
if (present_state = s0) then
    output_a <= '1';
elsif (present_state = s1) then
    output_b <= '1';
else       -- current_state = s3
    output_c <= '1';
end if;
```

This is how you may mistakenly write code if you intend output_a to be asserted only in state *s0*, output_b to be asserted only in state *s1*, and output_c to be asserted only in state *s2*. What this code really implies is that output_a is assigned 1 in state *s0*, and *it keeps whatever value it currently has in every other state*. Figure 5-14 shows a logic implementation for this code. The logic shows that after present_state becomes *s0* once, the value of output_a is always a 1.

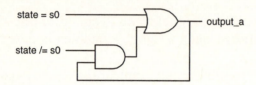

Figure 5-14   Implied memory

To avoid having a latch synthesized for output_a, output_b, and output_c, the above code should be rewritten, initializing the signals at the beginning of the process, as follows:

```
output_a <= '0';
output_b <= '0';
output_c <= '0';
if (current_state = s0) then
    output_a <= '1';
elsif (current_state = s1) then
    output_b <= '1';
else        -- current_state = s3
    output_c <= '1';
end if;
```

This will guarantee that the logic implementing these outputs is strictly a combinatorial decode of the state bits.

5.7   Summary

Writing VHDL code to implement a functionally accurate state machine can be simple. You can translate a state flow diagram using case-when and if-then-else statements. Often, your initial design will satisfy all of your requirements (time-to-market, performance, and cost). If the performance or cost requirements are not immediately met, you can quickly modify your design to meet the timing requirements and to fit most efficiently into the target architecture.

Some of the techniques that we discussed in this chapter include:

- decoding state machine outputs combinatorially from state registers,
- decoding state machine outputs in parallel output registers,
- encoding state machine outputs in the state registers,
- encoding state machines as one-hot, and
- designing fault-tolerant state machines.

You are now aware of multiple coding styles, state encoding schemes, and design trade-offs, which will enable you to more quickly arrive at the optimal solution for your designs.

Problems

5.1. Design a state machine that detects, starting with the left-most bit, the sequence "1110101101".

a. Draw the state flow diagram.

b. Code the design as a two-process FSM using an enumeration type to define the states.

c. Compile and synthesize the design, targeting a CY7C371. Simulate the design.

5.2. Use a synthesis directive to force a one-hot implementation of the state machine in Problem 5.1.

a. Implement the design in an FPGA and a CPLD.
b. Compare the performance and resource utilization for each device.

5.3. Design the state machine of Figure 5-15. Compile and synthesize the design, targeting a CY7C371.

a. Use an enumeration type to define the states.

b. Use constants to define the states so that the outputs can be encoded within the state bits in order to minimize the clock-to-output delays.

c. Compare the resource utilization and performance of implementations (a) and (b).

(a)

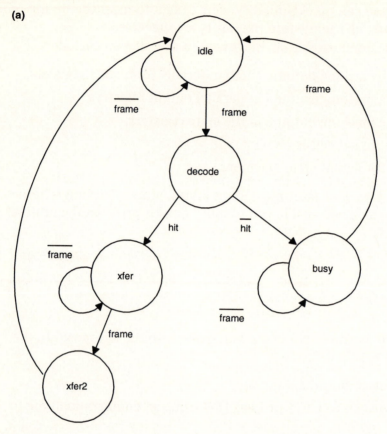

(b)

state	OE	GO	ACT
idle	0	0	0
decode	0	0	0
busy	0	0	1
xfer	1	1	1
xfer2	1	0	1

Figure 5-15   (a) State flow diagram and (b) state output table

5.4. The encoding for states read2 through read4 in Listing 5-5 is such that the two least significant bits are arbitrarily "00". Implement the design of Listing 5-5 with two different encodings for states read2 through read5, and compare resource utilization.

5.5. Rewrite the code for the memory controller shown in Figure 5-6 to handle the synchronous reset in each state transition. Compare the merits and demerits of using this modified version instead of the original version, which used an asynchronous reset signal. You may want to synthesize the design to compare the differences.

5.6. Build a 16-state counter using a state machine, not the + operator. Implement the design in a CY7C371. Compare one-hot encoding with sequential encoding, which is the default encoding used for states defined with an enumeration type. Draw the schematics for each, and compare to a shift register.

5.7. Give a specific example of where one-hot-zero encoding provides an advantage over one-hot-one.

5.8. Improve the fault tolerance of the design in Breakout Exercise 5-2. Add logic to detect whether more than one state is active at a time. Detection may span multiple clock cycles. Use this signal, after synchronizing it, to assert the asynchronous reset of all state flip-flops. Why should this signal be synchronized before it is used as a reset? What are the implications of allowing the detection to span multiple clock cycles?

5.9. Extend the collision detector shown on page 286 to include all 18 states. Rewrite the code using a for-generate or for-loop statement. You will need to change individual std_logics to std_logic_vectors. For example, colin1 will become colin(1).

Chapter 6

Hierarchy in Large Designs

6.1   Introduction

In the last three chapters, we covered entities, architectures, three basic coding styles, many VHDL language constructs, differences in how these constructs are synthesized, and several design topics including counters, bidirectional signals, multiplexers, decoders, and state machines. In this chapter we use two case studies to illustrate effective use of hierarchy in large designs. In the first we use VHDL to design the AM2901 4-bit microprocessor slice. Although it is not cost-efficient to implement a design for which there is already an off-the-shelf ASIC, the AM2901 serves as an excellent framework for a discussion of design decomposition, the importance of design hierarchy, reusable libraries, packages, and parameterized components. Breaking a design into manageable units creates **hierarchy.** The advantages of hierarchy are that it allows you to

- define the details of one portion of the design at a time (preferably in parallel with other engineers),
- focus on a manageable portion of a system, leading to fewer initial errors and quicker debugging time,
- verify each component individually (if a VHDL simulator is available), and
- build the design in stages, interfacing the constituent components one at a time.

In the second case study we use VHDL to design the core logic of a 100BASE-T4 network repeater, which shows the complexity of designs that VHDL synthesis tools are intended to handle, and programmable logic devices are intended to implement.

These case studies illustrate how programmable logic and VHDL can be used for **proof-of-concept**—the rapid prototyping that demonstrates the viability of a design. Programmable logic and VHDL also combine to provide excellent time-to-market and low initial cost. Time-to-market in the competitive electronics industry can often mean the difference between success and failure. If a product is clearly successful, then production volumes may warrant converting the design from a PLD to an ASIC, in which case the same VHDL code can be used.

6.2   Case Study: The AM2901

The AM2901 is a 4-bit microprocessor slice. Its full data-sheet description is readily available from Advanced Micro Devices datasheets. We have decomposed its architecture into the block diagram shown in Figure 6-1. The functional units, or components, are:

- RAM_REGS. This is the two-address RAM array used to read and write data. Taking the liberty to modify the design, we implement this RAM with a register file made of flip-flops. FPGA architectures that contain on-board RAM may be able to implement the register file using less area. However, using RAM may require that a vendor-specific RAM component be instantiated into the design, which may render the design nonportable across VHDL simulation and synthesis tools unless there is a synthesizable, behavioral VHDL model that accompanies the component. A shifter is used to load f, f/2, or f*2 into the ram array; ram0 and ram3 are bidirectional signals used for the shift-in and shift-out values. This shifter is also built into the RAM_REGS component.

- Q_REG. This is a one-word register used primarily for shifting in multiplication and division procedures, or as an accumulator. A shifter is used to load f, f/2, or f*2 into the Q register; qs0 and qs3 are bidirectional signals used for the shift-in and shift-out values. This shifter is built into the Q_REG component.

- SRC_OP. This design unit defines the source operand multiplexers.

- ALU. This design unit defines the arithmetic logic unit (ALU). It performs three arithmetic operations and five logic functions of two operands.

- OUT_MUX. The output multiplexer selects between the ALU output and the ad data word of the register array.

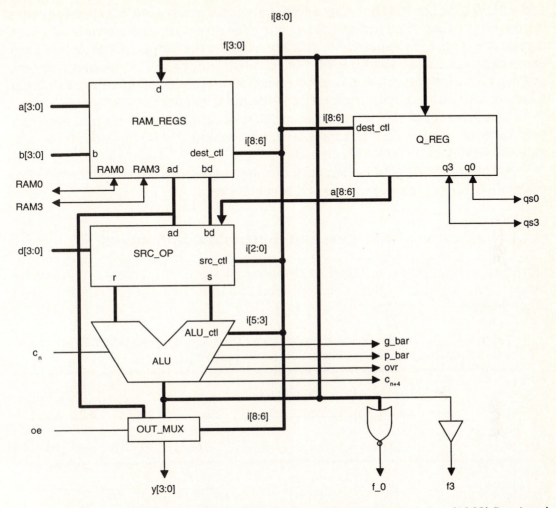

Figure 6-1 AM2901 block diagram [© Advanced Micro Devices, Inc. (1983) Reprinted with permission of copyright owner. All rights reserved.]

The a and b 4-bit addresses are used to address the 16-word register file. These addresses determine which words ad and bd are read from the register file. When the register file is enabled, the b address also indicates which address location is written to. Signals r and s are 4-bit words that are inputs, along with the carry-in, c_in, to the ALU. The multiplexers for the source operands to the ALU select from signals ad, bd, d, q, and logical 0. Signal d is a direct input to the r source operand multiplexer. Signal q represents the contents of Q_REG, and feeds the s source operand multiplexer. Signals ad and f feed the output multiplexer that has three-state enable. Signal f is also fed back to the input of both Q_REG and RAM_REGS. The ALU has four additional outputs: carry-out c_n4, carry-generate (inverted) g_bar, carry-propagate p_bar (also inverted), and overflow ovr. Two signals, f_0 and f_3, respectively, indicate whether the output of the ALU is zero and whether the most significant bit is asserted. Output f_0 is an open-collector output. These outputs allow you to determine if an arithmetic operation results in a zero or a negative number without enabling the three-state output of y.

The function of the microprocessor slice is defined by a 9-bit microinstruction. Three bits each define the source operands (Table 6-1), ALU function (Table 6-2), and ALU destination (Table 6-3, on page 298).

Before proceeding to design each of the components, we introduce the concepts of libraries, packages, and reusable components.

6.2.1   Libraries, Packages, and Reusable Components

Libraries and packages are used to declare and store components, type declarations, functions, procedures, and so forth, so that they can be reused later in other designs.

Table 6-1   ALU source operand [© Advanced Micro Devices, Inc. (1983) Reprinted with permission of copyright owner. All rights reserved.]

Mnemonic	Microcode				ALU source operands	
	I_2	I_1	I_0	Octal code	R	S
AQ	0	0	0	0	A	Q
AB	0	0	1	1	A	B
ZQ	0	1	0	2	O	Q
ZB	0	1	1	3	O	B
ZA	1	0	0	4	O	A
DA	1	0	1	5	D	A
DQ	1	1	0	6	D	Q
DZ	1	1	1	7	D	O

Table 6-2   ALU function [© Advanced Micro Devices, Inc. (1983)
Reprinted with permission of copyright owner. All rights reserved.]

Mnemonic	Microcode				ALU function
	I_5	I_4	I_3	Octal code	
ADD	0	0	0	0	R + S
SUBR	0	0	1	1	S - R
SUBS	0	1	0	2	R - S
OR	0	1	1	3	R OR S
AND	1	0	0	4	R AND S
NOTRS	1	0	1	5	(NOT R) AND S
EXOR	1	1	0	6	R XOR S
EXNOR	1	1	1	7	R XNOR S

Libraries. A library is a place—call it a directory for now—to which design units may be compiled. For example, entity declaration and architecture body pairs may be compiled to a library. The compiled format may be an internal vendor-specific format of the design unit. Design units (entities, for example) within a library may be used within other entities, provided that the library and design unit are visible. Multiple design units can be placed in a file; however, we typically place no more than an entity declaration and an architecture body in one file. Keeping separate design units in separate files may help for organizational purposes.

We have already been using two libraries in our designs to this point: the `ieee` and `work` libraries. Both are predefined. The `ieee` library is a storage place for IEEE standard design units (above and beyond those defined for IEEE standard 1076) such as the packages `std_logic_1164`, `numeric_std`, and `numeric_bit`. In order to use design units from a package, the library must be made visible by way of a `library` clause, as in

library `ieee;`

This clause makes the library accessible. It does not, however, allow you to immediately begin to use design units or items within that library. You must first make those components, packages, declarations, functions, procedures, and so forth visible via a `use` clause. The name of a library is not necessarily the name of a directory. For example, `ieee` does not necessarily represent a directory in your home or root directory. Rather, it is a logical name for a storage place (usually a

Table 6-3 ALU destination [© Advanced Micro Devices, Inc. (1983) Reprinted with permission of copyright owner. All rights reserved.]

Mnemonic	Microcode				RAM function		Q-REG function		Y Output	RAM shifter		Q shifter	
	I_8	I_7	I_6	Octal code	Shift	Load	Shift	Load		RAM_0	RAM_3	Q_0	Q_3
QREG	0	0	0	0	X	NONE	NONE	F->Q	F	X	X	X	X
NOP	0	0	1	1	X	NONE	X	NONE	F	X	X	X	X
RAMA	0	1	0	2	NONE	F->B	X	NONE	A	X	X	X	X
RAMF	0	1	1	3	NONE	F->B	X	NONE	F	X	X	X	X
RAMQD	1	0	0	4	DOWN	F/2->B	DOWN	Q/2 ->Q	F	F_0	IN_3	Q_0	IN_3
RAMD	1	0	1	5	DOWN	F/2->B	X	NONE	F	F_0	IN_3	Q_0	X
RAMQU	1	1	0	6	UP	2F->B	UP	2Q->Q	F	IN_0	F_3	IN_0	Q_3
RAMU	1	1	1	7	UP	2F->B	X	NONE	F	IN_0	F_3	X	Q_3

X = Don't care.
B = Register addressed by B inputs.
UP is toward MSB, DOWN is toward LSB.

directory) where the synthesis or simulation tool stores the ieee standard design units (in ASCII or a VHDL internal format, VIF). For example, Warp stores the ieee library design units in a subdirectory of the Warp install directory named lib\ieee.

The work library is a storage place for the designs you are currently working with, and it is the default place to which a VHDL processing tool compiles design units. The work, or working, library is a place in which to compile designs while they are in development. After verifying the accuracy of a design unit that is currently in the work library and that you wish to reuse in subsequent designs or as part of a team project, you may want to compile the design into an appropriate library. When teams work on large designs, they may have golden libraries in which to compile, or check-in, finished work, and individuals may keep their own working libraries. The work library is implicitly visible in *all* designs, so you are never required to use a library clause to make the work library visible.

Packages. A **package** is a design unit that can be used to make its type, component, function, and other declarations visible to design units other than itself. This is in contrast to an architecture declarative region, for which its type, component, function, and other declarations cannot be made visible to other design units.

A package consists of a package declaration and, optionally, a package body. A **package declaration** is used to declare items such as types, components, functions, and procedures. A **package body** is where the functions and procedures in a package declaration are defined. A package body that does not declare any functions or procedures does not need an associated package body.

A package is made visible with a use clause of the form

```
use library_name.package_name.item;
```

If you wish all items in the package to be visible, you can use the reserved word all, as we have done in previous listings. Unless there were a specific item in a package that conflicted with the definition of an item in another package, it is unlikely that you would specify anything but all. Making all items visible should not increase synthesis compile times.

By this point it should be obvious that the package std_logic_1164 declares several types and defines several functions. Library and use clauses are necessary to make its declarations visible to other design units.

Warp automatically places several packages in every work library. These include std_arith and several vendor-specific packages. The packages are not physically visible in the directory, which is created every time a work library is set up; they are linked into the library as necessary. (The library name is symbolic only). Because these packages are automatically added to each work library, to make them visible to a design unit no separate `library` clause is required before a use clause (all that is needed, for example, is use `work.std_arith.all;`).

Components. Components are design entities that are used in other design entities. But before an entity can be used in another entity, it and its **component declaration** must be made visible. A component declaration defines an interface for instantiating a component. Component declarations permit top-down design. For example, each of the components in the AM2901 design could be declared in a package, and a separate design unit could then use the declarations of that package to define a netlist that connects the components together. A component declaration may be declared in a package, as explained above, or in an architecture declarative region. For organizational purposes, we make most of our component declarations in package declarations. An example of a component declaration for a design entity named `dflop` is shown in Listing 6-1.

```
library ieee;
use ieee.std_logic_1164.all;
package my_package is
    component dflop port (
        d, clk:   in std_logic;
        q:        out std_logic);
    end component;
end my_package;

library ieee;
use ieee.std_logic_1164.all;
entity dflop is port(
    d, clk:   in std_logic;
    q:        out std_logic);
end dflop;
architecture archdflop of dflop is
begin
    process
        wait until clk = '1';
            q <= d;
    end;
end;
```

Listing 6-1 Two primary design units in one file

The entity declaration, architecture body, and package declaration are all design units, but all are contained in one file, as is permitted. Because the entity declaration and package declaration are primary design units, they have separate library and use clauses. The library and use clauses at the top of Listing 6-1 make the contents of std_logic_1164 visible to my_package but not to dflop. The type std_logic must be made visible to both primary design units. The architecture body is a secondary design unit, so any declarations visible to the associated entity are also visible to it.

To use this component in another entity, the design entity and its component declaration must be made visible. Listing 6-2 is a design that simply instantiates two of these dflops in series, assuming that my_package and dflop have been compiled into the work library.

```
library ieee;
use ieee.std_logic_1164.all;
use work.my_package.all;
entity my_design is port(async, clock:   in std_logic;
                         filt:           out std_logic);
end my_design;
architecture my_design of my_design is
   signal tmp: std_logic;
begin
u1: port map (clk => clock, d => async, q => tmp);
u2: port map (tmp, clock, filt);
end my_design;
```

Listing 6-2 Component instantiation with required use clauses

U1 and u2 are instantiation labels. In the first instantiation, the => symbol is used in **named association** to map (associate) the **actuals** (the signals async, clock, and tmp, which carry the data in this entity) with the **locals** (the ports d, clk, and q, which define the component interface template). In the second instantiation, **positional association** is used to map tmp with d, clock with clk, and filt with q. In this case, each actual is associated with a local by way of its positions within the port map.

6.2.2   Building a Library of Components

We need to use several basic components in the AM2901 and network repeater core logic designs (more are required in the core logic design than the AM2901 design), so we start the design process by building a library of components. We call this library basic, and in it we place several packages. Each package contains a set of common component types, such as flip-flops, registers, counters, or synchronizers. Each class of components is defined for several widths. To define them this way we parameterize the components via generics.

Generics and Parameterized Components. We begin with the design of D-type flip-flops with asynchronous resets. We want to create flip-flops of multiple widths. We need a 1-bit-wide flip-flop, but we don't know what other widths we may need in these and future designs. This leads us to design **parameterized components,** for which the sizes (widths) and feature sets may be defined by values of the instantiation parameters.

The design of a parameterized component is similar to that of any other component, except that a parameter, or **generic,** may be used to define the size (and, optionally, the feature set) of the component. We could parameterize components by simply using unconstrained arrays for ports, but generics make the parameterization explicit. In Listing 6-3, we define two entities (entity declaration and architecture body pairs): a 1-bit D-type flip-flop with asynchronous reset, and an n-bit–wide (where n is defined by the generic size) bank of D-type flip-flops with common clock and asynchronous reset. We will explain how their component declarations are placed in packages and used by higher-level design units later in the chapter.

In order to facilitate **team design,** we use mode buffer with all ports that are outputs, even if we could get away with mode out. We do this because of the restriction on ports of mode buffer: If the port of a component is mode buffer and the actual associated with that port is itself a port, then that actual must also be of mode buffer. Another approach to outputs is to always use mode out and employ internal signals in cases where mode buffer would otherwise be required. Figure 6-2 illustrates these two approaches.

```
--        Set of D-Type Flip-Flops
--
--        sizes: (1, size)
--
--  clk     -- posedge clock input
--  reset   -- asynchronous reset
--  d       -- register input
--  q       -- register output
-----------------------------------------
library ieee;
use ieee.std_logic_1164.all;
entity rdff1 is port (
    clk, reset:  in std_logic;
    d:           in std_logic;
    q:           buffer std_logic);
end rdff1;
```

```
component and2 port(
   i,j: in std_logic;
     k: buffer std_logic);
end component;

component or2 port(
   i,j: in std_logic;
     k: buffer std_logic);
end component;
```

Standardizing on mode **buffer**

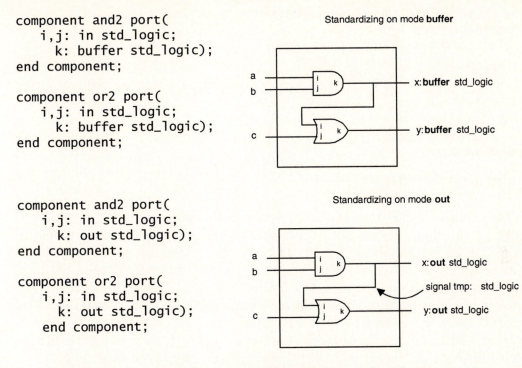

```
component and2 port(
   i,j: in std_logic;
     k: out std_logic);
end component;

component or2 port(
   i,j: in std_logic;
     k: out std_logic);
     end component;
```

Standardizing on mode **out**

Figure 6-2 Standardize on mode buffer or mode out for all outputs

```
architecture archrdff1 of rdff1 is
begin
p1: process (reset, clk) begin
     if reset = '1' then
         q <= '0';
     elsif (clk'event and clk='1') then
         q <= d;
     end if;
   end process;
end archrdff1;
----------------------------------------
library ieee;
use ieee.std_logic_1164.all;
entity rdff is
   generic (size: integer := 2);
   port ( clk, reset:in std_logic;
       d:                in std_logic_vector(size-1 downto 0);
       q:                buffer std_logic_vector(size-1 downto 0));
end rdff;
```

```vhdl
architecture archrdff of rdff is
begin
p1:     process (reset, clk) begin
            if reset = '1' then
                q <= (others => '0');
            elsif (clk'event and clk='1') then
                q <= d;
            end if;
        end process;
end archrdff;
```

Listing 6-3 Set of D-type flip-flops

These entity declaration and architecture body pairs are placed in the same design file, although they do not need to be. The generic `size` is given a default value of 2. If an instantiation of the `rdff` component does not specify a `generic map` (used to map an actual value to the generic of the component), then the component will have the default size of 2. `Size` is used to define the width of the `std_logic_vectors` for d and q. A separate component has been created for a 1-bit wide `rdff1`. This is not only because we will be using this width more frequently than other widths, but also because if `size` were equal to 1, we would need to pass in a one-element wide vector such as "0", a `std_logic_vector(0 downto 0)`.

We will also design a set of registers (made of D-type flip-flops) with synchronous enables and asynchronous resets. Again, we will need a 1-bit register but do not know what other widths will be required in these and future designs. The designs of two components, a 1-bit register and an *n*-bit register with common enable, are defined in Listing 6-4.

```vhdl
--      Set of registers
--      sizes: (1,size)
--
--      clk     -- posedge clock input
--      reset   -- asynchronous reset
--      load    -- active high input loads rregister
--      d       -- register input
--      q       -- register output
-------------------------------------------------------
library ieee;
use ieee.std_logic_1164.all;
entity rreg1 is port(
        clk, reset, load:   in std_logic;
        d:                  in std_logic;
        q:                  buffer std_logic);
end rreg1;
```

```
architecture archrreg1 of rreg1 is
begin
        p1: process (reset, clk) begin
                if reset = '1' then
                        q <= '0';
                elsif (clk'event and clk='1') then
                        if load = '1' then
                                q <= d;
                        end if;
                end if;
        end process;
end archrreg1;


--------------------------------------------------
library ieee;
use ieee.std_logic_1164.all;
entity rreg is
        generic (size: integer := 2);
        port (clk, reset, load: in std_logic;
                d:              in std_logic_vector(size-1 downto 0);
                q:              buffer std_logic_vector(size-1 downto 0));
end rreg;
architecture archrreg of rreg is
begin
        p1: process (reset,clk) begin
                if reset = '1' then
                        q <= (others => '0');
                elsif (clk'event and clk='1') then
                        if load = '1' then
                                q <= d;
                        end if;
                end if;
        end process;
end archrreg;
```

Listing 6-4 Set of registers with reset

Having designed both D-type flip-flops and registers with asynchronous reset, we would now like to create an "all-purpose" register with asynchronous reset and preset, as well as synchronous load. We create one parameterized component for this (Listing 6-5).

```
--          Register Set
--          sizes: (size) a generic
--
--          clk      -- posedge clock input
--          rst      -- asynchronous reset
--          pst      -- asynchronous preset
--          load     -- active high input loads register
--          d        -- register input
--          q        -- register output
-------------------------------------------------------
library ieee;
use ieee.std_logic_1164.all;
entity reg is generic ( size: integer := 2);
    port( clk, load:     in std_logic;
        rst, pst:        in std_logic;
        d:               in std_logic_vector(size-1 downto 0);
        q:               buffer std_logic_vector(size-1 downto 0));
end reg;
architecture archreg of reg is
begin
    p1: process (clk) begin
        if rst = '1' then
            q <= (others => '0');
        elsif pst = '1' then
            q <= (others => '1');
        elsif (clk'event and clk='1') then
            if load = '1' then
                q <= d;
            else
                q <= q;
            end if;
        end if;
    end process;
end archreg;
```

Listing 6-5 Set of all-purpose registers

When instantiating the component, size is used to indicate the width of the register. This component cannot be used with size equal to 1, because the code q <= (others => '1'), implies that q is an **aggregate,** or an array of more than one element. Normally the actuals associated with the locals will act as controls to the reset, preset, and load logic. Alternatively, the actuals associated with the locals can be signals that never change value so that features may be permanently enabled (such as the load) or disabled (such as the reset). For example, if the signals vdd and vss were permanently assigned the values '1' and '0', respectively, then synthesis of an instantiation of reg with the load permanently enabled and the preset permanently disabled (see below) would result in a register without unnecessary load and preset logic. The instantiation for this component is

```
u1: reg generic map(4) port map(myclk, vdd, reset, vss, data, mysig);
```

Synthesis of the following code will result in no logic at all:

```
u2: reg generic map(4) port map(myclk, vss, vss, vss, data, mysig);
```

In this instantiation, the load is permanently disabled. If the register never loads data, and is never set or preset, then it doesn't serve any purpose.

As noted earlier, the generic map is used to map an actual value to the generic of the component. The generic map may be omitted if a default value is specified in the generic declaration of the component definition. In this case the generic map specified the size of the register to be 4 bits wide.

Although the reg component is versatile, we will instantiate the other components in our design units where applicable. This will improve the readability of the code because it will keep the reader from having to look for the details of the generic and port maps.

Unconnected outputs—those outputs that are not needed—may be associated with the reserved word open. Assuming that the c_out port of the add component below represents the carry_out, then c_out can be associated with the reserved word open if this output is not needed:

```
u3: add port map (a => r; b => s; sum => f; c_out => open);
```

Results of synthesizing such a component yields an adder without the carry logic. Inputs may not be left open.

Next, we create a set of counters. The counters have asynchronous resets and synchronous initialization and enables. We do not create separate sets of counters without enables, resets, or both. If we require the use of such counters in a higher-level design unit, then we'll simply assign the port maps to enable or disable the functions as appropriate. The code for the counters is in Listing 6-6.

```
--      Synchronous Counter of Generic Size
--
--      CounterSize -- size of counter
--
--    clk     -- posedge clock input
--    areset -- asynchronous reset
--    sreset -- active high input resets counter to 0
--    enable -- active high input enables counting
--    count   -- counter output
------------------------------------------------
library ieee;
use ieee.std_logic_1164.all;
use work.std_arith.all;
entity ascount is
    generic (CounterSize: integer := 2);
    port(clk, areset, sreset, enable: in std_logic;
        count: buffer std_logic_vector(counterSize-1 downto 0));
end ascount;
architecture archascount of ascount is
begin
p1: process (areset, clk) begin
    if areset = '1' then
        count <= (others => '0');
    elsif (clk'event and clk='1') then
        if sreset='1' then
            count <= (others => '0');
        elsif enable = '1' then
            count <= count + 1;
        else
            count <= count;
        end if;
    end if;
  end process;
end archascount;
```

Listing 6-6 Set of counters

We now create two synchronization components (Listing 6-7), which consist of two D-type flip-flops in series. These components are used to synchronize an asynchronous inputs to the system clock. Two flip-flops are used to increase the MTBF for metastable events. One synchronizer component has an asynchronous reset; the other has an asynchronous preset.

```
--      Synchronizers
--
--
--      clk    -- posedge clock input
--      reset  -- asynchronous reset (rsynch)
--      preset -- asynchronous preset (psynch)
--      d      -- signal to synchronize
--      q      -- synchronized
-------------------------------------------------
library ieee;
use ieee.std_logic_1164.all;
entity rsynch is port (
    clk, reset:     in std_logic;
    d:              in std_logic;
    q:              buffer std_logic);
end rsynch;

architecture archrsynch of rsynch is
    signal temp: std_logic;
begin
p1:process (reset, clk) begin
      if reset = '1' then
         q <= '0';
      elsif (clk'event and clk='1') then
         temp <= d;
         q <= temp;
      end if;
   end process;
end archrsynch;


----------------------
library ieee;
use ieee.std_logic_1164.all;
entity psynch is port (
    clk, preset:    in std_logic;
    d:              in std_logic;
    q:              buffer std_logic);
end psynch;

architecture archpsynch of psynch is
  signal temp: std_logic;
begin
p1: process (preset, clk) begin
      if preset = '1' then
         q <= '1';
```

```
        elsif (clk'event and clk='1') then
            temp <= d;
            q <= temp;
        end if;
    end process;
end archpsynch;
```

Listing 6-7 Synchronizers

Because we have already defined the `rdff` component, the architecture for `rsynch` could be replaced by the following code, provided that the `rdff1` component is declared and visible to this architecture description:

```
u1: rdff1 port map(clk, preset, d, temp);
u2: rdff1 port map(clk, preset, temp, q);
```

This netlist description is succinct and may be easier to understand if you have a logic design background. However, it does create an additional level of hierarchy, and someone not familiar with the function of an `rdff1` component would need to find its description, which is likely in a different file.

So far, all of the components have ports of the types `std_logic` and `std_logic_vector`. Because we want to use the `numeric_std` package and the type `unsigned` in the AM2901 design, we create one last component:

```
--        Set of registers (unsigned)
--        sizes: (1,size)
--
--        clk      -- posedge clock input
--        reset    -- asynchronous reset
--        load     -- active high input loads rregister
--        d        -- register input
--        q        -- register output
-------------------------------------------------------
library ieee;
use ieee.std_logic_1164.all;
use work.numeric_std.all;
entity ureg is
        generic (size: integer := 2);
        port(clk, reset, load:in std_logic;
            d:                  in unsigned(size-1 downto 0);
            q:                  buffer unsigned(size-1 downto 0));
end ureg;
architecture archureg of ureg is
```

```
        begin
                p1: process (reset,clk) begin
                        if reset = '1' then
                                q <= (others => '0');
                        elsif (clk'event and clk='1') then
                                if load = '1' then
                                        q <= d;
                                else
                                        q <= q;
                                end if;
                        end if;
                end process;
        end archureg;
```

Listing 6-8 Parameterized registers for type unsigned

Now we are ready to group the component declarations for the design entities defined above into packages. We will then compile these packages into a library symbolically known as basic. We will create three packages: regs_pkg, counters_pkg, and synch_pkg. These packages are all contained in the same design file, but they don't have to be; we combine them here only to save space.

```
library ieee;
use ieee.std_logic_1164.all;
use work.numeric_std.all;
package regs_pkg is
    component rdff1 port (
        clk, reset: in std_logic;
        d:          in std_logic;
        q:          buffer std_logic);
    end component;
    component rdff
        generic (size: integer := 2);
        port (clk, reset: in std_logic;
            d:              in std_logic_vector(size-1 downto 0);
            q:              buffer std_logic_vector(size-1 downto 0));
    end component;
    component rreg1 port(
            clk, reset, load:in std_logic;
            d:                  in std_logic;
            q:                  buffer std_logic);
    end component;
```

```vhdl
    component rreg
      generic (size: integer := 2);
      port (clk, reset, load:in std_logic;
            d:                  in std_logic_vector(size-1 downto 0);
            q:                  buffer std_logic_vector(size-1 downto 0));
    end component;
    component reg generic ( size: integer := 2);
    port(  clk, load:  in std_logic;
       rst, pst:       in std_logic;
       d:              in std_logic_vector(size-1 downto 0);
       q:              buffer std_logic_vector(size-1 downto 0));
    end component;
    component ureg
        generic (size: integer := 2);
        port(   clk, reset, load:in std_logic;
            d:                  in unsigned(size-1 downto 0);
            q:                  buffer unsigned(size-1 downto 0));
    end component;
end regs_pkg;

library ieee;
use ieee.std_logic_1164.all;
package counters_pkg is
    component ascount
        generic (CounterSize: integer := 2);
        port(clk, areset, sreset, enable: in std_logic;
            count:    buffer std_logic_vector(counterSize-1 downto 0));
    end component;
end counters_pkg;

library ieee;
use ieee.std_logic_1164.all;
package synch_pkg is
    component port (
        clk, reset:     in std_logic;
        d:              in std_logic;
        q:              buffer std_logic);
    end component;
    component psynch port (
        clk, preset:    in std_logic;
        d:              in std_logic;
        q:              buffer std_logic);
    end component;
end synch_pkg;
```

Listing 6-9 Package declarations compiled into library basic

Once these packages are compiled into the basic library, we will be able to access them via library and use clauses. For example, to make the rreg1 component declaration visible (and the design entity to which it is bound by default) we could write:

```
library basic;              -- makes basic library accessible
use basic.regs_pkg.rreg1;   -- makes rreg1 component declaration visible
```

or

```
library basic;              -- makes all declarations in regs_pkg visible
use basic.regs_pkg.all;
```

Armed with a library of components, we are now ready to design each of the components in the AM2901.

Breakout Exercise 6-1

Purpose: To compile a package of commonly used components into a library called basic so that this library and its components can be reused in subsequent designs.

Refer to Chapter 4, "Galaxy," of the Warp on-line user's guide for more information on any of the instructions in this Breakout Exercise. Perform the following steps.

1. Create a project named c:\vhdlbook\ch6\basic\basic.

2. Select **Add** from the **Files** menu. Add all files to the project list. Examine the contents of each, but do not modify any of them.

3. Select **Libraries** from the **Files** menu. This opens Galaxy's library manager. No libraries have been created yet.

4. Select **Create Library** from the **File** menu of the library manager. In the dialog box, type basic. This will create a directory named basic in the current project directory. This is where design units that are compiled to the basic library will be stored.

5. Click on the **Done** button.

6. Choose **Select all** from the **Files** menu. Then, click on the **File** button in the **Synthesis options** panel. A window will appear. The file name in the title bar of this window will be one of the files in the project list. Make selections such that the Top Design for Chip box is not checked, the Other Destination

Library box is checked, and the library `basic` is selected. Click on **OK**. Another window, for the next file in the project list will appear. Make the above selections for each of the files in the list (Figure 6-3).

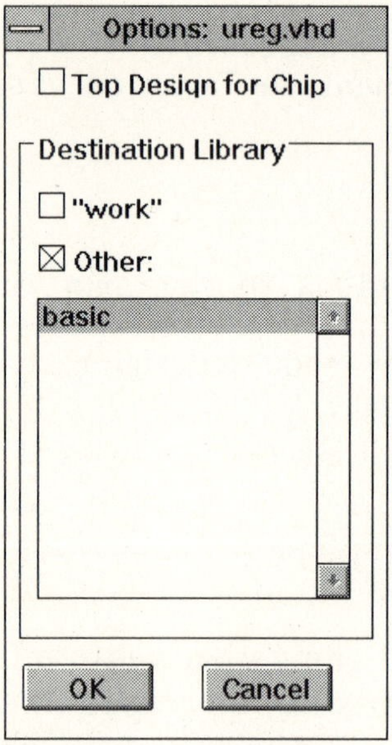

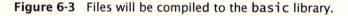

Figure 6-3   Files will be compiled to the `basic` library.

7. Select **Save** from the **File** menu to ensure that these settings are saved.

8. Click the **Smart** button to compile to each of the design units to the `basic` library.

9. Select **Libraries** from the **Files** menu. This opens Galaxy's library manager. Notice that several designs now exist in the `basic` library. Click once on each of several of the designs to see which design units they hold.

The `basic` library will be used in subsequent designs. Do not delete any files from this project or library.

6.2.3 Designing the AM2901 Components

Before defining the details of each of the functional units that make up this design, we first need to settle on the data types to be used. We will use `std_logic` for all control inputs and outputs. For the microinstruction i we will use a `std_logic_vector`. We will use the type `unsigned`, defined in `numeric_std`, for addresses and data. This includes internal data ad, bd, r, s, f, and q. We may have wished to use the type `signed`; however, in Release 4.0, Warp does not support arithmetic operator inferencing (module generation) for `signed` types. (Operator inferencing and module generation will be discussed in Chapter 7.) This will not prevent us from performing explicit signed arithmetic on an unsigned type, because the number representation of a binary integer and the operations performed on it can be independent.

Also, before we begin to design any of the components of the AM2901, we will create a package to be placed in the work library. This package will contain 24 constant declarations, one for each of the ALU source operand control mnemonics, ALU function control mnemonics, and ALU destination control mnemonics. When decoding the instructions, we will use the mnemonics rather than the equivalent binary in our VHDL code. The package `mnemonics` is shown below.

```vhdl
library ieee;
use ieee.std_logic_1164.all;
package mnemonics is
-- ALU source operand control mnemonics
    constant aq:  std_logic_vector(2 downto 0) := "000";
    constant ab:  std_logic_vector(2 downto 0) := "001";
    constant zq:  std_logic_vector(2 downto 0) := "010";
    constant zb:  std_logic_vector(2 downto 0) := "011";
    constant za:  std_logic_vector(2 downto 0) := "100";
    constant da:  std_logic_vector(2 downto 0) := "101";
    constant dq:  std_logic_vector(2 downto 0) := "110";
    constant dz:  std_logic_vector(2 downto 0) := "111";
-- ALU function control mnemonics
    constant add:  std_logic_vector(2 downto 0) := "000";
    constant subr: std_logic_vector(2 downto 0) := "001";
    constant subs: std_logic_vector(2 downto 0) := "010";
    constant orrs: std_logic_vector(2 downto 0) := "011";
    constant andrs:std_logic_vector(2 downto 0) := "100";
    constant notrs:std_logic_vector(2 downto 0) := "101";
    constant exor: std_logic_vector(2 downto 0) := "110";
    constant exnor:std_logic_vector(2 downto 0) := "111";
```

```
-- ALU destination control mnemonics
    constant qreg:   std_logic_vector(2 downto 0) := "000";
    constant nop:    std_logic_vector(2 downto 0) := "001";
    constant rama:   std_logic_vector(2 downto 0) := "010";
    constant ramf:   std_logic_vector(2 downto 0) := "011";
    constant ramqd:  std_logic_vector(2 downto 0) := "100";
    constant ramd:   std_logic_vector(2 downto 0) := "101";
    constant ramqu:  std_logic_vector(2 downto 0) := "110";
    constant ramu:   std_logic_vector(2 downto 0) := "111";
end mnemonics;
```

Listing 6-10 The mnemonics package defines several constants

RAM_REGS. Figure 6-4 illustrates how we will implement the RAM_REGS component. The RAM array (register file) is made up of 16 4-bit wide registers. We will use the `ureg` component compiled in the `basic` library because its data and output ports are of type `unsigned`. Thus, we will not have to use a type conversion function when mapping actuals to locals for a component that does something as simple as registering data. The shifter on the input to the register file is implemented with three-to-one multiplexers. The destination-control mnemonic is used to determine whether to shift f up, down, or not at all. Address b is decoded to determine which of the registers in the register file should be written to. Writing to a register location is enabled for certain values of the destination-control microinstructions. The a and b addresses are also used to select which registers to read from. The code that implements RAM_REGS is shown in Listing 6-11.

```
library ieee, basic;
use ieee.std_logic_1164.all;
use work.numeric_std.all;
use work.mnemonics.all;
use basic.regs_pkg.all;
entity ram_regs is port (
    clk, rst:    in std_logic;
    a, bf:       in unsigned(3 downto 0);
    dest_ctl:    in std_logic_vector(2 downto 0);
    ram0, ram3:  inout std_logic;
    ad, bd:      buffer unsigned(3 downto 0));
end ram_regs;
architecture ram_regs of ram_regs is
    signal ram_en:std_logic;
    signal data:unsigned(3 downto 0);
    signal en:std_logic_vector(15 downto 0);
    type ram_array is array (15 downto 0) of unsigned(3 downto 0);
    signal ab_data: ram_array;
```

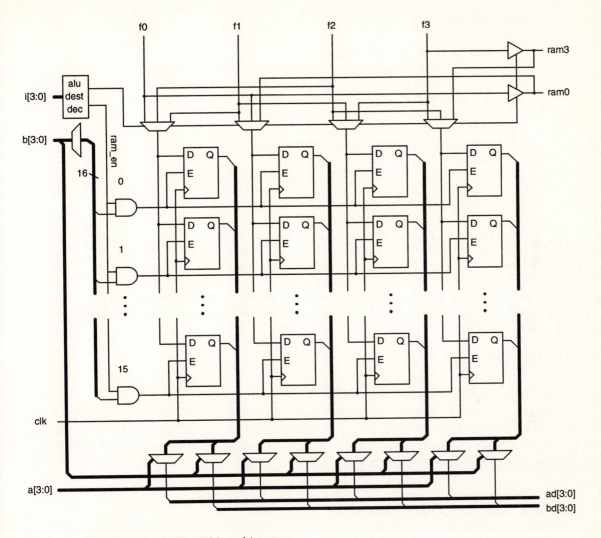

Figure 6-4   RAM_REGS architecture

```
begin
-- define register array:
gen: for i in 15 downto 0 generate
     ram: ureg generic map (4)
             port map (clk, rst, en(i), data, ab_data(i));
     end generate;
-- decode b to determine which register is enabled:
with dest_ctl select
    ram_en <='0' when qreg | nop,
             '1' when others;
```

```vhdl
decode_b: process (b)
    begin
        for i in 0 to 15 loop
            if to_integer(b) = i then en(i) <= ram_en;
                else en(i) <= '0';
            end if;
        end loop;
    end process;
-- define data input to register array:
with dest_ctl select
    data <=(f(2), f(1), f(0), ram0) when ramqu | ramu, -- shift up
           (ram3, f(3), f(2), f(1)) when ramqd | ramd, -- shift down
           f when rama | ramf,
           "----" when others;
-- define reg_array output for a and b regs:
    ad <= ab_data(to_integer(a));   -- to_integer defined in
    bd <= ab_data(to_integer(b));   -- numeric_std (See Ch 7)
-- define ram0 and ram3 inouts:
ram3 <= f(3) when (dest_ctl = ramu or dest_ctl = ramqu) else 'Z';
ram0 <= f(0) when (dest_ctl = ramd or dest_ctl = ramqd) else 'Z';
end ram_regs;
```

Listing 6-11 RAM_REGS design

Q_REG. The Q_REG component implements a simple one-word register that is 4 bits wide (Figure 6-5). For this register, we use the ureg component compiled in the basic library. Like the RAM_REG, this component has a shifter that is controlled by the destination-control microinstruction (Table 6-3). The code used for this component is shown in Listing 6-12.

```vhdl
library ieee, basic;
use ieee.std_logic_1164.all;
use work.numeric_std.all;
use work.mnemonics.all;
use basic.regs_pkg.all;
entity q_reg is port(
    clk, rst: in std_logic;
    f:        in unsigned(3 downto 0);
    dest_ctl: in std_logic_vector(2 downto 0);
    qs0, qs3: inout std_logic;
    q:        buffer unsigned(3 downto 0));
end q_reg;
architecture q_reg of q_reg is
    signal q_en:std_logic;
    signal data:unsigned(3 downto 0);
```

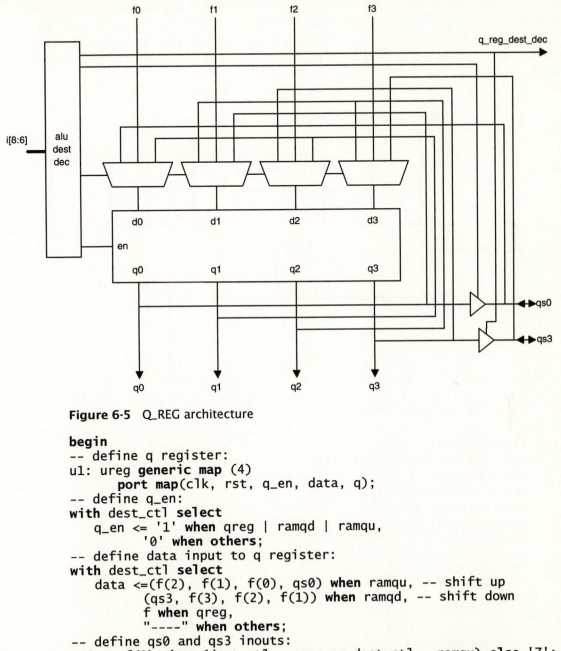

Figure 6-5   Q_REG architecture

```
begin
-- define q register:
u1: ureg generic map (4)
      port map(clk, rst, q_en, data, q);
-- define q_en:
with dest_ctl select
    q_en <= '1' when qreg | ramqd | ramqu,
          '0' when others;
-- define data input to q register:
with dest_ctl select
    data <=(f(2), f(1), f(0), qs0) when ramqu, -- shift up
          (qs3, f(3), f(2), f(1)) when ramqd, -- shift down
          f when qreg,
          "----" when others;
-- define qs0 and qs3 inouts:
qs3 <= f(3) when (dest_ctl = ramu or dest_ctl = ramqu) else 'Z';
qs0 <= f(0) when (dest_ctl = ramd or dest_ctl = ramqd) else 'Z';
end q_reg;
```

Listing 6-12 Q_REG design

SRC_OP. The block diagram of this design component is simply two multiplexers with select lines that are decoded from the source control instruction (Figure 6-6). The inputs to the multiplexer for r are ad, d, and logic 0. The inputs to the multiplexer for s are ad, bd, q, and logic 0. The code for this component is shown in Listing 6-13.

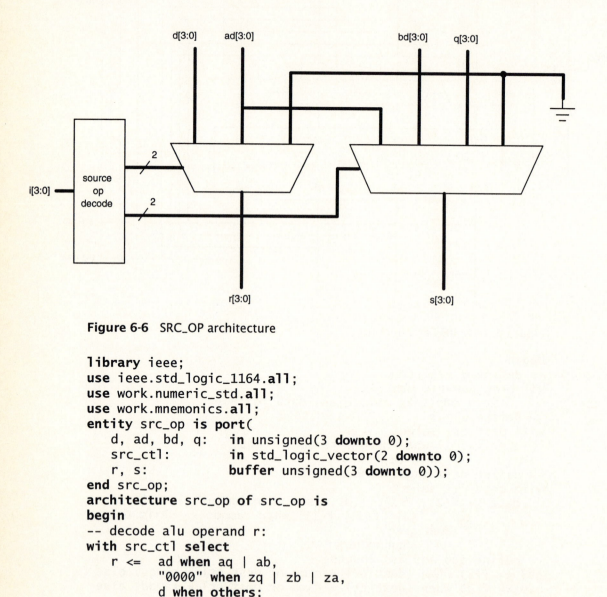

Figure 6-6 SRC_OP architecture

```
library ieee;
use ieee.std_logic_1164.all;
use work.numeric_std.all;
use work.mnemonics.all;
entity src_op is port(
    d, ad, bd, q:    in unsigned(3 downto 0);
    src_ctl:         in std_logic_vector(2 downto 0);
    r, s:            buffer unsigned(3 downto 0));
end src_op;
architecture src_op of src_op is
begin
-- decode alu operand r:
with src_ctl select
    r <=    ad when aq | ab,
            "0000" when zq | zb | za,
            d when others;
```

```
    with src_ctl select
        s <=  q when aq | zq | dq,
              bd when ab | zb,
              ad when za | da,
              "0000" when others;
    end src_op;
```

Listing 6-13 SRC_OP design

ALU. The design of the ALU is shown in Listing 6-14. First, the r and s operands are reassigned to unsigned vectors that are 5 bits wide so that we can track carry and overflow conditions. This is necessary because the + operation is defined in numeric_std such that the return value is a vector the size of the larger of the two operands. To implement the ALU functions, we use a process that is sensitive to r, s, c_n, and to the ALU function control microinstruction. A case statement indicates what set of statements to execute based on the microinstruction value. For example, when the mnemonic is add, then r1, s1, and the value of the carry are summed together to produce f1; when the mnemonic is subr, then the 2's complement of s1 is added to r1. Signal f is assigned the lower four bits of f1, and the carry out c_n4 is assigned f1(4). An overflow is detected if the most significant bit (the sign bit) of f and the carry-out are not the same. Carry generate and propagate equations are also shown in the code.

```
library ieee;
use ieee.std_logic_1164.all;
use work.numeric_std.all;
use work.mnemonics.all;
entity alu is port (
    r, s:             in unsigned(3 downto 0);
    c_n:              in std_logic;
    alu_ctl:          in std_logic_vector(2 downto 0);
    f:                buffer unsigned(3 downto 0);
    g_bar, p_bar:     buffer std_logic;
    c_n4:             buffer std_logic;
    ovr:              buffer std_logic);
end alu;
architecture alu of alu is
    signal r1, s1, f1: unsigned(4 downto 0);
begin
    r1 <= ('0', r(3), r(2), r(1), r(0));
    s1 <= ('0', s(3), s(2), s(1), s(0));
alu: process (r1, s1, c_n, alu_ctl)
```

```vhdl
    begin
      case alu_ctl is
        when add =>
          if c_n = '0' then
            f1 <= r1 + s1;
          else
            f1 <= r1 + s1 + 1;
          end if;
        when subr => -- subtraction same as 2's comp addn
          if c_n = '0' then
            f1 <= r1 + not(s1);
          else
            f1 <= r1 + not(s1) + 1;
          end if;
        when subs =>
          if c_n = '0' then
            f1 <= s1 + not(r1) + 1;
          else
            f1 <= s1 + r1;
          end if;
        when orrs => f1 <= r1 or s1;
        when andrs => f1 <= r1 and s1;
        when notrs =>f1 <= not r1 and s1;
        when exor =>f1 <= r1 xor s1;
        when exnor =>f1 <= not( r1 xor s1);
        when others => f1 <= "-----";
      end case;
  end process;
f <= f1(3 downto 0);
c_n4 <= f1(4);
g_bar <= not (
  (r(3) and s(3)) or
  ((r(3) or s(3)) and (r(2) and s(2))) or
  ((r(3) or s(3)) and (r(2) or s(2)) and (r(1) and s(1))) or
  ((r(3) or s(3)) and (r(2) or s(2)) and (r(1) or s(1)) and
  (r(0) and s(0))));
p_bar <= not (
  (r(3) or s(3)) and (r(2) or s(2)) and (r(1) and s(1)) and
  (r(0) and s(0)));
ovr <= '1' when (f1(4) /= f1(3)) else '0';
end alu;
```

Listing 6-14 ALU design

OUT_MUX. The OUT_MUX component contains a two-to-one multiplexer with select lines that are decoded by the destination-control microinstruction. The three-state output is also controlled by a dedicated output enable. The design is shown in Listing 6-15.

```
library ieee;
use ieee.std_logic_1164.all;
use work.numeric_std.all;
use work.mnemonics.all;
entity out_mux is port(
    ad, f:    in unsigned(3 downto 0);
    dest_ctl: in std_logic_vector(2 downto 0);
    oe:       in std_logic;
    y:        buffer unsigned(3 downto 0));
end out_mux;
architecture out_mux of out_mux is
    signal y_int: unsigned(3 downto 0);-- output before tri-state
                                       -- buffer
begin
    y_int <= ad when dest_ctl = rama else f;
    y <= y_int when oe = '0' else "ZZZZ";
end out_mux;
```

Listing 6-15 OUT_MUX design

AM2901 Top Level. We are now almost ready to tie the components together as shown in Figure 6-1. However, we must first declare each component for each of the entity/architecture pairs just created. We do this in Listing 6-16.

```
library ieee;
use ieee.std_logic_1164.all;
use work.numeric_std.all;
package am2901_comps is
    component ram_regs port (
        clk, rst:    in std_logic;
        a, b:        in unsigned(3 downto 0);
        f:           in unsigned(3 downto 0);
        dest_ctl:    in std_logic_vector(2 downto 0);
        ram0, ram3:  inout std_logic;
        ad, bd:      buffer unsigned(3 downto 0));
    end component;
    component q_reg port(
        clk, rst:    in std_logic;
        f:           in unsigned(3 downto 0);
        dest_ctl:    in std_logic_vector(2 downto 0);
```

```
        qs0, qs3:      inout std_logic;
        q:             buffer unsigned(3 downto 0));
    end component;
    component src_op port(
        d, ad, bd, q:   in unsigned(3 downto 0);
        src_ctl:        in std_logic_vector(2 downto 0);
        r, s:           buffer unsigned(3 downto 0));
    end component;
    component alu port (
        r, s:           in unsigned(3 downto 0);
        c_n:            in std_logic;
        alu_ctl:        in std_logic_vector(2 downto 0);
        f:              buffer unsigned(3 downto 0);
        g_bar, p_bar:   buffer std_logic;
        c_n4:           buffer std_logic;
        ovr:            buffer std_logic);
    end component;
    component out_mux port(
        ad, f:          in unsigned(3 downto 0);
        dest_ctl:       in std_logic_vector(2 downto 0);
        oe:             in std_logic;
        y:              buffer unsigned(3 downto 0));
    end component;
end am2901_comps;
```

Listing 6-16 Component declarations

Now we can instantiate the individual components and connect them to ports
of the AM2901 entity or with intermediate signals declared in its architecture. The
signal f_0 is defined as an open-collector output by turning a three-state buffer on
and driving to ground when f equals 0. Otherwise, an external pull-up pulls this
signal high (Figure 6-7). Depending on the size of the pull-up resistor, the rise time
may be significant. The code for the AM2901 top level is shown in Listing 6-17.

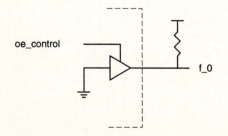

Figure 6-7 Open-collector output using external pull-up

```vhdl
library ieee;
use ieee.std_logic_1164.all;
use work.numeric_std.all;
use work.am2901_comps.all;
entity am2901 is port(
    clk, rst:       in std_logic;
    a, b:           in unsigned(3 downto 0);      -- address inputs
    d:              in unsigned(3 downto 0);      -- direct data
    i:              in std_logic_vector(8 downto 0);
                                                  -- micro instruction
    c_n:            in std_logic;                 -- carry in
    oe:             in std_logic;                 -- output enable
    ram0, ram3:     inout std_logic;              -- shift lines to ram
    qs0, qs3:       inout std_logic;              -- shift lines to q
    y:              buffer unsigned(3 downto 0);  -- data outputs (3-state)
    g_bar,p_bar:    buffer std_logic;             -- carry generate, propagate
    ovr:            buffer std_logic;             -- overflow
    c_n4:           buffer std_logic;             -- carry out
    f_0:            buffer std_logic;             -- f = 0
    f3:             buffer std_logic);            -- f(3) w/o 3-state
end am2901;
architecture am2901 of am2901 is
    alias dest_ctl: std_logic_vector(2 downto 0) is i(8 downto 6);
    alias alu_ctl:  std_logic_vector(2 downto 0) is i(5 downto 3);
    alias src_ctl:  std_logic_vector(2 downto 0) is i(2 downto 0);
    signal ad, bd:unsigned(3 downto 0);
    signal q:unsigned(3 downto 0);
    signal r, s:unsigned(3 downto 0);
    signal f:unsigned(3 downto 0);
begin
-- instantiate and connect components
u1: ram_regs port map(clk => clk, rst => rst, a => a, b => b, f => f,
                dest_ctl => dest_ctl, ram0 => ram0, ram3 => ram3,
                ad => ad, bd => bd);
u2: q_reg port map(clk => clk, rst => rst, f => f, dest_ctl => dest_ctl,
                qs0 => qs0, qs3 => qs3, q => q);
u3: src_op port map(d => d, ad => ad, bd => bd, q => q,
                src_ctl => src_ctl, r => r, s => s);
u4: alu port map(r => r, s => s, c_n => c_n, alu_ctl => alu_ctl,
                f => f, g_bar => g_bar, p_bar => p_bar,
                c_n4 => c_n4, ovr => ovr);
u5: out_mux port map(ad => ad, f => f, dest_ctl => dest_ctl,
                oe => oe, y => y);
-- define f_0 and f3 outputs
f_0 <= '0' when f = "0000" else 'Z';
f3 <= f(3);
end am2901;
```

Listing 6-17 AM2901 Top level

6.2.4   Design Implementation

Implementation of the AM2901 design is left as an exercise for the reader. In Chapters 7 and 9 we also explain how to optimize portions of the design. For now we move on to a significantly more complex design.

Breakout Exercise 6-2

Purpose: To compile and synthesize the AM2901 to a 4,000-gate FPGA.

Perform the following steps.

1. Create a project named `c:\vhdlbook\ch6\am2901\am2901`.
2. Add all of the files to the project list, but be sure that they are ordered properly. For example, `mnemonics.vhd` must be compiled before `alu.vhd` or any other design that makes use of the mnemonics package.
3. Select `am2901.vhd` as the top-level design.
4. Select the CY7C385A device as the target. Reduce node cost to 4.
5. Select **Libraries** from the **Files** menu.
6. Select **Assign Library** from the **File** menu, and select **Add** from the dialog box.
7. Traverse the directories to `c:\vhdlbook\ch6\basic\basic`. The path will appear in the upper-right of the dialog box when Warp recognizes that this directory is a library. Type the name `basic` for Library in the upper-left of the dialog box. Select **OK**. This creates a link to the `basic` library.
8. Return to the Galaxy project. Compile and synthesize the design.
9. Place and route the design. Record the utilization and performance. Save these results; they will be compared later against a modification of the design.

6.3   Case Study: A 100BASE-T4 Network Repeater

The network repeater design will provide a practical example of design hierarchy. It requires many of the design constructs that are frequently implemented with programmable logic devices: counters, communicating state machines, multiplexers, small FIFOs, and control logic. It uses a "real-world" design to elaborate on many of the concepts presented in previous chapters. We start at the top, breaking the network repeater into design units. Then we build each of the design units from the bottom up. Before launching into the design specifications for the network repeater, we provide some background on Ethernet.

Background. Ethernet is the most popular local area network (LAN) in use today for communication between networking equipment and groups of computers, servers, and peripherals. Ethernet is the trade name for a set of networking standards adopted by the International Standards Organization (ISO) and IEEE 802.3 as the CSMA/CD Network Standard. The standard embodies specifications for network media, physical interfaces, signaling, and network-access protocol. Initial work on Ethernet was pioneered in the early 1980s by researchers at Xerox, DEC, and Intel. Since then, Ethernet has evolved to meet market demands by including standards for new cabling types and faster data rates. A recent successful effort in the Ethernet standard working groups was to bring Ethernet to 100 megabits per second (Mb/s) over several media types. Figure 6-8 illustrates a typical work-group environment that is connected via several Ethernet media types.

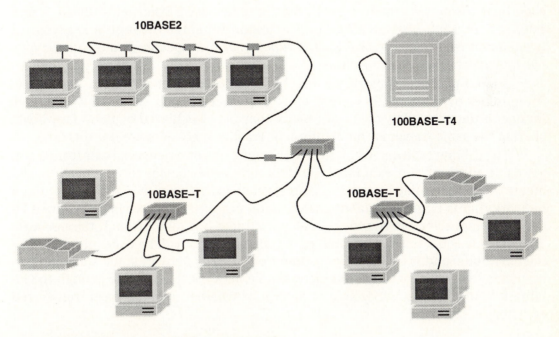

Figure 6-8 A typical Ethernet network

6.3.1   Ethernet Networks

Ethernet allows the creation of flexible and inexpensive networks that accommodate various media types and hundreds of host-station connections in a single network. Ethernet network architecture is based on a few simple concepts and configuration rules. The primary elements of the network are the medium, adaptor cards (transceivers), and hubs.

Shared Medium. Ethernet is based on the idea that the network should behave as a shared medium. Every host station on the network listens to all network traffic and processes only data intended for it. Only one host may transmit data at a time. Other hosts wishing to transmit must wait until they detect that the medium is quiet before they can start transmitting data onto the network. If two hosts transmit at the same time, then a collision occurs and both hosts must back off of the network and try to resend their data after an arbitrary waiting period. This technique for accessing the network is called **carrier sense, multiple access with collision detection** (CSMA/CD), and is the distinguishing feature of Ethernet.

The concept of a shared medium is inherent in the coaxial implementations of Ethernet (10BASE5 and 10BASE2) for which a common coaxial cable connects to each host through a transceiver. In twisted-pair-based Ethernet (10BASE-T and 100BASE-T), each host attaches to a common repeater through a segment of twisted pair cable (see Figure 6-8). *The function of the repeater is to create the logical equivalent of a shared medium.*

Several practical constraints limit the size of Ethernet networks. The first is the number of hosts—1,024—that may be connected to a single network. This number is determined by the performance that can be achieved by that many hosts sharing the same transmission medium. In practice, networks are not this large.

The cabling type determines the maximum size of a network built from a single cable segment. For example, 10BASE2 limits the coaxial cable length to 185 meters. Repeaters may be used to connect network segments together to build a network that is larger in total diameter. Total network diameter is determined by the maximum tolerable round-trip delay that data can take through the network. This delay is equal to the minimum data-frame size that can be transmitted by any host (512 bits) and is called the **slot time** (for 10 Mb/s networks, the slot-time corresponds to approximately 2,000 meters). In a network that is large enough to violate the slot-time, it is impossible to determine whether data has been transferred collision-free.

Adaptors and Transceivers. Adaptor cards interface computers, servers, or peripheral devices to the network medium. They are based on standard buses such as ISA, PCI, or PCMCIA. On an adaptor card, a media access controller (MAC) builds data frames from user data, recognizes frames addressed to it, and performs media-access management (CSMA/CD). Adaptor cards may have an RJ45 connector for twisted-pair–based Ethernet such as 10BASE-T or 100BASE-T4. They may also have an AUI (attachment unit interface) connector for interfacing coaxial transceivers for 10BASE2 or 10BASE5; however, only one network connection may be active at a time. Figure 6-9 shows a typical adaptor card.

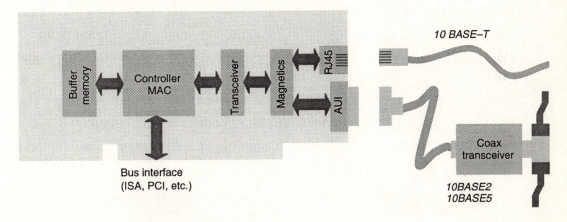

Figure 6-9 A typical Ethernet adaptor card

Hubs. Hub is a generic name for repeaters, bridges, and routers. Hubs are used to expand the size of the network and allow interoperation among various media (coaxial cable, fiber optics, and so forth) and network types (Token Ring and FDDI, for instance). Smart hubs such as routers, learning bridges, and switches can route traffic among various networks based on addresses associated with the data. These devices ease network congestion and improve bandwidth.

Ethernet over twisted pair requires the use of a repeater hub in order to provide connectivity between all of the host cable segments.

Repeaters, the simplest type of hub, logically join cable segments to create a larger network while providing the equivalent of a shared medium. Repeaters improve reliability and performance because they isolate hosts with faulty network connections, keeping them from disrupting the network. Repeaters may have management functions so that remote hosts or a local terminal can configure the network or query network performance statistics. An Ethernet network built with repeaters is shown in Figure 6-10. The basic objectives for a repeater are to:

- Detect carrier activity on ports and receive Ethernet frames on active ports
- Restore the shape, amplitude, and timing of the received frame signals prior to retransmission
- Forward the Ethernet frame to each of the active ports
- Detect and signal a collision event throughout a network
- Extend a network's physical dimensions
- Protect a network from failures of stations, cables, ports, and so forth
- Allow the installation and removal of stations without network disruption
- Support interoperability of various physical layers (10BASE2, 10BASE-T, and so on)
- Provide centralized management of network operations and statistics
- Provide for low-cost network installation, growth, and maintenance
- Partition bad segments

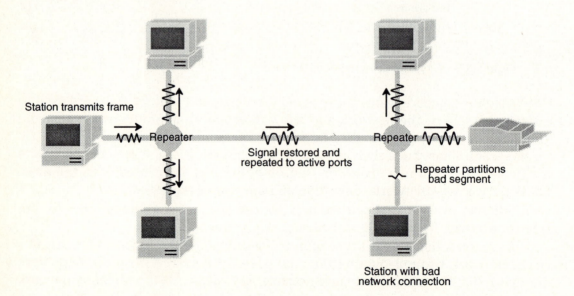

Figure 6-10   Ethernet network built with repeaters

Although our focus will be on the functionality and design of the digital logic to support a repeater, below we provide a brief description of bridges and routers to satisfy the curious reader. You may wish to proceed to the next section, "Design Specifications for the Core Logic of an 8-Port Repeater."

Bridges are used to connect distinct networks. This requires that data be reframed for the standard data frames of the appropriate networks. For example, an Ethernet network can be connected to a Token Ring network through a bridge that converts Ethernet frames to Token Ring frames. A bridge may also be used to connect distinct Ethernet networks to increase the overall network's physical dimension. A bridge used in this manner isolates the collisions between the attached networks and avoids the slot-time constraint. Figure 6-11 shows a bridge used to connect dissimilar networks.

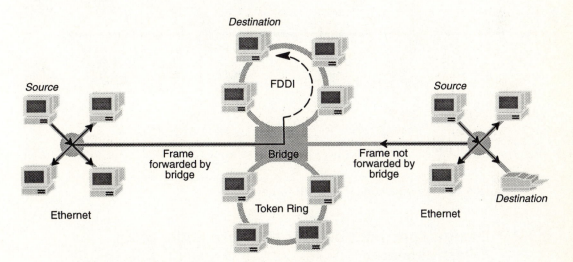

Figure 6-11   Network connected with bridges

Bridges may forward all frames between connected networks or they may selectively forward frames based on the frame's MAC address. To selectively forward frames, a bridge must know the network addresses that can be accessed by each of the attached networks. **Learning bridges** monitor the network traffic in order to learn addresses dynamically.

Bridges also increase network bandwidth. A bridge will isolate Ethernet traffic inside a local work group so that bandwidth isn't wasted in attached networks. The other local work groups attached to the bridge do not have to wait for foreign traffic to clear before sending data. Only nonlocal traffic crosses the bridge en route to its destination.

Routers work much like bridges except that they *forward* a packet based on its network layer address. Routers are thus able to transfer packets between different network protocols and media types (for example, TCP/IP -> X.25, Ethernet -> FDDI). Figure 6-12 shows routers transferring data among different media types and network protocols.

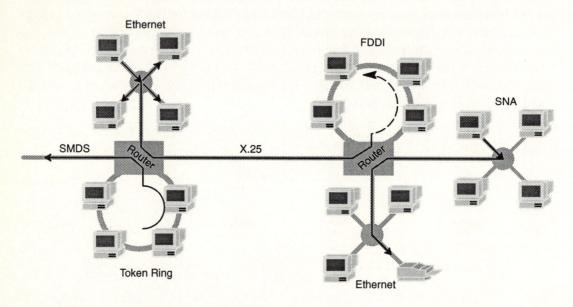

Figure 6-12   Network connected with routers

6.3.2   Design Specifications for the Core Logic of an 8-Port Repeater

Although we have made efforts to ensure the accuracy of the repeater core design, you should consult the IEEE 802.3 standard before attempting to use this design in a commercial product.

Interface. The basic function of a repeater is to retransmit data that is received from one port to all other ports. 100BASE-T4 is the 100 Mb/s Ethernet standard that operates over four pairs of category 3, 4, or 5 UTP (unshielded, twisted pair) cable. The architecture of a 100BASE-T4 repeater is shown in Figure 6-13. Transceivers, such as the CY7C971, perform the electrical functions needed to interface the ports to the repeater core logic. We will not be concerned with the functions or operation of the transceivers. Rather, we will focus on the functions of the repeater core logic. This requires that we understand the transceiver-repeater core interface.

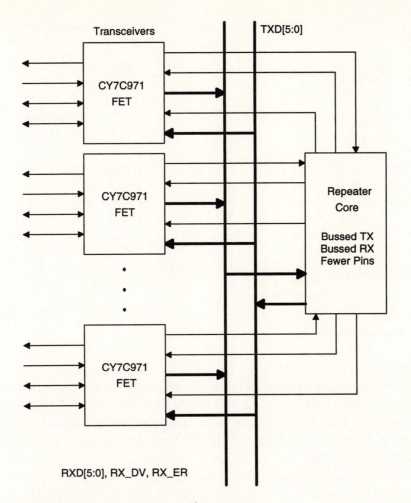

Figure 6-13   T4 repeater architecture

Figure 6-14 illustrates the transceiver interfaces to the repeater core. Each port is capable of receiving data and provides the following signals to the core logic:

- carrier sense (crs)
- receive clock (rx_clk)
- receive data valid (rx_dv)
- receive data error (rx_er)
- three pairs of data, (rxd0–rxd5)

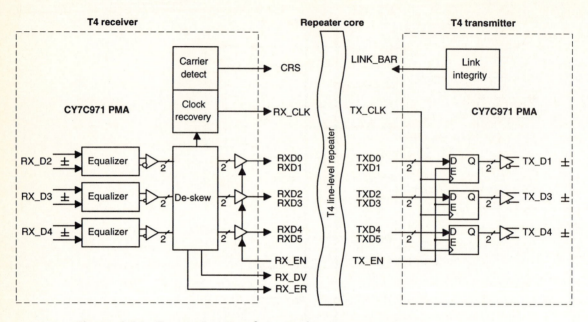

Figure 6-14 Transceiver interfaces to the repeater core

Signal crs indicates that data is being received by the transceiver. rx_clk is the clock recovered from the incoming data by the transceiver; it is used to synchronize the incoming data, rxd0–rxd5. Signal rx_dv indicates that received data is valid. It is asserted at a data frame's start of frame delimiter (SFD) and is deasserted at the end of a frame. Signal rx_er indicates that the transceiver detected an error in the reception of data.

The core logic provides only one signal to the receive side of each transceiver: rx_en (receive enable). It is used to control which port is driving the bus. All ports share a common receive bus for rxd0–rxd5, rx_dv, and rx_er (Figure 6-13).

The core logic provides several signals to the transmit side of each port: tx_clk (transmit clock), tx_en (transmit enable), and txd0–txd5 (transmit data).

An additional signal, link_bar (link integrity), indicates the integrity of the link between the repeater and a node on the network.

Protocol. Upon reception of a **carrier sense** (crs) from any port, the core logic must buffer the incoming data frame and retransmit this frame to all other functional ports, provided that (1) there is not a collision, (2) the port is not jabbering, and (3) the port is not partitioned.

A collision occurs if at any time more than one carrier sense becomes active, in which case a **jam** symbol must be generated and transmitted to all ports, including the one previously sending data. Those nodes that caused the collision will stop sending data, wait for an arbitrary length of time, and then attempt to resend data when the network is quiet.

If `crs` is not asserted by any of the ports, then **idle** symbols are generated and transmitted on all ports.

If the receiving port asserts `rx_er` while the repeater is retransmitting data to the other ports, then **bad** symbols (symbols that indicate that the transmission has gone bad) are generated and transmitted to all other ports until `crs` is deasserted or a collision occurs.

A port is **jabbering** if it continually transmits data for 40,000 to 75,000 bit times. If a port is jabbering, the repeater will inhibit `rx_en` (that is, it will stop receiving data from this port). Therefore, it will not retransmit data from this to the other ports. Instead, the repeater will free up the network for other ports to send data, retransmitting this data to all other ports except the one jabbering. The port will be considered to have ceased jabbering after `crs` is deasserted.

A port must be partitioned from the network if it causes 60 or more consecutive collisions, because continued collisions will bring all network communication to a halt. A broken cable or faulty connection is a likely source of these collisions. When a port is partitioned, the repeater will stop receiving data from that port. It will, however, continue to transmit data to this port. A partitioned port will be "reconnected" to the repeater if activity on another port occurs for 450 to 560 bit times without a `crs` from the partitioned port.

The transceiver detects a carrier by identifying the preamble of the incoming data frame. By the time the carrier is detected and the clock recovered, some of the preamble is lost, but the data to be transmitted to the other ports has not been lost. Before retransmitting the data, however, the preamble must be regenerated so that receiving nodes can sense a carrier and recover the clock prior to receiving the actual data being transmitted. The frame structure is described below.

Data Frame Structure. Data transmitted on the Ethernet is encapsulated in standard frames. The frame format is shown in Figure 6-15. The following are frame components:

- Preamble: Used by the receiving hosts to detect the presence of a carrier and initiate clock recovery.

- Start of frame delimiter (SFD): Indicates to the receiving hosts that the next group of bits is the actual data to be transmitted.

- Destination address: A 48-bit address that uniquely identifies which host on the network should receive the frame. A host address is created by taking the 24-bit organizationally unique identifier (OUI) assigned to each organization. The remaining 24 bits are determined internally by network administrators.

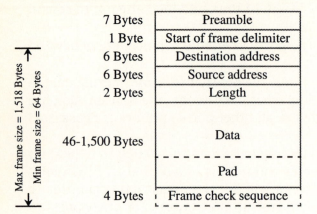

7 Bytes	Preamble	1010...for PLL synchronization
1 Byte	Start of frame delimiter	Indicates end of preamble and start of frame
6 Bytes	Destination address	Unique address of destination or broadcast
6 Bytes	Source address	Unique address of source
2 Bytes	Length	Length of the data field in bytes
46–1,500 Bytes	Data	Data to be transferred. If fewer than 46 bytes of data, add pad characters.
	Pad	
4 Bytes	Frame check sequence	32-bit CRC used for error detection

Max frame size = 1,518 Bytes
Min frame size = 64 Bytes

Figure 6-15   Ethernet MAC data frame

- Source address: A 48-bit address that uniquely identifies which host is sending the frame.

- Length: Two bytes long; determines how many bytes of data are in the data field.

- Data: The minimum data-field size is 46 bytes. If fewer than 46 bytes of data need to be sent, additional characters are added to the end of the data field. The maximum data field size is 1,500 bytes.

- Frame check sequence (FCS): The FCS is a 32-bit cyclic redundancy check (CRC) computed from a standard CRC polynomial. The receiving host computes a CRC from the bits it receives and compares the value to the FCS embedded in the frame to see whether the data was received error-free.

In order to transmit 100 Mb/s over 4 pairs, the frequency of operation must be 25 MHz. The repeater does not ensure that the minimum frame size is sent by a node but merely retransmits the data ("good data in, good data out; garbage in, garbage out").

6.3.3   Block Diagram

To summarize the functions of the repeater: (1) In general, the repeater receives data from one port and retransmits it to other ports; (2) it detects collisions, activity, and errors, generating and transmitting the appropriate symbols under these conditions; and (3) it detects jabbering and partition conditions, asserting tx_en and rx_en as appropriate. To accomplish these functions, the incoming data must be buffered and the symbols generated. The buffered data must be multiplexed with other symbols, depending on which data should be transmitted to the active ports. From this summary, we can construct the block diagram of Figure 6-16 to illustrate the top-level functionality of the core logic. At this point, we'll break this design down into manageable units.

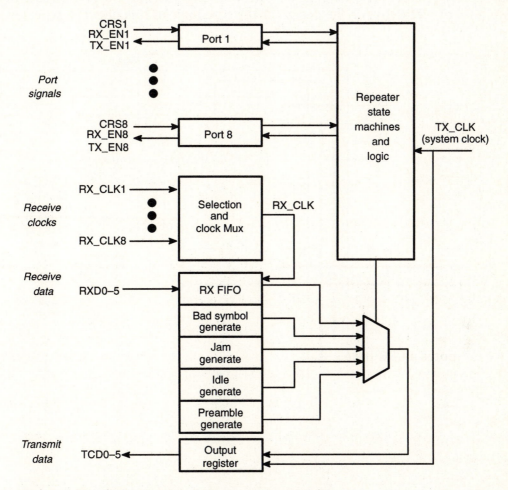

Figure 6-16   Block diagram of the repeater core logic

The block diagram of Figure 6-16 and the design specifications give us some good clues as to how we may want to structure the hierarchy. Each port interfaces to a transceiver that, in turn, interfaces to the core logic. Thus, the logic for each port is clearly a good candidate for a design unit, as we do not want to redesign it many times. We will also make design units for the repeater state machines and the FIFO. The port selection and clock multiplexer will be divided into two design units, one for each task. The final design unit will be a symbol generator and output multiplexer. We can start to draw out our first level of hierarchy, but we first need to more clearly define the function of each unit so that we can define the interfaces between the units and the top-level I/O. After reading through the descriptions of the following units, you will see that Figure 6-17 represents the first level of hierarchy for the design of the core logic of this network repeater.

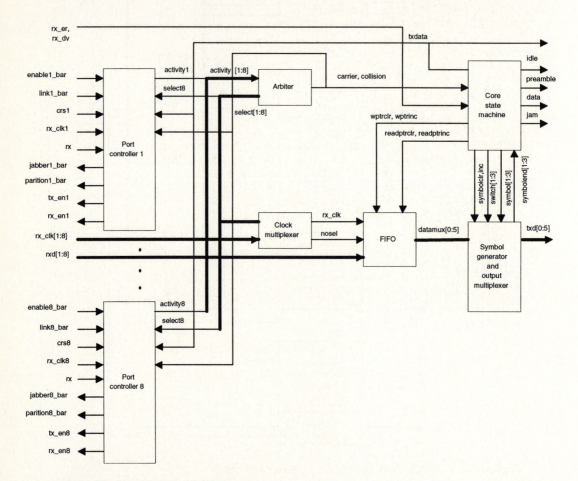

Figure 6-17 First level of hierarchy

Port Controller. There will be eight port controllers, one for each port of the repeater. On the receive side, each port controller will synchronize crs, link_bar, and enable_bar to tx_clk. Once a carrier has been detected and synchronized, activity is asserted. This signal is used by the arbiter to select a port from which to receive data. Rx_en is asserted by a port controller if its port is selected as the receiving port, as long as there is not a collision. On the transmit side, each port will assert tx_en if the core controller indicates that txdata (transmit data) is ready, provided that this port is not the receiving port (link_bar must also be present and the port cannot be jabbering). Tx_en will also be asserted in the event of a collision so that jam characters may be transmitted to all hosts. Jabber_bar and partition_bar are driven by the port controller to indicate that the port is either jabbering or partitioned. These signals can be used to light LEDs. To determine whether the port is jabbering, the port controller uses a timer to determine how long crs has been asserted. If crs has been asserted 40,000 to 75,000 bit times, then jabber_bar is asserted until crs is deasserted. To determine whether the port should be partitioned, the port controller counts the number of consecutive collisions. If the number of collisions is greater than 60, then partition_bar is asserted to prevent the port from halting network communication. To determine whether the port should be reconnected after being partitioned, the port controller monitors port activity. If another port is active for more than 450 to 560 bit times without this port's crs being asserted, then the port controller deasserts partition_bar. These conditions will be determined by the state of collision and carrier as well as by whether or not the port is selected. An additional input, enable_bar, will be usable by the implementers of the repeater core logic. In the event that eight ports are not required, enable_bar may be hard-wired as deasserted for the unused ports.

Arbiter. The arbiter will use the activity signals of each of the port controllers to supply eight selected signals to the port controllers and clock multiplexer. These signals will indicate which port is receiving data. They will be used to gate the rx_en of that port and to choose the appropriate clock for writing to the FIFO. The arbiter also supplies carrier and collision for use by the port controllers and the core controller. Nosel is supplied to the clock multiplexer, indicating that no port is receiving a transmission. Under this condition, idle characters are transmitted by all ports of the repeater.

Clock Multiplexer. The inputs to the clock multiplexer are the eight receive clocks (rx_clk7–rx_clk0), the eight selected lines from the arbiter, and nosel from the arbiter. Selected and nosel signals are used to select one of the receive clocks as *the* receive clock, rx_clk, for use by the FIFO.

FIFO. The FIFO will capture incoming data on the receive side, storing six bits of data (rxd5–rxd0) on the rising edge of rx_clk. Wptrclr (write-pointer clear), wptrinc (write-pointer increment), rptrclr (read-pointer clear), and rptrinc (read-pointer increment) are used to advance or clear the FIFO and to indicate which register to read for the outputs dmuxout5–dmuxout0.

Symbol Generator and Output Multiplexer. The character symbol generator and output multiplexer will generate symbols. These symbols are the

- bad characters, transmitted to indicate a receive error,
- jam characters, transmitted to indicate a collision,
- idle characters, transmitted to indicate that there is no activity on the network, and
- preamble characters, transmitted to allow for carrier sensing and clock recovery by the receiving nodes.

There are six output multiplexers (one for each of the transmit signals of the three transmit pairs). The multiplexers are paired with the transmit pairs, each pair sharing the same select lines. There are five inputs to each multiplexer, so three select lines per pair are required. This is a total of nine select lines for all multiplexers. The outputs are the transmit signals `txd5-txd0`.

Core Controller. The core controller controls the FIFO read and write pointers as well as symbol generation. It also asserts `tx_data` to indicate to the ports that data is ready. The core controller determines what data to transmit: data in the FIFO or preamble, idle, jam, or bad characters. To do this, the core controller requires `carrier`, `collision`, `rx_dv`, and `rx_er` as inputs and asserts the FIFO and multiplexer control lines.

Before proceeding to design the individual units, we need to know how the signals will be synchronized. In this design, there are basically five input signals (`crs`, `rx_dv`, `rx_er`, `link_bar`, and `enable_bar`) that will each need to be synchronized to the system transmit clock, `txclk`. These signals will be synchronized with two flip-flops in order to increase the mean time between failures (MTBF). The incoming data is aligned to the incoming clock `rxclk` and stored in a FIFO, and the outgoing data is synchronized to the transmit clock.

6.3.4   Designing the Units

In this design, we define the ports at the top level of the hierarchy to be individual `std_logics` or `std_logic_vectors`. We do this to make it easy to switch between simulating the source code and simulating the postlayout model, which will have individual `std_logics` as ports rather than vectors. Even if the tool has a utility to bus common signals, we would like to avoid any potential problems. This is a good idea particularly if you will be using several different tools, perhaps, one for synthesis, another for place and route, and yet another for simulation. We're certain that we could bus signals together and eventually get the interfaces to work (perhaps not seamlessly), but experience tells us that unless we test the flow with a smaller design, we should stick with what we know will work to avoid any unnecessary headaches. Interfaces between tools are notorious for not being seamless, as many experienced designers can attest. Because the top-level port is specified signal-by-signal, this will tend to permeate through other levels of hierarchy. We will use buses (vectors) occasionally.

Port Controller. We begin our design of the core logic for the network repeater with the port controller. The entity declaration is shown below, with the name porte. "Controller" was removed to avoid a cumbersome name (port_controller), and an "e" was added to *port* to avoid a conflict with a reserved word. Comments to the right may provide some additional information about the signals.

```
library ieee, basic;
use ieee.std_logic_1164.all;
use basic.regs_pkg.all;
use basic.synch_pkg.all;
use basic.counters_pkg.all;
entity porte is port (
        txclk:              in std_logic; -- TX_CLK
        areset:             in std_logic; -- Asynch reset
        crs:                in std_logic; -- Carrier sense
        enable_bar:         in std_logic; -- Port enable
        link_bar:           in std_logic; -- PMA_link_OK
        selected:           in std_logic; -- Arbiter select
        carrier:            in std_logic; -- Arbiter carrier
        collision:          in std_logic; -- Arbiter collision
        jam:                in std_logic; -- Control jam
        txdata:             in std_logic; -- Control transmit data
        prescale:           in std_logic; -- counter prescale
        rx_en:              buffer std_logic;   -- RX_EN
        tx_en:              buffer std_logic;   -- TX_EN
        activity:           buffer std_logic;   -- Activity
        jabber_bar:         buffer std_logic;   -- Jabber
        partition_bar:      buffer std_logic); -- Partition
end porte;
```

Looking back at the description of the port controller, we see that crs, link_bar, and enable_bar must be synchronized to tx_clk, so we will use the synchronizer components. We will use the synchronizer with an asynchronous reset for the active high signal, crs, and will use the one with an asynchronous preset for the active low signals (those ending in _bar). Using the synchronizers requires that we create three signals (crsdd, link_bardd, and enable_bardd) for the outputs of the synchronizers. The suffix "dd" indicates that these signals are twice-registered. Three components are instantiated:

```
u0: rsynch     port map (txclk, areset, crs, crsdd);
u1: psynch     port map (txclk, areset, link_bar, link_bardd);
u2: psynch     port map (txclk, areset, enable_bar, enable_bardd);
```

Instantiation of these components requires that they have been declared and are visible to the architecture. These components are declared in a package named synch_pkg, the contents of which are made visible to this entity through a library and use clause:

```
library basic;
use basic.synch_pkg.all;
```

Alternatively, the statement use basic.all; will make all design units in basic visible. Making all design units visible may, however, require longer compile times and more memory. Next, we create an equation for activity, which is asserted if a carrier is present, the link is established, and the port is not partitioned or jabbering. Carpres—carrier presence—is equivalent to crsdd gated by enable-bardd.

```
carpres <= crsdd and not enable_bardd;
activity <= carpres and not link_bardd and jabber_bar and partition_bar;
```

Here, we chose to define carpres and activity with Boolean equations because, in this case, other dataflow constructs do not enhance the readability of the code.

Rx_en and tx_eni will also be defined with Boolean equations. Tx_eni is the value of tx_en before it is registered; it is asserted when txdata is received from the core controller, indicating that this port should transmit data (if it is not jabbering). It must be delayed one clock cycle to synchronize it with the output data. Tx_eni must be declared as a signal local to this architecture. The logic is described below.

```
rx_en   <= not enable_bardd and not link_bardd and selected and  collision;
tx_eni  <= not enable_bardd and not link_bardd and jabber_bar and transmit;

u3: rdff1      port map (txclk, areset, tx_eni, tx_en);
```

Transmit is the logical AND of two quantities. The first signal is txdata, which indicates that the core controller state machine is ready to send data or jam characters. The second is the result of the logical OR of collision and a signal (copyd), which indicates that the arbiter has detected a carrier but that this port is not the selected port. In other words, the port should transmit jam characters (if a collision occurs) or data characters (to copy, or repeat, data received from another port). All signals must be synchronized. Txdata is one clock cycle behind the other signals because it is triggered by them (see the "Core Controller" section later in this chapter). Therefore, the other signals must be delayed:

```
u4: rdff1      port map (txclk, areset, copyin, copyd);
u5: rdff1      port map (txclk, areset, collision, collisiond);

copyin <= carrier and not selected;
transmit <= txdata and (copyd or collisiond);
```

There are two remaining functions of the port controller that we must design: jabber_bar and partition_bar. Jabber_bar should be asserted if the carrier is present for anywhere between 40,000 and 75,000 bit times. Forty-thousand bit times over four pairs requires 10,000 clock cycles (75,000 bit times requires 18,750 clock cycles). We will use a counter while the carrier is present. If it counts approximately 10,000 clock cycles, then jabber_bar will be asserted. The counter will be reset when the carrier is not present.

Counting to 10,000 requires a 14-bit counter. However, we don't want the counter to be replicated eight times, once for each port, because it would consume device resources unnecessarily. Therefore, we use a common counter, placing it in the core controller, to count to 1K. This counter runs continuously. In each of the port controllers, we place a 4-bit **prescaled counter** that is enabled each time the 10-bit counter rolls over, or reaches its maximum value. When the 4-bit counter reaches 12, we know the carrier has been present for 12K, plus or minus 1K, clock cycles ($10K < 12K +/- 1K < 18.75K$). For the design of the port controller, this requires the instantiation of a 4-bit counter and the definition of the counter enable and clear signals as well as jabber_bar.

```
u6: ascount  generic map (4)
             port map (txclk, areset, jabberclr, jabberinc, jabcnt);

jabber_bar <= not  (jabcnt(3) and jabcnt(2));    -- jabcnt=12
jabberclr <= not carpres;
jabberinc <= carpres and prescale and jabber_bar;
```

Jabber_bar is asserted when jabcnt reaches 12, which is 1100 in binary, or jabcnt(3) AND jabcnt(2). When jabcnt reaches this value, jabber_bar is asserted (low), causing the counter to be disabled. If the counter were to continue to be enabled, it could roll over and inadvertently cause jabber_bar to be deasserted.

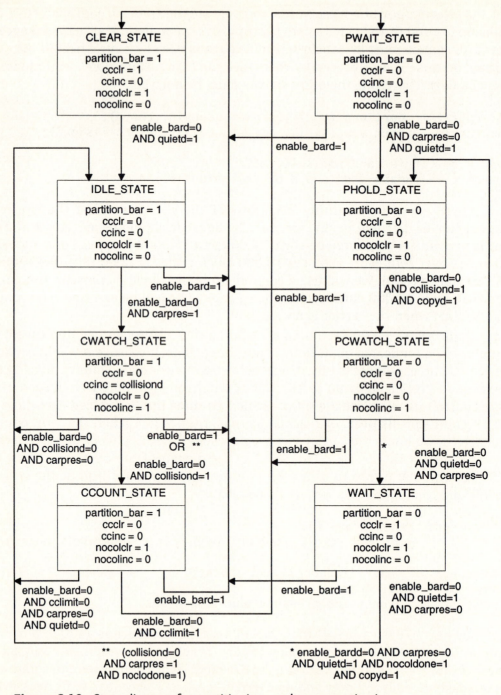

Figure 6-18 State diagram for partitioning and reconnecting†

The conditions for which a port is partitioned or reconnected have been described previously and are defined by a state diagram in the IEEE 802.3 standard. This state diagram has been modified for our purposes and is illustrated in Figure 6-18. The states on the left-hand side of the diagram are used to determine whether the port should be partitioned. The port is partitioned in the states on the right-hand side, indicated by `partition_bar` being asserted low. The states on the right-hand side are used to determine whether the port should be reconnected. The clearing and enabling of two counters are controlled by this state machine: one that counts collisions (the collision counter) and another that counts the number of consecutive clock cycles without a collision (the no-collision counter). Several signals are inputs to this state machine:

- `copyd` indicates that another port is active and that the port should repeat data being received on another port;
- `quietd` indicates that no other port is active—it is the opposite of `copyd`;
- `carpres` indicates that the carrier sense of this port is active;
- `collisiond` indicates a collision;
- `nocoldone` is asserted when the no-collision counter reaches 128 (128 clock cycles is between 450 and 560 bit times, the approximate size of the minimum data frame—each clock cycle represents four bit times, one for each of the transmit and receive pairs); and
- `cclimit` is asserted when 64 consecutive collisions have occurred.

The counters are cleared in the `clear_state`. The machine enters this state after a system reset or if a collision does not occur for approximately one minimum data-frame size while `carpres` is asserted. The `idle_state` resets the no-collision counter. In the collision-watch state, `cwatch_state`, if a collision occurs, the collision counter is incremented and the state machine transitions to the collision count state, `ccount_state`. As long as a collision does not occur, the state machine remains in the `cwatch_state` until `nocoldone` is asserted, after which the state machine transitions to the `clear_state` and both counters are reset.

†Adapted from IEEE Std 802.3u-1995 IEEE Standards for Local and Metropolitan Area Networks: Supplement to Carrier Sense Multiple Access with Collision Detection (CSMA/CD) Access Method and Physical Layer Specifications: Media Access Control (MAC) Parameters, Physical Layer, Medium Attachment Units, and Repeater for 100 Mb/s Operation, © 1995 by the Institute of Electrical and Electronics Engineers, Inc. The IEEE disclaims any responsibility or liability resulting from the placement and use in this publication. Information is adapted and reprinted with the permission of the IEEE.

The ccount_state is entered upon a collision. If the collision counter reaches its limit (64), then the port is to be partitioned and the state machine transitions to the pwait_state. If the collision counter does not reach its limit, then the machine waits for the offending nodes to back off of the network, transitioning to the idle_state when the network is quiet again. From this point, transitions through the states will continue; either additional collisions will be counted or the counters will be cleared.

The pwait_state indicates that the collision counter limit has been reached and that the port is partitioned. This state is used to wait until the collision ceases. Once the network is quiet again, the state machine transitions to the partition hold state, phold_state. This state and the next, the partition collision-watch state (pcwatch_state), are used to count consecutive clock cycles during which there is no collision and another port is active (copyd asserted). If the port does not cause a collision for 450 to 560 bit times while another port is active, then the state machine transitions to the wait_state. The wait_state is used to wait until the active port is quiet before transitioning to the idle_state.

As with many state machines, we will code this one using an enumeration type and a case-when construct, specifying the state machine outputs and transitions in the same process. The complete architecture is found in Listing 6-18.

```vhdl
architecture archporte of porte is

    type states is (CLEAR_STATE, IDLE_STATE, CWATCH_STATE, CCOUNT_STATE,
        PWAIT_STATE, PHOLD_STATE, PCWATCH_STATE, WAIT_STATE);
    attribute state_encoding of states:type is one_hot_one;
    signal state, newstate: states;

    signal  crsdd, link_bardd, enable_bardd: std_logic;
    signal  tx_eni, carpres, transmit,
            copyd, copyin, collisiond: std_logic;
    signal  jabcnt: std_logic_vector(3 downto 0);
    signal  jabberclr, jabberinc: std_logic;
    signal  quietd: std_logic;
    signal  cccnt: std_logic_vector(6 downto 0);
    signal  cclimit, nocoldone: std_logic;
    signal  nocolcnt: std_logic_vector(7 downto 0);
    signal  ccclr, ccinc, nocolclr, nocolinc: std_logic;
begin
--      Components
u0: rsynch      port map (txclk, areset, crs, crsdd);
u1: psynch      port map (txclk, areset, link_bar, link_bardd);
u2: psynch      port map (txclk, areset, enable_bar, enable_bardd);
u3: rdff1       port map (txclk, areset, tx_eni, tx_en);
u4: rdff1       port map (txclk, areset, copyin, copyd);
```

```
u5: rdff1        port map (txclk, areset, collision, collisiond);
u6: ascount      generic map (4) port map (txclk, areset, jabberclr,
                                           jabberinc, jabcnt);
u7: ascount      generic map (7) port map (txclk, areset, ccclr, ccinc,
                                           cccnt);
u8: ascount      generic map (8) port map (txclk, areset, nocolclr,
                                           nocolinc, nocolcnt);


carpres      <= crsdd and not enable_bardd;
activity     <= carpres and not link_bardd and jabber_bar and
                partition_bar;
rx_en        <= not enable_bardd and not link_bardd and selected and
                collision;
tx_eni       <= not enable_bardd and not link_bardd and jabber_bar and
                transmit;
copyin       <= carrier and not selected;
transmit     <= txdata and (copyd or collisiond);
jabber_bar   <= not (jabcnt(3) and jabcnt(2));
jabberclr    <= not carpres;
jabberinc    <= carpres and prescale and jabber_bar;
quietd       <= not copyd;
cclimit      <= cccnt(6);
nocoldone    <= nocolcnt(7);

--      Partition State Machine
p1: process (state, carpres, collisiond, copyd, quietd,
        nocoldone, cclimit, enable_bardd) begin
   case (state) is
   when CLEAR_STATE=>
           partition_bar    <= '1'  ;
           ccclr            <= '1'  ;
           ccinc            <= '0'  ;
           nocolclr         <= '1'  ;
           nocolinc         <= '0'  ;
           if (enable_bardd = '1') then
              newstate      <= CLEAR_STATE;
           elsif (quietd = '1')       then
              newstate      <= IDLE_STATE;
           else
              newstate      <= CLEAR_STATE;
           end if;

   when IDLE_STATE=>
           partition_bar    <= '1'  ;
           ccclr            <= '0'  ;
           ccinc            <= '0'  ;
           nocolclr         <= '1'  ;
```

```
        nocolinc          <= '0'  ;
        if (enable_bardd = '1') then
            newstate      <= CLEAR_STATE;
        elsif (carpres = '1')     then
            newstate      <= CWATCH_STATE;
        else
            newstate      <= IDLE_STATE;
        end if;

    when CWATCH_STATE=>
        partition_bar     <= '1'  ;
        ccclr             <= '0'  ;
        ccinc             <= collisiond;
        nocolclr          <= '0'  ;
        nocolinc          <= '1'  ;
        if (enable_bardd = '1') then
            newstate      <= CLEAR_STATE;
        elsif (collisiond = '1') then
            newstate      <= CCOUNT_STATE;
        elsif (carpres = '0') then
            newstate      <= IDLE_STATE;
        elsif (nocoldone = '1') then
            newstate      <= CLEAR_STATE;
        else
            newstate      <= CWATCH_STATE;
        end if;

    when CCOUNT_STATE=>
        partition_bar     <= '1'  ;
        ccclr             <= '0'  ;
        ccinc             <= '0'  ;
        nocolclr          <= '1'  ;
        nocolinc          <= '0'  ;
        if (enable_bardd = '1') then
            newstate      <= CLEAR_STATE;
        elsif (cclimit = '1')     then
            newstate      <= PWAIT_STATE;
        elsif (carpres = '0' and quietd = '1') then
            newstate      <= IDLE_STATE;
        else
            newstate      <= CCOUNT_STATE;
        end if;

    when PWAIT_STATE=>
        partition_bar     <= '0'  ;
        ccclr             <= '0'  ;
        ccinc             <= '0'  ;
```

```vhdl
            nocolclr          <= '1'  ;
            nocolinc          <= '0'  ;
            if (enable_bardd = '1') then
                newstate      <= CLEAR_STATE;
            elsif (carpres = '0' and quietd = '1') then
                newstate      <= PHOLD_STATE;
            else
                newstate      <= PWAIT_STATE;
            end if;

when PHOLD_STATE=>
            partition_bar     <= '0'  ;
            ccclr             <= '0'  ;
            ccinc             <= '0'  ;
            nocolclr          <= '1'  ;
            nocolinc          <= '0'  ;
            if (enable_bardd = '1') then
                newstate      <= CLEAR_STATE;
            elsif (collisiond = '1' or copyd = '1') then
                newstate      <= PCWATCH_STATE;
            else
                newstate      <= PHOLD_STATE;
            end if;

when PCWATCH_STATE=>
            partition_bar     <= '0'  ;
            ccclr             <= '0'  ;
            ccinc             <= '0'  ;
            nocolclr          <= '0'  ;
            nocolinc          <= '1'  ;
            if (enable_bardd = '1') then
                newstate      <= CLEAR_STATE;
            elsif (carpres = '1') then
                newstate      <= PWAIT_STATE;
            elsif (quietd = '0') then
                newstate      <= PHOLD_STATE;
            elsif (nocoldone = '1' and copyd = '1') then
                newstate      <= WAIT_STATE;
            else
                newstate      <= PCWATCH_STATE;
            end if;

when WAIT_STATE=>
            partition_bar     <= '0'  ;
            ccclr             <= '1'  ;
            ccinc             <= '0'  ;
            nocolclr          <= '1'  ;
```

```
                nocolinc          <= '0'  ;
                if (enable_bardd = '1') then
                    newstate      <= CLEAR_STATE;
                elsif (carpres = '0' and quietd = '1') then
                    newstate      <= IDLE_STATE;
                else
                    newstate      <= WAIT_STATE;
                end if;
        end case;
    end process;


--          State Flip-Flop for Synthesis
p1clk: process (txclk,areset)
    begin
        if areset = '1' then
            state <= clear_state;
        elsif (txclk'event and txclk = '1') then
            state <= newstate;
        end if;
    end process;
end archporte;
```

Listing 6-18 Port controller architecture

The state machine was quickly translated from the state diagram to VHDL code. Careful evaluation of the code shows that it models the description above.

Some designers would prefer to describe a design like this one by entering a bubble diagram, leaving the VHDL translation to a software tool. There are tools that will perform this task. We find, however, that at least as much time (if not more) is spent in entering a bubble diagram as would be spent entering the VHDL code directly.

The porte design may be synthesized to a device if the appropriate packages have been precompiled to the basic library.

Arbiter. The entity declaration for the arbiter is shown below, with the name arbiter8. Comments to the right may provide some additional information about the signals. The arbiter ensures that only one port is selected as the active receiving port, and identifies collisions as well as an absence of activity. The design does not present any surprises. The output signals are defined with Boolean equations. The activityin signals could have been described with an if-then construct, and the collision signal could have been defined with an algorithm using loops, but the Boolean equations are clear and easy to follow.

This arbiter does not use a fairness scheme, in which each port has equal priority for selection. Instead, activity1 has the highest priority and activity8 has the lowest. This means that the lower order ports will be selected over higher order ports if activity occurs on multiple ports at about the same time. For this application, this scheme is acceptable because if multiple ports are active a collision will occur anyway.

A bank of registers is used to create a pipeline stage. The carrier, collision, and nosel will be used in multiple modules and will propagate through several levels of logic, generating the need for a pipeline stage to reduce loading and to maintain a high frequency of operation. The other signals are pipelined to maintain synchronization. Fortunately, latency is not an issue in this design, thereby permitting its use. Chapter 9 discusses pipelining in greater detail. The complete code for arbiter is shown in Listing 6-19.

```vhdl
library ieee, basic;
use ieee.std_logic_1164.all;
use basic.regs_pkg.all;
entity arbiter8 is port(
    txclk:          in std_logic;        -- TX_CLK
    areset:         in std_logic;        -- Asynch reset
    activity1:      in std_logic;        -- Port activity 1
    activity2:      in std_logic;        -- Port activity 2
    activity3:      in std_logic;        -- Port activity 3
    activity4:      in std_logic;        -- Port activity 4
    activity5:      in std_logic;        -- Port activity 5
    activity6:      in std_logic;        -- Port activity 6
    activity7:      in std_logic;        -- Port activity 7
    activity8:      in std_logic;        -- Port activity 8
    sel1:           buffer std_logic;    -- Port select 1
    sel2:           buffer std_logic;    -- Port select 2
    sel3:           buffer std_logic;    -- Port select 3
    sel4:           buffer std_logic;    -- Port select 4
    sel5:           buffer std_logic;    -- Port select 5
    sel6:           buffer std_logic;    -- Port select 6
    sel7:           buffer std_logic;    -- Port select 7
    sel8:           buffer std_logic;    -- Port select 8
    nosel:          buffer std_logic;    -- No port selected
    carrier:        buffer std_logic;    -- Carrier detected
    collision:      buffer std_logic);   -- Collision detected
end arbiter8;

architecture archarbiter8 of arbiter8 is
    --      Signals
    signal  colin, carin: std_logic;
    signal  activityin1, activityin2, activityin3, activityin4: std_logic;
```

```
    signal  activityin5, activityin6, activityin7, activityin8: std_logic;
    signal  noactivity: std_logic;

    begin
--        Components

u1: rdff1 port map  (txclk, areset, activityin1, sel1);
u2: rdff1 port map  (txclk, areset, activityin2, sel2);
u3: rdff1 port map  (txclk, areset, activityin3, sel3);
u4: rdff1 port map  (txclk, areset, activityin4, sel4);
u5: rdff1 port map  (txclk, areset, activityin5, sel5);
u6: rdff1 port map  (txclk, areset, activityin6, sel6);
u7: rdff1 port map  (txclk, areset, activityin7, sel7);
u8: rdff1 port map  (txclk, areset, activityin8, sel8);

u9: pdff1 port map  (txclk, areset, noactivity, nosel);

u10: rdff1 port map (txclk, areset, colin, collision);
u11: rdff1 port map (txclk, areset, carin, carrier);

--        Arbitration Select Logic
   activityin1  <= activity1;

   activityin2  <= activity2
            and not activity1;

   activityin3  <= activity3
            and not(activity1 or activity2);

   activityin4  <= activity4
            and not(activity1 or activity2 or activity3);

   activityin5  <= activity5
            and not(activity1 or activity2 or activity3 or activity4);

   activityin6  <= activity6
            and not(activity1 or activity2 or activity3 or activity4 or
         activity5);

   activityin7  <= activity7
            and not(activity1 or activity2 or activity3 or activity4 or
         activity5 or activity6);

   activityin8  <= activity8
            and not(activity1 or activity2 or activity3 or activity4 or
         activity5 or activity6 or activity7);
```

```
noactivity    <= not(activity1 or activity2 or activity3 or activity4 or
               activity5 or activity6 or activity7 or activity8);

colin         <= (activity1 and (activity2 or activity3 or activity4 or
                 activity5 or activity6 or activity7 or activity8)) or

              (activity2 and (activity1 or activity3 or activity4
                or activity5 or activity6 or activity7 or activity8)) or

              (activity3 and (activity1 or activity2 or activity4
                or activity5 or activity6 or activity7 or activity8)) or

              (activity4 and (activity1 or activity2 or activity3
                or activity5 or activity6 or activity7 or activity8)) or

              (activity5 and (activity1 or activity2 or activity3
                or activity4 or activity6 or activity7 or activity8)) or

              (activity6 and (activity1 or activity2 or activity3
                or activity4 or activity5 or activity7 or activity8)) or

              (activity7 and (activity1 or activity2 or activity3
                or activity4 or activity5 or activity6 or activity8)) or

              (activity8 and (activity1 or activity2 or activity3
                or activity4 or activity5 or activity6 or activity7)) ;

carin         <= activity1 or activity2 or activity3 or activity4
                 or activity5 or activity6 or activity7 or activity8 ;
end archarbiter8;
```

Listing 6-19 Arbiter selects which port is active.

Clock Multiplexer. The entity declaration for the clock multiplexer is shown in Listing 6-20, with the name clockmux8. The design of the glitch-free clock-multiplexer circuit is left as an exercise for the reader. Figure 6-19 illustrates a potential solution, the use of product-term clocking. Be careful when using the output of a combinational function as a clock input. Doing so may cause false clocks due to inputs transitioning at slightly different times or propagating with slightly different delays, even if the simulation indicates that the delays are balanced. In most cases, use the output of one flip-flop as the product-term clock for another flip-flop.

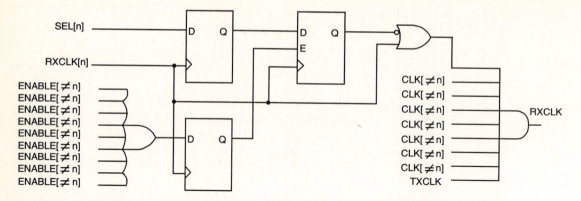

Figure 6-19   Glitch-free clock multiplexer circuit

```vhdl
library ieee, basic;
use ieee.std_logic_1164.all;
use basic.regs_pkg.all;

entity clockmux8 is port (
    areset          : in std_logic;            -- Asynch reset
    sreset          : in std_logic;            -- Synch  reset
    clk1            : in std_logic;            -- Clock 1
    clk2            : in std_logic;            -- Clock 2
    clk3            : in std_logic;            -- Clock 3
    clk4            : in std_logic;            -- Clock 4
    clk5            : in std_logic;            -- Clock 5
    clk6            : in std_logic;            -- Clock 6
    clk7            : in std_logic;            -- Clock 7
    clk8            : in std_logic;            -- Clock 8
    clk9            : in std_logic;            -- Clock 9 (txclk)
    sel1            : in std_logic;            -- Clock select 1
    sel2            : in std_logic;            -- Clock select 2
    sel3            : in std_logic;            -- Clock select 3
    sel4            : in std_logic;            -- Clock select 4
    sel5            : in std_logic;            -- Clock select 5
    sel6            : in std_logic;            -- Clock select 6
    sel7            : in std_logic;            -- Clock select 7
    sel8            : in std_logic;            -- Clock select 8
    sel9            : in std_logic;            -- Clock select 9
    rxclk           : buffer std_logic);       -- RX clock
end clockmux8;
```

Listing 6-20 Entity declaration for clock multiplexer

FIFO. Our approach to the design of this FIFO differs from the design of the FIFO in Chapter 4. In this design, Listing 6-21, rather than use an array of std_logic_vectors and a process to access the vectors, we instantiate eight 6-bit-wide registers. Accessing the registers with read and write pointers is handled in the same way as it was with the FIFO in Chapter 4.

The depth of the FIFO was chosen as eight to account for the latency between write and read cycles. This latency is caused by the port selection, state transition, and data path. Observation of the read and write pointers during simulation (discussed in Chapter 10) indicates that the depth is sufficient. A worst-case analysis for the depth of the FIFO is left as an exercise for the reader.

```
library ieee, basic;
use ieee.std_logic_1164.all;
use basic.regs_pkg.all; use basic.rreg;
use basic.counters_pkg.all; use basic.ascount
entity fifo is port(
        rxclk:       in std_logic;     -- from clock mux circuit
        txclk:       in std_logic;     -- Reference TX_CLK
        areset:      in std_logic;     -- Asynch reset
        sreset:      in std_logic;     -- Synch reset
        wptrclr:     in std_logic;     -- FIFO write pointer clear
        wptrinc:     in std_logic;     -- FIFO write pointer incr
        rptrclr:     in std_logic;     -- FIFO read pointer clear
        rptrinc:     in std_logic;     -- FIFO read pointer incr
        rxd5:        in std_logic;     -- FIFO data input
        rxd4:        in std_logic;     -- FIFO data input
        rxd3:        in std_logic;     -- FIFO data input
        rxd2:        in std_logic;     -- FIFO data input
        rxd1:        in std_logic;     -- FIFO data input
        rxd0:        in std_logic;     -- FIFO data input
        dmuxout:     buffer std_logic_vector(5 downto 0);
                                       -- FIFO mux output
        wptr2:       buffer std_logic;    -- write pointer
        wptr1:       buffer std_logic;    -- write pointer
        wptr0:       buffer std_logic;    -- write pointer
        rptr2:       buffer std_logic;    -- read pointer
        rptr1:       buffer std_logic;    -- read pointer
        rptr0:       buffer std_logic);   -- read pointer
end fifo;

architecture archfifo of fifo is
   -- signals
   signal rptr, wptr: std_logic_vector(2 downto 0);
   signal qout0, qout1, qout2, qout3, qout4, qout5,
        qout6, qout7, rxd: std_logic_vector(5 downto 0);
   signal en: std_logic_vector(7 downto 0);
```

```vhdl
begin
--        Components
         --FIFO array
u1: rreg generic map (6) port map (rxclk, areset, en(0), rxd, qout0);
u2: rreg generic map (6) port map (rxclk, areset, en(1), rxd, qout1);
u3: rreg generic map (6) port map (rxclk, areset, en(2), rxd, qout2);
u4: rreg generic map (6) port map (rxclk, areset, en(3), rxd, qout3);
u5: rreg generic map (6) port map (rxclk, areset, en(4), rxd, qout4);
u6: rreg generic map (6) port map (rxclk, areset, en(5), rxd, qout5);
u7: rreg generic map (6) port map (rxclk, areset, en(6), rxd, qout6);
u8: rreg generic map (6) port map (rxclk, areset, en(7), rxd, qout7);

-- Write pointer
u10: ascount    generic map (3)
                port map (rxclk, areset, wptrclr, wptrinc, wptr);
-- Read pointer
u11: ascount    generic map (3)
                port map (txclk,  areset, rptrclr, rptrinc, rptr);

  rxd <= (rxd5, rxd4, rxd3, rxd2, rxd1, rxd0);
  wptr2 <= wptr(2);
  wptr1 <= wptr(1);
  wptr0 <= wptr(0);
  rptr2 <= rptr(2);
  rptr1 <= rptr(1);
  rptr0 <= rptr(0);


--        8:1 Data mux
with rptr select
   dmuxout <=
       qout0 when "000",
       qout1 when "001",
       qout2 when "010",
       qout3 when "011",
       qout4 when "100",
       qout5 when "101",
       qout6 when "110",
       qout7 when others;

--        FIFO register selector decoder (wptr)
with wptr select
   en <=
       "00000001" when "000",
       "00000010" when "001",
       "00000100" when "010",
       "00001000" when "011",
       "00010000" when "100",
```

```
    "00100000" when "101",
    "01000000" when "110",
    "10000000" when others;

end archfifo;
```

Listing 6-21 FIFO design

The receive data is bused together internal to the architecture by concatenating the individual rxd bits:

```
rxd <= (rxd5, rxd4, rxd3, rxd2, rxd1, rxd0);
```

Because the read and write pointers are propagated to the top level, they are sent as individual std_logics rather than as a std_logic_vector:

```
wptr2 <= wptr(2);
wptr1 <= wptr(1);
wptr0 <= wptr(0);
rptr2 <= rptr(2);
rptr1 <= rptr(1);
rptr0 <= rptr(0);
```

Core Controller. Before discussing the design of the core controller, we will digress to explain how a host on the network transmits data.

The MAC-to-transceiver interface is shown at a high level in Figure 6-20. The transceiver takes nibble-wide data from the MAC each clock cycle. Over two clock cycles, the transceiver stores the first nibble in one register and the second in another. Eight bits of data are then encoded using the 8B6T ternary code of the IEEE 802.3 standard. Three shift registers used to serialize the data are loaded with the 8B6T code groups (Figure 6-21). One shift register is loaded while another byte is converted to an 8B6T code group. Therefore, the second register is loaded two clock cycles after the first. The third register is loaded two clock cycles after the second. Two clock cycles later, data in the first register has been transmitted, so it can be loaded with a new 8B6T code group. This interface results in the data-frame structure of Figure 6-22. The third transmit pair is the first to begin transmitting data, the first transmit pair is the second to transmit data, and the second pair is the last to transmit data. This transmission scheme is used to avoid latency and increase total system performance.

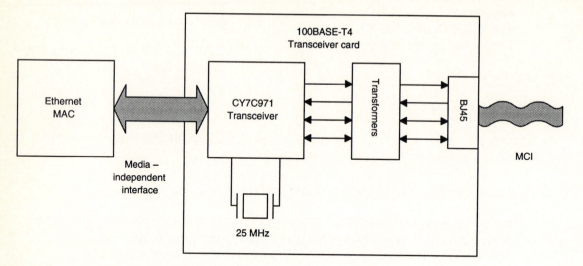

Figure 6-20   MAC-to-transceiver interface

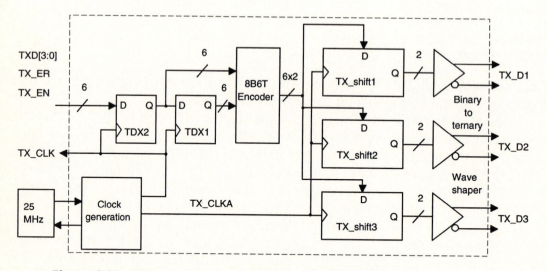

Figure 6-21   Mac-to-transceiver interface data frame structure

The repeater receives data with this structure and is responsible for retransmitting the data with the same structure. The preamble and SFD symbols (SOSA and SOSB) must be regenerated because the initial portion of the preamble is lost during the reception while clock recovery is performed. When the SFD symbol is received by the repeater, data is stored in the FIFO. Initial data is valid, however,

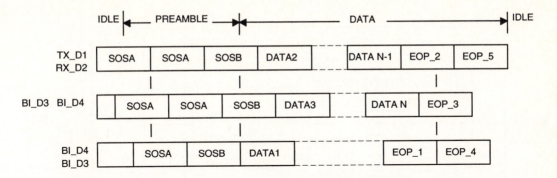

Figure 6-22   Data-frame structure [Adapted from IEEE Std 802.3u-1995 IEEE Standards for Local and Metropolitan Area Networks: Supplement to Carrier Sense Multiple Access with Collision Detection (CSMA/CD) Access Method and Physical Layer Specifications: Media Access Control (MAC) Parameters, Physical Layer, Medium Attachment Units, and Repeater for 100 Mb/s Operation, © 1995 by the Institute of Electrical and Electronics Engineers, Inc. The IEEE disclaims any responsibility or liability resulting from the placement and use in this publication. Information is adapted and reprinted with the permission of the IEEE.]

for only the third pair at first, then the first and third pairs, and finally all pairs (Figure 6-22). All data is stored in the FIFO for all pairs, even if it is not valid for all pairs. On the retransmission of data, only those pairs that are valid will be transmitted—the other transmit pairs will continue to transmit preamble, conforming to the data-frame structure. Now, we will return to the design of the core controller.

The function of the core controller is illustrated in Figure 6-23. The state machines interact primarily with the symbol generator and output multiplexer. There is a state machine for each of the transmit pairs. Although the symbol generation is shown in Figure 6-23 as three separate design units, it is designed as one unit in order to control the timing of transmit pairs (the multiplexers inside of this design unit are separate, however). A 3-bit counter is used to time the transmission of the SFD (start of frame delimiter) symbol and subsequent data on transmit pairs. One pair is transmitted when the counter reaches the decimal value of 1; the next pair begins at 3, and the next at 5. The counter continuously counts, rolling over after counting through 6, to indicate symbol boundaries and ensure that the data transmitted is separated by two clock cycles. Two clock cycles are required for the 8B6T encoding.

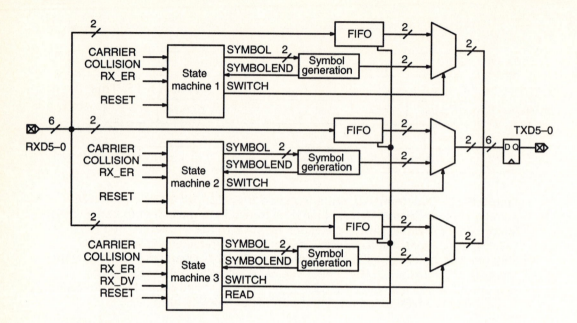

Figure 6-23 Core controllers

Each of the state machines follows the state transition diagram of Figure 6-24. The preamble state actually consists of three preamble substates for the first and third transmit pairs (Figure 6-25); the second transmit pair has four preamble states (three to transmit SOSA and one to transmit SOSB). Transitions from one preamble state to the next are based on the symbolend for each of the pairs. The symbolend is a symbol boundary that is generated from the 3-bit counter dis-

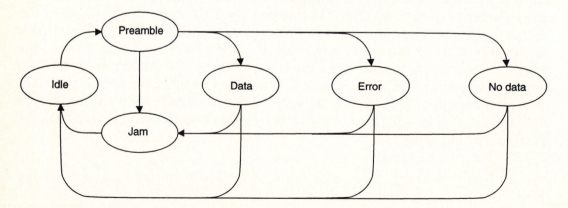

Figure 6-24 State transition diagram for core state machines

cussed in the previous paragraph. Symbolend1 indicates where the symbol boundaries are for the first transmit pair; symbolend2 is for the second transmit pair, and
symbolend3 is for the third. The symbol boundaries are separated by two clock
cycles, with symbolend2 starting at 1, symbolend3 starting at 3, and symbolend1
starting at 5 to conform to the data-frame structure of Figure 6-15. This is easiest
to see on the right-hand side of Figure 6-22, where the symbols end. The
symbolend counter will be placed in the symbol generator design unit because its
value is required in the generation of symbols.

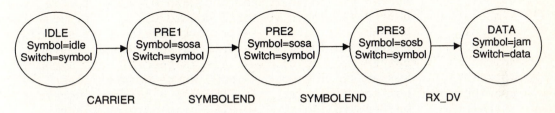

Figure 6-25   Preamble generation for pairs 1 and 3

The state machines use rx_dv and rx_er as inputs (they are bused together).
These signals transition from the high-impedance state and are gated with
carrierd to filter out glitches. Because rx_dv and rx_er are asynchronous to the
transmit clock, they must be synchronized to the rest of the system.

The FIFO read and write pointers and resets are all controlled by the core
controller. The FIFO read and write pointers are continuously incremented. Carrier
is an output of the arbiter and indicates that a port is active. However, the write
pointer is cleared until valid data is identified, and the read pointer is cleared until
the state machine enters a data state.

Finally, the prescale counter shared by the port controllers is placed in this
design unit. A prescale output is generated when the counter reaches its limit.

Listing 6-22 is a partial code listing of the core controller. It includes all logic
except for two of the state machines. The designs of those state machines are similar to that of the first, and are left as exercises for the reader.

```
library ieee, basic;
use ieee.std_logic_1164.all;
use basic.regs_pkg.all;
use basic.synch_pkg.all;
use basic.counters_pkg.all;


entity control is port(
        txclk:          in std_logic;      -- Reference TX_CLK
        areset:         in std_logic;      -- Async reset
```

```
        carrier:        in std_logic;      -- indicates carrier asserted
        collision:      in std_logic;      -- indicates collision condition
        rx_error:       in std_logic;      -- indicates RX PMA error
        rx_dv:          in std_logic;      -- indicates SFD found in data
        symbolend1:     in std_logic;      -- indicates end of symbol line 1
        symbolend2:     in std_logic;      -- indicates end of symbol line 2
        symbolend3:     in std_logic;      -- indicates end of symbol line 3
        symbolclr:      buffer std_logic;   -- resets symbol counter
        symbolinc:      buffer std_logic;   -- increments symbol counter
        symbol1:        buffer std_logic_vector(1 downto 0);   -- selects
        symbol2:        buffer std_logic_vector(1 downto 0);   -- special
        symbol3:        buffer std_logic_vector(1 downto 0);   -- symbols
        switch1:        buffer std_logic;   -- selects special/data symbols
        switch2:        buffer std_logic;   -- selects special/data symbols
        switch3:        buffer std_logic;   -- selects special/data symbols
        wptrclr:        buffer std_logic;   -- FIFO write pointer clear
        wptrinc:        buffer std_logic;   -- FIFO write pointer increment
        rptrclr:        buffer std_logic;   -- FIFO read pointer clear
        rptrinc:        buffer std_logic;   -- FIFO read pointer increment
        txdata:         buffer std_logic;   -- txdata is ready
        idle:           buffer std_logic;   -- indicates idle generation
        preamble:       buffer std_logic;   -- indicates preamble generation
        data:           buffer std_logic;   -- indicates data generation
        col:            buffer std_logic;   -- indicates jam generation
        prescale:       buffer std_logic);  -- prescale output to port
end control;


architecture archcontrol of control is
type states1 is (IDLE_STATE1, PRE1_STATE1, PRE2_STATE1, PRE3_STATE1,
        DATA_STATE1, JAM_STATE1, NOSFD_STATE1, ERROR_STATE1);
--attribute state_encoding of states1:type is one_hot_one;

type states2 is (IDLE_STATE2, PRE1_STATE2, PRE2_STATE2, PRE3_STATE2,
        DATA_STATE2, JAM_STATE2, NOSFD_STATE2, ERROR_STATE2, PRE4_STATE2);
--attribute state_encoding of states2:type is one_hot_one;

type states3 is (IDLE_STATE3, PRE1_STATE3, PRE2_STATE3, PRE3_STATE3,
        DATA_STATE3, JAM_STATE3, NOSFD_STATE3, ERROR_STATE3);
--attribute state_encoding of states3:type is one_hot_one;

signal state1, newstate1: states1;
signal state2, newstate2: states2;
signal state3, newstate3: states3;

signal  carrierd, carrierdd: std_logic;
signal  error, rx_dv_in, rx_error_in: std_logic;
signal  no_sfd, no_sfd_in, no_data, data_valid: std_logic;
```

```vhdl
signal  prescale_in: std_logic;
signal  pout: std_logic_vector(9 downto 0);

constant jam:    std_logic_vector(1 downto 0) := "00";
constant pre:    std_logic_vector(1 downto 0) := "00";
constant sosb:   std_logic_vector(1 downto 0) := "01";
constant bad:    std_logic_vector(1 downto 0) := "10";
constant zero:   std_logic_vector(1 downto 0) := "11";
constant fifodata:      std_logic := '1';
constant symboldata:    std_logic := '0';
signal vdd:std_logic := '1';
signal vss:    std_logic := '0';

begin
--       Components
u1: rsynch port map (txclk, areset, carrier, carrierdd);
u3: rsynch port map (txclk, areset, rx_error_in, error);
u5: rdff1 port map (txclk, areset, rx_dv_in, data_valid);
u7: rdff1 port map (txclk, areset, no_sfd_in, no_data);
u8: ascount generic map(10) port map (txclk, areset, vss, vdd, pout);
u9: rdff1 port map(txclk, areset, prescale_in, prescale);

rx_dv_in    <= carrierdd and rx_dv;      -- filter out glitches
rx_error_in <= carrierdd and rx_error; -- filter out glitches
wptrclr     <= not(rx_dv_in and not collision);
no_sfd_in   <= (no_sfd or no_data) and carrier;
prescale_in <= '1' when pout = "1111111111" else '0';

wptrinc <= '1';
rptrinc <= '1';
symbolinc <= '1';

--       State machine controllers
--       State machine controller Line 3

p3: process (carrier, collision, symbolend3, data_valid, error,
                state3)
   begin

      case (state3) is

      when IDLE_STATE3 =>

            symbol3<= zero;
            switch3 <= symboldata;
            symbolclr <= '1';
            rptrclr <= '1';
            preamble<= '0';
```

```vhdl
            data  <= '0';
            no_sfd<= '0';
            idle  <= '1';
            col   <= '0';
            txdata<= '0';
            if (collision = '1') then
                newstate3 <= JAM_STATE3;
            elsif (carrier = '1') then
                newstate3 <= PRE1_STATE3;
            else
                newstate3 <= IDLE_STATE3;
            end if;

        when PRE1_STATE3 =>
            symbol3<= pre;
            switch3 <= symboldata;
            symbolclr <= '0';
            rptrclr <= '1';
            preamble<= '1';
            data  <= '0';
            no_sfd<= '0';
            idle  <= '0';
            col   <= '0';
            txdata<= '1';
            if (carrier = '0') then
                newstate3 <= IDLE_STATE3;
            elsif (collision = '1') then
                newstate3 <= JAM_STATE3;
            elsif (symbolend3 = '1') then
                newstate3 <= PRE2_STATE3;
            else
                newstate3 <= PRE1_STATE3;
            end if;

        when PRE2_STATE3 =>
            symbol3<= pre;
            switch3 <= symboldata;
            symbolclr <= '0';
            rptrclr <= '1';
            preamble<= '1';
            data  <= '0';
            no_sfd<= '0';
            idle  <= '0';
            col   <= '0';
            txdata<= '1';
            if (carrier = '0') then
                newstate3 <= IDLE_STATE3;
```

```
        elsif (collision = '1') then
            newstate3 <= JAM_STATE3;
        elsif (symbolend3 = '1') then
            newstate3 <= PRE3_STATE3;
        else
            newstate3 <= PRE2_STATE3;
        end if;

    when PRE3_STATE3 =>
        symbol3<= sosb;
        switch3 <= symboldata;
        symbolclr <= '0';
        rptrclr <= '1';
        preamble<= '1';
        data   <= '0';
        no_sfd<= '0';
        idle   <= '0';
        col    <= '0';
        txdata<= '1';
        if (carrier = '0') then
            newstate3 <= IDLE_STATE3;
        elsif (collision = '1') then
            newstate3 <= JAM_STATE3;
        elsif (symbolend3 = '1' and error = '1') then
            newstate3 <= ERROR_STATE3;
        elsif (symbolend3 = '1' and data_valid = '0') then
            newstate3 <= NOSFD_STATE3;
        elsif (symbolend3 = '1' and data_valid = '1') then
            newstate3 <= DATA_STATE3;
        else
            newstate3 <= PRE3_STATE3;
        end if;

    when DATA_STATE3 =>
        symbol3<= jam;
        switch3 <= fifodata;
        symbolclr <= '0';
        rptrclr <= '0';
        preamble<= '0';
        data   <= '1';
        no_sfd<= '0';
        idle   <= '0';
        col    <= '0';
        txdata<= '1';
        if (carrier = '0') then
            newstate3 <= IDLE_STATE3;
```

```vhdl
    elsif (collision = '1') then
        newstate3 <= JAM_STATE3;
    elsif (symbolend3 = '1' and error = '1') then
        newstate3 <= ERROR_STATE3;
    else
        newstate3 <= DATA_STATE3;
    end if;

when JAM_STATE3 =>
    symbol3<= jam;
    switch3 <= symboldata;
    symbolclr <= '0';
    rptrclr <= '1';
    preamble<= '0';
    data   <= '0';
    no_sfd<= '0';
    idle   <= '0';
    col    <= '1';
    txdata<= '1';
    if (carrier = '0') then
        newstate3 <= IDLE_STATE3;
    else
        newstate3 <= JAM_STATE3;
    end if;

when NOSFD_STATE3 =>
    symbol3<= jam;
    switch3 <= symboldata;
    symbolclr <= '0';
    rptrclr <= '0';
    preamble<= '0';
    data   <= '1';
    no_sfd<= '1';
    idle   <= '0';
    col    <= '0';
    txdata<= '1';
    if (carrier = '0') then
        newstate3 <= IDLE_STATE3;
    elsif (collision = '1') then
        newstate3 <= JAM_STATE3;
    elsif (symbolend3 = '1' and error = '1') then
        newstate3 <= ERROR_STATE3;
    else
        newstate3 <= NOSFD_STATE3;
    end if;
```

```
    when ERROR_STATE3 =>
        symbol3<= bad;
        switch3 <= symboldata;
        symbolclr <= '0';
        rptrclr <= '0';
        preamble<= '0';
        data   <= '1';
        no_sfd<= '0';
        idle   <= '0';
        col    <= '0';
        txdata<= '1';
        if (carrier = '0') then
            newstate3 <= IDLE_STATE3;
        elsif (collision = '1') then
            newstate3 <= JAM_STATE3;
        else
            newstate3 <= ERROR_STATE3;
        end if;
    end case;
end process;

p3clk: process (txclk,areset)
    begin
        if areset = '1' then
            state3 <= idle_state3;
        elsif (txclk'event and txclk='1') then
            state3 <= newstate3;
        end if;
    end process;
end archcontrol;
```

Listing 6-22 Core controller code

There are several outputs in each state. Symbolclr is used to clear the 3-bit counter that controls the symbol boundaries, preamble indicates that the core controller is generating preamble, data indicates that the core controller is transmitting data, no_sfd indicates that no data was found, idle indicates that the network is idle, and col indicates that there is a collision and jam characters are being transmitted. All of these signals are propagated to the top level for observation. Txdata is used in each of the port controllers to assert tx_en. These signals do not need to be repeated in the design of the two additional state machines that control the other two transmit pairs.

The symbol and switch outputs are used to control two output multiplexers for each transmit pair. Symbol indicates which symbol to generate. Switch indicates whether the symbol or FIFO data is selected to transmit to the outputs. The symbol and switch signals are separate for each pair so that one transmit pair may transmit symbols while another transmits data.

Symbol Generator and Output Multiplexer. Listing 6-23 is the design of the symbol generator and output multiplexer. The jam, SOSB2, and bad characters for each of the transmission pairs are defined by the IEEE 802.3 standard. The values of the symbol counter and multiplexers are used to generate these symbols. Two multiplexers for each transmit pair are used. The first multiplexer selects a symbol, and the second selects either the symbol or data from the FIFO.

```vhdl
library ieee, basic;
use ieee.std_logic_1164.all;
use basic.regs_pkg.all;
use basic.counters_pkg.all;
entity symbolmux is port(
        txclk:      in std_logic;               -- Reference TX_CLK
        areset:     in std_logic;               -- Async reset
        symbolclr:  in std_logic;               -- Symbol counter clear
        symbolinc:  in std_logic;               -- Symbol counter increment
        switch1:    in std_logic;               -- Line 1 D/S switch control
        switch2:    in std_logic;               -- Line 2 D/S switch control
        switch3:    in std_logic;               -- Line 3 D/S switch control
        symbol1:    in std_logic_vector(1 downto 0);  -- Line 1 symbol
                                                -- mux control
        symbol2:    in std_logic_vector(1 downto 0);  -- Line 2 symbol
                                                -- mux control
        symbol3:    in std_logic_vector(1 downto 0);  -- Line 3 symbol
                                                -- mux control
        dmuxout:    in std_logic_vector(5 downto 0);  -- FIFO data input
        symbolend1: buffer std_logic;           -- End of line 1 symbol
        symbolend2: buffer std_logic;           -- End of line 2 symbol
        symbolend3: buffer std_logic;           -- End of line 3 symbol
        txd5:       buffer std_logic;           -- Data
        txd4:       buffer std_logic;           -- Data
        txd3:       buffer std_logic;           -- Data
        txd2:       buffer std_logic;           -- Data
        txd1:       buffer std_logic;           -- Data
        txd0:       buffer std_logic);          -- Data
end symbolmux;

architecture archsymbolmux of symbolmux is
-- signals
signal   clearcount: std_logic;
signal   symbolcount: std_logic_vector(2 downto 0);
```

```
signal    sosb1, sosb2, sosb3, bad1, bad2, bad3, jam: std_logic_vector
          (1 downto 0);
signal    txd, muxout, smuxout: std_logic_vector(5 downto 0);

-- Constants
constant plus : std_logic_vector(1 downto 0) := "10";
constant zero : std_logic_vector(1 downto 0) := "00";
constant minus: std_logic_vector(1 downto 0) := "01";

begin
-- Components

u1: ascount generic map(CounterSize => 3)-- Symbol count
        port map (txclk, areset, clearcount, symbolinc, symbolcount);
u2: rdff generic map (size => 6)            -- Output latch
      port map (txclk, areset, muxout, txd);

txd5 <= txd(5);
txd4 <= txd(4);
txd3 <= txd(3);
txd2 <= txd(2);
txd1 <= txd(1);
txd0 <= txd(0);

symbolend1<= symbolcount(0) and not symbolcount(1) and  symbolcount(2);
symbolend2<= symbolcount(0) and not symbolcount(1) and not symbolcount(2);
symbolend3<= symbolcount(0) and  symbolcount(1) and not symbolcount(2);
clearcount<= symbolend1 or symbolclr;

-- Special symbol mux
with symbol1 select
    smuxout(1 downto 0) <=
        jam   when "00",
        sosb1 when "01",
        bad1  when "10",
        zero  when others;

-- Line 1 switch mux
with switch1 select
        muxout(1 downto 0) <=
            smuxout(1 downto 0) when '0',
            dmuxout(1 downto 0) when others;

-- Special symbol mux (Line 2)
with symbol2 select
    smuxout(3 downto 2) <=
        jam   when "00",
        sosb2 when "01",
        bad2  when "10",
        zero  when others;
```

```
-- Line 2 switch mux
with switch2 select
      muxout(3 downto 2) <=
          smuxout(3 downto 2) when '0',
          dmuxout(3 downto 2) when others;

-- Special symbol mux (Line 3)
with symbol3 select
    smuxout(5 downto 4) <=
        jam   when "00",
        sosb3 when "01",
        bad3  when "10",
        zero  when others;

-- Line 3 switch mux
with switch3 select
      muxout(5 downto 4) <=
          smuxout(5 downto 4) when '0',
          dmuxout(5 downto 4) when others;

-- Jam/preamble generation (all lines)
with symbolcount(0) select
    jam <=
        plus  when '0',
        minus when others;

-- SOSB generation (line 1)
with symbolcount select
    sosb1 <=
        plus  when "000",
        minus when "001",
        plus  when "010",
        minus when "011",
        minus when "100",
        plus  when "101",
        zero  when others;

-- SOSB generation (line 2)
with symbolcount select
    sosb2 <=
        minus when "000",
        plus  when "001",
        plus  when "010",
        minus when "011",
        plus  when "100",
        minus when "101",
        zero  when others;
```

```
-- SOSB generation (line 3)
with symbolcount select
    sosb3 <=
        plus  when "000",
        minus when "001",
        minus when "010",
        plus  when "011",
        plus  when "100",
        minus when "101",
        zero  when others;

-- Bad code generation (line 1)
with symbolcount select
    bad1 <=
        minus when "000",
        minus when "001",
        minus when "010",
        plus  when "011",
        plus  when "100",
        plus  when "101",
        zero  when others;

-- Bad code generation (line 2)
with symbolcount select
    bad2 <=
        plus  when "000",
        plus  when "001",
        minus when "010",
        minus when "011",
        minus when "100",
        plus  when "101",
        zero  when others;

-- Bad code generation (line 3)
with symbolcount select
    bad3 <=
        minus when "000",
        plus  when "001",
        plus  when "010",
        plus  when "011",
        minus when "100",
        minus when "101",
        zero  when others;
end archsymbolmux;
```

Listing 6-23 Symbol generator and output multiplexer code

Top-Level Design. Before the design units can be connected in the top-level of the design hierarchy, a package, coretop_pkg, is created (not shown) in which the design units are declared as components. Once the components are declared and made visible to the top-level design, they can be instantiated. Listing 6-24 is the design of the repeater core logic in which the design units are interfaced on another and to the top-level I/O.

```vhdl
library ieee;
use ieee.std_logic_1164.all;

entity core is port(
    reset           : in std_logic;        -- Global reset
    clk             : in std_logic;        -- to CKTPAD for TX_CLK
    rxd5            : in std_logic;        -- RXD5
    rxd4            : in std_logic;        -- RXD4
    rxd3            : in std_logic;        -- RXD3
    rxd2            : in std_logic;        -- RXD2
    rxd1            : in std_logic;        -- RXD1
    rxd0            : in std_logic;        -- RXD0
    rx_dv           : in std_logic;        -- RX_DV
    rx_er           : in std_logic;        -- RX_ER

    clk1            : in std_logic;        -- RX_CLK1
    crs1            : in std_logic;        -- CRS1
    enable1_bar     : in std_logic;        -- ENABLE1
    link1_bar       : in std_logic;        -- LINK1

    clk2            : in std_logic;        -- RX_CLK2
    crs2            : in std_logic;        -- CRS2
    enable2_bar     : in std_logic;        -- ENABLE2
    link2_bar       : in std_logic;        -- LINK2

    clk3            : in std_logic;        -- RX_CLK3
    crs3            : in std_logic;        -- CRS3
    enable3_bar     : in std_logic;        -- ENABLE3
    link3_bar       : in std_logic;        -- LINK3

    clk4            : in std_logic;        -- RX_CLK4
    crs4            : in std_logic;        -- CRS4
    enable4_bar     : in std_logic;        -- ENABLE4
    link4_bar       : in std_logic;        -- LINK4

    clk5            : in std_logic;        -- RX_CLK5
    crs5            : in std_logic;        -- CRS5
    enable5_bar     : in std_logic;        -- ENABLE5
    link5_bar       : in std_logic;        -- LINK5
```

```vhdl
clk6              : in std_logic;          -- RX_CLK6
crs6              : in std_logic;          -- CRS6
enable6_bar       : in std_logic;          -- ENABLE6
link6_bar         : in std_logic;          -- LINK6

clk7              : in std_logic;          -- RX_CLK7
crs7              : in std_logic;          -- CRS7
enable7_bar       : in std_logic;          -- ENABLE7
link7_bar         : in std_logic;          -- LINK7

clk8              : in std_logic;          -- RX_CLK8
crs8              : in std_logic;          -- CRS8
enable8_bar       : in std_logic;          -- ENABLE8
link8_bar         : in std_logic;          -- LINK8

rx_en1            : buffer std_logic;      -- RX_EN1
tx_en1            : buffer std_logic;      -- TX_EN1
partition1_bar    : buffer std_logic;      -- PARTITION1
jabber1_bar       : buffer std_logic;      -- JABBER1

rx_en2            : buffer std_logic;      -- RX_EN2
tx_en2            : buffer std_logic;      -- TX_EN2
partition2_bar    : buffer std_logic;      -- PARTITION2
jabber2_bar       : buffer std_logic;      -- JABBER2

rx_en3            : buffer std_logic;      -- RX_EN3
tx_en3            : buffer std_logic;      -- TX_EN3
partition3_bar    : buffer std_logic;      -- PARTITION3
jabber3_bar       : buffer std_logic;      -- JABBER3

rx_en4            : buffer std_logic;      -- RX_EN4
tx_en4            : buffer std_logic;      -- TX_EN4
partition4_bar    : buffer std_logic;      -- PARTITION4
jabber4_bar       : buffer std_logic;      -- JABBER4

rx_en5            : buffer std_logic;      -- RX_EN5
tx_en5            : buffer std_logic;      -- TX_EN5
partition5_bar    : buffer std_logic;      -- PARTITION5
jabber5_bar       : buffer std_logic;      -- JABBER5

rx_en6            : buffer std_logic;      -- RX_EN6
tx_en6            : buffer std_logic;      -- TX_EN6
partition6_bar    : buffer std_logic;      -- PARTITION6
jabber6_bar       : buffer std_logic;      -- JABBER6
```

```
    rx_en7              : buffer std_logic;        -- RX_EN7
    tx_en7              : buffer std_logic;        -- TX_EN7
    partition7_bar      : buffer std_logic;        -- PARTITION7
    jabber7_bar         : buffer std_logic;        -- JABBER7

    rx_en8              : buffer std_logic;        -- RX_EN8
    tx_en8              : buffer std_logic;        -- TX_EN8
    partition8_bar      : buffer std_logic;        -- PARTITION8
    jabber8_bar         : buffer std_logic;        -- JABBER8

    txd5                : buffer std_logic;        -- TXD5
    txd4                : buffer std_logic;        -- TXD4
    txd3                : buffer std_logic;        -- TXD3
    txd2                : buffer std_logic;        -- TXD2
    txd1                : buffer std_logic;        -- TXD1
    txd0                : buffer std_logic;        -- TXD0

    txdata              : buffer std_logic;        -- TX_ENall
    idle                : buffer std_logic;        -- Idle generation
    preamble            : buffer std_logic;        -- Preamble generation
    data                : buffer std_logic;        -- Data generation
    jam                 : buffer std_logic;        -- Jam generation
    collision           : buffer std_logic;        -- Collision indication
    wptr2               : buffer std_logic;        -- Write pointer2
    wptr1               : buffer std_logic;        -- Write pointer1
    wptr0               : buffer std_logic;        -- Write pointer0
    rptr2               : buffer std_logic;        -- Read pointer2
    rptr1               : buffer std_logic;        -- Read pointer1
    rptr0               : buffer std_logic);       -- Read pointer0
end core;

use work.coretop_pkg.all;

architecture archcore of core is
    signal txclk1, nosel, areset, sel1, sel2, sel3, sel4: std_logic;
    signal sel5, sel6, sel7, sel8, rxclk, txclk: std_logic;
    signal activity1, activity2, activity3, activity4: std_logic;
    signal activity5, activity6, activity7, activity8: std_logic;
    signal carrier: std_logic;
    signal wptrclr, wptrinc, rptrclr, rptrinc,symbolinc:std_logic;
    signal switch1, switch2, switch3: std_logic;
    signal symbolend1, symbolend2, symbolend3: std_logic;
    signal symbolclr : std_logic;
    signal symbol1, symbol2, symbol3: std_logic_vector(1 downto 0);
    signal dmuxout: std_logic_vector(5 downto 0);
    signal prescale: std_logic;
```

```
begin
--      Components
u1: clockmux8 port map
    (areset,
    clk1, clk2, clk3, clk4, clk5, clk6, clk7, clk8, txclk1,
    sel1, sel2, sel3, sel4, sel5, sel6, sel7, sel8, nosel,
    rxclk);

u2: arbiter8 port map
    (txclk, areset,
    activity1, activity2, activity3, activity4,
    activity5, activity6, activity7, activity8,
    sel1, sel2, sel3, sel4, sel5, sel6, sel7, sel8,
    nosel, carrier, collision);

u3: fifo port map
    (rxclk, txclk, areset, wptrclr, wptrinc, rptrclr,
    rptrinc, rxd5, rxd4, rxd3, rxd2, rxd1, rxd0,
    dmuxout,  wptr2, wptr1, wptr0, rptr2, rptr1, rptr0);

u4: symbolmux port map
    (txclk, areset,
    symbolclr, symbolinc, switch1, switch2, switch3, symbol1,
    symbol2, symbol3, dmuxout, symbolend1, symbolend2,
    symbolend3, txd5, txd4, txd3, txd2, txd1, txd0);

u5: control port map
    (txclk, areset, carrier, collision, rx_er, rx_dv,
    symbolend1, symbolend2, symbolend3, symbolclr, symbolinc,
    symbol1, symbol2, symbol3, switch1, switch2, switch3,
    wptrclr, wptrinc, rptrclr, rptrinc, txdata, idle,
    preamble, data, jam, prescale);

u6: porte port map
    (txclk, areset,
    crs1, enable1_bar, link1_bar,
    sel1, carrier, collision, jam, txdata, prescale, rx_en1, tx_en1,
    activity1, jabber1_bar, partition1_bar);

u7: porte port map
    (txclk, areset,
    crs2, enable2_bar, link2_bar,
    sel2, carrier, collision, jam, txdata, prescale, rx_en2, tx_en2,
    activity2, jabber2_bar, partition2_bar);

u8: porte port map
    (txclk, areset,
```

```
          crs3, enable3_bar, link3_bar,
          sel3, carrier, collision, jam, txdata, prescale, rx_en3, tx_en3,
          activity3, jabber3_bar, partition3_bar);

    u9: porte port map
          (txclk, areset,
          crs4, enable4_bar, link4_bar,
          sel4, carrier, collision, jam, txdata, prescale, rx_en4, tx_en4,
          activity4, jabber4_bar, partition4_bar);

    u10: porte port map
          (txclk, areset,
          crs5, enable5_bar, link5_bar,
          sel5, carrier, collision, jam, txdata, prescale, rx_en5, tx_en5,
          activity5, jabber5_bar, partition5_bar);

    u11: porte port map
          (txclk, areset,
          crs6, enable6_bar, link6_bar,
          sel6, carrier, collision, jam, txdata, prescale, rx_en6, tx_en6,
          activity6, jabber6_bar, partition6_bar);

    u12: porte port map
          (txclk, areset,
          crs7, enable7_bar, link7_bar,
          sel7, carrier, collision, jam, txdata, prescale, rx_en7, tx_en7,
          activity7, jabber7_bar, partition7_bar);

    u13: porte port map
          (txclk, areset,
          crs8, enable8_bar, link8_bar,
          sel8, carrier, collision, jam, txdata, prescale, rx_en8, tx_en8,
          activity8, jabber8_bar, partition8_bar);

    txclk  <= clk;
    txclk1 <= clk;
    areset <= reset;

end archcore;
```

Listing 6-24 Top-level repeater core-logic design code

Listing 6-24 completes the design of the repeater core logic. In Chapter 8, we discuss issues concerning the synthesis of this design for implementation in an FPGA. In Chapter 10, we explain how to create a VHDL test bench to simulate both the source code and the postsynthesis and place and route models.

Problems

6.1. Create entity declaration and architecture body pairs for:

a. and2   h.   nor2

b. and4   i.   nor4

c. and8   j.   nor8

d. or2   k.   nand2

e. or4   l.   nand4

f. or8   m.   nand8

g. xor2

6.2. Use generics to create parameterized entity declaration and architecture body pairs for:

a. andn

b. orn

c. norn

d. nandn

6.3. Create a package with component declarations for the entities defined in Problems 6.1 and 6.2.

6.4. Compile the design units of Problems 6.1, 6.2, and 6.3 into a library named logic.

6.5. Create a new project in a new directory. Implement the equation x = ab + c, using the components in the logic library created in Problem 6.4.

6.6. Modify the ALU design so that it uses only two + operands in the entire description. Set node cost to 4.

6.7. Recompile the AM2901 design after incorporating the change in Problem 6.6. Compare results to those of Breakout Exercise 6-2.

6.8. The 14-bit counters described on page 343 are built with a 10-bit base counter and 4-bit prescaled counters. Redesign the jabber counters to use 11-bit base counters and 3-bit prescaled counters. What is the accuracy now? Are any other combinations possible? How many logic cells are required for each? Develop an algorithm for accuracy and resources based on using an n-bit base counter and m-bit prescaled counters, with $n + m = 14$.

6.9. Rewrite the `arbiter8` code in Listing 6-19 to use `std_logic_vectors` instead of individual `std_logics` for `activity`, `activityin`, and `sel`. Use a for-generate or `for-loop` construct to define the equations for `activityin`.

6.10. Design the glitch-free clock multiplexer circuit of Figure 6-19.

6.11. Complete the partial code presented in Listing 6-22 by including the other two state machines.

6.12. After completing Problems 6.10 and 6.11, compile, synthesize, place, and route the complete network repeater. Target the CY7C388A FPGA.

6.13. Do a worst-case analysis to determine whether the depth of the FIFO is adequate.

6.14. What recommendations and changes would you make to improve the performance of the network repeater?

6.15. Presently, all of the state machine outputs of the core controller come from the third state machine, which unnecessarily loads its state bits. Move some of the outputs to the other state machines. (Was this one of your recommendations in response to Problem 6.13?) Synthesize, place, and route the original control design, then the modified version. Compare results.

6.16. Recompile, synthesize, place, and route the repeater design with the modification from Problem 6.15. Compare results to those of Problem 6.11.

Chapter 7

Functions and Procedures

7.1   Introduction

In Chapter 6 we brought together many of the language constructs that were introduced in earlier chapters to construct two complex designs that served as case studies—a microprocessor slice and the core logic of a network repeater. Each design was decomposed into smaller and more manageable functional units. Design hierarchy was used to create simple components that combined to create larger components. Some components were parameterized so that each instance could be tailored to its application. Packages were used to make declarations—including component declarations, which serve as interface templates for the entity that a component represents—visible to other design units. Collections of entity declarations, architecture bodies, and packages were compiled into libraries for reuse in future designs.

In this chapter we introduce subprograms: functions and procedures. We introduce subprograms late in our study of VHDL, after our case studies, (1) to de-emphasize their use in models for synthesis, and (2) to illustrate how functions and procedures could have been used as short-hand notation for some of the component instantiations.

Used frequently in models for simulation, **functions** and **procedures** are high-level design constructs that compute values or define processes for type conversions, operator overloading, or as an alternative to component instantiation. Although all of these have applications for synthesis, the functions of most use have already been defined in the IEEE 1076, 1164, and 1076.3 standards.

We begin our discussion of subprograms by introducing type conversion functions. The functions `to_integer`, `to_signed`, and `to_unsigned`—defined in `numeric_std`—prove useful when combining types in arithmetic operations. We illustrate how to define and use your own type conversion functions by analyzing an example that describes how to convert a signal of type `Boolean` to type `bit`. Next, we illustrate how functions can be used as short-hand for instantiation of simple components. We show how to overload operators and other functions, then we discuss standard functions and overloaded operators and explain how to interpret a few of the functions in the IEEE 1076.3 and 1164 standards. We introduce the concept of operator inferencing and module generation and contrast this with the processing of behavioral models of functions by simulators. Finally, we describe procedures, the differences between functions and procedures, and how procedures can be used as short-hand for more complex component instantiations.

7.2   Functions

bl2bit (Boolean to Bit). Listing 7-1 shows a type conversion function.

```
1  function bl2bit(a:BOOLEAN) return BIT is
2    begin
3      if a then
4        return '1';
5      else
6        return '0';
7      end if;
8  end bl2bit;
```

Listing 7-1 A `Boolean` to `bit` type conversion function

Listing 7-1 describes a function that is used to convert a signal of type `Boolean` to type `bit`. `Boolean` and `bit` are both predefined by the IEEE 1076 standard. Line 1 declares the function `bl2bit` and defines the input parameter as type `Boolean` and the return type as `bit`. Lines 2 and 8 begin and end the function definition. All statements within the function definition must be sequential statements. Lines 3 through 7 are sequential statements that define the return value based on the Boolean condition a. If a is true, then the return value is '1'; otherwise, the return value is '0' (the return type is `bit`). Other often-used type conversion functions are `bit` to `Boolean`, `bit` to `std_logic`, and `bit_vector` to `std_logic_vector`. You'll have an opportunity to write a couple of these conversion functions in the exercises at the end of the chapter.

A `bit` to `Boolean` (or `Boolean` to `bit`) type conversion function can be helpful in writing Boolean equations or evaluation clauses. For example, if the signal `clk` is of type `Boolean`, you can write

```
wait until clk;
```

rather than

```
wait until clk='1';
```

or

```
if (clk'event and clk) then...
```

rather than

```
if (clk'event and clk='1') then...
```

Likewise

```
if ((A and B) xor (C and D)) then...
```

can be substituted for

```
if (((A and B) xor (C and D))='1') then...
```

One way is not necessarily better than the other. For the designer writing VHDL models for synthesis, `std_logic` is the preferred type. For the designer writing VHDL models for simulation, `std_logic` may be a poor choice because it is a subtype that has an associated resolution function. Each time an assignment is made to an object of a resolved type, the resolution function must be called, which slows simulation. All of the designs in this book are insignificantly small to be concerned about simulation time, especially because synthesis is our primary concern. Regardless of the type you choose to use, VHDL provides the flexibility to meet various coding styles by allowing you to write type conversion functions.

Function Parameters. Function parameters can only be inputs; therefore, the parameters cannot be modified. The parameter a in Listing 7-1 is an input only. By default, all parameters are of mode `in`, so it does not need to be explicitly declared. Functions can return only one argument. (Procedures, as you'll see later, can return multiple arguments.) As mentioned in the explanation of the example above, all statements within the function definition are sequential. In addition, no new signals can be declared in functions; however, variables may be declared in a function's declaration region and assigned values within the function definition.

We'll take a look at a couple of examples to help you understand how to create your own functions. After that, we'll explain where to declare and define your functions and how to use them.

7.2.1   Type Conversion Functions

bv2i (Bit_vector to Integer). Read through Listing 7-2 to determine how this function works.

```
1    -- bv2i
2    --   Bit_vector to Integer.
3    --   In:      bit_vector.
4    --   Return: integer.
5    --
6    function bv2I (bv : bit_vector) return integer is
7      variable result, abit : integer := 0;
8      variable  count        : integer := 0;
9    begin   --   bv2i
10     bits : for I in bv'low to bv'high loop
11       abit := 0;
12       if ((bv(I) = '1')) then
13          abit := 2**(I - bv'low);
14       end if;
15          result := result + abit;        -- Add in bit if '1'.
16       count := count + 1;
17       exit bits when count = 32;         -- 32 bits max.
18     end loop bits;
19     return (result);
20   end bv2I;
```

Listing 7-2 A type conversion function

Lines 1 through 5 of Listing 7-2 are comment lines that document the function name, describe the type conversion function, and indicate the input parameter and return type. This function takes as its input a bit_vector; it performs a binary to decimal conversion and returns an integer. Line 6 has an input parameter that is unconstrained because the widths of the bit_vectors that will be passed into this function are not known a priori. But the widths of the vector in the calling function must be known at compile time: Because signals represent a collection of wires connected to gates, the widths of those signals must be defined.

Lines 7 and 8 make up the function's declarative region, in which variables can be declared; it is similar to the declarative region of a process. In this bv2i function, three variables are declared as integers and initialized to zero. All of the integers could have been declared with one variable declaration, but the declarations are separate to emphasize the various purposes that the variables serve. The function definition is enclosed between the begin and end statements of lines 9 and 20. Line 10 begins a loop that starts with the lowest order bit of the bit_vector bv. The attributes 'low and 'high are predefined VHDL attributes that are used here to return the lowest and highest indices of the bit_vector that are passed into the function as a parameter. Therefore, regardless of the order of bit_vector bv—(x downto y) or (y to x)—y will be considered the least significant bit, and the integer value created for the bit_vector will reflect that y is the LSB and x is the MSB. For example. the two bit_vectors, a and b, may be defined as follows:

```
signal a: bit_vector(13 downto 6);
signal b: bit_vector(6 to 13);
```

For each of these bit_vectors, a(6) and b(6) will be considered the LSB. The function could have been written to always interpret the value on the left as the MSB, but that is left as an exercise for the reader.

The loop is used to ascend the bit_vector from LSB to MSB, with the variable i used to index the bit_vector. Line 11 initializes the variable abit to zero for each iteration of the loop. For each bit of bv that is asserted, abit is assigned the appropriate power of two determined by its position in the bit_vector. The position is determined by subtracting the lowest index for the bit_vector ('low) from the current index. Consider our bit_vector a(13 downto 6): If a(8) is a '1', then abit is assigned the integer value 4 because i is 8, bv'low is 6, I - bv'low is 2, and 2**2 is 4. This represents the binary number 100. The value of abit is added to result for each iteration of the loop. Count is used to determine the width of the bit_vector being converted to an integer. The range of integers that a VHDL tool must support extends to 2^{32}, so count ensures that the integer returned is within the valid range. When the loop finishes or is exited, result is returned (line 19), and the bit_vector-to-integer conversion is complete.

i2bv (Integer to Bit_vector). Function i2bv performs the opposite conversion: integer to bit_vector. Read through Listing 7-3 to understand how this conversion is accomplished.

```
--  i2bv
--   Integer to Bit_vector.
--   In:     integer, value and width.
--   Return: bit_vector, with right bit the most significant.
```

```
    --
    function i2bv   (VAL, width : INTEGER) return BIT_VECTOR is
        variable result : BIT_VECTOR (0 to width-1) := (others=>'0');
        variable bits   : INTEGER := width;
    begin
        if (bits > 32) then                -- Avoid overflow errors.
          bits := 32;
        else
          ASSERT 2**bits > VAL REPORT
            "Value too big for BIT_VECTOR width"
            SEVERITY WARNING;
        end if;

        for i in 0 to bits - 1 loop
            if ((val/(2**i)) MOD 2 = 1) then
                result(i) := '1';
            end if;
        end loop;

        return (result);
    end i2bv;
```

Listing 7-3 An integer to bit_vector type conversion function

This function takes as its inputs an integer value and the size (width) of the bit_vector that is to be returned. The function performs a decimal to binary conversion and returns the value of the integer as a bit_vector.

In the function declaration, result is declared as a variable of type bit_vector whose size is determined by the value of width. The variable bits is declared as an integer and is initialized to the value of width. Bits may be modified in the function, and therefore it is used rather than width. Width is a parameter to this function; it must be mode in, and cannot be modified.

The function definition begins by evaluating the size of the bit_vector to be returned. If it is greater than 32 (the largest integer that VHDL-processing tools must handle is 2^{32}), then the size of the bit_vector is truncated to 32. Otherwise, the integer value val is evaluated to determine whether it can be converted to a bit_vector of size bits. If the width of the bit_vector is too small to handle the integer, then the assertion condition is true and a severity warning is issued.

Next, result is computed by assigning a '1' to each bit of the bit_vector if val divided by 2^i (where i is the current index of the bit_vector) has a remainder of 1. After all iterations of the loop, result is returned and the conversion is complete.

7.2.2   Functions as Shorthand for Simple Components

Functions are sometimes used in place of component instantiations because they provide a way to write concise, C-like code. Functions are restricted to substituting for components with one output. They cannot have `wait` statements, and can contain only sequential statements. We cover a few potentially useful functions and then a problematic function description.

inc_bv (Increment Bit_vector). Examine Listing 7-4 to determine how it accomplishes an incrementing function. This function could substitute for a component that serves the same purpose.

```
-- inc_bv
--   Increment bit_vector.
--   In:     bit_vector.
--   Return: bit_vector.
--
function inc_bv   (a : bit_vector) return bit_vector is
    variable s        : bit_vector (a'range);
    variable carry    : bit;
begin
    carry    := '1';
    for i in a'low to a'high loop
        s(i)           := a(i) xor carry;
        carry          := a(i) and carry;
    end loop;
    return  (s);
end inc_bv;
```

Listing 7-4 A function for incrementing `bit_vectors`

Function `inc_bv` takes as its input a `bit_vector`, increments the value of that `bit_vector`, and returns a `bit_vector` of the same size as the input `bit_vector`.

The attribute `'range` is a predefined VHDL attribute that returns the range of an array. It enables variable `s` to be declared as a `bit_vector` with the same range—(x downto y) or (y to x)—as the input vector `a`. `Carry` is defined as a bit.

The function definition sets the first carry input to be a '1' in order to increment the vector. The value of `a(i)` exclusive-or `carry` is assigned to `s(i)` for each bit of the input vector `a`. `Carry` is initially '1' and is recomputed for each bit of the vector. The result of adding 1 to the `bit_vector` `a` is therefore `bit_vector` `s`. We will discuss the **synthetic** of this description—the result of synthesizing this description—later in the chapter.

majority. Our next function returns a bit that is asserted if the majority of the signals that are inputs to the function are asserted.

```
function majority (a, b, c: bit) return bit is
begin
    return ((a and b) or (a and c) or (b and c));
end majority;
```

Listing 7-5 Majority function for three inputs

Before explaining how to use these functions, we will consider a function that may pose problems for synthesis.

7.2.3   Problematic Function Descriptions

Functions can provide an elegant and succinct way to describe the behavior of an operation, but some descriptions may be problematic in that they cannot be handled by synthesis tools. Listing 7-6 is a description of a majority function for a bit_vector with a width that is determined by the width of the bit_vector in the function call. This function uses a loop with which to determine the number of '1's in the bit_vector passed to it. A counter variable is used to keep track of the number of '1's. Next, the value of this variable is compared with the value equal to one half of the width of the bit_vector. For a bit_vector of an odd length, the value is rounded up to the next highest integer. If the value of the counter variable is greater than this value, then the function returns a '1'; otherwise, it returns a '0'.

```
function maj(vec: bit_vector) return bit is
    variable tmp: integer;
begin
    tmp := 0;
    for i in vec'range loop
        if vec(i) = '1' then
            tmp := tmp + 1;
        end if;
    end loop;
    if tmp > (vec'high)/2 then return ('1');
                           else return ('0');
    end if;
end maj;
```

Listing 7-6 Majority function for a bit_vector *n*-bits wide

Warp accurately synthesizes this function to logic that behaves as this model behaves under simulation. Nonetheless, this functional description may be too abstract, too far removed from the hardware it describes. As noted in Chapter 3, the synthesis of variables is not well defined. It is not clear how the `tmp` variable should be synthesized. Certainly, it should not be used as a sequential logic circuit that counts the number of '1's in a vector (as one might infer from the + operator). After all, the function does not even contain a clock. It does contain the division operator (/). Again, we do not want the synthesis tool to generate a divider. Rather, we want it to consider `vec'high/2` as a constant known at compile time. An example of a function that can clearly be synthesized is `inc_bv`: when the loop is unraveled, the resulting equations are well defined. A good test to determine whether a description can be synthesized is to attempt to use the code to write equations yourself. That is, think like the synthesis tool will have to think. If you cannot determine the equations from the code, then it is likely the code is too far removed from the hardware it describes. At the least, its implementation may be suspect, in that it may take more area or propagation time than anticipated. This does not necessarily apply to type conversion functions that change only the representation of a signal, not its value.

Now that we've looked at how functions are created, we'll explore how to use them within design entities and architectures.

7.2.4   Using Functions

A function may be defined in the declarative region of an architecture, in which case the function definition also serves as the function declaration. Alternatively, a package may be used to declare a function with the definition of that function occurring in the associated package body. You may wish to create a collection of type conversion and component substitution functions, place them in a package, and compile that package into a library so that you can easily use them in any design. A function declared in the declarative region of an architecture is visible only to that architecture. A function declared in a package can be made visible, with a `use` clause, to other designs. Also, if one function requires the use of another function, you will likely find it less cumbersome to have those function declarations and definitions in a package rather than in the architecture of the entity you are describing. We'll take a look at both ways of declaring functions; you can decide which method meets your particular style and needs.

To begin with, let's use the first `majority` function of Listing 7-5 in the full-adder design of Listing 7-7. We will use this function to compute the carry-out. The function definition is located in the architecture declarative region, and also serves as the function declaration.

```
entity full_add is port(
    a, b, carry_in: in bit;
    sum, carry_out: out bit);
end full_add;
architecture full_add of full_add is
    function majority (a, b, c: bit) return bit is
    begin
        return ((a and b) or (a and c) or (b and c));
    end majority;
begin
  sum <= a xor b xor carry_in;
  carry_out <= majority(a, b, carry_in);
end;
```

Listing 7-7 Design of full_add using majority function

Alternatively, the function can be declared in a package declaration and defined in the associated package body. Other declarations may also be part of this package. In our case, we'll move the majority function as well as the inc_bv and i2bv functions into a package (Listing 7-8).

```
package my_package is
    function majority (a, b, c: bit) return bit;
    function inc_bv (a: bit_vector) return bit_vector;
    function i2bv (val, width : integer) return bit_vector;
end my_package;

package body my_package is
    function majority (a, b, c: bit) return bit is
    begin
        return ((a and b) or (a and c) or (b and c));
    end majority;

    -- inc_bv
    -- Increment bit_vector.
    -- In:     bit_vector.
    -- Return: bit_vector.
    --
    function inc_bv    (a: bit_vector) return bit_vector is
        variable s      : bit_vector (a'range);
        variable carry  : bit;
    begin
        carry   := '1';
```

```
        for i in a'low to a'high loop
            s(i)            := a(i) xor carry;
            carry           := a(i) and carry;
        end loop;

        return (s);
    end inc_bv;

    -- i2bv
    -- Integer to Bit_vector.
    -- In:     integer, value and width.
    -- Return: bit_vector, with right bit the most significant.
    --
    function i2bv    (val, width : integer) return bit_vector is
        variable result : bit_vector (0 to width-1) := (others=>'0');
        variable bits   : integer := width;
    begin
        if (bits > 32) then                 -- Avoid overflow errors.
          bits := 32;
        else
          ASSERT 2**bits > VAL REPORT
            "Value too big for BIT_VECTOR width"
            SEVERITY WARNING;
        end if;

        for i in 0 to bits - 1 loop
            if ((val/(2**i)) MOD 2 = 1) then
                result(i) := '1';
            end if;
        end loop;

        return (result);
    end i2bv;

end my_package;
```

Listing 7-8 Package containing four type conversion functions

The package declaration only declares the function. This function declaration provides an interface template for designs that call this function; the function definition is contained in the package body. Listing 7-9 makes this package visible in order to make the function declarations and definitions visible. It is assumed that the package is compiled to the work library.

```
entity full_add is port(
    a, b, carry_in: in bit;
    sum, carry_out: out bit);
end full_add;

use work.my_package.majority -- could specify .all, but not needed
architecture full_add of full_add is
begin
  sum <= a xor b xor carry_in;
  carry_out <= majority(a, b, carry_in);
end;
```

Listing 7-9 Using functions declared in a package

The placement of the use clause before the architecture makes it visible to the architecture, but not to the entity declaration. This can be significant if there is more than one architecture for a given entity declaration. VHDL supports the use of configuration statements to bind a specific architecture description to an entity declaration. Release 4.0 of Warp does not support such configuration statements or multiple architectures for one entity; configuration statements are not discussed in this text. Refer to nearly any of the VHDL books that focus on modeling for simulation for a discussion of configuration statements.

7.2.5   Overloading Operators

A powerful use of functions is to overload operators. An overloaded operator is one for which there is a user-defined function that handles an operation for various data types. Many overloaded operators are also defined in the IEEE 1164 and 1076.3 standards. In previous chapters, you've seen how overloaded operators provided by a synthesis tool vendor can be used. In this section, we'll discuss how to define your own overloaded operator. Later in the chapter, we will contrast the synthesis of user-defined overloaded operators with the synthesis of both IEEE standard and vendor supplied overloaded operators.

The + operator is defined by the IEEE 1076 standard to operate on numeric types (integer, floating point, and physical types) but not with enumeration types like std_logic or bit_vector. To add a constant integer to a signal of type std_logic, an overloaded operator is required. The overloaded operator uses a function that defines the operator for the given types. Listing 7-10 is a design in which an integer is added to a bit_vector. Other useful addition operations include, among others, the addition of a bit_vector to an integer, a bit_vector to a bit, a std_logic_vector to an integer, or a std_logic_vector to a std_logic.

```
entity counter is port(
        clk, rst, pst, load,counten:   in bit;
        data:                          in bit_vector(3 downto 0);
        count:                         buffer bit_vector(3 downto 0));
end counter;

use work.myops.all;
architecture archcounter of counter is
begin
upcount: process (clk, rst, pst)
            begin
                if rst = '1' then
                        count <= "0000";
                elsif pst = '1' then
                        count <= "1111";
                elsif (clk'event and clk= '1') then
                        if load = '1' then
                                count <= data;
                        elsif counten = '1' then
                                count <= count + 1;
                        end if;
                end if;
            end process upcount;
end archcounter;
```

Listing 7-10 A counter in which the + operator has operands of types bit_vector and integer

The code in Listing 7-10 uses the + operator for the statement count <= count + 1;. The native VHDL operator will not handle this addition because the operands are bit_vector and integer. The overloaded operator must come from within the package myops.

You can create several functions that define the same operation for different types (this is called **overloading a function**). VHDL synthesis and simulation tools are required to perform template matching—to look for the function (or operator, in this case) with the same number and type of parameters as the calling function.

Listing 7-11 contains a package declaration and package body that declare and define two operator overloads for the + operator.

```
package myops is
    function "+"          (a, b   : BIT_VECTOR)              return BIT_VECTOR
    function "+"     (a  : BIT_VECTOR; b : INTEGER)          return BIT_VECTOR
end myops;

use work.my_package.all;
package body myops is
    -- "+"
    -- Add overload for:
    -- In:     two bit_vectors.
    -- Return: bit_vector.
    --
    function "+" (a, b   : bit_vector)              return bit_vector is
        variable s      : bit_vector (a'range);
        variable carry  : bit;
        variable bi     : integer;        -- Indexes b.
    begin
            carry      := '0';

        for i in  a'low to a'high loop
            bi := b'low + (i - a'low);
            s(i)  := (a(i) xor b(bi)) xor carry;
            carry := ((a(i) or b(bi)) and carry) or (a(i) and b(bi));
        end loop;

        return  (s);
    end "+";                                    -- Two bit_vectors.

    -- "+"
    -- Overload "+" for bit_vector plus integer.
    -- In:     bit_vector and integer.
    -- Return: bit_vector.
    --
    function "+" (a  : bit_vector; b : integer) return bit_vector is
    begin
        return (a + i2bv(b, a'length));
    end "+";
end myops;
```

Listing 7-11 Declaring and defining operator overloading functions

This package also includes a use clause to make my_package visible to this design unit. The i2bv function is required for the second + function. The return expression for this second + function first converts the integer that is passed in as a parameter to a bit_vector. Next, the two bit_vectors are added together. This is done by using the + operator defined in the first + overload definition. The first + overloaded operator may be used by this design because all declarations in a package declaration are implicitly visible to a package body; as long as it does not cause recursion, those declarations can be used within the package body. After adding the two bit_vectors together, the result is returned.

The following line of code from the first overload function is used to ensure that the most significant bit of one vector is added to the most significant (not least significant) bit of the other vector:

```
bi := b'low + (i - a'low);
```

When declaring and defining the function, the addition operator is enclosed in quotation marks to indicate that it is an operator. When it is used as in the counter-example of Listing 7-10, the compiler must search for the addition function with matching operand types for the statement count <= count + 1; (where count is a bit_vector and 1 is an integer). If integers are being added, then the native VHDL addition operator is used. In the case of Listing 7-10, the second version of the + operator defined in the package myops is used.

Listing 7-10 can be written such that the counter uses the inc_bv function defined earlier. The line

```
count <= count + 1;
```

is then replaced by

```
count <= inc_bv(count);
```

The first implementation (the one using the + operator) provides more readable code. Even without documentation (comments), it is unambiguous what is accomplished with the statement count <= count + 1;. What is accomplished with the statement count <= inc_bv(count); may be completely obvious to the original designer, but it may not be intuitive for someone else reading the code. The inc_bv function may require the reader to delve into the function definition or documentation. If you use an overloaded operator, there is no need to maintain and document yet another function, and if your design is transferred to another designer, it will be easily understood. As you'll learn later in this chapter, using the native operators and vendor-supplied (but standardized) overloaded operators will also likely result in a more efficient implementation of your circuit.

7.2.6   Overloading Functions

Operators are not the only functions that can be overloaded; you can overload any function. Take, for example, the functions declared in the package `majority` in Listing 7-12.

```
package majorities is
    -- majority for 3 single bit/std_logic inputs
    function majority (a, b, c: bit) return bit;
    function majority (a, b, c: std_logic) return std_logic;
    -- majority for 4 single bit/std_logic inputs
    function majority (a, b, c, d: bit) return bit;
    function majority (a, b, c, d: std_logic) return std_logic;
    -- majority for 2, 3, or 4 inputs as bit_vector/std_logic_vector
    function majority (vec: bit_vector) return bit;
    function majority (vec:std_logic_vector) return std_logic;
end majorities;

package body majorities is
    -- majority for 3 single bit/std_logic inputs
    -- Function #1
    function majority (a, b, c: bit) return bit is
    begin
        return ((a and b) or (a and c) or (b and c));
    end majority;


    -- Function #2
    function majority (a, b, c: std_logic) return std_logic is
    begin
        return ((a and b) or (a and c) or (b and c));
    end majority;


    -- majority for 4 single bit/std_logic inputs
    -- Function #3
    function majority (a, b, c, d: bit) return bit is
    begin
        return ((a and b and c) or (a and b and d) or
                (a and c and d) or (b and c and d));
    end majority;


    -- Function #4
    function majority (a, b, c, d: std_logic) return std_logic is
    begin
        return ((a and b and c) or (a and b and d) or
                (a and c and d) or (b and c and d));
    end majority;
```

```vhdl
-- majority for 2, 3, or 4 bit_vector/std_logic_vector inputs
-- Function #5
function majority (vec: bit_vector) return bit is
    variable a: bit_vector(vec'length - 1 downto 0);
begin
    a := vec;
    if a'length = 2 then
        return (a(0) or a(1));
    elsif a'length = 3 then--a'length mut excl.; no priority
        return ((a(0) and a(1)) or (a(0) and a(2)) or (a(1) and a(2)));
    elsif a'length = 4 then
        return ((a(0) and a(1) and a(2)) or (a(0) and a(1) and a(3)) or
            (a(0) and a(2) and a(3)) or (a(1) and a(2) and a(3)));
    else
        assert (false)
            report "Majority function only supports 2, 3, or 4 inputs."
            severity warning;
            return ('0');
    end if;
end majority;

-- Function #6
function majority (a:std_logic_vector) return std_logic;
    variable a: bit_vector(vec'length - 1 downto 0);
begin
    a := vec;
    if a'length = 2 then
        return (a(0) or a(1));
    elsif a'length = 3 then--a'length mut excl.; no priority
        return ((a(0) and a(1)) or (a(0) and a(2)) or (a(1) and a(2)));
    elsif a'length = 4 then
        return ((a(0) and a(1) and a(2)) or (a(0) and a(1) and a(3)) or
            (a(0) and a(2) and a(3)) or (a(1) and a(2) and a(3)));
    else
        assert (false)
            report "Majority function only supports 2, 3, or 4 inputs."
            severity warning;
            return('0');
    end if;
end majority;

end mygates;
```

Listing 7-12 Overloading the majority function for various numbers and types of inputs

Six functions of the same name have been declared and defined. Each function, however, defines the majority operation for a different number of inputs or types. When the `majority` functions are used in Listing 7-13, the compiler must choose the appropriate function for the function call.

```vhdl
library ieee;
use ieee.std_logic_1164.all;
entity find_majority is port(
    a, b, c, d: in bit;
    e: in bit_vector(1 downto 0);
    f: in bit_vector(2 downto 0);
    g: in bit_vector(3 downto 0);
    h, i, j, k: in std_logic;
    l: in std_logic_vector(1 downto 0);
    m: in std_logic_vector(2 downto 0);
    n: in std_logic_vector(3 downto 0);
    o: in bit_vector(4 downto 0);
    p: in std_logic_vector(7 downto 0);
    x1, x3, x5, x6, x7, x11: bit;
    x2, x4, x8, x9, x10, x12: std_logic);
end find_majority;
architecture find_majority of find_majority is
begin
-- requires function #1:
x1 <= majority(a, b, c);
-- requires function #2:
x2 <= majority(h, i, j);
-- requires function #3:
x3 <= majority(a, b, c, d);
-- requires function #4:
x4 <= majority(h, i, j, k);
-- require function #5:
x5 <= majority(e);
x6 <= majority(f);
x7 <= majority(g);
-- require function #6:
x8 <= majority(l);
x9 <= majority(m);
x10 <= majority(n);
-- require function #5 or function #6, but result in compile
-- time warning and function always returning '0':
x11 <= majority(o);
x12 <= majority(p);
end;
```

Listing 7-13 Using the overloaded majority functions

Listing 7-13 demonstrates that functions can be used as an alternative to certain types of component instantiations (particularly for combinational functions). The listing also illustrates that the `majority` function can be overloaded to accept various numbers and types of input parameters and various types of return values. The compiler must do template matching to determine which function definition applies.

It is not necessarily a good idea to overload all operators to handle several types, because having the compiler find type mismatches may be useful in some cases.

7.2.7   Standard Functions

Fortunately, standard functions have been established since the first version of the VHDL Language Reference Manual (IEEE standard 1076) was released in 1987. Standard packages have been defined that include operator overloading for multiple types. This eliminates the need for each tool vendor to provide a proprietary package with unique function names. VHDL code that makes use of these standard packages—rather than vendor-supplied packages—is portable from one tool to another, provided that the tool supports the standard. For example, the `std_logic_1164` package provides a standard data type system that, because it is supported by multiple tool vendors, enables you to use the data types defined in this package by including the following `library` and `use` clause:

```
library ieee;
use ieee.std_logic_1164.all;
```

For every synthesis or simulation tool vendor that supports this package, you will be able to use your code with that tool without any modifications to your code. If each tool vendor required you to use proprietary packages to have access to useful data types or operators, then you would not be able to easily port your code from one system to another.

The IEEE 1164 standard defines a package that not only declares a standard datatype system but also defines standard overloaded operators and type conversion functions for use with that data type system. Among other things, the `std_logic_1164` package includes common subtypes of `std_logic_1164`: X01 and X01Z. It overloads the logical operators (AND, OR, and so forth), and it provides some commonly used type conversion functions:

```
function To_bit ( s : std_ulogic; xmap : BIT := '0') return bit;

function To_bitvector        ( s : std_logic_vector ; xmap : bit := '0')
                               return bit_vector;

function To_bitvector        ( s : std_ulogic_vector; xmap : bit := '0')
                               return bit_vector;

function To_StdULogic        ( b : bit)
                               return std_ulogic;

function To_StdLogicVector   ( b : bit_vector)
                               return std_logic_vector;

function To_StdLogicVector   ( s : std_ulogic_vector)
                               return std_logic_vector;

function To_StdULogicVector  ( b : bit_vector)
                               return std_ulogic_vector;

function To_StdULogicVector  ( s : std_logic_vector)
                               return std_ulogic_vector;
```

To_bitvector, To_StdLogicVector, and To_StdULogicVector are all over-loaded for different input parameter types.

Another important standard for synthesis is IEEE 1076.3. This standard specifies "two packages that define vector types for representing signed and unsigned arithmetic values, and that define arithmetic, shift, and type conversion operations on those types." The packages are numeric_std and numeric_bit, which we have discussed. An example of just one of the arithmetic operators that this standard defines is given in Listing 7-14. (You won't want to read this in detail but rather in general, to understand that the operators such as the + operator have been over-loaded to accommodate the addition of data objects of many types.) For a com-plete copy of the standard, contact the IEEE or VHDL International via the World Wide Web at http:// www.vhdl.org.

The following declarations are from the numeric_bit package:

```
type UNSIGNED is array (NATURAL range <> ) of BIT;
type SIGNED is array (NATURAL range <> ) of BIT;

-- Id: A.3
function "+" (L, R: UNSIGNED) return UNSIGNED;
-- Result subtype: UNSIGNED(MAX(L'LENGTH, R'LENGTH)-1 downto 0).
-- Result: Adds two UNSIGNED vectors that may be of different lengths.
```

```
-- Id: A.4
function "+" (L, R: SIGNED) return SIGNED;
-- Result subtype: SIGNED(MAX(L'LENGTH, R'LENGTH)-1 downto 0).
-- Result: Adds two SIGNED vectors that may be of different lengths.

-- Id: A.5
function "+" (L: UNSIGNED; R: NATURAL) return UNSIGNED;
-- Result subtype: UNSIGNED(L'LENGTH-1 downto 0).
-- Result: Adds an UNSIGNED vector, L, with a non-negative INTEGER, R.

-- Id: A.6
function "+" (L: NATURAL; R: UNSIGNED) return UNSIGNED;
-- Result subtype: UNSIGNED(R'LENGTH-1 downto 0).
-- Result: Adds a non-negative INTEGER, L, with an UNSIGNED vector, R.

-- Id: A.7
function "+" (L: INTEGER; R: SIGNED) return SIGNED;
-- Result subtype: SIGNED(R'LENGTH-1 downto 0).
-- Result: Adds an INTEGER, L(may be positive or negative), to a SIGNED
--          vector, R.

-- Id: A.8
function "+" (L: SIGNED; R: INTEGER) return SIGNED;
-- Result subtype: SIGNED(L'LENGTH-1 downto 0).
-- Result: Adds a SIGNED vector, L, to an INTEGER, R.
```

Listing 7-14 Some overloaded operators defined in numeric_bit*

The following declarations are from the numeric_std package:

```
type UNSIGNED is array (NATURAL range <> ) of STD_LOGIC;
type SIGNED is array (NATURAL range <> ) of STD_LOGIC;

-- Id: A.3
function "+" (L, R: UNSIGNED) return UNSIGNED;
-- Result subtype: UNSIGNED(MAX(L'LENGTH, R'LENGTH)-1 downto 0).
-- Result: Adds two UNSIGNED vectors that may be of different lengths.
```

*[VHDL code in Listings 7-14 through 7-17 are reprinted from IEEE Draft Standard P1076.3, dated February 13, 1995 Draft Standard VHDL Synthesis Package, © 1995 by the Institute of Electrical and Electronics Engineers, Inc. The IEEE disclaims any responsibility or liability resulting from the placement and use in this publication. This is an unapproved draft of a proposed IEEE Standard, subject to change. Use of information contained in the unapproved draft is at your own risk. Information is reprinted with the permission of the IEEE.]

```
-- Id: A.4
function "+" (L, R: SIGNED) return SIGNED;
-- Result subtype: SIGNED(MAX(L'LENGTH, R'LENGTH)-1 downto 0).
-- Result: Adds two SIGNED vectors that may be of different lengths.

-- Id: A.5
function "+" (L: UNSIGNED; R: NATURAL) return UNSIGNED;
-- Result subtype: UNSIGNED(L'LENGTH-1 downto 0).
-- Result: Adds an UNSIGNED vector, L, with a non-negative INTEGER, R.

-- Id: A.6
function "+" (L: NATURAL; R: UNSIGNED) return UNSIGNED;
-- Result subtype: UNSIGNED(R'LENGTH-1 downto 0).
-- Result: Adds a non-negative INTEGER, L, with an UNSIGNED vector, R.

-- Id: A.7
function "+" (L: INTEGER; R: SIGNED) return SIGNED;
-- Result subtype: SIGNED(R'LENGTH-1 downto 0).
-- Result: Adds an INTEGER, L(may be positive or negative), to a SIGNED
--         vector, R.

-- Id: A.8
function "+" (L: SIGNED; R: INTEGER) return SIGNED;
-- Result subtype: SIGNED(L'LENGTH-1 downto 0).
-- Result: Adds a SIGNED vector, L, to an INTEGER, R.
```

Listing 7-15 Some overloaded operators defined in `numeric_std`

As you can imagine, having standard packages to define these overloaded operators greatly increases the power, flexibility, and portability of VHDL for both synthesis and simulation. It is usually better to use the standard packages from the library specified by the standard or vendor than to create your own. Creating your own may provide functionally equivalent code; however, vendors may provide unique implementations that will provide better synthesis.

Another important function defined in `numeric_std` is `std_match`. The function is overloaded for several types:

```
-- Id: M.1
function STD_MATCH (L, R: STD_ULOGIC) return BOOLEAN;
-- Result subtype: BOOLEAN
-- Result: terms compared per STD_LOGIC_1164 intent

-- Id: M.2
function STD_MATCH (L, R: UNSIGNED) return BOOLEAN;
-- Result subtype: BOOLEAN
```

```
-- Result: terms compared per STD_LOGIC_1164 intent
 -- Id: M.3
function STD_MATCH (L, R: SIGNED) return BOOLEAN;
-- Result subtype: BOOLEAN
-- Result: terms compared per STD_LOGIC_1164 intent

-- Id: M.4
function STD_MATCH (L, R: STD_LOGIC_VECTOR) return BOOLEAN;
-- Result subtype: BOOLEAN
-- Result: terms compared per STD_LOGIC_1164 intent

-- Id: M.5
function STD_MATCH (L, R: STD_ULOGIC_VECTOR) return BOOLEAN;
-- Result subtype: BOOLEAN
-- Result: terms compared per STD_LOGIC_1164 intent
```

Listing 7-16 Std_match function declarations

The first two std_match functions (Id M.1 and M.2) are defined in Listing 7-17.

```
-- support constants for STD_MATCH:

type BOOLEAN_TABLE is array(STD_ULOGIC, STD_ULOGIC) of BOOLEAN;

constant MATCH_TABLE: BOOLEAN_TABLE := (
-------------------------------------------------------------------
-- U     X     0     1     Z     W     L     H     -
-------------------------------------------------------------------
(FALSE, FALSE, FALSE, FALSE, FALSE, FALSE, FALSE, FALSE,  TRUE), -- | U |
(FALSE, FALSE, FALSE, FALSE, FALSE, FALSE, FALSE, FALSE,  TRUE), -- | X |
(FALSE, FALSE,  TRUE, FALSE, FALSE, FALSE,  TRUE, FALSE,  TRUE), -- | 0 |
(FALSE, FALSE, FALSE,  TRUE, FALSE, FALSE, FALSE,  TRUE,  TRUE), -- | 1 |
(FALSE, FALSE, FALSE, FALSE, FALSE, FALSE, FALSE, FALSE,  TRUE), -- | Z |
(FALSE, FALSE, FALSE, FALSE, FALSE, FALSE, FALSE, FALSE,  TRUE), -- | W |
(FALSE, FALSE,  TRUE, FALSE, FALSE, FALSE,  TRUE, FALSE,  TRUE), -- | L |
(FALSE, FALSE, FALSE,  TRUE, FALSE, FALSE, FALSE,  TRUE,  TRUE), -- | H |
( TRUE,  TRUE,  TRUE,  TRUE,  TRUE,  TRUE,  TRUE,  TRUE,  TRUE)  -- | - |
 );

-- Id: M.1
function STD_MATCH (L, R: STD_ULOGIC) return BOOLEAN is
  variable VALUE: STD_ULOGIC;
begin
  return MATCH_TABLE(L, R);
end STD_MATCH;
```

```
-- Id: M.2
function STD_MATCH (L, R: UNSIGNED) return BOOLEAN is
  alias LV: UNSIGNED(1 to L'LENGTH) is L;
  alias RV: UNSIGNED(1 to R'LENGTH) is R;
begin
  if ((L'LENGTH < 1) or (R'LENGTH < 1)) then
    assert NO_WARNING
        report "NUMERIC_STD.STD_MATCH: null detected, returning FALSE"
        severity WARNING;
    return FALSE;
  end if;
  if LV'LENGTH /= RV'LENGTH then
    assert NO_WARNING
        report "NUMERIC_STD.STD_MATCH: L'LENGTH /= R'LENGTH, returning
FALSE"
        severity WARNING;
    return FALSE;
  else
    for I in LV'LOW to LV'HIGH loop
      if not (MATCH_TABLE(LV(I), RV(I))) then
        return FALSE;
      end if;
    end loop;
    return TRUE;
  end if;
end STD_MATCH;
```

Listing 7-17 Two overloaded std_match functions

The first function returns a Boolean value based on whether two data objects of type std_ulogic match according to don't-care conditions. For example, the function as overloaded for std_ulogic_vectors allows the comparison of "1--1" to a signal of type std_ulogic_vector (of width 4) to evaluate to true as long as the first and last elements of the vector are '1,' regardless of the value of the middle two.

The following comparison will evaluate to false, for all values of a except "1--1":

```
if a = "1--1" then ...
```

Although '-' represents the don't-care value, the = operator cannot be used to identify don't-care conditions. The LRM defines the = operator for enumeration types such as std_logic to result in a Boolean evaluation of true only if the left-hand-side expression is equivalent to the right-hand-side expression. The don't-care value, '-', is the 'high value of the std_ulogic type. A comparison of '-' to '0' or to '1' using the = operator evaluates false. The `std_match` function, on the other hand, returns true for the comparison of '-' to '0' or '1'. The constant `match_table` on page 401 can be used to determine the result of comparing two `std_ulogic` values using the `std_match` function. Find one of the values you wish to compare in the row contained in a comment line at the top of the table. Find the other value in the right-hand column. The result of the comparison is the Boolean value listed at the intersection of the row and column of the two values that you are comparing. To use the function, you will need to include the appropriate `use` clause, and write code similar to the following:

```
if std_match(a, "1--1") then ...
```

A similar type of table is in the `std_logic_1164` package to resolve multiple drivers for the subtype `std_logic`.

Shift Operations. `Shift_left`, `shift_right`, `rotate_left`, and `rotate_right` operators are also defined in `numeric_std`. These functions, or the `sll`, `srl`, `rol`, `ror` operators, can be used to shift vectors. The `shift_left` function is used to shift a vector to the left, replacing the bits on the right-hand side with zeros. The `shift_right` function is used to shift a vector to the right, replacing the bits on the left-hand side with zeros. The `rotate_left` and `rotate_right` functions are also used for shifting, where the bits shifted out are used to replace those left empty on the opposite side. The number of bits shifted is specified by the second operand, which can be a constant or another signal. For example, if a is a `std_logic_vector(7 downto 0)`, then the statements,

```
x <= a sll 2;
y <= a rol 2;
```

are equivalent to,

```
x   <= a(5 downto 0)  & "00";
y <= a(5 downto 0) & a(7 downto 6);
```

7.2.8   Standard versus User-Defined Functions

If you were to use the `inc_bv` function of Listing 7-4 or the overloaded + operator of Listing 7-11 to describe an incrementer or adder, the resulting synthetic would simply be a mapping of the equations generated by these functions to the target architecture. It is not likely that these generic implementations of incrementers and adders would be the most efficient for a given device architecture. Data path operations should be optimized for the specific resources of a given device architecture. Data path optimization techniques are discussed in Chapter 9.

Operator Inferencing. If you were to use one of the overloaded + operators from the copy of the synthesis packages that the vendor supplies, then the implementation would be a device-specific rendering of the circuit (if the synthesis tool that you are using provides operator inferencing). This is because a package supplied by the vendor may be built in such a way that it allows the synthesis tool to "cheat": When one of these operators is called, rather than synthesizing the behavioral description used by simulators, the synthesis tool may substitute an optimized, device-specific implementation of the circuit.

Operator inferencing is the process by which a VHDL synthesis tool infers an operation from a design description and produces an optimized, device-specific component for that structure. This process is also referred to as **module generation.**

Two components can be inferred from the following VHDL code fragment:

```
if a=b then
    q <= q;
else
    q <= x + y;
end if;
```

The synthesis software can infer from this code that an equality comparator should be instantiated for if a = b and an adder for q <= x + y;. Operator inferencing produces the logic shown in Figure 7-1. How is this different from not using operator inferencing to implement this design? Without module generation, the synthesis tool would create a Boolean equation for each bit of q and then map that

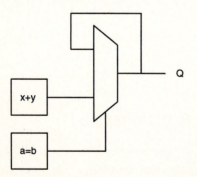

Figure 7-1   Example result of operator inferencing

logic to the device architecture. Module generation is used to identify arithmetic structures and implement hand-tuned, vendor-specific macros. The implementations of a few adders are discussed in Chapter 9.

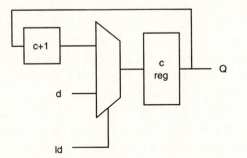

Figure 7-2 Implementation resulting from operator inferencing of a loadable counter

Let's take another look at module generation. What logic do you suppose synthesizing the code in Listing 7-18 produces?

```
library ieee;
use ieee.std_logic_1164.all;
use work.std_arith.all;
entity cnt16 is port(
    clk, rst: in std_logic;
    ld:       in std_logic;
    d:        in std_logic_vector(3 downto 0);
    c:        inout std_logic_vector(3 downto 0));
end cnt16;

architecture archcnt16 of cnt16 is
begin
counter: process (clk, rst)
    begin
        if rst = '1' then
            c <= (others => '0');
        elsif (clk'event and clk='1') then
            if ld = '1' then c <= d; else c <= c + 1; end if;
        end if;
    end process counter;
end archcnt16;
```

Listing 7-18 Counter design; how does operator inferencing help with the implementation of this design?

Does this code cause the compiler to infer, or identify, a 16-bit counter with synchronous load? Probably not. To identify this as a 16-bit counter with synchronous load would require more than operator inferencing; it would truly require a robust module generator. We are not aware of any compilers or synthesis tools that recognize such code as a 16-bit counter (that is, that provide this level of module generation). One reason for the lack of such tools is that VHDL permits a designer to write numerous possible constructs from which it is extremely difficult for a tool to pick out regular components. Certainly a tool can publish a list of recognizable constructs, but this limits VHDL coders to strict templates, defeating the purpose of a high-level description language. Such templates are not standard across tools. Instead of interpreting the code of Listing 7-18 as a 16-bit counter with synchronous load, most synthesis tools recognize the +1 adder (incrementer), implementing the logic as in Figure 7-2 and then optimizing it as necessary for the target architecture.

We'll use the code of Listing 7-19 to illustrate the difficulty of inferring the optimal logic from a high-level description:

```vhdl
library ieee;
use ieee.std_logic_1164.all; use work.myops.all;
entity wierdcnt16 is port(
    clk, rst:            in std_logic;
    en,up,by2,by3,by5:   in std_logic;
    d:                   in std_logic_vector(3 downto 0);
    c:                   inout std_logic_vector(3 downto 0));
end wierdcnt16;

architecture archwierdcnt16 of wierdcnt16 is
begin
counter: process (clk, rst)
    begin
        if rst = '1' then
            c <= (others => '0');
        elsif (clk'event and clk='1') then
            if en = '1' then
                if up = '1' then
                    if by2 = '1' then
                        c <= c + 2;
                    elsif  by3 = '1' then
                        c <= c + 3;
                    elsif by5 = '1' then
                        c <= c + 5;
                    else
                        c <= c + d;
                    end if;
```

```
        elsif by2 =  '1' then
           c <= c - 2;
        elsif by3 = '1' then
           c <= c - 3;
        elsif by5 = '1' then
           c <= c - 5;
        else
           c <= c - d;
        end if;
     else
        c <= c;
     end if;
  end if;
end process counter;
end archwierdcnt16;
```

Listing 7-19 A unique counter: Operator inferencing can identify modules but not the optimal hand-tuned construct

No compiler or synthesis tool today or in the near future will be able to produce the optimal implementation for the `wierdcnt16` of Listing 7-19 that is achievable by manual design. Instead, operator inferencing produces an implementation similar to that in the example above. That is, the +2, +3, +5, +d, −2, −3, −4, and −d adders and subtracters would be inferred and the results multiplexed based on the values of en, up, by2, by3, and by5.

Directive-Driven Module Generation. Directives may be used to direct the implementation of a module. In other words, there may be multiple possible implementations for a component, such as a 16-bit adder. You may want this component to be optimized to be area-efficient, speed-efficient, or a balance of the two. Directives can provide that level of control, enabling you to control the critical and noncritical portions of a design. The code of Listing 7-19, as ludicrous as it may seem, is instructive: the 16-bit adder for c + d is the most complex logic, so the critical path in this circuit will be from the c registers through this adder and back to the input of the c registers. Paths through the other adders will not be nearly so complex. Therefore, while you may want to direct this adder to be speed-optimized in order to reduce the delay of the critical path, you will likely want to optimize the other adders to be area-efficient. Because they are not in the critical path, creating speed-optimized components would be of no advantage.

Recalling the ALU design of Listing 6-14, we can see that a more efficient description would result in fewer modules being generated. Some of the more mature synthesis tools will recognize that the same adder can be shared, but

Release 4.0 of Warp instantiates separate adders for each of the + operators, as indicated in the report file:

```
alu.vhd (line 24, col 20):  Note: Substituting module 'warp_add_2s_us' for '+'.
alu.vhd (line 26, col 21):  Note: Substituting module 'warp_add_2s_us' for '+'.
alu.vhd (line 26, col 24):  Note: Substituting module 'warp_add_1s1c_us' for '+'.
alu.vhd (line 30, col 25):  Note: Substituting module 'warp_add_2s_us' for '+'.
alu.vhd (line 32, col 26):  Note: Substituting module 'warp_add_2s_us' for '+'.
alu.vhd (line 32, col 29):  Note: Substituting module 'warp_add_1s1c_us' for '+'.
alu.vhd (line 36, col 26):  Note: Substituting module 'warp_add_2s_us' for '+'.
alu.vhd (line 36, col 29):  Note: Substituting module 'warp_add_1s1c_us' for '+'.
alu.vhd (line 38, col 20):  Note: Substituting module 'warp_add_2s_us' for '+'.
```

The different names of the adders `2s_us` and `1s1c_us` indicate that the adders are either for two signals that are unsigned or for one unsigned signal and one `unsigned` constant. It is left as an exercise for the reader to rework Listing 6-14 to use only one adder.

Vendor-Supplied Packages. Some of the designs in this text use the `std_arith` package to add operands of type `std_logic` and integer, for example. These are nonstandard overloaded operators that are supplied by Warp because some designers do not want to deal with the overhead of the types signed and unsigned. Other synthesis vendors supply similar kinds of packages, which will also ensure that module generation takes place. If you want to use a nonstandard operator overload, check to make sure the synthesis vendor supplies a package for this purpose before writing your own operator overloading function.

Breakout Exercise 7-1

Purpose: To verify module generation for arithmetic components.

Modify Listing 7-19 to use the `std_arith` package. Compile and synthesize the design to a CY7C371. Use the report file to verify that modules have been detected for each of the + and – operators. Does the report file indicate that the logic can be further reduced? Simulate the design.

7.3   Procedures

Like functions, procedures are high-level design constructs to compute values or define processes that you can use for type conversions or operator overloading, or as an alternative to component instantiation.

Procedures differ from functions in a few ways. To begin with, a procedure can return more than one value. This is accomplished with parameters: If a parameter is declared as mode out or inout, then the parameter is returned to the actual parameter of the calling procedure. A parameter in a function, however, can only be of mode in. Another difference between a procedure and a function is that a procedure can have a wait statement, whereas a function cannot.

As with functions, all statements within a procedure must be sequential statements, and procedures cannot declare signals. But variables can be declared in the declarative region of a procedure.

Procedures and functions are declared and defined in the same way: either in the architecture's declarative region or in a package with the associated definition in the package body.

Now that we've defined the rules for procedures, let's take a look at how to put those rules to use.

```
library ieee;
use ieee.std_logic_1164.all;
package myflops is
    procedure dff ( signal d: bit_vector;
                    signal clk: bit;
                    signal q: out bit_vector);
    procedure dff ( signal d: bit_vector;
                    signal clk, rst: bit;
                    signal q: out bit_vector);
    procedure dff ( signal d: bit_vector;
                    signal clk, rst, pst: bit;
                    signal q: out bit_vector);
    procedure dff ( signal d: bit_vector;
                    signal clk, rst: bit;
                    signal q, q_bar: out bit_vector);
    procedure dff ( signal d: std_logic_vector;
                    signal clk: std_logic;
                    signal q: out std_logic_vector);
    procedure dff ( signal d: std_logic_vector;
                    signal clk, rst: std_logic;
                    signal q: out std_logic_vector);
    procedure dff ( signal d: std_logic_vector;
                    signal clk, rst, pst: std_logic;
                    signal q: out std_logic_vector);
    procedure dff ( signal d: std_logic_vector;
                    signal clk, rst: std_logic;
                    signal q, q_bar: out std_logic_vector);
end myflops;
```

```vhdl
package body myflops is
procedure dff ( signal d: bit_vector;
                signal clk: bit;
                signal q: out bit_vector) is
begin
    if clk'event and clk = '1' then
        q <= d;
    end if;
end procedure;

procedure dff ( signal d: bit_vector;
                signal clk, rst: bit;
                signal q: out bit_vector) is
begin
    if rst = '1' then q <= (others => '0');
    elsif clk'event and clk = '1' then
        q <= d;
    end if;
end procedure;

procedure dff ( signal d: bit_vector;
                signal clk, rst, pst: bit;
                signal q: out bit_vector) is
begin
    if rst = '1' then q <= (others => '0');
    elsif pst = '1' then q <= (others => '1');
    elsif clk'event and clk = '1' then
        q <= d;
    end if;
end procedure;

procedure dff ( signal d: bit_vector;
                signal clk, rst: bit;
                signal q, q_bar: out bit_vector) is
begin
    if rst = '1' then q <= (others => '0');
    elsif clk'event and clk = '1' then
        q <= d; q_bar <= not d;
    end if;
end procedure;

procedure dff ( signal d: std_logic_vector;
                signal clk: std_logic;
                signal q: out std_logic_vector) is
begin
    if clk'event and clk = '1' then
        q <= d;
```

```
      end if;
  end procedure;

  procedure dff ( signal d: std_logic_vector;
                  signal clk, rst: std_logic;
                  signal q: out std_logic_vector) is
  begin
      if rst = '1' then q <= (others => '0');
      elsif clk'event and clk = '1' then
          q <= d;
      end if;
  end procedure;

  procedure dff ( signal d: std_logic_vector;
                  signal clk, rst, pst: std_logic;
                  signal q: out std_logic_vector) is
  begin
      if rst = '1' then q <= (others => '0');
      elsif pst = '1' then q <= (others => '1');
      elsif clk'event and clk = '1' then
          q <= d;
      end if;
  end procedure;

  procedure dff ( signal d: std_logic_vector;
                  signal clk, rst: std_logic;
                  signal q, q_bar: out std_logic_vector) is
  begin
      if rst = '1' then q <= (others => '0');
      elsif clk'event and clk = '1' then
          q <= d; q_bar <= not d;
      end if;
  end procedure;

  end myflops;
```

Listing 7-20 A procedure defining eight flip-flops

Listing 7-20 declares eight procedures named dff overloaded for various types and numbers of parameters. When the number of parameters to the procedures are the same, they are differentiated by the types of each parameter. Each parameter is either bit, bit_vector, std_logic, or std_logic_vector. A function could not serve the role of the procedures defined above that return multiple parameters. The width of these flip-flops is defined by the width of the vector in the calling procedure.

The procedure parameters were explicitly declared as signals. If the class of data object is not defined and the mode is out or inout, the class defaults to variable. Using the procedure is quite easy, as demonstrated in Listing 7-21.

```
entity flop8 is port(
        clk, rst, pst:   in bit;
        data_in:         in bit_vector(7 downto 0);
        data:            out bit_vector(7 downto 0));
end flop8;

use work.myflops.all;
architecture archflop8 of flop8 is
begin
        dff8(data_in,clk,rst,pst,data);
end archflop8;
```

Listing 7-21 Using the procedure defined in Listing 7-20

The calling procedure returns a value in data. The types of the actuals in this procedure call are types bit and bit_vector. There are five actuals that are passed in. They are associated with the **formals**—the parameters of the subprogram definition—positionally. The compiler must perform template matching to distinguish between these two procedures, each with five parameters of types bit and bit_vector.

```
procedure dff ( signal d: bit_vector;
                signal clk, rst, pst: bit;
                signal q: out bit_vector);
procedure dff ( signal d: bit_vector;
                signal clk, rst: bit;
                signal q, q_bar: out bit_vector);
```

7.2.10 About Subprograms

Subprograms (functions and procedures) can greatly add to the readability of code, making VHDL both powerful and flexible. Use subprograms carefully, however, to ensure that the circuit you are describing will be implemented in such a way as to achieve your design objectives (performance and capacity).

Use vendor-supplied standard overloaded operators before defining your own. Often, these operators come in the form of standard packages such as the std_logic_1164, numeric_bit, or numeric_std packages. You can create your own overloaded operators, and the implementation will be logically correct. Nonetheless, synthesis and simulation tool vendors may have optimized package bodies for use with their tools.

Rest assured, however, that there are many more uses for subprograms—some we have explored, others we leave for you to discover—in which the function has not already been standardized or defined.

Problems

7.1. Create an i2std (integer to std_logic_vector) function similar to the one for i2bv function.

7.2. Overload the + operator for operands of type std_logic_vector (see myops package, page 392)

7.3. Compile and synthesize the following design, using the myops package of Listing 7-11.

```
use work.myops.all;
entity add is port(
    a, b:  bit_vector(15 downto 0);
    x:     out bit_vector(15 downto 0));
end add;
architecture add of add is
begin
    s <= a + b;
end;
```

7.4. Compile and synthesize the design of Problem 7.3, modified to use Warp's bit_arith package. Compare the results with those of Problem 7.3. Does module generation provide an advantage?

7.5. Create a procedure for decrementing bit_vectors. Also, create an underflow output for the procedure.

7.6. What are the disadvantages of using a procedure versus instantiating a component?

7.7. Rewrite the bv2i function shown in Listing 7-2 to interpret the value on the left of the bit-vector as the MSB.

7.8. Write a procedure to perform a 16-bit even parity check. Synthesize this design for a MAX340 CPLD. Select retain XORs under device options.

7.9. Write a function to replace the synchronizer component of the network repeater design.

7.10. Write a procedure to create a random number generator. Can you synthesize this procedure? Explain.

Chapter 8

Synthesis and Design Implementation

8.1   Introduction

Up to this point, we have discussed writing VHDL code to create device-independent designs. In this chapter, we examine the processes of synthesis and fitting (placing and routing for FPGAs) to illustrate how designs are implemented in specific device architectures. We show that synthesis and fitting produce the best results—in terms of resource utilization, achievable performance, and meeting design objectives—when they use information about the target device to make decisions about how to optimize and implement logic circuits. To demonstrate how designs are realized and optimized for different architectures, we present case studies using FLASH370 CPLDs and pASIC380 FPGAs; we implement designs to illustrate the architectural strengths and weaknesses of each. These case studies help us to:

- understand how a design description is realized in a target device,

- write code, or use synthesis directives, to take advantage of particular architectural features, and

- determine whether a CPLD or FPGA architecture is best suited to a particular application and set of design objectives.

In the previous chapter, we identified a few synthesis issues such as mutually exclusive signal selection, conditional signal selection, memory element creation, intentional implicit memory, unintentional implicit memory, state machine coding schemes, and operator inferencing. We haven't yet discussed how a VHDL description is synthesized and the resulting logic fitted to a limited resource. Designers beginning to write VHDL code for programmable logic devices frequently forget that the PLD, CPLD, or FPGA has limited resources; the resources have specific features; and not every design will fit in every architecture.

VHDL provides powerful language constructs that enable you to describe a large amount of logic quickly and easily. Even a small code listing can describe a design that requires a large number of gates to implement. The language also allows you to describe numerous types of constructs such as product-term clocks and internal three-states, but not all architectures have these features. For each of your designs, you will have to choose a programmable logic device with the appropriate capacity and feature set. Choosing an appropriate device can be easy, because VHDL allows you to benchmark designs in different devices: You can use the same code for implementation in multiple architectures or devices. You can then easily compare the implementation results and choose the device that best meets design objectives.

Be that as it may, most designers do not have the luxury of selecting a device so late in the design process; they usually need to select a device earlier so that board layout and board-level design can continue in parallel. Thus, it's important for you to understand the processes of synthesis, fitting, and place and route, so that you will know which resources will be required of a given design and whether a particular device will provide the requisite features, capacity, and performance. Without this understanding you risk choosing a device that may not be best suited for an application, which may cause schedule slips, lost time-to-market, reduced design functionality or speed, or the necessity for redesign in a new device with a new board layout. Granted, in many applications any of several devices may be well suited for the job; but if you intend to push the limits of performance or capacity, the potential for problems increases.

8.2   Design Implementation: An Example

Following is a simple design example that requires specific device resources. It shows that even with a simple design, an appropriate device must be selected. In our discussion back in Chapter 4 about creating registered elements using different templates for asynchronous reset and preset, we didn't discuss how a device's available resources affect the final realization of the described logic. Now that we want to target the design description to a specific device, we need to consider these issues. Take, for instance, the code shown in Listing 8-1:

```vhdl
library ieee;
use ieee.std_logic_1164.all;
use work.std_arith.all;
entity counter is port(
    clk, reset: in std_logic;
    count:       buffer std_logic_vector(3 downto 0));
end counter;

architecture archcounter of counter is
begin
upcount: process (clk, reset)
    begin
        if reset = '1' then
            count <= "1010";
        elsif (clk'event and clk= '1') then
            count <= count + 1;
        end if;
    end process upcount;
end archcounter;
```

Listing 8-1 A 4-bit counter that resets to "1010"

The code describes a 4-bit counter that is reset asynchronously to "1010" when rst is asserted. Could this design fit in a logic block like that shown in Figure 8-1? At first glance, you may think not. After all, the logic block is like the 22V10 shown in Figure 2-6, in that all of the macrocells share a common asynchronous reset. A counter with registers sharing a common reset will reset the counter to "0000", not "1010", as shown in Figure 8-2, right? But after more thought, you may realize the design *can* still fit if inverters are placed between the registers and pins of the second and fourth macrocells, as shown in Figure 8-3. This way, the registers will be reset to "0000" when rst is asserted, but the counter output pins will read "1010". If you read the fine print in Figure 8-1, you will find that either polarity of each register may be propagated to a device pin (as in a 22V10). Table 8-1 and Figure 8-3 indicate that slight design modifications are also necessary.

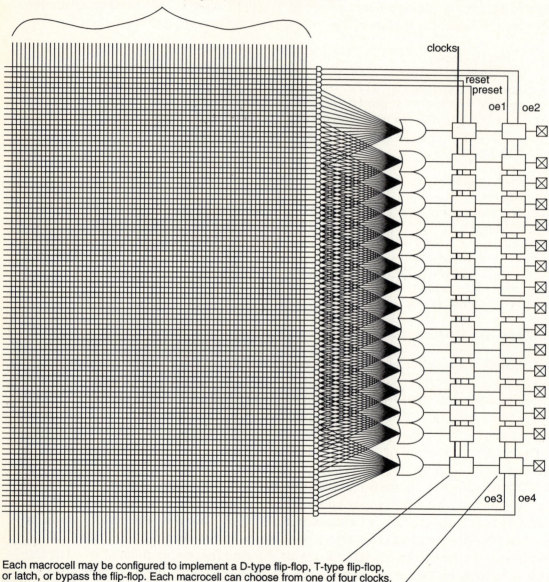

36 signals (and complements) from programmable interconnect matrix

clocks

reset
preset

oe1   oe2

oe3   oe4

Each macrocell may be configured to implement a D-type flip-flop, T-type flip-flop,
or latch, or bypass the flip-flop. Each macrocell can choose from one of four clocks.
The output of the macrocell can be inverted and is fed back to the programmable
Interconnect matrix.

Each I/O cell can be configured to be always an input, always an output, or
a three-state or bidirectional I/O by using one of two output-enable product
terms. All I/Os, whether input or output, are fed back to the programmable
interconnect matrix.

Figure 8-1   Logic block of the FLASH370 family of CPLDs

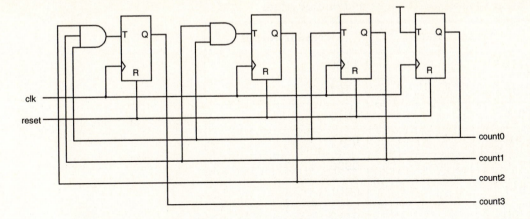

Figure 8-2   Counter that resets to "0000"

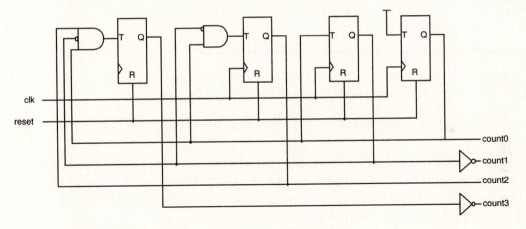

Figure 8-3   Counter that resets to "1010" at pins

Table 8-1   State and output values

Present state	Present output
0000	1010
0001	1011
0010	1000
0011	1001
0100	1110
0101	1111

Table 8-1 (continued)   State and output values

Present state	Present output
0110	1100
0111	1101
1000	0010
1001	0011
1010	0000
1011	0001
1100	0110
1101	0111
1110	0100
1111	0101

If we use a device that has two of the logic blocks shown in Figure 8-1, such as the CY7C371, then the design can be synthesized and fit by

- inserting inverters between registers and output pins (the method described above),
- working around the preset/reset conditions of the logic blocks—partitioning the design into the two logic blocks by placing the first and third counter bits in one logic block (with a common reset) and the second and fourth counter bits in the other (with a common preset), or
- combining the two methods.

The chosen method will affect the availability of resources for additional logic that may need to be implemented in the device. For example, with the second method, all registers in one logic block must share the same reset, and all registers in the other logic block must share the same preset. Logic that is added to this device must work around this placement and allocation of logic resources: all registers must conform to make use of the same preset and reset as the counter does. In most cases, the first method is preferred because all registers can be placed in the same logic block with one common reset signal, leaving the second logic block's reset and preset signals available for additional logic.

This example demonstrates that a device architecture indeed affects how a design will finally be realized in the device. It also demonstrates that not every design can fit in every architecture. Fortunately, state-of-the-art synthesis and fitting algorithms can try many options in a short time, automatically finding an efficient implementation in most cases.

Having examined a simple example, we will now introduce in more detail the task of synthesis and fitting for CPLDs and FPGAs. With an understanding of how VHDL designs are realized in devices, you will be equipped to choose the most suitable devices and optimize your designs for resource utilization and performance requirements. Your understanding will enable you to squeeze out the last product-term, logic cell, or nanosecond from a design because you will be able to write efficient VHDL code and provide human creativity, which no synthesis or fitting tool can match.

8.3   Synthesis and Fitting

Besides being tightly coupled to a device architecture, the synthesis and fitting processes must work closely together. Although these are two separate tasks from a software point of view, they are in effect on a continuum; where one stops, the other must pick up. Ideally, the processes communicate in a feedback loop, where information in optimization and fitting can be used to automatically resynthesize critical portions of a circuit for optimal implementation.

Whereas synthesis is the process of creating logic equations or netlists from the VHDL code, fitting is the process of finding a way to fit the logic those equations or netlists describe into a programmable logic device. Device-specific optimization can occur in synthesis, fitting, or both (Figure 8-4).

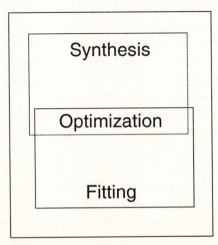

Figure 8-4 Optimization can occur in synthesis, fitting, or both; ideally, the processes are on a continuum

In this section, we have used the term "fitting" to mean the same as the phrase "placing and routing." Fitting, usually associated with CPLDs, describes how logic is partitioned into logic blocks and how signals are routed in the programmable interconnect to connect the logic blocks and I/O. Placing and routing, usually associated with FPGAs, is used to describe how logic is placed in an FPGA's array of logic cells and how signals are routed between those logic cells and the I/O.

The synthesis process can pass to the fitter a design's logic equations in a way that indicates precisely which resources should be used. Alternatively, the synthesis process can pass nonoptimized equations, leaving the optimization task to the fitter. The designer doesn't care where the device-specific optimization takes place, just as long as it does. What is important is that the synthesis and fitting processes interface well—that the fitter receives information from the synthesis in a way that enables the fitter to produce the best possible implementation. If the fitter does not perform any optimization, then the synthesis process should pass logic equations and information in such a way that the fitter simply places the logic. However, if the fitter does provide optimization, then information should be passed from the synthesis process in a way that does not restrict the fitter from performing the appropriate optimization.

Having acquired a general understanding of the synthesis and fitting issues, we will now introduce our first case study, the FLASH370 CPLD.

8.4   CPLDs: A Case Study

In this section, we will examine the task of synthesizing and fitting several designs to the FLASH370 architecture shown in Figure 8-5. This examination will expose you to many issues common to synthesizing and fitting designs to CPLDs. For a review of CPLD architectures, refer to Chapter 2. For a complete description of the FLASH370 CPLD family architecture, refer to Appendix A for instructions on viewing and printing the data sheet. Below is a summary of its architecture

The FLASH370 architecture consists of logic blocks that communicate with each other through a programmable interconnect matrix (PIM). PIM is the Cypress Semiconductor term for what we have previously referred to as the programmable interconnect (PI). All signals (except the clocks) route through the PIM. Each logic block can be configured to receive up to 36 inputs from the PIM. These signals and their complements are used to produce up to 86 product terms, of which 80 are allocated to 16 macrocells and six are allocated to output enables, asynchronous presets, and asynchronous resets. All macrocell and I/O signals feed back to the PIM. Figure 8-1 illustrates the architecture of a logic block.

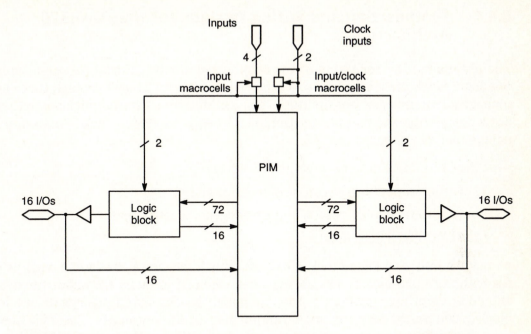

Figure 8-5   Block diagram of the 32-macrocell member of the FLASH370 family of CPLDs

Each I/O macrocell (see Figure 2-28) can sum from zero to 16 product terms; product terms can be individually allocated from one macrocell to the next or shared among multiple macrocells. The sum of product terms at the macrocell can be used as a combinational output, combinational **buried node** (a node that is not an output of the device but is used to feed a function back to the PIM to be used as an input to a logic block), registered output, registered buried node, latched output, or latched buried node. If the macrocell is configured for registering, the register can be a D-type register or T-type register with asynchronous reset and set lines. The output of any macrocell, in any mode, can be fed back to the programmable interconnect. The output of a nonburied macrocell can also drive an I/O cell (I/O cells may be configured for input, output, or bidirectional signals), in which case the output may be inverted. Each macrocell can be configured to use one of several clocks that are allocated to the logic block.

Some of the pins in this family of devices function as dedicated inputs (that is, these cells cannot be configured as output or bidirectional cells). Some of the dedicated inputs also serve as clock inputs (clock pins). The input/clock macrocells are shown in Figure 2-29 and described on page 64.

8.4.1   Synthesizing and Fitting Designs for the FLASH370 Architecture

The example at the beginning of the chapter demonstrated that fitting designs in one logic block presents problems that may be difficult, but for which there are a manageable number of possibilities—one can determine fairly quickly whether or not a design fits. The method for finding a fit with one logic block is to assign signals to macrocells based on

- the product-term requirements of each signal,
- how the product terms can be steered or shared,
- how output enables, resets, and presets can be used, and
- the clocking requirements.

With only one logic block, there are only a few ways that some designs can fit. With multiple logic blocks, designs can often fit in many ways, but the design should be carefully partitioned among the logic blocks. Grouping signals in a logic block (partitioning) based on one condition may affect how another resource may be used. In the first part of the chapter, we looked at fitting the counter of Listing 8-1 into a device with two logic blocks. We decided that the second method we considered restricted the way in which additional logic could fit in the device. Partitioning logic into multiple logic blocks must satisfy the limits imposed by

- the number of macrocells per logic block,
- the number of product terms per logic block,
- the possible preset/reset combinations within a logic block,
- the possible output-enable combinations within a logic block,
- the number of inputs from the programmable interconnect to a logic block, and
- the possible clocking schemes within a logic block.

Partitioning a design into groups of signals assigned to separate logic blocks should be based on a balance of these considerations; otherwise, the capacity of the device may be unnecessarily restricted. Next we briefly explain the level of difficulty in partitioning based on each of the six limitations listed above.

- Partitioning logic based on the number of macrocells is easily accomplished. Each logic block can hold 16 macrocells. These macrocells may contain registered or combinational signals.

- Partitioning based on the second limitation, the number of product terms that are available in a logic block compared to the number of product terms required by a group of signals, is more complicated. This is because the number of required product terms depends on which combination of flip-flop type and polarity is used to implement an equation: D-type and positive, D-type and negative, T-type and positive, or T-type and negative. For example, the complement of a large sum of individual terms ($X = A + B + C + D + E + F$) may be expressed as one product term ($\overline{X} = \overline{A}\,\overline{B}\,\overline{C}\,\overline{D}\,\overline{E}\,\overline{F}$).

- Partitioning based on the number of reset and preset combinations allowed in a logic block compared to the number required by a group of signals is not simply a matter of counting the number of resets or presets described in a design's source code. As our example at the beginning of the chapter illustrated, the number of required resets or presets is also dependent upon whether the positive or negative polarity of an equation is used. That is, if an inverter is introduced between a macrocell and an I/O cell (or the feedback path to the PI), it may be possible to convert a reset equation to a preset (or vice versa). However, doing this also requires that the logic for the complement of that signal be implemented in the product-term array. This may have the side effect of increasing the product-term count. Thus, the limitations above are coupled in some cases.

- Partitioning based on the number of inputs to a logic block means that all of the signals, or functions, that are placed in a logic block's macrocells can have only a certain total number of inputs. The FLASH370 CPLDs have a relatively large number of inputs, 36, compared to other CPLDs. Although this is fewer than three inputs per function on average, most collections of signals can share some common inputs. This means that the software fitter should group together signals that can share common inputs. If signals cannot be shared, the capacity of a logic block may be affected and preassigned pinouts may be difficult to support, as we will explain later in the chapter.

- Partitioning based on the number of output-enable combinations for the FLASH370 family means that four separate output-enable equations are allowed per logic block—two for the top half and two for the bottom half. Thus, in the I/O-intensive versions of these CPLDs, each group of eight I/Os has two output-enable equations available, excluding programming for always on and always off, which do not require separate product terms. Partitioning based on output-enable conditions affects how pin assignments can be supported.

• Partitioning based on the number of clocking schemes requires that the registered or latched signals in a logic block do not exceed the total number of clocks allowed in a logic block. The CY7C371 and CY7C372 can have two clocks per logic block. The remaining members of the family can have four clocks per logic block. The polarity of a clock is selectable at the macrocell. However, both polarities of the same clock are not allowed in the same logic block. If both polarities of a clock are required for a design, then the macrocells clocked on the positive rising edge must be in logic blocks separate from the macrocells clocked on the falling edge.

This discussion illustrates that partitioning logic into logic blocks—fitting in general—is a nontrivial task. The partitioning limitations are interrelated. If the software's first attempt at partitioning fails, other groupings are attempted based on what the software knows about the current grouping and the availability of resources. The partitioning algorithms must include decisions such as: (1) Can the signal be moved to another logic block (or traded with a signal in another logic block) without upsetting that logic block's preset/reset or output-enable combinations? (2) Can the polarity of a signal be reversed in order to maintain consistent preset/reset combinations while meeting the conditions listed above? (3) Finally, can the signal fit in the present logic block while taking multiple passes?

This information foreshadows a point that will be elucidated throughout the chapter: that it is usually best to allow the fitter to choose a pin-assignment the first time through a design cycle; otherwise, you could inadvertently choose a pin assignment that violates one of the partitioning restrictions or that forces an implementation that is neither resource nor speed efficient. In the next several sections, we explore a few of these partitioning decisions.

Allowable Asynchronous Preset/Reset Combinations. All CPLDs have particular feature sets that affect the way in which designs may be implemented. In the next several examples, we look at the asynchronous reset and preset resources of the CY7C371 CPLD and discuss how this resource can and cannot be used. The one preset product term and one reset product term (see the top-right of Figure 8-1) of each logic block usually provide enough flexibility, since asynchronous resets and presets tend to be global. However, there are cases in which this limitation must be worked around or will not suffice for a design's requirements.

Listing 8-2 shows two 16-bit counters with synchronous load that asynchronously reset to two different values based on the signals rsta and rstb. How can this design be partitioned into a CY7C371? Intuitively, you may want to partition the counters into separate logic blocks; in fact, this is the only way that these two counters can be partitioned into this device. Rsta must be used as an asynchronous reset for cnta, and therefore resets all of the registers within that logic block. The resetting of cntb is not controlled by rsta, and therefore all cntb registers must be in a logic block separate from the cnta registers.

```vhdl
library ieee;
use ieee.std_logic_1164.all;
use work.std_arith.all;
entity counter is port(
clk, rsta,rstb,lda,ldb: in std_logic;
        cnta, cntb:      buffer std_logic_vector(15 downto 0));
end counter;

architecture archcounter of counter is
begin

upcnta: process (clk, rsta)
        begin
                if rsta = '1' then             --async reset #1
                        cnta <= x"3261";
                elsif (clk'event and clk= '1') then
                        if lda = '1' then
                            cnta <= cntb;
                        else
                            cnta <= cnta + 1;
                        end if;
                end if;
        end process upcnta;

upcntb: process (clk, rstb)
        begin
                if rstb = '1' then             --async reset #2
                        cntb <= x"5732";
                elsif (clk'event and clk= '1') then
                        if ldb = '1' then
                                cntb <= cntb;
                        else
                                cntb <= cntb + 1;
                        end if;
                end if;
        end process upcntb;
end archcounter;
```

Listing 8-2 Two 16-bit counters with synchronous load

The two counters could be defined in one process, but are described here with two processes for readability. Read through Listing 8-3 and determine how this design can fit into a CY7C371.

```
library ieee;
use ieee.std_logic_1164.all;
use work.std_arith.all;
entity counter is port(
        clk, rsta, rstb, rstc:  in std_logic;
        cnta, cntb, cntc:       buffer std_logic_vector(7 downto 0));
end counter;

architecture archcounter of counter is
begin

upcnta: process (clk, rsta)
        begin
                if rsta = '1' then                 --async reset #1
                        cnta <= (others => '0');
                elsif (clk'event and clk= '1') then
                        cnta <= cnta + 1;
                end if;
        end process upcnta;

upcntb: process (clk, rstb)
        begin
                if rstb = '1' then                 --async reset #2
                        cntb <= (others => '0');
                elsif (clk'event and clk= '1') then
                        cntb <= cntb + 1;
                end if;
        end process upcntb;

upcntc: process (clk, rstc)
        begin
                if rstc = '1' then                 --async reset #3
                        cntc <= (others => '0');
                elsif (clk'event and clk= '1') then
                        cntc <= cntc + 1;
                end if;
        end process upcntc;

end archcounter;
```

Listing 8-3 Three 8-bit counters with separate asynchronous resets

Even though there are enough macrocells to store all the register values, this design will not fit into two logic blocks because three asynchronous resets are required. Each asynchronous reset must reset all registers within a logic block. Therefore, this design requires three logic blocks and will not fit in a CY7C371. Modifying the design as shown in Listing 8-4 to use two synchronous resets permits the design to easily fit. The entity declaration is the same and is not repeated.

```vhdl
architecture archcounter of counter is
begin
upcnta: process (clk, rsta)
    begin
        if rsta = '1' then                    --async reset #1
            cnta <= (others => '0');
        elsif (clk'event and clk= '1') then
            cnta <= cnta + 1;
        end if;
    end process upcnta;

upcntb: process (clk, rstb)
    begin
        if (clk'event and clk= '1') then
            if rstb = '1' then                --synchronous reset
                cntb <= (others => '0');
            else
                cntb <= cntb + 1;
            end if;
        end if;
    end process upcntb;

upcntc: process (clk, rstc)
    begin
        if (clk'event and clk= '1') then
            if rstc = '1' then                --synchronous reset
                cntc <= (others => '0');
            else
                cntc <= cntc + 1;
            end if;
        end if;
    end process upcntc;

end archcounter;
```

Listing 8-4 Three 8-bit counters: one with asynchronous reset, two with synchronous reset

Listing 8-4 uses a synchronous reset for the second and third counter. The synchronous resets use additional product terms but eliminate the need for three separate logic blocks.

The logic block of Figure 8-1 indicates that the asynchronous reset and preset lines are product terms. The design in Listing 8-5 will make use of a product-term reset.

```vhdl
library ieee;
use ieee.std_logic_1164.all;
use work.std_arith.all;
entity counter is port(
        clk, rsta, rstb:        in std_logic;
        cnta, cntb:             buffer std_logic_vector(15 downto 0));
end counter;

architecture archcounter of counter is
begin

upcnta: process (clk, rsta,rstb)
        begin
                if (rsta = '1' and rstb = '1') then --product term reset
                        cnta <= x"0001";
                elsif (clk'event and clk= '1') then
                        cnta <= cnta + 1;
                end if;
        end process upcnta;

upcntb: process (clk, rsta, rstb)
        begin
                if (rsta = '1' and rstb = '1') then --PT async reset
                        cntb <= x"0002";
                elsif (clk'event and clk= '1') then
                        cntb <= cntb + 1;
                end if;
        end process upcntb;
end archcounter;
```

Listing 8-5 A design with product-term asynchronous reset

The asynchronous set and reset product terms have polarity control, which allows the registers to be set or reset based on an AND expression (product term) or an OR expression (sum term). If the reset signal is the sum of two literals, such as rsta OR rstb, then the product term ((rsta)' AND (rstb)')' may be used. Thus, the reset logic of the code shown in Listing 8-6 may be implemented as shown in Figure 8-6.

```
library ieee;
use ieee.std_logic_1164.all;
use work.std_arith.all;
entity counter is port(
        clk, rsta, rstb:in std_logic;
        cnta, cntb:        buffer std_logic_vector(15 downto 0));
end counter;

architecture archcounter of counter is
begin

upcnta: process (clk, rsta, rstb)
        begin
                if (rsta = '1' or rstb = '1') then   --OR term async rst
                        cnta <= x"0001";
                elsif (clk'event and clk= '1') then
                        cnta <= cnta + 1;
                end if;
        end process upcnta;

upcntb: process (clk, rsta, rstb)
        begin
                if (rsta = '1' or rstb = '1') then   --OR term async rst
                        cntb <= x"0002";
                elsif (clk'event and clk= '1') then
                        cntb <= cntb + 1;
                end if;
        end process upcntb;
end archcounter;
```

Listing 8-6 A design with an OR term reset

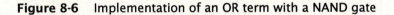

Figure 8-6   Implementation of an OR term with a NAND gate

The report file generated by synthesizing Listing 8-6 to a CY7C371 indicates that the OR term asynchronous reset is implemented as an AND term, using DeMorgan's theorem to transform the equation:

```
/cntb_0.AR =
        /rsta * /rstb
```

Sometimes more complicated reset conditions are required. In these cases, the resulting equation cannot be implemented in one OR or AND term. Instead, an intermediate signal placed on a macrocell must be used to generate the reset equation. This requires two passes through the product-term array and an incremental delay on the order of several nanoseconds is incurred. Listing 8-7 is an example of a complex reset condition. Because the reset equation requires the use of a macrocell, the size of at least one of the counters had to be reduced in order for this design to fit in a 32-macrocell device. Because the size of the counter is no longer a multiple of four, the hexadecimal base specifier (x) cannot be used in the assignment statement for the next condition. Instead, aggregates were used. The first aggregate indicates that cnta(0) is assigned '1', and all other elements are assigned '0'. The second aggregate indicates that cntb(1) is assigned '1' and all other elements are assigned '0'.

```
library ieee;
use ieee.std_logic_1164.all;
use work.std_arith.all;
entity counter is port(
        clk, rsta, rstb:          in std_logic;
        cnta, cntb:               buffer std_logic_vector(14 downto 0));
end counter;

architecture archcounter of counter is
begin
upcnta: process (clk, rsta, rstb)
        begin
                if ((rsta xor rstb) = '1') then   --complex async rst
                        cnta <= (0 => '1', others => '0'); --aggregate
                elsif (clk'event and clk= '1') then
                        cnta <= cnta + 1;
                end if;
        end process upcnta;
upcntb: process (clk, rsta, rstb)
        begin
                if ((rsta  xor rstb) = '1') then --complex async rst
                        cntb <= (1 => '1', others => '0');
                elsif (clk'event and clk= '1') then
                        cntb <= cntb + 1;
                end if;
        end process upcntb;
end archcounter;
```

Listing 8-7 Description of a complex reset condition that requires two passes through product-term array

The report file confirms that the reset equation must be placed on a macro-cell and that this causes an incremental delay. You should always read the timing report to verify that a design implementation produces the expected results.

```
cnta_14.T =
      cnta_4.Q * cnta_3.Q * cnta_2.Q * cnta_1.Q * cnta_0.Q * cnta_9.Q *
      cnta_8.Q * cnta_7.Q * cnta_6.Q * cnta_5.Q * cnta_13.Q *
      cnta_12.Q * cnta_11.Q * cnta_10.Q
cnta_14.AP =
      GND
cnta_14.AR =
      cnta_14_AR.CMB
cnta_14.C =
      clk

cnta_14_AR =
      rsta * /rstb
    + /rsta * rstb
```

```
TIMING PATH ANALYSIS        (23:50:13) using Package: CY7C371-143JC
Messages:
----------------------------------------------------------------------
Signal Name | Delay Type |    tmax    | Path Description
----------------------------------------------------------------------
reg::cnta_14[24]
inp::cnta_4.Q
            tSCS          7.0 ns      1 pass
inp::rsta
---->cnta_14_AR
            tRO           18.5 ns     2 passes
out::cnta_14
            tCO           6.0 ns
----------------------------------------------------------------------
```

Breakout Exercise 8-1

Purpose: To illustrate how reset signals can be transformed to preset signals in order to achieve a fit.

Compile the following design to a CY7C371 device. The design is located in c:\vhdlbook\ch8\cntrp.vhd. After synthesis, review the equations. Verify that grst is actually used as the preset signal for all counter flip-flops. To maintain correct polarity at the output pins, the inputs to some of the flip-flops must be the inverse logic.

```vhdl
library ieee;
use ieee.std_logic_1164.all;
use work.numeric_std.all;
entity cnt8 is port(
        txclk, grst:        in std_logic;
        enable, load:       in std_logic;
        data:               in unsigned(7 downto 0);
        cnt:                buffer unsigned(7 downto 0));
end cnt8;

architecture archcnt8 of cnt8 is
begin
count: process (grst, txclk)
  begin
        if grst = '1' then
          cnt <= "11001100";
        elsif (txclk'event and txclk='1') then
                if load = '1' then
                        cnt <= data;
                elsif enable = '1' then
                        cnt <= cnt + 1;
                end if;
        end if;
  end process count;
end archcnt8;
```

Routing Architectures and Pin Assignment. Ideally, concurrent engineering enables multiple parallel efforts, which reduces cost and time-to-market. An often practiced example of concurrent engineering is parallel board-level and chip-level design. The idea is that board-level design, layout, and manufacturing can proceed in parallel with the design of the logic to be implemented in a PLD (or ASIC). This type of parallel effort requires that critical issues are understood before the work begins. Misunderstandings can lead to rework, additional costs, and missed schedules.

Of course, the most important issue is design functionality. The function of the logic to be implemented in the PLD must be clearly defined. Its interface to the rest of the board design—including pin assignments—must also be clearly defined. However, as the examples in the previous section show, you must understand logic placement and routing restrictions to be assured that your design will fit. A design may not fit if you make pin assignments yourself rather than allow the fitter to choose how to place logic. For example, if the counters cnta and cntb in Listing 8-2 are preassigned to pins associated with the same logic block, the design will fit only if

1. additional macrocells are available (for Listing 8-2 implemented in the CY7C371, additional macrocells are not available; you would need to use the 64-macrocell CY7C372), and
2. the counter registers of each counter are implemented in the macrocells of separate logic blocks, but the outputs of these macrocells are routed through the programmable interconnect to the other logic block, and combinatorially through a macrocell to its assigned pin (Figure 8-7).

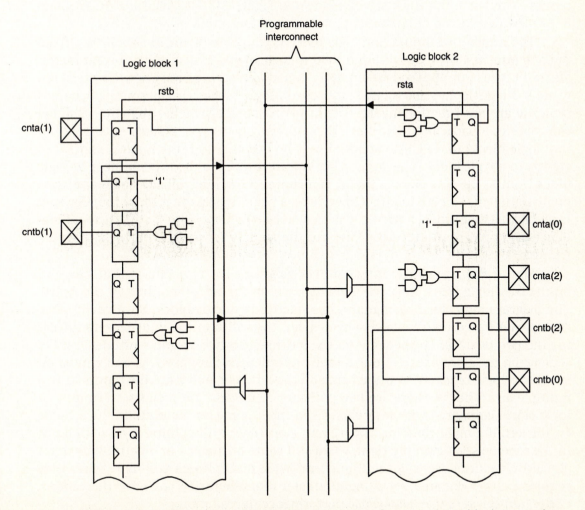

Figure 8-7 Working around limitations by routing from one logic block to another

This way the reset and preset limitations are not violated and the design can fit, even if inefficiently (using extra macrocells and a second pass, resulting in a clock-to-output of t_{CO2}). Although this fitting solution is inefficient, it may get you out of trouble in a bind.

Routing and product-term distribution schemes can also affect how well a fixed pin assignment can be supported. Let's look at routing schemes first. Logic blocks have only a certain number of inputs. For example, FLASH370 CPLDs have 36 inputs per logic block; this is the total number of inputs that can be routed into a logic block for all functions to be implemented in that logic block. If a fixed pin assignment is such that implementation of the equations for a given logic block requires more than 36 inputs, then buried macrocells must be used in other logic blocks—similar to the work around shown in Figure 8-7—to achieve a fit. Problem 8–14 provides you an opportunity to try this work-around.

The number of inputs to a logic block is only one factor in supporting fixed pin assignments. How signals are routed to logic blocks is also an important factor. Most CPLDs use multiplexer-based interconnect or routing pools (see Chapter 2) to route I/O signals and macrocell feedbacks to logic blocks. These routing schemes typically are not functionally equivalent to crosspoint switches. Whether a signal can route to a particular logic block depends on which other signals must route to that logic block; that is, it may not always be possible to route a *particular set* of signals to a logic block. The larger a set is with respect to the total number of logic block inputs, the less chance that it can route to the logic block. If you specify a pin assignment, you are in effect specifying a set of signals that must route to that logic block. Oftentimes, however, you may not know how many or which set of signals is required to produce the logic for the signals for which you are specifying a pinout.

Figure 8-8 shows the interconnect schemes for two CPLDs that have 36 inputs to a logic block (one scheme is shown on the left, the other on the right). The diagram indicates how signals are routed into a logic block. Both devices use multiplexer-based interconnect schemes, but the width of the multiplexers differs for the two devices. The scheme on the left uses 36 two-to-one multiplexers; the scheme on the right uses 36 four-to-one multiplexers. Suppose x, y, and z must all route to a logic block. With the scheme on the left, x, y, and z are the inputs to two multiplexers. That is, there are two paths, or "chances," for a signal to route to a logic block, compared with four chances in the scheme on the right. In the scheme on the left, if x must route on input2 and z on input3, then there is no path for y. In the scheme shown on the right, y can still route on input4 or input5. Why don't all silicon vendors use wider multiplexers? Wide multiplexers and more wires may require a larger die area, resulting in greater manufacturing costs for the vendor. Wider multiplexers may also cause performance degradation.

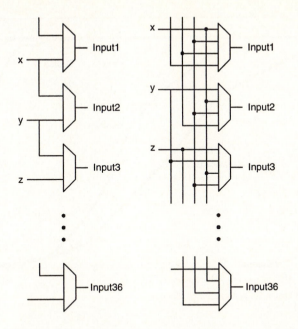

Figure 8-8 Multiplexer-based interconnect schemes

The number of inputs to a logic block and the scheme used to route signals into a logic block determines a device's **routability,** its capability to route signals through the programmable interconnect and into a logic block.

In Figure 8-9, device A is different from the rest; it has 22 inputs from the programmable interconnect to each logic block, whereas each of the other devices has 36. Because device A has only 22 inputs to a logic block, it follows that the probability of routing any set of more than 22 signals into a logic block is zero. (A corollary is that functions of greater than 22 signals require more than one pass through the logic array in this device.) If we assume that the devices compared in Figure 8-9 use multiplexer-based interconnect schemes, then we can conclude that devices D and E have wider multiplexers than devices B and C. This accounts for the fact that a larger number of unique sets of signals (signals from I/Os or macro-cells) can route to a logic block in devices E and D. For example, if 35 signals are required to route to a logic block, upward of 90 percent of the unique sets of 35 signals can route in devices D and E, whereas fewer than 5 percent of the unique sets of 35 signals can route in devices B and C. This does not mean that fewer than 5 percent of designs requiring 35 signals per logic block will fit in devices B and C, but it does mean that if you specify which sets of 35 signals must be routed to the logic block (by specifying a pinout, for example), the chance of finding a fit is less than 5 percent.

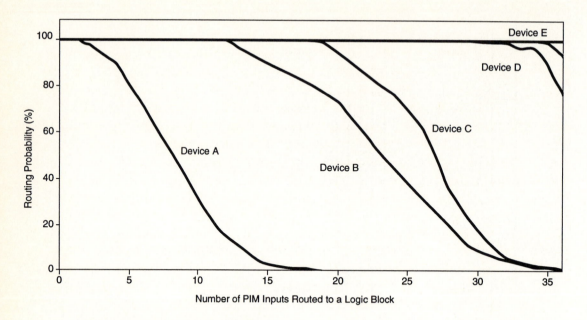

Figure 8-9   Routability of CPLDs

Because assigning a pinout defines a set of signals that must route to a logic block, designing a board layout prior to finishing the PLD design for devices B and C would be ill-advised. Beware of this pitfall: a design that fits with a software-chosen pin assignment may not fit with the same pin assignment after a small change, because a design change may require a different set of signals—perhaps only slightly different—to route to a logic block. Often, a design change is required after a bug is discovered in testing or quality assurance. Obviously, you'd like the design to fit with the same pinout so that you won't need to modify the board. If the design change is small, the inputs to the logic block may not change at all. However, if a different set of signals is required and the probability of routing signals to the logic block is low, you may have to make changes to the board.

The design in Listing 8-8 consists of two 16-bit counters with synchronous load and enable. These count by one or by two depending on the value of signal by1. If you were to attempt to fit this design into the CY7C371, you would find that the two counters can be partitioned into logic blocks in only one way—each counter must be in a separate logic block. This is because each counter requires all 36 inputs to the logic block: 16 for the counter bits (the present count value is required to determine the next count value), 16 for the load bits, and one each for rst, by1, ld, and the enable. Counter bits from one counter cannot be placed in the logic block of the other counter because that requires the other counter's enable signal (either ena or enb) to also route to that logic block. This design example demonstrates that although you are free to specify the pinout for the counters within each logic block, you are not able to specify a pinout that requires different bits of a counter to be in separate logic blocks (the CY7C371 is device E in Figure 8-9, so defining a set of signals to route to a logic block rarely presents a problem). Additionally, if you use a different 32-macrocell CPLD that is divided into two logic blocks having fewer than 36 inputs, the design does not fit at all.

Unless a CPLD specifically guarantees a crosspoint switch for the interconnection of logic blocks and the interconnection of macrocells to I/O pins, preassigning a pinout or making a logic change after the fitter has chosen a pinout introduces a subsequent fitting constraint for which it may not be possible to find a solution given your design's resource and feature-set requirements. Even with a crosspoint switch, a fit will not be possible if a design change requires that more signals route to a logic block than there are inputs to that logic block. If you must preassign a pinout, be sure you understand all of the issues involved with the architectural features that will affect your design's ability to fit into the target architecture. Understanding the routability of signals through the programmable interconnect and to the logic blocks (as quantified in Figure 8-9) will also help you to judge whether it will be possible to make design changes and keep the same pinout.

```vhdl
library ieee;
use ieee.std_logic_1164.all;
entity counter is port(
    clk, rsta,rstb:     in std_logic;
    ld, ena, enb, by1:  in std_logic;
    cnta, cntb:         buffer std_logic_vector(15 downto 0));
end counter;

use work.std_math.all;
architecture archcounter of counter is
begin

upcnta: process (clk, rsta)
    begin
        if rsta = '1' then
            cnta <= x"0000";
        elsif (clk'event and clk= '1') then
            if ld = '1' then
                cnta <= cntb;
```

```
                    elsif en = '1' then
                        if by1 = '1' then
                            cnta <= cnta + 1;
                        else
                            cnta <= cnta + 2;
                        end if;
                    else
                        cnta <= cnta;
                    end if;
                end if;
            end process upcnta;

    upcntb: process (clk, rstb)
        begin
            if rstb = '1' then
                cntb <= x"0000";
            elsif (clk'event and clk= '1') then
                if ld = '1' then
                    cntb <= cntb;
                elsif enb = '1' then
                    if by1 = '1' then
                        cntb <= cntb + 1;
                    else
                        cntb <= cntb + 2;
                    end if;
                else
                    cntb <= cntb;
                end if;
            end if;
        end process upcntb;
    end archcounter;
```

Listing 8-8 Counters that count by1 or by2

Product-Term Distribution and Pin Assignments. The product-term distribution scheme can also affect the ability of a device to support a preassigned pinout. For example, suppose two signals, a and b are neighbors (in both pinout and macrocell location). If one signal, a, requires many product terms, then depending on the product-term allocation scheme, neighboring macrocells (including b) may have to give up product terms—in which case it may not be possible to allocate product terms for b (see Figure 8-10). If a requires five product terms, for instance, b must give up all of its available product terms, because the product-term allocation scheme steers product terms in groups of four. If macrocells neighboring b cannot forfeit their product terms, then b is left without any, in which case the design may not fit with this preassignment of pins and macrocells.

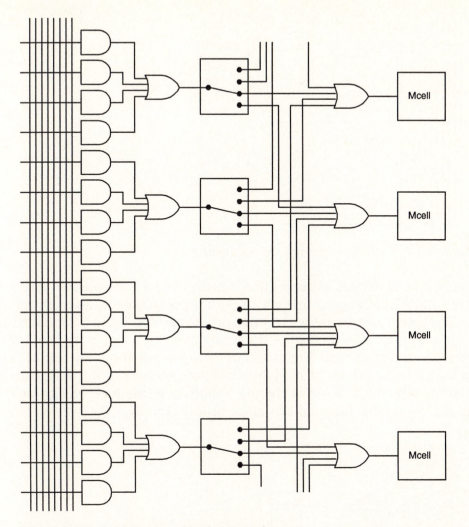

Figure 8-10   Product-term distribution scheme 1

Figure 8-11 shows another product-term distribution scheme in which product terms may be steered (in groups of five) from one macrocell to another. This scheme also makes use of several additional expander product terms, which may be used with any macrocell at the expense of an incremental delay. This scheme avoids the need for neighboring macrocells to give up all product terms in all cases in which more than five are needed on any given macrocell. If a macrocell has a high product-term requirement, however, then neighboring macrocells may have to forfeit their product terms, reducing the possibility of a fit with a pre-assigned pinout.

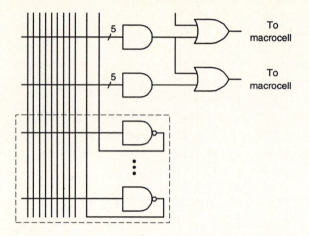

Figure 8-11   Product-term distribution scheme 2

Figure 8-12 illustrates a distribution scheme in which the product terms may be steered individually, permitting a fit with a preassigned pinout in the case where a and b each require more than five product terms (up to a combined total of 20). What happens if 16 product terms are required for a and more than four are required for b, or if more than 20 product terms are required for any pair of macrocells? In such a scenario, this architecture could not permit signal b to be placed on a neighboring pin, unless a was at the top or bottom of the logic block where two adjacent macrocells are allocated 22 unique product terms.

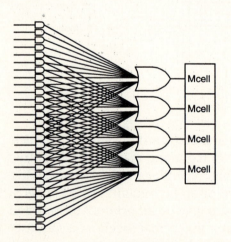

Figure 8-12   Product-term distribution scheme 3

Forcing Signals to Macrocells. Figure 8-7 illustrates a possible work-around for cases where equations cannot be placed on macrocells associated with specific device pins due to reset, preset, product-term, or logic-block input limitations. In this section we use two examples to illustrate similar design issues, one involving inputs to a logic block, the other involving product-term count. Before we begin these examples, we discuss **virtual substitution.**

In the following code fragment, signal x is considered to be a **virtual** node because it is not an input to a macrocell (registered or combinational) or to an I/O cell. Signal y, on the other hand, is considered a device node because it is an input to an I/O cell.

```vhdl
library ieee; use ieee.std_logic_1164.all;
entity substitute is port(
    a, b, c:  in std_logic;
    y:          buffer std_logic);
end substitute;
architecture substitute of substitute is
    signal x: std_logic;
begin
    x <= a or b or c;
    y <= x or d;
end;
```

Because x is a virtual node, not a device node, the expression for it may be substituted into the equation for y. Hence, the result of synthesizing this code is the equation

```
/y =
     /a * /b * /c * /d
```

You can see from this equation that signal x has been substituted out because it is a nonessential node. In many synthesis tools you can retain signal x as a device node, by using a synthesis directive. In Warp the synthesis_off directive can be applied as an attribute to achieve this control, as in the following code.

```vhdl
library ieee; use ieee.std_logic_1164.all;
entity substitute is port(
    a, b, c: in std_logic;
    y:          buffer std_logic);
end substitute;
architecture substitute of substitute is
    signal x: std_logic;
    attribute synthesis_off of x:signal is true;   -- retain node
```

```
begin
    x <= a or b or c;
    y <= x or d;
end;
```

The results of synthesizing this code are the equations and timing information below, which show that signal x is retained as a device node, causing a two-
pass delay. The first pass through the product-term array is to produce x (the AND
of a, b, and c). The second pass is to produce y (the AND of x and d).

```
/y =
    /d * /x.CMB

/x =
    /a * /b * /c
```

TIMING PATH ANALYSIS   (03:32:22) using Package: CY7C371-143JC

Messages:

```
---------------------------------------------------------------------
Signal Name | Delay Type  |    tmax    | Path Description
---------------------------------------------------------------------
cmb::y[24]
inp::a
---->x
                    tPD        13.0 ns      2 passes
---------------------------------------------------------------------
```

In this case, there is no advantage to forcing signal x to a device node: it
requires additional resources and results in a slower implementation. However,
we need this kind of control in our next two examples, which illustrate first, a
28-bit counter with synchronous load, and second, saving product terms, macrocells, and speed.

Implementing a 28-bit counter with synchronous load in a 32 macrocell
CY7C371, which has 36 inputs into each logic block, presents a design obstacle. In
a CY7C371, counters are typically implemented with T-type flip-flops. If the
counter is not being loaded, then the least significant flip-flop toggles every clock
cycle, and all subsequent bits toggle only when all of the lesser significant bits are
asserted. For example, the equation for the fifth bit of a counter with synchronous
load is:

```
cnt_4.T =
      cnt_2.Q * cnt_1.Q * cnt_0.Q * /ld * cnt_3.Q
    + ld * cnt_4.Q * /data_4
    + ld * /cnt_4.Q * data_4
```

From the first product term of this equation, we can deduce that the fifth bit will toggle when the load signal is deasserted and cnt(3), cnt(2), cnt(1), and cnt(0) are asserted. From the last two product terms of this equation, we can deduce that the bit will also toggle if $\overline{\text{load}}$ is asserted and the current cnt(4) value is different than the data(4) value being loaded.

The twenty-eighth bit of the counter cannot be implemented in quite the same way; that is, the first product term cannot be a product of $\overline{\text{load}}$ and the previous 27 bits of the counter. Additional bits of the counter must also be implemented in this same logic block (there are only two logic blocks for all 28 bits), and each of these bits requires an input for the load data. Thus, the total of all the counter bits plus the load bits is in excess of the 36 allowed inputs, if we plan to simply AND all previous bits to determine when the MSBs should toggle. To get around this, we can implement the first 15 bits of the counter in the first logic block, passing to the next logic block a token that represents the product of these 15 bits. By forcing the token to a device node, the sixteenth bit, cnt(15), is enabled by this one signal rather than by a product of 15 signals. In effect, this is creating a cascaded AND gate, where one AND gate is in the first logic block, and subsequent ones are in the next logic block (Figure 8-13). The code to implement this design is shown in Listing 8-9.

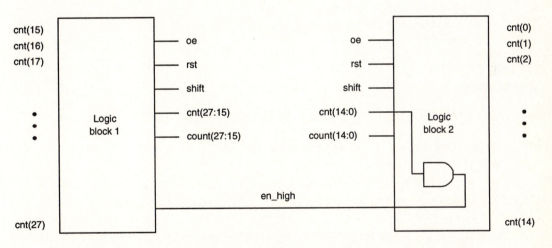

Figure 8-13   Implementation of a 28-bit counter that uses token passing

```vhdl
library ieee;
use ieee.std_logic_1164.all;
use work.std_arith.all;
entity cnt28 is port(
    clk, rst, oe, shift:  in std_logic;
    count:                buffer std_logic_vector(27 downto 0));
end cnt28;
architecture cnt28 of cnt28 is
    signal en_high: std_logic;
    attribute synthesis_off of en_high:signal is true;  -- explained below
    signal cnt: std_logic_vector(27 downto 0);
    alias lowcnt: std_logic_vector(14 downto 0) is cnt(14 downto 0);
    alias highcnt: std_logic_vector(12 downto 0) is cnt(27 downto 15);
begin
p1: process (clk, rst)
    begin
        if rst = '1' then
            cnt <= (others => '0');
        elsif (clk'event and clk='1') then
            if shift = '1' then
                cnt <= count(26 downto 0) & count (27);
            else
                lowcnt <= lowcnt + 1;
                if en_high = '1' then
                    highcnt <= highcnt + 1;
                end if;
            end if;
        end if;
    end process;

en_high <= '1' when lowcnt = "111111111111111" else '0';

count <= cnt when oe = '1' else (others => 'Z');

end;
```

Listing 8-9 Description of a 28-bit counter that uses token passing

The signal en_high is the result of ANDing the first 15 bits, count(0) through count(14). The upper order bits of the counter are enabled by en_high. The equations for en_high, cnt(15), and cnt(16) illustrate this:

```
en_high =
        count_0.Q * count_1.Q * count_2.Q * count_3.Q * count_4.Q *
        count_5.Q * count_6.Q * count_7.Q * count_8.Q * count_9.Q *
        count_10.Q * count_11.Q * count_12.Q * count_13.Q * count_14.Q
```

```
count_15.D =
      /shift * en_high.CMB * /count_15.Q
    + /shift * /en_high.CMB * count_15.Q
    + shift * count_14

count_16.T =
      /shift * en_high.CMB * count_15.Q
    + shift * /count_16.Q * count_15
    + shift * count_16.Q * /count_15
```

By default, the synthesis and optimization software eliminates en_high as a virtual node, and simply substitutes the equation for en_high into each counter-bit equation. The result, substituting the equivalent expression for en_high into the equation for cnt(16), is:

```
count_16.T =
      /shift * count_0.Q * count_1.Q * count_2.Q * count_3.Q *
      count_4.Q * count_5.Q * count_6.Q * count_7.Q * count_8.Q *
      count_9.Q * count_10.Q * count_11.Q * count_12.Q * count_13.Q *
      count_14.Q * count_15
    + shift * count_16 * /count_16.Q
    + shift * /count_16 * count_16.Q
```

To ensure that en_high is made a device node and not substituted out, the synthesis_off directive is used. This token-passing scheme introduces an incremental delay because it requires two passes through the logic array—one for each AND function. An alternate token-passing scheme that requires only one pass through the logic array is one in which en_high is registered. The input to the register is the value of the counter one clock cycle before it will cause count(15) to toggle. This implementation is left as an exercise for the reader. It is also left as an exercise to compare the results of synthesizing Listing 8-9 to the results of synthesizing this 28-bit counter without token passing. This exercise will give you an opportunity to better understand Warp's module generation.

Although many equations are best implemented in CPLDs when they are flattened to a minimal sum of products, the equation shown in Listing 8-10 is an exception. If the expression for x is flattened, its implementation requires 362 product terms split over 23 macrocells (an average of 16 product terms per macrocell), with one additional macrocell used to sum each of the partial sums. The resource-utilization summary extracted from the report file is shown below.

	Required	Max (Available)
Macrocells Used	24	32
Unique Product Terms	363	160

```vhdl
library ieee;
use ieee.std_logic_1164.all;
entity p_terms is port(
    a, b, c, d, e, f, g, h, i, j, k, l:    in std_logic;
    x:                                     out std_logic);
end p_terms;
architecture p_terms of p_terms is
begin
    x <=  (a and b) xor (c or d) xor (e and f) xor (g or h) xor
        (i and j) xor (k or l);
end;
```

Listing 8-10 Description of a complex function. If flattened, the equation for *x* requires many product terms

This design obviously won't fit in a 32-macrocell device if implemented in this manner. But if a synthesis directive that controls the flattening of an expression is used to create factoring points, then the product-term and macrocell requirements can be reduced. In Listing 8-11, three factoring points (x1, x2, and x3) are created to implement smaller expressions. These smaller expressions are then XORed together without substitution.

```vhdl
library ieee;
use ieee.std_logic_1164.all;
entity p_terms is port(
    a, b, c, d, e, f, g, h, i, j, k, l:in std_logic;
    x:                                out std_logic);
end p_terms;
architecture p_terms of p_terms is
    signal x1, x2, x3: std_logic;
    attribute synthesis_off of x1,x2,x3:signal is true;
begin
    x1 <= (a and b) xor (c or d);
    x2 <= (e and f) xor (g or h);
    x3 <= (i and j) xor (k and l);
    x <= x1 xor x2 xor x3;
end;
```

Listing 8-11 Alternative implementation for Listing 8-10.

The equations generated by synthesizing this description require considerably fewer product terms. They are reprinted as follows to show that the signals x1, x2, and x3 were forced to device nodes due to the synthesis directive. This implementation can easily fit in the CY7C371:

```
x =
      x1.CMB * /x2.CMB * /x3.CMB
   + /x1.CMB *  x2.CMB * /x3.CMB
   + /x1.CMB * /x2.CMB *  x3.CMB
   +  x1.CMB *  x2.CMB *  x3.CMB
x3 =
      i * j * /l
   + /j * k * l
   + /i * k * l
   +  i * j * /k
/x2 =
      /f * /g * /h
   + /e * /g * /h
   +  e *  f *  h
   +  e *  f *  g
/x1 =
      /b * /c * /d
   + /a * /c * /d
   +  a *  b *  d
   +  a *  b *  c
```

	Required	Max (Available)
Macrocells Used	4	32
Unique Product Terms	16	160

Clocking. Most CPLDs have synchronous clocks—with dedicated pins—not only because synchronous clocks are inherently faster, but also because asynchronous clocking is not a standard design practice. Some CPLDs include product-term (gated) clocks for asynchronous clocking to accommodate those designs that may require them. Implementation of a gated clock should always be similar to that shown in Figure 6-19 or from the Q output of a register, *never* from combinational gates that may introduce glitches due to gate-delay imbalances. If your design uses gated clocks, the programmable logic device you choose must support this clocking scheme. The clock multiplexer circuit of the network repeater is a design that uses product-term clocking.

An interesting feature of the FLASH370 devices is their ability to select either polarity for a clock on a logic-block-by-logic-block basis. This feature allows state machines, counters, and other logic to run at twice the system clock frequency—though it consumes twice the resources, since the logic must be replicated in separate logic blocks. It does not, however, mean that you can run the device above its maximum speed rating—propagation delays from register to register remain the same.

Take for example a DRAM controller that operates on a 20 MHz system clock (see Figure 8-14 and Listing 8-12). The system address is captured on the rising edge of a clock, during which the address strobe is asserted. The upper bits of the system address are examined to determine whether the address is for a memory location. This address comparison is evaluated in the `address_detect` state. Subsequent states place the row and column addresses on the bus and assert at the proper time the RAS and CAS lines for the bank of DRAMs. The timing diagram for interfacing to an asynchronous DRAM controller is shown in Figure 8-15. The block diagram for the DRAM controller is shown in Figure 8-16.

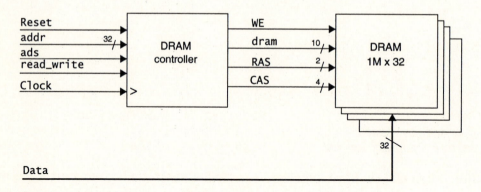

Figure 8-14   DRAM controller interfacing to an asynchronous DRAM

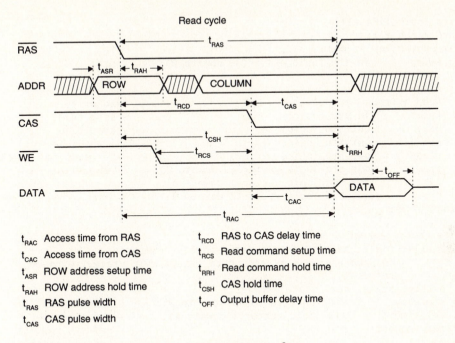

Figure 8-15   Timing diagram for DRAM interface

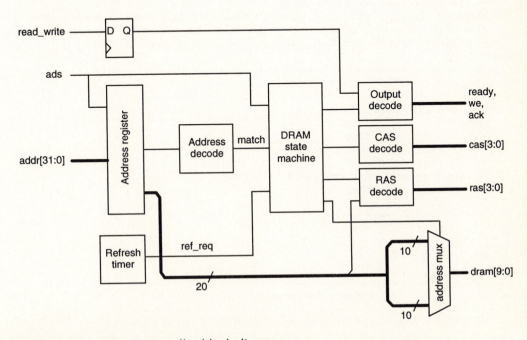

Figure 8-16   DRAM controller block diagram

```vhdl
library ieee;
use ieee.std_logic_1164.all;
use work.std_arith.all;
entity dram_controller is port (
            addr:        in std_logic_vector(31 downto 0);  -- system address
            clock,                                          -- clock 20MHz
            ads,                                            -- address strobe
            read_write,                                     -- read/write
            reset:       in std_logic;                      -- system reset
            ack:         out std_logic;                     -- acknowledge
            we:          out std_logic;                     -- write enable
            ready:       out std_logic;                     -- data ready for latching
            dram:        out std_logic_vector (9 downto 0);  -- DRAM address
            ras:         out std_logic_vector(1 downto 0);   -- row address strobe
            cas:         out std_logic_vector(3 downto 0));  -- column address strobe
end dram_controller;

architecture controller of dram_controller is
    type states is (idle, address_detect, row_address, ras_assert,
                    col_address, cas_assert, data_ready, wait_state, refresh0,
                    refresh1);
    signal present_state, next_state: states;
    signal stored:          std_logic_vector(31 downto 0);   -- latched addr
    signal ref_timer:       std_logic_vector(8 downto 0);    -- refresh timer
    signal ref_request:     std_logic;                       -- refresh request
    signal match:           std_logic;                       -- address match
    signal read:            std_logic;                       -- latched read_write
    -- row and column address aliases
    alias row_addr:     std_logic_vector(9 downto 0) is stored(19 downto 10);
    alias col_addr: std_logic_vector(9 downto 0) is stored(9 downto 0);
    --attribute synthesis_off of match,ref_request: signal is true;
begin
----------------------------------------------------------------
--                   Capture Address      --
----------------------------------------------------------------
capture: process (reset, clock)
    begin
        if reset = '1' then
            stored <= (others => '0');
            read <= '0';
        elsif (clock'event and clock='1') then
          if ads = '0' then
            stored <= addr;
            read <= read_write;
          end if;
        end if;
    end process;


----------------------------------------------------------------
--                   Address Comparator    --
----------------------------------------------------------------
-- The address comparator determines if memory is being accessed

  match <= '1' when stored(31 downto 21) = "00000000000" else '0';
```

```
-------------------------------------------------------------
--                   Address Multiplexer               --
-------------------------------------------------------------
-- The address multiplexer selects the row, column, or refresh
-- address depending on the current cycle

multiplexer: process (row_addr, col_addr, present_state)
    begin
        if ( present_state = row_address or present_state = ras_assert) then
            dram <= row_addr;
        else
            dram <= col_addr;
        end if;
    end process;


-------------------------------------------------------------
--          Refresh Counter & Refresh Timer            --
-------------------------------------------------------------
-- The refresh timer is used to initiate refresh cycles.
-- A refresh request is generated every 312 clock cycles.
-- Refresh_req is asserted until a refresh cycle begins

synchronous: process (reset, clock)
    begin
        if reset = '1' then
            ref_timer <= (others => '0');
        elsif clock'event and clock = '1' then
            if (ref_timer = "100111000") then  -- start request at 312
                ref_timer <= (others => '0');
            else
                ref_timer <= ref_timer + 1;
            end if;
        end if;
    end process;

    ref_request <= '1' when (ref_timer = "100111000" or
                (ref_request = '1' and present_state /= refresh0))
        else '0';


-------------------------------------------------------------
--          DRAM State Machine                         --
-------------------------------------------------------------
-- The DRAM controller state machine controls the state of
-- the address multiplexer select lines as well as the
-- state of RAS and CAS

state_tr: process (present_state, ref_request, ads, match)
    begin
        case present_state is
    when idle =>
        if ref_request = '1' then
            next_state <= refresh0;
        elsif ads = '0' then
            next_state <= address_detect;
```

```vhdl
            else
                next_state <= idle;
            end if;
        when address_detect =>
            if match = '1' then
                next_state <= row_address;
            else
                next_state <= idle;
            end if;
        when row_address =>
            next_state <= ras_assert;
        when ras_assert =>
            next_state <= col_address;
        when col_address =>
            next_state <= cas_assert;
        when cas_assert =>
            next_state <= data_ready;
        when data_ready =>
            next_state <= wait_state;
        when wait_state =>
            next_state <= idle;
        when refresh0 =>
            next_state <= refresh1;
        when refresh1 =>
            next_state <= idle;
            end case;
        end process;

    clocked: process (reset, clock)
        begin
            if reset = '1' then
                present_state <= idle;
            elsif (clock'event and clock = '1') then
                present_state <= next_state;
            end if;
        end process;

    with present_state select
        cas <=      "0000" when cas_assert | data_ready | wait_state |
                                refresh0 | refresh1,
                    "1111" when others;

    ras <=      "00" when (present_state = refresh1)
                else "01" when ((present_state = ras_assert or
                                 present_state = col_address or
                                 present_state = cas_assert or
                                 present_state = data_ready or
                                 present_state = wait_state) and stored(20)='1')
                else "10" when ((present_state = ras_assert or
                                 present_state = col_address or
                                 present_state = cas_assert or
                             present_state = data_ready or
                             present_state = wait_state) and stored(20)='0')
        else "11";
```

```
    we <=  '0' when ((present_state = col_address or
                      present_state = cas_assert or
                      present_state = data_ready) and read = '0')
           else '1';

    ack <=     '0' when (present_state = address_detect and match = '1')
               else '1';

    ready <=   '0' when (read = '1' and (present_state = data_ready or
                         present_state = wait_state))
               else '1';

end controller;
```

Listing 8-12 DRAM controller

While the design is functionally accurate, the interface to the DRAM may be slower than the maximum specification of the DRAM. With a 20MHz clock, RAS and CAS are asserted 50 ns apart. What if the DRAMs are 60-ns DRAMs (that is, data is valid 60 ns after RAS is asserted)? To take advantage of the faster DRAM access times, we would need to run the state machine at twice the current frequency. One solution is to use a two-phase clock (possibly obtained using a programmable skew clock buffer such as the CY7B991). Another solution is to clock registers on both the rising and falling edges, as allowed in some CPLDs. This requires that two state machines and outputs that are multiplexed based on the current state of the clock as shown in Figure 8-17 and Listing 8-13. One state machine looks at the present state of the other to determine its next state. Two sets of outputs are produced, and are multiplexed based on `clock`. The capture address and refresh controller and timer processes do not change.

This design illustrates the concept of clocking a state machine on both the rising and falling edges of a clock, but it would need to be modified before being used with an asynchronous DRAM. Care must be taken to ensure that there is no glitching on any of the asynchronous interface signals. Glitching could cause erroneous accesses or unpredictable behavior of the DRAM. Inserting a delay in the multiplexer select line will ensure that the output of the multiplexer switches only after the inputs to the multiplexer are stable.

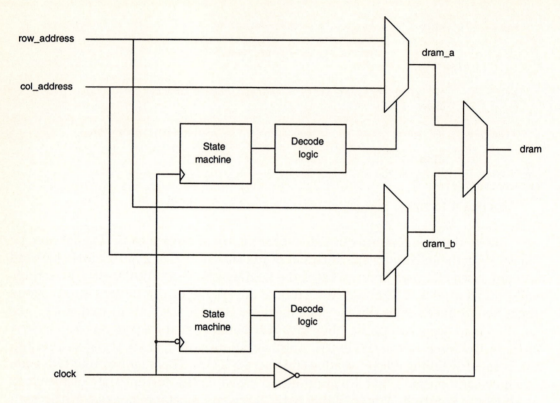

Figure 8-17 Implementation of a DRAM controller that uses both the rising and falling edges of a clock

```
library ieee;
use ieee.std_logic_1164.all;
use work.std_arith.all;
entity dram_controller is port (
    addr: in std_logic_vector(31 downto 0);        -- system address
    clock,                                         -- clock 20MHz
    ads,                                           -- address strobe
    read_write,                                    -- read/write
    reset: in std_logic;                           -- system reset
    ack: out std_logic;                            -- acknowledge
    we: out std_logic;                             -- write enable
    ready: out std_logic;                          -- data ready for latching
    dram:out std_logic_vector (9 downto 0);        -- DRAM address
    ras: out std_logic_vector(1 downto 0);         -- row address strobe
    cas: out std_logic_vector(3 downto 0));        -- column address strobe
end dram_controller;

architecture controller of dram_controller is
    type states is (idle, address_detect, row_address, ras_assert,
                    col_address, cas_assert, data_ready, wait_state, refresh0,
                    refresh1);
```

```vhdl
    signal present_state_a, next_state_a: states;
    signal present_state_b, next_state_b: states;
    signal dram_a, dram_b: std_logic_vector(9 downto 0);
    signal ras_a, ras_b: std_logic_vector(1 downto 0);
    signal cas_a, cas_b: std_logic_vector(3 downto 0);
    signal we_a, we_b, ack_a, ack_b, ready_a, ready_b: std_logic;
    signal stored: std_logic_vector(31 downto 0);          -- latched addr
    signal ref_timer:std_logic_vector(8 downto 0);         -- refresh timer
    signal ref_request: std_logic;                         -- refresh request
    signal match: std_logic;                               -- address match
    signal read: std_logic;                                -- latched read_write
    -- row and column address aliases
    alias row_addr: std_logic_vector(9 downto 0) is stored(19 downto 10);
    alias col_addr: std_logic_vector(9 downto 0) is stored(9 downto 0);
    --attribute synthesis_off of match,ref_request: signal is true;
begin
-----------------------------------------------------------------
--                    Capture Address      --
-----------------------------------------------------------------
capture: process (reset, clock)
    begin
        if reset = '1' then
            stored <= (others => '0');
            read <= '0';
        elsif (clock'event and clock='1') then
          if ads = '0' then
            stored <= addr;
            read <= read_write;
          end if;
        end if;
    end process;


-----------------------------------------------------------------
--                    Address Comparator      --
-----------------------------------------------------------------
-- The address comparator determines whether memory is being accessed

    match <= '1' when stored(31 downto 21) = "00000000000" else '0';


-----------------------------------------------------------------
--                    Address Multiplexers                  --
-----------------------------------------------------------------
-- The address multiplexer selects the row, column, or refresh
-- address depending on the current cycle

multiplexer_a: process (row_addr, col_addr, present_state_a)
begin
    if (present_state_a = row_address or present_state_a = ras_assert) then
        dram_a <= row_addr;
    else
        dram_a <= col_addr;
    end if;
end process;
```

```
multiplexer_b: process (row_addr, col_addr, present_state_b)
 begin
    if ( present_state_b = row_address or present_state_b = ras_assert) then
        dram_b <= row_addr;
    else
        dram_b <= col_addr;
    end if;
 end process;


---------------------------------------------------------------
--              Refresh Counter & Refresh Timer              --
---------------------------------------------------------------
-- The refresh timer is used to initiate refresh cycles.
-- A refresh request is generated every 312 clock cycles.
-- Refresh_req is asserted until a refresh cycle begins

synchronous: process (reset, clock)
    begin
        if reset = '1' then
            ref_timer <= (others => '0');
        elsif clock'event and clock = '1' then
            if (ref_timer = "100111000") then   -- start request at 312
                ref_timer <= (others => '0');
            else
                ref_timer <= ref_timer + 1;
            end if;
        end if;
    end process;

  ref_request <= '1' when (ref_timer = "100111000" or
                (ref_request = '1' and present_state_a /= refresh0))
            else '0';


---------------------------------------------------------------
--          DRAM State Machine A                             --
---------------------------------------------------------------
-- The DRAM controller state machine controls the state of
-- the address multiplexer select lines as well as the
-- state of RAS and CAS

state_tr_a: process (present_state_b, ref_request, ads, match)
begin
    case present_state_b is            --next_state_a depends on present_state_b
    when idle =>
        if ref_request = '1' then
            next_state_a <= refresh0;
        elsif ads = '0' then
            next_state_a <= address_detect;
        else
            next_state_a <= idle;
        end if;
```

```vhdl
        when address_detect =>
            if match = '1' then
                next_state_a <= row_address;
            else
                next_state_a <= idle;
            end if;
        when row_address =>
            next_state_a <= ras_assert;
        when ras_assert =>
            next_state_a <= col_address;
        when col_address =>
            next_state_a <= cas_assert;
        when cas_assert =>
            next_state_a <= data_ready;
        when data_ready =>
            next_state_a <= wait_state;
        when wait_state =>
            next_state_a <= idle;
        when refresh0 =>
            next_state_a <= refresh1;
        when refresh1 =>
            next_state_a <= idle;
        end case;
end process;

clocked_a: process (reset, clock)
    begin
        if reset = '1' then
            present_state_a <= idle;
        elsif (clock'event and clock = '1') then
            present_state_a <= next_state_a;
        end if;
    end process;

    with present_state_a select
    cas_a <=        "0000" when cas_assert | data_ready |
                            wait_state | refresh0 | refresh1,
                    "1111" when others;

    ras_a <=        "00" when (present_state_a = refresh1)
                    else "01" when ((present_state_a = ras_assert or
                            present_state_a = col_address or
                            present_state_a = cas_assert or
                            present_state_a = data_ready or
                            present_state_a = wait_state) and stored(20)='1')
                    else "10" when ((present_state_a = ras_assert or
                            present_state_a = col_address or
                            present_state_a = cas_assert or
                            present_state_a = data_ready or
                            present_state_a = wait_state) and stored(20)='0')
                    else "11";
```

```vhdl
    we_a <=      '0' when ((present_state_a = col_address or
                            present_state_a = cas_assert or
                            present_state_a = data_ready or
                            present_state_a = wait_state) and read = '0')
            else '1';

    ack_a <=     '0' when (present_state_a = address_detect and match = '1')
            else '1';

    ready_a <=      '0' when (read = '1' and (present_state_a = data_ready or
                        present_state_a = wait_state))
                else '1';

-------------------------------------------------------------
--          DRAM State Machine B                           --
-------------------------------------------------------------
state_tr_b: process (present_state_a, ref_request, ads, match)
begin
    case present_state_a is          --next_state_b depends on present_state_a
    when idle =>
        if ref_request = '1' then
            next_state_b <= refresh0;
        elsif ads = '0' then
            next_state_b <= address_detect;
        else
            next_state_b <= idle;
        end if;
    when address_detect =>
        if match = '1' then
            next_state_b <= row_address;
        else
            next_state_b <= idle;
        end if;
    when row_address =>
        next_state_b <= ras_assert;
    when ras_assert =>
        next_state_b <= col_address;
    when col_address =>
        next_state_b <= cas_assert;
    when cas_assert =>
        next_state_b <= data_ready;
    when data_ready =>
        next_state_b <= wait_state;
    when wait_state =>
        next_state_b <= idle;
    when refresh0 =>
        next_state_b <= refresh1;
    when refresh1 =>
        next_state_b <= idle;
    end case;
end process;
```

```
clocked_b: process (reset, clock)
    begin
        if reset = '1' then
            present_state_b <= idle;
        elsif (clock'event and clock = '0') then
            present_state_b <= next_state_b;
        end if;
    end process;

    with present_state_b select
    cas_b <=        "0000" when cas_assert | data_ready | wait_state |
                            refresh0 | refresh1,
                    "1111" when others;

    ras_b <=        "00" when (present_state_b = refresh1)
                    else "01" when ((present_state_b = ras_assert or
                            present_state_b = col_address or
                            present_state_b = cas_assert or
                            present_state_b = data_ready or
                            present_state_b = wait_state) and stored(20)='1')
                    else "10" when ((present_state_b = ras_assert or
                            present_state_b = col_address or
                            present_state_b = cas_assert or
                            present_state_b = data_ready or
                            present_state_b = wait_state) and stored(20)='0')
                        else "11";

    we_b <=     '0' when ((present_state_b = col_address or
                            present_state_b = cas_assert or
                            present_state_b = data_ready) and read = '0')
                else '1';

    ack_b <=    '0' when (present_state_b = address_detect and match = '1')
                else '1';

    ready_b <=      '0' when (read = '1' and (present_state_b = data_ready or
                            present_state_b = wait_state))
                    else '1';
```

```
--------------------------------------------------------
-- Output Multiplexers
--------------------------------------------------------
    cas   <= cas_a when clock = '1' else cas_b;
    ras   <= ras_a when clock = '1' else ras_b;
    we    <= we_a  when clock = '1' else we_b;
    ack   <= ack_a when clock = '1' else ack_b;
    dram  <= dram_a when clock = '1' else dram_b;
    ready <= ready_a when clock = '1' else ready_b;

end controller;
```

Listing 8-13 Description of DRAM controller operating on both the rising and falling edges of the clock.

Falling-edge clocks can also be used to align data that is transferred between two buses operating at different speeds, or to work around a race condition between data and a buffered clock, among other possibilities.

Implementing Network Repeater Ports in a CY7C374. In this section, we examine the implementation of three network-repeater port controllers in a 128-macrocell member of the FLASH370 family of devices. We begin by analyzing the design to determine how many and which resources it requires. We then synthesize the design and examine the report file to compare our expectations with the realization of the circuit.

Listing 6-20 in Chapter 6 defines one port controller of the repeater core logic. The design of this port controller is modular so that ports can be added or removed easily from the top level design. In Chapter 6, the network repeater has eight ports, and the design is implemented in one FPGA. An alternate methodology for implementation is to place the port controllers in external devices, leaving the FIFO, core controller, clock multiplexer, and so forth in a smaller FPGA. Listing 8-14 is the code required to implement three repeater port controllers in one device.

Reviewing Listing 6-20, we can determine the required number of macrocells to implement one repeater with fairly good precision. Determining the number of required macrocells requires that we understand how many registers and combinatorial outputs are needed, as well as whether any of the combinatorial logic exceeds 16 product terms (in which case, it would require two passes through the logic array and more than one macrocell). Each of the three repeater ports requires:

- 19 buried registers to hold the current state of the counters,
- three buried registers for an 8-state state machine,
- six input registers (double registers) to synchronize `crs`, `link_bar`, and `enable_bar`,
- two registers for `copyin` and `collision`, and
- five output macrocells for outputs (one registered, four combinational).

This is a total of 35 I/O macrocells for each port controller, or 105 for three controllers. There are six clock/input macrocells on the device. One will be used for clocking, leaving five available to replace 10 I/O macrocells for synchronizing external signals. One input macrocell can replace two I/O macrocells because the input macrocells, designed to synchronize asynchronous signals, contain two registers. Thus we expect that a minimum of 95 I/O macrocells and 10 input macrocells will be required. More than three macrocells may be required for the state machine if the state transition logic is sufficiently complex. The product-term requirements are considerably more difficult to estimate, but here is our attempt:

- 57 product terms for all counter bits (three product terms per counter bit, assuming an implementation with T-type flip-flops and a counter with enable and synchronous clear).

- 24 product terms for the state machine (an average of eight for each port). This is a guess based on past experience.

- eight product terms for all of the outputs. Based on the descriptions, most outputs (except partition_bar) are simple decodes of registers.

This is a total of 89 product terms for each port controller, or 267 total product terms; well below the 640 available.

```
library ieee;
use ieee.std_logic_1164.all;
entity port3 is port(
        txclk, areset:                        in std_logic;
        crs1, enable1_bar, link1_bar, sel1:   in std_logic;
        carrier, collision, jam, txdata,prescale: in std_logic;
        rx_en1, tx_en1, activity1:            inout std_logic;
        jabber1_bar, partition1_bar:          buffer std_logic;
        crs2, enable2_bar, link2_bar, sel2:   in std_logic;
        rx_en2, tx_en2, activity2:            buffer std_logic;
        jabber2_bar, partition2_bar:          buffer std_logic;
        crs3, enable3_bar, link3_bar, sel3:   in std_logic;
        rx_en3, tx_en3, activity3:            buffer std_logic;
        jabber3_bar, partition3_bar:          buffer std_logic);
end port3;

use work.coretop_pkg.all;
architecture archport3 of port3 is
begin

u1: porte port map
        (txclk, areset,
        crs1, enable1_bar, link1_bar,
        sel1, carrier, collision, jam, txdata, prescale, rx_en1, tx_en1,
        activity1, jabber1_bar, partition1_bar);

u2: porte port map
        (txclk, areset,
        crs2, enable2_bar, link2_bar,
        sel2, carrier, collision, jam, txdata, prescale, rx_en2, tx_en2,
        activity2, jabber2_bar, partition2_bar);
```

```
u3: porte port map
        (txclk, areset,
        crs3, enable3_bar, link3_bar,
        sel3, carrier, collision, jam, txdata, prescale, rx_en3, tx_en3,
        activity3, jabber3_bar, partition3_bar);

end archport3;
```

Listing 8-14 Description of three network repeater ports to be implemented in a CPLD

Below is a summary from the report file showing the utilization of the realized circuit after synthesis and fitting:

```
                                    Required      Max (available)
CLOCK/LATCH ENABLE signals             1                 4
Input REG/LATCH signals                5                 5
Input PIN signals                      0                 0
Input PIN signals using I/O cells      7                 7
Output PIN signals                    95               121

Total PIN signals                    108               134
Macrocells used                       95               128
Unique product terms                 254               640
```

The circuit realization meets our expectations for macrocell utilization (95 I/O macrocells and five input macrocells). Fewer product terms were required than expected, due to an overestimate on our part or to the ability of some product terms to be shared among multiple macrocells. There is a substantial amount of resources available for additional logic or for significant design changes if required.

The following diagram is an excerpt from a report file; it illustrates how the product terms in one logic block were assigned. The logic block's 80 product terms are numbered at the top from zero to 79. The 16 macrocells are listed on the left, numbered from zero to 15, with the signal name just to the right of the macrocell number. Each macrocell's allotment of product terms (16) is shown in the row directly below the macrocell number and name. A plus sign (+) indicates an unused product term. An X represents a used product term. Most product terms may be shared by several macrocells. For example, product terms 18, 19, 20, and 21 can all be shared by macrocells 1, 2, 3, and 4. This does not mean, however, that because product term 18 is used by macrocell 4 that it *must* be used by macrocells 1, 2, and 3. The diagram illustrates that this is not the case. (An X is placed in product-term location 18 for macrocell 4, and a + is placed in location 18 for the other macrocells.) This logic block was the most heavily used in the device, yet there are still several product terms available. This placement can easily accommodate a design change that requires the macrocells to use additional product terms.

```
_____     1111111111222222222233333333334444444444555555555566666666667777777777
           01234567890123456789012345678901234567890123456789012345678901234567890123456789
_____
| 0 |(u2_stateSBV_2)
XXXXXXX+XX++++++..............................................................
| 1 |(u3_crsdd)
......+X+++++++++++++.........................................................
| 2 |partition2_bar
.........X+XX++++++++++++......................................................
| 3 |(u2_cccnt_1)
...........X+XX++++++++++++....................................................
| 4 |(u2_cccnt_3)
..............X+XX++++++++++++.................................................
| 5 |(u2_cccnt_5)
.................X+XX++++++++++++..............................................
| 6 |(u2_jabcnt_0)
....................X+XX++++++++++++...........................................
| 7 |(u2_jabcnt_3)
.......................X+XX++++++++++++.........................................
| 8 |(u2_jabcnt_2)
..........................X+XX++++++++++++......................................
| 9 |(u2_jabcnt_1)
.............................X+XX++++++++++++...................................
|10 |(u2_cccnt_6)
................................X+XX++++++++++++...............................
|11 |(u2_cccnt_4)
...................................X+XX++++++++++++............................
|12 |(u2_cccnt_2)
......................................X+XX++++++++++++.........................
|13 |(u2_cccnt_0)
.........................................X+XX++++++++++++.........
|14 |jabber2_bar
............................................X+++++++++++++++++......
|15 |(u2_stateSBV_1)
.............................................XXXXXXX+XX++++++
_____
Total product terms to be assigned   =  56
Max product terms used / available   =  56 / 80  = 70.1 %
```

The following diagram is an excerpt from the report file that illustrates the signals that were routed to the logic block (on the left) and the macrocell placements (on the right). Macrocells for which the outputs are not driven to I/O buffers are shown in parentheses; those for which outputs propagate to the pins are shown without parentheses. Of the 36 inputs to the logic block, 23 were required. Design changes that require additional inputs to the logic block should not present a problem.

Logic Block 5

```
-----------------------------------------------------
|    |= >jabber2_bar                      |   |
|    |= >prescale                         |   |
|    |= >u2_enable_b..                     |   |
|    |= >u2_jabcnt_2.Q                    | 63|= (u2_stateSBV_2)
|    |= >u2_cccnt_0.Q                     |   |
|    |= >u2_cccnt_6.Q                     | 64|= (u3_crsdd)
|    |= >areset                           |   |
|    |= >u2_jabcnt_3.Q                    | 65|= partition2_bar
|    |= >u2_stateSBV..                     |   |
|    |= >u2_copyd.Q                       | 66|= (u2_cccnt_1)
|    |= >partition2_..                     |   |
|    |= >u3_collisio..                     | 67|= (u2_cccnt_3)
|    |= >u2_jabcnt_0.Q                    |   |
|    |= >u2_crsdd.Q                       | 68|= (u2_cccnt_5)
|    |= >u2_cccnt_4.Q                     |   |
|    |> not used:333                      | 69|= (u2_jabcnt_0)
|    |> not used:334                      |   |
|    |> not used:335                      | 70|= (u2_jabcnt_3)
|    |= >u2_nocolcnt..                     |   |
|    |= >u2_cccnt_1.Q                     | 72|= (u2_jabcnt_2)
|    |> not used:338                      |   |
|    |= >u2_stateSBV..                     | 73|= (u2_jabcnt_1)
|    |> not used:340                      |   |
|    |= >u2_cccnt_3.Q                     | 74|= (u2_cccnt_6)
|    |> not used:342                      |   |
|    |> not used:343                      | 75|= (u2_cccnt_4)
|    |> not used:344                      |   |
|    |> not used:345                      | 76|= (u2_cccnt_2)
|    |= >u2_jabcnt_1.Q                    |   |
|    |> not used:347                      | 77|= (u2_cccnt_0)
|    |> not used:348                      |   |
|    |= >u2_cccnt_2.Q                     | 78|= jabber2_bar
|    |> not used:350                      |   |
|    |> not used:351                      | 79|= (u2_stateSBV_1)
|    |= >crs3.QI                          |   |
|    |= >u2_cccnt_5.Q                     |   |

-----------------------------------------------------
```

Below is a summary of the worst-case performance metrics. The worst-case combinational propagation delay is 12.0 ns. This indicates that all combinational logic can be implemented in one level of logic (one pass through the product-term array). The worst-case setup time with respect to the clock is 7.0 ns. The worst-case register-to-register delay is 10 ns (which supports 100MHz operation, well above the required 25MHz). The worst-case clock-to-output delay is 15.0 ns. This clock-to-output delay (listed as tCO in the report file below) represents t_{CO2} rather than t_{CO} because the partition outputs are decoded from the state bits, which requires an additional level of logic.

```
Worst Case Path Summary
-----------------------
Worst case COMB,    tmax = 12.0 ns for activity1
Worst case PIN->D, tS   = 7.0 ns for tx_en2.D
Worst case Q->Q,    tmax = 10.0 ns for tx_en2.D
Worst case CLK->Q, tCO  = 15.0 ns for partition2_bar.C
```

Our case study of the FLASH370 identifies the relationship between synthesis and fitting, illustrates how to take advantage of CPLD resources, points out differences in capability among various CPLDs, and enables resource utilization and performance estimations.

Having covered these issues, we will now turn our attention to designing with FPGAs.

8.5   FPGAs: A Case Study

FPGAs are usually more akin to semicustom gate arrays than CPLDs are. The tasks of synthesizing, placing, and routing designs for FPGAs does not center around algorithms to partition logic among logic blocks, route signals through a programmable interconnect, and steer or share logic block resources, as it does for CPLDs; rather, it centers around optimizing logic and signal paths for the device architecture in order to achieve the appropriate balance (as directed by the designer) between density and speed trade-offs. In this section, we explore some of the issues involved with targeting designs to FPGAs. We continue this discussion in the next chapter, where we cover optimizing datapaths. Before proceeding, you may want to review some of the differences between CPLDs and FPGAs discussed in Chapter 2.

A block diagram of the pASIC380 FPGA architecture that we will be using for our discussion is shown in Figure 8-18. As with most other FPGAs, it consists of an array of logic cells that communicate with one another and the I/O through routing wires within the routing channels. The logic cell (see Figure 8-19) consists of a flip-flop, three two-to-one multiplexers (which may be cascaded as a four-to-one multiplexer), and AND gates for the multiplexer select lines and inputs. The logic cell has multiple outputs that may be used at the same time. The flip-flop clock, asynchronous set, and asynchronous reset signals may be driven by any internal signal or by a signal from one of the dedicated low-skew, high-performance distribution trees.

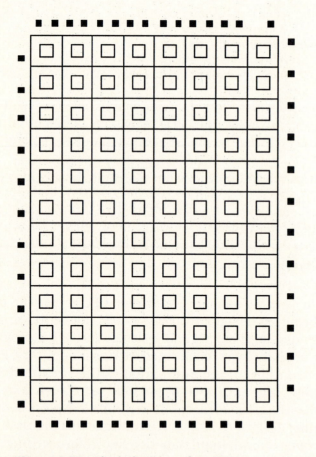

Figure 8-18   Block diagram of an FPGA

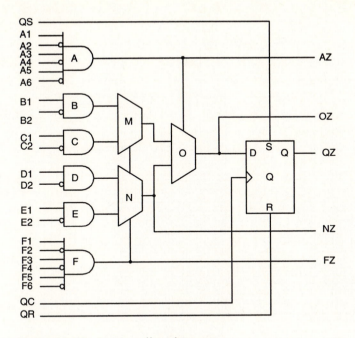

Figure 8-19 Logic cell architecture

A theoretical architecture model consisting of two logic cells is shown in Figure 8-20. The smallest of this family of devices, the CY7C381, has 96 logic cells (an array of eight by 12), with 22 signal-routing wires in each of the vertical routing channels and 12 routing wires in each of the horizontal routing channels. For a complete description of the pASIC380 family architecture, refer to Appendix A for instructions on viewing and printing the data sheets.

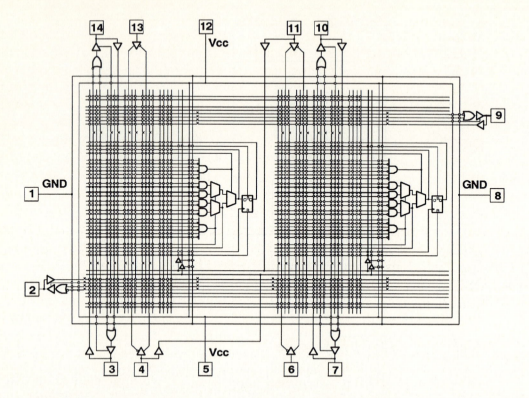

Figure 8-20   Model architecture of an FPGA with two logic cells

8.5.1   Synthesizing, Placing, and Routing Designs for the pASIC380 Architecture

Determining the optimal design implementation for an FPGA is not as easy as you might think. For one, there may be multiple solutions that are comparable in performance and capacity. Also, "optimal" is not well defined—it can be different for two designers or two designs. A designer may be concerned with performance for one design, and with another design, for cost reasons, the same designer may be concerned only with fitting the design into the smallest FPGA. Often, the design must fit in a device of a particular size, but certain signal paths must meet specific performance criteria. This means that some logic should be packed in as tightly as possible with little concern for performance, while other portions of logic should be placed and routed for high performance with less concern for resource conservation. In achieving the density and performance requirements of a particular design, two of the most challenging tasks for FPGA synthesis and fitting tools are to (1) optimize logic for the FPGA logic cell architecture and (2) make the appropriate trade-offs while placing and routing the logic by prioritizing the placement of critical portions of logic.

Optimizing logic for FPGA resources is more challenging than it is for most CPLDs because the architecture does not lend itself easily to a sum-of-products (SP) implementation. Most software logic minimization algorithms begin with SP equations that they then map to a device's resources. (Other algorithms may use binary decision diagrams to map directly to logic cells.) With CPLDs, the task of mapping SP equations is easy—the products are mapped to the product-term array, and these products are summed at each macrocell. Some CPLDs have XOR gates included in macrocells (one input to the XOR gate is the sum of a variable number of product terms and the other is one product term), but software can work with the logic to determine whether the XOR can provide any logic reduction. If not, an XOR input with one product term is tied low. For FPGAs, software must have special mapping technologies to optimize logic for the device resources. Take, for instance, the logic cell shown in Figure 8-19. The three two-to-one multiplexers can be cascaded to create a four-to-one multiplexer. A 2^n-to-one multiplexer is a universal logic module that can implement any function of $n + 1$ variables, provided that both the true and complement of each variable are available; thus, this logic cell can implement any function of three variables. But using an algorithm that assumes that this is the *most* logic that can be implemented in this logic cell would potentially waste many of its resources. After all, many other functions can be implemented: a 7-input AND gate, a 7-input OR gate, a 14-input AND gate (with half of the inputs inverted), a sum of three small products, a two-to-four decoder, or multiple functions at the same time, among other logic circuits (see Figure 8-21). Each synthesis tool vendor or silicon vendor must create algorithms for mapping logic into FPGA device architectures.

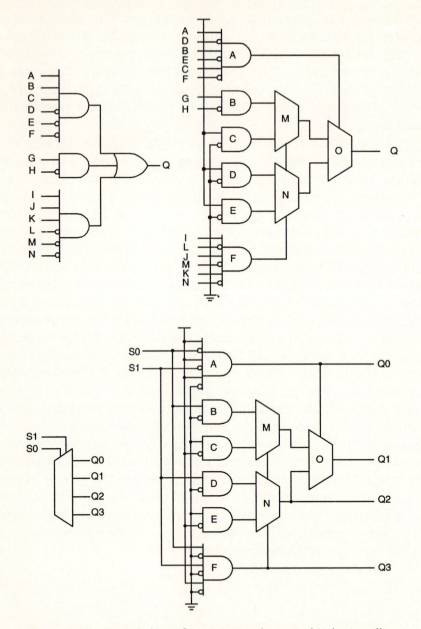

Figure 8-21   Sample logic functions implemented in logic cells

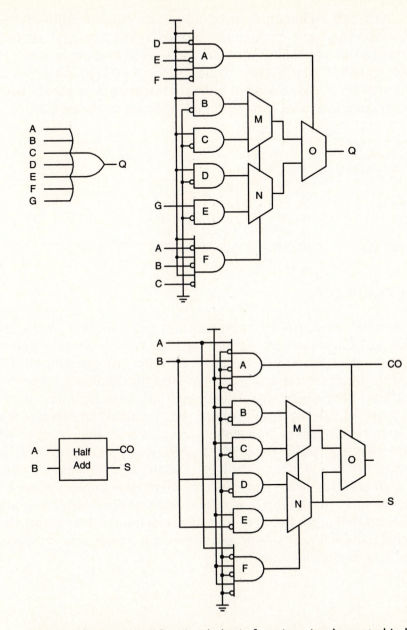

Figure 8-21(continued) Sample logic functions implemented in logic cells

Because the pASIC380 architecture does not have a sum-of-products logic array, expressions (either implicitly or explicitly defined in VHDL) are not flattened into a two-level sum of products. Rather, they are factored to find expressions that can be easily implemented in multiplexers. Thus, Listing 8-10 is synthesized and optimized nicely in this FPGA. The resource utilization summary is shown below, and the physical view from the place and route tool is shown in Figure 8-22.

```
+++++++++++++++++++++++++++++
| Utilization Information |
+++++++++++++++++++++++++++++
Utilized cells:          4 of      96  (  4.2%)
Partially free cells:    1
Input only cells:        0 of       6  (  0.0%)
Clock only cells:        0 of       2  (  0.0%)
Bi directional cells:   13 of      32  ( 40.6%)
```

8.5.2   Design Trade-Offs

Although one of the tasks of synthesis and place and route tools is to use logic resources efficiently, packing as much logic into the logic cells as possible may not produce the results the designer wants. We pose the following question to make this point: Which of the implementations of a D-type flip-flop shown in Figure 8-23 on page 476 is optimal? (Obviously, we're assuming that there isn't any requirement for logic in front of the flip-flop.) Again, the "optimal" implementation depends on the design requirements. Implementation (a) allows the six input AND gates to be used for other logic in the design (if the AND gates aren't required, then the inputs can be tied off to any value). Implementation (a) is the optimal choice unless you have a high performance requirement, in which case implementation (b) is optimal because the input to the flip-flop will be ready sooner. Implementation (a) requires that the flip-flop input fan-in to four logic cell inputs. This greater load means that the signal rises and falls slower and is available at the input to the flip-flop later than it is with implementation (b).

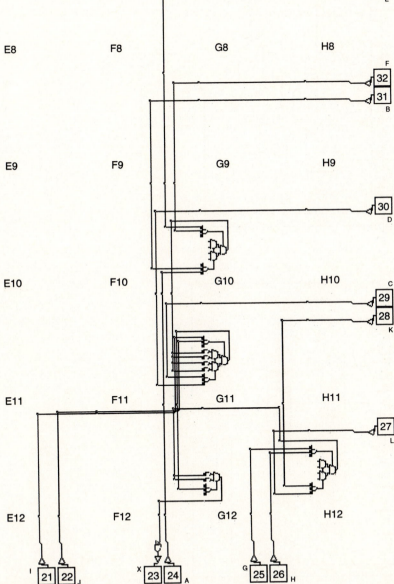

Figure 8-22 Physical view of the implementation of the design described in
Listing 8-10

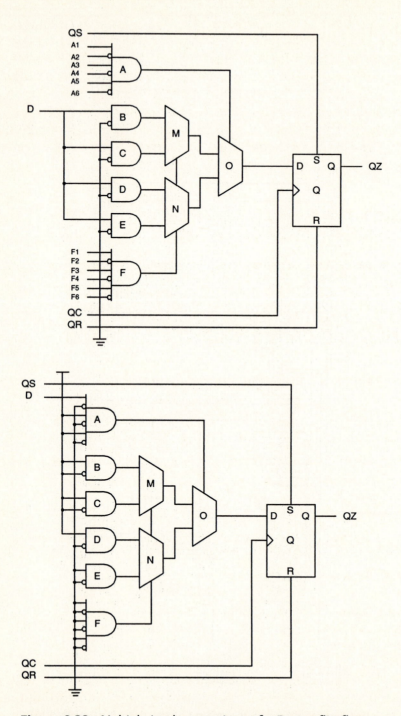

Figure 8-23   Multiple implementations of a D-type flip-flop

Propagation delays from logic cell to logic cell, I/O to logic cell, or logic cell to I/O depend not only on the fan-out (of the source) and the number of logic cell levels (that is, the number of logic cells through which a signal must pass), but also on the available routing resources and how far signals must route. This points to another difference between CPLDs and FPGAs: that predicting propagation delays before implementing a design in CPLDs is usually easier because delays are less dependent upon fan-out, logic placement, and routing resources. Figure 8-24 illustrates the worst-case path for signal x in Figure 8-22 when it is broken into its constituent I/O cell, routing, and logic cell propagation delays.

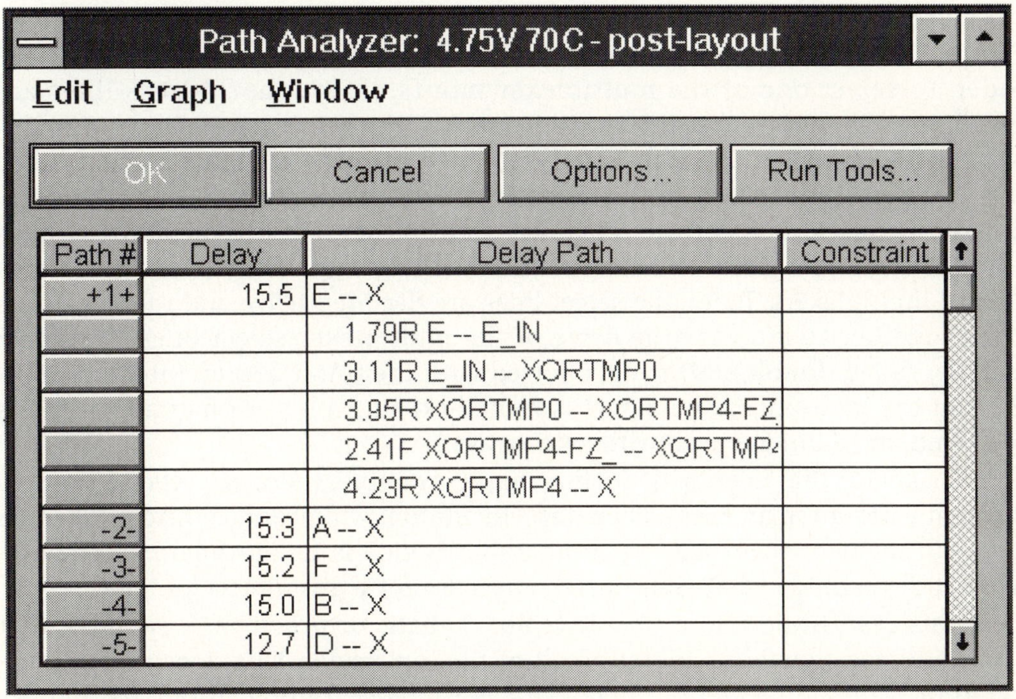

Path Analyzer: 4.75V 70C - post-layout

Edit Graph Window

| OK | | Cancel | | Options... | | Run Tools... |

Path #	Delay	Delay Path	Constraint
+1+	15.5	E -- X	
		1.79R E -- E_IN	
		3.11R E_IN -- XORTMP0	
		3.95R XORTMP0 -- XORTMP4-FZ_	
		2.41F XORTMP4-FZ_ -- XORTMP4	
		4.23R XORTMP4 -- X	
-2-	15.3	A -- X	
-3-	15.2	F -- X	
-4-	15.0	B -- X	
-5-	12.7	D -- X	

Figure 8-24 Constituent delays of critical path

As a starting point, synthesis tools will often use just one algorithm to reduce logic so that it can be implemented in the fewest possible logic cells. This implementation usually produces the highest-performance solution—except where fan-outs are excessively high or signals must travel a long distance—because there is a correlation between the total number of logic cells and the number of logic cell levels required to implement a function. (A signal that must pass through many logic cell levels typically has a greater propagation delay than one that passes through few levels.)

Adding levels of logic can help to split the fan-out through several buffers, but the additional propagation delay through a buffer must be made up by quicker rise times. Faster rise times may be possible due to a smaller load per buffer. For example, consider 32 two-to-one multiplexers that have the same select line:

```
signal address: std_logic_vector(3 downto 0);
signal a, b, x: std_logic_vector(31 downto 0);
...
with address select
x <= a when "10110",
     b when others;
```

Figure 8-25 shows five possible implementations for these 32 multiplexers. In Figure 8-25 (a), the address lines are used in each logic cell where they are decoded to select one of the multiplexer inputs. In (b), the address lines are decoded once, then the resulting signal is used as the select line for the 32 multiplexers. In (c), the select line is decoded once, and then the resulting signal is used as the select line for a couple of the multiplexers and as an input to several buffers that drive the select lines of the remaining multiplexers. In (d), the address lines are decoded multiple times and each of the resulting signals drive the select lines of several multiplexers. In (e), the select lines are decoded twice and these outputs are tied together to increase the drive of the multiplexer select lines. (This is a technique, called **double-buffering,** allowed with the pASIC380 architecture, provided that the multiply driven signal is routed on an express or a quad wire; it is also a common technique used with gate arrays.)

You can see that even with such a simple example, there are several ways to implement a design in an FPGA. Each implementation will produce different timing results, but many of them may be comparable. Which is the optimal implementation? That depends on what your design goals are for a given piece of logic.

In this case, option (a) probably is not realistic or practical. It requires that the four address signals be routed to all of the logic cells. This doesn't gain anything. In fact, this implementation consumes valuable routing resources that are better used by a critical signal. Option (b) is viable, but the select line will have a slow rise time and a fair amount of skew between the time it triggers the select input of the first and last multiplexers. If your design can operate under these conditions, then after considering the alternatives, you may choose to proceed with this implementation.

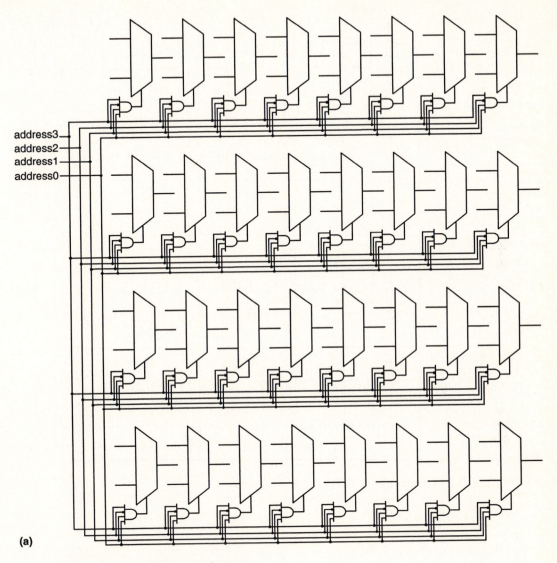

address3
address2
address1
address0

(a)

Figure 8-25 Buffering techniques

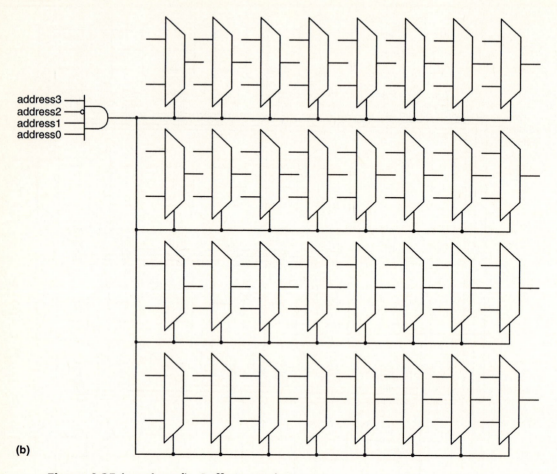

Figure 8-25 (continued)   Buffering techniques

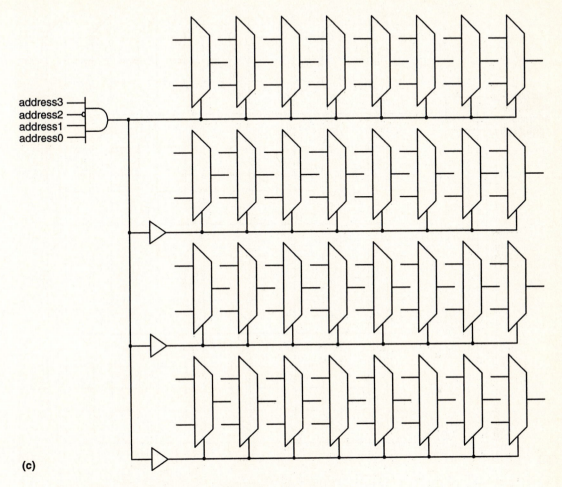

Figure 8-25 (continued)   Buffering techniques

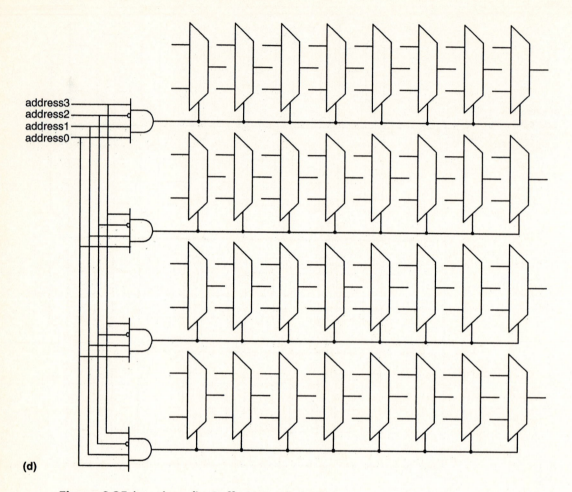

Figure 8-25 (continued)   Buffering techniques

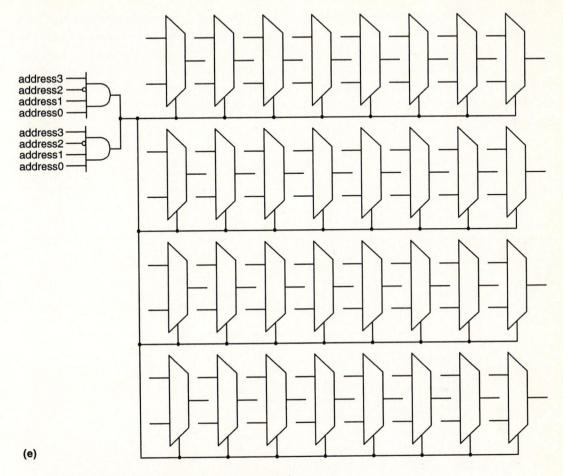

Figure 8-25 (continued)   Buffering techniques

Buffering the select line, as in options (c), (d), and (e), reduces the time it takes for all select lines to switch on transitions of address. Option (d) differs from (c) in that the select logic is replicated multiple times. Transitions in the select lines relative to transitions in address are closer together in option (d), whereas these transitions will be spread out in time for option (c). Option (d) is probably preferred over option (c), unless option (d) causes the lines to transition slower due to additional loading on address. Depending on whether or not the address signals must route elsewhere, using them as inputs to multiple buffers may increase the load on these lines such that the total propagation delay from the sources of the address lines to the multiplexer selection inputs is greater than the total propagation delay when the signals are buffered, as in option (c). In option (d), the three buffers can be implemented with one logic cell (Figure 8-26). Option (e) may provide the best results, but it requires that a specific device resource be available.

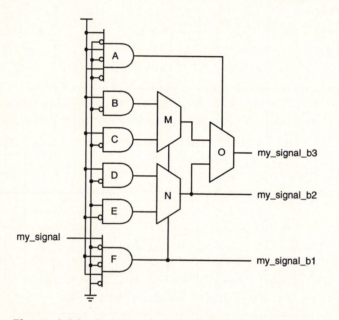

Figure 8-26   Creating three buffers with one logic cell

With all of these options, which implementation does synthesis choose? Writing algorithms to try all the combinations for every unique netlist would be impossible. Fortunately, in architectures such as the pASIC380, many of the implementations are comparable, enabling synthesis software developers to reduce the number of algorithms for optimizing designs. Choosing the "correct" implementation is also a matter of understanding the goals for a design or subdesign. Synthesis must be guided (by you) in these instances, as we'll discuss next. Because there are so many variables involved, a technique may prove more successful in one application than in another. When you push the limits of the technology, you may need to evaluate multiple implementations. Some of these implementations can be evaluated by the synthesis software and do not require user interaction. Others may require you to change the source code to include pipelines (as we'll discuss in the next chapter).

8.5.3   Directive-Driven Synthesis

Optimizing a set of equations to use the fewest logic cells may be a starting point for FPGA synthesis, but more sophisticated software will also allow you to direct the synthesis process to achieve area or speed optimization or specific control over implementation. Area and speed optimization directives may be applied globally (for the entire design), or locally (to particular portions of logic). This way, the design may have a global area optimization goal, but small portions of logic in the critical path can be optimized for speed. Directives may come in the form of attributes, command line switches, GUI options, or a synthesis tool vendor's proprietary language. In FPGA designs, synthesis directives are often used to control the buffering of high fan-out signals, floor-planning, and module generation.

We've already seen several buffering techniques. Rather than describing (and redescribing) those implementations in VHDL each time you want to find the results of using a particular buffering technique, you can use synthesis directives to quickly alter the buffering scheme, specifying the maximum load on a signal. Some of the more mature synthesis tools allow you to merely specify the target propagation delay for a critical path in a circuit, and the synthesis tool will choose a buffering technique in an attempt to meet the timing goal. We discussed fan-out buffering above. Below, we introduce the idea of floor planning and elaborate on the topic of module generation, which was introduced in the last chapter. After these brief discussions we move on to two examples that put a couple synthesis directives to use. Synthesis tools usually support many more directives than we will discuss, and their implementations may differ. But the directives that we discuss will likely provide the greatest impact without convoluting the synthesis or place and route processes.

Automatic Floor-Planning. The "fitter" for an FPGA is a place and route tool. Whereas fitters for CPLDs often perform the design optimization and partitioning, place and route tools typically do little, if any, logic optimization. A synthesis tool will convert a VHDL description into logic equations, optimize those equations for implementation in logic cells, and create a device-specific netlist (one that can be directly mapped to the device architecture). The place and route tool then places the logic cells and routes them along with the I/O to complete the design implementation. The place and route tool may perform some additional logic optimization. For example, it may also insert buffers in the critical paths of signals that have a high fan-out.

Place and route tools can have a large impact on performance, because propagation delays can depend significantly on how closely logic cells are placed to each other and which routing resources are used to connect the logic cells. Signals that must route long distances will usually have larger propagation delays, because to route a signal a long distance requires a longer wire. This wire will have a larger total capacitance, not only because of its length but also its incremental fuse capacitance (if multiple wires are connected to create a longer wire). Therefore, place and route tools may include algorithms to attempt to place critical portions of a circuit close together.

Many place and route tools use a process called **simulated annealing** to determine how to place logic within the available cells. In simulated annealing, the placer first places logic semirandomly within the array of logic cell locations (for example, in the CY7C381A, there are 96 logic cell locations in which the logic cells can be placed). The placement is semirandom because those logic cells used to capture inputs or propagate outputs are usually given preference for locations around the periphery of the logic cell matrix. This reduces setup and clock-to-output delays. After the initial semirandom placement, the router determines the cost of routing with this placement. The cost is typically estimated by determining how far signals must travel, which is a good determinant of speed. Next, the placer shuffles logic cells around, trying to reduce the overall cost. If an exchange or movement of logic cell placements increases the cost, then the cells are moved back to their previous locations. As long as the placer continues to make good progress in reducing the cost, the process goes on. When the placer determines that the cost savings return is diminishing, that it is asymptotically approaching an optimal placement, it settles on a solution. A user setting usually specifies the amount of "effort" the placer must make. Once a final placement is selected, routing begins. Routers typically attempt to use the type of routing resource and path that adds the least capacitance to a signal path.

Simulated annealing can be quite successful with designs of 10K gates or fewer. However, with very large devices, the large number of logic cell locations and the exponential number of combinations of possible logic cell placements may cause the simulated annealing approach to require considerable time to settle on an appropriate solution. Pure simulated annealing algorithms also tend to optimize the "average" paths, as opposed to the critical ones. Better approaches exist in parallel with simulated annealing: (1) timing-constraint-driven place and route, and (2) floor planning.

Timing-constraint-driven place and route combines simulated annealing with user direction to indicate which paths in a design are critical. Figure 8-27 plots signal paths (numbered 1 through 100) versus the delay (in nanoseconds) for each path. The paths are listed in order of descending delays, with the first path having the worst delay. The first few paths have delays of greater than 20 nanoseconds, whereas most of the other paths have delays well under 20 ns. Suppose that you had a design requirement stipulating that all of the paths listed must have delays under 20 ns. If the requirement did not further stipulate that some of these paths

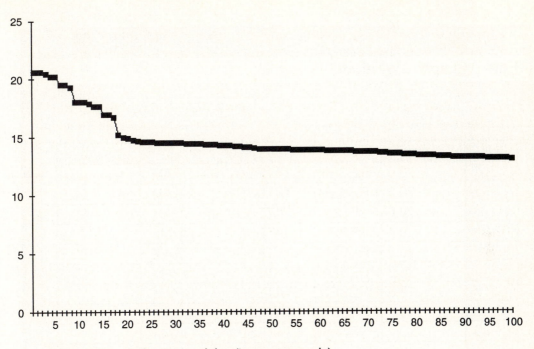

Figure 8-27 Paths versus delay (in nanoseconds)

must meet even smaller delays, you would be willing to give up some of the margin on those delays that easily meet the 20 ns target in order to get the first few signals under 20 ns. This is essentially what timing-driven placing and routing does; it allows you to insert timing constraints for paths, as shown on the right-hand side of Figure 8-28. On the left of this figure is the current actual delay, and on the right is what you may enter as a constraint to indicate the desired goal. After running the timing-driven place and route tools, we find that the delays are all under 20 ns (Figure 8-29). The tool was able to give up the margin in some of the noncritical paths to meet the specification of 20 ns for the first few paths. More precisely, the timing constraints indicated to the tool to give precedence to placement of the constrained logic over the nonconstrained logic. This means that the sources and destinations of these signals may be able to be placed slightly closer together to reduce routing delays. This, however, may be at the expense of other signal delays.

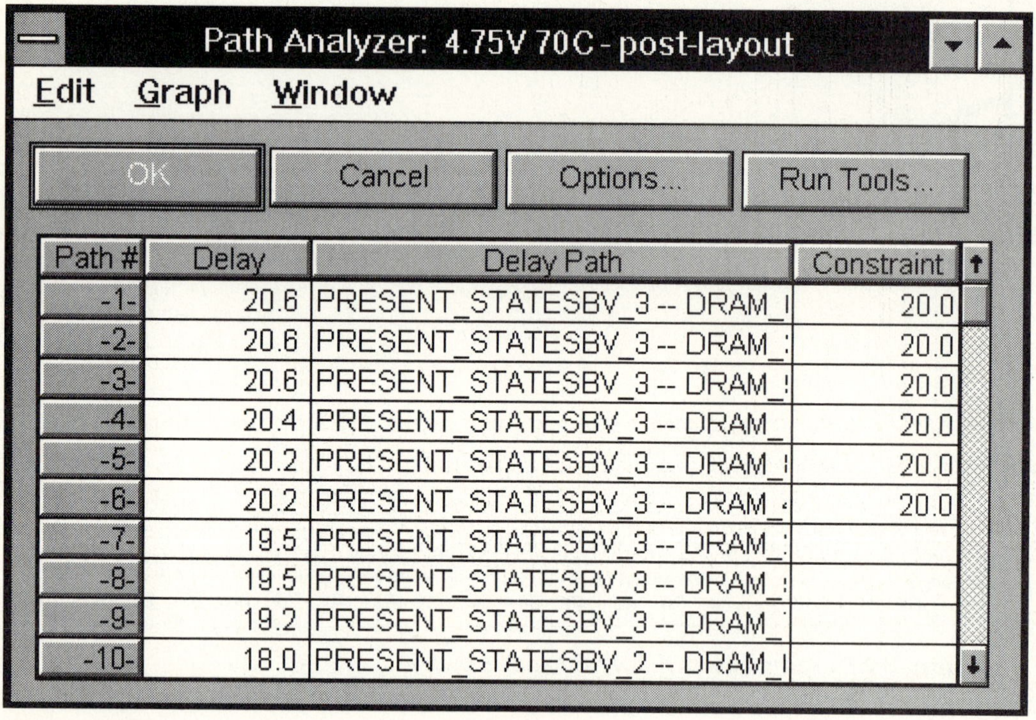

Path Analyzer: 4.75V 70C - post-layout	▼	▲

Edit   Graph   Window

OK	Cancel	Options...	Run Tools...

Path #	Delay	Delay Path	Constraint	↑
-1-	20.6	PRESENT_STATESBV_3 -- DRAM_I	20.0	
-2-	20.6	PRESENT_STATESBV_3 -- DRAM_	20.0	
-3-	20.6	PRESENT_STATESBV_3 -- DRAM_	20.0	
-4-	20.4	PRESENT_STATESBV_3 -- DRAM_	20.0	
-5-	20.2	PRESENT_STATESBV_3 -- DRAM_	20.0	
-6-	20.2	PRESENT_STATESBV_3 -- DRAM_	20.0	
-7-	19.5	PRESENT_STATESBV_3 -- DRAM_		
-8-	19.5	PRESENT_STATESBV_3 -- DRAM_		
-9-	19.2	PRESENT_STATESBV_3 -- DRAM_		
-10-	18.0	PRESENT_STATESBV_2 -- DRAM_I		↓

Figure 8-28 Constraining out-of-spec delays

Floor planning is based on the assumption that large designs are typically broken up into functional units (for instance, a state machine, counter, comparator, controller, FIFO, and so forth). An optimal placement is one that keeps the logic that makes up these functional units close together (rather than shuffling this logic randomly and placing it with the logic of other components). With floor planning, functional units may be locally optimized within a specified bounding box. The relative placement of the logic cells within these functional units may then be "frozen" and the functional units moved, as a whole, to the portion of the FPGA that makes the most sense. Obviously, if the functional block interfaces with the chip I/O, it should be placed near the periphery of the logic cell matrix. If it controls internal logic, then it will likely be best placed internal to the matrix. After the global optimization process places the functional units, routing may be performed.

With automatic floor planning, units are identified as such either because they are library components, as in a schematic or an inferred module, or because a user directive has been attached, indicating that certain signals are logically related and should therefore be placed in proximity to one another. Automatic

Path Analyzer: 4.75V 70C – post-layout

Edit   Graph   Window

OK   Cancel   Options...   Run Tools...

Path #	Delay	Delay Path	Constraint
-1-	19.5	PRESENT_STATESBV_3 -- DRAM_	
-2-	19.5	PRESENT_STATESBV_3 -- DRAM_I	20.0
-3-	19.4	PRESENT_STATESBV_3 -- DRAM_	20.0
-4-	19.1	PRESENT_STATESBV_3 -- DRAM_	20.0
-5-	19.1	PRESENT_STATESBV_3 -- DRAM_	
-6-	18.9	PRESENT_STATESBV_3 -- DRAM_	
-7-	18.8	PRESENT_STATESBV_3 -- DRAM_	20.0
-8-	16.8	PRESENT_STATESBV_3 -- DRAM_	20.0
-9-	16.7	PRESENT_STATESBV_2 -- DRAM_	
-10-	16.7	PRESENT_STATESBV_2 -- DRAM_I	

Figure 8-29   Results of constraint-driven place and route

floor planning can greatly reduce the randomness of results of placing and routing. It can enable a tool to come to an optimal solution quickly while focusing on critical portions of a circuit. Automatic floor planning requires tight coupling between the synthesis and place and route processes.

Ideally, designers would like to be able to specify the required operating frequency, setup times, clock-to-output delays, and propagation delays of a design, leaving the software tool to synthesize, place, and route the design so that it meets the specifications. This describes the combined processes of timing-driven synthesis and timing-driven place and route. Timing-driven place and route and floor planning are only intermediate steps to the ideal design flow. But timing-driven place and route and floor planning allow the designer to provide clues to the software based on information the designer has that software algorithms may not be able to infer. As true timing-driven synthesis and place and route technology evolves, there will be less need for user intervention. Today's place and route technology is usually fully automatic, though at times (especially for routing-constrained architectures), manual intervention is required.

Directive-Driven Module Generation. We introduced the concepts of operator inferencing and module generation in the previous chapter. Here, we wish only to expand the notion of module generation to include directive-driven, speed- or area-optimized module generation. This concept is that a synthesis directive can be used to specify whether an area-efficient or speed-efficient implementation of an inferred module should be implemented. For example, a directive that specifies that the module generation goal is "area" will cause implementations that are area efficient but perhaps not speed efficient. In the next chapter we will take a look at trading off speed versus area in a few arithmetic components. For now, we simply note that directives are available to allow us access to these different implementations, and that the synthesis directives apply to both CPLDs and FPGAs.

8.5.4   Design Tuning: The DRAM Controller

In this section we apply a few synthesis directives to see how they affect the implementation of the DRAM controller of Listing 8-12. We focus on using directives in our case study of FPGAs because timing results for a design implemented in an FPGA tend to vary from one placement and routing to the next. This variation is in part due to the smaller grained logic cell (in comparison to the CPLD macrocells and associated product terms) and routing.

First we synthesize the design using only the default options in Warp, targeting a CY7C382A device. The default options will insert buffers only if a signal's fan-out is 13 or greater. The default is also to place high fan-out input signals on the special-purpose (clock or high-drive) input pads. In this case, no signals were buffered, the clock was placed on a clock pad, and the address strobe, ads, was placed on a high-drive pad because of its high internal fan-out. The setup time, register-to-register delay, and clock-to-output delay are shown in the table below, along with the number of required logic cells.

Table 8-2 First pass: Default options

Area (logic cells)	69
t_S (ns)	10.0
t_{SCS} (ns)	15.3
t_{CO} (ns)	21.9
limiting parameter	t_{CO}

This data indicates that the limiting factor in system operating frequency is the clock-to-output delay. If the devices that are sampling the outputs of this DRAM controller were to have setup times similar to the required setup times for the inputs of this device (the asynchronous DRAMs don't have setup times with respect to the clock—we pursue this line of reasoning only to illustrate a point), then the system operating frequency would be the reciprocal of the sum of the clock-to-output, the sampling devices setup time, and about 1 ns for trace delay (propagation of the signals on the PCB). In this case, that is about 1/32.9 ns, or 30 MHz, which is 30 MHz less than the frequency that the internal register-to-register delays would permit.

Next, we use a few directives to improve the setup time and clock-to-output time, hoping to balance the allowable internal and external frequencies. The first directive that we use causes the state machine to be encoded as a one-hot state machine. This machine is only 10 states, so it may not help, but it shouldn't hurt. This directive may improve register-to-register delays (or the logic cell count, if the next-state decoding is complex). We also use a directive that will place the ads signal on two high-drive input pins and tie the internal inputs together. Although this will require two device pin resources, it will increase the drive of this signal for its 33 loads. Finally, we use a directive to decrease the maximum load that any of the synthesis-generated state-bit signals can have before the software tool inserts buffers, as in option (c) of Figure 8-22. We change the maximum load limit from 13 to 4 in hope of reducing the delay caused by decoding the state bits to produce the outputs. The results of this "tuning" cycle are shown below, along with the first-pass results.

Table 8-3 Second pass: One-hot encoding, buffering, high drive pads

	Second pass	First pass
Area (logic cells)	68	69
t_S (ns)	5.5	10.0
t_{SCS} (ns)	15.2	15.3
t_{CO} (ns)	25.9	21.9
limiting parameter	t_{CO}	t_{CO}

The results of the second pass indicate that the setup time was decreased by about 5 ns, the register-to-register delays remained nearly the same, and the clock to output worsened by about 4 ns. Seeing these results leads us to believe that we chose too low a number for the maximum load for buffering. We decide to try a third time, with the same directives, except for reducing the maximum loading for the state bits. This way, fewer variables are changing—perhaps this should have been our second pass, as it is a good idea to limit the number of directives being introduced on any given pass. The results of this pass are shown below, along with the first two.

Table 8-4   Third pass: One-hot encoding, high drive pads

	Third pass	Second pass	First pass
Area (logic cells)	67	68	69
t_S (ns)	5.3	5.5	10.0
t_{SCS} (ns)	15.2	15.5	15.3
t_{CO} (ns)	22.6	25.9	21.9
limiting parameter	t_{CO}	t_{CO}	t_{CO}

The results of this third pass show essentially the same setup time as the second pass, about the same register-to-register delays, and a clock-to-output delay similar to that of the first pass. This permits a system operating frequency of just under 35 MHz, an improvement of about 5 MHz over the initial implementation. Experience tells us that additional combinations of directives (or place and route timing constraints) will not likely yield an improvement in the clock-to-output delay of more than another 5 percent. The design easily fits into the 1K device, with about 30 percent of the resource still available.

In the next chapter we will revisit this design and use pipelining to reduce the clock-to-output delay and increase system operating frequency.

8.5.5   Implementing the Network Repeater in an 8K FPGA

In this section, we examine the implementation of the 8-port network repeater that we designed in Chapter 6. We begin by analyzing the design to determine the amount of resources we think it will require. We then synthesize, place, and route the design, and examine the report file and path analyzer to compare our expectations with the realization of the design.

Resource estimations are somewhat more difficult to make for FPGAs than for CPLDs because the logic cells contain less logic on average than a macrocell and its associated product terms. FPGAs are said to have a "finer grained" architecture. An estimation of the logic cell count follows:

clockmux8 (37)

- 27 for registers and the enable equations
- nine for the clock selection
- one for rxclk

arbiter8 (13)

- 11 for registers
- one for the collision signal
- one for the carryin signal

FIFO (110)

- 48 for eight 6-bit registers for the FIFO
- six for the counters (read and write pointers)
- 48 for six eight-to-one FIFO output multiplexers
- eight for the decoding of the write pointer

symbolmux (24)

- three for the symbol counter
- six for the output registers
- 12 for the output multiplexers (two for each line)
- three for symbolend signals

core controller (47)

- four for synchronization of inputs
- three for synchronization of internal signals
- 10 for the counter
- 25 for the three state machines
- five for the outputs

port controller ($8 \times 40 = 320$)

- six for synchronization of inputs
- two to synchronize internal signals

- 19 for the three counters
- eight for the one-hot state machine
- five for output signals

As with nearly any speed-critical FPGA design, load limiting will be an important issue in this design. Several signals will fan out to several logic cells. Some of these signals may be generated by synthesis (the state-bit signals, for example). In this implementation we use the default buffer generation and load limit. Following is an excerpt from the report file, listing the buffers that are created during synthesis:

```
-----------------------------------------------------------
Begin Buffer Generation.
-----------------------------------------------------------
[max_load = 13, fanout = 51] Created 3 buffers [Duplicate] for 'rxclk'
[max_load = 13, fanout = 18] Created 1 buffers [Duplicate] for 'WFAC17'
[max_load = 13, fanout = 18] Created 1 buffers [Duplicate] for 'WFAC18'
[max_load = 13, fanout = 18] Created 1 buffers [Duplicate] for 'WFAC19'
[max_load = 13, fanout = 18] Created 1 buffers [Duplicate] for 'WFAC20'
[max_load = 13, fanout = 18] Created 1 buffers [Duplicate] for 'WFAC21'
[max_load = 13, fanout = 18] Created 1 buffers [Duplicate] for 'WFAC22'
[max_load = 13, fanout = 18] Created 1 buffers [Duplicate] for 'WFAC23'
[max_load = 13, fanout = 18] Created 1 buffers [Duplicate] for 'WFAC24'
[max_load = 13, fanout = 25] Created 2 buffers [Normal    ] for 'carrier'
[max_load = 13, fanout = 15] Created 2 buffers [Normal    ] for 'u4_symbolcount_0'
[max_load = 13, fanout = 19] Created 2 buffers [Normal    ] for 'u5_state3SBV_0'
[max_load = 13, fanout = 15] Created 2 buffers [Normal    ] for 'u5_state3SBV_1'
[max_load = 13, fanout = 16] Created 2 buffers [Normal    ] for 'u5_state3SBV_2'
[max_load = 13, fanout = 48] Created 4 buffers [Normal    ] for 'u6_collisiond'
[max_load = 13, fanout = 20] Created 2 buffers [Normal    ] for 'collision_OUT'
```

While buffering may solve the performance problem for many signals, other optimization techniques may be required. In this design we anticipated the need to pipeline to maintain 40 MHz operation. Illustrative examples of pipelining are given in Chapter 9, "Optimizing Data Paths." In this design, the outputs of the arbiter have been pipelined because the collision and carrier signals are used in several design units and would propagate through several levels of logic cells if the pipeline were absent. In a design such as that of the repeater, pipeline registers may be added for some signals (jabber_bar and partition_bar, for example) without having to add pipeline registers for the others. This is because a clock cycle of latency between these signals and others does not pose a problem. For example, jabber_bar can be asserted for a range of counter values, so adding a pipeline register will not affect the function of the design.

The common outputs (txdata, idle, jam) for the core controller state machines are all generated from the third state machine. This unnecessarily places a higher load on the state registers for the third state machine. Since the common outputs can be decoded from any of the state machines and all state machines must run at 40 MHz, it may make sense to balance the loading of all state machine registers. Of course, the state machines should be one-hot, designed for maximum performance. But if logic is added to the one-hot state machine to check for transitions to illegal states, then a comparison of the performance of this state machine versus a sequentially encoded state machine may prove that one is not better than the other.

Special-purpose pads can aid in the performance of a design. The pASIC380 has two clock pads and six high-drive pads. Signals assigned to a clock pad make use of a high-performance, low-skew clock distribution tree. Clocks on one of these trees can be propagated to all logic cells in about 5 ns with a skew of less than 1 ns. A systemwide clock that does not use a clock distribution tree has a considerably larger distribution time. With this design, the system clock is the transmit clock. The clock distribution tree may also be used for the sets and resets of flip-flops. The reset in this design has a fanout of 343, so the clock distribution tree is the best choice.

High-drive inputs provide about twice the internal input driving current of normal I/Os configured as inputs. High fan-out signals coming from off-chip should make use of these special-purpose pads. Following is the list of automatic pad selection.

```
------------------------------------------------------------
Begin PAD Generation
------------------------------------------------------------
Created CLKPAD for signal 'reset'
    Above signal drives   0 Clocks, 343 Set/Resets. Total = 343
Created CLKPAD for signal 'clk'
    Above signal drives 294 Clocks,   0 Set/Resets. Total = 294
    And    1 other inputs (active high).
    Above signal consumed 1 express wire
Created HD1PAD  for signal 'rxd5'
    Above signal drives  0 Clocks,  0 Set/Resets,  8 other inputs. Total =  8
Created HD1PAD  for signal 'rxd4'
    Above signal drives  0 Clocks,  0 Set/Resets,  8 other inputs. Total =  8
Created HD1PAD  for signal 'rxd3'
    Above signal drives  0 Clocks,  0 Set/Resets,  8 other inputs. Total =  8
Created HD1PAD  for signal 'rxd2'
    Above signal drives  0 Clocks,  0 Set/Resets,  8 other inputs. Total =  8
Created HD1PAD  for signal 'rxd1'
    Above signal drives  0 Clocks,  0 Set/Resets,  8 other inputs. Total =  8
Created HD1PAD  for signal 'rxd0'
    Above signal drives  0 Clocks,  0 Set/Resets,  8 other inputs. Total =  8
```

Gated clocks are used with the FIFO. To ensure a small clock delay and skew, floor planning may be required for the FIFO. Simulated annealing may not find the optimal placement for the FIFO registers. The optimal placement for the flip-flops that make up the FIFO is to have one flip-flop on top of the other in the array of logic cell locations. This is the optimal placement because the outputs of the pASIC logic cell feed back to the left side of the logic cell, where the vertical routing channel is. Placing each of the registers (six flip-flops) in a vertical column ensures that the gated clocks need to route to only one column per register.

Above we estimated that this implementation requires 551 logic cells, not including those needed for buffering. After place and route, the total logic cell count is listed as 604, which is within reach of our estimation. The discrepancy is probably in the number of logic cells that we estimated for the state machines. It is left as an exercise for the reader to implement the individual units to determine more precisely the resource requirements of each. Performance is difficult to estimate. The post-place-and-route worst-case delays for register-to-register operation are shown in Figure 8-30. The worst-case delay of 36.5ns will support 25 MHz operation.

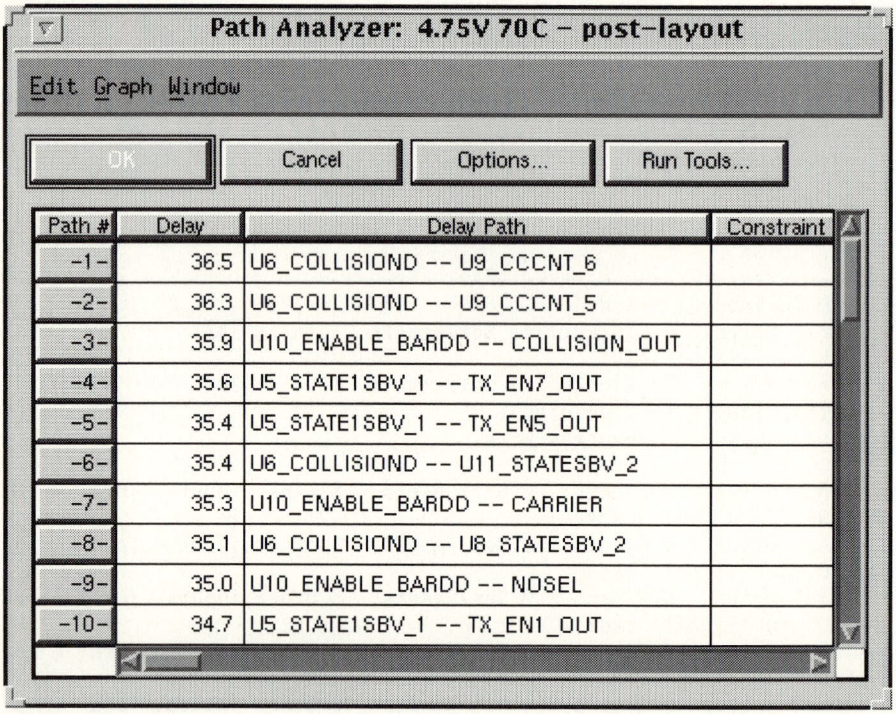

Path Analyzer: 4.75V 70C – post–layout

Edit Graph Window

| OK | Cancel | Options... | Run Tools... |

Path #	Delay	Delay Path	Constraint
-1-	36.5	U6_COLLISIOND -- U9_CCCNT_6	
-2-	36.3	U6_COLLISIOND -- U9_CCCNT_5	
-3-	35.9	U10_ENABLE_BARDD -- COLLISION_OUT	
-4-	35.6	U5_STATE1SBV_1 -- TX_EN7_OUT	
-5-	35.4	U5_STATE1SBV_1 -- TX_EN5_OUT	
-6-	35.4	U6_COLLISIOND -- U11_STATESBV_2	
-7-	35.3	U10_ENABLE_BARDD -- CARRIER	
-8-	35.1	U6_COLLISIOND -- U8_STATESBV_2	
-9-	35.0	U10_ENABLE_BARDD -- NOSEL	
-10-	34.7	U5_STATE1SBV_1 -- TX_EN1_OUT	

Figure 8-30 Worst-case register-to-register delays

8.5.6   Preassigning Pinouts

Preassigning pinouts in FPGAs is usually possible because fewer restrictions are placed on where device resources may be accessed. Some FPGAs are better than others in this respect. Those with many routing resources and smaller timing variations from implementation to implementation do a better job of supporting an assigned pinout. Routability in some FPGAs may be limited as the amount of logic placed in the device increases. Always check vendor claims before pursuing a board design in an FPGA.

8.6   To Use a CPLD or an FPGA?

This chapter has illustrated that CPLDs and FPGAs both have their strengths and weaknesses. CPLDs usually provide the highest performance, but they also contain fewer registers than FPGAs. CPLDs can implement large functions in one pass through the logic array. Most have deterministic timing, which can simplify timing analysis. A CPLD's resources are partitioned into logic blocks, imposing restrictions on how they may be used. FPGAs have a finer grained architecture. They perform well in pipelined designs, but can also implement longer datapaths by cascading multiple logic cells. FPGAs contain arrays of logic cells, and are less partitioned than CPLDs. This makes device features more accessible, but this accessibility may be at the expense of more difficult optimization and timing analysis. Before selecting a device, you should understand a design's functionality and the resources that will be required of the design. You should also understand your performance objectives, cost objectives, and packaging requirements. If time to market is a critical requirement, you will want the architecture you choose to support design changes in the same pinout (just in case hardware bugs are discovered late in the design cycle). With all of your requirements written down, you can then compare your needs with what a given device has to offer, using any available benchmark data to help. Before final selection you should make sure the software tools are available and user-friendly, and fit into your system design environment.

▼

Breakout Exercise 8-2

Purpose: To become familiar with synthesis directives and the tuning cycle.

Read Chapter 9 of the on-line user's guide. The chapter takes you through the tuning cycle for two designs implemented in both FPGAs and CPLDs.

▲

Problems

8.1. Determine whether the following designs can fit in a 22V10:

   a. an 8-bit counter with synchronous load

   b. an 11-bit counter

   c. a 4-bit counter that asynchronously resets to 1010

8.2. In Figure 8-1, if the second macrocell from the top is allocated eight product terms, how many unique product terms may be allocated to the macrocells directly above and below it?

   a. What if 10 product terms were allocated to the second macrocell?

   b. 12 product terms?

   c. 16 product terms?

8.3. The output-enable product terms in a CY7C371 do not have polarity control. How would (a AND b) and (a OR b) differ as enabling conditions when fitted? Compare resource usage and timing.

8.4. Convert the following expression to a canonical sum of products:

   x <= (a **or** b) **xor** (c **and** d)

8.5. Why does synthesis_off help with the following equation?

   x <= (a **or** b) **xor** (c **and** d) **xor** e **xor** f **xor** g **xor** h;

8.6. What are the concerns a designer must keep in mind when selecting a device?

8.7. What are the typical constraints a designer must keep in mind when targeting CPLDs?

8.8. What are the typical constraints a designer must keep in mind when targeting FPGAs?

8.9. Discuss the trade-offs you would consider in using a synchronous or an asynchronous reset. Be sure to include resource requirements, timing, and simulation issues.

8.10. Would a CPLD fitter handle a design better if:

a. signals are assigned to specific pins, and equations are specified for implementation in a specific I/O or buried macrocell, or

b. signals are assigned to specific pins only, or

c. equations are specified for implementation in a specific I/O or buried macrocell, or

d. no assignments are made?

Are there generalizations that can be made? When might one method work better than another?

8.11. Given that the final implementation of a design is device-specific, discuss the issues involved in the portability of VHDL designs over various FPGA and CPLD families. What can you do to maintain a high degree of portability?

8.12. Create a scheme of your own to achieve product term (asynchronous) clocking in FLASH370 CPLDs.

8.13. Present scenarios that could benefit from each of the buffering techniques described in Section 3.2.1 of the on-line user's guide.

8.14. Attempt to synthesize and fit the following design to a CY7C371 in the 44-pin PLCC package.

```
entity many_signals is port(
    a,b:  in bit_vector (23 downto 0);
    x,y:  out bit);
attribute pin_numbers of many_signals:entity is "x:3 y:4";
end many_signals
architecture hard-to-fit of many_signals is

begin

proc1: process (a,b)
        variable j,k: bit;
      begin
        j:='0'; k:='0';
        for i in a'range loop
            j:=j or a(i);
            k:=k or b(i);
        end loop;
```

```
                x<=j;
                y<=k;
            end process;
        end hard_to_fit;
```

a. Why doesn't this design fit as it's written?

b. Modify the design—without changing the pinout—so that the design will fit. (Hint: Use a buried macrocell.)

c. Compare propagation delays for x and y.

8.15. Attempt to synthesize and fit the following design to a CY7C371 in the 44-pin PLCC package.

```
entity product_terms is port(
    a0, b0, c0, d0, e0:in bit;
    a1, b1, c1, d1, e1:in bit;
    x,y: out bit);
attribute pin_numbers of product_terms:entity is "x:3 y:4";
end product_terms;
architecture p_terms of product_terms is
begin
    x<= a0 xor b0 xor c0 xor d0 xor e0;
    y<= a1 xor b1 xor c1 xor d1 xor e1;
end;
```

a. Why doesn't this design fit as it is written?

b. Modity the design—without changing the pinout—so that the design will fit.

c. Compare propagation delays for x and y.

8.16. a. Synthesize and fit the design of Listing 8-9, targeting a CY7C371.

b. Modify the design so that the token is registered (for improved register-to-register delays). Ensure that the counter counts properly.

c. Compare timing for the designs in (a) and (b).

8.17. a. How often is the DRAM refreshed by the DRAM controller (Listing 8-13)?

b. Modify the design to refresh the DRAM every 4 ns.

Chapter 9

Optimizing Data Paths

9.1   Introduction

In Chapter 2, we introduced our implementation methodology: programmable logic. In Chapters 3, 4, 5, 6, and 7, we learned to write code that synthesizes efficiently, covering a breadth of language constructs and design issues. In Chapter 8, we illustrated how designs can be implemented in CPLDs and FPGAs, discussing several fitting and optimization options. In this chapter, we discuss design techniques.

Most designs can be implemented in any of several ways; you must make implementation decisions based on design requirements. Although the order of the following list can vary greatly from design to design, it enumerates, in general, the critical requirements of almost any design. In the commercial sector, design requirements are based on business decisions and forecasts of the profitability of a product with a given set of requirements.

- The design must be finished by a certain date. This ensures that the product comes to market in a timely manner in order to establish a greater market share.

- The design must be functional, without hardware bugs, and with minimum features.

- The design must be able to operate at a specified minimum operating frequency.

- The design cannot cost more than a specified amount; it must fit in a device no larger than cost allows.

- The design must fit in a certain type of package, because of space, cost, or military requirements.

The order of the requirements can help you make implementation decisions. For example, if time to market is the most important requirement, you do not spend additional time optimizing a design that already meets the other requirements. If the operating frequency of a design is more critical than its cost, you don't spend time optimizing a design for reduced area if it already meets performance requirements.

This chapter discusses several trade-offs in performance- and area-optimized implementations of designs. Sometimes speed- and area-optimized implementations oppose each other. That is, a speed-optimized implementation may require more resources than an area-optimized implementation, and an area-optimized implementation may be slower than a speed-optimized implementation. We'll discuss several design techniques (such as pipelining, resource sharing, carry lookahead schemes, and taking advantage of early arriving signals) that you can apply to your designs.

We begin the chapter by revisiting the DRAM controller from the last chapter, where while attempting to optimize the design, we soon discovered that we were limited by the clock-to-output delay. In this chapter we show that introducing a pipeline stage enables an increase of system frequency from 37 to 60 MHz. Next, we revisit the ALU design used in the AM2901 of Chapter 6 to see how one adder can be shared by all of the arithmetic operations. We also illustrate where pipeline stages can be introduced for increased performance. Several implementations of adders are discussed next: ripple carry adders, pipelined ripple carry adders, carry lookahead adders, and carry select adders. Here, we also discuss the difference between static timing analysis and dynamic timing simulation. We illustrate two designs for magnitude comparators. We end the chapter by illustrating methods for designing fast counters, including up/down counters.

9.2   Pipelining

The idea behind pipelining is to take a large data-path operation that is currently executed over one clock cycle and break it up into smaller operations that are executed over multiple shorter clock cycles.

Figure 9-1 illustrates a large data-path operation broken into three smaller data-path operations. If the t_{PD} of the large data-path operation is x, the maximum operating frequency of this circuit is $1/x$. If we break the large data path into three

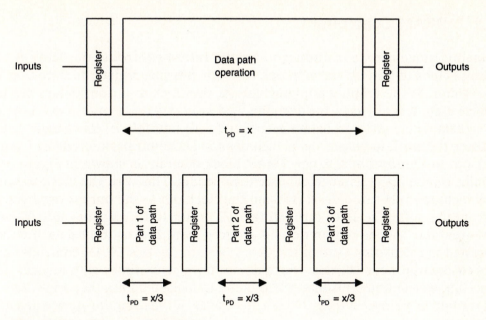

Figure 9-1 Concept of pipelining

equal parts, then (ideally) each part has a t_{PD} of $x/3$, which permits a system frequency that is three times greater than the original. Of course, this calculation does not take into account the clock-to-output and setup times of the pipeline registers, so the number $x/3$ is somewhat inflated. Neglecting these delays, we see that the pipeline gives a threefold increase in **throughput**—the amount of data processed in a given period of time. However, the increased throughput is also at the expense of three clock cycles of **latency.** That is, the outputs of the pipelined circuit are available three clock cycles later than in the original implementation. This may require that the system design be modified to account for this latency.

The advantage of pipelining is increased performance—but the increased performance is at the expense of latency and sometimes additional logic resources for registering. However, most FPGAs have flip-flops in every logic cell, which facilitates pipelining. CPLDs usually have considerably more gates per flip-flop than FPGAs, so pipelining is implemented less often in CPLDs. CPLDs also tend to be able to perform larger operations in one pass through the logic array than FPGAs can in one level of logic cells. This means that in general, CPLDs can perform larger operations in one clock cycle than FPGAs can within the same clock period, so there is less need to implement pipelines in CPLD implementations.

9.2.1   DRAM Controller

A pipeline stage can be introduced into the DRAM controller of Figure 8-16 to decrease clock-to-output times. In this case, the pipeline register is simply an output register. In the original implementation, the clock-to-output delays are large because state bits are used for decoding and selecting (via a multiplexer) the output signals. This results in delays associated with multiple levels of logic cells. In addition, the clock-to-output delay includes the signal propagation delay from the clock pin to the flip-flops. A new DRAM block diagram is shown in Figure 9-2. It contains a pipeline register to capture the outputs. This way, the clock-to-output delay includes only two delays: (1) from the clock pin to the output registers, and (2) from the output register through the I/O buffer to the output pins. Table 9-1 shows that the clock-to-output delay is reduced from 21.9 ns to 11.6 ns. If we were interested in calculating system frequency (we aren't—this DRAM controller interfaces to asynchronous DRAMs, which do not have setup times with respect to the clock—but we continue this line of reasoning to make a point), then we would find that it could be increased from 37 MHz to 60 MHz, if the sampling device had a 5 ns setup time.

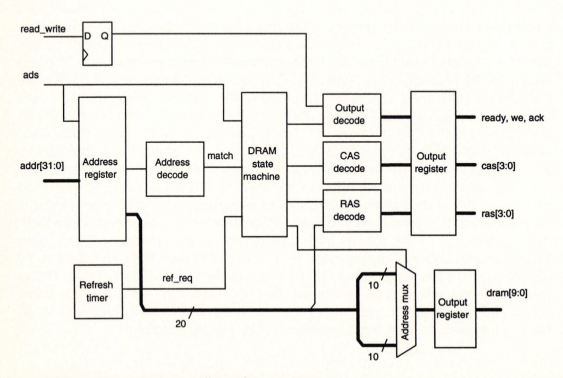

Figure 9-2   DRAM controller with output register

Table 9-1   Comparison of DRAM controllers

	Nonpipelined	Pipelined
Area (logic cells)	69	74
t_S (ns)	10.0	5.4
t_{SCS}	15.3	16.7
t_{CO} (ns)	21.9	11.6

Describing this pipeline in VHDL is relatively simple. First, we give new names to the output signals, so that we can continue to use the previous output signal names within the architecture to describe the signals feeding the output register.

```
ack_q:    out std_logic;                    -- acknowledge
we_q:     out std_logic;                    -- write enable
ready_q:  out std_logic;                    -- data ready for latching
dram_q:   out std_logic_vector (9 downto 0); -- DRAM address
ras_q:    out std_logic_vector(1 downto 0);  -- row address strobe
cas_q:    out std_logic_vector(3 downto 0)); -- column address strobe
```

Next, because we will use the names previously used for the output signals in the architecture, we need to declare these signals in the architecture declarative region:

```
signal ack, we, ready: std_logic;
signal dram: std_logic_vector(9 downto 0);
signal ras: std_logic_vector(1 downto 0);
signal cas: std_logic_vector(3 downto 0);
```

Within the body of the architecture we describe the output register. The signal names previously used for the outputs are now used for the inputs to the output register:

```
------------------------------------------------------------------
--                     Output Registers                        --
------------------------------------------------------------------
regd: process (reset, clock)
    begin
        if reset = '1' then
            ack_q <= '1'; we_q <= '1'; ready_q <= '1';
            cas_q <= "1111"; ras_q <= "11";
            dram_q <= (others => '0');
```

```
    elsif clock'event and clock = '1' then
        ack_q <= ack; we_q <= we; ready_q <= ready;
        cas_q <= cas; ras_q <= ras; dram_q <= dram;
    end if;
end process;
```

9.3 Resource Sharing

The idea behind resource sharing is to use the same data-path execution units, and schedule or select the inputs to the execution unit as appropriate. For example, consider the code:

```
r <= (a + b) when source = '1' else (c + d);
```

This circuit can be implemented as shown in Figure 9-3 or Figure 9-4. If the critical path is from a, b, c, or d to f, the implementation of Figure 9-3 is optimal. If the critical path is from the source to f—and the implementation of Figure 9-3 does not satisfy the requirements—then the implementation of Figure 9-4 is optimal. Some synthesis tools that have directives for specifying the requirements for a critical path will infer the appropriate implementation. In Release 4.0, Warp's module generator will infer two adders from the above code, producing the imple-

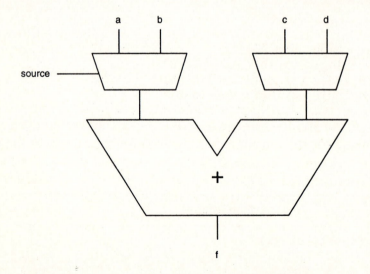

Figure 9-3 Resource sharing (one adder inferred)

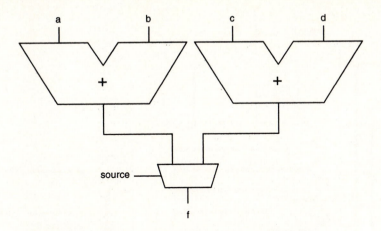

Figure 9-4 No resource sharing (two adders inferred)

mentation of Figure 9-4. To obtain the alternate implementation from Warp, the code may be rewritten as:

```
r <= a when source = '1' else c;
s <= b when source = '1' else d;
f <= r + s;
```

9.3.1 The AM2901

In Problem 6-6, we asked you to rewrite the code for the ALU because as it is written in Listing 6-14, Warp infers and generates several adder modules. Instead we would like only two adders inferred: one optimized for adding two signals, and another optimized for adding one signal and one constant, as shown in Figure 9-5. One description for this logic is given in Listing 9-1. The process operands is used to define the r1 and s1 operands, based on the value of alu_ctl. For most operations, '0' is prepended to these vectors so that the value returned by the + operation will contain an extra bit for indicating an overflow. If the ALU operation is a subtraction, one of the operands is also inverted. The adders are described using two concurrent signal assignment statements. The outputs of the arithmetic and logical operations are then multiplexed to f1.

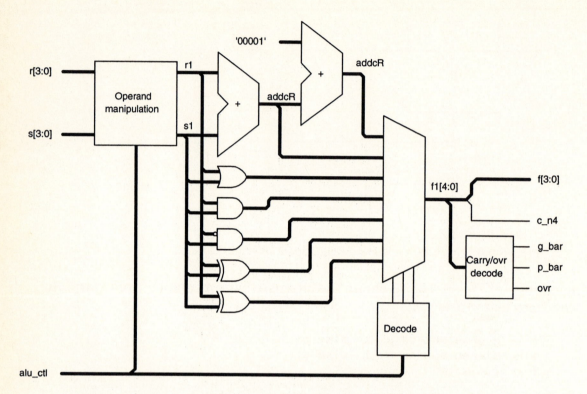

Figure 9-5 Block diagram of ALU using two adder components

```vhdl
architecture alu of alu is
    signal r1, s1: unsigned(4 downto 0);
    signal addR, addcR, f1: unsigned(4 downto 0);
begin
-- define the operands to the adder
operands: process (r, s, c_n, alu_ctl)
    begin
        case alu_ctl is
            when subr => -- subtraction same as 2's comp addn
                    r1 <= ('0', r(3), r(2), r(1), r(0));
                    s1 <= not ('0', s(3), s(2), s(1), s(0));
            when subs =>
                    r1 <= not ('0', r(3), r(2), r(1), r(0));
                    s1 <= ('0', s(3), s(2), s(1), s(0));
            when others =>
                    r1 <= ('0', r(3), r(2), r(1), r(0));
                    s1 <= ('0', s(3), s(2), s(1), s(0));
        end case;
    end process;
-- describe the arithmetic operations
    addR <= r1 + s1;
    addcR <= addR + 1;
```

```
-- multiplex the results for desired output
mux: process (r1, s1, addr, addcR, alu_ctl)
    begin
        case alu_ctl is
            when add =>
                if c_n = '0' then
                    f1 <= addR;
                else
                    f1 <= addcR;
                end if;
            when subr => -- subtraction same as 2's comp addn
                if c_n = '0' then
                    f1 <= addR;
                else
                    f1 <= addcR;
                end if;
            when subs =>
                if c_n = '0' then
                    f1 <= addcR;
                else
                    f1 <= addr;
                end if;
            when orrs => f1 <= r1 or s1;
            when andrs => f1 <= r1 and s1;
            when notrs =>f1 <= not r1 and s1;
            when exor =>f1 <= r1 xor s1;
            when exnor =>f1 <= r1 xnor s1;
            when others => f1 <= "-----";
        end case;
    end process;
f <= f1(3 downto 0);
c_n4 <= f1(4);
g_bar <= not (
        (r(3) and s(3)) or
        ((r(3) or s(3)) and (r(2) and s(2))) or
        ((r(3) or s(3)) and (r(2) or s(2)) and (r(1) and s(1))) or
        ((r(3) or s(3)) and (r(2) or s(2)) and (r(1) or s(1)) and (r(0) and s(0))));
p_bar <= not (
(r(3) or s(3)) and (r(2) or s(2)) and (r(1) and s(1)) and (r(0) and s(0)));
ovr <= '1' when (f1(4) /= f1(3)) else '0';
end alu;
```

Listing 9-1 ALU code rewritten for resource sharing

The design of the AM2901 has exceptionally long clock-to-output and register-to-register delays. The clock-to-output data path extends from the ab, bd, q, and d inputs through the source operand multiplexer, the ALU, and the output multiplexer to the output pins. The register-to-register delay extends from the ab, bd, q, and d inputs through the source operand multiplexer and ALU, then back to the register array or the Q register. These long data paths could benefit from a pipeline register at the outputs of the ALU, as shown in Figure 9-6. If a pipeline stage is inserted at the output of the ALU, then a pipeline register is also necessary for the carry and overflow signals in order to maintain data coherency. Introducing these pipeline registers alters the functionality of the design, introducing a cycle of latency, but improves the clock-to-output delay and effective operating frequency.

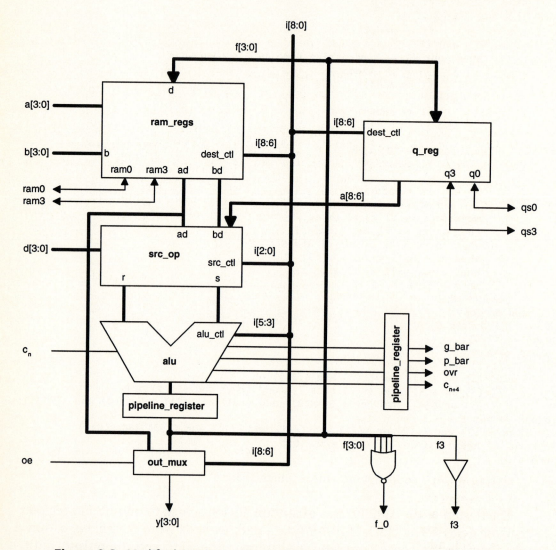

Figure 9-6 Modified AM2901 with pipeline register

9.3.2   Adders

Increasingly, programmable logic devices are being used in DSP (digital signal processing) applications that require arithmetic operations on data. In this section we discuss several versions of adders. The design concepts presented in this section can be extended to other circuits.

Ripple Carry Adders. A ripple carry adder starts with the full adder circuit shown in Figure 9-7, which is used to produce the sum and carry of two bits and a carry-in. The sum signal is the exclusive-OR of a, b, and ci, the carry-in. The exclusive-OR of an odd number of signals is true if an odd number of those signals is asserted. The signal co, carry-out, is asserted if both a and b are asserted, or if one of these signals is asserted and the carry-in is asserted. A multibit adder is built from full-adder components by connecting the carry-out of one full adder to the carry-in of the next, as in the 8-bit ripple carry adder shown in Figure 9-8. The VHDL equivalent of this 8-bit adder is given in Listing 9-2. First, the full_adder is defined in a separate entity, then the 8-bit ripple carry adder is defined. The full_adder component is declared in the architecture declarative region of the ripadd_8 component; otherwise it would not be visible to this design unit.

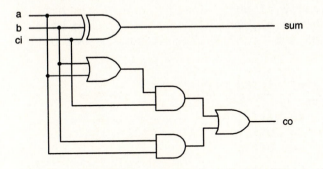

Figure 9-7 Full adder circuit

```
entity full_adder is
    port (ci:          in bit;
          a,b:         in  bit;
          sum, co:     out bit);
end full_adder;
architecture full_adder of full_adder is
begin
    sum <= a xor b xor ci;
    co <= ((a or b) and ci) or (a and b);
end;
```

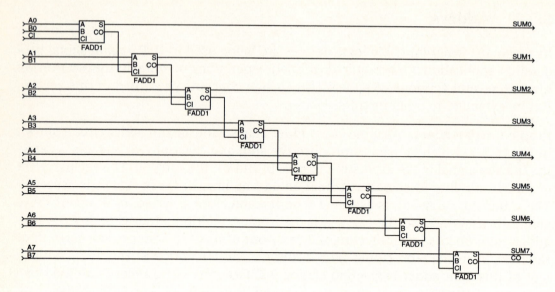

Figure 9-8   An 8-bit ripple carry adder

```
entity ripadd_8 is
    port (CI:                                          in bit;
        a7,a6,a5,a4,a3,a2,a1,a0:                        in bit;
        b7,b6,b5,b4,b3,b2,b1,b0:                        in bit;
        sum7,sum6,sum5,sum4,sum3,sum2,sum1,sum0:        out bit;
        co: out bit);
end ripadd_8;
architecture ripadd_8 of ripadd_8 is
    component full_adder
        port (ci:       in bit;
            a,b:        in bit;
            sum, co:    out bit);
    end component;
    signal c1, c2, c3, c4, c5, c6, c7: bit;
begin
    u1: full_adder port map(ci, a0, b0, sum0, c1);
    u2: full_adder port map(c1, a1, b1, sum1, c2);
    u3: full_adder port map(c2, a2, b2, sum2, c3);
    u4: full_adder port map(c3, a3, b3, sum3, c4);
    u5: full_adder port map(c4, a4, b4, sum4, c5);
    u6: full_adder port map(c5, a5, b5, sum5, c6);
    u7: full_adder port map(c6, a6, b6, sum6, c7);
    u8: full_adder port map(c7, a7, b7, sum7, co);
end;
```

Listing 9-2 An 8-bit ripple carry adder

If this design is targeted for a FLASH370 CPLD, then the synthesis software will attempt to "flatten" the design into two levels of logic for easy implementation in the product-term array. However, as illustrated in the previous chapter, XOR expansion results in a large number of product terms. In this design, flattening the equation for c4 results in the equation:

```
c4 = ((a0 * b3 * b2 * b1 * b0)
    + (ci * b3 * b2 * b1 * b0)
    + (ci * a0 * b3 * b2 * b1)
    + (a1 * a0 * b3 * b2 * b0)
    + (ci * a1 * b3 * b2 * b0)
    + (ci * a1 * a0 * b3 * b2)
    + (a1 * b3 * b2 * b1)
    + (a2 * a0 * b3 * b1 * b0)
    + (ci * a2 * b3 * b1 * b0)
    + (ci * a2 * a0 * b3 * b1)
    + (a2 * a1 * a0 * b3 * b0)
    + (ci * a2 * a1 * b3 * b0)
    + (ci * a2 * a1 * a0 * b3)
    + (a2 * a1 * b3 * b1)
    + (a2 * b3 * b2)
    + (a3 * a0 * b2 * b1 * b0)
    + (ci * a3 * b2 * b1 * b0)
    + (ci * a3 * a0 * b2 * b1)
    + (a3 * a1 * a0 * b2 * b0)
    + (ci * a3 * a1 * b2 * b0)
    + (ci * a3 * a1 * a0 * b2)
    + (a3 * a1 * b2 * b1)
    + (a3 * a2 * a0 * b1 * b0)
    + (ci * a3 * a2 * b1 * b0)
    + (ci * a3 * a2 * a0 * b1)
    + (a3 * a2 * a1 * a0 * b0)
    + (ci * a3 * a2 * a1 * b0)
    + (ci * a3 * a2 * a1 * a0)
    + (a3 * a2 * a1 * b1)
    + (a3 * a2 * b2)
    + (a3 * b3));
```

Because c4 is a virtual node, its expression is substituted into the equation for sum5. When this expression is XORed with a5 and b5, the result of flattening is an equation with a very large number of product terms. When completely flattened, this adder implementation requires 88 macrocells (most for sum-splitting) and 1,218 unique product terms. If signals c3 and c6 are made device nodes (that is, if the equations for these signals are implemented in macrocells to avoid flattening), then only 15 macrocells and 129 product terms are required. The worst-case delay in this implementation requires three passes through the logic array: one pass to generate c3, one to generate c6, and one to generate the outputs sum7 and co. Signals c3 and c6 can be made device nodes by using the synthesis_off directive. This 8-bit ripple carry adder is a reasonable implementation, but for larger adders a carry lookahead scheme usually provides a more area- and speed-efficient implementation in CPLDs.

The full adder circuit shown in Figure 9-7 requires two logic cells for implementation in the pASIC380 FPGA: one for the sum output, and one for the carry output. The 8-bit adder shown in Figure 9-8 and Listing 9-2 requires 16 logic cells and has a propagation delay of 34.7 ns (delays in FPGAs are place and route specific; your results may vary). The code of Listing 9-2 can be synthesized without the synthesis_off directive, because the optimization algorithms for FPGA synthesis factor out expressions rather than flatten them. This 8-bit ripple-carry adder is a reasonable implementation, but for larger adders, a carry select scheme usually provides an improved speed-efficient implementation in FPGAs.

9.3.3   Pipelined Ripple Carry Adders

The 8-bit ripple carry adder shown in Figure 9-8 represents a large data path. The critical path is from the least significant bits, a0, b0, and ci, to sum7 and co. This data path, which is eight logic cell levels deep, could benefit from pipelining, as illustrated in Figure 9-9. Four pipeline registers, including an output register, are inserted. The data path is broken every two full adders, or two logic cell delays.

Pipelining results in a clock-to-output delay of 10 ns, and an operating frequency of 89 MHz in the pASIC380 FPGA. The register-to-register delay represents a more than three-fold improvement over the pin-to-pin delay of the nonpipelined ripple carry adder. Figure 9-10 illustrates a latency of four clock cycles from input to output.

To take advantage of this 89 MHz operation, the sum of the trace delay and setup time of the sampling device cannot exceed 1.2 ns. This is because 1/89 MHz = 11.2 ns, and the clock-to-output delay is 10 ns. Alternatively, the sampling device could be clocked slightly later than the FPGA. Intentional skew can be controlled with a programmable skew clock buffer such as Cypress's CY7C991.

The increased performance in this pipelined implementation is at the expense of an additional 32 logic cells, or one-third of the 1,000 gate device. If performance is critical, this may be the best implementation; it is most efficient when numbers are continually being added (that is, if the pipeline is always kept full). If numbers are added only occasionally, this implementation would be a poor choice because the result would not be available until four clock cycles after data was entered into the adder. Four clock cycles of 11.2 ns is greater than the pin-to-pin delay of the nonpipelined version.

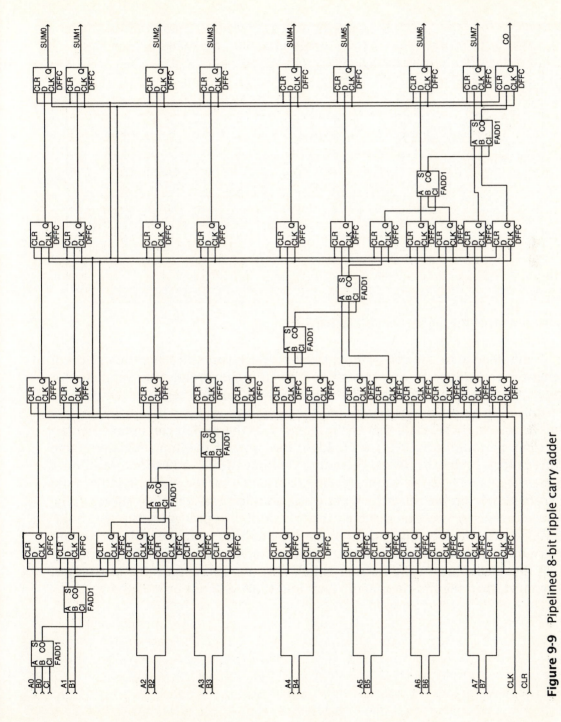

Figure 9-9 Pipelined 8-bit ripple carry adder

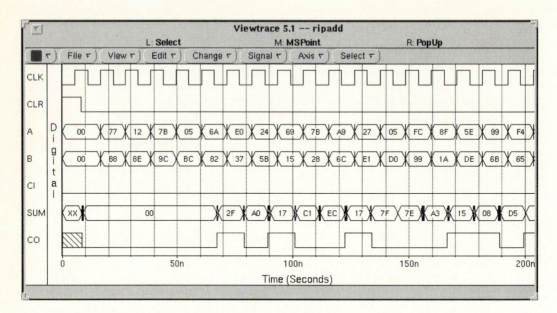

Figure 9-10   Timing simulation illustrates latency

If you choose to use the nonpipelined version, you still have the option of running the remainder of your design at a much higher frequency. Suppose, for example, that the inputs to the adder come from an on-chip register, the outputs are captured in an on-chip register, and the propagation delay through this data path is 25 ns. Suppose, also, that the remainder of the design can operate with a 10 ns clock period (Figure 9-11). By holding the value of the input register stable for three clock cycles, or 30 ns, the adder will have time to produce valid data (Figure 9-12). As long as the output register is disabled for the same period of time and enabled only on the third clock cycle, the addition can complete successfully. The output register must be disabled for this period to prevent setup and hold-time violations, which could cause the flip-flops to become metastable (to go into indeterminate states) for an indeterminate (but statistically predictable) period of time. If the enable line of the register is held low (by a state machine or counter, for example), then the flip-flops setup and hold times will not be violated.

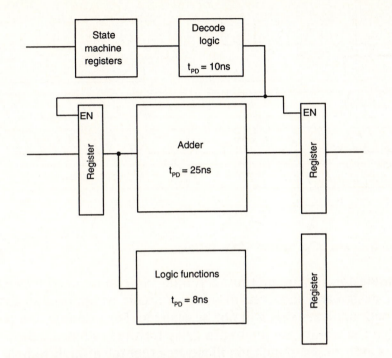

Figure 9-11   Point-to-point delays

Static Timing Analysis. The design technique explained in the previous paragraph provides an excellent example to explain the limitations of a static timing-path analyzer. Path analyzers of place and route tools usually provide static timing information only. That is, they provide point-to-point delay information based on the worst-case signal transition, either rising or falling edge. For the design example described in the previous paragraph, the path analyzer would indicate that the worst-case register-to-register delay is 25 ns. Although you would normally use the worst-case register-to-register delay to calculate operating frequency, in this case you must filter out all of the paths through the adder because the system is designed to give these paths three clock cycles. Because the enable lines of the input and output registers will be carefully controlled for addition operations, the clock frequency of this design is calculated from other register-to-register paths in this circuit, with 10 ns being the worst case.

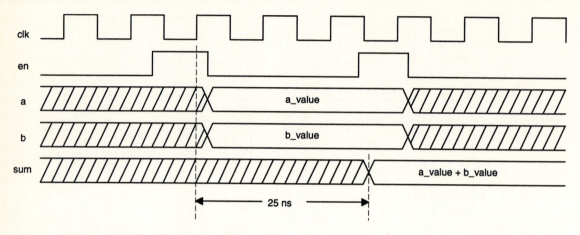

Figure 9-12   Using a slow data path in a fast system

Dynamic Timing Simulation. Dynamic timing simulation can be used to verify the functionality of a design and show real delays in a circuit, as opposed to those delays listed in the path analyzer that will not be realized. For example, the path analyzer indicates that the worst-case pin-to-pin delay for the nonpipelined ripple carry adder is 34.7 ns, but timing simulation illustrates that for a small sample of operands (200 at random), the worst-case delay is 30.84 ns (Figure 9-13). Further simulation may reveal a combination of operands that result in propagation delay of 34.7 ns. Sometimes, however, the combinations of inputs are controlled such that the worst-case path predicted by the static path analyzer is never realized.

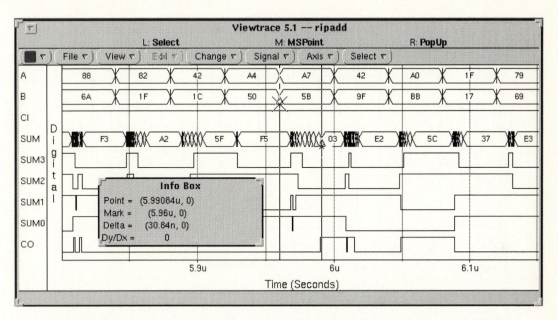

Figure 9-13 Dynamic timing simulation indicates that the worst-case delay is 30.84 ns in a sample of 200 operands

9.3.4   Carry Lookahead Adders

Carry lookahead schemes are used to reduce delays associated with carry chains. Figure 9-14 illustrates the construction of an adder of xn bits. The size of the n-bit group adders affects the area and performance of the carry lookahead logic. For example, the carry logic for a 16-bit adder with 2-bit group adders requires more gates (and potentially, additional propagation time) than the carry logic for a 16-bit adder with 4-bit group adders, because the design with 2-bit group adders requires more carry terms. The trade-off is that the 4-bit group adder requires more gates (and propagation time) than the 2-bit group adders. The optimal size for the group adders depends on the size of the adder and the target technology. We illustrate the results of using 2-, 3-, and 4-bit group adders in an 8-bit adder, targeting a pASIC380 FPGA.

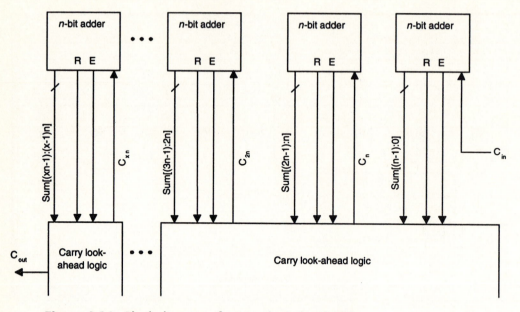

Figure 9-14 Block diagram of a carry lookahead adder

Each *n*-bit group adder has three outputs: a sum, carry generate, and carry propagate. A **carry generate** indicates that the group adder produced a carry-out to the next stage, regardless of the value of the carry-in to this group. A **carry propagate** indicates that the group adder produces a carry-out to the next stage only if the value of the carry-in to this stage is '1'. The equations for a 1-bit carry generate and propagate, (G and P), respectively, and the carry-out to the next stage are:

$$G = A \bullet B$$
$$P = A + B$$

and

$$C_{out} = G + C_{in}P$$

We distinguish 1-bit carry generate and propagate terms from *n*-bit carry generate and propagate terms by using the letters E and R, for group generate and group propagate. The code for an 8-bit adder with 2-bit group adders is in Listing 9-3. First we define the 2-bit group adder in a separate entity, then we define the 8-bit carry lookahead adder. The fcadd2 component is declared in the architecture declarative region of the fcadd8_2 component; otherwise it would not be visible to this design unit. The synthesis_off directive is used to ensure that carry generate and propagate terms are not substituted into equations.

```vhdl
entity fcadd2 is
    port (ci                : in bit;
          a1,a0,b1,b0       : in  bit;
          sum1,sum0         : out bit;
          e,r               : out bit);
end fcadd2;

architecture archfcadd2 of fcadd2 is
begin
    sum0 <= a0 xor b0 xor ci;
    sum1 <= a1 xor b1 xor ((a0 and b0) or (a0 and ci) or (b0 and ci));

    e <= (a1 and b1) or ((a1 or b1) and (a0 and b0));
    r <= (a1 or b1) and (a0 or b0);
end archfcadd2;


entity fcadd8_2 is
    port (ci : in bit;
          a7,a6,a5,a4,a3,a2,a1,a0:                    in bit;
          b7,b6,b5,b4,b3,b2,b1,b0:                    in bit;
          sum7,sum6,sum5,sum4,sum3,sum2,sum1,sum0 : out bit;
          co: out bit);
end fcadd8_2;
architecture archfcadd8_2 of fcadd8_2 is
    component fcadd2 port(
          ci                : in bit;
          a1,a0,b1,b0       : in  bit;
          sum1,sum0         : out bit;
          e,r               : out bit);
    end component;
        signal c2,c4,c6 : bit;
        attribute synthesis_off of c2,c4,c6 : signal is true;
        signal e0,e1,e2,e3 : bit;
        attribute synthesis_off of e1,e2,e3 : signal is true;
        signal r0,r1,r2,r3 : bit;
        attribute synthesis_off of r1,r2,r3 : signal is true;
begin
    U1: fcadd2 port map (ci,a1,a0,b1,b0,sum1,sum0,e0,r0);
    U2: fcadd2 port map (c2,a3,a2,b3,b2,sum3,sum2,e1,r1);
    U3: fcadd2 port map (c4,a5,a4,b5,b4,sum5,sum4,e2,r2);
    U4: fcadd2 port map (c6,a7,a6,b7,b6,sum7,sum6,e3,r3);
```

```
    c2 <= e0 or (r0 and ci);
    c4 <= e1 or (r1 and e0) or (r1 and r0 and ci);
    c6 <= e2 or (r2 and e1) or (r2 and r1 and e0) or
              (r2 and r1 and r0 and ci);
    co <= e3 or (r3 and e2) or (r3 and r2 and e1) or
              (r3 and r2 and r1 and e0) or (r3 and r2 and r1 and r0 and ci);
end archFCADD8_2;
```

Listing 9-3 An 8-bit carry lookahead adder with 2-bit group adders

The carry term c2, the carry-in to the second group adder, is asserted if the first group adder generates a carry or propagates its carry-in. The carry term c4, the carry-in to the third group adder, is asserted if the second group adder generates a carry or propagates a carry that is either generated or propagated by the first group. The carry term c6, the carry-in to the fourth group adder, is asserted if the third group adder generates a carry or propagates a carry that is (1) generated by the second group, or (2) propagated by the second group due to either the first group generating or propagating a carry.

In Listing 9-4, we define an 8-bit carry lookahead adder with two 3-bit group adders and one 2-bit group adder. It is assumed that the fcadd2 entity declaration and architecture body described in Listing 9-3 have been compiled to the work library.

```
entity fcadd3 is port (
            ci                      : in bit;
            a2,a1,a0,b2,b1,b0       : in  bit;
            sum2, sum1,sum0         : out bit;
            e,r                     : out bit);
end fcadd3;

architecture archfcadd3 of fcadd3 is
    signal c1, c2: bit;
begin
    sum0 <= a0 xor b0 xor ci;
    sum1 <= a1 xor b1 xor c1;
    sum2 <= a2 xor b2 xor c2;

    c1 <= (a0 and b0) or ((a0 or b0) and ci);
    c2 <= (a1 and b1) or ((a1 or b1) and (a0 and b0)) or
        ((a1 or b1) and (a0 or b0) and ci);

    e <= (a2 and b2) or ((a2 or b2) and (a1 and b1)) or
    ((a2 or b2) and (a1 or b1) and (a0 and b0));
    r <= (a2 or b2) and (a1 or b1) and (a0 or b0);
end archfcadd3;
```

```vhdl
entity fcadd8_3 is
    port (ci : in bit;
        a7,a6,a5,a4,a3,a2,a1,a0:                     in bit;
        b7,b6,b5,b4,b3,b2,b1,b0:                     in bit;
        sum7,sum6,sum5,sum4,sum3,sum2,sum1,sum0 : out bit;
        co: out bit);
end fcadd8_3;
architecture archfcadd8_3 of fcadd8_3 is
    component fcadd3 port(
            ci                  : in bit;
            a2,a1,a0,b2,b1,b0   : in  bit;
            sum2, sum1,sum0     : out bit;
            e,r                 : out bit);
    end component;
    component fcadd2 port(
            ci                  : in bit;
            a1,a0,b1,b0         : in  bit;
            sum1,sum0           : out bit;
            e,r                 : out bit);
    end component;
        signal c3,c6 : bit;
        attribute synthesis_off of c3,c6 : signal is true;
        signal e0,e1,e2 : bit;
        attribute synthesis_off of e1,e2 : signal is true;
        signal r0,r1,r2 : bit;
        attribute synthesis_off of r1,r2 : signal is true;
        signal vss : bit := '0';
begin
    u1: fcadd3 port map (ci,a2,a1,a0,b2,b1,b0,sum2,sum1,sum0,e0,r0);
    u2: fcadd3 port map (c3,a5,a4,a3,b5,b4,b3,sum5,sum4,sum3,e1,r1);
    u3: fcadd2 port map (c6,a7,a6,b7,b6,sum7,sum6,e2,r2);

    c3 <= e0 or (r0 and ci);
    c6 <= e1 or (r1 and e0) or (r1 and r0 and ci);
    co <= e2 or (r2 and e1) or (r2 and r1 and e0) or
          (r2 and r1 and r0 and ci);
end archFCADD8_3;
```

Listing 9-4 An 8-bit carry lookahead adder

The carry terms are defined in a similar manner as described for the 2-bit group adders. The results of synthesizing, placing, and routing this design are listed in Table 9-2. The code for an 8-bit adder using 4-bit group adders is left as an exercise for the reader.

Table 9-2   Area and speed variations with size of group adders

	2-bit group adders	3-bit group adders	4-bit group adders
Area (logic cells)	24	24	22
t_{PD} (ns)	37.9	33.7	34.5

These results illustrate that in this FPGA, the use of a carry lookahead adder provides no advantage over the ripple carry adder for an adder size of 8; the carry lookahead scheme requires more resources and the propagation delay is longer. Carry lookahead schemes work well, however, in CPLD architectures. It is left as an exercise for the reader to compile the results of implementing carry lookahead adders in a CPLD. Another technique for adder implementations is illustrated next.

Carry Select Adders. Carry select adders are not area-efficient, but may provide improved performance. The block diagram of a 12-bit adder is shown in Figure 9-15. The size of the group adders is chosen as 4 bits. For each stage of the counter (except the first), two 4-bit group adders sum the inputs. One of the group adders has its carry-in tied low, the other is tied high. The carry out of the previous stage is used to select, via a multiplexer, the appropriate output. This way, the critical path is not through the carry-in. The carry-out of a group adder for which the carry-in is tied low represents a carry generate; the carry-out of a group adder for which the carry-in is tied high represents a carry propagate.

Breakout Exercise 9-1

Purpose: To verify that the implementation of Listing 9-3 uses the factoring points specified in the code with the synthesis-off directive.

Compile, synthesize, and fit the design fcadd8_2.vhd to a CY7C371. Verify that the design equations maintain the integrity of the factoring specified in the code. How many product terms and macrocells are required?

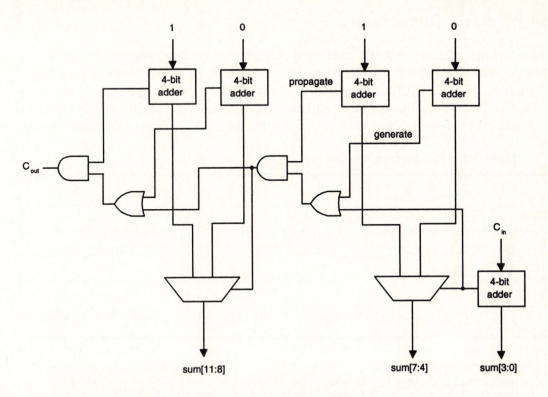

Figure 9-15 Block diagram of a carry select adder

9.4 Magnitude Comparators

In this section, we design a basic magnitude comparator, point out how this design can be optimized by buffering, and illustrate the design of a pipelined magnitude comparator. The techniques described here are not new, but are applied to a new application.

9.4.1   Basic Comparators

Table 9-3 illustrates the truth tables for comparing two bits. We will design an "*a* greater than *b*" comparator. The comparison of more than two bits can be accomplished via the algorithm described in Listing 9-5. However, because synthesis tools do not usually support next and exit statements for conditions that are not determinate at compile time, we cannot use this listing to generate the comparator.

Table 9-3   Two bit comparisons

AB	A > B	A < B	A ≥ B	A ≤ B	A = B
00	0	0	1	1	1
01	0	1	0	1	0
10	1	0	1	0	0
11	0	0	1	1	1
	$A\overline{B}$	$\overline{A}B$	$A + \overline{B}$	$\overline{A} + B$	$\overline{A \oplus B}$

```
library ieee;
use ieee.std_logic_1164.all;
use work.std_arith.all;
entity magnitude is port(
    a, b:in std_logic_vector(7 downto 0);
    agrb:buffer std_logic);
end magnitude;
architecture comparator of magnitude is
begin
p1: process (a, b)
        variable agtb: std_logic;
    begin
        agtb := '0';
        for i in a'range loop
            if a(i) = b(i) then next;
            elsif a(i) > b(i) then agtb := '1'; exit;
            else agtb := '0'; exit;
            end if;
        end loop;
        agrb <= agtb;
    end process;
end;
```

Listing 9-5 Nonsynthesizable magnitude comparator description

The circuit for a basic magnitude is shown in Figure 9-16. Examining this circuit diagram, you can see that the design works like this: if the most significant bit of a is greater than the most significant bit of b, then agrb is asserted. Subsequent bits of a and b will cause agrb to be asserted only if all previous bits cause the assertion of the appropriate agreb (a greater than or equal to b) line.

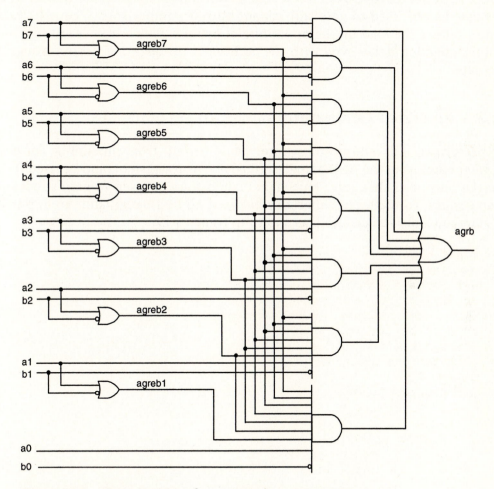

Figure 9-16 Block diagram of a magnitude comparator

When implemented in a pASIC380 FPGA, this design requires five logic cells, and has a propagation delay of 16.6 ns. Examining the circuit diagram, you can see that the most significant bits have a large fan-out. For a larger comparator, this could be of concern. Synthesis directives and buffering techniques can be employed to deal with fan-out problems. Perhaps a better solution than inserting buffers is to use an AND gate for several of the agreb signals. The output of this AND gate can be used to gate subsequent bitwise comparisons. The AND gate is used to reduce the load on the upper bits of a and b, which may result in a lower total propagation delay even with the additional propagation delay through the AND gate.

9.4.2   Pipelined Comparators

The performance of a large comparator could benefit from pipelining. For example, after employing the AND gate described above, a register could be used to capture the output of this gate. This signal could then be used to gate subsequent comparisons. To maintain coherency between all bits being compared, pipeline registers must also be inserted, as shown in Figure 9-17.

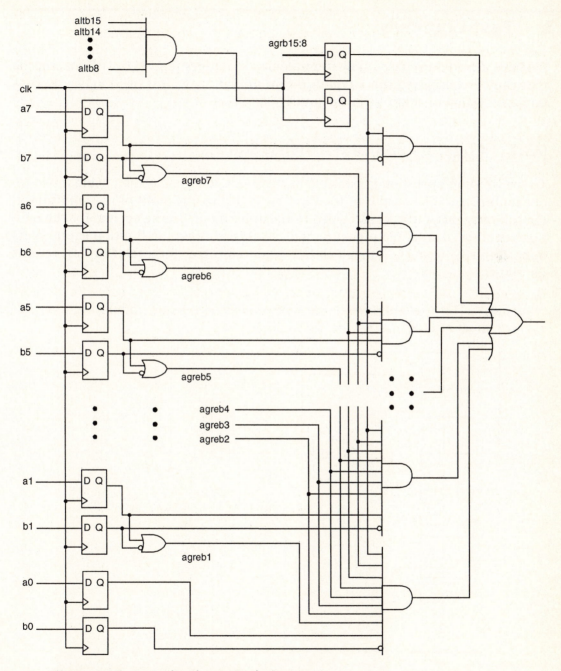

Figure 9-17 A pipelined magnitude comparator

9.5   **Fast Counters**

We have already discussed how to implement counters in CPLDs with macrocells that can be configured for T-type flip-flop operation. In this section, we discuss implementation of counters in the pASIC380 FPGAs.

9.5.1   **Counters and Late-Arriving Signals**

T-type flip-flop operation is possible in the pASIC380 logic cell by using a two-to-one multiplexer. The output of the flip flow is tied to one input of the multiplexer; the complement of this signal is tied to the other input. The select line for the multiplexer is the T input (Figure 9-18). If T is asserted, then the flip-flop captures its opposite value (that is, T toggles). If T is not asserted, then the flip-flop retains its value.

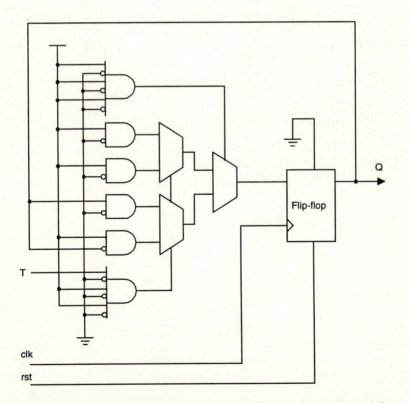

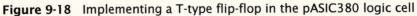

Figure 9-18   Implementing a T-type flip-flop in the pASIC380 logic cell

A 7-bit counter can be implemented in one level of logic cells, because a 6-bit AND gate can be combined with the T-type flip-flop operation (Figure 9-19). The signal count6 will toggle only if all of the previous counter bits are asserted.

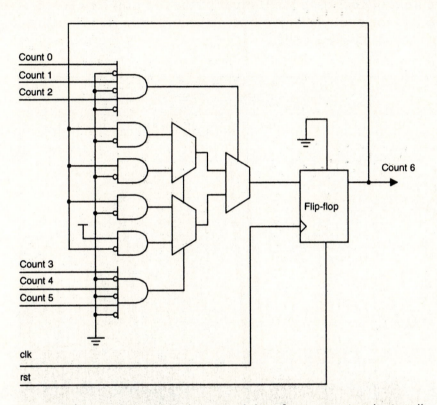

Figure 9-19 Implementing the seventh bit of a counter in a logic cell

The critical path for this seventh bit of the counter is from the least significant bit, count0, to the input of the flip-flop for count6. This is because count0 toggles with the greatest frequency (every clock cycle), while count1 toggles only every two clock cycles, count3 every four, count4 every eight, and so forth. Thus, signals count1 through count5 are **early arriving signals.** That is, they will be stable well before clock0 arrives. The signal count5 is especially early, as it will be asserted for many clock cycles before the lower bits of the counter (Figure 9-20). So even if the static path analyzer indicates, for example, that the delay from count3 to the input of the flip-flop for count6 is greater than the delay from count0 to the input of the flip-flop for count6, this delay can be filtered out—it is not the critical path. The critical paths for this 7-bit counter are (1) from count0 to the input of any other flip-flop and (2) from the output of any flip-flop to the input of the logic cell containing that flip-flop. Immediately after the value of the counter changes from "0111111" to "1000000", count0 to count6 is a critical path to ensure that the flip-flop does not toggle in the subsequent clock cycle. The other critical path is from the output of count6 to the D-input of the flip-flop for count6. It must propagate back to the multiplexer input to prevent the flip-flop from latching in the value from the wrong clock cycle.

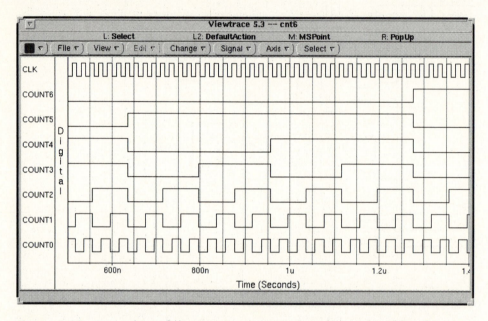

Figure 9-20   Upper bits of the counter arrive early at the input of flip-flops

You can take advantage of early arriving signals in the design of larger counters that require multiple logic cell levels. Figure 9-21 illustrates a 12-bit counter, which requires two levels of logic. The early arriving signals are placed on the second-level logic cell. Even though they will take longer to propagate to the input of the first logic cell level, they will be stable long before the lower bits of the counter. That is, cascade will be asserted well before the signals count4, count3, count2, count1, and count0 are all asserted in the same clock cycle. Thus the critical paths for this counter are (1) from count0 to any other counter bit, and (2) from any counter bit to itself. The latter paths are critical in ensuring that a counter bit (other than count0) does not toggle in two consecutive clock cycles. All other paths listed in a static path analyzer should be filtered out.

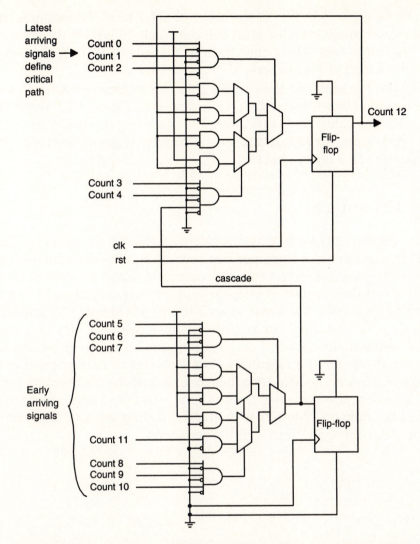

Figure 9-21 Implementing the twelfth bit of a counter in two logic cells

9.5.2 Pipelined Counters

In the implementations that we have discussed so far, count0 must propagate to the logic cells of all bits in the counter, count1 to all but one, count2 to all but two, and so forth. In order to limit the loading on the least significant bits of the counter, a couple of schemes can be used.

One scheme is to replicate a few of the lower counter bits. For example, in a 16-bit counter the lower significant bit must fan out to all 16 bits of the counter, but if this bit is replicated four times, then each of these least significant bits of the counter will have a load of four or five.

Another scheme is to break up the counter into two separate counters, using one flip-flop to cascade between them. This is illustrated in Figure 9-22. When the lower counter reaches the value "1111110", then the cascading flip-flop is asserted in the next clock cycle. Thus, the LSB of this second counter toggles one clock cycle after the lower counter value is "1111111".

9.5.3   One-Hot Counters

Because FPGAs are register-intensive, with considerably fewer logic gates per flip-flop than in a CPLD, one-hot state machines can provide an effective implementation for a small counter. Suppose you needed a counter to assert a terminal count when it reached 11, and then restart. A one-hot counter that counts to 11 can be implemented with 11 logic cells. The input to each flip-flop is simply the output of the previous flip-flop. The terminal count output comes from the eleventh state bit. An equivalent sequentially encoded counter requires only four flip-flops for the counter and one to decode the terminal count. However, it may not run at as high a speed as the one-hot implementation, because each of the counter bits has a greater load. In addition, the terminal count signal will take longer to decode because it depends not only on state bits with greater loading but also on an additional propagation delay through a logic cell for decoding.

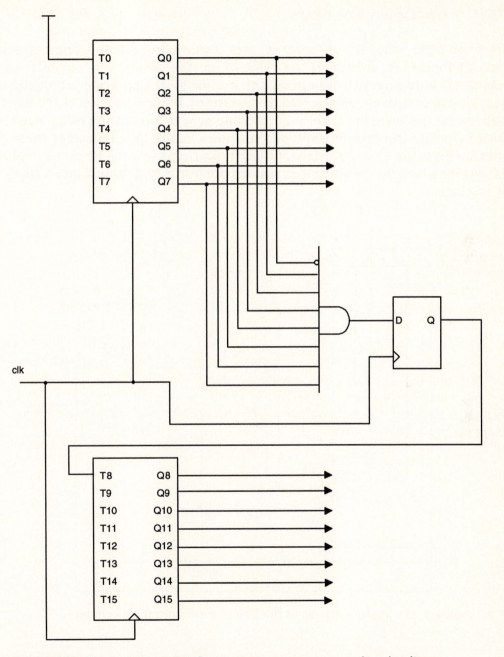

Figure 9-22 Introducing a flip-flop between counters to reduce loading

9.5.4   Up/Down Counters

The truth table for a 3-bit up/down counter is shown in Table 9-4. The least significant bit toggles regardless of the value of up. The second bit toggles if up and count0 are both asserted, or both deasserted; the most significant bit toggles if up, count1, and count0 are all asserted or deasserted. Implementation of the most significant bit is shown in Figure 9-23. Module generation, on the other hand, may create separate incrementers and decrementers, rather than flattening these operations. This is not always the case, however, particularly if the target technology is a CPLD for which the resulting expressions can be easily flattened into a small sum of products.

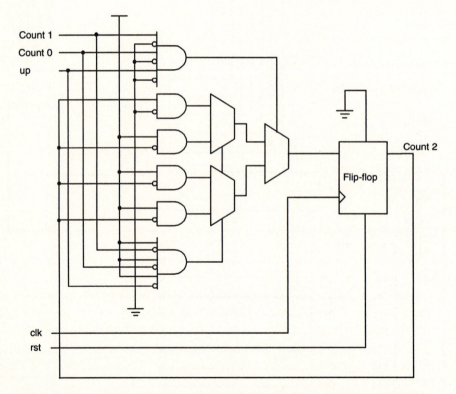

Figure 9-23   Implementation of third bit in a 3-bit up/down counter

Table 9-4   Up/down counter truth table

Present value	up = '1'	up = '0'
000	001	111
001	010	000
010	011	001
011	100	010
100	101	011
101	110	100
110	111	101
111	000	110

This concludes our study of synthesis, optimization, fitting (place and route), and design-optimization issues. In our final chapter we illustrate how to create test benches for combinational and synchronous logic.

Problems

9.1. Generate the appropriate adders and complete two copies of the following table: one for a CY7C375–100 and one for a CY7C386P–2.

Table 9-5   Ripple carry adders

	8-bit	16-bit	24-bit	32-bit
Area				
t_{PD}				

9.2. Generate the appropriate adders and complete two copies of the following table: one for a CY7C375–100 and one for a CY7C386P–2.

Table 9-6   Pipelined ripple carry adders

	16-bit			32-bit		
Pipeline stages	2	4	8	2	4	8
Area						
t_{SU}						
t_{SCS}						
t_{CO}						

9.3. Generate the appropriate adders and complete two copies of the following table: one for a CY7C375–100 and one for a CY7C386P–2.

Table 9-7   Carry lookahead adders

	16-bit			32-bit		
Group adder size	2	4	8	2	4	8
Area						
t_{PD}						

9.4. Generate the appropriate adders and complete two copies of the following table: one for a CY7C375–100 and one for a CY7C386P–2.

Table 9-8   Carry select adders

	16-bit			32-bit		
Group adder size	2	4	8	2	4	8
Area						
t_{PD}						

9.5. Create a 16-bit pipelined carry lookahead adder using 4-bit group adders.

9.6. Create a 16-bit pipelined carry select adder using 4-bit group adders.

9.7. Design a 4-bit multiplier for implementation in the CY7C375–100.

9.8. Design a 4-bit multiplier for implementation in the CY7C386P–2.

9.9. A magnitude comparator can also be implemented with a subtractor—the sign bit indicates whether a is greater than b. Compare this implementation for a 16-bit comparator with that of the basic comparator described in the text. Compare performance and area.

9.10. Using VHDL, create a 16-bit counter with synchronous load. Synthesize, place, and route the design in a CY7C386P–2. Reverse engineer the counter implementation. Describe the critical path, and determine the maximum operating frequency.

Chapter 10

Creating Test Benches

10.1   Introduction

The focus of this text has been to assist readers in writing VHDL code that can be efficiently synthesized for use with programmable logic. The intended audience has been those interested in VHDL primarily as a design language, rather than those interested in VHDL as a language for modeling devices and systems for simulation. Nonetheless, much of the content of chapters 3, 4, 5, 6, and 7 is directly applicable to modeling for simulation. In particular, we spent considerable time discussing the simulation cycle and the differences between synthesis and simulation results. Even though our focus has been on design, our VHDL models are still portable to simulation software.

A crucial and sometimes time-consuming part of the design process is design verification, but the ability to simulate a VHDL model can greatly increase efficiency; it allows for the functional verification of a design before synthesis and place and route. With traditional design methodologies, functional simulation of the design source was impossible; verification came only after implementation. With VHDL, functional verification can be performed prior to spending time on implementation. Granted, with today's VHDL synthesis and placement and routing technologies, implementation only takes anywhere from less than a minute to several hours, depending upon the size of the design and efficiency of the software. But because the initial realization of the design may not yield the required performance and resource-utilization goals, subsequent runs of the software processes may be required to tune the design. If functional verification is not performed until after iterations of synthesis and place and route, then the time spent implementing may be wasted, since a design error—particularly one that significantly changes the design—may require that the tuning process begin anew. Simulation of a VHDL model can bring out design errors at a much earlier stage of the process, allowing them to be corrected *before* implementation.

On the other hand, it is not necessarily wise to spend an inordinate amount of time with functional verification before a first pass through synthesis. After all, if the initial pass through synthesis yields unacceptable speed or area results, then significant design modification may be required even if the design is functionally correct. Such design modifications require that the model be tested again.

In this chapter, the models that we focus on writing are **test benches.** Most VHDL simulators allow real-time interaction—values of inputs can be assigned, simulation time can be executed, and the values of outputs can be inspected by looking at waveforms. This cycle can be repeated until the designer is satisfied that the model functions as expected. Alternatively, a test bench (sometimes referred to as a **test fixture**) can be used to verify a design's functionality. It allows input test vectors to be applied to a design (the unit under test) and output test vectors to be either observed by waveform, recorded in an output vector file, or compared within the test bench against the expected values.

A test bench provides several advantages over interactive simulation: (1) It allows the input and output test vectors to be easily documented. (2) This in turn provides a more methodical approach than would relying on interactively entering and inspecting test vectors. (3) Once the test bench has been built and the test vectors defined, the same functional tests can be repeated during iterations of design changes. That is, little time is required after a design change to rerun tests. (4) The same test bench used to verify the functionality described in the VHDL source code can be used to verify the functionality and timing described by a postfit model.

Many fitters and place and route tools produce postfit or postlayout VHDL models. These models are representations of a design as fitted in a device architecture. The actual model bears little resemblance to the source code. Instead, it typically consists of component instantiations of device architecture features and signals connecting the components. The models also usually have timing information so that a simulation run can detect setup violations and outputs can be observed to propagate according to the device's AC timing specifications. These models will have the same I/O as the original source code, so the same test bench used to evaluate the functionality of the source code can be used to verify both the functionality and the timing of the postfit model. Figure 10-1 illustrates the use of one test bench to verify both source and postlayout models.

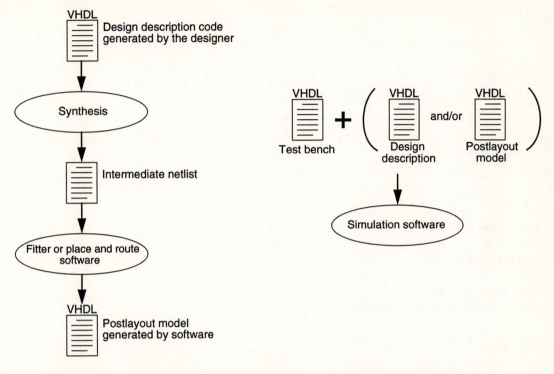

Figure 10-1   One test bench for both source and postimplementation

10.2   Approaches to Writing Test Benches

In this section, we illustrate three approaches to creating test benches. The first uses a table of test vectors embedded within the test bench, the second uses a table of test vectors contained in a separate file, and the third uses an algorithm to compute expected outputs and compare with actual outputs.

10.2.1 Tabular Approach

Listing 10-1 is a 3-bit counter for which we will create a test bench.

```
library ieee;
use ieee.std_logic_1164.all;
package mycntpkg is
  component count port(clk, rst: in std_logic;
                             cnt:        inout std_logic_vector(2 downto 0));
    end component;
end mycntpkg;

library ieee;
use ieee.std_logic_1164.all;
entity count is port(clk, rst:  in std_logic;
                          cnt:        inout std_logic_vector(2 downto 0));
end count;

use work.std_arith.all;
architecture archcount of count is
begin
counter: process (clk, rst)
begin
        if rst = '1' then
                cnt <= (others => '0');
        elsif (clk'event and clk= '1') then
                cnt <= cnt + 1;
        end if;
end process;
end archcount;
```

Listing 10-1 Source code of a 3-bit counter

The component declaration is made for the count entity so that it can be instantiated in the test bench as the unit under test.

Listing 10-2 is the text bench that we use with the source code and with the postfit model. In this listing, we include the test vectors for the unit under test in the source code of the test fixture.

The entity declaration for testcnt does not include any ports because there are no inputs or outputs to the test bench—it is self-contained. Signals are declared for each port of the unit under test. We choose signal names that match the local signal names of the component. The type test_vector is defined as a record. Each test_vector has elements for the clk, rst, and cnt signals. The type test_vector_array is defined as an array of test_vector. A constant, `test_vectors`, is defined to be of the type `test_vector_array`, and its value defines the set of test vectors to be applied to the unit under test as well as to the expected output.

The `count` component is instantiated as the unit under test. Inside a process, a loop is used to sequence through the `test_vectors` array. For each vector in the array, the clock and reset stimulus are assigned to the `clk` and `rst` signals. Because the signal assignments are to signals, they are not immediate but are scheduled. The signals assume the values of the present value of the variables only after a delta delay or if any simulation time transpires. In this case, the very next statement calls for 20 ns of simulation time to elapse. But before any simulation time elapses, all signals that are not explicitly initialized are, by default, initialized to the 'LEFT value (for `std_logic` that's the 'U', or uninitialized, value), and signals are evaluated. Thus, the `counter` process is executed once before any simulation time. Because neither the `if` nor `elsif` condition is true, the value of `cnt` remains "UUU" (all array elements uninitialized).

The statement, `wait for 20 ns;` causes the next simulation cycle to be executed; so the `clk` and `rst` signals assume the values that were scheduled in their projected output waveforms. The changes in values for `clk` and `rst` cause the `counter` process to execute once again. This time `cnt` is assigned "000" as a result of `rst` being '1'. Twenty nanoseconds elapse, and then the value of `cnt` is compared with the expected result (`vector.cnt`). If `cnt` is not the expected value, then the assertion statement causes the simulation software to issue a report: `cnt is wrong value`. The report is issued if the assertion statement is false. The assertion is hard-coded as false, because the comparison of `cnt` to the test vector was accomplished with an `if-then` construct. An unexpected value of `cnt` also causes the variable `errors` to be asserted. The loop continues for the remainder of the vectors, following the sequence of events described above with the exception of initialization. Once the loop has ended, two mutually exclusive assertion statements are evaluated. If the value of `errors` is false, then the report `Test vectors passed` is issued; otherwise, the report `Test vectors failed` is issued.

```
library ieee;
use ieee.std_logic_1164.all;
entity testcnt is
end testcnt;

use work.mycntpkg.all;
architecture mytest of testcnt is
  signal clk, rst: std_logic;
  signal cnt: std_logic_vector(2 downto 0);
```

```vhdl
    type test_vector is record
         clk: std_logic;
         rst: std_logic;
         cnt: std_logic_vector(2 downto 0);
    end record;
    type test_vector_array is array(natural range <>) of test_vector;
    constant test_vectors: test_vector_array := (
      -- reset the counter
         (clk => '0', rst => '1', cnt => "000"),
         (clk => '1', rst => '1', cnt => "000"),
         (clk => '0', rst => '0', cnt => "000"),
      -- clock the counter several times
         (clk => '1', rst => '0', cnt => "001"),
         (clk => '0', rst => '0', cnt => "001"),
         (clk => '1', rst => '0', cnt => "010"),
         (clk => '0', rst => '0', cnt => "010"),
         (clk => '1', rst => '0', cnt => "011"),
         (clk => '0', rst => '0', cnt => "011"),
         (clk => '1', rst => '0', cnt => "100"),
         (clk => '0', rst => '0', cnt => "100"),
         (clk => '1', rst => '0', cnt => "101"),
         (clk => '0', rst => '0', cnt => "101"),
         (clk => '1', rst => '0', cnt => "110"),
         (clk => '0', rst => '0', cnt => "110"),
         (clk => '1', rst => '0', cnt => "111"),
         (clk => '0', rst => '0', cnt => "111"),
         (clk => '1', rst => '0', cnt => "000"),
         (clk => '0', rst => '0', cnt => "000"),
         (clk => '1', rst => '0', cnt => "001"),
         (clk => '0', rst => '0', cnt => "001"),
         (clk => '1', rst => '0', cnt => "010"),
      -- reset the counter
         (clk => '0', rst => '1', cnt => "000"),
         (clk => '1', rst => '1', cnt => "000"),
         (clk => '0', rst => '0', cnt => "000"),
      -- clock the counter several times
         (clk => '1', rst => '0', cnt => "001"),
         (clk => '0', rst => '0', cnt => "001"),
         (clk => '1', rst => '0', cnt => "010"),
         (clk => '0', rst => '0', cnt => "010")
    );
  begin
  -- instantiate unit under test
  uut: count port map(clk => clk, rst => rst, cnt => cnt);
```

```vhdl
-- apply test vectors and check results
verify: process
        variable vector: test_vector;
        variable errors: boolean := false;
begin
        for i in test_vectors'range loop
                -- get vector i
                vector := test_vectors(i);

                -- schedule vector i
                clk <= vector.clk;
                rst <= vector.rst;

                -- wait for circuit to settle
                wait for 20 ns;

                -- check output vectors
                if cnt /= vector.cnt then
                        assert false
                                report "cnt is wrong value ";
                        errors := true;
                end if;
        end loop;

        -- assert reports on false
        assert not errors
          report "Test vectors failed."
          severity note;
        assert errors
          report "Test vectors passed."
          severity note;
        wait;
  end process;
end;
```

Listing 10-2 Design used to run test vectors

The unit under test was instantiated with the actuals associated with the locals by using named association rather than by positional association. This was done so that the component of the postfit model, which will not likely have the ports listed in the same order, can be instantiated in the same test bench.

10.2.2   File I/O Approach

Sometimes it will be easier to simply apply the input test vectors and observe the output vectors in a waveform. However, you may want to record these output vectors and compare them with those of the postfit model. Also, if you will need to apply a large number of vectors, then you likely will not want to list those vectors in the source code; you may wish to list them in a file and read them into the source code. This approach allows you to use the same test fixture to run multiple tests simply by changing the file.

Eight procedure calls will be used to read in a line from a file, to read `std_logics` or `std_logic_vectors` from a line, to write `std_logics` or `std_logic_vectors` to a line, and to write a line to a file. The procedure declarations for these functions are:

```
procedure Readline (F:in Text; L:out Line);
procedure Writeline(F:out Text; L:in Line);
procedure Read (L: inout Line; Value: out std_logic; Good: out
                boolean);
procedure Read (L: inout Line; Value: out std_logic);
procedure Read (L: inout Line; Value: out std_logic_vector;
                Good: out boolean);
procedure Read (L: inout Line; Value: out std_logic_vector);
procedure Write (L: inout Line; Value: in std_logic;
                 Justified:in Side := Right; Field: in Width := 0);
procedure Write (L: inout Line; Value: in std_logic_vector;
                 Justified:in Side := Right; Field: in Width := 0);
```

The first procedure declaration is for a procedure that reads in a line from a file. The second is for a procedure that writes a line to a file. These two procedures are from the `textio` package that is defined by the IEEE 1076 standard.

The third procedure declaration is for a procedure that attempts to read a `std_logic` value from the beginning of the line. If the value read is a `std_logic` value, then good returns the value true; otherwise, it returns the value false. The fourth procedure declaration is for a procedure that reads a `std_logic` value from a line. The next two procedure declarations are for procedures that perform the same jobs for `std_logic_vectors`. The two write functions are for writing `std_logics` and `std_logic_vectors` to a line.

Unfortunately, whereas there are standard read and write procedures for characters, strings, and bits, there are no standard procedures for the last of the six procedure declarations listed above. We have overloaded the standard procedure calls with ones for `std_logics` and `std_logic_vectors`. The content of these procedures is listed at the end of the chapter. For now, we can proceed with generating a test bench for the state machine of Listing 5-1. We will make the above procedures visible to our test bench by including a use clause.

First, we place the following test vectors in a file. These vectors will be read into the test bench and applied to the memory_controller. Some of the inputs are the don't-care value '–'.

```
-- test vectors for memory controller

reset   r/w   ready   burst    bus_id
  1      0      0       0      00000000  -- reset
  1      0      0       0      00000000  -- reset
  1      0      0       0      00000000  -- reset
  0      0      0       0      00000000  -- wrong address
  0      0      0       0      10101010  -- wrong address
  0      1      0       0      10101010  -- wrong address
  0      0      1       1      10101010  -- wrong address
  0      0      0       0      10101010  -- wrong address
  0      0      1       0      10101010  -- wrong address
  0      0      1       0      10101010  -- wrong address
  0      0      1       0      10101010  -- wrong address
  0      0      0       0      11110011  -- right address, go to decision
  0      1      0       0      --------  -- go to read1
  0      0      0       0      --------  -- stay in read1, not ready
  0      0      1       1      --------  -- go to read2, it's a burst
  0      0      1       0      --------  -- go to read3
  0      0      0       0      --------  -- stay in read3, not ready
  0      0      1       0      --------  -- go to read4
  0      0      1       0      --------  -- go to idle
  0      0      0       0      00111011  -- wrong address
  0      0      0       0      00111011  -- wrong address
  0      0      0       0      00111011  -- wrong address
  0      0      0       0      11110011  -- right address, go to decision
  0      1      0       0      --------  -- go to read1
  0      0      0       0      --------  -- stay in read1, not ready
  0      0      0       0      --------  -- stay in read1, not ready
  0      0      1       0      --------  -- go to idle
  0      0      0       0      11110011  -- right address, go to decision
  0      0      0       0      --------  -- go to write
  0      0      1       0      --------  -- go to idle
  0      0      0       0      11110011  -- right address, go to decision
  0      1      0       0      --------  -- go to read1
  0      0      1       1      --------  -- go to read2, it's a burst
  0      0      1       0      --------  -- go to read3
  1      0      1       0      --------  -- reset -- go to idle
  0      0      0       0      11110011  -- right address, go to decision
  0      1      0       0      --------  -- go to read1
  0      0      1       1      --------  -- go to read2, it's a burst
  0      0      1       0      --------  -- go to read3
  0      0      1       0      --------  -- go to read4
  0      0      1       0      --------  -- go to idle
  0      0      1       0      00111011  -- wrong address
  0      0      1       0      00111011  -- wrong address
```

```
0        0        1        0        00111011  -- wrong address
0        0        1        0        00111011  -- wrong address
0        0        0        0        11110011  -- right address, go to decision
0        0        0        0        11110011  -- go to write
0        0        0        0        11110011  -- stay in write, not ready
0        0        0        0        11110011  -- stay in write, not ready
0        0        0        0        11110011  -- stay in write, not ready
0        0        0        0        11110011  -- stay in write, not ready
0        0        1        0        11110011  -- go to idle
```

The test bench for the memory controller is shown in Listing 10-3. Signals are declared to match the ports of the unit under test. This time, the clock is initialized to zero because we will be controlling it from within the test fixture rather than from the vectors. The unit under test is instantiated, and a process is used to read in the vectors, apply the vectors, and control clocking. The procedure calls expect variables in the port maps, so variables are declared to match the signal names of the component ports. As long as the file is not empty, a line is read from the input vector file. A character is taken from the beginning of the line and placed in the variable ch. If the attempt to read the first value of the line does not return a valid character, or if the character is not a tab, then the next iteration of the loop starts. If the line starts with a tab character, the next value is read. It is expected to be a std_logic value, so it is taken from the line and placed into the variable vreset. If the value is not a std_logic, the next iteration of the loop begins. If it is a std_logic, we are confident that we have found a line containing a test vector. Tab characters and vector elements are read according to the test vectors listed above.

After reading in the test vector, we force 10 ns of simulation time before scheduling the inputs. We want to apply the vectors 10 ns before the rising edge of the clock. If the clock has a 40 ns clock period and starts out at zero, then we wait 10 ns, apply the vectors, wait 10 ns, clock the circuit, wait 20 ns (for a 50 percent duty cycle clock), and transition the clock back to zero before reading in the next vector. We record the present outputs 10 ns before the rising edge of the clock.

```
-------------------------------------------------------------------------
-- test fixture for memory controller
-- reads file "memory.inp" ; writes file "memory.out"
-------------------------------------------------------------------------
entity test_fixture_of_memory is end;
library ieee;
use ieee.std_logic_1164.all;
use std.textio.all;
use work.myio.all;
use work.memory_pkg.all;
architecture testmemory of test_fixture_of_memory is
    signal clk: std_logic := '0';
```

```vhdl
    signal reset, read_write, ready, burst, oe, we : std_logic;
    signal bus_id: std_logic_vector(7 downto 0);
    signal addr: std_logic_vector(1 downto 0);
begin
    -- instantiate the unit under test
    uut: memory_controller port map(
        reset => reset,
        read_write => read_write,
        ready => ready,
        burst => burst,
        clk => clk,
        bus_id => bus_id,
        oe => oe,
        we => we,
        addr => addr );

test: process
    file vector_file : text is in "memory.inp";
    file output_file : text is out "memory.out";
    variable invecs, outvecs : line;
    variable good : boolean;
    variable ch : character;
    variable vbus_id: std_logic_vector(7 downto 0);
    variable vreset, vread_write, vready, vburst : std_logic;
    variable out_vec: std_logic_vector(3 downto 0);
begin
    while not endfile(vector_file) loop
        -- read a line from the file
        readline(vector_file, invecs);

    --skip line if it does not begin with a tab
    read(invecs, ch, good);
    if not good or ch /= HT then next; end if;

    -- skip line if next value is not a std_logic
    read(invecs, vreset, good);
    next when not good;

    -- found a vector
    -- read vreset, vread_write, vready, vburst, vbus_id
    -- with tabs in between
    read(invecs,ch);
    read(invecs,vread_write);
    read(invecs,ch);
    read(invecs,vready);
    read(invecs,ch);
    read(invecs,vburst);
```

```
    read(invecs,ch);
    read(invecs,vbus_id);

    -- wait 10 ns before scheduling the vector (we want to
    -- introduce skew between the vectors and clock edges)
    wait for 10 ns;

    -- schedule vectors
    reset <= vreset;
    read_write <= vread_write;
    ready <= vready;
    burst <= vburst;
    bus_id <= vbus_id;

    -- apply vectors with plenty of setup time
    -- also, record the current output vector
    -- we will record output vectors 10 ns before rising
    -- edge of clock for each clock cycle
    wait for 10 ns;
    out_vec := oe & we & addr;
    write(outvecs, out_vec); writeline(output_file, outvecs);

    -- schedule and execute clock transition
    clk <= not (clk);
    wait for 20 ns;

    -- schedule and ensure execution of next clock transition
    clk <= not (clk) after 0 ns;

  end loop;

  assert false report "Test complete";
  end process;
end;
```

Listing 10-3 Test fixture for memory controller

The signals could have been scheduled by appending the words after 10 ns to the assignment statement, but since we need to record the outputs at same time that we are scheduling the inputs, we used the simple wait statement.

The output vectors are stored in a file called memory.out; presynthesis simulation results can be compared with postlayout simulation results by comparing the output files. On a UNIX system, the diff command can be used to ensure that the contents of two files are the same. Alternatively, you could use a VHDL design to read in both files and compare results.

10.2.3   Procedural Approach

Tables and files of vectors can work fine if you need to apply a particular sequence of test vectors or if the number of test vectors is small enough that they can be generated in a reasonable amount of time. Another approach is to embed algorithms within the test bench itself to determine if the output of the unit under test is valid. Listing 10-4 uses the procedural approach. A concurrent signal assignment statement is used to schedule transactions on the clock for every 50 ns (a 100 ns clock period). The first loop in the process is used to fill the RAM_REG array with data: the destination control is set to the RAM_REG array, the ALU operation is set to ADD, and the source operands are the D-input and zero. The second loop verifies that the addition function operates properly. The third loop contains a nested loop. Together, these loops are used to check all eight instructions, using the contents of all locations of the a and b registers. The data is put back into the current address of the a and b registers. The final loop is used to verify operation for all combinations of the operands sources. The output is shown in waveform for observation.

```vhdl
library ieee;
use ieee.std_logic_1164.all;
use work.numeric_std.all;
use work.mnemonics.all;
entity testbench is end;
architecture testbench of testbench is
component am2901 port(
    clk, rst:     in std_logic;
    a, b:         in unsigned(3 downto 0);          -- address inputs
    d:            in unsigned(3 downto 0);          -- direct data
    i:            in std_logic_vector(8 downto 0);  -- micro instruction
    c_n:          in std_logic;                     -- carry in
    oe:           in std_logic;                     -- output enable
    ram0, ram3:   inout std_logic;                  -- shift lines to ram
    q0, q3:       inout std_logic;                  -- shift lines to q
    y:            buffer unsigned(3 downto 0);      -- data outputs (3-state)
    g_bar,p_bar:  buffer std_logic;                 -- carry gen.,prop.
    ovr:          buffer std_logic;                 -- overflow
    c_n4:         buffer std_logic;                 -- carry out
    f_0:          buffer std_logic;                 -- f = 0
    f3:           buffer std_logic);                -- f(3) w/o 3-state
end component;
    signal clk: std_logic := '0';
    signal rst: std_logic := '1';
    signal a, b: unsigned(3 downto 0) := "0000";
    signal d:unsigned(3 downto 0) := "0000";
```

```vhdl
    signal i: std_logic_vector(8 downto 0);
    signal c_n: std_logic := '0';
    signal oe: std_logic := '0';
    signal ram0, ram3: std_logic;
    signal q0, q3: std_logic;
    signal y: unsigned(3 downto 0);
    signal g_bar, p_bar: std_logic;
    signal ovr:std_logic;
    signal c_n4:std_logic;
    signal f_0:std_logic;
    signal f3:std_logic;
    alias dest_ctl: std_logic_vector(2 downto 0) is i(8 downto 6);
    alias alu_ctl:  std_logic_vector(2 downto 0) is i(5 downto 3);
    alias src_ctl:  std_logic_vector(2 downto 0) is i(2 downto 0);

begin
u1: am2901 port map (clk => clk, rst => rst, a => a, b => b,
     d => d, i => i, c_n => c_n, oe => oe, ram0 => ram0,
     ram3 => ram3, q0 => q0, q3 => q3, y => y,
     g_bar => g_bar, p_bar => p_bar, ovr => ovr, f_0 => f_0,
     f3 => f3);
clk <= not(clk) after 50 ns;
verify: process
    begin
        -- fill ram_reg array
        for i in 0 to 15 loop
            wait until clk = '1';
                rst <= '0';
                b <= to_unsigned(i,4);
                d <= to_unsigned(i,4);
                dest_ctl <= ramf;
                alu_ctl <= add;
                src_ctl <= dz;
        end loop;
        -- add a + b; check output
        for i in 0 to 15 loop
            wait until clk = '1';
                a <= to_unsigned(i,4);
                b <= to_unsigned(i,4);
                src_ctl <= a + b;
        end loop;
        -- check all 8 alu instructions for ab regs;
        for j in 0 to 8 loop
```

```
            for i in 0 to 15 loop
                wait until clk = '1';
                    a <= to_unsigned((15 - i), 4);
                    b <= to_unsigned(i, 4);
                    alu_ctl <= std_logic_vector(to_unsigned(j,3));
            end loop;
        end loop;
        -- check all 8 src operand combinations
        for i in 0 to 8 loop
            wait until clk = '1';
                a <= "1100";
                b <= "1010";
                d <= "0101";
                src_ctl <= std_logic_vector(to_unsigned(i, 3));
        end loop;
    end process;
end;
```

Listing 10-4 Test bench for the AM2901 design

10.3   Overloaded Read and Write Procedures

The following are the overloaded read and write procedures used in the test fixture above, overloaded for the type std_logic. Keep an eye on the World Wide Web (http://www.vhdl.org) to see if standard read and write procedures become available.

```
library ieee;
use ieee.std_logic_1164.all;
use std.textio.all;

package myio is
    procedure Read (L: inout Line; Value: out std_logic; Good: out boolean);
    procedure Read (L: inout Line; Value: out std_logic);
    procedure Read (L: inout Line; Value: out std_logic_vector; Good: out boolean);
    procedure Read (L: inout Line; Value: out std_logic_vector);
    procedure Write (L: inout Line; Value: in std_logic;
                          Justified:in Side := Right; Field: in Width := 0);
    procedure Write (L: inout Line; Value: in std_logic_vector;
                          Justified:in Side := Right; Field: in Width := 0);
    type std_logic_chars is array (character) of std_logic;
    constant to_stdlogic: std_logic_chars :=
          ('U' => 'U', 'X' => 'X', '0' => '0', '1' => '1', 'Z' => 'Z',
           'W' => 'W', 'L' => 'L', 'H' => 'H', '-' => '-', others => 'X');
    type character_chars is array (std_logic) of character;
```

```vhdl
   constant to_character: character_chars :=
        ('U' => 'U', 'X' => 'X', '0' => '0', '1' => '1', 'Z' => 'Z',
         'W' => 'W', 'L' => 'L', 'H' => 'H', '-' => '-');
end myio;

package body myio is

   procedure Read (L: inout Line; Value: out std_logic; Good: out boolean) is
     variable temp: character;
     variable good_character: boolean;
   begin
        read(L, temp, good_character);
        if good_character = true then
            good := true;
            value := to_stdlogic(temp);
        else
          good := false;
        end if;
   end Read;

   procedure Read (L: inout Line; Value: out std_logic) is
     variable temp: character;
     variable good_character: boolean;
   begin
        read(L, temp, good_character);
        if good_character = true then
          value := to_stdlogic(temp);
        end if;
   end Read;

   procedure Read (L: inout Line; Value: out std_logic_vector; Good: out boolean) is
     variable temp: string(value'range);
     variable good_string: boolean;
   begin
        read(L, temp, good_string);
        if good_string = true then
            good := true;
            for i in temp'range loop
              value(i) := to_stdlogic(temp(i));
            end loop;
        else
          good := false;
        end if;
   end Read;
   procedure Read (L: inout Line; Value: out std_logic_vector) is
     variable temp: string(value'range);
     variable good_string: boolean;
   begin
        read(L, temp, good_string);
        if good_string = true then
          for i in temp'range loop
              value(i) := to_stdlogic(temp(i));
          end loop;
        end if;
   end Read;
```

```
    procedure Write (L: inout Line; Value: in std_logic;
                        Justified:in Side := Right; Field: in Width := 0) is
      variable write_value: character;
    begin
        write_value := to_character(value);
        write(L, write_value, Justified, Field);
    end Write;

    procedure Write (L: inout Line; Value: in std_logic_vector;
                        Justified:in Side := Right; Field: in Width := 0) is
      variable write_value: string(value'range);
    begin
        for i in value'range loop
          write_value(i) := to_character(value(i));
        end loop;
        write(L, write_value, Justified, Field);
    end Write;

end myio;
```

Each of the type conversions in the above code was accomplished using the to_stdlogic or to_character look-up table. An alternative approach follows, but it is less efficient, because the simulator will have to execute the case statement.

```
procedure Read (L: inout Line; Value: out std_logic; Good: out boolean) is
  variable temp: character;
  variable good_character: boolean;
begin
      read(L, temp, good_character);
      if good_character = true then
  good := true;
          case temp is
              when 'U' => value := 'U';
              when 'X' => value := 'X';
              when '0' => value := '0';
              when '1' => value := '1';
              when 'Z' => value := 'Z';
              when 'W' => value := 'W';
              when 'L' => value := 'L';
              when 'H' => value := 'H';
              when '-' => value := '-';
              when others => good := false;
          end case;
      else
        good := false;
      end if;
end Read;
```

Breakout Exercise 10-1

Purpose: To run a presynthesis simulation using a test bench.

If you have access to a VHDL simulator, use the file `c:\vhdlbook\ch10\test.vhd` as a test bench for the ALU design of Chapter 6.

Problems

10.1. List the advantages of performing presynthesis simulation.

10.2. Should you perform an exhaustive presynthesis simulation, even if it is time-consuming and you have not performed an initial synthesis and fit to determine whether the design will have adequate performance? Explain.

10.3. Create a comprehensive test fixture for a 16-bit carry-lookahead adder.

10.4. Create a comprehensive test fixture for an 8-bit up/down counter with three-state outputs. Verify the functionality of the counter with your test fixture. Ensure that your test fixture has the ability to evaluate setup-time violations.

10.5. Can you synthesize a postlayout model produced by fitter and place and route software? Explain.

10.6. Can you synthesize a test bench? Explain.

10.7. Use the read and write procedures to read in two files and compare results.

Afterword

Review

The intent of this book was to thoroughly motivate and involve the readers by presenting numerous design issues, examples, and techniques, so that they forgot they were simultaneously learning a new design language. The book established its framework and pedagogy early: VHDL was to be learned through its application in synthesis and design with programmable logic devices, and programmable logic devices were to be understood through a series of design issues, examples, and techniques. Chapter 1, "Introduction" whetted the appetite of the reader by explaining how modern engineering uses programmable logic devices and synthesizable languages to rapidly develop complex systems. Chapter 2, "Programmable Logic Primer" introduced the implementation methodology—designing with programmable logic devices—discussing the advantages and limitations of CPLD and FPGA architectures. Chapter 3 introduced the basics to VHDL modeling, explaining differences between models written for simulation and those written for synthesis. Chapter 4 covered several language constructs, illustrating how they can be reduced to logic circuits through synthesis. Chapter 5 was devoted to state machine design, illustrating several design trade-offs and descriptions styles. Chapter 6, in the context of two case studies, explained the concepts of libraries, packages, and reusable components. Chapter 7 introduced a high-level modeling technique, subprograms, discussing operator overloading and some of the IEEE standard packages. Chapter 8, "Synthesis and Design Implementation" covered many of the issues involved with synthesizing device-independent designs to devices with specific architectural features, namely CPLDs and FPGAs. Chapter 9, "Optimizing Data Paths" discussed several design-optimization techniques that allow speed and area trade-offs. Chapter 10, "Creating Test Benches" illustrated how to create test benches for the design verification of source code and postlayout VHDL models.

Reading this book and doing the problems and exercises in it should provide you with sufficient knowledge to design with programmable logic using VHDL, understand synthesis issues unique to designs, and write test benches. The best way to solidify your understanding and skills is to apply what you have learned to new designs.

Where to Go from Here

Depending on your interests and motivation for reading this text, you may be interested in learning more about VHDL as a simulation language, programmable logic devices, synthesizable design languages, or design techniques.

This text covered only briefly simulation issues such as the simulation cycle and creation of test benches. Several of the books listed in the bibliography can help you to understand more about the simulation cycle, event-driven simulation, cycle-based simulation, and writing efficient models for processing by VHDL simulation software tools. As with learning VHDL in a synthesis framework, learning VHDL within a simulation framework is best done hands-on. Acquiring a VHDL simulator such as the one in Warp3 will facilitate your learning new concepts.

As mentioned in Chapter 2, "Programmable Logic Primer", the best way to learn more about a particular device architecture or offering from a programmable logic vendor is to acquire the appropriate datasheets. The World Wide Web site for PREP is at http://www.prep.org; another useful PLD website is at http://www.pldsite.com, and the news group address for discussions is comp.arch.fpga. Most vendors of programmable logic devices also have Web sites that can easily be searched for. Cypress Semi-conductor's is http://www.cypress.com.

Verilog is another popular and powerful language for simulation and synthesis. It is now an IEEE Standard (1364). Some of its strengths are that it is often more concise than VHDL; however, this is sometimes at the expense of the richness of the language. Verilog benefits from having established a set of sign-off-quality ASIC libraries for simulation. Users of VHDL had to scramble to bring out VITAL (VHDL initiative toward ASIC libraries), which leverages off of the SDF (standard delay format) of Verilog. Proprietary languages appear to be slowly disappearing because few designers want to learn a language that is not portable among vendors. As with the number of books on VHDL, the number of Verilog books continues to grow as design methodologies that include synthesizable languages become the norm rather than the exception. Of course, an available Verilog synthesis or simulation software tool will facilitate your learning. Internet World Wide Web and news groups that may be of interest include VHDL International (http://www.vhdl.org), Synthesis news group (comp.cad.synthesis), VHDL news group (comp.lang.vhdl), and Verilog news group (comp.lang.verilog).

There are numerous ways to increase your repertoire of design techniques. Textbooks on logic design and computer organization are a good source, but learning from colleagues is perhaps more effective. Old and new design ideas are also often presented in electronic trade journals such as *Electronic Design News*. The applications handbooks of vendors of programmable logic devices and other devices illustrate interesting design techniques, although they are often specific to a particular device or architecture. And, of course, there's no substitute for trying out an idea of your own to discover whether or not it works.

Appendix A   Installing Warp and Viewing On-line Documentation

Installing Warp On a PC (Windows 95, Windows 3.1, or Windows NT)

Warp installation is automated. Simply insert the CD-ROM, start the Warp setup program \pc\setup.exe, and follow the on-screen instructions. You will be prompted for a serial number. The serial number for the Warp2 product that accompanies this book is 1051. Other Warp products reside on the CD-ROM; however, you are not licensed for these products, nor is a serial number provided. Although you may not need them, detailed installation instructions may be found in the text file \warppc.txt in the root directory of the CD-ROM. These instructions, as well as installation trouble-shooting information, are also located in the Warp user's guide on-line documentation. To view the user's guide, you must install the Adobe Acrobat reader.

Installing Warp On a Sun SPARCstation (SunOS 4.1.x or Solaris 2.5)

Detailed installation instructions may be found in the text file /warpunix.txt. These instructions explain local and remote installation procedures for Solaris and SunOS 4.1.x. You will be prompted for a serial number, which is 1051.

Viewing On-line Documentation

Warp documentation is available on-line and can be viewed using the Adobe Acrobat reader shipped with the CD-ROM. Documentation includes the Warp user's guide and reference manual, located in the \doc directory of the CD-ROM. This documentation may be transferred to your hard drive during the installation process. Data sheets for Cypress's programmable logic products are also included, and are located in the \doc\databook directory. Instructions for installing the Acrobat reader follow. The Acrobat reader may be installed before or after installation of the Warp software.

　　　For a PC (Windows 95, Windows 3.1, or Windows NT), start the Adobe Acrobat reader installation program \pc\acroread\disk1\setup.exe and follow the on-screen instructions. To view on-line documentation, start the Acrobat reader and load the appropriate file. For a Sun SPARCstation (SunOS 4.1.x or Solaris 2.5), the text file /sunos/warp.txt contains instructions for installing the Acrobat reader.

Appendix B Reserved Words

Below are the **reserved words,** or key words, that have special meaning in VHDL. A reserved word cannot be used as an identifier, such as a signal name. Not all reserved words are meaningful for synthesis.

abs	downto	library	postponed	srl
access	else	linkage	procedure	subtype
after	elsif	literal	process	then
alias	end	loop	pure	to
all	entity	map	range	transport
and	exit	mod	record	type
architecture	file	nand	register	unaffected
array	for	new	reject	units
assert	function	next	rem	until
attribute	generate	nor	report	use
begin	generic	not	return	variable
block	group	null	rol	wait
body	guarded	of	ror	when
buffer	if	on	select	while
bus	impure	open	severity	with
case	in	or	signal	xnor
component	inertial	others	shared	xor
configuration	inout	out	sla	
constant	is	package	sll	
disconnect	label	port	sra	

Appendix C Quick Reference Guide

This quick reference guide is not meant to be an exhaustive guide to the VHDL language. Rather, it is intended to be used as a reference to help you quickly build VHDL descriptions for use with synthesis tools.

The right columns of all tables contain brief examples. Constructs that are simplified and modified versions of the BNF (Backus-Naur form) syntax categories found in Annex A of the IEEE Std. 1076-1993 *Language Reference Manual* (LRM) are contained in the left column. The BNF syntax categories are simplified and modified so as to present only those constructs most useful in creating VHDL designs for use with synthesis tools and to combine a syntax category used in another syntax category. In BNF, boldface words are reserved words and lowercase words represent syntax categories. A vertical bar, |, represents a choice between items; square brackets, [ ], enclose optional items; and braces, { }, contain items that may be optionally repeated (except for boldface items immediately following an opening brace—these must be included). The left column may also contain brief descriptions and editorial comments to indicate the usefulness of the item in creating simple designs.

Building Blocks

Entity Declaration . . . page 109

Description	Example

entity entity_name is
port (
  [signal] identifier {, identifier}: [mode] signal_type
  {; [signal] identifier {, identifier}: [mode] signal_type});
end [entity] [entity_name];
	entity register8 is
	  port (
	    clk, rst, en: in std_logic;
	    data: in std_logic_vector(7 downto 0);
	    q: out std_logic_vector(7 downto 0));
	end register8;

Entity Declaration with Generics . . . page 303

Description	Example

entity entity_name is
generic (
  [signal] identifier {, identifier}: [mode] signal_type
    [:=static_expression]
  {; [signal] identifier {, identifier}: [mode] signal_type
    [:=static_expression]});
port (
  [signal] identifier {, identifier}: [mode] signal_type
  {; [signal] identifier {, identifier}: [mode] signal_type});
end [entity] [entity_name];
	entity register_n is
	  generic (
	    width: integer := 8);
	  port (
	    clk, rst, en: in std_logic;
	    data: in std_logic_vector(width-1 downto 0);
	    q: out std_logic_vector(width-1 downto 0));
	end register_n;

Architecture Body . . . page 112

Description	Example

architecture architecture_name **of** entity_name **is**
  type_declaration
  | signal_declaration
  | constant_declaration
  | component_declaration
  | alias_declaration
  | attribute_specification
  | subprogram_body
begin
  {process_statement
  | concurrent_signal_assignment_statement
  | component_instantiation_statement
  | generate_statement}
end [**architecture**] [architecture_name];
	architecture archregister8 **of** register8 **is**
	begin
	  process (rst, clk)
	  begin
	    if (rst = '1') **then**
	      q <= (others => '0');
	    elsif (clk'event and clk = '1') **then**
	      if (en = '1') **then**
	        q <= data;
	      else
	        q <= q;
	      end if;
	    end if;
	  end process;
	end archregister8;
	
	architecture archfsm **of** fsm **is**
	type state_type **is** (st0, st1, st2);
	signal state: state_type;
	signal y, z: std_logic;
	begin
	  process begin
	    wait until clk' = '1';
	    case state **is**
	      when st0 =>
	        state <= st1;
	        y <= '1';
	      when st1 =>
	        state <= st2;
	        z <= '1';
	      when others =>
	        state <= st3;
	        y <= '0';
	        z <= '0';
	    end case;
	  end process;
	end archfsm;

Declaring a Component ... page 296

Description	Example

<pre>component component_name
port (
[signal] identifier {, identifier}: [mode] signal_type
{; [signal] identifier {, identifier}: [mode] signal_type});
end component [component_name];</pre>
	<pre>component register8
	port (
	clk, rst, en: in std_logic;
	data: in std_logic_vector(7 downto 0);
	q: out std_logic_vector(7 downto 0));
	end component;</pre>

Declaring a Component with Generics ... page 302

Description	Example

<pre>component compnent_name
generic (
[signal] identifier {, identifier}: [mode] signal_type
       [:=static_expression]
{; [signal] identifier {, identifier]}: [mode] signal_type
       [:=static_expression]});
port (
[signal] identifier {, identifier}: [mode] signal_type
{; [signal] identifier {, identifier}: [mode] signal_type});
end component [component_name];</pre>
	<pre>component register8
	generic (
	width: integer := 8);
	port (
	clk, rst, en: in std_logic;
	data: in std_logic_vector(width-1 downto 0);
	q: out std_logic_vector(width-1 downto 0));
	end component;</pre>

Component Instantiation (named association) ... page 301

Description	Example

<pre>instantiation_label:
component_name
port map (
port_name =>   signal_name
               | expression
               | variable_name
               | open
{, port_name => signal_name
               | expression
               | variable_name
               | open});</pre>
	<pre>architecture archreg8 of reg8 is
	signal clock, reset, enable: std_logic;
	signal data_in, data_out: std_logic_vector(7 downto 0);
	begin
	   First_reg8:
	   register8
	      port map (
	         clk => clock,
	         rst => reset,
	         en => enable,
	         data => data_in,
	         q => data_out);
	end archreg8;</pre>

Component Instantiation with Generics (named association) . . . page 307

Component Instantiation with Generics (named association) . . . page 307

Description	Example

<pre>instantiation_label:
component_name
generic map(
generic_name =>   signal_name
                 | expression
                 | variable_name
                 | open
{, generic_name => signal_name
                 | expression
                 | variable_name
                 | open}
 	
port map (
port_name =>   signal_name
                 | expression
                 | variable_name
                 | open
{, port_name =>   signal_name
                 | expression
                 | variable_name
                 | open});</pre>
	<pre>architecture archreg5 of reg5 is
	signal clock, reset, enable: std_logic;
	signal data_in, data_out: std_logic_vector(7 downto 0);
	begin
	   First_reg5:
	      register_n
	      generic map (width => 5) --no semicolon here
	      port map (
	         clk => clock,
	         rst => reset,
	         en => enable,
	         data => data_in,
	         q => data_out);
	end archreg5;</pre>

Component Instantiation (positional association) . . . page 301

Component Instantiation (positional association) . . . page 301

Description	Example

<pre>instantiation_label:
component_name
port map (signal_name | expression
         | variable_name | open
{, signal_name | expression
 | variable_name | open});</pre>
	<pre>architecture archreg8 of reg8 is
	signal clock, reset, enable: std_logic;
	signal data_in, data_out: std_logic_vector(7 downto 0);
	begin
	   First_reg8:
	      register8
	      port map (clock, reset, enable, data_in, data_out);
	end archreg8;</pre>

Component Instantiation with Generics (positional association) . . . page 307

Description	Example

instantiation_label:
component_name
generic map (signal_name | expression
  | variable_name | **open**
{, signal_name | expression
  | variable_name | **open**})
port map (signal_name | expression
  | variable_name | **open**
{, signal_name | expression
  | variable_name | **open**});
	architecture archreg5 **of** reg5 **is**
	  signal clock, reset, enable: std_logic;
	  signal data_in, data_out: std_logic_vector(7 **downto** 0);
	begin
	First_reg5:
	register_n
	  generic map (5)
	  port map (clock, reset, enable, data_in, data_out);
	end archreg5;

Concurrent Statements

Boolean Equations . . . page 163

Description	Example

relation { **and** relation}
| relation { **or** relation }
| relation { **xor** relation }
| relation { **nand** relation }
| relation { **nor** relation }
	v <= (a **and** b **and** c) **or** d; --parenthesis req'd w/ 2-level logic
	w <= a **or** b **or** c;
	x <= a **xor** b **xor** c;
	y <= a **nand** b **nand** c;
	z <= a **nor** b **nor** c;

when-else Conditional Signal Assignment . . . page 167

Description	Example

{expression **when** condition **else**} expression;	x <= '1' **when** b = c **else** '0';
	y <= j **when** state = idle **else**
	    k **when** state = first_state **else**
	    l **when** state = secon_state **else**
	    m **when others**;

with-select-when Selected Signal Assignment . . . page 165

Description	Example

with selection_expression select
{identifier <= expression when
  identifier | expression | discrete_range | others,}
identifier <= expression when
  identifier | expression | discrete_range | others;
	architecture archfsm of fsm is
	type state_type is (st0, st1, st2, st3, st4, st5, st6, st7, st8);
	signal state: state_type;
	signal y, z: std_logic_vector(3 downto 0);
	begin
	  with state select
	      x <="0000" when st0 | st1; -- st0 "or" st1
	      "0010" when st2 | st3;
	      y when st4;
	      z when others;
	end archfsm;

Generate Scheme for Component Instantiation or Equations . . . page 209

Description	Example

generate_label: (for identifier in discrete_range)
| (if condition) generate
  {concurrent_statement}
end generate [generate_label] ;
	g1: for i in 0 to 7 generate
	    reg1: register8 port map (clock, reset, enable,
	      data_in(i), data_out(i));
	    end generate g1;
	
	g2: for j in 0 to 2 generate
	    a(j) <= b(j) xor c (j);
	    end generate g2;

Sequential Statements

Process Statement . . . page 113

Description	Example

[process_label:]
process (sensitivity_list)
{type_declaration
  | constant_declaration
  | variable_declaration
  | alias_declaration}
begin
  {wait_statement
  | signal_assignment_statement
  | variable_assignment_statement
  | if_statement
  | case_statement
  | loop_statement}
end process [process_label];
	my_process:
	process (rst, clk)
	  constant zilch : std_logic_vector(7 **downto** 0) :=
	  "0000_0000";
	begin
	  wait until clk = '1';
	  if (rst = '1') **then**
	    q <= zilch;
	  elsif (en = '1') **then**
	    q <= data;
	  else
	    q <= q;
	  end if;
	end my_process;

if-then-else Statement . . . page 177

Description	Example

if condition **then** sequence_of_statements
{**elsif** condition **then** sequence_of_statements}
[**else** sequence_of_statements]
end if;
	if (count = "00") **then**
	  a <= b;
	elsif (count = "10") **then**
	  a <= c;
	else
	  a <= d;
	end if;

case-when Statement ... page 183

Description	Example
| ```
case expression is
  {when identifier | expression | discrete_range | others =>
    sequence_of_statements}
end case;
``` | ```
case count is
  when "00" =>
    a <= b;
  when "10" =>
    a <= c;
  when others =>
    a <= d;
end case;
``` |

for-loop Statement ... page 214

Description	Example
| ```
[loop_label:]
for identifier in discrete_range loop
  {sequence_of_statements}
end loop [loop_label];
``` | ```
my_for_loop:
for i in 3 downto 0 loop
  if reset(i) = '1' then
    data_out(i) := '0';
  end if;
end loop my_for_loop;
``` |

while-loop Statement ... page 214

Description	Example
| ```
[loop_label:]
while condition loop
  {sequence_of_statements}
end loop [loop_label];
``` | ```
count := 16;
my_while_loop:
while (count > 0) loop
  count := count - 1;
  result <= result + data_in;
end loop my_while_loop;
``` |

Describing Synchronous Logic Using Processes

No Reset (Assume clock is of type std_logic) . . . page 188

Description	Example
| ```
[process_label:]
process (clock)
begin
  if clock'event and clock = '1' then  -- or rising_edge
    synchronous_signal_assignment_statement;
  end if;
end process [process_label];
---------------------or-------------------
[process_label:]
process
begin
  wait until clock = '1';
  synchronous_signal_assignment_statement;
end process [process_label];
``` | ```
reg8_no_reset:
process (clk)
begin
  if clk'event and clk = '1' then
    q <= data;
  end if;
end process reg8_no_reset;
-----------------------or-----------------
reg8_no_reset:
process
begin
  wait until clock = '1';
  q <= data;
end process reg8_no_reset;
``` |

Synchronous Reset . . . page 194

Description	Example
| ```
[process_label:]
process (clock)
begin
  if clock'event and clock = '1' then
    if synch_reset_signal = '1' then
      synchronous_signal_assignment_statement;
    else
      synchronous_signal_assignment_statement;
    end if;
  end if;
end process [process_label];
``` | ```
reg8_sync_reset:
process (clk)
begin
  if clk'event and clk = '1' then
    if sync_reset = '1' then
      q <= "0000_0000";
    else
      q <= data;
    end if;
  end if;
end process;
``` |

Asynchronous Reset or Preset . . . page 193

Description	Example

``[process_label:]
process (reset, clock)
begin
  if reset = '1' then
    asynchronous_signal_assignment_statement;
  elsif clock'event and clock = '1' then
    synchronous_signal_assignment_statement;
  end if;
end process [process_label];```
	``reg8_async_reset:
	process (asyn_reset, clk)
	begin
	  if async_reset = '1' then
	    q <= (others => '0');
	  elsif clk'event and clk = '1' then
	    q <= data;
	  end if;
	end process reg8_async_reset;```

Asynchronous Reset and Preset . . . page 201

Description	Example

``[process_label:]
process (reset, preset, clock)
begin
  if reset = '1' then
    asynchronous_signal_assignment_statement;
  elsif preset = '1' then
    asynchronous_signal_assignment_statement;
  elsif clock'event and clock = '1' then
    synchronous_signal_assignment_statement;
  end if;
end process [process_label];```
	``reg8_async:
	process (asyn_reset, async_preset, clk)
	begin
	  if async_reset = '1' then
	    q <= (others => '0');
	  elsif async_preset = '1' then
	    q <= (others => '1');
	  elsif clk'event and clk = '1' then
	    q <= data;
	  end if;
	end process reg8_async;```

Conditional Synchronous Assignment (enables) . . . page 194

Description	Example

``[process_label:]
process (reset, clock)
begin
  if reset = '1' then
    asynchronous_signal_assignment_statement;
  elsif clock'event and clock = '1' then
    if enable = '1' then
      synchronous_signal_assignment_statement;
    else
      synchronous_signal_assignment_statement;
    end if;
  end if;
end process [process_label];```
	``reg8_sync_assign:
	process (rst, clk)
	begin
	  if rst = '1' then
	    q <= (others => '0');
	  elsif clk'event and clk = '1' then
	    if enable = '1' then
	      q <= data;
	    else
	      q <= q;
	    end if;
	  end if;
	end process reg8_sync_assign;```

573

Translating a State Flow Diagram to a Two-Process FSM Description . . . page 235

Description

state	outputs oe	we
idle	0	0
decision	0	0
write	0	1
read	1	0

Example

```vhdl
architecture state_machine of example is
  type StateType is (idle, decision, read, write);
  signal present_state, next_state : StateType;
begin
state_comb:process(present_state, read_write, ready) begin
  case present_state is
    when idle =>     oe <= '0'; we <= '0';
      if ready = '1' then
        next_state <= decision;
      else
        next_state <= idle;
      end if;
    when decision => oe <= '0'; we <= '0';
      if (read_write = '1') then
        next_state <= read;
      else
        --read_write='0'
        next_state <= write;
      end if;
    when read =>     oe <= '1'; we <= '0';
      if (ready = '1') then
        next_state <= idle;
      else
        next_state <= read;
      end if;
    when write =>    oe <= '0'; we <= '1';
      if (ready = '1') then
        next_state <= idle;
      else
        next_state <= write;
      end if;
  end case;
end process state_comb;

state_clocked:process(clk) begin
  if (clk'event and clk='1') then
    present_state <= next_state;
  end if;
end process state_clocked;
end state_machine;
```

Data Objects

Signals . . . page 140

Description	Example
· Signals are the most commonly used data object in synthesis designs. · Nearly all basic designs, and many large designs as well, can be fully described using signals as the only kind of data object. · Signals have projected output waveforms. · Signal assignments are scheduled, not immediate; they update projected output waveforms.	```architecture architernal_counter of internal_counter is
signal count, data:std_logic_vector(7 downto 0);
begin
process (clk)
begin
if (clk'event and clk = '1') then
if en = '1' then
count <= data;
else
count <= count + 1;
end if;
end if;
end process;
end archinternal_counter;```

Constants . . . page 140

Description	Example
Constants are used to hold a static value; they are typically used to improve the readability and maintenance of code.	```my_process:
process (rst, clk)
constant zilch : std_logic_vector(7 downto 0) := "0000_0000";
begin
wait until clk = '1';
if (rst = '1') then
q <= zilch;
elsif (en = '1') then
q <= data;
else
q <= q;
end if;
end my_process;```

Variables . . . page 142

Description	Example

· Variables can be used in processes and subprograms—that is, in sequential areas only.
· The scope of a variable is the process or subprogram.
· A variable in a subprogram does not retain its value between calls.
· Variables are most commonly used as the indices of loops or for the calculation of intermediate values, or immediate assignment.
· To use the value of a variable outside of the process or subprogram in which it was declared, the value of the variable must be assigned to a signal.
· Variable assignment is immediate, not scheduled.
	`architecture archloopstuff of loopstuff is`
	`    signal data:    std_logic_vector (3 downto 0);`
	`    signal result:  std_logic;`
	`begin`
	`process (data)`
	`    variable tmp:        std_logic;`
	`begin`
	`    tmp := '1';`
	`    for i in a'range downto 0 loop`
	`        tmp := tmp and data(i);`
	`    end loop;`
	`    result <= tmp;`
	`end process;`
	`end archloopstuff;`

Data Types and Subtypes

std_logic . . . page 145

Description	Example

· Values are:
  `'U',` -- Uninitialized
  `'X',` -- Forcing unknown
  `'0',` -- Forcing 0
  `'1',` -- Forcing 1
  `'Z',` -- High impedance
  `'W',` -- Weak unknown
  `'L',` -- Weak 0
  `'H',` -- Weak 1
  `'-',` -- Don't care
· The standard multivalue logic system for VHDL model inter-operability.
· A resolved type (i.e., a resolution function is used to determine the value of a signal with more than one driver).
· To use it must include the following two lines:
`library ieee;`
`use ieee.std_logic_1164.all;`
	`signal x, data, enable:  std_logic;`
	`. . .`
	`x <= data when enable = '1' else 'Z';`

std_ulogic . . . page 145

Description	Example

· Values are:
 	
  'U', -- Uninitialized
  'X', -- Forcing unknown
  '0', -- Forcing 0
  '1', -- Forcing 1
  'Z', -- High impedance
  'W', -- Weak unknown
  'L', -- Weak 0
  'H', -- Weak 1
  '-', -- Don't care
 	
· An unresolved type (i.e., a signal of this type may have only one driver).
· Along with its subtypes, std_ulogic should be used over user-defined types to ensure interoperability of VHDL models among synthesis and simulation tools.
· To use must include the following two lines:
  library ieee;
  use ieee.std_logic_1164.all;
	signal x, data, enable: std_ulogic;
	. . .
	x <= data **when** enable = '1' **else** 'Z';

std_logic_vector and std_ulogic_vector . . . page 147

Description	Example

· Are arrays of types std_logic and std_ulogic.
· Along with its subtypes, std_logic_vector should be used over user-defined types to ensure interoperability of VHDL models among synthesis and simulation tools.
· To use must include the following two lines:
  library ieee;
  use ieee.std_logic_1164.all;
	signal mux: std_logic_vector(7 **downto** 0);
	. . .
	if state = address **or** state = ras **then**
	  mux <= dram_a;
	else
	  mux <= (**others** => 'Z');
	end if;

bit and bit_vector . . . page 147

Description	Example

· Bit values are: '0' and '1'.
· Bit_vector is an array of bits.
· Pre-defined by the IEEE 1076 standard.
· This type was used extensively prior to the introduction and synthesis-tool vendor support of std_logic_1164.
· Useful when metalogic values not required.
	``
	signal x: bit;
	
	. . .
	if x = '1' then
	    state <= idle;
	else
	    state <= start;
	end if;
	``

Boolean . . . page 145

Description	Example

· Values are TRUE and FALSE.
· Often used as return value of function.
	``
	signal a: boolean;
	
	. . .
	if a = '1' then
	    state <= idle;
	else
	    state <= start;
	end if;
	``

Integer . . . page 146

Description	Example

· Values are the set of integers.
· Data objects of this type are often used for defining widths of signals or as an operand in an addition or subtraction.
· The types std_logic_vector and bit_vector work better than integer for components such as counters because the use of integers may cause "out of range" run-time simulation errors when the counter reaches its maximum value.
	``
	entity counter_n is
	    generic (
	        width: integer := 8);
	    port (
	        clk, rst: in std_logic;
	        count: out std_logic_vector(width-1 downto 0));
	end counter_n;
	. . .
	    process(clk)
	    begin
	        if (rst = '1') then
	            count <= 0;
	        elsif (clk'event and clk='1') then
	            count <= count + 1;
	        end if;
	    end process;
	``

Enumeration Types . . . page 144

Description	Example
| · Values are user-defined.<br>· Commonly used to define states for a state machine. | ```
architecture archfsm of fsm is
  type state_type is (st0, st1, st2);
  signal state:  state_type;
  signal y, z:   std_logic;
begin
  process
  begin
    wait until clk'event = '1';
    case state is
      when st0 =>
        state <= st2;
        y <= '1'; z <= '0';
      when st1 =>
        state <= st3;
        y <= '1'; z <= '1';
      when others =>
        state <= st0;
        y <= '0'; z <= '0';
    end case;
  end process;
end archfsm;
``` |
```

Modes

In, out, buffer, inout . . . page 110

Description	Example
| · **In:** Used for signals (ports) that are inputs-only to an entity.<br>· **Out:** Used for signals that are outputs-only and for which the values are not required internal to the entity.<br>· **Buffer:** Used for signals that are outputs, but for which the values are required internal to the given entity. Caveat with usage: If the local port of an instantiated component is of mode buffer, then if the actual is also a port, it must be of mode buffer as well. For this reason, some designers standardize on mode buffer.<br>· **Inout:** Used for signals that are truly bidirectional. May also be used for signals that are inputs-only or outputs-only, at the expense of code readability. | ```vhdl
entity counter_4 is
port (
    clk, rst, ld:  in std_logic;
    term_cnt:      buffer std_logic;
    count:         inout std_logic_vector(3 downto 0));
end counter_4;

architecture archcounter_4 of counter_4 is
    signal int_rst:    std_logic;
    signal int_count:  std_logic_vector(3 downto 0);
begin
    process(int_rst, clk)
    begin
        if (int_rst = '1') then
            int_count <= "0000";
        elsif (clk'event and clk='1') then
            if (ld = '1') then
                int_count <= count;
            else
                int_count <= int_count + 1;
            end if;
        end if;
    end process;

    term_cnt <= count(2) and count(0);
                        -- term_cnt is 3
    int_rst <= term_cnt or rst;
                        -- resets at term_cnt
    count <= int_count when ld = '0' else "ZZZZ";
                        -- count is bidirectional

end archcounter_4;
``` |
```

Operators

All operators of the same class have the same level of precedence. The classes of operators are listed here in order of decreasing precedence. Many of the operators are overloaded in the `std_logic_1164`, `numeric_bit`, and `numeric_std` packages.

Miscellaneous Operators . . . page 164

Description	Example

· Operators: `**`, abs, not.
 · The not operator is used frequently, the other two are rarely used for designs to be synthesized.
 · Predefined for any integer type (`**`), any numeric type (abs), and either bit and Boolean (not).
	```signal a, b, c:bit;```
	 ``. . .``
	 ```a <= not (b and c);```

Multiplying Operators . . . page 196

Description	Example

· Operators: `*`, `/`, mod, rem.
 · The `*` operator is occasionally used for multipliers; the other three are rarely used in synthesis.
 · Predefined for any integer type (`*`, `/`, mod, rem), and any floating point type (`*`,`/`).
	```variable a, b:integer range 0 to 255;```
	 ``. . .``
	 ```a <= b * 2;```

Sign

Description	Example

· Operators: `+`, `−`.
 · Rarely used for synthesis.
 · Predefined for any numeric type (floating-point or integer).
	```variable a, b, c:integer range 0 to 255;```
	 ``. . .``
	 ```a <= − (b + 2);```

Adding Operators . . . page 196

Description	Example
| · Operators: +, – <br> · Used frequently to describe incrementers, decrementers, adders, and subtractors. <br> · Predefined for any numeric type. | ```
signal count:  integer range 0 to 255;
. . .
    count <= count + 1;
``` |

Shift Operators . . . page 403

Description	Example
| · Operators: sll, srl, sla, sra, rol, ror. <br> · Used occasionally. <br> · Predefined for any one-dimensional array with elements of type bit or Boolean. Overloaded for std_logic arrays. | ```
signal a, b:  bit_vector(4 downto 0);
signal c:     integer range 0 to 4;
. . .
    a <= b sll c;
``` |

Relational Operators . . . page 173

Description	Example
| · Operators: =, /=, <, <=, >, >=. <br> · Used frequently for comparisons. <br> · Predefined for any type (both operands must be of same type). | ```
signal a, b:  integer range 0 to 255;
signal agtb:  std_logic;
. . .
    if a >= b then
        agtb <= '1';
    else
        agtb <= '0';
``` |

Logical Operators . . . page 164

Description	Example
| · Operators: and, or, nand, nor, xor, xnor. <br> · Used frequently to generate Boolean equations. <br> · Predefined for types bit and Boolean. Std_logic_1164 overloads these operators for std_ulogic and its subtypes. | ```
signal a, b, c:std_logic;
. . .
    a <= b and c;
``` |

Glossary

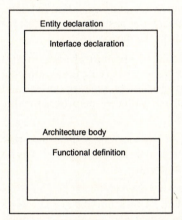

Entity

Figure G-1 Relationship between a design entity and its entity declaration and architecture body

```
entity top is port(
    i, j, k: in bit; z: out bit);
end top;
architecture top of top is
    signal h: bit;
begin
u1: and2 port map(a => i, b => j, x => h);
u2: or2 port map(a => h, b => k, y => z);
end;
```

Listing G-1 Port map shows actuals and locals

Actual A signal that is mapped to a port of a component. In Listing G-1, signals h, i, j, k, and z are actuals. *See* local.

Alias A substitute name for a signal.

Antifuse The opposite of a fuse. An antifuse initially provides insulation between two conductors, but when a sufficient programming voltage is applied across it, a conducting path forms.

Architecture body A design unit that describes the behavior or structure of a design entity. An entity declaration is paired with an architecture body to form a complete design entity (see Figure G-1).

ASIC Application-specific integrated circuit. A semiconductor device custom designed to perform a specific function. ASICs are not field-programmable, but are manufactured for a particular application. Development of an ASIC requires an NRE expense, and the manufacturing of the first device can take many weeks (even many months).

Component A design entity instantiated in another design entity. Components are used to create hierarchy.

Component declaration A template that defines the interface of a component. At the time of synthesis, a component must be bound to a specific entity declaration and architecture body pair.

Die The semiconductor silicon device found inside a device package. Multiple silicon devices are formed on a single silicon wafer, which is then cut into individual dice for packaging.

Die size The area of the rectangular piece of silicon that makes up the semiconductor device, usually measured in mil^2.

Entity An abstraction of a system, board, chip, component, or logic gate. An entity, or design entity, is defined by an entity declaration and architecture body (see Figure G-1).

Entity declaration A design unit that defines a design entity's interface. It is paired with an architecture body to form a complete design entity (see Figure G-1).

Fault tolerance A quality that describes a system's resistance to failure. A fault-tolerant system is one that is designed to self-correct and continue operation under many circumstances. The Space Shuttle's computer is an example of a fault-tolerant system. The term is also used to describe a state machine that forces itself into a known state whenever an unforeseen condition or hardware glitch is encountered.

FIFO First-in, first-out buffer. A semiconductor memory device that stores information in the order in which it was received and then releases that information starting with the first element received and progressing sequentially. FIFOs have a depth and width related to the number and size of words that may be stored in them.

Fitting The process of transforming a gate-level or sum-of-products representation of a circuit into a file used for programming a PLD or CPLD device. This process typically occurs after synthesis, and the resulting file is typically a JEDEC file. *See* place and route, synthesis.

Generic A component interface item used to parameterize a component instance for a particular size, features set, operation, and so forth.

Glitch A voltage spike on a signal. A short unintended pulse.

Hold time The minimum time an input to a digital logic storage element must remain stable after the triggering edge of a clock has occurred. *See* metastability, setup time.

Library A collection of VHDL design units, typically used to hold reusable components and type declarations.

Local In a component instantiation, the port associated with the underlying entity and component declarations. In Listing G-1, ports a, b, and x in the and2 component instantiation, and ports a, b, and y in the or2 component instantiation, are locals. *See* actuals.

Logic block Similar in nature and capability to a small PLD such as the 22V10, it contains product terms, a product-term distribution scheme, configurable macrocells, and I/O cells. A CPLD has two or more logic blocks that communicate through the programmable interconnect.

Logic cell A replicated element of logic within an FPGA device. It usually contains a register and additional logic that forms the basic building block for implementing logic in the device.

Macrocell A replicated element of logic in PLD and CPLD architectures that typically contains a configurable memory element, polarity control, and one or more feedback paths to the programmable interconnect.

Mealy machine A state machine with outputs that may change asynchronously with respect to the clock. *See* Moore machine.

Metalogical value A value of 'U', 'X', 'W', or '-' as defined in the IEEE 1164 standard for the type std_logic. These values are intended for simulation of VHDL models, and represent signal logic values of uninitialized, forcing unknown, weak unknown, and don't-care, respectively. The IEEE 1076.3 standard distinguishes between metalogical values and the high-impedance value, whereas in this text we also consider the high-impedance value a metalogic value because it represents neither the high nor low logic states ("meta" means in-between).

Metastability In-between states. An undesirable output condition of digital logic storage elements caused by the violation of setup or hold times. Metastability can be seen as an output that transitions to the wrong state, remains indeterminate, or oscillates for an indeterminate (but statistically predictable) period of time.

Mode Associated with ports declared in an entity declaration. A mode defines the direction of signal communication for an entity, and whether a signal is readable, writable, or both.

Moore machine A state machine in which outputs change synchronously with respect to the clock. *See* Mealy machine.

NRE Nonrecurring engineering. Refers to the time and money required to perform nonrecurring tasks. For example, the design effort and manufacturing costs for developing an ASIC are nonrecurring. Many projects have low NRE expense requirements.

One-hot-one encoding A method of state encoding that uses one register for each state. Only one bit is asserted, or "hot," for each state. The hot state can be asserted as a logic value of zero or one, but is typically a logical one.

One-hot-zero encoding Similar to one-hot-one encoding except that the reset, or idle, state is encoded with all logic zero levels. This is typically done to allow the use of dedicated hardware register resets to easily place the state machine in a known reset or idle state.

Package A design unit often used to gather related component, type, constant, and subprogram declarations. Packages are compiled to libraries. *See* library.

Performance The maximum clock frequency at which a design can operate, determined by its implementation in a particular programmable logic device. Performance is measured in Hertz (typically MHz) for clock frequency; its reciprocal is the clock period, measured in seconds (typically ns).

Place and route The process of transforming a gate-level representation of a circuit into a programming file that may be used to program an FPGA device. This process requires two steps: one to place the required logic into logic cells, and one to route signals that connect logic cells and I/O via horizontal and vertical routing wires. *See* fitting, logic cell, synthesis.

Postlayout (postfit) model A VHDL model produced by place and route (or fitter) software. The description is of a circuit as implemented in a device. When simulated, it can be used to verify the function and timing of a design.

Product-term distribution The method of distributing logic in the form of AND terms (product terms) to macrocells. PLDs have various product-term distribution schemes.

Programmable interconnect Refers to the communication network within a CPLD architecture that provides communication between logic blocks and I/O pins. It can also refer to the technology used to connect two wires via a programmable fuse (or antifuse).

Routability A measure of probability that a signal will successfully be connected from one location within a device to another location. Routability within FPGA devices is affected by the number of horizontal and vertical routing wires and the architecture of the logic cells. Routability within CPLD devices refers to the probability that a set of logic signals can be successfully routed through the programmable interconnect and into a logic block.

Setup time The minimum time an input to a digital logic storage element must remain stable before the triggering edge of a clock occurs. *See* hold time, metastability.

Synthesis The process of converting a high-level design description into a lower level representation (such as a set of equations or a netlist) of a circuit. *See* fitting, place and route.

Test bench A simulation model used to apply vectors to a design entity and verify its output. A test bench can be used to simulate either a presynthesis or a postlayout design description.

Type A quality of a data object that defines the values the object can hold. Examples of types are bit and std_logic. Objects of type bit can hold values '0' or '1'. Objects of type std_logic can hold values of 'U', 'X', '0', '1', 'Z', 'W', 'L', 'H', or '-'.

Selected Bibliography

The following is a list of books and articles about VHDL, programmable logic, and design techniques. It is intended to point you to further reading that can help you become skilled in the use of VHDL simulation and synthesis tools, and knowlegeable of programmable logic and design techniques.

Advanced Micro Devices, Inc. *Bipolar Microprocessor Logic and Interface Data Book.* Sunnyvale, Calif.: Advanced Micro Devices, Inc., 1983.

——. *PAL Device Data Book and Design Guide.* Sunnyvale, Calif.: Advanced Micro Devices, Inc., 1995.

Altera Corporation. *Data Book.* San Jose, Calif.: Altera Corporation, 1995.

Armstrong, J. R. *Chip-Level Modeling with VHDL.* Englewood Cliffs, N.J.: Prentice Hall, 1988.

——, et al. "The VHDL Validation Suite." *Proceedings: 27th Design Automation Conference.* June 1990, pp. 2–7.

Ashenden, Peter. *The Designer's Guide to VHDL.* San Francisco: Morgan Kaufmann, 1995.

——. *VHDL Cookbook.* Available via ftp://ftp.cs.adelaide.edu.au/pub/VHDL/.

Aylor, J., R. Waxman, and C. Scarratt. "VHDL: Feature Description and Analysis." *IEEE Design & Test of Computers,* April 1986.

Barton, David. "Behavioral Descriptions in VHDL." *VLSI Systems Design,* June 1988.

——. "A First Course in VHDL." *VLSI Systems Design,* January 1988.

Bhasker, J. *A VHDL Primer.* Revised Edition, Englewood Cliffs, N.J.: Prentice Hall, 1992.

——. "Process-Graph Analyzer: A Front-End Tool for VHDL Behavioral Synthesis." *Software Practice and Experience,* vol. 18, no. 5, May 1988.

——. "An Algorithm for Microcode Compaction of VHDL Behavioral Descriptions." *Proceedings: 20th Microprogramming Workshop,* December 1987.

Brown, Stephen, *Field-Programmable Devices,* second edition, Los Gatos, Calif.: Stan Baker Associates, 1995.

Carlson, S. *Introduction to HDL-Based Design Using VHDL.* Mountain View, Calif.: Synopsys Inc., 1991.

Chan, Pak, and Samiha Mourad. *Digital System Design Using Field Programmable Gate Arrays.* Englewood Cliffs, N.J.: Prentice Hall, 1994.

Chaney, T. "Comments on 'A note on Synchronizer or Interlock Maloperation.'" *IEEE Trans. Computing,* October 1979.

Coelho, David. *The VHDL Handbook.* Boston: Kluwer Academic, 1989.

——. "VHDL: A Call for Standards." *Proceedings: 25th Design Automation Conference,* June 1988.

Coppola, A., and J. Lewis. "VHDL for Programmable Logic Devices." *1993 Programmable Logic Devices Conference,* Santa Clara, Calif.: March 1993.

Coppola, A., et al. "Tokenized State Machines for PLDs and FPGAs." *Proceedings of IFIP WG10.2/WG10.5 Workshop on Control-Dominated Synthesis from a Register-Transfer-Level Description*. G. Saucier and J. Trilhe, editors. Grenoble, France: Elsevier Science Publisher, September 1992.

——— "VHDL Synthesis of Concurrent State Machines to a Programmable Logic Device." *Proceedings of the IEEE VHDL International User's Forum*. Scottsdale, Ariz.: May 1992.

Coppola, A., and M. Perkowski. "A State Machine PLD and Associated Minimization Algorithms," *Proceedings of the FPGA'92 ACM/SIGDA First International Workshop on Field-Programmable Gate Arrays*. Berkeley, Calif.: February 1992.

Cypress Semiconductor Corporation. *Applications Handbook*. San Jose, Calif.: Cypress Semiconductor Corporation, 1994.

——— . *Data Book*. San Jose, Calif.: Cypress Semiconductor Corporation, 1995.

——— . *Programmable Logic Data Book*. San Jose, Calif.: Cypress Semiconductor Corporation, 1996.

Dewey, Allen, and Anthony Gadient. "VHDL Motivation" *IEEE Design & Test of Computers*. New York: IEEE, April 1986.

Dillinger, T. E., et al., "A Logic Synthesis System for VHDL Design Description." *IEEE ICCAD-89*. Santa Clara, Calif.: 1989.

Dingman, Sean. "Determine PLD Metastability to Derive Ample MTBFs." *EDN*. August 5, 1991.

Euzent, Bruce, et al. *Reliability Aspects of a Floating Gate E^2PROM*. Santa Clara, Calif.: Intel Corporation, 1981.

Farrow, R., and A. Stanculescu. "A VHDL Compiler Based on Attribute Grammar Methodology." *SIGPLAN 1989*.

Gilman, Alfred. "The Designer Environment." *IEEE Design & Test of Computers*. New York: IEEE, April 1986.

——— . "Logic Modeling in WAVES." *IEEE Design and Test of Computers*. New York: IEEE, June 1990, pp. 49–55.

Hamacher, Carl, Zvonko Vranesic, and Safwat Zaky. *Computer Organization,* third edition. New York: McGraw-Hill, 1990.

Hands, J. P., "What Is VHDL?" *Computer-Aided Design*. vol. 22, no. 4, May 1990.

Harr, Randolph, et al. *Applications of VHDL to Circuit Design,* Boston: Kluwer Academic, 1991.

Higgins, Richard. *Digital Signal Processing in VLSI*. Englewood Cliffs, N.J.: Prentice Hall, 1990.

Hines, J. "Where VHDL Fits Within the CAD Environment." *Proceedings: 24th Design Automation Conference*, 1987.

IEEE. *IEEE Standard VHDL Language Reference Manual, Std 1076-1993*. New York: IEEE, 1993.

——— . *IEEE Standard Multivalue Logic System for VHDL Model Interoperability (Std_logic_1164), Std IEEE 1164-1993*. New York: IEEE, 1993.

——— . *MAC Parameters, Physical Layer, Medium Attachment Units and Repeater for 100 Mb/s Operation, Supplement to Std IEEE 802.3-1993.* New York: IEEE, 1995.

Intel Corporation. *E^2PROM Family Applications Handbook*. Santa Clara, Calif.: Intel Corporation, 1981.

Jenkins, Jesse. *Designing with CPLDs and FPGAs*. Englewood Cliffs, N.J.: Prentice Hall, 1994.

Kapusta, Richard. "Options Dot the Programmable Logic Landscape." *EDN*. July 6, 1995.

Katz, Randy. *Contemporary Logic Design*. Redwood City, Calif.: Benjamin/Cummings: 1994.

Kim, K., and J. Trout. "Automatic Insertion of BIST Hardware Using VHDL," *Proceedings, 25th Design Automation Conference,* 1988.

Koren, Israel. *Computer Arithmetic Algorithms.* Englewood Cliffs, N.J.: Prentice Hall, 1993.

Lala, Parag. *Practical Digital Design and Testing.* Englewood Cliffs, N.J.: Prentice Hall, 1996.

Langholz, Gideon, Abraham Kandel, and Joe Mott. *Digital Logic Design.* Dubuque, Iowa: Wm. C. Brown Publishers, 1988.

Leung, Steven, and Michael Shanblatt. *ASIC System Design With VHDL: A Paradigm.* Boston: Kluwer Academic, 1989.

Lipsett, Roger, Erich Marschner, and Moe Shahdad. "VHDL: The Language." *IEEE Design & Test of Computers.* New York: IEEE, April 1986.

Lipsett, Roger, Carl Schaefer, and Cary Ussery. *VHDL: Hardware Description and Design.* Boston: Kluwer Academic, 1989.

Lowenstein, Al, and Greg Winter. "VHDL's Impact on Test." *IEEE Design & Test of Computers.* New York: IEEE, April 1986.

Mazor, Stanley, and Patricia Langstraat. *A Guide to VHDL.* Boston: Kluwer Academic, 1992.

McCluskey, Edward. *Logic Design Principles, with Emphasis on Testable Semicustom Circuits.* Englewood Cliffs, N.J.: Prentice Hall, 1986.

Moughzail, M., et al., "Experience with the VHDL Environment." *Proceedings: 25th Design Automation Conference,* June 1988.

Nash, J., and L. Saunders. "VHDL Critique." *IEEE Design & Test of Computers.* New York: IEEE, April 1986.

Navabi, Zainalabedin. *VHDL Analysis and Modeling of Digital Systems.* New York: McGraw-Hill, 1993.

Perry, Douglas. *VHDL,* second edition. New York: McGraw-Hill, 1994.

Proceedings: PLDCON95. Manhasset, N.Y.: CMP Publications, 1995.

Prince, Betty, and Gunnar Due-Gundersen. *Semiconductor Memories.* Chichester, England: John Wiley & Sons, 1983.

Proceedings: VHDL International Users' Forum Fall 1995 Conference. Newton, Mass.: VIUF, 1995.

Prosser, F., and D. Winkel. *The Art of Digital Design,* second edition. Englewood Cliffs, N.J.: Prentice Hall, 1987.

Roth, Charles. *Fundamentals of Logic Design.* fourth edition. St. Paul, Minn.: West Publishing, 1992.

Saunders, L. "The IBM VHDL Design System." *Proceedings 24th Design Automation Conference,* 1987.

Schoen, J. M. *Performance and Fault Modeling with VHDL.* Englewood Cliffs, N.J.: Prentice Hall, 1992.

Tanenbaum, Andrew. *Computer Networks.* second edition. Englewood Cliffs, N.J.: Prentice Hall, 1988.

Tutorials: VHDL International Users' Forum Fall 1995 Conference. Newton, Mass.: VIUF, 1995.

Sternheim, Eli, et al. *Digital Design and Synthesis.* San Jose, Calif.: Automa, 1993.

Wakerly, John. *Digital Design Principles and Practice.* Englewood Cliffs, N.J.: Prentice Hall, 1990.

Ward, P. C., and J. Armstrong. "Behavioral Fault Simulation in VHDL." *Proceedings, 27th Design Automation Conference,* June 1990, pp. 587–593.

Wolf, Wayne. *Modern VLSI Design: A System's Approach.* Englewood Cliffs, N.J.: Princeton Hall, 1994.

Xilinx Inc., *Programmable Logic Data Book,* San Jose, Calif.: Xilinx Inc., 1994.

Index